Your Companion Site — Even More Help for Studying!

bedfordstmartins.com/roarkunderstanding

FREE Online Study Guide—
Improve Your Understanding!

Get immediate feedback on your progress with

- Quizzing
- Key terms review
- Map and visual activities
- Timeline activities
- Note-taking outlines
- Chapter study guide steps

FREE History Research and Writing Help

Refine your research skills, evaluate sources, and organize your findings with

- A database of useful images, maps, documents and more at *Make History*
- A guide to online sources for history
- Help with writing history papers
- A tool for building a bibliography
- Tips on avoiding plagiarism

Understanding the American Promise

A BRIEF HISTORY

Understanding the American Promise

A BRIEF HISTORY

Volume II
From 1865

James L. Roark
Emory University

Michael P. Johnson
Johns Hopkins University

Patricia Cline Cohen
*University of California,
Santa Barbara*

Sarah Stage
Arizona State University

Alan Lawson
Boston College

Susan M. Hartmann
The Ohio State University

Bedford/St. Martin's
Boston • New York

For Bedford/St. Martin's

Publisher for History: Mary Dougherty
Executive Editor for History: William J. Lombardo
Director of Development for History: Jane Knetzger
Developmental Editor: Kathryn Abbott
Senior Production Editor: Bridget Leahy
Assistant Production Manager: Joe Ford
Executive Marketing Manager: Jenna Bookin Barry
Editorial Assistant: Robin Soule
Copy Editor: Linda McLatchie
Indexer: Leoni Z. McVey
Photo Researcher: Picture Research Consultants, Inc.
Permissions Manager: Kalina Ingham Hintz
Senior Art Director: Anna Palchik
Text Designer: Jerilyn Bockorick
Cover Designer: Donna Lee Dennison
Cover Photo: Dwight and Mamie Eisenhower. Courtesy Dwight D. Eisenhower Library.
Cartography: Mapping Specialists Limited
Composition: Nesbitt Graphics, Inc.
Printing and Binding: RR Donnelley and Sons

President: Joan E. Feinberg
Editorial Director: Denise B. Wydra
Director of Marketing: Karen R. Soeltz
Director of Production: Susan W. Brown
Associate Director, Editorial Production: Elise S. Kaiser
Managing Editor: Elizabeth M. Schaaf

Library of Congress Control Number: 2010936410

Manufactured in the United States of America.

6   5   4   3   2   1
f   e   d   c   b   a

For information, write: Bedford/St. Martin's, 75 Arlington Street, Boston, MA 02116
(617-399-4000)

ISBN: 978–0–312–64518–2   (combined edition)
ISBN: 978–0–312–64519–9   (Vol. I)
ISBN: 978–0–312–64520–5   (Vol. II)

PREFACE

In *Understanding the American Promise,* we set out solve a couple of problems that had come to us over the years. First, we knew that, although many students dutifully read their survey texts, they came away confused. They couldn't tell what was most important and they felt overwhelmed. At the same time, their instructors felt that some texts didn't show students what was so exciting and even fun about history. These teachers wanted a way to give their students a grounding in the basics and to show how historians think and work, a text that would show that history is a discipline based upon inquiry, interpretation, and debate. With these issues in mind, we took a hard look at the survey course from all directions. We reflected on our own classes and students and how they've changed. We reviewed state-of-the-art scholarship on effective teaching. We consulted learning experts and instructional designers. We talked to students. And, most importantly, we talked to you—instructors teaching the course—and asked about your needs. *Understanding the American Promise* is the product of these efforts.

With *Understanding the American Promise*, we offer something new—an abridged narrative of U.S. history that concentrates on important developments, combined with an innovative design and pedagogy orchestrated to work together to foster students' comprehension and historical thinking. This brief narrative and distinctive format will help your students grasp important developments and begin to think like historians.

This means that, in *Understanding,* design, pedagogy and narrative work together to help students learn, and then reinforce and retain their knowledge. We started with *The American Promise,* our full-length survey textbook acclaimed for its effective braiding together of political and social history, and reduced the length by over thirty percent. This abridged narrative will better help students discern overarching trends and connect them with the individuals—from Presidents to pipefitters and sharecroppers to suffragettes—that animate the past.

Then, we joined our prose with an innovative pedagogy and a well-crafted design to make a compelling new teaching and learning tool. *Understanding's* chapter architecture supports students' comprehension and helps them to grasp key themes and ideas. To this end, all chapters open with a succinct, single paragraph–length statement about the main themes and events of the chapter, designed to establish clear learning outcomes. At the beginning of each chapter, we also ask students a "Did You Know?" question to invite them to connect what they already know (or think they know) to each chapter's big theme. Chapters are then organized into three to six main sections, with all section titles crafted as big questions to facilitate active reading and to emphasize that history is an inquiry-based discipline. These main sections end with quick review questions that prompt students to check their comprehension and reflect on what they've read. Throughout, chronology boxes show the sequence of events, and marginal definitions highlight key terms, providing on-the-page reinforcement and a handy tool for review. We hope that this structure will help students to grasp meaning as they read and also model how historians think, how they pose questions, and how they answer those questions with evidence and interpretation.

We've also reconsidered the traditional review that comes at the end of the chapter. We've provided a three-step chapter review that will help students with the basic material but also help them go beyond a basic understanding of what happened. In step one, students identify key terms and explain why each matters. In step two, they apply their understanding of basic terms to questions about cause and effect, change over time, and comparison. And in step three, students pull it all together with analytical and synthetic questions that treat the whole chapter. Finally, an active recitation question asks students to consider what is truly important to understand about what they have just read.

As teachers, our guiding principle is to promote intelligent engagement as a catalyst toward historical understanding. This means giving our students an effective textbook that is enjoyable to read and that provides the tools to help them develop their skills of historical analysis and interpretation, and it is our hope that this new approach provides just such a tool. It is our article of faith that when we empower students to engage meaningfully with the past, we encourage habits of thinking essential for a well-rounded general education at any college or university—and beyond. Historical knowledge and the ability to think critically provide a rock-solid foundation for informed and active citizenship, whether that citizen was born in the United States or is a first generation immigrant, as many of our students are.

As always, our use of *American Promise* in our title reflects our emphasis on human agency and our conviction that American history is an unfinished story. For millions, the nation has held out the promise of a better life, unfettered worship, representative government, democratic politics, and other freedoms seldom found elsewhere. But none of these promises has come with guarantees. As we see it, much of American history is a continuing struggle over the definition and realization of the nation's promise. Abraham Lincoln, in the midst of what he termed the "fiery trial" of the Civil War, pronounced the nation "the last best hope of Earth." Kept alive by countless sacrifices, that hope has been marred by compromises, disappointments, and denials, but it lives still. We hope that *Understanding the American Promise* will help students become aware of the legacy of hope bequeathed to them by previous generations of Americans stretching back nearly four centuries, a legacy that is theirs to preserve and build on.

We trust you'll agree that *Understanding the American Promise* achieves its goal of giving students a smart alternative for *understanding* American history. If we help you stir in your students a lifelong passion for history and the habits of critical thinking, the pleasure is ours.

Acknowledgments

We gratefully acknowledge all the helpful suggestions from those who have read and taught from previous editions of *The American Promise: A History of the United States* and *The American Promise: A Compact History*. We would like specifically to acknowledge those scholars and teachers who gave their time and expertise to the draft for this first edition of *Understanding the American Promise*: Cary W. Blankenship, *University of Kentucky;* Roland Frankum Jr., *Millersville*

University; Cecilia Gowdy-Wygant, *Front Range Community College;* Pauline S. Johnson, *Mars Hill College;* Carol A. Keller, *San Antonio College;* Tracy A. Lai, *Seattle Central Community College;* Peggy Lambert, *Lone Star College-Kingwood;* John Mack, *Labette Community College;* Anne Paulet, *Humboldt State University,* Jeffrey Smith, *Lindenwood University;* and Julie Winch, *University of Massachusetts-Boston.*

A project as complex as this requires the talents of many individuals. First, we would like to acknowledge our families for their support, forbearance, and toleration of our textbook responsibilities. Pembroke Herbert and Sandi Rygiel of Picture Research Consultants, Inc., contributed their unparalleled knowledge, soaring imagination, and diligent research to make possible the extraordinary illustration program. Pauline Johnson of Mars Hill College reviewed each chapter's pedagogy with the astute eye of a lifelong teacher.

We would also like to thank the many people at Bedford/St. Martin's who have been crucial to this project. Developmental editor Kathryn Abbott oversaw the development of each chapter and added value at every step. Thanks also go to editorial assistant Robin Soule, who provided unflagging assistance and who coordinated the review program and the turnover of manuscript. We are also grateful to Jane Knetzger, director of development for history, William Lombardo, executive editor, and Mary Dougherty, publisher, for their support and guidance. For their imaginative and tireless efforts to promote the book, we want to thank Jenna Bookin Barry, executive marketing manager, Sally Constable, market development manager, John Hunger, senior history specialist, Sean Blest, eastern history specialist, and Stephen Watson, marketing assistant. With great skill and professionalism, Bridget Leahy, senior production editor, pulled together the many pieces related to copyediting, design, and typesetting, with the able assistance of Lidia MacDonald-Carr and Laura Winstead and the guidance of managing editor Elizabeth Schaaf and assistant managing editor John Amburg. Assistant production manager Joe Ford oversaw the manufacturing of the book. Designer and page makeup artist Jerilyn Bockorick, copyeditor Linda McLatchie, and proofreaders Jan Cocker and Melissa Clark attended to the myriad details that help make the book shine. Leoni McVey provided an outstanding index. The book's covers were designed by Donna Dennison. New media editor Marissa Zanetti, associate editor Jack Cashman, and media producer Nancy Hiney, made sure that *Understanding the American Promise: A Brief History* remains at the forefront of technological support for students and instructors. Editorial director Denise Wydra provided helpful advice throughout the course of the project. Finally, Charles H. Christensen, former president, took a personal interest in *The American Promise* from the start, and Joan E. Feinberg, president, has guided all editions through every stage of development.

James Roark
Michael Johnson
Patricia Cohen
Sarah Stage
Alan Lawson
Susan Hartmann

BRIEF CONTENTS

CONTENTS

16
RECONSTRUCTING A NATION
1863–1877 *427*

17
CONTESTING THE WEST
1870–1900 *455*

18
DEFINING THE GILDED AGE OF BUSINESS AND POLITICS
1870–1895 *481*

19
THE GROWTH OF AMERICA'S CITIES
1870–1900 *509*

20
A DECADE OF DISSENT, DEPRESSION, AND WAR
1890–1900 *537*

30
THE CONSERVATIVE TURN
1969–1989 *829*

31
FACING THE CHALLENGES OF A CHANGING WORLD
SINCE 1989 *857*

MAPS, FIGURES, AND TABLES

VERSIONS AND SUPPLEMENTS

Understanding the American Promise: A Brief History is supported by loads of resources—study tools for students, instructor materials, and many options for packaging the book with documents readers, trade books, atlases, and other guides—for free or at a substantial discount. Descriptions follow, but for more information, visit the book's catalog site at bedfordstmartins.com/roarkunderstanding/catalog or contact your local Bedford/St. Martin's sales representative.

Available Versions of This Book

To accommodate different course lengths and course budgets, this title is available in several different formats. The e-books are available at a substantial discount.

Combined Volume (Chapters 1–31)—available in paperback and e-book formats
Volume I: To 1877 (Chapters 1–16)—available in paperback and e-book formats
Volume II: From 1865 (Chapters 16–31)—available in paperback and e-book formats

With our innovative e-books your students get the content you want in a convenient format—for about half the cost of a print book. **Bedford/St. Martin's e-Books** have been optimized for reading and studying online. **CourseSmart e-Books** can be downloaded or used online, whichever is more convenient for your students.

Companion site at bedfordstmartins.com/roarkunderstanding

Our new companion sites gather free and premium resources, giving students a way to extend their Bedford book, online. These book-specific sites provide one destination to practice, read, write, and study—and to find and access quizzes and activities, study aids, and history research and writing help.

▶ **FREE Online Study Guide.** Available at the companion site, this popular resource provides students with self-review quizzes and activities for each chapter, including a multiple-choice self-test that focuses on important concepts; an identification quiz that helps students remember key people, places, and events; a flashcard activity that tests students' knowledge of key terms; and map activities intended to strengthen students' geography skills. It also includes downloadable versions of the textbook chapter study guides. Instructors can monitor students' progress through an online Quiz Gradebook or receive email updates.

▶ **FREE History Research and Writing Help.** Also available on the companion site, this resource includes the textbook authors' *Suggested References* organized by chapter; *History Research and Reference Sources,* with links to history-related databases, indexes, and journals; *More Sources and How to Format a History*

Paper, with clear advice on how to integrate primary and secondary sources into research papers and how to cite and format sources correctly; ***Build a Bibliography,*** a simple Web-based tool that generates bibliographies in four commonly used documentation styles; and ***Tips on Avoiding Plagiarism,*** an online tutorial that reviews the consequences of plagiarism and features exercises to help students practice integrating sources and recognize acceptable summaries.

Instructor Resources

Bedford/St. Martin's has developed a wide range of teaching resources for this book and for this course. They range from lecture and presentation materials to assessment tools and course management options. Most can be downloaded or ordered at bedfordstmartins.com/roarkunderstanding/catalog.

▶ *HistoryClass for Understanding the American Promise. HistoryClass,* a Bedford/St. Martin's Online Course Space, puts the online resources available with this textbook in one convenient place—an interactive e-book and primary sources reader; maps, images, documents and links; chapter review quizzes; interactive multimedia exercises; and research and writing help. Get into HistoryClass and get all our premium content and tools in one completely customizable course space; then assign, rearrange, and mix our resources with yours. For more information visit yourhistoryclass.com.

▶ **Bedford/St. Martin's Course Cartridges.** Whether you use Blackboard, WebCT, Desire2Learn, Angel, Sakai, or Moodle, we have free content and support available for you to plug our content into your course management system. Registered instructors can download cartridges with no hassle, no strings attached. Content includes our most popular free resources and book-specific content for this title. Visit bedfordstmartins.com/cms to get a demo, find your versions, or download your cartridge.

▶ **NEW PowerPoint Maps, Images, Lecture Outlines, and i>clicker Content.** Look good and save time with *The Bedford Lecture Kit.* These presentation materials are downloadable individually from the Media and Supplements tab at bedfordstmartins.com/roarkunderstanding/catalog, and they are available on *The Bedford Lecture Kit Instructor's Resource CD-ROM.* They include ready-made and fully customizable PowerPoint multimedia presentations built around lecture outlines that are embedded with maps, figures, and selected images from the textbook and are supplemented by more detailed instructor notes on key points. Also available are maps and selected images in JPEG and PowerPoint format; content for i>clicker, a classroom response system, in Microsoft Word and PowerPoint formats; the Instructor's Resource Manual in Microsoft Word format; and outline maps in PDF format for quizzing or handouts. All files are suitable for copying onto transparency acetates.

▶ **Instructor's Resource Manual.** The instructor's manual offers both experienced and first-time instructors tools for presenting textbook material in engaging ways. It includes chapter review material, teaching strategies, and a guide to chapter-specific supplements available for the text.

▶ **Computerized Test Bank.** The test bank includes a mix of fresh, carefully crafted multiple-choice, fill-in-the-blank, short-answer, and essay questions for each chapter. The questions appear in Microsoft Word format and in easy-to-use test bank software that allows instructors to easily add, edit, re-sequence, and print questions and answers. Instructors can also export questions into a variety of formats, including WebCT and Blackboard.

▶ *Make History*—**Free Documents, Maps, Images, and Web Sites.** *Make History* combines the best Web resources with hundreds of maps and images, to make finding the source material you need simple. Browse the collection of thousands of resources by course or by topic, date, and type. Each item has been carefully chosen and helpfully annotated to make it easy to find exactly what you need. Available at bedfordstmartins.com/makehistory.

▶ *Reel Teaching* **Video clips.** This DVD provides a large collection of short video clips for classroom presentation. Designed as engaging "lecture launchers" varying in length from 1 to 15 or more minutes, the 59 documentary clips were carefully chosen for use in both semesters of the U.S. survey course. The clips feature compelling images, archival footage, personal narratives, and commentary by noted historians.

▶ **NEW** *America in Motion: Video clips for U.S. History.* Set history in motion with *America in Motion*, an instructor DVD containing dozens of short digital movie files of twentieth-century American historical events. From the wreckage of the battleship *Maine*, to FDR's Fireside Chats, to Oliver North testifying before Congress, *America in Motion* engages your students with dynamic scenes from key events and challenges them to think critically. All files are classroom-ready, edited for brevity, and easily integrated with PowerPoint or other presentation software for electronic lectures or assignments. An accompanying guide provides each clip's historical context, ideas for use, and suggested questions.

▶ **Videos and Multimedia.** A wide assortment of videos and multimedia CD-ROMs on various topics in U.S. history is available to qualified adopters through your Bedford/St. Martin's sales representative.

Packaging Opportunities

Save your students money and package your favorite text with more! For information on free packages and discounts up to 50%, contact your local Bedford/St. Martin's sales representative.

▶ **e-Book.** The e-book for this title can be packaged with the print text at no additional cost. For a complete list of titles, visit bedfordstmartins.com/ebooks/catalog.

▶ *Reading the American Past: Selected Historical Documents*, **Fourth Edition.** Edited by Michael P. Johnson (Johns Hopkins University), one of the authors of *The American Promise,* and designed to complement the textbook, *Reading the American Past* provides a broad selection of over 150 primary source documents, as well as editorial apparatus to help students analyze the sources. Emphasizing the important social, political, and economic themes of U.S. history courses, these documents provide a wide range of perspectives on environmental, western, ethnic, and gender history. Available free when packaged with the text. For more information, visit bedfordstmartins.com/roarksources/catalog.

▶ *Reading the American Past e-Book.* The reader is available as an e-book. When packaged with the print or electronic version of the textbook, it is available for free. For more information, visit bedfordstmartins.com/ebooks/catalog.

▶ *Rand McNally Atlas of American History.* This collection of more than eighty full-color maps illustrates key events and eras from early exploration, settlement, expansion, and immigration to U.S. involvement in wars abroad an on U.S. soil. Introductory pages for each section include brief overview, timelines, graphs, and photos to quickly establish a historical context. Available for $3.00 when packaged with the text. For a complete list of titles, visit bedfordstmartins.com/americanatlas/catalog.

▶ *Maps in Context: A Workbook for American History.* Written by historical cartography expert Gerald A. Danzer (University of Illinois at Chicago), this skill-building workbook helps students comprehend essential connections between geographic literacy and historical understanding. Organized to correspond to the typical U.S. history survey course, Maps in Context presents a wealth of map-centered projects and convenient pop quizzes that give students hands-on experience working with maps. Available free when packaged with the text. For a complete list of titles, visit bedfordstmartins.com/mapsincontext/catalog.

▶ *The Bedford Glossary for U.S. History.* This handy supplement for the survey course gives students historically contextualized definitions for hundreds of terms—from *abolitionism* to *zoot suit*—that students will encounter in lectures, reading, and exams. Available free when packaged with the text. For a complete list of titles, visit bedfordstmartins.com/usgloss/catalog.

▶ *U.S. History Matters: A Student Guide to World History Online.* This resource, written by Alan Gevinson, Kelly Schrum, and the late Roy Rosenzweig (all of George Mason University), provides an illustrated and annotated guide to 250 of the most useful Web sites for student research in U.S. history as well as advice on evaluating and using Internet sources. This essential guide is based on the acclaimed "History Matters" Web site developed by the American Social History Project and the Center for History and New Media. Available free when packaged with the text. For a complete list of titles, visit bedfordstmartins.com/ushistorymatters/catalog.

▶ **The Bedford Series in History and Culture.** More than one hundred titles in this highly praised series combine first-rate scholarship, historical narrative, and important primary documents for undergraduate courses. Each book is brief, inexpensive, and focused on a specific topic or period. For a complete list of titles, visit bedfordstmartins.com/history/series. Package discounts are available.

▶ **Trade Books.** Titles published by sister companies Hill and Wang; Farrar, Strauss and Giroux; Henry Holt and Company; St. Martin's Press; Picador; and Palgrave Macmillan are available at a 50 percent discount when packaged with Bedford/St. Martin's textbooks. For more information, visit bedfordstmartins.com/tradeup.

▶ *Going to the Source: The Bedford Reader in American History.* Developed by Victoria Bissell Brown and Timothy J. Shannon, this reader's strong pedagogical framework helps students learn how to ask fruitful questions in order to evaluate documents effectively and develop critical reading skills. The reader's wide variety of chapter topics that complement the survey course and its rich diversity of sources—from personal letters to political cartoons—provoke students' interest as it teaches them the skills they need to successfully interrogate historical sources. Package discounts are available. For more information, visit bedfordstmartins.com/brownshannon/catalog.

▶ *America Firsthand.* With its distinctive focus on ordinary people, this primary documents reader, by Robert D. Marcus, David Burner, and Anthony Marcus, offers a remarkable range of perspectives on America's history from those who lived it. Popular Points of View sections expose students to different perspectives on a specific event or topic, and Visual Portfolios invite analysis of the visual record. Package discounts are available. For more information, visit bedfordstmartins.com/marcusburner/catalog.

▶ *A Pocket Guide to Writing in History.* This portable and affordable reference tool by Mary Lynn Rampolla provides reading, writing, and research advice useful to students in all history courses. Concise yet comprehensive advice on approaching typical history assignments, developing critical reading skills, writing effective history papers, conducting research, using and documenting sources, and avoiding plagiarism—enhanced with practical tips and examples throughout—have made this slim reference a best-seller. Package discounts are available. For more information, visit bedfordstmartins.com/rampolla/catalog.

▶ *A Student's Guide to History.* This complete guide to success in any history course provides the practical help students need to be effective. In addition to introducing students to the nature of the discipline, author Jules Benjamin teaches a wide range of skills from preparing for exams to approaching common writing assignments, and he explains the research and documentation process with plentiful examples. Package discounts are available. For more information, visit bedfordstmartins.com/benjamin/catalog.

How to use this book to figure out what's **really** important

Memorizing facts and dates for a history class won't get you very far. That's because history isn't just about "facts." It's also about understanding cause-and-effect and the significance of people, places, and events from the past that still have relevance to your world today. This textbook is designed to help you focus on what's truly significant in U.S. history and to give you practice in thinking like a historian.

The opening page gives you a preview of the entire chapter.

16

RECONSTRUCTING A NATION

1863–1877

The title tells you the subject of the chapter and identifies the time span that will be covered.

> This chapter explores the period known as Reconstruction, in which the nation struggled to define the defeated South's status within the Union and the meaning of freedom for ex-slaves. Despite the end of the Civil War, the nation entered one of its most violent eras, as victorious Northerners, defeated white Southerners, and newly freed African

The opening paragraph identifies the themes that will be explored, such as the continuing struggle between North and South, the meaning of freedom for ex-slaves, and erupting violence.

> What were Lincoln's plans for wartime reconstruction?

> What vision did Andrew Johnson have for presidential reconstruction?

> How radical was congressional reconstruction?

> How was the battle over reconstruction fought in the South?

> Why did reconstruction collapse?

> Conclusion: What were the achievements and failures of reconstruction?

Each question opens a new section of the chapter and will be addressed in turn on the following pages.

SAML. DOVE wishes to know of the whereabouts of his mother, Areno, his sisters Maria, Neziah, and Peggy, and his brother Edmond, who were owned by Geo. Dove, of Rockingham county, Shenandoah Valley, Va. Sold in Richmond, after which Sami, and Edmond were taken to Nashville, Tenn., by Joe Mick; Areno was left at the Eagle Tavern, Richmond
Respectfully yours,
SAML. DOVE.
Utica, New York, Aug. 5, 1865–3m

U. S. CHRISTIAN COMMISSION,
NASHVILLE, TENN., July 19, 1865.

DID YOU KNOW?

The priorities for newly freed African Americans were to locate family members, acquire land, and worship in their own churches.

Voting day, June 5, 1867. Black freedmen line up to vote in Washington, D.C.

427

Each section has tools that help you focus on what's important.

> ## What vision did Andrew Johnson have for presidential reconstruction?

The Black Codes

Titled "Selling a Freeman to Pay His Fine at Monticello, Florida," this 1867 drawing from a northern magazine equates black codes with the reinstitution of slavery. The ascension of Andrew Johnson to the presidency emboldened many southern states to pass laws severely restricting blacks' freedom. *Granger Collection.*

The question in red is the specific topic discussed in this section.

Marginal key terms give you background on important people, ideas, and events. Use them for reference while you read but also pay attention to which terms are emphasized.

Andrew Johnson

▶ President of the United States from 1865 to 1869, Vice President Johnson became president after the assassination of Abraham Lincoln. Like Lincoln, Johnson sought the quick restoration of civil government in the South and pardoned most ex-Confederates. Johnson battled with Congress over the course of Reconstruction and was the first president in U.S. history to be impeached by the House of Representatives. He barely escaped removal from office by the Senate.

WITH ABRAHAM LINCOLN'S death on April 15, 1865, Vice President Andrew Johnson of Tennessee became the new president. Congress had adjourned in March and would not reconvene until December. Thus, throughout the summer and fall, Johnson drew up and executed a plan of reconstruction without congressional advice.

Congress reconvened in December to find that, as far as the president and former Confederates were concerned, reconstruction was completed. Most Republicans, however, thought Johnson's puny demands of ex-rebels encouraged the rebirth of the Old South at the expense of black liberty. They proceeded to dismantle Johnson's program and substitute a program of their own.

Johnson's Program of Reconciliation

Born in 1808 in Raleigh, North Carolina, **Andrew Johnson** was the son of illiterate parents. Self-educated and ambitious, Johnson moved to Tennessee, where he built a career in politics championing the South's common white people and assailing its "illegitimate, swaggering, bastard, scrub aristocracy." The only senator from a Confederate state to remain loyal to the Union, Johnson held the planter class responsible for secession.

A Democrat all his life, Johnson occupied the White House only because the Republican Party in 1864 had needed a vice presidential candidate who would appeal to loyal, Union-supporting Democrats. Johnson vigorously defended states' rights (but not secession) and opposed Republican efforts to expand the power of the federal government. A steadfast supporter of slavery, Johnson grudgingly accepted emancipation more because he hated planters than because he sympathized with slaves. "Damn the negroes," he said. "I am fighting those traitorous aristocrats, their masters." The new president harbored unshakable racist convictions. Africans, Johnson said, were "inferior to the white man in point of intellect—better calculated in physical structure to undergo drudgery and hardship."

CHAPTER LOCATOR | What were Lincoln's plans for wartime reconstruction?

Like Lincoln, Johnson stressed the rapid restoration of civil government in the South. Like Lincoln, he promised to pardon most, but not all, ex-rebels. Johnson recognized the state governments created by Lincoln but set out his own requirements for restoring the other rebel states to the Union. All that the citizens of a state had to do was to renounce the right of secession, deny that the debts of the Confederacy were legal and binding, and ratify the Thirteenth Amendment, abolishing slavery, which became part of the Constitution in December 1865.

Johnson also returned to pardoned ex-Confederates all confiscated and abandoned land, even if it was in the hands of freedmen. Reformers were shocked. Instead of punishing planters as Republicans expected, his instructions canceled the promising beginnings made by General Sherman and the Freedmen's Bureau to settle blacks on land of their own. As one freedman observed, "Things was hurt by Mr. Lincoln getting killed."

White Southern Resistance and Black Codes

In the summer of 1865, delegates across the South gathered to draw up the new state constitutions required by Johnson's plan of reconstruction. Rather than accept Johnson's plan, delegates balked at even the president's mild requirements to renounce secession, disown their war debts, and ratify the Thirteenth Amendment. Despite this defiance, Johnson did nothing. White Southerners began to think that by standing up for themselves they could define the terms of reconstruction.

State governments across the South adopted a series of laws known as **black codes**, which made a travesty of black freedom. The codes sought to keep ex-slaves subordinate to whites by subjecting them to every sort of discrimination.

Black Codes

Several states made it illegal for blacks to own a gun.

Mississippi made insulting gestures and language by blacks a criminal offense.

The codes barred blacks from jury duty.

Not a single southern state granted any black the right to vote.

At the core of the black codes, however, lay the matter of labor and the desire to force freedmen back to the plantations. South Carolina attempted to limit blacks to either farmwork or domestic service by requiring them to pay annual taxes of $10 to $100 to work in any other occupation. Mississippi declared that blacks who did not possess written evidence of employment could be declared vagrants and be subject to involuntary plantation labor. Under so-called apprenticeship laws, courts bound thousands of black children—orphans and others whose parents they deemed unable to support them—to work for planter "guardians."

CHRONOLOGY

1865
- President Abraham Lincoln is shot; dies on April 15; is succeeded by Andrew Johnson.
- Johnson carries out rapid restoration of civil government in the South.
- Johnson returns confiscated and abandoned land to pardoned ex-Confederates.
- Southern states enact black codes.
- The Thirteenth Amendment, abolishing slavery, becomes part of Constitution.

1866
- Civil Rights Act nullifies black codes and extends civil rights to blacks.

black codes
▶ Laws passed by state governments in the South in 1865 that sought to keep ex-slaves subordinate to whites. At the core of the black codes lay the desire to force freedmen back to the plantations.

Chronologies for each major section show the sequence of events in this section.

The quick review helps you check your recall of the section.

QUICK REVIEW

Why and how did the aims of Congress and the president diverge? What specifically were the issues over which they clashed?

| What vision did Andrew Johnson have for presidential reconstruction? | How radical was congressional reconstruction? | How was the battle over reconstruction fought in the South? | Why did reconstruction collapse? | Conclusion: What were the achievements and failures of reconstruction? |

433

The chapter locator at the bottom of the page puts this section in the context of the chapter as a whole, so you can see how this section relates to what's coming next.

The Chapter Study Guide provides a 3-step process that will build your understanding and your historical skills.

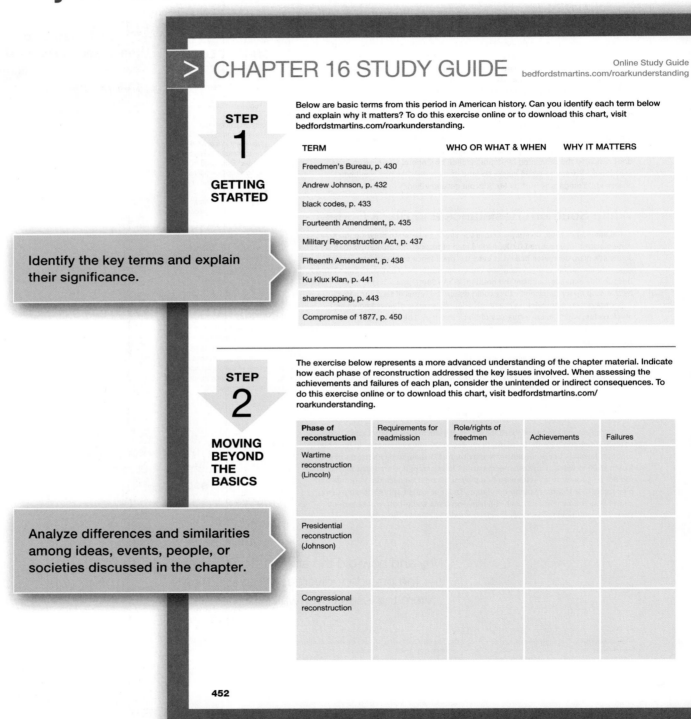

Online Study Guide
bedfordstmartins.com/roarkunderstanding

STEP 1

GETTING STARTED

Below are basic terms from this period in American history. Can you identify each term below and explain why it matters? To do this exercise online or to download this chart, visit bedfordstmartins.com/roarkunderstanding.

TERM	WHO OR WHAT & WHEN	WHY IT MATTERS
Freedmen's Bureau, p. 430		
Andrew Johnson, p. 432		
black codes, p. 433		
Fourteenth Amendment, p. 435		
Military Reconstruction Act, p. 437		
Fifteenth Amendment, p. 438		
Ku Klux Klan, p. 441		
sharecropping, p. 443		
Compromise of 1877, p. 450		

Identify the key terms and explain their significance.

STEP 2

MOVING BEYOND THE BASICS

The exercise below represents a more advanced understanding of the chapter material. Indicate how each phase of reconstruction addressed the key issues involved. When assessing the achievements and failures of each plan, consider the unintended or indirect consequences. To do this exercise online or to download this chart, visit bedfordstmartins.com/roarkunderstanding.

Phase of reconstruction	Requirements for readmission	Role/rights of freedmen	Achievements	Failures
Wartime reconstruction (Lincoln)				
Presidential reconstruction (Johnson)				
Congressional reconstruction				

Analyze differences and similarities among ideas, events, people, or societies discussed in the chapter.

452

Now that you've reviewed various parts of the chapter, take a step back and try to see the big picture by answering these questions. Remember to use specific examples from the chapter in your answers. To do this exercise online, visit bedfordsmartins.com/roarkunderstanding.

Answer the big-picture questions using specific examples or evidence from the chapter.

PRESIDENTIAL AND CONGRESSIONAL RECONSTRUCTION

▶ What role did the black codes play in shaping the course of reconstruction?

▶ What steps did Congress take between 1865 and 1869 to assist ex-slaves in their lives as freedmen? How effective were these actions?

SOUTHERN RECONSTRUCTION IN ACTION

▶ How did white Southerners respond during Reconstruction? Consider both Democrats and Republicans in your response.

▶ How did southern African Americans attempt to shape their own lives during Reconstruction?

LOOKING BACKWARD, LOOKING AHEAD

▶ How did long-held racial views among whites, in both the South and the North, shape Reconstruction?

▶ What were the lasting accomplishments of Reconstruction? What were its most important failures?

THE END OF RECONSTRUCTION

▶ How and why did the decline of northern support for Reconstruction help southern Democrats "redeem" the South?

▶ Why did white supremacy become the foundation of southern politics in the 1870s?

IN YOUR OWN WORDS

Imagine that you must explain chapter 16 to someone who hasn't read it. What would be the most important points to include and why?

Explain the important points in your own words to make sure you have a firm grasp of the chapter material.

Understanding
the
American Promise

A BRIEF HISTORY

16
RECONSTRUCTING A NATION

1863–1877

> This chapter explores the period known as Reconstruction, in which the nation struggled to define the defeated South's status within the Union and the meaning of freedom for ex-slaves. Despite the end of the Civil War, the nation entered one of its most violent eras, as victorious Northerners, defeated white Southerners, and newly freed African Americans battled to shape the postwar South.

> What were Lincoln's plans for wartime reconstruction?

> What vision did Andrew Johnson have for presidential reconstruction?

> How radical was congressional reconstruction?

> How was the battle over reconstruction fought in the South?

> Why did reconstruction collapse?

> Conclusion: What were the achievements and failures of reconstruction?

SAML. DOVE wishes to know of the whereabouts of his mother, Areno, his sisters Maria, Neziah, and Peggy, and his brother Edmond, who were owned by Geo. Dove, of Rockingham county, Shenandoah Valley, Va. Sold in Richmond, after which Saml. and Edmond were taken to Nashville, Tenn., by Joe Mick; Areno was left at the Eagle Tavern, Richmond
Respectfully yours,
SAML. DOVE.
Utica, New York, Aug. 5, 1865–3m

U. S. CHRISTIAN COMMISSION,
NASHVILLE, TENN., July 19, 1865.

DID YOU KNOW?

The priorities for newly freed African Americans were to locate family members, acquire land, and worship in their own churches.

Voting day, June 5, 1867. Black freedmen line up to vote in Washington, D.C.

What vision did Andrew Johnson have for presidential reconstruction?

The Black Codes

Titled "Selling a Freeman to Pay His Fine at Monticello, Florida," this 1867 drawing from a northern magazine equates black codes with the reinstitution of slavery. The ascension of Andrew Johnson to the presidency emboldened many southern states to pass laws severely restricting blacks' freedom. Granger Collection.

WITH ABRAHAM LINCOLN'S death on April 15, 1865, Vice President Andrew Johnson of Tennessee became the new president. Congress had adjourned in March and would not reconvene until December. Thus, throughout the summer and fall, Johnson drew up and executed a plan of reconstruction without congressional advice.

Congress reconvened in December to find that, as far as the president and former Confederates were concerned, reconstruction was completed. Most Republicans, however, thought Johnson's puny demands of ex-rebels encouraged the rebirth of the Old South at the expense of black liberty. They proceeded to dismantle Johnson's program and substitute a program of their own.

Johnson's Program of Reconciliation

Andrew Johnson

▶ President of the United States from 1865 to 1869, Vice President Johnson became president after the assassination of Abraham Lincoln. Like Lincoln, Johnson sought the quick restoration of civil government in the South and pardoned most ex-Confederates. Johnson battled with Congress over the course of Reconstruction and was the first president in U.S. history to be impeached by the House of Representatives. He barely escaped removal from office by the Senate.

Born in 1808 in Raleigh, North Carolina, **Andrew Johnson** was the son of illiterate parents. Self-educated and ambitious, Johnson moved to Tennessee, where he built a career in politics championing the South's common white people and assailing its "illegitimate, swaggering, bastard, scrub aristocracy." The only senator from a Confederate state to remain loyal to the Union, Johnson held the planter class responsible for secession.

A Democrat all his life, Johnson occupied the White House only because the Republican Party in 1864 had needed a vice presidential candidate who would appeal to loyal, Union-supporting Democrats. Johnson vigorously defended states' rights (but not secession) and opposed Republican efforts to expand the power of the federal government. A steadfast supporter of slavery, Johnson grudgingly accepted emancipation more because he hated planters than because he sympathized with slaves. "Damn the negroes," he said. "I am fighting those traitorous aristocrats, their masters." The new president harbored unshakable racist convictions. Africans, Johnson said, were "inferior to the white man in point of intellect—better calculated in physical structure to undergo drudgery and hardship."

CHAPTER LOCATOR | What were Lincoln's plans for wartime reconstruction?

Like Lincoln, Johnson stressed the rapid restoration of civil government in the South. Like Lincoln, he promised to pardon most, but not all, ex-rebels. Johnson recognized the state governments created by Lincoln but set out his own requirements for restoring the other rebel states to the Union. All that the citizens of a state had to do was to renounce the right of secession, deny that the debts of the Confederacy were legal and binding, and ratify the Thirteenth Amendment, abolishing slavery, which became part of the Constitution in December 1865.

Johnson also returned to pardoned ex-Confederates all confiscated and abandoned land, even if it was in the hands of freedmen. Reformers were shocked. Instead of punishing planters as Republicans expected, his instructions canceled the promising beginnings made by General Sherman and the Freedmen's Bureau to settle blacks on land of their own. As one freedman observed, "Things was hurt by Mr. Lincoln getting killed."

White Southern Resistance and Black Codes

In the summer of 1865, delegates across the South gathered to draw up the new state constitutions required by Johnson's plan of reconstruction. Rather than accept Johnson's plan, delegates balked at even the president's mild requirements to renounce secession, disown their war debts, and ratify the Thirteenth Amendment. Despite this defiance, Johnson did nothing. White Southerners began to think that by standing up for themselves they could define the terms of reconstruction.

State governments across the South adopted a series of laws known as **black codes**, which made a travesty of black freedom. The codes sought to keep ex-slaves subordinate to whites by subjecting them to every sort of discrimination.

Black Codes

Several states made it illegal for blacks to own a gun.
Mississippi made insulting gestures and language by blacks a criminal offense.
The codes barred blacks from jury duty.
Not a single southern state granted any black the right to vote.

At the core of the black codes, however, lay the matter of labor and the desire to force freedmen back to the plantations. South Carolina attempted to limit blacks to either farmwork or domestic service by requiring them to pay annual taxes of $10 to $100 to work in any other occupation. Mississippi declared that blacks who did not possess written evidence of employment could be declared vagrants and be subject to involuntary plantation labor. Under so-called apprenticeship laws, courts bound thousands of black children—orphans and others whose parents they deemed unable to support them—to work for planter "guardians."

Johnson, a staunch defender of states' rights and white supremacy, refused to intervene. His stance was politically advantageous. A conservative Tennessee Democrat at the head of a northern Republican Party, he had begun to look southward for political allies. By pardoning powerful whites, by accepting governments even when they failed to satisfy his minimal demands, and by acquiescing in the black codes, he won useful southern friends.

In the fall elections of 1865, white Southerners dramatically expressed their mood. To represent them in Congress, they chose former Confederates, many of whom had

CHRONOLOGY

1865
- President Abraham Lincoln is shot; dies on April 15; is succeeded by Andrew Johnson.
- Johnson carries out rapid restoration of civil government in the South.
- Johnson returns confiscated and abandoned land to pardoned ex-Confederates.
- Southern states enact black codes.
- The Thirteenth Amendment, abolishing slavery, becomes part of Constitution.

1866
- Civil Rights Act nullifies black codes and extends civil rights to blacks.

black codes
▶ Laws passed by state governments in the South in 1865 that sought to keep ex-slaves subordinate to whites. At the core of the black codes lay the desire to force freedmen back to the plantations.

What vision did Andrew Johnson have for presidential reconstruction?	How radical was congressional reconstruction?	How was the battle over reconstruction fought in the South?	Why did reconstruction collapse?	Conclusion: What were the achievements and failures of reconstruction?

been high-ranking military and government officials in the Confederacy. As one Georgian remarked, "It looked as though Richmond had moved to Washington."

Expansion of Federal Authority and Black Rights

Southerners had assumed that what Andrew Johnson was willing to accept, Republicans would accept as well. But southern intransigence compelled even moderate Republicans to conclude that ex-rebels were still untrustworthy and dangerous. The black codes became a symbol of southern intentions to "restore all of slavery but its name." "We tell the white men of Mississippi," the *Chicago Tribune* roared, "that the men of the North will convert the State of Mississippi into a frog pond before they will allow such laws to disgrace one foot of the soil in which the bones of our soldiers sleep and over which the flag of freedom waves."

The moderate majority of the Republican Party did not champion black equality, the confiscation of plantations, or black voting, as did the radicals. But southern obstinacy had succeeded in forging temporary unity among Republican factions. In December 1865, Republicans refused to seat the southern representatives elected in the fall elections. Rather than accept Johnson's claim that the "work of restoration" was done, Congress challenged his executive power.

Republican senator Lyman Trumbull declared that the president's policy meant that ex-slaves would "be tyrannized over, abused, and virtually reenslaved without some legislation by the nation for [their] protection." Early in 1866, the moderates produced two bills that strengthened the federal shield. The first, the Freedmen's Bureau bill, prolonged the life of the agency established by the previous Congress. Arguing that the Constitution never contemplated a "system for the support of indigent persons," President Andrew Johnson vetoed the bill. Congress failed by a narrow margin to override the president's veto.

The moderates designed their second measure, the Civil Rights Act, to nullify the black codes by affirming African Americans' rights to "full and equal benefit of all laws and proceedings for the security of person and property as is enjoyed by white citizens." The act required the end of racial discrimination in state laws and represented an extraordinary expansion of black rights and federal authority. The president argued that the civil rights bill amounted to "unconstitutional invasion of states' rights" and vetoed it.

In April 1866, an incensed Republican Congress passed the civil rights bill again and overrode the presidential veto. In July, it passed another Freedmen's Bureau bill and overrode Johnson's veto. For the first time in American history, Congress had overridden presidential vetoes of major legislation. As a worried South Carolinian observed, Johnson had succeeded in uniting the Republicans and probably touched off "a fight this fall such as has never been seen."

> **QUICK REVIEW**

When the southern states passed the black codes, how did President Andrew Johnson respond? How did congressional Republicans respond?

CHAPTER LOCATOR | What were Lincoln's plans for wartime reconstruction?

State Convention at Richmond, Virginia

Between 1867 and 1869, every southern state except Tennessee held a convention to draft a new constitution. In Virginia, where blacks were more than 40 percent of the population, they made up about 20 percent of the convention. Richmond History Center.

BY THE SUMMER OF 1866, President Andrew Johnson and Congress were locked in a battle unprecedented in American history. Johnson made it clear that he would not budge on either constitutional issues or policy. Moderate Republicans responded by amending the Constitution. But the obstinacy of Johnson and white Southerners pushed Republican moderates ever closer to the radicals and to acceptance of additional federal intervention in the South. Congress also voted to impeach the president. In time, Congress debated whether to make voting rights color-blind, while women sought to make voting sex-blind as well.

The Fourteenth Amendment and Escalating Violence

In June 1866, Congress passed the **Fourteenth Amendment** to the Constitution, and two years later the states ratified it. The most important provisions of this complex amendment made all native-born or naturalized persons American citizens and prohibited states from abridging the "privileges and immunities" of citizens, depriving them of "life, liberty, or property without due process of law," and denying them "equal protection of the laws." By making blacks national citizens, the amendment provided a national guarantee of equality before the law. In essence, it protected blacks against violation by southern state governments.

Fourteenth Amendment

▶ Constitutional amendment ratified in 1868 that made all native-born or naturalized persons U.S. citizens and prohibited states from abridging the rights of national citizens. The amendment hoped to provide a guarantee of equality before the law for black citizens.

1866

– Congress approves Fourteenth Amendment, granting citizenship and equal rights to former slaves.
– Elizabeth Cady Stanton and Susan B. Anthony found the American Equal Rights Association to support woman suffrage.

1867

– Military Reconstruction Act initiates military occupation of the South and, with black suffrage and the disfranchisement of many ex-rebels, guarantees Republican governments in the South.

1868

– Impeachment trial of President Andrew Johnson.

1869

– Congress approves Fifteenth Amendment, making it illegal to deny voting rights on the basis of race.

The Fourteenth Amendment also dealt with voting rights. It gave Congress the right to reduce the congressional representation of states that withheld suffrage from some of its adult male population. In other words, white Southerners could either allow black men to vote or see their representation in Washington slashed.

The Fourteenth Amendment's suffrage provisions ignored the small band of women who had emerged from the war demanding "the ballot for the two disenfranchised classes, negroes and women." Founding the American Equal Rights Association in 1866, Susan B. Anthony and Elizabeth Cady Stanton lobbied for "a government by the people, and the whole people; for the people and the whole people." They felt betrayed when their old antislavery allies refused to work for their goals. "It was the Negro's hour," Frederick Douglass explained. Senator Charles Sumner suggested that woman suffrage could be "the great question of the future."

The Fourteenth Amendment provided for punishment of any state that excluded voters on the basis of race but not on the basis of sex. The amendment also introduced the word *male* into the Constitution when it referred to a citizen's right to vote. Stanton predicted that "if that word 'male' be inserted, it will take us a century at least to get it out."

Tennessee approved the Fourteenth Amendment in July, and Congress promptly welcomed the state's representatives and senators back. Had President Johnson counseled other southern states to ratify this relatively mild amendment, they might have listened. Instead, Johnson advised Southerners to reject the Fourteenth Amendment and to rely on him to trounce the Republicans in the fall congressional elections.

Johnson had decided to make the Fourteenth Amendment the overriding issue of the 1866 elections and to gather its white opponents into a new conservative party, the National Union Party. The president's strategy suffered a setback

Andrew Johnson Cartoon

Appearing in 1868 during President Andrew Johnson's impeachment trial, this cartoon includes captions that read: "This little boy would persist in handling books above his capacity" and "And this was the disastrous result." The cartoonist's portrait of Johnson being crushed by the Constitution refers to the president's flouting of the Tenure of Office Act, which caused Republicans to vote for his impeachment.
Granger Collection.

THIS LITTLE BOY WOULD PERSIST IN HANDLING BOOKS ABOVE HIS CAPACITY.

AND THIS WAS THE DISASTROUS RESULT.

CHAPTER LOCATOR | What were Lincoln's plans for wartime reconstruction?

when whites in several southern cities went on rampages against blacks. The mob violence shocked Northerners and renewed skepticism about Johnson's claim that southern whites could be trusted. "Who doubts that the Freedmen's Bureau ought to be abolished forthwith," a New Yorker observed sarcastically, "and the blacks remitted to the paternal care of their old masters, who 'understand the nigger, you know, a great deal better than the Yankees can.'"

The 1866 elections resulted in an overwhelming Republican victory. Johnson had bet that Northerners would not support federal protection of black rights and that a racist backlash would blast the Republican Party. But the war was still fresh in northern minds, and as one Republican explained, southern whites "with all their intelligence were traitors, the blacks with all their ignorance were loyal."

Radical Reconstruction and Military Rule

When Johnson continued to urge Southerners to reject the Fourteenth Amendment, every southern state except Tennessee voted it down. "The last one of the sinful ten," thundered Representative James A. Garfield of Ohio, "has flung back into our teeth the magnanimous offer of a generous nation." After the South rejected the moderates' program, the radicals seized the initiative.

Each act of defiance by southern whites had boosted the standing of the radicals within the Republican Party. Radicals such as Massachusetts senator Charles Sumner and Pennsylvania representative Thaddeus Stevens did not speak with a single voice, but they united in demanding civil and political equality for ex-slaves. Southern states were "like clay in the hands of the potter," Stevens declared in January 1867, and he called on Congress to begin reconstruction all over again.

In March 1867, Congress overturned the Johnson state governments and initiated military rule of the South. The **Military Reconstruction Act** (and three subsequent acts) divided the ten unreconstructed Confederate states into five military districts. Congress placed a Union general in charge of each district and instructed him to "suppress insurrection, disorder, and violence" and to begin political reform. After the military had completed voter registration, which would include black men, voters in each state would elect delegates to conventions that would draw up new state constitutions. Each constitution would guarantee black suffrage. When the voters of each state had approved the constitution and the state legislature had ratified the Fourteenth Amendment, the state could submit its work to Congress. If Congress approved, the state's senators and representatives could be seated, and political reunification would be accomplished.

Radicals proclaimed the provision for black suffrage "a prodigious triumph," for it extended far beyond the limited suffrage provisions of the Fourteenth Amendment. When combined with the disfranchisement of thousands of ex-rebels, it promised to cripple any neo-Confederate resurgence and guarantee Republican state governments in the South.

Despite its bold suffrage provision, the Military Reconstruction Act of 1867 disappointed those who also advocated the confiscation and redistribution of southern plantations to ex-slaves. Thaddeus Stevens agreed with the freedman who said, "Give us our own land and we take care of ourselves, but without land, the old masters can hire us or starve us, as they please." But most Republicans

Reconstruction Military Districts, 1867

Military Reconstruction Act

▶ Congressional act of March 1867 that initiated military rule of the South. Congressional reconstruction divided the ten unreconstructed Confederate states into five military districts, each under the direction of a Union general. It also established the procedure by which unreconstructed states could reenter the Union.

What vision did Andrew Johnson have for presidential reconstruction?

How radical was congressional reconstruction?

How was the battle over reconstruction fought in the South?

Why did reconstruction collapse?

Conclusion: What were the achievements and failures of reconstruction?

believed they had provided blacks with what they needed: equal legal rights and the ballot. If blacks were to get land, they would have to gain it themselves.

Declaring that he would rather sever his right arm than sign such a formula for "anarchy and chaos," Andrew Johnson vetoed the Military Reconstruction Act, but Congress quickly overrode his veto. With the passage of the Reconstruction Acts of 1867, congressional reconstruction was virtually completed. Congress left whites owning most of the South's land but, in a departure that justified the term "radical reconstruction," had given black men the ballot.

Impeaching a President

Despite his defeats, Andrew Johnson had no intention of yielding control of reconstruction. In a dozen ways, he sabotaged Congress's will and encouraged southern whites to resist. He issued a flood of pardons, waged war against the Freedmen's Bureau, and replaced Union generals eager to enforce Congress's Reconstruction Acts with conservative men eager to defeat them. Johnson claimed that he was merely defending the "violated Constitution." At bottom, however, the president subverted congressional reconstruction to protect southern whites from what he considered the horrors of "Negro domination."

Radicals argued that Johnson's abuse of constitutional powers and his failure to fulfill constitutional obligations to enforce the law were impeachable offenses. But moderates disagreed, arguing that only actual violations of criminal statutes were impeachable offenses. As long as Johnson refrained from breaking the law, impeachment (the process of formal charges of wrongdoing against the president or other federal official) remained stalled.

Then in August 1867, Johnson suspended Secretary of War Edwin M. Stanton from office. As required by the Tenure of Office Act, which demanded the approval of the Senate for the removal of any government official who had been appointed with Senate approval, the president requested the Senate to consent to the dismissal. When the Senate balked, Johnson removed Stanton anyway. "Is the President crazy, or only drunk?" asked a dumbfounded Republican moderate. "I'm afraid his doings will make us all favor impeachment."

News of Johnson's open defiance of the law convinced every Republican in the House to vote for a resolution impeaching the president. Supreme Court chief justice Salmon Chase presided over the Senate trial, which lasted from March until May 1868. When the critical vote came, thirty-five senators voted guilty and nineteen not guilty. The impeachment forces fell one vote short of the two-thirds needed to convict.

After his trial, Johnson called a truce, and for the remaining ten months of his term, congressional reconstruction proceeded unhindered by presidential interference. Without interference from Johnson, Congress revisited the suffrage issue.

The Fifteenth Amendment and Women's Demands

In February 1869, Republicans passed the **Fifteenth Amendment** to the Constitution, which prohibited states from depriving any citizen of the right to vote

Fifteenth Amendment
▶ Constitutional amendment ratified in 1870 prohibiting states from depriving any citizen of the right to vote because of "race, color, or previous condition of servitude." The Reconstruction Acts of 1867 already required black suffrage in the South; the Fifteenth Amendment extended black suffrage nationwide. Woman suffrage advocates, in particular Susan B. Anthony and Elizabeth Cady Stanton, were disappointed with the Fifteenth Amendment's failure to extend voting rights to women.

CHAPTER LOCATOR | What were Lincoln's plans for wartime reconstruction?

CHAPTER 16
438 RECONSTRUCTING A NATION, 1863–1877

because of "race, color, or previous condition of servitude." The Reconstruction Acts of 1867 already required black suffrage in the South; the Fifteenth Amendment extended black voting nationwide.

Some Republicans, however, found the final wording of the Fifteenth Amendment "lame and halting." Rather than absolutely guaranteeing the right to vote, the amendment merely prohibited exclusion on the grounds of race. The distinction would prove to be significant. In time, white Southerners would devise tests of literacy and property and other apparently nonracial measures that would effectively disfranchise blacks yet not violate the Fifteenth Amendment. But an amendment that fully guaranteed the right to vote courted defeat outside the South. Rising antiforeign sentiment—against the Chinese in California and European immigrants in the Northeast—caused states to resist giving up total control of suffrage requirements. In March 1870, after three-fourths of the states had ratified it, the Fifteenth Amendment became part of the Constitution. Republicans generally breathed a sigh of relief, confident that black suffrage was "the last great point that remained to be settled of the issues of the war."

Woman suffrage advocates, however, were sorely disappointed with the Fifteenth Amendment's failure to extend voting rights to women. Elizabeth Cady Stanton and Susan B. Anthony condemned the Republicans' "negro first" strategy and pointed out that women remained "the only class of citizens wholly unrepresented in the government." Stanton wondered aloud why ignorant black men should legislate for educated and cultured white women. The Fifteenth Amendment severed the early feminist movement from its abolitionist roots. Over the next several decades, feminists established an independent suffrage crusade that drew millions of women into political life.

Republicans took enough satisfaction in the Fifteenth Amendment to promptly scratch the "Negro question" from the agenda of national politics. Even that steadfast crusader for equality Wendell Phillips concluded that the black man now held "sufficient shield in his own hands. . . . Whatever he suffers will be largely now, and in future, his own fault." Northerners had no idea of the violent struggles that lay ahead.

QUICK REVIEW

Why and how did the aims of Congress and the president diverge? What specifically were the issues over which they clashed?

| What vision did Andrew Johnson have for presidential reconstruction? | **How radical was congressional reconstruction?** | How was the battle over reconstruction fought in the South? | Why did reconstruction collapse? | Conclusion: What were the achievements and failures of reconstruction? |

> How was the battle over reconstruction fought in the South?

Black Woman in Cotton Fields, Thomasville, Georgia

Few images of everyday black women during the Reconstruction era survive. This photograph was taken in 1895, but it nevertheless goes to the heart of the labor struggle after the Civil War. Before emancipation, black women worked in the fields; after emancipation, white landlords wanted them to continue working there. Freedom allowed some women to escape field labor, but not this Georgian, who probably worked to survive. Courtesy, Georgia Department of Archives and History, Atlanta, Georgia.

NORTHERNERS BELIEVED THEY HAD discharged their responsibilities with the Reconstruction Acts and the amendments to the Constitution, but Southerners knew that the battle had just begun. Black suffrage established the foundation for the rise of the Republican Party in the South. Gathering together outsiders and outcasts, southern Republicans won elections, wrote new state constitutions, and formed new state governments.

Challenging the established class for political control was dangerous business. Equally dangerous were the confrontations that took place on southern farms and plantations, where blacks sought to give economic meaning to their newly won legal and political equality. Freedom remained contested territory, and Southerners fought pitched battles with one another to determine the contours of their new world.

Freedmen, Yankees, and Yeomen

African Americans made up the majority of southern Republicans. After gaining voting rights in 1867, nearly all eligible black men registered to vote as Republicans. Southern blacks did not have identical political priorities, but they united in their desire for education and equal treatment before the law.

Northern whites who made the South their home after the war were a second element of the South's Republican Party. Conservative white Southerners called

CHAPTER LOCATOR | What were Lincoln's plans for wartime reconstruction?

them carpetbaggers, opportunistic men who put all their belongings in a single carpet-sided suitcase and headed south to "fatten on our misfortunes." But most Northerners who moved south were young men who looked upon the South as they did the West—as a promising place to make a living. Northerners in the southern Republican Party consistently supported programs that encouraged vigorous economic development along the lines of the northern free-labor model.

Southern whites made up the third element of the South's Republican Party. Approximately one out of four white Southerners voted Republican. The other three condemned the one who did as a traitor to his region and his race and called him a scalawag, a term for runty horses and low-down, good-for-nothing rascals. Yeoman farmers accounted for the majority of southern white Republicans. Some were Unionists who emerged from the war with bitter memories of Confederate persecution. Others were small farmers who wanted to end state governments' favoritism toward plantation owners. Yeomen supported initiatives for public schools and for expanding economic opportunity in the South.

The South's Republican Party, then, was made up of freedmen, Yankees, and yeomen—an improbable coalition. The mix of races, regions, and classes inevitably meant friction as each group maneuvered to define the party. But Reconstruction represents an extraordinary moment in American politics: Blacks and whites joined together in the Republican Party to pursue political change. Formally, of course, only men participated in politics—casting ballots and holding offices—but white and black women also played a part in the political struggle by joining in parades and rallies, attending stump speeches, and even campaigning.

Most whites in the South condemned southern Republicans as illegitimate and felt justified in doing whatever they could to stamp them out. Violence against blacks—the "white terror"—took brutal institutional form in 1866 with the formation in Tennessee of the **Ku Klux Klan**, a social club of Confederate veterans that quickly developed into a paramilitary organization supporting Democrats. The Klan went on a rampage of murder and mayhem to defeat Republicans and restore white supremacy. Rapid demobilization of the Union army after the war left only twenty thousand troops to patrol the entire South. Without effective military protection, southern Republicans had to take care of themselves.

Republican Rule

In the fall of 1867, southern states held elections for delegates to state constitutional conventions, as required by the Reconstruction Acts. About 40 percent of the white electorate stayed home because they had been disfranchised or because they had decided to boycott politics. Republicans won three-fourths of the seats. About 15 percent of the Republican delegates to the conventions were Northerners who had moved south, 25 percent were African Americans, and 60 percent were white Southerners. As a British visitor observed, the delegate elections reflected "the mighty revolution that had taken place in America."

The reconstruction constitutions introduced two broad categories of changes in the South: those that reduced aristocratic privilege and increased democratic equality and those that expanded the state's responsibility for the general welfare. In the first category, the constitutions adopted universal male suffrage, abolished property qualifications for holding office, and made more offices elective and fewer appointed. In the second category, they enacted prison reform; made

CHRONOLOGY

1866
- Ku Klux Klan is founded.

1867
- Southern African Americans gain voting rights under the Military Reconstruction Act.
- In elections for state constitutional convention delegates, Republicans win three-fourths of the seats.

1875
- One-half of South Carolina's and Mississippi's children, the majority of whom are black, are attending school.
- Sharecropping is the dominant labor system for rural southern blacks.

Ku Klux Klan

▶ A paramilitary organization formed in Tennessee in 1866 that supported Democrats. With too few Union troops in the South to control the region, the Klan went on a rampage of murder and mayhem to defeat Republicans and restore white supremacy. Legislative efforts by Congress to suppress violence in the South were undermined by failures of enforcement.

What vision did Andrew Johnson have for presidential reconstruction?

How radical was congressional reconstruction?

How was the battle over reconstruction fought in the South?

Why did reconstruction collapse?

Conclusion: What were the achievements and failures of reconstruction?

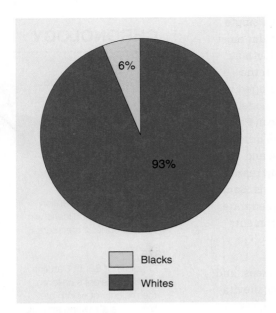

FIGURE 16.1 ■ Southern Congressional Delegations, 1865–1877
The statistics contradict the myth of black domination of congressional representation during Reconstruction.

the state responsible for caring for orphans, the insane, and the deaf and mute; and exempted debtors' homes from seizure.

To Democrats, however, these forward-looking state constitutions looked like wild revolution. Democrats were blind to the fact that no constitution confiscated and redistributed land, as virtually every former slave wished, or disfranchised ex-rebels wholesale, as most southern Unionists advocated. And they were convinced that the new constitutions initiated "Negro domination" in politics. In fact, although 80 percent of Republican voters were black men, only 6 percent of Southerners in Congress during Reconstruction were black (**Figure 16.1**). And no state legislature experienced "Negro rule," despite black majorities in the populations of some states.

Southern voters ratified the new constitutions and swept Republicans into power. When the former Confederate states ratified the Fourteenth Amendment, Congress readmitted them. Southern Republicans then turned to the staggering array of problems that faced them. The southern landscape and economy lay in ruins. Making matters worse, racial harassment and reactionary violence dogged Southerners who sought reform. It was in this context that Republicans struggled to reform and rebuild the region.

Activity focused on three areas—education, civil rights, and economic development. Every state inaugurated a system of public education. Before the Civil War, whites had deliberately kept slaves illiterate, and planter-dominated governments rarely spent tax money to educate the children of yeomen. By 1875, half of Mississippi's and South Carolina's eligible children (the majority of whom were black) were attending school. Although schools were underfunded, literacy rates rose sharply. Public schools were racially segregated, but education remained for many blacks a tangible, deeply satisfying benefit of freedom and Republican rule.

State legislatures also attacked racial discrimination and defended civil rights. Republicans especially resisted efforts to segregate blacks from whites in public transportation. Mississippi levied fines of up to $1,000 and three years in jail for railroads and steamboats that pushed blacks into "smoking cars" or to lower decks. A Mississippian complained: "Money cannot buy for a colored man or woman decent treatment and the comforts that white people claim and can obtain." But passing color-blind laws was one thing; enforcing them was another. Despite the laws, segregation—later called Jim Crow—developed at white insistence and became a feature of southern life long before the end of the Reconstruction era.

Republican governments also launched ambitious programs of economic development. They envisioned a South of diversified agriculture, roaring factories, and booming towns. State legislatures chartered scores of banks and industrial companies, appropriated funds to fix ruined levees and drain swamps, and went on a railroad-building binge. These efforts fell far short of solving the South's economic troubles, however. Republican spending to stimulate economic growth also meant rising taxes and enormous debt, which drained funds from schools and other programs.

The southern Republicans' record, then, was mixed. To their credit, the biracial party took up an ambitious agenda to change the South. Their agenda, however, faced difficult obstacles. Money was scarce, the Democrats continued

CHAPTER LOCATOR | What were Lincoln's plans for wartime reconstruction?

their harassment, and factionalism and corruption threatened the Republican Party from within. Despite shortcomings, however, the Republican Party made headway in its efforts to purge the South of aristocratic privilege and racist oppression. Republican governments had less success in overthrowing the long-established white oppression of black farm laborers in the rural South.

White Landlords, Black Sharecroppers

Ex-slaves who wished to escape slave labor and ex-masters who wanted to reinstitute old ways clashed repeatedly. Except for having to pay subsistence wages, planters had not been required to offer many concessions to emancipation. They continued to believe that African Americans would not work without coercion. Whites moved quickly to restore work regimes that were as close to those of slavery as possible.

Ex-slaves resisted every effort to turn back the clock. They argued that if any class could be described as "lazy," it was the planters, who, as one ex-slave noted, "lived in idleness all their lives on stolen labor." Land of their own would anchor their economic independence, they believed, and end planters' interference in their personal lives. They could then, for example, make their own decisions about whether women and children would labor in the fields. Indeed, within months after the war, perhaps one-third of black women abandoned field labor to work on chores in their own cabins just as poor white women did. Hundreds of thousands of black children enrolled in school. But without their own land, ex-slaves had little choice but to work on plantations.

Although forced to return to the planters' fields, freedmen resisted efforts to restore slavelike conditions. Instead of working for wages, a South Carolinian observed, "the negroes all seem disposed to rent land," which increased their independence from whites. Out of this tug-of-war between white landlords and black laborers emerged a new system of southern agriculture.

Sharecropping was a compromise that offered both ex-masters and ex-slaves something but satisfied neither. Under the new system, planters divided their cotton plantations into small farms that freedmen rented, paying with a share of each year's crop, usually half. Sharecropping gave blacks more freedom than did the system of wages and labor gangs and released them from the day-to-day supervision of whites. Black families abandoned the old slave quarters and scattered over plantations, building separate cabins for themselves on the patches of land they rented (**Map 16.1**). Still, most blacks remained dependent on white landlords, who had the power to expel them at the end of each growing season. For planters, sharecropping offered a way to resume agricultural production, but it did not restore the old slave plantation.

Sharecropping introduced a new figure—the country merchant—into the agricultural equation. Landlords supplied sharecroppers with land, mules, seeds, and tools, but blacks also needed credit to obtain essential food and clothing before they harvested their crops. Thousands of small crossroads stores sprang up to offer credit. Under an arrangement called a crop lien, a merchant would advance goods to a sharecropper in exchange for a lien, or legal claim, on the farmer's future crop. Some merchants charged exorbitant rates of interest, as much as 60 percent, on the goods they sold. At the end of the growing season, after the landlord had taken half of the farmer's crop for rent, the merchant took most of the

sharecropping

▶ System of southern agriculture that emerged in the decade following the Civil War. Under the system, planters divided their cotton plantations into small farms that freedmen rented, paying with a share of each year's crop. Sharecropping gave blacks more freedom than did the system of wages and labor gangs and released them from the day-to-day supervision of whites. White landowners, however, used a variety of tactics, particularly debt, to restrict the freedom of sharecroppers.

What vision did Andrew Johnson have for presidential reconstruction?

How radical was congressional reconstruction?

How was the battle over reconstruction fought in the South?

Why did reconstruction collapse?

Conclusion: What were the achievements and failures of reconstruction?

443

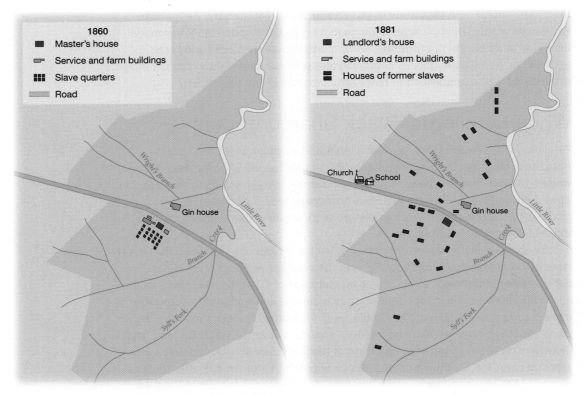

MAP 16.1 ■ A Southern Plantation in 1860 and 1881

These maps of the Barrow plantation in Georgia illustrate some of the ways in which ex-slaves expressed their freedom. Freedmen and freedwomen deserted the clustered living quarters behind the master's house, scattered over the plantation, built family cabins, and farmed rented land. The former Barrow slaves also worked together to build a school and a church.

▶ FOR MORE HELP ANALYZING THIS MAP, see the map activity for this chapter in the Online Study Guide at bedfordstmartins.com/roarkunderstanding.

rest. Sometimes, the farmer's debt to the merchant exceeded the income he received from his remaining half of the crop, and the farmer would have no choice but to borrow more from the merchant and begin the cycle all over again.

An experiment at first, sharecropping spread quickly and soon dominated the cotton South. Lien merchants forced tenants to plant cotton, which was easy to sell, instead of food crops. The result was excessive production of cotton and falling cotton prices, developments that cost thousands of small white farmers their land and pushed them into the ranks of sharecroppers. The new sharecropping system of agriculture took shape just as the political power of Republicans in the South began to buckle under Democratic pressure.

> **QUICK REVIEW**

How did politics and economics shape
the lives of postwar blacks in the South?

CHAPTER LOCATOR | What were Lincoln's plans for wartime reconstruction?

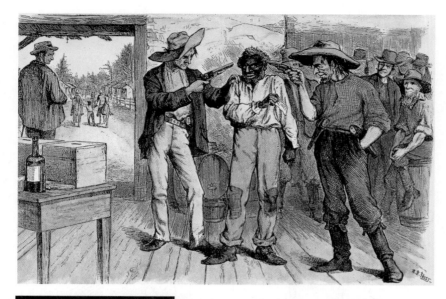

"Of Course He Wants to Vote the Democratic Ticket"

This Republican cartoon from the October 21, 1876, issue of *Harper's Weekly* comments sarcastically on the possibility of honest elections in the South. The caption reads, "You're free as air, ain't you? Say you are or I'll blow yer black head off."
Granger Collection.

> ▶ FOR MORE HELP ANALYZING THIS IMAGE, see the visual activity for this chapter in the Online Study Guide at bedfordstmartins.com/roarkunderstanding.

BY 1870, after a decade of war and reconstruction, Northerners wanted to put "the southern problem" behind them. While northern commitment to defend black freedom eroded, southern commitment to white supremacy intensified. Without northern protection, southern Republicans were no match for the Democrats' economic coercion, political corruption, and bloody violence. The election of 1876 both confirmed and completed the collapse of reconstruction.

Grant's Troubled Presidency

In 1868, the Republican nominee for president was Ulysses S. Grant. Hero of the Civil War and a supporter of congressional reconstruction, Grant was the obvious choice. His Democratic opponent, Horatio Seymour of New York, ran on a platform that blasted congressional reconstruction as "a flagrant usurpation of power . . . unconstitutional, revolutionary, and void." The Republicans answered by waving the bloody shirt—that is, they reminded voters that the Democrats were "the party of rebellion." Grant won a narrow 309,000-vote margin in the popular vote and a substantial victory (214 votes to 80) in the electoral college (**Map 16.2**).

The talents Grant had demonstrated on the battlefield—decisiveness, clarity, and resolution—were less obvious in the White House. He surrounded himself with friends and family

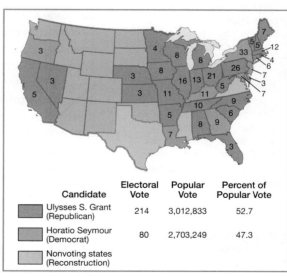

Candidate	Electoral Vote	Popular Vote	Percent of Popular Vote
Ulysses S. Grant (Republican)	214	3,012,833	52.7
Horatio Seymour (Democrat)	80	2,703,249	47.3
Nonvoting states (Reconstruction)			

MAP 16.2 ■ The Election of 1868

What vision did Andrew Johnson have for presidential reconstruction?

How radical was congressional reconstruction?

How was the battle over reconstruction fought in the South?

Why did reconstruction collapse?

Conclusion: What were the achievements and failures of reconstruction?

1868
- Republican Ulysses S. Grant is elected president.

1871
- Ku Klux Klan Act makes interference with voting rights a felony.

1872
- Liberal Party is formed; calls for end of government corruption and the end of reconstruction.
- President Grant is reelected.

1873
- Economic depression sets in for the remainder of the decade.
- In the *Slaughterhouse* cases, the U.S. Supreme Court rules that the Fourteenth Amendment protects only those rights that stem from the federal government.

1874
- Democrats win majority in House of Representatives.

1875
- Civil Rights Act outlaws racial discrimination in transportation, public accommodations, and juries.

1876
- In *United States v. Cruikshank*, the U.S. Supreme Court rules that the reconstruction amendments give Congress the power to legislate against discrimination by states but not by individuals.

1877
- Republican Rutherford B. Hayes assumes presidency; Reconstruction era ends.

Grant and Scandal

This anti-Grant cartoon by Thomas Nast, the nation's most celebrated political cartoonist, shows the president falling headfirst into the barrel of fraud and corruption that tainted his administration. Library of Congress.

▶ FOR MORE HELP ANALYZING THIS IMAGE, see the visual activity for this chapter in the Online Study Guide at bedfordstmartins.com/roarkunderstanding.

and made a string of dubious appointments that led to a series of damaging scandals. Charges of corruption tainted his vice president, Schuyler Colfax, and brought down two of his cabinet officers. Though never personally implicated in any scandal, Grant was seemingly blind to the rot that filled his administration.

In 1872, anti-Grant Republicans bolted and launched the Liberal Party. To clean up the graft and corruption, Liberals proposed the creation of a nonpartisan civil service commission that would oversee competitive examinations for appointment to government offices. Liberals also demanded that the federal government remove its troops from the South and restore "home rule" (southern white control). Democrats liked the Liberals' southern policy and endorsed the Liberal presidential candidate, Horace Greeley, the longtime editor of the *New York Tribune*. The nation, however, still felt enormous affection for the man who had saved the Union and reelected Grant with 56 percent of the popular vote.

Northern Resolve Withers

Although Grant genuinely wanted to see blacks' civil and political rights protected, he understood that most Northerners had grown weary of reconstruction

CHAPTER LOCATOR | What were Lincoln's plans for wartime reconstruction?

and were increasingly willing to let southern whites manage their own affairs. Citizens wanted to shift their attention to other issues, especially after the nation slipped into a devastating economic depression in 1873. More than eighteen thousand businesses collapsed, leaving more than a million workers on the streets. Northern businessmen wanted to invest in the South but believed that recurrent federal intrusion was itself a major cause of instability in the region. Republican leaders began to question the wisdom of their party's alliance with the South's lower classes—its small farmers and sharecroppers. One member of Grant's administration proposed allying with the "thinking and influential native southerners . . . the intelligent, well-to-do, and controlling class."

Congress, too, wanted to leave reconstruction behind, but southern Republicans made that difficult. When the South's Republicans begged for federal protection from Klan violence, Congress enacted three laws in 1870 and 1871 that were intended to break the back of white terrorism. The severest of the three, the Ku Klux Klan Act (1871), made interference with voting rights a felony. Federal marshals arrested thousands of Klansmen and came close to destroying the Klan, but they did not end all terrorism against blacks. Congress also passed the Civil Rights Act of 1875, which boldly outlawed racial discrimination in transportation, public accommodations, and juries. But federal authorities never enforced the law aggressively, and segregated facilities remained the rule throughout the South.

By the early 1870s, the Republican Party had lost its leading champions of African American rights to death or defeat at the polls. Other Republicans concluded that the quest for black equality was mistaken or hopelessly naive. In May 1872, Congress restored the right of officeholding to all but three hundred ex-rebels. Many Republicans had come to believe that traditional white leaders offered the best hope for honesty, order, and prosperity in the South.

Underlying the North's abandonment of reconstruction was unyielding racial prejudice. Northerners had learned to accept black freedom during the war, but deep-seated prejudice prevented many from accepting black equality. Even the actions they took on behalf of blacks often served partisan political advantage. Northerners generally supported Indiana senator Thomas A. Hendricks's harsh declaration that "this is a white man's Government, made by the white man for the white man."

The U.S. Supreme Court also did its part to undermine reconstruction. The Court issued a series of decisions that significantly weakened the federal government's ability to protect black Southerners. In the *Slaughterhouse* cases (1873), the Court distinguished between national and state citizenship and ruled that the Fourteenth Amendment protected only those rights that stemmed from the federal government, such as voting in federal elections and interstate travel. Since the Court decided that most rights derived from the states, it sharply curtailed the federal government's authority to defend black citizens. Even more devastating, the *United States v. Cruikshank* ruling (1876) said that the reconstruction amendments gave Congress the power to legislate against discrimination only by states, not by individuals. The "suppression of ordinary crime," such as assault, remained a state responsibility. The Supreme Court did not declare reconstruction unconstitutional but eroded its legal foundation.

The mood of the North found political expression in the election of 1874, when for the first time in eighteen years the Democrats gained control of the House of Representatives. As one Republican observed, the people had grown

| What vision did Andrew Johnson have for presidential reconstruction? | How radical was congressional reconstruction? | How was the battle over reconstruction fought in the South? | **Why did reconstruction collapse?** | Conclusion: What were the achievements and failures of reconstruction? |

tired of the "negro question, with all its complications, and the reconstruction of Southern States, with all its interminable embroilments." Reconstruction had come apart. Rather than defend reconstruction from its southern enemies, Northerners steadily backed away from the challenge. By the early 1870s, southern Republicans faced the forces of reaction largely on their own.

White Supremacy Triumphs

Republican governments in the South attracted more hatred than any other political regimes in American history. To most whites, Republican rule meant an intolerable reversal of what they saw as the natural racial hierarchy. The northern retreat from reconstruction permitted southern Democrats to set things right.

Taking the name Redeemers, they promised to replace "bayonet rule" (a few federal troops continued to be stationed in the South) with "home rule." They promised that honest, thrifty Democrats would supplant the corrupt and irresponsible tax-and-spend Republicans. Above all, Redeemers swore to save southern civilization from a descent into "African barbarism." As one man put it, "We must render this either a white man's government, or convert the land into a Negro man's cemetery."

Southern Democrats adopted a multipronged strategy to overthrow Republican governments. First, they sought to polarize the parties around color. They went about gathering all the South's white voters into the Democratic Party, leaving the Republicans to depend on blacks, who made up a minority of population in almost every southern state. To dislodge whites from the Republican Party, Democrats fanned the flames of racial prejudice. A South Carolina Democrat crowed that his party appealed to the "proud Caucasian race, whose sovereignty on earth God has proclaimed." Local newspapers published the names of whites who kept company with blacks, and neighbors ostracized offenders.

Democrats also exploited the severe economic plight of small white farmers by blaming it on Republican financial policy. Government spending soared during reconstruction, and small farmers saw their tax burden skyrocket. "This is tax time," a South Carolinian reported. "We are nearly all on our head about them. They are so high & so little money to pay with" that farmers were "selling every egg and chicken they can get." In 1871, Mississippi reported that one-seventh of the state's land—3.3 million acres—had been forfeited for nonpayment of taxes. The small farmers' economic distress had a racial dimension. Because few freedmen succeeded in acquiring land, they rarely paid taxes. In Georgia in 1874, blacks made up 45 percent of the population but paid only 2 percent of the taxes. From the perspective of a small white farmer, Republican rule meant that he was paying more taxes and paying them to aid blacks.

If racial pride, social isolation, and financial hardship proved insufficient to drive yeomen from the Republican Party, Democrats turned to terrorism. "Night riders" targeted white Republicans as well as blacks for murder and assassination. Whether white or black, a "dead Radical is very harmless," South Carolina Democratic leader Martin Gary told his followers.

But the primary victims of white violence were black Republicans. The object was to "kill out the leading men of the republican party," a black Republican from Florida declared. But violence targeted all black voters, not just leaders. And it escalated to unprecedented levels. In 1873, a clash between black militiamen and

CHAPTER LOCATOR | What were Lincoln's plans for wartime reconstruction?

whites in Louisiana killed two white men and an estimated seventy black men. The whites slaughtered half of the black men after they surrendered. Although the federal government indicted more than one hundred of the white men, local juries failed to convict even one.

Even before adopting the all-out white supremacist tactics of the 1870s, Democrats had taken control of the governments of Virginia, Tennessee, and North Carolina. The new campaign brought fresh gains. The Redeemers retook Georgia in 1871, Texas in 1873, and Arkansas and Alabama in 1874. As the state election in Mississippi approached in 1876, Governor Adelbert Ames appealed to Washington for federal troops to control Democratic violence, only to hear from the attorney general that the "whole public are tired of these annual autumnal outbreaks in the South." Abandoned, Mississippi Republicans succumbed to the Democratic onslaught in the fall elections. By 1877, only three Republican state governments survived in the South (**Map 16.3**).

An Election and a Compromise

The year 1876 witnessed one of the most tumultuous elections in American history. The election took place in November, but not until March 2 of the following year did the nation know who would be inaugurated president on March 4. The Democrats nominated New York's governor, Samuel J. Tilden, who immediately targeted the corruption of the Grant administration and the "despotism" of Republican reconstruction. The Republicans put forward Rutherford B. Hayes, governor of Ohio. Privately, Hayes considered "bayonet rule" a mistake but concluded that waving the bloody shirt remained the Republicans' best political strategy.

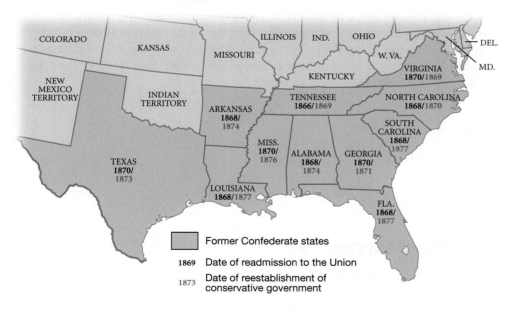

MAP 16.3 ■ The Reconstruction of the South
Myth has it that Republican rule of the former Confederacy was not only harsh but long. In most states, however, conservative southern whites stormed back into power in months or just a few years. By the election of 1876, Republican governments could be found in only three states, and they soon fell.

| What vision did Andrew Johnson have for presidential reconstruction? | How radical was congressional reconstruction? | How was the battle over reconstruction fought in the South? | **Why did reconstruction collapse?** | Conclusion: What were the achievements and failures of reconstruction? |

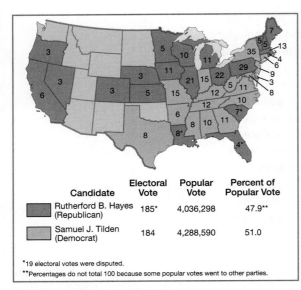

Candidate	Electoral Vote	Popular Vote	Percent of Popular Vote
Rutherford B. Hayes (Republican)	185*	4,036,298	47.9**
Samuel J. Tilden (Democrat)	184	4,288,590	51.0

*19 electoral votes were disputed.
**Percentages do not total 100 because some popular votes went to other parties.

MAP 16.4 ■ The Election of 1876

Compromise of 1877

▶ Political compromise that delivered the presidency to Rutherford B. Hayes. In exchange for a Democratic promise not to block Hayes's inauguration and to deal fairly with the freedmen, Hayes vowed to refrain from using the army to uphold the remaining Republican regimes in the South and to provide the South with substantial federal subsidies for internal improvements. The Compromise of 1877 effectively brought Reconstruction to an end.

On election day, Tilden tallied 4,288,590 votes to Hayes's 4,036,000. But in the all-important electoral college, Tilden fell one vote short of the majority required for victory. The electoral votes of three states—South Carolina, Louisiana, and Florida, the only remaining Republican governments in the South— remained in doubt because both Republicans and Democrats in those states claimed victory. To win, Tilden needed only one of the nineteen contested votes. Hayes had to have all of them.

Congress had to decide who had actually won the elections in the three southern states and thus who would be president. The Constitution provided no guidance for this situation. Moreover, Democrats controlled the House, and Republicans controlled the Senate. Congress created a special electoral commission to arbitrate the disputed returns. All of the commissioners voted their party affiliation, giving every state to the Republican Hayes and putting him over the top in electoral votes (**Map 16.4**).

Some outraged Democrats vowed to resist Hayes's victory. Rumors flew of an impending coup and renewed civil war. But the impasse was broken when negotiations behind the scenes resulted in an informal understanding known as the **Compromise of 1877**. In exchange for a Democratic promise not to block Hayes's inauguration and to deal fairly with the freedmen, Hayes vowed to refrain from using the army to uphold the remaining Republican regimes in the South and to provide the South with substantial federal subsidies for internal improvements.

Stubborn Tilden supporters bemoaned the "stolen election" and damned "His Fraudulency," Rutherford B. Hayes. Old-guard radicals such as William Lloyd Garrison denounced Hayes's bargain as a "policy of compromise, of credulity, of weakness, of subserviency, of surrender." But the nation as a whole celebrated, for the country had weathered a grave crisis. The last three Republican state governments in the South fell quickly once Hayes abandoned them and withdrew the U.S. Army. Reconstruction came to an end.

> **QUICK REVIEW**

How did the decline of northern support for reconstruction help southern Democrats "redeem" the South?

CHAPTER LOCATOR | What were Lincoln's plans for wartime reconstruction?

450 CHAPTER 16 RECONSTRUCTING A NATION, 1863–1877

The Granger Collection, New York.

Conclusion: What were the achievements and failures of reconstruction?

MOST WHITE SOUTHERNERS resisted the passage from slavery to free labor, from white racial despotism to equal justice, and from white political monopoly to biracial democracy. The old elite wanted as little change as possible, while African Americans and some whites were eager to exploit the revolutionary implications of emancipation.

The northern-dominated Republican Congress pushed the revolution along. Congress employed constitutional amendments to require ex-Confederates to accept legal equality and share political power with black men. Conservative southern whites fought ferociously to recover their power and privilege. When Democrats regained control of politics, whites used both state power and private violence to wipe out many of the gains of Reconstruction.

Yet Northern victory in the Civil War ensured that ex-slaves no longer faced the auction block and could send their children to school, worship in their own churches, and work independently on their own rented farms. Sharecropping, with all its hardships, provided more autonomy and economic welfare than bondage had.

The Civil War and emancipation set in motion the most profound upheaval in the nation's history. War destroyed the largest slave society in the New World and gave birth to a modern nation-state. Washington increased its role in national affairs, and the victorious North set the nation's compass toward the expansion of industrial capitalism and the final conquest of the West.

Despite massive changes, however, the Civil War remained only a "half accomplished" revolution. By not fulfilling the promises the nation seemed to hold out to black Americans at war's end, reconstruction represents a tragedy of enormous proportions. The failure to protect blacks and guarantee their rights had enduring consequences. It was the failure of the first reconstruction that made the modern civil rights movement necessary.

> SAML. DOVE wishes to know of the whereabouts of his mother, Areno, his sisters Maria, Neziah, and Peggy, and his brother Edmond, who were owned by Geo. Dove, of Rockingham county, Shenandoah Valley, Va. Sold in Richmond, after which Saml. and Edmond were taken to Nashville, Tenn., by Joe Mick; Areno was left at the Eagle Tavern, Richmond
> Respectfully yours,
> SAML. DOVE.
> Utica, New York, Aug. 5, 1865—3m
> U. S. CHRISTIAN COMMISSION,
> NASHVILLE, TENN., July 19, 1865.

SO NOW YOU KNOW

Even though newly freed African Americans had their own ideas of freedom—family, land, and independence—the politics of Reconstruction in both the North and South and the violent reaction of many white Southerners undermined these hopes. By the end of the era, political rights for most southern blacks were restricted, and economic independence was rare.

What vision did Andrew Johnson have for presidential reconstruction?

How radical was congressional reconstruction?

How was the battle over reconstruction fought in the South?

Why did reconstruction collapse?

Conclusion: What were the achievements and failures of reconstruction?

CHAPTER 16 STUDY GUIDE

STEP 1

GETTING STARTED

Below are basic terms from this period in American history. Can you identify each term below and explain why it matters? To do this exercise online or to download this chart, visit bedfordstmartins.com/roarkunderstanding.

TERM	WHO OR WHAT & WHEN	WHY IT MATTERS
Freedmen's Bureau, p. 430		
Andrew Johnson, p. 432		
black codes, p. 433		
Fourteenth Amendment, p. 435		
Military Reconstruction Act, p. 437		
Fifteenth Amendment, p. 438		
Ku Klux Klan, p. 441		
sharecropping, p. 443		
Compromise of 1877, p. 450		

STEP 2

MOVING BEYOND THE BASICS

The exercise below represents a more advanced understanding of the chapter material. Indicate how each phase of reconstruction addressed the key issues involved. When assessing the achievements and failures of each plan, consider the unintended or indirect consequences. To do this exercise online or to download this chart, visit bedfordstmartins.com/roarkunderstanding.

Phase of reconstruction	Requirements for readmission	Role/rights of freedmen	Achievements	Failures
Wartime reconstruction (Lincoln)				
Presidential reconstruction (Johnson)				
Congressional reconstruction				

Now that you've reviewed various parts of the chapter, take a step back and try to see the big picture by answering these questions. Remember to use specific examples from the chapter in your answers. To do this exercise online, visit bedfordsmartins.com/roarkunderstanding.

SOUTHERN RECONSTRUCTION IN ACTION

▶ How did white Southerners respond during Reconstruction? Consider both Democrats and Republicans in your response.

▶ How did southern African Americans attempt to shape their own lives during Reconstruction?

PRESIDENTIAL AND CONGRESSIONAL RECONSTRUCTION

▶ What role did the black codes play in shaping the course of reconstruction?

▶ What steps did Congress take between 1865 and 1869 to assist ex-slaves in their lives as freedmen? How effective were these actions?

LOOKING BACKWARD, LOOKING AHEAD

▶ How did long-held racial views among whites, in both the South and the North, shape Reconstruction?

▶ What were the lasting accomplishments of Reconstruction? What were its most important failures?

THE END OF RECONSTRUCTION

▶ How and why did the decline of northern support for Reconstruction help southern Democrats "redeem" the South?

▶ Why did white supremacy become the foundation of southern politics in the 1870s?

IN YOUR OWN WORDS

Imagine that you must explain chapter 16 to someone who hasn't read it. What would be the most important points to include and why?

17
CONTESTING THE WEST

1870–1900

> This chapter explores the westward expansion of the late nineteenth century. It examines the impact of expansion on Native Americans, the role mining played in the creation of the American West, and Americans' settlement and exploitation of western lands. Finally, it considers the enduring power of the mythic West in American memory.

> What did American expansion mean for Native Americans?

> How did mining motivate and shape American expansion?

> Who fought for control of the land and resources of the American West?

> Conclusion: What is the meaning of the mythic West?

DID YOU KNOW?

It took the United States less than 40 years to gain control of the western half of the country.

Cliffs of the Upper Colorado, 1882. When artist Thomas Moran arrived in Wyoming Territory in 1871, these towering buttes were his first sight.

What did American expansion mean for Native Americans?

WHILE THE EUROPEAN POWERS expanded their authority and wealth through imperialism and colonialism, establishing far-flung empires abroad, the United States focused its attention on the West. Expansion in the American West involved the conquest, displacement, and rule over native peoples. Removed to Indian Territory or confined on reservations, Indians became wards of the federal government, their culture assaulted by policies designed to force assimilation (**Map 17.1**). Through the lens of colonialism, we can see how the United States' commitment to an imperialist, expansionist ideology resulted in the displacement of Native Americans and the establishment of new territories and eventually states. The colonizing of the West was a dynamic process in which Native Americans actively resisted, contested, and adapted to colonial rule.

Indian Removal and the Reservation System

Manifest destiny—the belief that the United States had a "God-given" right to aggressively spread the values of white civilization and expand the nation from ocean to ocean—dictated U.S. policy. In the name of manifest destiny, Americans forced the removal of the Five Civilized Tribes to Oklahoma; colonized Texas and won its independence from Mexico in 1836; conquered California, Arizona, New Mexico, and parts of Utah and Colorado in the Mexican-American War of 1846–1848; and invaded Oregon in the 1840s.

By midcentury, settlers in unprecedented numbers crossed the Great Plains on their way to the goldfields of California or the rich farmland of Washington and Oregon. In their path stood a solid wall of Indian land, stretching from Minnesota

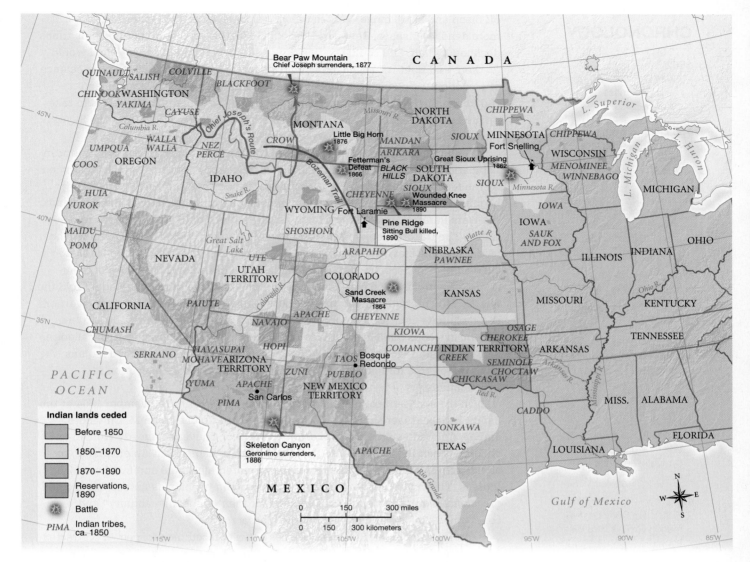

MAP 17.1 ■ The Loss of Indian Lands, 1850–1890

By 1890, western Indians were isolated on small, scattered reservations. Native Americans had struggled to retain their land in major battles, from the Great Sioux Uprising in Minnesota in 1862 to the massacre at Wounded Knee, South Dakota, in 1890.

▶ FOR MORE HELP ANALYZING THIS MAP, see the map activity for this chapter in the Online Study Guide at bedfordstmartins.com/roarkunderstanding.

to Texas, much of it granted through the policy of Indian removal. The "Indian problem" needed to be solved—through treaties if possible or coercion if necessary. In 1851, some ten thousand Plains Indians came together at Fort Laramie in Wyoming to negotiate a treaty that ceded a wide swath of their land to allow passage of the wagon trains. In return, the government promised that the rest of the Indian land would remain inviolate.

The Indians who "touched the pen" to the 1851 Treaty of Fort Laramie hoped to preserve their culture in the face of the white onslaught on their people and land. White invaders cut down trees, miners polluted streams, and hunters killed

CHAPTER LOCATOR | What did American expansion mean for Native Americans? | How did mining motivate and shape American expansion? | Who fought for control of the land and resources of the American West? | Conclusion: What is the meaning of the mythic West?

457

CHRONOLOGY

1862
- Great Sioux Uprising leads to the largest mass execution in American history.

1864
- Sand Creek Massacre, in which Colorado militiamen kill 270 Cheyenne Indians.

1867
- Treaty of Medicine Lodge negotiates peace with southern Plains Indians.

1868
- Sioux victories on the northern plains lead to U.S. concessions at the second Treaty of Fort Laramie.

1876
- At the Battle of the Little Big Horn, Sioux forces decimate the U.S. cavalry led by George Armstrong Custer.

1882
- Indian Rights Association, composed of whites sympathetic to the Indian cause, is formed.

1883
- Buffalo Bill Cody begins touring with his Wild West show.

1887
- Dawes Allotment Act provides for the breakup of reservation lands.

1889
- The Ghost Dance movement, a spiritual revival, spreads among Indians across the West.

1890
- At Wounded Knee, South Dakota, U.S. cavalry massacre more than two hundred Sioux followers of the Ghost Dance.

off bison and small game. Whites brought alcohol, guns, and something even more deadly—disease. Between 1780 and 1870, the population of the Plains tribes declined by half. "If I could see this thing, if I knew where it came from, I would go there and fight it," a Cheyenne warrior anguished. Disease shifted the balance of power on the plains from Woodland agrarian tribes like the Mandan and Hidatsa to the Lakota (Western) Sioux, who fled the contagion of villages to take up life as equestrian (horse-riding) nomads on the western plains. As the Sioux pushed west, they displaced weaker tribes.

The Indian wars in the West marked the last resistance of a Native American population devastated by disease and demoralized by the removal policy pursued by the federal government. More accurately called "settlers' wars" (since they began with "peaceful settlers," often miners, overrunning Native American land), the wars flared up again only a few years after the signing of the Fort Laramie treaty. The Dakota Sioux in Minnesota went to war in 1862. For years, under the leadership of Chief Little Crow, the Dakota, also known as the Santee, had pursued a policy of accommodation, ceding land in return for the promise of annuities. But with his people on the verge of starvation (the local Indian agent told the hungry Dakota, "Go and eat grass"), Little Crow reluctantly led his angry warriors in a desperate campaign against the intruders, killing more than 1,000 settlers. American troops quelled what was called the Great Sioux Uprising (also called the Santee Uprising) and marched 1,700 Sioux to Fort Snelling, where 400 Indians were put on trial for murder and 38 died in the largest mass execution in American history.

On the southern plains, the conflict reached its nadir in November 1864 at the Sand Creek Massacre in Colorado Territory. There Colonel John M. Chivington and his Colorado militia descended on a village of Cheyenne, mostly women and children. Their leader, Black Kettle, raised a white flag and an American flag to signal surrender, but the charging cavalry ignored his signal and butchered 270 Indians. The city of Denver treated Chivington and his men as heroes, but a congressional inquiry castigated the soldiers for their "fiendish malignity" and condemned the "savage cruelty" of the massacre.

After the Civil War, President Ulysses S. Grant faced the prospect of protracted Indian war on the Great Plains. Reluctant to spend more money and sacrifice more lives in battle, Grant adopted a "peace policy" designed to segregate and control the Indians while opening up land to white settlers. The government sought control of Indian lands and promised in return to pay annuities and put the Indians on lands reserved for their use—reservations. This policy won the support of both friends of the Indians, who feared for their survival, and Indian haters, who coveted their land and wished to confine them to the least desirable areas in the West. General William Tecumseh Sherman summed up the new Indian policy succinctly: "Remove all to a safe place and then reduce them to a helpless condition."

Poverty and starvation stalked the reservations (see Map 17.1, page 457). Confined by armed force, the Indians eked out an existence on stingy government rations. They found themselves dependent on government handouts and the assistance of Indian agents who, in the words of Paiute Sarah Winnemucca, did "nothing but fill their pockets." Winnemucca launched a lecture campaign in the United States and Europe denouncing the government's reservation policy.

Indian reservations soon became cultural battlegrounds. Reservations closely resembled colonial societies where native populations, ruled by outside bureau-

crats, saw their culture assaulted, their religious practices outlawed, their children sent away to school, and their way of life attacked in the name of progress and civilization. Self-styled "friends of the Indians," many of them easterners with little experience in the West, maintained that reservations would provide a classroom of civilization where Indians could be taught to speak English, to worship a Christian god, to give up hunting for farming, and to reject tribal ways.

The white reformers also proposed that Indian children be sent to off-reservation boarding schools. At these schools, children as young as seven were forced to adopt white dress, manners, culture, and language. While many boarding schools were in the West, a few—including the famous Carlisle Indian School in Pennsylvania—were hundreds of miles from the reservations. To a large extent, the plan, in the words of Carlisle founder Richard Henry Pratt, to "kill the Indian and save the man" failed. Instead, Indian children from different tribes formed bonds and a new sense of pan-Indian identity. In the face of this assault on their cultures, Indians found ways to resist, adapt, and hold on to their cultural identity.

The Decimation of the Great Bison Herds and the Fight for the Black Hills

By the nineteenth century, more than two hundred years of contact with whites had utterly transformed Native American societies. Indians had been pushed off their lands east of the Mississippi and moved west. Through trade with the Spaniards and French, Indians had acquired horses and guns. The Sioux, hunting on horseback, staked their survival on the buffalo (American bison). But the great herds, once numbering as many as thirty million, fell into decline. A host of environmental and human factors contributed to the destruction of the bison. By the 1850s, a combination of drought and buffalo hunting had driven the great herds onto the far western plains.

After the Civil War, the accelerating pace of industrial expansion brought about the near extinction of the bison. Industrial demand for heavy leather belting

CHAPTER LOCATOR | What did American expansion mean for Native Americans? | How did mining motivate and shape American expansion? | Who fought for control of the land and resources of the American West? | Conclusion: What is the meaning of the mythic West?

459

used in machinery and the development of larger, more accurate rifles combined to hasten the slaughter of the bison. At the same time, the nation's growing transcontinental rail system cut the range in two and divided the herds. "It will not be long before all the buffaloes are extinct near and between the railroads," Ohio senator John Sherman predicted in 1868. The army took credit for the conquest of the Plains Indians, but victory came about largely as a result of the decimation of the great bison herds. General Philip Sheridan acknowledged as much when he applauded white hide hunters for "destroying the Indians' commissary." With their food supply gone, Indians had to choose between starvation and the reservation. "A cold wind blew across the prairie when the last buffalo fell," the great Sioux leader **Sitting Bull** lamented, "a death wind for my people."

On the southern plains in 1867, more than five thousand warring Comanches, Kiowas, and Southern Arapahos gathered at Medicine Lodge Creek in Kansas to negotiate a treaty. Satak, or Sitting Bear, a prominent Kiowa chief and medicine man, explained why the Indians sought peace: "In the far-distant past . . . the world seemed large enough for both the red man and the white man." But, he observed, "its broad plains seem now to contract, and the white man grows jealous of his red brother." To preserve their land from white encroachment, the Indians signed the Treaty of Medicine Lodge, agreeing to move to a reservation. But after 1870, hide hunters poured into the region, and within a decade, they had nearly exterminated the southern bison herds. Luther Standing Bear recounted the sight and stench: "I saw the bodies of hundreds of dead buffalo lying about, just wasting, and the odor was terrible. . . . They were letting our food lie on the plains to rot."

On the northern plains, gold sparked the conflict between Indians and Euro-Americans. In 1866, the Cheyenne united with the Sioux in Wyoming to protect their hunting grounds in the Powder River valley, which were threatened by the construction of the Bozeman Trail connecting Fort Laramie with the goldfields in Montana. Impressive Sioux victories led to the **1868 Treaty of Fort Laramie**, in which the United States agreed to abandon the Bozeman Trail and guaranteed the Indians control of the Black Hills, land sacred to the Lakota Sioux. The treaty was vague and full of contradictions. Nonetheless, some tribes accepted it. The great Sioux chief Red Cloud led many of his people onto the reservation. Red Cloud soon regretted his decision. "Think of it!" he told a visitor to the Pine Ridge Reservation. "I, who used to own . . . country so extensive that I could not ride through it in a week . . . must tell Washington when I am hungry. I must beg for that which I own." Several Sioux chiefs, among them Crazy Horse of the Oglala band and Sitting Bull of the Hunkpapa, refused to sign the treaty. Crazy Horse said that he wanted no part of the "piecemeal penning" of his people.

In 1874, the discovery of gold in the Black Hills of the Dakotas led the government to break its promise to Red Cloud. At first, the government offered to purchase the Black Hills. But to the Lakota Sioux, the Black Hills were sacred—"the heart of everything that is." They refused to sell. The army responded by issuing an ultimatum ordering all Lakota Sioux and Northern Cheyenne bands onto the Pine Ridge Reservation and threatening to hunt down those who refused.

In the summer of 1876, the army launched a three-pronged attack led by Lieutenant Colonel George Armstrong Custer, General George Crook, and Colonel John Gibbon. Crazy Horse stopped Crook at the Battle of the Rosebud. Custer,

Sitting Bull

▶ Great Sioux leader of the second half of the nineteenth century. Sitting Bull was among those who refused to sign the two Treaties of Fort Laramie (1851 and 1868). Along with Crazy Horse, he led Indian forces at the Battle of Little Big Horn. Sitting Bull surrendered in 1881. When, in 1890, Sitting Bull joined the Ghost Dance, he was killed by Indian police as they tried to arrest him.

1868 Treaty of Fort Laramie

▶ Treaty with the Sioux in which the United States agreed to abandon the Bozeman Trail and guarantee Sioux control of the Black Hills. The treaty was signed following a brief war with the Sioux on the northern plains.

leading the second prong of the army's offensive, divided his troops and ordered an attack. On June 25, he spotted signs of the Indians' camp and, crying "Hurrah Boys, we've got them," led 265 men of the Seventh Cavalry into the largest Indian camp ever assembled on the Great Plains. Indian warriors led by Sitting Bull and Crazy Horse set upon Custer and his men and quickly annihilated them. "It took us about as long as a hungry man to eat his dinner," the Cheyenne chief Two Moons recalled.

"Custer's Last Stand," as the **Battle of the Little Big Horn** was styled in myth, turned out to be the last stand for the Sioux. The bands that had massed at the Little Big Horn scattered, and the army hunted them down. "Wherever we went," wrote the Oglala holy man Black Elk, "the soldiers came to kill us." In 1877, Crazy Horse was captured and killed. Four years later, in 1881, Sitting Bull surrendered. The government took the Black Hills and confined the Lakota to the Great Sioux Reservation. The Sioux never accepted the loss of the Black Hills. In 1923, they filed suit, demanding the return of the land taken illegally from them. After a protracted court battle lasting nearly sixty years, the U.S. Supreme Court ruled in 1980 that the government had illegally abrogated the Treaty of Fort Laramie and upheld an award of $122.5 million in compensation to the tribes. The Sioux refused the settlement and continue to press for the return of the Black Hills.

The Dawes Act and Indian Land Allotment

In the 1880s, the practice of rounding up Indians and herding them onto reservations lost momentum in favor of allotment—a new policy designed to encourage assimilation through farming and the ownership of private property. Pressure for this shift in policy came both from white Americans who coveted reservation lands and from those who were appalled at the desperate poverty on the reservations and feared for the Indians' survival. Helen Hunt Jackson, in her classic work *A Century of Dishonor* (1881), convinced many readers that the Indians had been treated unfairly. "Our Indian policy," *the New York Times* concluded, "is usually spoliation behind the mask of benevolence."

The Indian Rights Association, a group of mainly white easterners formed in 1882, campaigned for the dismantling of the reservations, now viewed as obstacles to progress. To "cease to treat the Indian as a red man and treat him as a man" meant putting an end to tribal communalism and fostering individualism. "Selfishness," declared Senator Henry Dawes of Massachusetts, "is at the bottom of civilization." Dawes called for "allotment in severalty"—the institution of private property.

In 1887, Congress passed the **Dawes Allotment Act**, dividing up reservations and allotting parcels of land to individual Indians as private property.

Provisions of the Dawes Allotment Act

Indian heads of household received an allotment of 160 acres from reservation lands.
Single persons over eighteen and orphans under eighteen received 80 acres.
Indians who took allotments earned U.S. citizenship.
The government reserved the right to sell "surplus" reservation lands to white settlers.

Battle of the Little Big Horn
▶ Battle between Sioux warriors led by Crazy Horse and Sitting Bull and American cavalry led by George Armstrong Custer. When Custer charged into a Sioux encampment, he and his men were killed. The Battle of Little Big Horn was a major military victory for the Sioux, but their success was shortlived.

Dawes Allotment Act
▶ 1887 law that divided up reservations and allotted parcels of land to individual Indians as private property. In the end, the American government sold almost two-thirds of Indian land to white settlers. The Dawes Act dealt a crippling blow to traditional tribal culture.

CHAPTER LOCATOR | What did American expansion mean for Native Americans? | How did mining motivate and shape American expansion? | Who fought for control of the land and resources of the American West? | Conclusion: What is the meaning of the mythic West?

461

As a result of the Dawes Act, Indian land dropped from 138 million acres in 1887 to a scant 48 million in 1934. The legislation, in the words of one critic, worked "to despoil the Indians of their lands and to make them vagabonds on the face of the earth." The Dawes Act completed the dispossession of the western Indian peoples and dealt a crippling blow to traditional tribal culture. It remained in effect until 1934, when the United States restored the right of Native Americans to own land communally (see chapter 24).

Indian Resistance and Survival

Faced with the extinction of their entire way of life, different groups of Indians responded in different ways in the waning decades of the nineteenth century. Some tribes, including the Crow, Arikara, Pawnee, and Shoshoni, fought along-side the U.S. Army against their old enemies, the Sioux. The Crow chief Plenty Coups explained why he allied with the United States: "Not because we loved the white man . . . or because we hated the Sioux . . . but because we plainly saw that this course was the only one which might save our beautiful country for us." The Crow and Shoshoni got to stay in their homelands and avoided the fate of other tribes shipped to reservations far away.

Indians who refused to stay on reservations risked being hunted down. The Nez Percé war of 1877 is perhaps the most harrowing example of the army's policy. In 1863, the government dictated a treaty drastically reducing Nez Percé land. Most of the chiefs refused to sign the treaty and did not move to the reservation. In 1877, the army issued an ultimatum—come in to the reservation or be hunted down. Some eight hundred Nez Percé people, many of them women and children, fled across the mountains of Idaho, Wyoming, and Montana, heading for the safety of Canada. Only 50 miles from the border, after a 1,300-mile journey, the army caught up with them and attacked. Yellow Wolf recalled their plight: "Children crying with cold. No fire. There could be no light. Everywhere the crying, the death wail." After a five-day siege, the Nez Percé leader, Chief Joseph, surrendered. His speech, reported by a white soldier, would become famous. "I am tired of fighting," he said as he surrendered his rifle. "Our chiefs are killed. It is cold and we have no blankets. The little children are freezing to death. . . . I am tired. My heart is sick and sad. From where the sun now stands, I will fight no more forever."

In the Southwest, the Apaches resorted to armed resistance. They roamed the Sonoran Desert of southern Arizona and northern Mexico, perfecting a hit-and-run guerrilla warfare in the 1870s and 1880s. General George Crook combined a policy of dogged pursuit with judicious diplomacy. Crook relied on Indian scouts to track the raiding parties, recruiting nearly two hundred, including Apaches along with Navajos and Paiutes. By 1882, Crook had succeeded in per-suading most of the Apaches to settle on the San Carlos Reservation in Arizona Territory. A desolate piece of desert inhabited by scorpions and rattlesnakes, San Carlos, in the words of one Apache, was "the worst place in all the great territory stolen from the Apaches."

Geronimo, a respected shaman (medicine man) of the Chiricahua Apache, refused to stay at San Carlos and repeatedly led raiding parties in the early 1880s. His warriors attacked ranches to obtain ammunition and horses. In the

Geronimo

▶ Chiricahua Apache shaman (medicine man) who refused to stay at the San Carlos Reservation and repeatedly led raiding parties in the early 1880s. Geronimo and his band were captured in September 1886. Although fewer than three dozen Apaches had been identified as "hostiles," the government rounded up nearly five hundred Apaches, including the scouts who had helped track Geronimo, and sent them as prisoners to Florida.

Ghost Dancers

Arapaho women at the Darlington Agency in Indian Territory (Oklahoma) participate in the Ghost Dance. Different tribes performed variations of the dance, but generally dancers formed a circle and danced until they reached the trancelike state shown here. National Anthropological Archives, Smithsonian Institution, Washington, D.C. (#81-9626).

spring of 1885, Geronimo and his followers went on a ten-month offensive, moving from the Apache sanctuary in the Sierra Madre to raid and burn ranches and towns on both sides of the Mexican border. General Crook caught up with Geronimo in the fall and persuaded him to return to San Carlos, only to have him slip away on the way back to the reservation. Chagrined, Crook resigned his post. General Nelson Miles, Crook's replacement, adopted a policy of hunt and destroy.

Geronimo's band of thirty-three Apaches, including women and children, managed to elude Miles's troops for more than five months. Eventually, Miles's scouts cornered Geronimo in 1886 at Skeleton Canyon. Caught between Mexican regulars and the U.S. Army, Geronimo agreed to march north with the soldiers and negotiate a settlement. "We have not slept for six months," he admitted, "and we are worn out." Although fewer than three dozen Apaches had been considered "hostile," when General Miles induced them to surrender, the government rounded up nearly five hundred Apaches, including the scouts who had helped track Geronimo, and sent them as prisoners to Florida.

On the plains, many tribes turned to a nonviolent form of resistance—a new religion called the **Ghost Dance**. The Paiute shaman Wovoka, drawing on a cult that had developed in the 1870s, combined elements of Christianity and traditional Indian religion to found the Ghost Dance religion in 1889. Wovoka claimed that he had received a vision in which the Great Spirit spoke through him to all

Ghost Dance

▶ New religion that served as a nonviolent form of resistance for Indians in the late nineteenth century. The Paiute shaman Wovoka combined elements of Christianity and traditional Indian religion to found the Ghost Dance religion in 1889. The Ghost Dance frightened whites and was violently suppressed.

CHAPTER LOCATOR | What did American expansion mean for Native Americans? | How did mining motivate and shape American expansion? | Who fought for control of the land and resources of the American West? | Conclusion: What is the meaning of the mythic West?

463

Indians, prophesying that if they would unite in the Ghost Dance ritual, whites would be destroyed in an apocalypse. This religion, born of despair and carrying a message of hope, spread like wildfire over the plains. The Ghost Dance was performed in Idaho, Montana, Utah, Wyoming, Colorado, Nebraska, Kansas, the Dakotas, and Indian Territory by tribes as diverse as the Sioux, Arapaho, Cheyenne, Pawnee, and Shoshoni.

The Ghost Dance was nonviolent, but it frightened whites, especially when the Sioux taught that wearing a white ghost shirt made Indians immune to soldiers' bullets. Soon whites began to fear an uprising. "Indians are dancing in the snow and are wild and crazy," wrote the Bureau of Indian Affairs agent at the Pine Ridge Reservation in South Dakota. Frantic, he pleaded for reinforcements. "We are at the mercy of these dancers. We need protection, and we need it now." President Benjamin Harrison dispatched several thousand federal troops to Sioux country.

In December 1890, when Sitting Bull joined the Ghost Dance, he was killed by Indian police as they tried to arrest him at his cabin on the Standing Rock Reservation. His people, fleeing the scene, joined with a larger group of Miniconjou Sioux, who were apprehended by the Seventh Cavalry near Wounded Knee Creek, South Dakota. As the Indians laid down their arms, a shot rang out, and the soldiers opened fire. In the ensuing melee, more than two hundred Sioux men, women, and children were killed. Settler Jules Sandoz surveyed the scene the day after the massacre at **Wounded Knee**. "Here in ten minutes an entire community was as the buffalo that bleached on the plains," he wrote. "There was something loose in the world that hated joy and happiness as it hated brightness and color, reducing everything to drab agony and gray." It had taken Euro-Americans 250 years to wrest control of the eastern half of the United States from the Indians. It took them less than 40 years to take the western half. The subjugation of the Native Americans marked the first chapter in a national mission of empire that would later lead to overseas imperialistic adventures in Asia, Latin America, the Caribbean, and the Pacific Islands.

Wounded Knee

▶ December 1890 massacre of Sioux Indians by American cavalry at Wounded Knee Creek, South Dakota. Sent to suppress the Ghost Dance, the soldiers opened fire on a group of Sioux as they attempted to surrender. More than two hundred Sioux men, women, and children were killed.

> ## QUICK REVIEW

How did U.S. policy toward Native Americans change between 1870 and 1900?

"Mining on the Comstock" This illustration, made at Gold Hill, Nevada, in 1876, shows a sectional view of a mine, including the tunnels, incline, cooling-off room, blower, and air shaft, along with a collection of miner's tools. University of California at Berkeley, Bancroft Library.

> ► FOR MORE HELP ANALYZING THIS IMAGE, see the visual activity for this chapter in the Online Study Guide at bedfordstmartins.com/ roarkunderstanding.

MINING STOOD AT THE CENTER of the United States' quest for empire in the West. The California gold rush of 1849 touched off the frenzy. The four decades following witnessed equally frenetic rushes for gold and other metals, most notably on the Comstock Lode in Nevada and later in New Mexico, Colorado, the Dakotas, Montana, Idaho, Arizona, and Utah. The diverse peoples drawn to the West by the promise of mining riches made the region the most cosmopolitan in the nation. A close look at mining on the Comstock Lode indicates some of the patterns and paradoxes of western mining. And a look at territorial government uncovers striking parallels with corruption and cupidity in politics east of the Mississippi (**Map 17.2**).

Mining on the Comstock Lode

By 1859, refugees from California's played-out goldfields flocked to the Washoe basin in Nevada. While searching for gold, Washoe miners stumbled on the richest vein of silver ore on the continent—the legendary **Comstock Lode**, named for prospector Henry Comstock. To exploit even potentially valuable silver claims required capital and expensive technology well beyond the means of the prospector. An active San Francisco stock market sprang up to finance operations on the Comstock. Shrewd businessmen soon recognized that the easiest way to get rich was not to mine at all but to sell their claims or to form mining companies and sell shares of stock. Speculation, misrepresentation, and outright thievery ran rampant. In twenty years, more than $300 million poured from the earth in Nevada alone, most of it going to speculators in California.

Comstock Lode
► Silver ore deposit discovered in 1859 in the Washoe basin in Nevada. Discovery of the Comstock Lode touched off an influx of people into the region and led to the establishment of a number of boomtowns, including Virginia City, Nevada. By 1875, Virginia City had a diverse population of about 25,000 people.

CHAPTER LOCATOR | What did American expansion mean for Native Americans? | **How did mining motivate and shape American expansion?** | Who fought for control of the land and resources of the American West? | Conclusion: What is the meaning of the mythic West?

465

CHRONOLOGY

1859
– Initial discovery of Comstock Lode in Nevada.

1870
– Women constitute 30 percent of the population of Virginia City, Nevada.

1873
– Miners uncover "Big Bonanza" on Comstock Lode.

1875
– Population of Virginia City, Nevada, reaches 25,000.

1882
– Chinese Exclusion Act effectively bars Chinese immigration.

MAP 17.2 ■ Western Mining, 1848–1890

Rich deposits of gold, silver, copper, lead, and iron larded the mountains of the West, from the Sierra Nevada of California to the Rockies of Colorado and the Black Hills of South Dakota. Miners from all over the world flocked to the West. Few struck it rich, but many stayed on as paid workers in the increasingly mechanized corporate mines. Source: After Francaviglia.

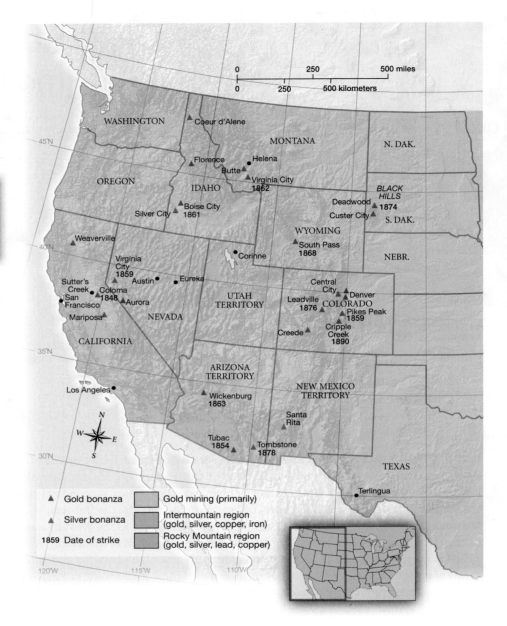

The promise of gold and silver drew thousands to the mines of the West. As Mark Twain observed, the Comstock attracted an international array of immigrants. "All the peoples of the earth had representative adventures in the Silverland," he wrote. Irish, Chinese, Germans, English, Scots, Welsh, Canadians, Mexicans, Italians, Scandinavians, French, Swiss, Chileans, and other South and Central Americans came to share in the bonanza. With them came a sprinkling of Russians, Poles, Greeks, Japanese, Spaniards, Hungarians, Portuguese, Turks, Pacific Islanders, and Moroccans, as well as other North Americans, African Americans, and American Indians. This polyglot population, typical of mining boomtowns, made Virginia City, Nevada (a boomtown created by the Comstock Lode), in the 1870s more cosmopolitan than New York or Boston. In the part of

Utah Territory that eventually became Nevada, as many as 30 percent of the people came from outside the United States, compared with 25 percent in New York and 21 percent in Massachusetts.

Irish immigrants formed the largest ethnic group in the mining district. In Virginia City, fully one-third of the population claimed at least one parent from Ireland. Irish and Irish American women constituted the largest group of women on the Comstock. As servants, boardinghouse owners, and washer-women, they made up a significant part of the workforce. In contrast, the Chinese community, numbering 642 in 1870, remained overwhelmingly male. Virulent anti-Chinese sentiment barred the men from work in the mines, but despite the violent anti-Asian rhetoric, the mining community came to depend on Chinese domestic labor.

The discovery of precious metals on the Comstock spelled disaster for the Indians. No sooner had the miners struck pay dirt than they demanded army troops to "hunt Indians" and establish forts to protect transportation to and from the diggings. This sudden and dramatic intrusion left Nevada's native tribes—the Northern Paiute and Bannock Shoshoni—exiles in their own land. At first they resisted, but over time they made peace with the invaders and proved resourceful in finding ways to adapt and preserve their culture and identity.

In 1873, Comstock miners uncovered a new vein of ore. This "Big Bonanza" speeded the transition from small-scale industry to corporate oligopoly, creating a radically new social and economic environment. The Comstock became a labora-tory for new mining technology. Huge stamping mills pulverized rock with piston-like hammers driven by steam engines. Enormous Cornish pumps sucked water from the mine shafts, and huge ventilators circulated air in the underground chambers. Virginia City quickly grew into an industrial center with more than 1,200 stamping mills working on average a ton of ore every day. Almost 400 men worked in milling, nearly 300 labored in manufacturing industries, and roughly 3,000 toiled in the mines. Most of the miners who came to the Comstock ended up as laborers for the big companies.

New technology eliminated some of the dangers of mining but often created new ones. In the hard-rock mines of the West, accidents in the 1870s disabled 1 out of every 30 miners and killed 1 in 80. Ross Moudy, who worked as a miner in Cripple Creek, Colorado, recalled how a stockholder visiting the mine nearly fell to his death. The terrified visitor told the miner next to him that "instead of being paid $3 a day, they ought to have all the gold they could take out." On the Com-stock Lode, because of the difficulty of obtaining skilled labor, the richness of the ore, and the need for a stable workforce, labor unions formed early and held con-siderable bargaining power. Comstock miners commanded $4 a day, the highest wage in the mining West.

The mining towns of the "Wild West" are often portrayed as lawless out-posts, filled with saloons and rough gambling dens and populated almost exclu-sively by men. The truth is more complex, as Virginia City's development attests. An established urban community built to serve an industrial giant, Virginia City in its first decade boasted churches, schools, theaters, an opera house, and hundreds of families. By 1870, women composed 30 percent of the population, and 75 percent of the women listed their occupation in the census as housekeeper. Mary McNair Mathews, a widow from Buffalo, New York, who lived on the Comstock in the 1870s, worked as a teacher, nurse, seamstress, laundress, and

CHAPTER LOCATOR | What did American expansion mean for Native Americans? | **How did mining motivate and shape American expansion?** | Who fought for control of the land and resources of the American West? | Conclusion: What is the meaning of the mythic West?

467

lodging-house operator. She later published a book on her adventures. By 1875, Virginia City boasted a population of 25,000 people, making it one of the largest cities between St. Louis and San Francisco.

The Diverse Peoples of the West

The West of the late nineteenth century was a polyglot place, as much so as the big cities of the East. The sheer number of peoples who mingled in the West produced a complex blend of racism and prejudice. One historian has noted, not entirely facetiously, that the West was home to at least eight oppressed "races"— Indians, Latinos, Chinese, Japanese, blacks, Mormons, strikers, and radicals.

African Americans who ventured out to the territories faced hostile settlers determined to keep the West "for whites only." In response, they formed all-black communities such as Nicodemus, Kansas. That settlement, founded by thirty black Kentuckians in 1877, grew to a community of seven hundred by 1880. Isolated and often separated by great distances, small black settlements grew up throughout the West, in Nevada, Utah, and the Pacific Northwest as well as in Kansas. Black soldiers who served in the West during the Indian wars often stayed on as settlers. Called buffalo soldiers because Native Americans thought their hair resembled that of the buffalo, these black troops numbered up to 25,000. In the face of discrimination, poor treatment, and harsh conditions, the buffalo soldiers served with distinction and boasted the lowest desertion rate in the army.

Hispanic peoples had lived in Texas and the Southwest since Juan de Oñate led pioneer settlers up the Rio Grande in 1598. Hispanics had occupied the Pacific coast since San Diego was founded in 1769. Overnight, they were reduced to a "minority" after the United States annexed Texas in 1845 and took land stretching to California after the Mexican-American War ended in 1848. At first, the Hispanic owners of large *ranchos* in California, New Mexico, and Texas greeted conquest as an economic opportunity. But racial prejudice soon ended their optimism. Californios (Mexican residents of California), who had been granted American citizenship by the Treaty of Guadalupe Hidalgo (1848), faced discrimination by Anglos who sought to keep them out of California's mines and commerce. Whites illegally squatted on *rancho* land while protracted litigation over Spanish and Mexican land grants forced the Californios into court. Although the U.S. Supreme Court eventually validated most of their claims, it took so long—seventeen years on average—that many Californios sold their property to pay taxes and legal bills.

Swindles, chicanery, and intimidation dispossessed scores of Californios. Many ended up segregated in urban barrios (neighborhoods) in their own homeland. Their percentage of California's population declined from 82 percent in 1850 to 19 percent in 1880 as Anglos migrated to the state. In New Mexico and Texas, Mexicans remained a majority of the population but became increasingly impoverished as Anglos dominated business and took the best jobs. Skirmishes between Hispanics and whites in northern New Mexico over the fencing of the open range lasted for decades. In Texas, violence along the Rio Grande pitted Tejanos (Mexican residents of Texas) against the Texas Rangers, who saw their role as "keeping Mexicans in their place."

Like the Mexicans, the Mormons faced prejudice and hostility. The followers of Joseph Smith, the founder and prophet of the Church of Jesus Christ of Latter-Day Saints, fled west to avoid religious persecution. They believed that they had a divine right to the land, and their messianic militancy contributed to making them outcasts. The Mormon practice of polygamy (a man taking more than one wife) became a convenient point of attack for those who hated and feared the group. After Smith was killed by an Illinois mob in 1844, Brigham Young led more than 20,000 Mormons over the Rockies to the valley of the Great Salt Lake in Utah Territory. The Mormons quickly set to work irrigating the desert. They relied on cooperation and communalism, a strategy that excluded competition from those outside the faith. By 1882, the Mormons had built Salt Lake City, a thriving metropolis of more than 150,000 residents.

The Mormon practice of polygamy (Brigham Young had twenty-seven wives) had come under attack as early as 1857, when U.S. troops occupied Salt Lake City (see chapter 12). To counter criticism of polygamy, the Utah territorial legislature gave women the right to vote in 1870, the first universal woman suffrage act in the nation. (Wyoming had granted suffrage to white women in 1869.) Although women's rights advocates argued that the newly enfranchised women would "do away with the horrible institution of polygamy," it remained in force. Not until 1890 did the church hierarchy give in to pressure to renounce polygamy. The fierce controversy over polygamy postponed statehood for Utah until 1896.

The Chinese suffered brutal treatment at the hands of employers and other laborers. Drawn by the promise of gold, more than 20,000 Chinese had joined the rush to California by 1852. Miners determined to keep "California for Americans" succeeded in passing prohibitive foreign license laws to keep the Chinese out of the mines. But Chinese immigration continued. In the 1860s, when white workers moved on to find riches in the mines of Nevada, Chinese laborers took jobs abandoned by the whites. Railroad magnate Charles Crocker hired Chinese gangs to work on the Central Pacific, reasoning that the race that built the Great Wall could lay tracks across the treacherous Sierra Nevada. Some 12,000 Chinese, representing 90 percent of Crocker's workforce, completed America's first transcontinental railroad in 1869.

Chinese Workers

Chinese section hands are shown here in 1898 shoveling dirt for the North Pacific Coast Railroad in Corte Madera, California. California Historical Society, FN-25345.

CHAPTER LOCATOR | What did American expansion mean for Native Americans? | **How did mining motivate and shape American expansion?** | Who fought for control of the land and resources of the American West? | Conclusion: What is the meaning of the mythic West?

469

By 1870, more than 63,000 Chinese immigrants lived in America, 77 percent of them in California. A 1790 federal statute that limited naturalization to "white persons" was modified after the Civil War to extend naturalization to blacks ("persons of African descent"). But the Chinese and other Asians continued to be denied access to citizenship. As perpetual aliens, they constituted a reserve army of transnational laborers that many saw as a threat to American labor. For the most part, the Chinese did not displace white workers but instead found work as railroad laborers, cooks, servants, and farmhands while white workers sought out more lucrative fields. In the 1870s, when California and the rest of the nation weathered a major economic depression, the Chinese became easy scapegoats. California workingmen rioted and fought to keep Chinese workers out of the state.

In 1876, the Workingmen's Party formed to fight for Chinese exclusion. Racial and cultural animosities stood at the heart of anti-Chinese agitation. Denis Kearney, the fiery San Francisco leader of the movement, made clear this racist bent when he urged legislation to "expel every one of the moon-eyed lepers." Nor was California alone in its anti-immigrant nativism. As the country confronted growing ethnic and racial diversity with the rising tide of global immigration in the decades following the Civil War, many questioned the principle of racial equality at the same time they argued against the assimilation of "nonwhite" groups. In this climate, Congress passed the **Chinese Exclusion Act** in 1882, effectively barring Chinese immigration and setting a precedent for further immigration restrictions. The Chinese Exclusion Act led to a sharp drop in the Chinese population—from 105,465 in 1880 to 89,863 in 1900—because Chinese immigrants, overwhelmingly male, did not have families to sustain their population. Eventually, Japanese immigrants, including women as well as men, replaced the Chinese, particularly in agriculture. As "nonwhite" immigrants, they could not become naturalized citizens, but their children born in the United States claimed the rights of citizenship. Japanese parents, seeking to own land, purchased it in their children's names. Although anti-Asian prejudice remained strong in California and elsewhere in the West, Asian immigrants formed an important part of the economic fabric of the western United States.

The American West in the nineteenth century witnessed more than its share of conflict and bloodshed. Violent prejudice against the Chinese and other Asian immigrants remained common. But violence also broke out between cattle ranchers and sheep ranchers, between ranchers and farmers, between striking miners and their bosses, among rival Indian groups, and between whites and Indians. At issue was who would control the vast resources of the emerging region.

Chinese Exclusion Act

▶ 1882 law that effectively barred Chinese immigration and set a precedent for further immigration restrictions. Racial and cultural animosities stood at the heart of the anti-Chinese agitation that led to the passage of the Exclusion Act. The Chinese Exclusion Act led to a sharp drop in the Chinese population in America.

> **QUICK REVIEW**

What role did mining play in shaping the society and economy of the American West?

Railroad Locomotive In the years following the Civil War, the locomotive replaced the covered wagon, enabling settlers to travel from Chicago or St. Louis to the West Coast in two days. The first transcontinental railroad, completed in 1869, soon led to the creation of competing systems, so that by the 1880s, travelers going west could choose from four railroad lines. Library of Congress.

IN THE THREE DECADES following 1870, more land was settled than in all the previous history of the country. Americans by the hundreds of thousands packed up and moved west, many drawn by the promise of owning land. The agrarian West shared with the mining West a persistent restlessness, an equally pervasive addiction to speculation, and a penchant for exploiting natural resources and labor.

Two factors stimulated the land rush in the trans-Mississippi West. The **Homestead Act of 1862** promised 160 acres free to any citizen or prospective citizen, male or female, who settled on the land for five years. Even more important, transcontinental railroads opened up new areas and actively recruited settlers. After the completion of the first transcontinental railroad in 1869, homesteaders abandoned the covered wagon, making the trip west in a matter of days.

Although the country was rich in land and resources, not all who wanted to own land achieved their goal. During the transition from the family farm to large commercial farming, small farms gave way to vast spreads worked by migrant labor or paid farmworkers. Just as industry corporatized and consolidated in the East, the period from 1870 to 1900 witnessed corporate consolidation in mining, ranching, and agriculture.

Homestead Act of 1862

▶ Act that promised 160 acres in the trans-Mississippi West free to any citizen or prospective citizen who settled on the land for five years. Between 1870 and 1900, hundreds of thousands of Americans moved west, many drawn by the promise of free land.

Homesteaders and Speculators

A Missouri homesteader remembered packing as her family pulled up stakes and headed west to Oklahoma in 1890. "We were going to God's Country," she wrote.

CHAPTER LOCATOR | What did American expansion mean for Native Americans? | How did mining motivate and shape American expansion? | **Who fought for control of the land and resources of the American West?** | Conclusion: What is the meaning of the mythic West?

471

1862
- Homestead Act promises free land in the West to American settlers.

1869
- First transcontinental railroad is completed.

1879
- More than fifteen thousand black Exodusters move to Kansas from the South.

1886–1888
- Severe blizzards decimate cattle herds.

1889
- Two million acres in Oklahoma are opened for settlement.

1893
- Last land rush takes place in Oklahoma Territory.

"You had to work hard on that rocky country in Missouri. I was glad to be leaving it. . . . We were going to a new land and get rich."

People who ventured west searching for "God's Country" faced hardship, loneliness, and deprivation. Hard work was no guarantee of success. Blizzards, tornadoes, grasshoppers, hailstorms, drought, prairie fires, accidental death, and disease were only a few of the catastrophes that could befall even the best farmer. Homesteaders on free land still needed as much as $1,000 for a house, a team of farm animals, a well, fencing, and seed. Poor farmers called "sodbusters" did without even these basics, living in dugouts carved into hillsides.

"Father made a dugout and covered it with willows and grass," one Kansas girl recounted. When it rained, the dugout flooded, and "we carried the water out in buckets, then waded around in the mud until it dried." Rain wasn't the only problem. "Sometimes the bull snakes would get in the roof and now and then one would lose his hold and fall down on the bed. . . . Mother would grab the hoe . . . and after the fight was over Mr. Bull Snake was dragged outside."

For women on the frontier, obtaining simple daily necessities such as water and fuel meant backbreaking labor. "A yoke was made to place across [Mother's] shoulders, so as to carry at each end a bucket of water," one daughter recollected, "and then water was brought a half mile from spring to house." Gathering fuel was another heavy chore. Without ready sources of coal or firewood, the most prevalent fuel was "chips"— chunks of dried cattle and buffalo dung, found in abundance on the plains.

Despite the hardships, some homesteaders succeeded in building comfortable lives. The sod hut made way for a more substantial house; the log cabin yielded to a white clapboard home with a porch and a rocking chair. For others, the promise of the West failed to materialize. Already by the 1870s, much of the best land had been taken. "There is plenty of land for sale in California," one migrant complained in 1870, but "the majority of the available lands are held by speculators, at prices far beyond the reach of a poor man." The railroads, flush from land grants provided by the state and federal governments, owned huge swaths of land in the West and actively recruited settlers. Altogether, the land grants totaled approximately 180 million acres—an area almost one-tenth the size of the United States (**Map 17.3**). Of the 2.5 million farms established between 1860 and 1900, homesteading accounted for only one in five; the vast majority of farmland sold for a profit.

As land grew scarce on the prairie in the 1870s, farmers began to push farther west, moving into western Kansas, Nebraska, and eastern Colorado—the region called the Great American Desert by settlers who had passed over it on their way to California and Oregon. Words of caution about insufficient rain were drowned out by the extravagant claims of western promoters, many employed by the railroads to sell off their land grants. "Rain follows the plow" became the slogan of western boosters, who insisted that cultivation would alter the climate of the region and bring more rainfall. Instead, drought followed the plow. Droughts were a cyclical fact of life on the Great Plains. Plowed up, the dry topsoil blew away in the wind. A protracted drought in the late 1880s and early 1890s sent starving farmers reeling back from the plains. Thousands left, some in wagons carrying the slogan "In God we trusted, in Kansas we busted."

Fever for fertile land set off a series of spectacular land runs in Oklahoma. When two million acres of land in former Indian Territory opened for settlement in 1889, thousands of homesteaders massed on the border. At the opening pistol shot, "with a shout and a yell the swift riders shot out, then followed the light buggies or wagons," a reporter wrote. "Above all, a great cloud of dust hover[ed]

Midwestern Settlement before 1862

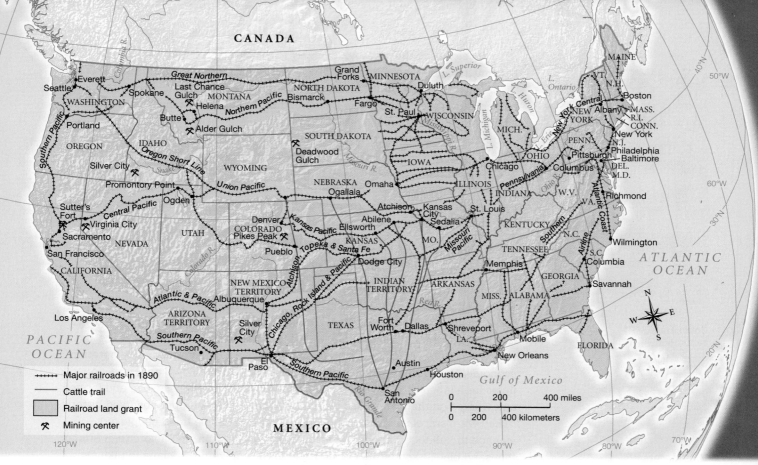

MAP 17.3 ■ Federal Land Grants to Railroads and the Development of the West, 1850–1900
Generous federal land grants meant that railroads could sell the desirable land next to the track at a profit or hold it for speculation. Railroads received more than 180 million acres, an area as large as Texas. Notice how the railroads connect with major cattle trailheads in Dodge City, Abilene, and Kansas City and to mining towns in Montana, Nevada, Colorado, and New Mexico.

like smoke over a battlefield." By nightfall, Oklahoma boasted two tent cities with more than ten thousand residents. As public land grew scarce, the hunger for land grew fiercer for both farmers and ranchers.

Ranchers and Cowboys

Cattle ranchers followed the railroads onto the plains, establishing a cattle kingdom from Texas to Wyoming between 1865 and 1885. Cowboys drove huge herds, as many as three thousand head of cattle that grazed on public lands as they followed cattle tracks like the Chisholm Trail from Texas to railheads in Kansas.

Barbed wire, invented in 1874, revolutionized the cattle business and sounded the death knell for the open range. As the largest ranches in Texas began to fence, fights broke out between big ranchers and "fence cutters," who resented the end of the free range. One old-timer observed, "Those persons, Mexicans and Americans, without land but who had cattle were put out of business by fencing." Fencing forced small-time ranchers who owned land but could not afford to buy barbed wire or sink wells to sell out for the best price they could get. The displaced ranchers, many of them Mexicans, ended up as wageworkers on the huge spreads owned by Anglos or by European syndicates.

CHAPTER LOCATOR | What did American expansion mean for Native Americans? | How did mining motivate and shape American expansion? | **Who fought for control of the land and resources of the American West?** | Conclusion: What is the meaning of the mythic West?

473

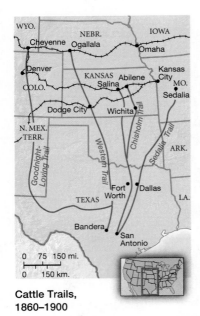

Cattle Trails, 1860–1900

On the range, the cowboy gave way to the cattle king and, like the miner, became a wage laborer. Many cowboys were African Americans (as many as five thousand in Texas alone). Writers of western literature chose to ignore the presence of black cowboys like Deadwood Dick (Nat Love), who was portrayed as a white man in the dime novels of the era.

By 1886, cattle overcrowded the range. Severe blizzards during the winters of 1886–87 and 1887–88 decimated the herds. "A whole generation of cowmen," wrote one chronicler, "went dead broke." Fencing worsened the situation. During blizzards, cattle stayed alive by keeping on the move. But when they ran up against barbed-wire fences, they froze to death. In the aftermath of the "Great Die Up," new labor-intensive forms of cattle ranching replaced the open-range model.

Tenants, Sharecroppers, and Migrants

In the post–Civil War period, as agriculture became a big business tied to national and global markets, an increasing number of laborers worked land that they would never own. In the southern United States, farmers labored under particularly heavy burdens (see chapter 16). The Civil War wiped out much of the region's capital, which had been invested in slaves, and crippled the plantation economy. Newly freed slaves rarely obtained land of their own and often ended up as farm laborers. "The colored folks stayed with the old boss man and farmed and worked on the plantations," a black Alabama sharecropper observed bitterly. "They were still slaves, but they were free slaves." Some freed people did manage to pull together enough resources to go west. In 1879, more than fifteen thousand black **Exodusters** moved from Mississippi and Louisiana to take up land in Kansas.

California's highly skilled Mexican cowboys, or *vaqueros*, commanded decent wages throughout the Southwest. But by 1880, as the coming of the railroads ended the long cattle drives and large feedlots began to replace the open range, the value of their skills declined. Many vaqueros ended up as migrant laborers, often on land their families had once owned. Similarly, in Texas, Tejanos found themselves displaced. After the heyday of cattle ranching ended in the late 1880s, cotton production rose in the southeastern regions of the state. Ranchers turned their pastures into sharecroppers' plots and hired displaced cowboys, most of them Mexicans, as seasonal laborers for as little as seventy-five cents a day, thereby creating a growing army of agricultural wageworkers.

Land monopoly and large-scale farming fostered tenancy and migratory labor on the West Coast. By the 1870s, less than 1 percent of California's population owned half the state's available agricultural land. The rigid economics of large-scale commercial agriculture and the seasonal nature of the crops spawned an army of migratory agricultural laborers. Most farm laborers were Chinese immigrants. After passage of the Chinese Exclusion Act of 1882, Mexicans, Filipinos, and Japanese immigrants filled the demand for migratory workers.

Commercial Farming and Industrial Cowboys

In the late nineteenth century, America's population remained overwhelmingly rural. The 1870 census showed that nearly 80 percent of the nation's people lived on farms and in villages of fewer than 8,000 inhabitants. By 1900, the figure had dropped to 66 percent (**Figure 17.1**). At the same time, the number of farms rose. Rapid growth in the West increased the number of the nation's farms from 2 million in 1860 to more than 5.7 million in 1900.

Despite the hardships individual farmers experienced, new technology and farming techniques revolutionized American farm life. Mechanized plows and reapers halved the time and labor cost of production and made it possible to cultivate vast tracts of land. Urbanization provided farmers with expanding markets for their produce, and railroads carried crops to markets thousands of miles away. Even before the start of the twentieth century, American agriculture had entered the era of what would come to be called agribusiness—farming as a big business—with the advent of huge commercial farms.

As farming moved onto the prairies and plains, mechanization took command. Horse-drawn implements gave way to steam-powered machinery. By 1880, a single combine could do the work of twenty men, vastly increasing the acreage a farmer could cultivate. This agricultural revolution meant that Americans raised more than four times the corn, five times the hay, and seven times the wheat and oats they had before the Civil War.

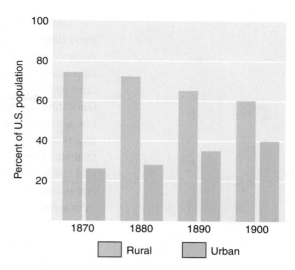

FIGURE 17.1 ■ **Changes in Rural and Urban Populations, 1870–1900**

Between 1870 and 1900, not only did the number of urban dwellers increase, but, even as the number of rural inhabitants fell, the number of farms increased. Mechanization made it possible to farm with fewer hands, fueling the exodus from farm to city throughout the second half of the nineteenth century.

Mechanical Corn Planter

Mechanical planters came into use in the 1860s. The Farmers Friend Manufacturing Company of Dayton, Ohio, advertised its lever and treadle corn planter in the early 1880s. Ohio History Society

▶ FOR MORE HELP ANALYZING THIS IMAGE, see the visual activity for this chapter in the Online Study Guide at bedfordstmartins.com/roarkunderstanding.

CHAPTER LOCATOR | What did American expansion mean for Native Americans? | How did mining motivate and shape American expansion? | Who fought for control of the land and resources of the American West? | Conclusion: What is the meaning of the mythic West?

475

Like cotton farmers in the South, western grain and livestock farmers increasingly depended on foreign markets for their livelihood. A fall in global market prices meant that a farmer's entire harvest went to pay off debts. In the depression that followed the panic of 1893, many heavily mortgaged farmers lost their land to creditors. As a Texas cotton farmer complained, "By the time the World Gets their Liveing out of the Farmer as we have to Feed the World, we the Farmer has nothing Left but a Bear Hard Liveing." Commercial farming, along with mining, represented another way in which the West developed its own brand of industrialism. The far West's industrial economy sprang initially from California gold and the vast territory that came under American control following the Mexican-American War. In the ensuing rush on land and resources, environmental factors interacted with economic and social forces to produce enterprises as vast in scale and scope as anything found in the East.

Two Alsatian immigrants, Henry Miller and Charles Lux, pioneered the West's mix of agriculture and industrialism. Beginning as meat wholesalers, Miller and Lux quickly expanded their business to encompass cattle, land, and land reclamation projects such as dams and irrigation systems. With a labor force of migrant workers, a highly coordinated corporate system, and large sums of investment capital, the firm of Miller & Lux became one of America's industrial behemoths. Eventually, these "industrial cowboys" grazed a herd of 100,000 cattle on 1.25 million acres of company land in California, Oregon, and Nevada and employed more than 1,200 migrant laborers on their corporate ranches. Miller & Lux attracted labor by offering free meals to migratory workers. When the company's Chinese cooks rebelled at washing the dishes resulting from the free meals, the migrant laborers were forced to eat after the ranch hands and use their dirty plates. By the 1890s, more than eight hundred migrants a year followed what came to be known as the "Dirty Plate Route" on Miller & Lux ranches throughout California.

Since the days of Thomas Jefferson, agrarian life had been linked with the highest ideals of a democratic society. Now agrarianism itself had been transformed. The farmer was no longer a self-sufficient yeoman but often a businessman or a wage laborer tied to a global market. And even as farm production soared, industrialization outstripped it. More and more farmers left the fields for urban factories or found work in the "factories in the fields" of the new industrialized agribusiness. Now that the future seemed to lie not with the small farmer but with industrial enterprises, was democracy itself at risk? This question would ignite a farmers' revolt in the 1880s and dominate political debate in the 1890s.

> **QUICK REVIEW**

Why did many homesteaders find it difficult to acquire good land in the West?

Smithsonian American Art Museum, Washington, D.C./Art Resource, NY.

Conclusion: What is the meaning of the mythic West?

EVEN AS THE OLD WEST was changing, the mythic West was being born. Buffalo Bill became its icon. Born William F. Cody, the masterful showman formed a touring Wild West company in 1883. Part circus, part theater, the Wild West extravaganza featured exhibitions of riding, shooting, and roping and presented dramatic reenactments of great moments in western lore. Highly dubious as history, as spectacle the Wild West show was unbeatable. At the World's Columbian Exposition in 1893, crowds numbering tens of thousands packed the bleachers to cheer. By the turn of the twentieth century, the high drama of the struggle for the West had become little more than a thrilling but harmless entertainment.

Across the fairgrounds historian Frederick Jackson Turner addressed the American Historical Association on "The Significance of the Frontier in American History." Turner noted that by 1890, the census could no longer discern a clear frontier line. His tone was elegiac: "The existence of an area of free land, its continuous recession, and the advance of settlement westward," he observed, "explained American development" and was inextricably linked to what was best and unique in America. Of course, land in the West had never been empty or free. And the pastoral agrarianism Turner celebrated belied the urban, industrial West found on the Comstock and in the commercial farms of California. Nevertheless, Turner's frontier thesis became one of the most enduring myths of the American West.

The real West was no less dramatic than the mythic West. In the decades following the Civil War, as the United States pursued empire in the American West, new problems replaced the old issues of slavery and sectionalism. The growing power of big business, the exploitation of labor and natural resources, corruption in politics, and ethnic and racial tensions exacerbated by colonial expansion and unparalleled immigration dominated the debates of the day in both the East and the West. As the nineteenth century ended, Americans had more questions than answers. Could the American promise survive in the new world of corporations, wage labor, and mushrooming cities? Neither out of place nor out of time, the West contributed its share to both the promise and the problems of the era Mark Twain would brand the Gilded Age.

SO NOW YOU KNOW

It took Euro-Americans 250 years to conquer the eastern half of what became the United States. In the second half of the nineteenth century, using new technology in both transportation and warfare, the United States was able to gain relatively quick possession of western lands.

CHAPTER LOCATOR | What did American expansion mean for Native Americans? | How did mining motivate and shape American expansion? | Who fought for control of the land and resources of the American West? | Conclusion: What is the meaning of the mythic West?

477

CHAPTER 17 STUDY GUIDE

Online Study Guide
bedfordstmartins.com/roarkunderstanding

STEP 1 GETTING STARTED

Below are basic terms from this period in American history. Can you identify each term below and explain why it matters? To do this exercise online or to download this chart, visit bedfordstmartins.com/roarkunderstanding.

TERM	WHO OR WHAT & WHEN	WHY IT MATTERS
Sitting Bull, p. 460		
1868 Treaty of Fort Laramie, p. 460		
Battle of the Little Big Horn, p. 461		
Dawes Allotment Act, p. 461		
Geronimo, p. 462		
Ghost Dance, p. 463		
Wounded Knee, p. 464		
Comstock Lode, p. 465		
Chinese Exclusion Act, p. 470		
Homestead Act of 1862, p. 471		
Exodusters, p. 474		

STEP 2 MOVING BEYOND THE BASICS

The exercise below represents a more advanced understanding of the chapter material. Fill in the chart below by describing the policies and goals of the federal government with respect to Indian peoples, natural resources, land, and the flow of migrants into the West. What connections were there among the policies in each of these four areas? To do this exercise online or to download this chart, visit bedfordstmartins.com/roarkunderstanding.

	Federal policies and legislation	Goals
Indian peoples		
Natural resources		
Land		
Migrants		

Now that you've reviewed the chapter, take a step back and try to see the big picture. Remember to use specific examples from the chapter in your answers. To do this exercise online, visit bedfordstmartins.com/roarkunderstanding.

INDIAN POLICY

▶ How did Indians respond to the flood of westward migration after the Civil War?

▶ How did federal Indian policy change over the course of the late nineteenth century, and what was the Indian reaction?

MINING AND THE WEST

▶ Why was mining such an important factor in promoting western expansion?

▶ How did mining affect the economy and society of the West and the nation?

WESTERNERS

▶ Who went west and why?

▶ How did racial and ethnic prejudice affect relations among westerners?

LOOKING BACKWARD, LOOKING AHEAD

▶ How did western expansion before the Civil War differ from western expansion after the Civil War?

▶ What new political issues and tensions did American expansion raise? What was the relationship between the East and the West in 1900?

IN YOUR OWN WORDS

Imagine that you must explain chapter 17 to someone who hasn't read it. What would be the most important points to include and why?

18
DEFINING THE GILDED AGE OF BUSINESS AND POLITICS

1870–1895

> This chapter examines the acceleration of industrialization and the growing interplay of business and politics in the era known as the Gilded Age. It details the practices of business pioneers from 1870 to 1895 and explores the impact of economic change on the political and cultural landscape of late-nineteenth-century America.

> How did the railroads stimulate big business?

> How did big business change at the end of the nineteenth century?

> What factors influenced political life in the late nineteenth century?

> What issues shaped presidential politics in the late nineteenth century?

> What role did the economy play in the politics of the 1880s and 1890s?

> Conclusion: Why was business so dominant in the Gilded Age?

DID YOU KNOW?

Author Mark Twain labeled the Gilded Age as an age of gaudy excess in a best-selling novel he wrote in 1873.

The Lost Bet, **1893.** Artist Joseph Klir painted the scene of a Chicago parade after a local Republican agreed to pull his Democratic friend if Grover Cleveland won the 1892 presidential election.

How did the railroads stimulate big business?

The power wielded by John D. Rockefeller and the Standard Oil Company is captured in this political cartoon by Horace Taylor, which appeared in the January 22, 1900, issue of the *Verdict*. Rockefeller is pictured holding the White House and the Treasury Department in the palm of his hand, while in the background the U.S. Capitol has been converted into an oil refinery. Collection of the New-York Historical Society.

> ▶ FOR MORE HELP ANALYZING THIS IMAGE, see the visual activity for this chapter in the Online Study Guide at bedfordstmartins.com/roarkunderstanding.

IN THE YEARS following the Civil War, the scale and scope of American industry expanded dramatically. Old industries transformed into modern corporations typified by the behemoth U.S. Steel. Discovery and invention stimulated new industries, from oil refining to electric light and power. The expansion of the nation's rail system in the decades after the Civil War played the key role in the transformation of the American economy. New rail lines created a national market that enabled businesses to expand from a regional to a nationwide scale. The railroads became America's first big business. Jay Gould, Andrew Carnegie, John D. Rockefeller, and other business leaders pioneered new strategies to seize markets and consolidate power in the rising railroad, steel, and oil industries and set the tone in the get-rich-quick era of freewheeling capitalism that Mark Twain labeled the Gilded Age.

Railroads: America's First Big Business

In the decades following the Civil War, the United States built the greatest railroad network in the world. The first transcontinental railroad was completed in 1869, linking new markets in the West to the nation's economy. Between 1870 and 1880, the amount of track in the country doubled, and it nearly doubled again in the following decade. By 1900, the nation boasted more than 193,000 miles of railroad track—more than in all of Europe and Russia combined (see **Map 18.1**, page 484, and "Global Comparison," page 486). To understand how the railroads developed and came to dominate American life, there is no better place to start than with the career of Jay Gould, who pioneered the expansion of America's railway system and became the era's most notorious speculator.

CHAPTER LOCATOR | How did the railroads stimulate big business?

Gould, by his own admission, knew little about railroads and cared less about their operation. Instead he operated in the stock market like a shark, looking for vulnerable railroads, buying enough stock to take control, and threatening to undercut his competitors until they bought him out at a high profit. In the 1880s, he moved to put together a second transcontinental railroad. To defend their interests, his competitors had little choice but to adopt his strategy of expansion and consolidation, which in turn encouraged railroad building and stimulated a national market.

The dramatic growth of the railroads created the country's first big business. Before the Civil War, even the largest textile mill in New England employed no more than 800 workers. In contrast, the Pennsylvania Railroad by the 1870s boasted a payroll of more than 55,000 workers, making it the largest private enterprise in the world.

The Republican Party, firmly entrenched in Washington, worked closely with business interests, subsidizing the transcontinental railroad system with land grants of 100 million acres of public land and $64 million in tax incentives and direct aid. States and local communities joined the railroad boom, with the combined federal and state giveaway amounting to more than 180 million acres, an area larger than Texas.

A revolution in communication accompanied and supported the growth of the railroads. Developed by Samuel F. B. Morse, the telegraph formed the "nervous system" of the new industrial order. Telegraph service transformed business by providing instantaneous communication. Again Jay Gould took the lead. In 1879, through stock manipulation, he seized control of Western Union, the company that monopolized the telegraph industry.

The railroads soon fell on hard times. Already by the 1870s, lack of planning led to overbuilding. On the eastern seaboard, railroads competed fiercely for business. A manufacturer in an area served by competing railroads could get substantially reduced shipping rates in return for promises of steady business. Because railroad owners lost money through this kind of competition, they tried to set up agreements to end competition by dividing up territory and setting rates. But these informal agreements invariably failed because men like Jay Gould, intent on undercutting all competitors, refused to play by the rules.

The public's alarm at the control wielded by the new railroad magnates provided a barometer of attitudes toward big business itself. When Gould died in 1892, he was, as he himself admitted shortly before his death, "the most hated man in America."

Andrew Carnegie, Steel, and Vertical Integration

If Jay Gould was the man Americans loved to hate, **Andrew Carnegie** became one of America's heroes. Unlike Gould, Carnegie turned his back on speculation and worked to build something enduring—Carnegie Steel, the biggest steel business in the world during the Gilded Age.

The growth of the steel industry proceeded directly from railroad building. The first railroads ran on iron rails. Steel, both stronger and more flexible than iron, remained too expensive for use in rails until Englishman Henry Bessemer

CHRONOLOGY

1869
– First transcontinental railroad is completed.

1870
– John D. Rockefeller incorporates Standard Oil Company.

1872
– Andrew Carnegie opens his steel mill outside of Pittsburgh and pioneers vertical integration.

1876
– Alexander Graham Bell demonstrates the telephone.

1882
– John D. Rockefeller develops the trust.

1880s
– Thomas Edison pioneers the use of electricity as an energy source.

Andrew Carnegie
▶ Investor and philanthropist who built Carnegie Steel, the biggest steel business in the world during the Gilded Age. Carnegie pioneered a system of business organization called vertical integration. Famed as a philanthropist, Carnegie espoused the gospel of wealth, calling on the rich to use their riches for the good of the people.

How did big business change at the end of the nineteenth century?

What factors influenced political life in the late nineteenth century?

What issues shaped presidential politics in the late nineteenth century?

What role did the economy play in the politics of the 1880s and 1890s?

Conclusion: Why was business so dominant in the Gilded Age?

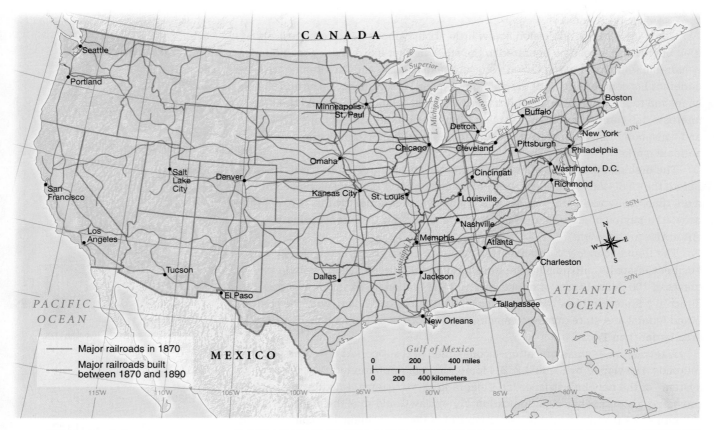

MAP 18.1 ■ Railroad Expansion, 1870–1890

Railroad mileage nearly quadrupled between 1870 and 1890, with the greatest growth occurring in the trans-Mississippi West. New transcontinental lines—the Great Northern, Northern Pacific, Southern Pacific, and Atlantic and Pacific—were completed in the 1880s. Small feeder lines such as the Oregon Short Line and the Atchison, Topeka, and Santa Fe fed into the great transcontinental systems, knitting the nation together.

▶ FOR MORE HELP ANALYZING THIS MAP, see the map activity for this chapter in the Online Study Guide at bedfordstmartins.com/roarkunderstanding.

developed a way to make steel more cheaply from pig iron. Andrew Carnegie came to dominate the emerging industry.

Carnegie, a Scottish immigrant, landed in New York in 1848 at the age of twelve. He rose from poverty to become one of the richest men in America. Before he died, he gave away more than $300 million, most notably to public libraries. His generosity, combined with his humble beginnings, burnished his public image.

When Carnegie was a teenager, his skill as a telegraph operator caught the attention of Tom Scott, superintendent of the Pennsylvania Railroad. Scott hired Carnegie and lent him the money for his first investments. A millionaire before his thirtieth birthday, Carnegie turned away from speculation and set out to reshape the iron and steel industry. "My preference was always manufacturing," he wrote. "I wished to make something tangible." By applying the lessons of cost accounting and efficiency that he had learned working for the Pennsylvania Railroad, Carnegie turned steel into the nation's first manufacturing big business. In 1872 he built the the most up-to-date steel plant in the nation outside of Pittsburgh (**Figure 18.1**).

Carnegie's formula for success was simple: "Cut the prices, scoop the market, run the mills full; watch the costs and profits will take care of themselves." To guarantee the lowest costs and the maximum output, Carnegie pioneered a system of business organization called vertical integration. All aspects of the business were under Carnegie's control—from the mining of iron ore, to its transport

CHAPTER LOCATOR | How did the railroads stimulate big business?

on the Great Lakes, to the production of steel. Vertical integration, in the words of one observer, meant that "from the moment these crude stuffs were dug out of the earth until they flowed in a stream of liquid steel in the ladles, there was never a price, profit, or royalty paid to any outsider."

The great productivity Carnegie encouraged came at a high price. He deliberately pitted his managers against one another, firing the losers and rewarding the winners with a share in the company. Workers achieved the output Carnegie demanded by enduring low wages, dangerous working conditions, and twelve-hour days six days a week. One worker, commenting on the contradiction between Carnegie's endowments to public libraries and his labor policies, observed, "After working twelve hours, how can a man go to a library?"

By 1900, Andrew Carnegie had become the best-known manufacturer in the nation, and the age of iron had yielded to an age of steel. As a captain of industry, Carnegie's only rival was the titan of the oil industry, John D. Rockefeller.

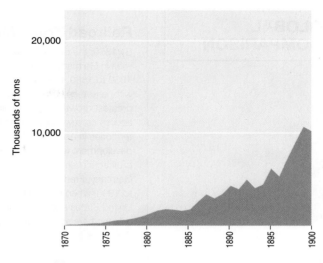

FIGURE 18.1 ■ Iron and Steel Production, 1870–1900
Iron and steel production in the United States grew from nearly none in 1870 to 10 million tons a year by 1900. The secrets to the great increase in steel production were the use of the Bessemer process and vertical integration, pioneered by Andrew Carnegie. By 1900, Carnegie's mills alone produced more steel than all of Great Britain. With corporate consolidation after 1900, the rate of growth in steel proved even more spectacular.

John D. Rockefeller, Standard Oil, and the Trust

In the days before the automobile and gasoline, crude oil was refined into lubricating oil for machinery and kerosene for lamps. The amount of capital needed to buy or build an oil refinery in the 1860s and 1870s remained relatively low. As a result, the new petroleum industry experienced riotous competition among many small refineries. Ultimately, **John D. Rockefeller** and his Standard Oil Company succeeded in controlling nine-tenths of the oil-refining business.

Rockefeller was the son of a peddler who taught him to drive a hard bargain. Rockefeller learned his lessons well. In 1865, at the age of twenty-five, he controlled the largest oil refinery in Cleveland. Like a growing number of business owners, Rockefeller abandoned partnership or single proprietorship to embrace the corporation as the business structure best suited to maximize profit and minimize personal liability. In 1870, he incorporated his oil business, founding the Standard Oil Company.

As the largest refiner in Cleveland, Rockefeller demanded secret rebates from the railroads in exchange for his steady business. Rebates enabled Rockefeller to drive out his competitors through predatory pricing. The railroads needed Rockefeller's business so badly that they gave him a share of the rates that his competitors paid. Secret deals, predatory pricing, and rebates enabled Rockefeller to undercut his competitors and pressure competing refiners to sell out or face ruin.

To gain legal standing for Standard Oil's secret deals, Rockefeller in 1882 pioneered a new form of corporate structure—the trust. The trust differed markedly from Carnegie's vertical approach in steel. Instead of attempting to control all

John D. Rockefeller
▶ Oil tycoon whose Standard Oil Company came to control 90 percent of the oil-refining business. Rockefeller used trusts, and later holding companies, to stifle competition and force railroads to offer him secret rebates. His business tactics were the subject of a scathing exposé written by Ida M. Tarbell.

How did big business change at the end of the nineteenth century?

What factors influenced political life in the late nineteenth century?

What issues shaped presidential politics in the late nineteenth century?

What role did the economy play in the politics of the 1880s and 1890s?

Conclusion: Why was business so dominant in the Gilded Age?

Railroad Track Mileage, 1890

By 1850, the railway network in Great Britain was already well established, and most of the main lines in Germany had been built. France was slower to invest in railroads, but during the period 1850 to 1860, the government invested heavily in laying track, and the French soon caught up with, and then bypassed, their European neighbors. Russia's railway development experienced its greatest growth in the late nineteenth century. This growth was driven by the country's need to access its newly developing industrial regions and the vast natural resources of its far-flung territories in Asia. Like Russia, most of India's railroad growth occurred late in the century. This development was financed by the British, who were eager to tap the economic potential of their profitable overseas colony. By 1890, the United States had laid more railroad track than Britain, Germany, France, Russia, and India combined. Most of this growth occurred in the period 1870 to 1890, when railroad mileage in the United States nearly quadrupled. The vast area of the United States and its western territories accounted for some of the disparity between railroad mileage here and in Europe. England, France, and Germany combined contained less land than the states east of the Mississippi River.

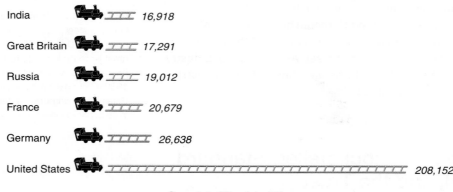

India　　　　　16,918

Great Britain　17,291

Russia　　　　19,012

France　　　　20,679

Germany　　　26,638

United States　208,152

Completed Track in Miles

aspects of the oil business, Rockefeller used horizontal integration to control the refining process. Several trustees held stock in various refinery companies "in trust" for Standard's stockholders. This elaborate stock swap allowed the trustees to coordinate policy among the refineries, giving Rockefeller a virtual monopoly on the oil-refining business. The Standard Oil trust, valued at more than $70 million, paved the way for trusts in sugar, whiskey, matches, and many other products.

When the federal government responded to public pressure to outlaw the trust as a violation of free trade, Standard Oil changed tactics and reorganized as a holding company. Instead of stockholders in competing companies acting through trustees to set prices and determine territories, the holding company simply brought competing companies under one central administration. No longer technically separate businesses, they could act in concert without violating anti-trust laws that forbade companies from forming "combinations in restraint of trade." By the 1890s, Standard Oil ruled more than 90 percent of the oil business, employed 100,000 people, and was the biggest, richest, most feared, and most admired business organization in the world.

John D. Rockefeller enjoyed enormous success in business, but he was not well liked by the public. Editor and journalist Ida M. Tarbell's "History of the Standard Oil Company," which ran for three years (1902–1905) in serial form in *McClure's*

CHAPTER LOCATOR | How did the railroads stimulate big business?

Magazine, largely shaped the public's harsh view of Rockefeller. Her history chronicled the methods Rockefeller had used to take over the oil industry. Publicly, Rockefeller refused to respond to her allegations. "If I step on that worm I will call attention to it," he explained. "If I ignore it, it will disappear." Yet by the time Tarbell finished publishing her story, Standard Oil and the man who created it had become the symbol of heartless monopoly.

New Inventions: The Telephone and Electricity

The second half of the nineteenth century was an age of invention (**Table 18.1**). Men like Thomas Alva Edison and Alexander Graham Bell became folk heroes. But no matter how dramatic the inventors or the inventions, the new electric and telephone industries pioneered by Edison and Bell soon eclipsed their inventors and fell under the control of bankers and industrialists.

Alexander Graham Bell came to America from Scotland at the age of twenty-four with a passion to find a way to teach the deaf to speak (his wife and mother were deaf). Instead, he developed a way to transmit voice over wire—the telephone. His invention astounded the world when he demonstrated it at the Philadelphia Bicentennial Exposition in 1876. In 1880, Bell's company, American Bell, pioneered "long lines" (long-distance telephone service), creating American Telephone and Telegraph (AT&T) as a subsidiary. Bell's invention proved a boon to business, contributing to speed and efficiency. The number of telephones soared, reaching 310,000 in 1895 and more than 1.5 million in 1900.

Even more than Alexander Graham Bell, inventor **Thomas Alva Edison** embodied the ingenuity and rugged individualism that Americans most admired. Self-educated, he worked twenty hours a day in his laboratory in Menlo Park, New Jersey, vowing to turn out "a minor invention every ten days and a big thing every six months or so." At the height of his career, he averaged a patent every eleven days and invented such "big things" as the phonograph, the motion picture camera, and the filament for the incandescent lightbulb.

Edison, in competition with George W. Westinghouse, pioneered the use of electricity as an energy source. By the late nineteenth century, electricity had become a part of American urban life. It powered trolley cars and lighted factories, homes, and office buildings. Indeed, electricity became so prevalent in urban life that it symbolized the city, whose bright lights contrasted with rural America, left largely in the dark because private enterprise judged it not profitable enough to run electric lines to outlying farms and ranches.

The day of the inventor quietly yielded to the heyday of the corporation. In 1892, the electric industry consolidated. Reflecting a nationwide trend in business, Edison General Electric dropped the name of its inventor, becoming simply General Electric (GE). For years, an embittered Edison refused to set foot inside a GE building. General Electric could afford to overlook the slight. A prime example of the trend toward business consolidation taking place in the 1890s, GE soon dominated the market.

TABLE 18.1 ■ Notable American Inventions 1865–1899

Year	Invention
1865	Railroad sleeping car
1867	Typewriter
1868	Railroad refrigerator car
1870	Stock ticker
1874	Barbed wire
1876	Telephone
1877	Phonograph
1879	Electric lightbulb
1882	Electric fan
1885	Adding machine
1886	Coca-Cola
1888	Kodak camera
1890	Electric chair
1891	Zipper
1895	Safety razor
1896	Electric stove
1899	Tape recorder

Thomas Alva Edison
▶ Self-educated American inventor who in the 1880s pioneered the use of electricity. Other inventions included the phonograph, the motion picture camera, and the filament for incandescent lightbulbs.

QUICK REVIEW

What tactics and strategies did America's business owners employ during the early years of the Gilded Age?

How did big business change at the end of the nineteenth century?	What factors influenced political life in the late nineteenth century?	What issues shaped presidential politics in the late nineteenth century?	What role did the economy play in the politics of the 1880s and 1890s?	Conclusion: Why was business so dominant in the Gilded Age?

How did big business change at the end of the nineteenth century?

Homestead Steelworks

The Homestead steelworks, outside Pittsburgh, is pictured shortly after J. P. Morgan bought out Andrew Carnegie and created U.S. Steel.
Hagley Museum & Library.

J. P. Morgan

▶ The preeminent finance capitalist of the late nineteenth century. Morgan acted as a power broker in the reorganization of the railroads and the creation of industrial giants such as General Electric and U.S. Steel. His efforts formed the model for corporate consolidation that would characterize the modern economy.

EVEN AS ROCKEFELLER and Carnegie built their empires, the era of the "robber barons," as they were dubbed by their detractors, was drawing to a close. Increasingly, businesses replaced partnerships and sole proprietorships with the anonymous corporate structure that would come to dominate the twentieth century. At the same time, mergers led to the creation of huge new corporations.

Banks and financiers played a key role in this consolidation, so much so that the decades at the turn of the twentieth century can be characterized as a period of finance capitalism—investment sponsored by banks and bankers. During these years, a new social philosophy based on the theories of naturalist Charles Darwin helped to justify consolidation and to inhibit state or federal regulation of business. A conservative Supreme Court further frustrated attempts to control business by consistently declaring that legislation designed to regulate railroads or to outlaw trusts and monopolies was unconstitutional.

J. P. Morgan and Finance Capitalism

John Pierpont Morgan, the preeminent finance capitalist of the late nineteenth century, sought whenever possible to eliminate competition by substituting consolidation and central control. **J. P. Morgan**'s passion for order made him the architect of business mergers. At the turn of the twentieth century, he dominated American banking, exerting an influence so powerful that his critics charged he controlled a vast "money trust."

CHAPTER LOCATOR | How did the railroads stimulate big business?

Morgan acted as a power broker in the reorganization of the railroads and the creation of industrial giants such as General Electric and U.S. Steel. When the railroads fell on hard times in the 1890s, Morgan quickly took over struggling railroads and moved to eliminate competition by creating what he called "a community of interest" among handpicked managers. By the time he finished reorganizing the railroads, Morgan had concentrated the nation's rail lines in the hands of a few directors who controlled two-thirds of the nation's track.

Banker control of the railroads rationalized, or coordinated, the industry. But stability came at a high price. To keep investors happy and to guarantee huge profits from the sale of stock, Morgan issued more shares than the assets of the company warranted. Overcapitalization hurt the railroads in the long run, saddling them with enormous debt. Equally harmful was the management style of the Morgan directors, who aimed at short-term profit and discouraged the continued technological and organizational innovation needed to run the railroads effectively.

In 1898, Morgan moved into the steel industry and, in 1901, purchased Carnegie Steel for $480 million (the equivalent of about $10 billion in today's currency). Morgan's acquisition of Carnegie Steel signaled the passing of the old entrepreneurial order personified by Andrew Carnegie and the arrival of a new, anonymous corporate world. Morgan quickly moved to pull together Carnegie's chief competitors to form a huge new corporation, United States Steel. Created in 1901 and capitalized at $1.4 billion, U.S. Steel was the largest corporation in the world.

Even more than Carnegie or Rockefeller, Morgan left his stamp on the twentieth century. His efforts formed the model for corporate consolidation that would characterize the modern economy. Economists and social scientists soon justified such consolidation with a new social theory known as social Darwinism.

Social Darwinism, Laissez-Faire, and the Supreme Court

John D. Rockefeller Jr., the son of the founder of Standard Oil, once remarked to his Baptist Bible class that the Standard Oil Company, like the American Beauty rose, resulted from "pruning the early buds that grew up around it." The elimination of smaller, inefficient units, he said, was "merely the working out of a law of nature and a law of God." The comparison of the business world to the natural world gave rise to a theory of society based on the law of evolution formulated by British naturalist Charles Darwin. In *On the Origin of Species* (1859), Darwin theorized that in the struggle for survival, adaptation to the environment triggered among species a natural selection process that led to evolution. Herbert Spencer in Britain and William Graham Sumner in the United States developed the theory of **social Darwinism**, which became popular in the 1880s. The social

CHRONOLOGY

1880s
– Herbert Spencer and William Graham Sumner espouse social Darwinism.

1889
– Andrew Carnegie publishes "Gospel of Wealth."

1901
– J. P. Morgan purchases Carnegie Steel for $480 million and creates U.S. Steel, America's first billion-dollar corporation.

social Darwinism
▶ Developed by Herbert Spencer and William Graham Sumner, social Darwinism gained favor in the late nineteenth century. Social Darwinists believed that wealth was a sign of "fitness" and poverty a sign of "unfitness" for survival. They argued that efforts to alleviate inequality were counterproductive and even destructive.

| How did big business change at the end of the nineteenth century? | What factors influenced political life in the late nineteenth century? | What issues shaped presidential politics in the late nineteenth century? | What role did the economy play in the politics of the 1880s and 1890s? | Conclusion: Why was business so dominant in the Gilded Age? |

Darwinists concluded that progress came about as a result of relentless competition in which the strong survived and the weak died out.

In social terms, the idea of the "survival of the fittest" had profound significance, as Sumner, a professor of political economy at Yale University, made clear in his book *What Social Classes Owe to Each Other* (1883). "The drunkard in the gutter is just where he ought to be, according to the fitness and tendency of things," Sumner insisted. Conversely, "millionaires are the product of natural selection," and although "they get high wages and live in luxury," Sumner claimed, "the bargain is a good one for society."

Social Darwinists equated wealth and power with "fitness" and believed that the unfit should be allowed to die off to advance the progress of humanity. Any efforts by the rich to aid the poor would only tamper with the rigid laws of nature and slow down evolution. Social Darwinism acted to curb social reform while at the same time glorifying great wealth and justifying economic inequality.

Andrew Carnegie softened some of the harshness of social Darwinism in his essay "The Gospel of Wealth," published in 1889. The millionaire, Carnegie wrote, acted as a "mere trustee and agent for his poorer brethren, bringing to their service his superior wisdom, experience, and ability to administer, doing for them better than they could or would do for themselves." Carnegie urged the rich to "live unostentatious lives" and "administer surplus wealth for the good of the people." His gospel of wealth earned much praise but won few converts.

Social Darwinism suited an age in which the gross inequalities accompanying industrialization seemed to cry out for action. Assuaging the nation's conscience, social Darwinism justified neglect of the poor in the name of "race progress." With so many of the poor coming from different races and ethnicities, social Darwinism fueled racism. A new "scientific racism" purported to prove "Anglo-Saxons" superior to all other groups. Social Darwinism buttressed the status quo and reassured comfortable, white Americans that all was as it should be.

Social Darwinism, with its emphasis on the free play of competition and the survival of the fittest, encouraged the economic theory of laissez-faire (French for "let it alone"). Business argued that government should not meddle in economic affairs, while ignoring the huge land grants and protective tariffs that benefited industry. During the 1880s and 1890s, a conservative Supreme Court in a series of landmark decisions used the Fourteenth Amendment—originally intended to protect freed slaves from state laws violating their rights—to protect corporations from taxation, regulation, labor organization, and antitrust legislation. Only in the arena of politics did Americans attempt to tackle the power of corporate capitalism.

> **QUICK REVIEW**

How did social Darwinism shape American society and business in the late nineteenth century?

What factors influenced political life in the late nineteenth century?

"Woman's Holy War"

This political cartoon styles the temperance campaign as "Woman's Holy War." Women's activism against alcohol in the 1870s led to the creation of the Woman's Christian Temperance Union in 1874. Picture Research Consultants & Archives.

▶ FOR MORE HELP ANALYZING THIS IMAGE, see the visual activity for this chapter in the Online Study Guide at bedfordstmartins.com/roarkunderstanding.

FOR MANY AMERICANS, politics provided a source of identity, a livelihood, and a form of entertainment. A variety of factors contributed to the complicated interplay of politics and culture. Patronage provided an economic incentive for voter participation (see **Figure 18.2**, page 492), but ethnicity, religion, sectional loyalty, race, and gender all influenced the political life of the period.

Political Participation and Party Loyalty

Patronage proved a strong motivation for party loyalty among many voters. Political parties in power doled out hundreds of thousands of federal, state, and local government jobs to their loyal supporters. Money greased the wheels of this system of patronage, dubbed the **spoils system** from the adage "to the victor go the spoils." With their livelihoods tied to their party identity, government employees in particular had an incentive to vote in great numbers.

Political affiliation provided a powerful sense of group identity for many voters. Democrats, who traced the party's roots back to Thomas Jefferson, called theirs "the party of the fathers." The Republican Party still claimed strong loyalties as a result of its alignment with the Union during the Civil War.

Religion and ethnicity also played a significant role in politics. In the North, Protestants from the old-line denominations, particularly Presbyterians and Methodists, flocked to the Republican Party, which championed a series of moral

spoils system
▶ The system in which government positions were distributed to the supporters of successful political candidates. Under this system, the political parties in power doled out hundreds of thousands of federal, state, and local government jobs to their loyal supporters. The assassination of President James Garfield in 1881 led to civil service reform.

1869
– National Woman Suffrage Association is founded.

1874
– Woman's Christian Temperance Union, an all-women reform organization, is founded.

1886
– *Atlanta Constitution* editor Henry Grady calls for a New South modeled on the industrial North.

1890
– General Federation of Women's Clubs is founded.

1892
– Ida B. Wells launches antilynching campaign.

reforms, including local laws requiring businesses to close in observance of the Sabbath. In the cities, the Democratic Party courted immigrants and working-class Catholic and Jewish voters and charged, rightly, that Republican moral crusades often masked attacks on immigrant culture.

Sectionalism and the New South

After the end of Reconstruction, most white voters in the former Confederate states remained loyal Democrats. Labeling the Republican Party the agent of "Negro rule," Democrats urged white southerners to "vote the way you shot." Yet the so-called solid South proved far from solid on the state and local levels. The economic plight of the South led to shifting political alliances and to third-party movements that challenged Democratic attempts to define politics along race lines and maintain the Democratic Party as the white man's party.

The South's economy, devastated by the war, foundered at the same time the North experienced an unprecedented industrial boom. Soon an influential group of southerners called for a **New South** modeled on the industrial North. Henry Grady, the editor of the *Atlanta Constitution*, used his paper's influence to exhort the South to use its natural advantages—cheap labor and abundant natural resources—to go head-to-head in competition with northern industry. Many southerners, men and women, black and white, joined the national migration from farm to city. And even as southern Democrats took back control of state governments (see chapter 16), they embraced northern promoters who promised prosperity and profits.

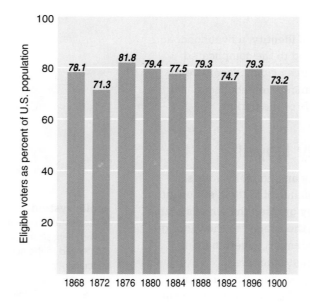

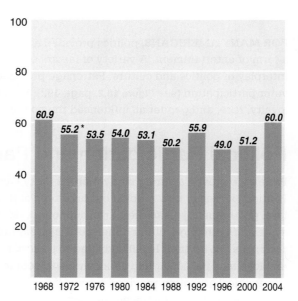

*Decrease because of expansion of eligibility with the enfranchisement of 18- to 21-year-olds.

FIGURE 18.2 ■ **Voter Turnout, 1868–1900 and 1968–2004**
Despite the weakness of the presidency and the largely undistinguished men who filled the office, people turned out in record numbers to vote in late-nineteenth-century elections. Compare the rate of voter participation to that of the late twentieth century. What factors do you think account for the differences?

CHAPTER LOCATOR | How did the railroads stimulate big business?

The railroads came first, opening up the region for industrial development. Southern railroad mileage grew fourfold from 1865 to 1890. The number of cotton spindles also soared as textile mill owners abandoned New England in search of the cheap labor and proximity to raw materials promised in the South. By 1900, the South had become the nation's leading producer of cloth, and more than 100,000 southerners, many of them women and children, worked in the region's textile mills.

The New South prided itself most on its iron and steel industry, which grew up in the area surrounding Birmingham, Alabama. Andrew Carnegie toured the region in 1889 and observed, "The South is Pennsylvania's most formidable industrial enemy." But southern industry remained controlled by northern investors. Elaborate mechanisms rigged the price of southern steel, inflating it, as one northern insider confessed, "for the purpose of protecting the Pittsburgh mills and in turn the Pittsburgh steel users." Similar policies also prevailed in the lumber and mining industries.

In practical terms, the industrialized New South proved an illusion. Much of the South remained agricultural, caught in the grip of the insidious crop lien system (see chapter 16). White southern farmers, desperate to get out of debt, sometimes joined with African Americans to pursue their goals politically. Between 1865 and 1900, voters in every southern state experimented with political alliances that crossed the color line. In Virginia, the "Readjusters," a coalition of blacks and whites determined to "readjust" (lower) the state debt and spend more money on public education, captured state offices from 1879 to 1883. In southern politics, the interplay of race and gender made coalitions like the Readjusters a potent threat to the status quo.

Gender, Race, and Politics

Gender—society's notion of what constitutes acceptable masculine or feminine behavior—influenced politics throughout the nineteenth century. From the early days of the Republic, citizenship had been defined in male terms. Citizenship and its prerogatives (voting and officeholding) served as a badge of manliness and rested on its corollary, patriarchy—the power and authority men exerted over their wives and families. With the advent of universal (white) male suffrage in the early nineteenth century, gender eclipsed class as the defining feature of citizenship. Once the public sphere of political participation became equated with manhood, women found themselves increasingly restricted to the private sphere of home and hearth.

Gender permeated politics in other ways, especially in the New South. Cross-racial alliances rested on the belief that universal political rights (voting, officeholding, patronage) could be extended to black males in the public sphere without eliminating racial barriers in the private sphere. Democrats fought back by trying to convince voters that black voting would inevitably lead to miscegenation (racial mixing). Black male political power and sexual power, they warned, went hand in hand. Ultimately their arguments prevailed, and many whites returned to the Democratic fold to protect "white womanhood" and with it white supremacy.

The notion that black men threatened white southern womanhood reached its most vicious form in the practice of lynching—the killing and mutilation of black men by white mobs. By 1892, the practice had become so prevalent that a

New South

▶ Vision of economic development of the South to mirror the industrial North. In the aftermath of the Civil War, Henry Grady, among others, promoted the virtues of a new industrial South. Despite some achievements, the industrialized New South, in practical terms, proved an illusion.

| How did big business change at the end of the nineteenth century? | What factors influenced political life in the late nineteenth century? | What issues shaped presidential politics in the late nineteenth century? | What role did the economy play in the politics of the 1880s and 1890s? | Conclusion: Why was business so dominant in the Gilded Age? |

493

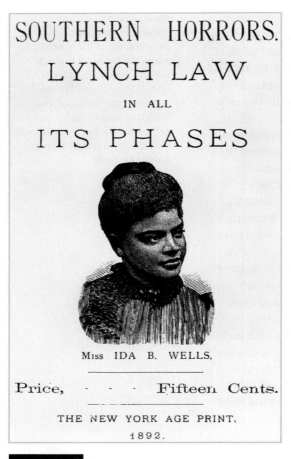

SOUTHERN HORRORS.

LYNCH LAW

IN ALL

ITS PHASES

Miss IDA B. WELLS,

Price, - - - Fifteen Cents.

THE NEW YORK AGE PRINT,
1892.

Ida B. Wells

Ida B. Wells began her antilynching campaign in 1892 after a friend's murder led her to examine the problem of lynching in the South. She spread her message in lectures and pamphlets like this one, distributed for fifteen cents. Manuscript, Archives and Rare Books Division, Schomburg Center for Research in Black Culture, The New York Public Library, Astor, Lenox, and Tilden Foundations.

Ida B. Wells

▶ Black female journalist who launched an antilynching crusade in the 1890s. Wells saw lynching as part of an effort by whites to protect the racial and economic status quo. Despite reprisals and death threats, Wells worked all her life to end lynching.

courageous black woman, **Ida B. Wells**, launched an antilynching movement. That year, a white mob lynched a friend of Wells's whose grocery store competed too successfully with a white-owned store. Wells shrewdly concluded that lynching served "as an excuse to get rid of Negroes who were acquiring wealth and property and thus keep the race terrorized." She began to collect data on lynching and discovered that in the decade between 1882 and 1892, lynching rose in the South by an overwhelming 200 percent, with more than 241 people killed. The vast increase in lynching testified to the retreat of the federal government following Reconstruction and to white southerners' determination to maintain supremacy through terrorism and intimidation.

Wells articulated lynching as a problem of race and gender. She insisted that the myth of black attacks on white southern women masked the reality that mob violence had more to do with economics and the shifting social structure of the South than with rape. She demonstrated in a sophisticated way how the southern patriarchal system, having lost its control over blacks with the end of slavery, used its control over women to circumscribe the liberty of black men.

Wells's strong stance immediately resulted in reprisal. While she was traveling in the North, vandals ransacked her office in Tennessee and destroyed her printing equipment. Yet the warning that she would be killed on sight if she ever returned to Memphis only stiffened her resolve. As she wrote in her autobiography, *Crusade for Justice* (1928), "Having lost my paper, had a price put on my life and been made an exile . . . , I felt that I owed it to myself and to my race to tell the whole truth now that I was where I could do so freely."

Lynching did not end during Wells's lifetime, but her forceful voice brought the issue to national and international prominence. At her funeral in 1931, black leader W. E. B. Du Bois eulogized Wells as the woman who "began the awakening of the conscience of the nation." Wells's determined campaign against lynching provided just one example of women's political activism during the Gilded Age. The suffrage and temperance movements, along with the growing popularity of women's clubs, dramatized how women refused to be kept out of politics.

Women's Activism

In 1869, Elizabeth Cady Stanton along with Susan B. Anthony formed the National Woman Suffrage Association (NWSA), the first independent women's rights organization in the United States. Although it would be many years before women gained suffrage, they found ways to act politically long before they voted and cleverly used their moral authority as wives and mothers to move from the domestic sphere into the realm of politics.

The extraordinary activity of women's clubs in the period following the Civil War provides just one example. Women's clubs proliferated from the 1860s to the 1890s, often in response to the exclusionary policies of men's organizations. In 1868, newspaper reporter Jane Cunningham Croly founded the Sorosis Club in

CHAPTER LOCATOR | How did the railroads stimulate big business?

New York City after the New York Press Club denied entry to women journalists wishing to attend a banquet honoring the British author Charles Dickens. In 1890, Croly brought state and local clubs together under the umbrella of the General Federation of Women's Clubs (GFWC). Not wanting to alienate southern women, the GFWC barred black women's clubs from joining, despite their vehement objections. Women's clubs soon turned from literary pursuits to politics and reform, endorsing an end to child labor, supporting the eight-hour workday, and helping pass pure food and drug legislation.

The temperance movement (the movement to end drunkenness) attracted by far the largest number of organized women in the late nineteenth century. During the winter of 1873–74, temperance women adopted a radical new tactic. Armed with Bibles and singing hymns, they marched on taverns and saloons and refused to leave until the proprietors signed a pledge to quit selling liquor. Known as the Woman's Crusade, the movement spread through small towns in Ohio, Indiana, Michigan, and Illinois and soon moved east into New York, New England, and Pennsylvania. Before it was over, more than 100,000 women had marched in more than 450 cities and towns.

The women's tactics may have been new, but the temperance movement dated back to the 1820s. Originally, the movement was led by Protestant men who organized clubs to pledge voluntary abstinence from liquor. By the 1850s, temperance advocates won significant victories when states, starting with Maine, passed laws to prohibit the sale of liquor. The Woman's Crusade dramatically brought the issue of temperance back into the national spotlight and led to the formation of a new organization, the **Woman's Christian Temperance Union (WCTU)**, in 1874. Composed entirely of women, the WCTU advocated total abstinence from alcohol.

Temperance provided women with a respectable outlet for their increasing resentment of women's inferior status and their growing recognition of women's capabilities. In its first five years, the WCTU relied on education and moral suasion, but when Frances Willard became president in 1879, she politicized the organization (see chapter 20). When the women of the WCTU joined with the Prohibition Party (formed in 1869 by a group of evangelical clergymen), one wag observed, "Politics is a man's game, an' women, childhern, and prohyibitionists do well to keep out iv it." By sharing power with women, the Prohibitionist men violated the old political rules and risked attacks on their honor and manhood.

Even though they could not yet vote, women found ways to affect the political process. Like men, they displayed strong party loyalties and rallied around traditional Republican and Democratic candidates. Third parties courted women, recognizing that their volunteer labor and support could be key assets in party building. Nevertheless, despite growing political awareness among women, politics, particularly presidential politics, remained an exclusively male prerogative.

Woman's Christian Temperance Union (WCTU)
▶ All-women organization founded in 1874 to advocate for total abstinence from alcohol. The WCTU became an important way for women to express their political views.

QUICK REVIEW <

How did race and gender influence politics in the late nineteenth century?

How did big business change at the end of the nineteenth century?

What factors influenced political life in the late nineteenth century?

What issues shaped presidential politics in the late nineteenth century?

What role did the economy play in the politics of the 1880s and 1890s?

Conclusion: Why was business so dominant in the Gilded Age?

> What issues shaped presidential politics in the late nineteenth century?

Civil Service Exam In the 1890s, prospective police officers in Chicago take the written civil service exam. Civil service meant that politicians and party bosses could no longer use jobs to reward their supporters. Chicago Historical Society.

UNTIL THE 1890s, few Americans thought the president or the national government had any role to play in addressing the problems accompanying the nation's industrial transformation. The dominant creed of laissez-faire, coupled with the dictates of social Darwinism, warned government to leave business alone. Still, presidents in the Gilded Age grappled with corruption and party strife and struggled toward the creation of new political ethics designed to replace patronage with a civil service system that promised to award jobs on the basis of merit, not party loyalty.

Corruption and Party Strife

The political corruption and party factionalism that characterized the administration of Ulysses S. Grant (1869–1877) (see chapter 16) continued to trouble the nation in the 1880s. The spoils system remained the driving force in party politics at all levels of government in the Gilded Age. Pro-business Republicans generally held a firm grip on the White House, while Democrats had better luck in Congress. Both parties relied on patronage to cement party loyalty.

A small but determined group of reformers championed a new ethics that would preclude politicians from getting rich from public office. The selection of U.S. senators particularly concerned them. Under the Constitution, senators were selected by state legislatures, not directly elected by the voters. Powerful business interests often controlled state legislatures and through them U.S. senators.

CHAPTER LOCATOR | How did the railroads stimulate big business?

As journalist Henry Demarest Lloyd quipped, Standard Oil "had done everything to the Pennsylvania legislature except to refine it." In this climate, a constitutional amendment calling for the direct election of senators faced stiff opposition from entrenched interests.

Republican president Rutherford B. Hayes, whose disputed election in 1876 signaled the end of Reconstruction in the South, tried to steer a middle course between spoilsmen and reformers. Hayes was a hardworking, well-informed executive who wanted peace, prosperity, and an end to party strife. Yet the Republican Party remained divided into three factions led by strong party bosses who boasted that they could make or break any president.

Republican Factions in 1880

Stalwarts	Supporters of the patronage system, led by master spoilsman Senator Roscoe Conkling of New York.
Half Breeds	Less openly corrupt than the Stalwarts, led by Conkling's archrival, Senator James G. Blaine of Maine.
Mugwumps	Reform-minded Republicans from Massachusetts and New York who deplored the spoils system and advocated civil service reform.

President Hayes's middle course pleased no one, and he soon managed to alienate all factions of his party. No one was surprised when he announced that he would not seek reelection in 1880. To avoid choosing among its factions, the Republican Party in 1880 nominated a dark-horse candidate, Representative James A. Garfield from Ohio. To appease Senator Roscoe Conkling (leader of the "Stalwart" faction), they picked Stalwart Chester A. Arthur as the vice presidential candidate. The Democrats made an attempt to overcome sectionalism and establish a national party by selecting an old Union general, Winfield Scott Hancock. But as one observer noted, "It is a peculiarly constituted party that sends rebel brigadiers to Congress because of their rebellion, and then nominates a Union General as its candidate for president because of his loyalty." Hancock received 155 electoral votes to Garfield's 214, although the popular vote was less lopsided.

Garfield's Assassination and Civil Service Reform

"My God," Garfield swore after only a few months in office, "what is there in this place that a man should ever want to get into it?" Garfield, like Hayes, faced the difficult task of remaining independent while pacifying the party bosses and placating the reformers. On July 2, 1881, less than four months after taking office, Garfield was shot and died two months later. His assailant, Charles Guiteau, though clearly insane, turned out to be a disappointed office seeker who claimed to be motivated by political partisanship. He told the police officer who arrested him, "I did it; I will go to jail for it; Arthur is president, and I am a Stalwart." The press almost universally condemned Republican factionalism for creating the political climate that produced Guiteau and led to the second political assassination in a generation.

After Garfield's assassination, attacks on the spoils system increased, and the public joined the chorus calling for reform. Both parties claimed credit for passage

CHRONOLOGY

1880
- Republican compromise candidate James A. Garfield is elected president.

1881
- Garfield is assassinated; Vice President Chester A. Arthur becomes president.

1883
- Pendleton Civil Service Act establishes a merit system for thousands of federal jobs to replace the spoils system.

1884
- Grover Cleveland becomes the first Democrat to be elected president since 1856.

| How did big business change at the end of the nineteenth century? | What factors influenced political life in the late nineteenth century? | **What issues shaped presidential politics in the late nineteenth century?** | What role did the economy play in the politics of the 1880s and 1890s? | Conclusion: Why was business so dominant in the Gilded Age? |

of the Pendleton Civil Service Act of 1883, which established a permanent Civil Service Commission consisting of three members appointed by the president. Some fourteen thousand jobs came under a merit system that required examinations for office and made it impossible to remove jobholders for political reasons. The new law also prohibited federal jobholders from contributing to political campaigns, thus drying up the major source of the party bosses' revenue. Soon, business interests stepped in to replace officeholders as the nation's chief political contributors. Ironically, **civil service reform** thus gave business an even greater influence in political life.

civil service reform

▶ Effort in the 1880s to do away with the spoils system. The assassination of President James Garfield in 1881 led to the passage of the Pendleton Civil Service Act of 1883, which established a permanent Civil Service Commission. Some fourteen thousand jobs came under a merit system that required examinations for office and made it impossible to remove jobholders for political reasons.

Reform and Scandal: The Campaign of 1884

When Conkling's political star fell after Garfield's assassination, James G. Blaine assumed leadership of the Republican Party and at long last captured the presidential nomination in 1884. But Mugwumps like editor Carl Schurz insisted that Blaine "wallowed in spoils like a rhinoceros in an African pool." They bolted the party and embraced the Democrats' presidential nominee, Grover Cleveland, reform governor of New York. Cleveland distinguished himself from an entire generation of politicians by the simple motto "A public office is a public trust." First

Campaign Pins, 1884

These gilt campaign pins from the election of 1884 show Republican candidate James G. Blaine, on the right, thumbing his nose at Democratic candidate Grover Cleveland. The gilt pins are a symbol for Gilded Age politics, an era characterized by corruption and party strife. Collection of Janice L. and David J. Frent.

CHAPTER LOCATOR | How did the railroads stimulate big business?

as mayor of Buffalo and later as governor of New York, he built a reputation for honesty, economy, and administrative efficiency. The Democrats, who had not won the presidency since 1856, had high hopes for his candidacy, especially after the Mugwumps threw their support to Cleveland, insisting that "the paramount issue this year is moral rather than political."

The Mugwumps soon regretted their words. The 1884 contest degenerated so far into scandal and nasty mudslinging that one disgusted journalist styled it "the vilest campaign ever waged." In July, Cleveland's hometown paper, the *Buffalo Telegraph*, revealed that the candidate had fathered an illegitimate child in an affair with a local widow. Cleveland, a bachelor, accepted responsibility for the child. Crushed by the scandal, the Mugwumps lost much of their enthusiasm. At public rallies, Blaine's partisans taunted Cleveland, chanting, "Ma, Ma, where's my Pa?"

Blaine set a new campaign style by launching a whirlwind national tour. On a last-minute stop in New York City, Blaine committed a misstep that may have cost him the election. He overlooked a remark by a supporter, a local clergyman who cast a slur on Catholic voters by styling the Democrats as the party of "Rum, Romanism, and Rebellion." Linking drinking (rum) and Catholicism (Romanism) offended Irish Catholic voters, whom Blaine had counted on to desert the Democratic Party and support him because of his Irish background.

With less than a week to go until the election, Blaine had no chance to recover from the negative publicity. He lost New York State by fewer than 1,200 votes and with it the election ending twenty-five years of Republican control of the presidency (**Map 18.2**). Cleveland's followers had the last word. To the chorus of "Ma, Ma, where's my Pa?" they retorted, "Going to the White House, ha, ha, ha."

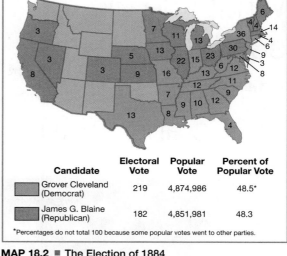

Candidate	Electoral Vote	Popular Vote	Percent of Popular Vote
Grover Cleveland (Democrat)	219	4,874,986	48.5*
James G. Blaine (Republican)	182	4,851,981	48.3

*Percentages do not total 100 because some popular votes went to other parties.

MAP 18.2 ■ The Election of 1884

QUICK REVIEW

How did the divisions within the Republican Party contribute to the outcome of the 1884 presidential election?

| How did big business change at the end of the nineteenth century? | What factors influenced political life in the late nineteenth century? | **What issues shaped presidential politics in the late nineteenth century?** | What role did the economy play in the politics of the 1880s and 1890s? | Conclusion: Why was business so dominant in the Gilded Age? |

499

What role did the economy play in the politics of the 1880s and 1890s?

FOUR YEARS LATER, in the election of 1888, voters turned Cleveland out, electing Republican Benjamin Harrison. Then, in the only instance in America's history when a president once defeated at the polls returned to office, the voters brought Cleveland back in the election of 1892. What factors account for such a surprising turnaround? The 1880s witnessed a remarkable political realignment as a set of economic concerns replaced appeals to Civil War sectional loyalties. The tariff, federal regulation of the railroads and trusts, and the campaign for free silver restructured American politics.

The Tariff and the Politics of Protection

The tariff became a potent political issue in the 1880s. The concept of a protective tariff to raise the price of imported goods and stimulate American industry dated back to Alexander Hamilton in the founding days of the Republic. The Republicans turned the tariff to political ends in 1861 by enacting a measure that both raised revenues for the Civil War and rewarded their industrial supporters, who wanted protection from foreign competition. After the war, the pro-business Republicans continued to revise and enlarge the tariff. By the 1880s, the tariff produced more than $2.1 billion in revenue and had created a huge surplus that sat idly in the Treasury's vaults while the government argued about how (or even whether) to spend it.

To many Americans, particularly southern and midwestern farmers who sold their crops in a world market but had to buy goods priced artificially high because of the protective tariff, the answer was simple: Reduce the tariff. Advocates of free trade and moderates agitated for tariff reform. But those who benefited from the tariff—industrialists insisting that America's "infant industries" needed protection and some westerners producing protected raw materials such as wool, hides, and lumber—firmly opposed lowering the tariff. Many argued that workers, too, benefited from high tariffs that protected American wages by giving American products an edge over imported goods.

The Republican Party seized on the tariff question to forge a new national coalition. "Fold up the bloody shirt and lay it away," Blaine advised a colleague in 1880. "It's of no use to us. You want to shift the main issue to protection." By encouraging an alliance among industrialists, labor, and western producers of raw materials—groups seen to benefit from the tariff—Blaine hoped to solidify the North, Midwest, and West against the solidly Democratic South. Although the tactic failed for Blaine in the presidential election of 1884, it worked for the Republicans four years later.

Cleveland, who had straddled the tariff issue in the election of 1884, startled the nation in 1887 by calling for tariff reform. Cleveland attacked the tariff as a tax levied on American consumers by powerful industries. And he pointed out that high tariffs impeded the expansion of American markets abroad at a time when American industries needed to expand if they were to keep growing. The Republicans countered by arguing that "tariff tinkering" would only unsettle prosperous industries, drive down wages, and shrink the farmers' home market. Republican Benjamin Harrison, who supported the high tariff, ousted Cleveland from the White House in 1888, carrying all the western and northern states except Connecticut and New Jersey.

Back in power, the Republicans passed the highest tariff in the nation's history in 1890. The new tariff, sponsored by Republican representative William McKinley of Ohio and signed into law by Harrison, stirred up protests across the United States. The American people had elected Harrison to preserve protection but not to enact a higher tariff. Democrats condemned the McKinley tariff and labeled the Republican Congress that passed it the "Billion Dollar Congress" for its spending, which depleted the nation's surplus by enacting a series of pork barrel programs designed to bring federal money to congressmen's own constituents. In the congressional election of 1890, angry voters swept the Republicans, including tariff sponsor McKinley, out of office. Two years later, Harrison himself was defeated, and Grover Cleveland returned to the White House.

Controversy over the tariff masked deeper divisions in American society. Conflict between workers and farmers on the one side and bankers and corporate giants on the other erupted throughout the 1880s and came to a head in the 1890s. Both sides in the tariff debate spoke to concern over class conflict when

CHRONOLOGY

1873
– Wall Street panic leads to major economic depression.

1887
– Interstate Commerce Act establishes the nation's first regulatory agency.

1890
– Congress passes the McKinley tariff, the highest in U.S. history.
– Sherman Antitrust Act forbids businesses from entering into agreements to restrict competition.

1893
– Wall Street panic touches off national depression.

1895
– Banker J. P. Morgan bails out U.S. Treasury.

How did big business change at the end of the nineteenth century?

What factors influenced political life in the late nineteenth century?

What issues shaped presidential politics in the late nineteenth century?

What role did the economy play in the politics of the 1880s and 1890s?

Conclusion: Why was business so dominant in the Gilded Age?

501

they insisted that their respective plans, whether McKinley's high tariff or Cleveland's tariff reform, would bring prosperity and harmony. For their part, many working people shared the sentiment voiced by one labor leader that the tariff was "only a scheme devised by the old parties to throw dust in the eyes of laboring men."

Railroads, Trusts, and the Federal Government

American voters may have divided on the tariff, but increasingly they agreed on the need for federal regulation of the railroads and federal legislation to curb the power of the "trusts" (a term loosely applied to all large business combinations). As early as the 1870s, angry farmers in the Midwest who suffered from the unfair shipping practices of the railroads organized to fight for railroad regulation. The Patrons of Husbandry, or the Grange, founded in 1867 as a social and educational organization for farmers, soon became an independent political movement. By electing Grangers to state office, farmers made it possible for several midwestern states to pass laws in the 1870s and 1880s regulating the railroads. At first, the Supreme Court ruled in favor of state regulation (*Munn v. Illinois*, 1877). But in 1886, the Court reversed itself, ruling that because railroads crossed state boundaries, they fell outside state jurisdiction (*Wabash v. Illinois*). With more than three-fourths of railroads crossing state lines, the Supreme Court's decision effectively quashed the states' attempts at railroad regulation.

Anger at the *Wabash* decision finally led to the first federal law regulating the railroads, the Interstate Commerce Act, passed in 1887 during Cleveland's first administration. The act established the nation's first federal regulatory agency, the Interstate Commerce Commission (ICC), to oversee the railroad industry. In its early years, however, the ICC was never strong enough to pose a serious threat to the railroads and was more important as a precedent than effective as a watchdog.

Sherman Antitrust Act

▶ 1890 act that outlawed pools and trusts, ruling that businesses could no longer enter into agreements to restrict competition. Government inaction, combined with the Supreme Court's narrow reading of the act in the *United States v. E. C. Knight Company* decision, undermined the law's effectiveness.

Concern over the growing power of the trusts led Congress to pass the **Sherman Antitrust Act** in 1890. The act outlawed pools and trusts, ruling that businesses could no longer enter into agreements to restrict competition. It did nothing to restrict huge holding companies such as Standard Oil, however, and proved to be a weak sword against the trusts. In the following decade, the government successfully struck down only six trusts but used the law four times against labor by outlawing unions as a "conspiracy in restraint of trade." In 1895, the conservative Supreme Court dealt the antitrust law a crippling blow in *United States v. E. C. Knight Company*. In its decision, the Court ruled that "manufacture" did not constitute "trade." The ruling drastically narrowed the law, in this case allowing the American Sugar Refining Company, which had bought out a number of other sugar companies (including E. C. Knight) and controlled 98 percent of the production of sugar, to continue its virtual monopoly.

Both the ICC and the Sherman Antitrust Act testified to the nation's concern about corporate abuses of power and to a growing willingness to use federal measures to intervene on behalf of the public interest. As corporate capitalism became more and more powerful, public pressure toward government intervention grew. Yet not until the twentieth century would more active presidents sharpen and use these weapons effectively against the large corporations.

The Fight for Free Silver

While the tariff and regulation of the trusts gained many backers, the silver issue stirred passions like no other issue of the day. On one side stood those who believed that gold constituted the only honest money. The government's support of the gold standard meant that anyone could redeem paper money for gold. Many who supported the gold standard were eastern creditors who did not wish to be paid in devalued dollars. On the opposite side stood a coalition of western silver barons and poor farmers from the West and South who called for **free silver**. The mining interests, who had seen the silver bonanza in the West drive down the price of the precious metal, wanted the government to buy silver and mint silver dollars. Farmers from the West and South who had suffered from deflation during the 1870s and 1880s hoped that increasing the money supply with silver dollars, thus causing inflation, would give them some debt relief by enabling them to pay off their creditors with cheaper dollars.

During the depression following the panic of 1873, critics of hard money organized the Greenback Labor Party, an alliance of farmers and urban wage laborers. The Greenbackers favored issuing paper currency not tied to the gold supply, citing the precedent of the greenbacks issued during the Civil War. The government had the right to define what constituted legal tender, the Greenbackers reasoned: "Paper is equally money, when . . . issued according to law." They proposed that the nation's currency be based on its wealth—land, labor, and capital—and not simply on its reserves of gold. The Greenback Labor Party captured more than a million votes and elected fourteen members to Congress in 1878. Although conservatives considered the Greenbackers dangerous cranks, their views eventually prevailed in the 1930s, when the country abandoned the gold standard.

After the Greenback Labor Party collapsed, proponents of free silver came to dominate the monetary debate in the 1890s. Advocates of free silver pointed out that until 1873, the country had enjoyed a system of bimetallism—the minting of both silver and gold into coins. In that year, at the behest of those who favored gold, the Republican Congress had voted to stop buying and minting silver, an act silver supporters denounced as the "crime of '73." By sharply contracting the money supply at a time when the nation's economy was burgeoning, the Republicans had enriched bankers and investors at the expense of cotton and wheat farmers and industrial wageworkers. In 1878 and again in 1890, with the Sherman Silver Purchase Act, Congress took steps to ease the tight money policy and appease advocates of silver by passing legislation requiring the government to buy silver and issue silver certificates. Though good for the mining interests, the laws did little to promote the inflation desired by farmers. Soon monetary reformers began to call for "the free and unlimited coinage of silver," a plan whereby nearly all the silver mined in the West would be minted into coins circulated at the rate of sixteen ounces of silver to one ounce of gold.

By the 1890s, the silver issue crossed party lines. The Democrats hoped to use it to achieve a union between western and southern voters. Unfortunately for them, Democratic president Grover Cleveland supported the gold standard as vehemently as any Republican. After a panic on Wall Street in the spring of 1893, Cleveland called a special session of Congress and bullied the legislature into repealing the

free silver

▶ Term used by opponents of the gold standard for their proposal that the government buy silver and use it to mint currency. Western silver barons and poor farmers from the West and South were the primary advocates of free silver. The latter hoped that such a policy would result in inflation, effectively providing them with debt relief.

How did big business change at the end of the nineteenth century?	What factors influenced political life in the late nineteenth century?	What issues shaped presidential politics in the late nineteenth century?	**What role did the economy play in the politics of the 1880s and 1890s?**	Conclusion: Why was business so dominant in the Gilded Age?

Silver Purchase Act because he believed it threatened economic confidence. Repeal proved disastrous for Cleveland, not only economically but also politically. It did nothing to bring prosperity and dangerously divided the country.

Panic and Depression

President Cleveland had scarcely begun his second term in office in 1893 when the country faced the worst depression it had yet seen. In the face of economic disaster, Cleveland clung to the gold standard. In the winter of 1894–95, the president walked the floor of the White House, sleepless over the prospect that the United States might go bankrupt. Individuals and investors, rushing to trade in their banknotes for gold, strained the country's monetary system. The Treasury's gold reserves dipped so low that the government faced a real risk of going bankrupt.

At this juncture, J. P. Morgan stepped in to purchase gold abroad and supply it to the Treasury. A storm of controversy erupted over the deal. The press claimed that Cleveland had lined his own pockets and rumored that Morgan had made $8.9 million. Neither allegation was true. Cleveland had not profited a penny, and Morgan made far less than the millions his critics claimed.

But if President Cleveland's action managed to salvage the gold standard, it did not save the country from hardship. The winter of 1894–95 was one of the worst times in American history. People faced unemployment, cold, and hunger. A firm believer in limited government, Cleveland insisted that nothing could be done to help. "I do not believe that the power and duty of the General Government ought to be extended to the relief of individual suffering which is in no manner properly related to the public service or benefit." Nor did it occur to Cleveland that his great faith in the gold standard prolonged the depression, favored creditors over debtors, and caused immense hardship for millions of Americans.

> **QUICK REVIEW**

What role did the gold standard play in the economic crisis of the 1890s?

Library of Congress.

Conclusion: Why was business so dominant in the Gilded Age?

THE GOLD DEAL between J. P. Morgan and Grover Cleveland underscored a dangerous reality: The federal government was so weak that its solvency depended on a private banker. This lopsided power relationship signaled the dominance of business in the era author Mark Twain satirically but accurately characterized as the Gilded Age. Perhaps no other era in American history spawned greed, corruption, and vulgarity on so grand a scale.

Nevertheless, the Gilded Age was not without its share of achievements. In these years, America made the leap into the industrial age. Factories and refineries poured out American steel and oil at unprecedented rates. Businessmen developed new strategies to consolidate American industry. New inventions, including the telephone and electric light and power, changed Americans' everyday lives. By the end of the nineteenth century, the country had achieved industrial maturity. It boasted the largest, most innovative, most productive economy in the world.

Yet the changes that came with these developments worried many Americans and gave rise to the era's political turmoil. Race and gender profoundly influenced American politics, leading to new political alliances. Ida B. Wells fought racism in its most brutal form—lynching. Women's organizations championed causes, notably suffrage and temperance, and challenged prevailing views of woman's proper place. Reformers fought corruption by instituting civil service. And new issues—the tariff, the regulation of the trusts, and currency reform—restructured the nation's politics.

The Gilded Age witnessed a nation transformed. Where dusty roads and cattle trails once sprawled across the continent, steel rails now bound the country together. Cities grew exponentially, not only with new inhabitants from around the globe but also with new bridges, subways, and skyscrapers. The nation's workers and the great cities they labored to build are the focus of chapter 19.

SO NOW YOU KNOW

Mark Twain accurately labeled the late nineteenth century the Gilded Age, but not everyone shared in the gaudy excess of the period. The gap between the rich and the poor grew ever larger.

How did big business change at the end of the nineteenth century?	What factors influenced political life in the late nineteenth century?	What issues shaped presidential politics in the late nineteenth century?	What role did the economy play in the politics of the 1880s and 1890s?	**Conclusion: Why was business so dominant in the Gilded Age?**

CHAPTER 18 STUDY GUIDE

Online Study Guide
bedfordstmartins.com/roarkunderstanding

STEP 1 GETTING STARTED

Below are basic terms from this period in American history. Can you identify each term below and explain why it matters? To do this exercise online or to download this chart, visit bedfordstmartins.com/roarkunderstanding.

TERM	WHO OR WHAT & WHEN	WHY IT MATTERS
Andrew Carnegie, p. 483		
John D. Rockefeller, p. 485		
Thomas Alva Edison, p. 487		
J. P. Morgan, p. 488		
social Darwinism, p. 489		
spoils system, p. 491		
New South, p. 493		
Ida B. Wells, p. 494		
Woman's Christian Temperance Union, p. 495		
civil service reform, p. 498		
Sherman Antitrust Act, p. 502		
free silver, p. 503		

STEP 2 MOVING BEYOND THE BASICS

The exercise below represents a more advanced understanding of the chapter material. Fill in the following chart by describing the positions that various political parties held on the key economic issues of the period and the regional differences in viewpoint on these issues. How did people in different parts of the country see these issues? To do this exercise online or to download this chart, visit bedfordstmartins.com/roarkunderstanding.

Key economic issues	Democrats	Republicans	Third parties	Regional differences
Tariffs				
Railroads				
Trusts				
Free silver				

Now that you've reviewed various parts of the chapter, take a step back and try to see the big picture by answering these questions. Remember to use specific examples from the chapter in your answers. To do this exercise online, visit bedfordstmartins.com/roarkunderstanding.

THE RISE OF BIG BUSINESS

▶ What role did railroads and new technologies play in the rise of American big business?

▶ How did the business pioneers of the late nineteenth century organize and grow their businesses?

LATE-NINETEENTH-CENTURY POLITICS

▶ How did ideas about gender and race shape late-nineteenth-century politics?

▶ How did new social philosophical theories justify business and political practices in the late nineteenth century?

LOOKING BACKWARD,
LOOKING AHEAD

▶ How did the role of business in politics in the late nineteenth century differ from its role in the first half of the century?

▶ How did the rise of big business affect the economic and political landscape of early-twentieth-century America? In what ways did Americans try to deal with the excesses of big business?

ECONOMIC ISSUES AND POLITICAL CONFLICT

▶ How did each Gilded Age president react to economic issues? How did Supreme Court decisions affect economic issues?

▶ What made free silver such a powerful and emotional issue in the late nineteenth century?

IN YOUR OWN WORDS

Imagine that you must explain chapter 18 to someone who hasn't read it. What would be the most important points to include and why?

NEW YORK
ILLUSTRATED

19
THE GROWTH OF AMERICA'S CITIES

1870–1900

> This chapter explores the rise of urban, industrial America. It examines urban growth and its consequences, focusing on the nature of industrial labor, tensions between workers and employers, the impact of urbanization on daily life, and the cities' efforts to respond to the demands of their fast-growing populations.

> Why did American cities grow so fast in the late nineteenth century?

> What kinds of work did people do in industrial America?

> What steps did workers take to organize in the 1870s and 1880s?

> How did industrialization transform home life and leisure?

> How did cities respond to the challenges of growth?

> Conclusion: Who built the cities?

DID YOU KNOW?

More than 40 percent of Americans have ancestors who came through Ellis Island.

Brooklyn Bridge. Completed in 1883, the Brooklyn Bridge realized John Roebling's dream of creating "a great work of art" as well as a superbly engineered bridge.

> Why did American cities grow so fast in the late nineteenth century?

Russian Immigrant Family

A Russian immigrant family is shown leaving Ellis Island in 1900. Notice the white slips of paper pinned to their coats indicating that they have been processed. An immigration official in uniform stands on the left. The original wooden structure burned down and was replaced with an elaborate stone building the year this photo was taken.
Keystone-Mast Collection, UCR/California Museum of Photography, University of California, Riverside.

"WE CANNOT ALL LIVE IN CITIES, yet nearly all seem determined to do so," New York editor Horace Greeley complained. The last three decades of the nineteenth century witnessed an urban explosion. Cities and towns grew more than twice as rapidly as the total population. Most of the nation's largest cities were east of the Mississippi, although St. Louis and San Francisco both ranked among the top ten urban areas in 1900. Patterns of global migration contributed to the surge in urban population. In the port cities of the East Coast, more than fourteen million people arrived, many from southern and eastern Europe.

The Urban Explosion, a Global Migration

Between 1870 and 1900, eleven million people moved into cities. Industrial centers such as Pittsburgh, Chicago, New York, and Cleveland acted as giant magnets, attracting workers from the countryside. But migrants to the cities were by no means only rural Americans. Worldwide in scope, the movement from rural areas to urban industrial centers attracted millions of immigrants to American shores.

By the 1870s, the world could be conceptualized as three interconnected geographic regions (**Map 19.1**). At the center stood an industrial core that included parts of North America and Europe. This core was surrounded by a vast agricultural domain. Capitalist development in the late nineteenth century shattered traditional patterns of economic activity in this rural periphery. As old patterns broke down, these rural areas exported, along with other raw materials, new recruits for the industrial labor force.

CHAPTER LOCATOR | Why did American cities grow so fast in the late nineteenth century?

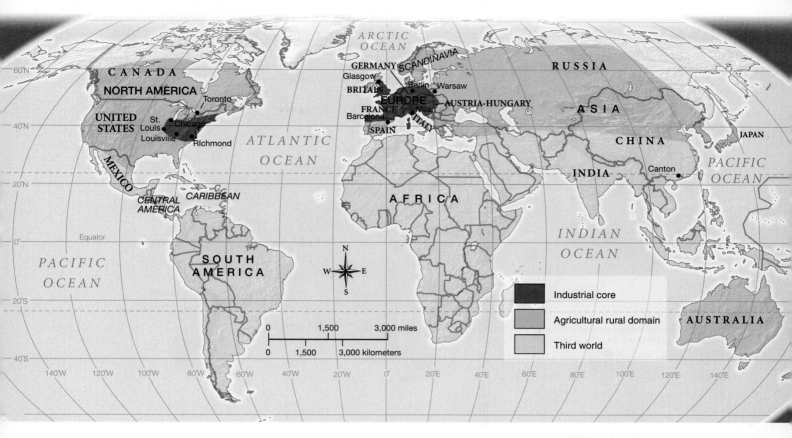

MAP 19.1 ■ **Economic Regions of the World, 1890s**

The global nature of the world economy at the turn of the twentieth century is indicated by three interconnected geographic regions. At the center stands the industrial core—western Europe and the northeastern United States. The second region—the agricultural periphery—supplied immigrant laborers to the industries in the core. Beyond these two regions lay a vast area tied economically to the industrial core by colonialism.

Beyond this second circle lay an even larger third world. Ties between this part of the world and the industrial core strengthened in the late nineteenth century, but most of the people living there stayed put. They worked on plantations and railroads, in mines and ports, as part of a huge export network managed by foreign powers that staked out spheres of influence and colonies.

In the 1870s, railroad expansion and low steamship fares gave the world's peoples a newfound mobility that enabled industrialists to draw on a global population for cheap labor. When Andrew Carnegie opened his first steel mill in 1872, his superintendent hired workers he called "buckwheats"—young American boys just off the farm. By the 1890s, however, Carnegie's workforce included rural Hungarians and Slavs who had migrated to the United States, willing to work for low wages.

Altogether, more than 25 million immigrants came to the United States between 1850 and 1920 (**Map 19.2**, page 512). Part of a worldwide migration, immigrants traveled to South America and Australia as well as to the United States. Yet more than 70 percent of all European immigrants chose North America as their destination. (See "Global Comparison," page 513.)

At first, the largest number of immigrants to the United States came from the British Isles and from German-speaking lands. The vast majority of immigrants were white; Asians accounted for fewer than one million immigrants, and other people of color numbered even fewer. Yet ingrained racial prejudices increasingly influenced the country's perception of immigration patterns. One of the classic formulations of the history of European immigration divided immigrants into two distinct waves that have been called the "old" and the "new" immigration. According to this theory, before 1880 the majority of immigrants came from northern and western Europe. After 1880, the pattern shifted, with more and more

| What kinds of work did people do in industrial America? | What steps did workers take to organize in the 1870s and 1880s? | How did industrialization transform home life and leisure? | How did cities respond to the challenges of growth? | Conclusion: Who built the cities? |

Immigrants: foreign-born and children of foreign or mixed parentage; by county

Less than 10%	50% to 75%
10% to 25%	More than 75%
25% to 50%	

N.Y. 2,748,011 Total foreign-born population in 1910

MAP 19.2 ■ The Impact of Immigration, to 1910

Immigration flowed in all directions—south from Canada, north from Mexico and Latin America, east from Asia to Seattle and San Francisco, and west from Europe to East Coast port cities, including Boston and New York.

▶ FOR MORE HELP ANALYZING THIS MAP, see the map activity for this chapter in the Online Study Guide at bedfordstmartins.com/roarkunderstanding.

ships carrying passengers from southern and eastern Europe. Implicit in the distinction was an invidious comparison between "old" pioneer settlers and "new" unskilled proletarians. Yet this sweeping generalization spoke more to perception than to reality. In fact, many of the earlier immigrants from Ireland, Germany, and Scandinavia came not as settlers or farmers, but as wage laborers, much like the Italians and Slavs who followed them.

The "new" immigration resulted from a number of factors. Improved economic conditions in western Europe coupled with increased immigration to Australia and Canada slowed the flow of immigrants coming into the United States from northern and western Europe. At the same time, economic depression in southern Italy, the persecution of Jews in eastern Europe, and a general desire to avoid conscription into the Russian army led many people from southern and eastern Europe to move to the United States. The need of America's industries for cheap, unskilled labor during prosperous years also stimulated immigration.

Steamship companies courted immigrants with low fares. By the 1880s, the price of a ticket from Liverpool had dropped to less than $25. Would-be immigrants eager for information about the United States relied on letters from friends and relatives, advertisements, and word of mouth—sources that were not always dependable or truthful. No wonder people left for the United States believing, as one Italian immigrant observed, "that if they were ever fortunate enough to reach America, they would fall into a pile of manure and get up brushing the diamonds out of their hair."

CHAPTER LOCATOR | Why did American cities grow so fast in the late nineteenth century?

CHAPTER 19

512 THE GROWTH OF AMERICA'S CITIES, 1870–1900

European Emigration, 1870–1890

A comparison of European emigrants and their destinations between 1870 and 1890 shows that emigrants from Germany and the British Isles (including England, Ireland, Scotland, and Wales) formed the largest group of out-migrants. The United States, which took in 63 percent of these emigrants, was by far the most popular destination. After 1890, the origin of European emigrants would tilt south and east, with Italians and eastern Europeans growing in number. Argentina proved a particularly popular destination for Italian emigrants, who found the climate and geography to their liking. What factors might account for why Europeans immigrated to the port cities of the eastern United States rather than to South America or Australia?

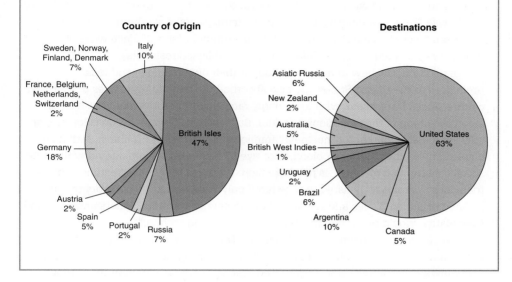

Country of Origin

Sweden, Norway, Finland, Denmark 7%
Italy 10%
France, Belgium, Netherlands, Switzerland 2%
British Isles 47%
Germany 18%
Austria 2%
Spain 5%
Portugal 2%
Russia 7%

Destinations

Asiatic Russia 6%
New Zealand 2%
Australia 5%
British West Indies 1%
Uruguay 2%
Brazil 6%
Argentina 10%
United States 63%
Canada 5%

Most of the newcomers stayed in the nation's cities. By 1900, almost two-thirds of the country's immigrant population resided in cities, many of the immigrants being too poor to move on. Although the foreign-born population rarely outnumbered the native-born population, taken together immigrants and their American-born children did constitute a majority, particularly in the nation's largest cities: Philadelphia, 55 percent; Boston, 66 percent; Chicago, 75 percent; and New York City, an amazing 80 percent in 1900.

Not all the newcomers came to stay. Perhaps eight million European immigrants—most of them young men—worked for a year or a season and then returned to their homelands. Immigration officers called these immigrants, many of them Italians, "birds of passage" because they followed a regular pattern of migration to and from the United States. By 1900, almost 75 percent of the new immigrants were young, single men. Women generally had less access to funds for travel and faced tighter family control. For these reasons, women most often came to the United States as wives, mothers, or daughters, not as single wage laborers. Only among the Irish did women immigrants outnumber men by a small margin.

Jews from eastern Europe most often came with their families and came to stay. Beginning in the 1880s, a wave of violent pogroms, or persecutions, in Russia and Poland prompted the departure of more than a million Jews in the next two decades. Most of the Jewish immigrants settled in the port cities of the East, creating distinct ethnic enclaves.

| What kinds of work did people do in industrial America? | What steps did workers take to organize in the 1870s and 1880s? | How did industrialization transform home life and leisure? | How did cities respond to the challenges of growth? | Conclusion: Who built the cities? |

1880s
- Immigration from southern and eastern Europe rises.

1890
- Jacob Riis publishes *How the Other Half Lives*, documenting in photographs the lives of tenement dwellers.

1890s
- African American migration from the South begins.

1892
- Ellis Island, a facility for processing new immigrants arriving in New York City, opens.

1896
- President Grover Cleveland vetoes immigrant literacy test.

Racism and the Cry for Immigration Restriction

Ethnic diversity and racism played a role in dividing skilled workers (those with a craft or specialized ability) from unskilled workers (those who supplied muscle or tended machines). As industrialists mechanized to replace skilled workers with lower-paid unskilled labor, they drew on immigrants, particularly those from southern and eastern Europe, who had come to the United States in the hope of bettering their lives. Skilled workers, frequently members of older immigrant groups, criticized the newcomers. Throughout the nineteenth century and into the twentieth, many Americans viewed ethnic and even religious differences as racial characteristics, referring to the Polish or the Jewish "race." Americans judged "new" immigrants of southern and eastern European "races" as inferior to those of Anglo-Teutonic "stock." Each wave of newcomers was deemed somehow inferior to the established residents.

In addition, the new immigrants brought their own religious and racial prejudices to the United States and also absorbed the popular prejudices of American culture. Social Darwinism, with its strongly racist overtones, decreed that whites stood at the top of the evolutionary ladder. But who was "white"? Skin color supposedly served as a marker for the "new" immigrants—"swarthy" Italians; dark-haired, olive-skinned Jews. But even blond, blue-eyed Poles were not considered white. The social construction of "race" is nowhere more apparent than in the testimony of an Irish dockworker who boasted that he hired only "white men," a category that he insisted excluded "Poles and Italians." For the new immigrants, Americanization and assimilation would prove inextricably part of becoming "white."

For African Americans, the cities of the North promised not just economic opportunity but also an end to institutionalized segregation and persecution. Jim Crow laws—restrictions that segregated blacks—became common throughout the South in the decades following Reconstruction. Intimidation and lynching terrorized blacks throughout the South (see chapter 18). "To die from the bite of frost is far more glorious than at the hands of a mob," proclaimed the *Defender*, Chicago's largest African American newspaper. In the 1890s, many blacks moved north, settling for the most part in the growing cities. Racism relegated them to poor jobs and substandard living conditions, but by 1900 New York, Philadelphia, and Chicago had the largest black communities in the nation.

On the West Coast, Asian immigrants became scapegoats of the changing economy. After California's gold rush, many Chinese who had come to work "on the gold mountain" found jobs on the country's transcontinental railroads. When the railroad work ended, they took work other groups shunned, including domestic service. But hard times in the 1870s made them a target for disgruntled workers. Prohibited from owning land, the Chinese migrated to the cities. The Chinese population of San Francisco continued to grow until passage of the Chinese Exclusion Act in 1882 (see chapter 17). For the first time in the nation's history, U.S. law excluded an immigrant group on the basis of race. In contrast, the nation's small Japanese community of about 3,000 expanded rapidly after 1890, until pressures to keep out all Asians led in 1910 to the creation of an immigration station at Angel Island in San Francisco Bay. Asian immigrants were detained there, sometimes for months, and many were deported as "undesirables."

On the East Coast, the volume of immigration from Europe in the last two decades of the century proved unprecedented. In 1888 alone, more than half a million Europeans landed in America, 75 percent of them in New York City. The Statue of Liberty, a gift from the people of France erected in 1886, stood sentinel

CHAPTER LOCATOR | Why did American cities grow so fast in the late nineteenth century?

CHAPTER 19
514 THE GROWTH OF AMERICA'S CITIES, 1870–1900

in the harbor. The tide of immigrants to New York City soon swamped the immigration office at Castle Garden in lower Manhattan. A new facility opened on **Ellis Island** in New York harbor in 1892. Its overcrowded halls became the gateway to the United States for millions.

To many Americans, the "new" immigrants seemed impossible to assimilate. "These people are not Americans," editorialized the popular journal *Public Opinion*, "they are the very scum and offal of Europe." Terence V. Powderly, head of the broadly inclusive Knights of Labor, complained that the newcomers "herded together like animals and lived like beasts." Blue-blooded Yankees led by Senator Henry Cabot Lodge of Massachusetts formed an unlikely alliance with organized labor to press for immigration restrictions. In 1896, Congress approved a literacy test for immigrants, but President Grover Cleveland promptly vetoed it. "It is said," the president reminded Congress, "that the quality of recent immigration is undesirable. The time is quite within recent memory when the same thing was said of immigrants, who, with their descendants, are now numbered among our best citizens." Cleveland's veto forestalled immigration restriction but did not stop anti-immigrant forces from pressing for restrictions until they achieved their goal in the 1920s (see chapter 23).

The Social Geography of the City

During the Gilded Age, cities experienced demographic and technological changes that greatly altered the social geography of the city. Cleveland, Ohio, provides a good example. In the 1870s, Cleveland was a small city in both population and area. Oil magnate John D. Rockefeller could, and often did, walk from his large brick house to his office downtown. On his way, he passed the small homes of his clerks and other middle-class families. Behind these homes ran alleys crowded with the dwellings of Cleveland's working class. Farther out, on the shores of Lake Erie, close to the factories and foundries, clustered the shanties of the city's poorest laborers.

Within two decades, the coming of mass transit had transformed this walking city. In its place emerged a central business district surrounded by concentric rings of residences organized by ethnicity and income. First the horsecar in the 1870s and then the electric streetcar in the 1880s made it possible for those who could afford the fare to work downtown and live in the "cool green rim" of the city, with its single-family homes, lawns, gardens, and trees. Social segregation— the separation of rich and poor, and of ethnic and old-stock Americans—was one of the major social changes engendered by the rise of the industrial metropolis, evident not only in Cleveland but in cities across the nation.

Race and ethnicity affected the way cities evolved. Newcomers to the nation's cities faced hostility and not surprisingly sought out their kin and country folk as they struggled to survive. Distinct ethnic neighborhoods often formed around a synagogue or church. Blacks typically experienced the greatest residential segregation, but every large city had its ethnic enclaves where English was rarely spoken.

Poverty, crowding, dirt, and disease constituted the daily reality of New York City's immigrant poor—a plight documented by photojournalist Jacob Riis in his best-selling book *How the Other Half Lives* (1890). Riis's photographs opened the nation's eyes to conditions in the city's slums. Many middle-class Americans worried equally about the excesses of the wealthy. They feared the class antagonism fueled by the growing inequality so visible in the nation's cities and shared

Ellis Island

▶ Immigration facility opened in 1892 in New York harbor that processed new immigrants coming into New York City. In the late nineteenth century, some 75 percent of European immigrants to America came through New York.

| What kinds of work did people do in industrial America? | What steps did workers take to organize in the 1870s and 1880s? | How did industrialization transform home life and leisure? | How did cities respond to the challenges of growth? | Conclusion: Who built the cities? |

515

The gap between the rich and the poor documented in Jacob Riis's best seller, *How the Other Half Lives*, is underscored here by juxtaposing the photographs of two women. Riis took the photograph of a "scrub" or washerwoman (left) in one of the notorious Police Station lodging houses, the shelters of last resort for the city's poor. On the right is Alice Vanderbilt costumed as the "Spirit of Electricity" for her sister-in-law Alva Vanderbilt's costume ball in 1883. Washerwoman: Museum of the City of New York; Vanderbilt: Collection of the New-York Historical Society.

► FOR MORE HELP ANALYZING THIS IMAGE, see the visual activity for this chapter in the Online Study Guide at bedfordstmartins.com/roarkunderstanding.

Riis's view that "the real danger to society comes not only from the tenements, but from the ill-spent wealth which reared them."

Such excesses were nowhere more visible than in the lifestyle of the Vanderbilts. With a fortune amassed in the railroads, the Vanderbilts spent their money on residences that sought to rival the palaces of Europe. In 1883, Alva (Mrs. William) Vanderbilt launched herself into New York society by throwing a costume party so lavish that not even old New York society, which turned up its nose at the nouveau riche, could resist an invitation. Her sister-in-law Alice Vanderbilt stole the show by appearing as that miraculous new invention, the electric light, in a white satin evening dress studded with diamonds (see photo). The *New York World* speculated that Alva Vanderbilt's party cost more than a quarter of a million dollars (more than $4 million today).

Such ostentatious displays of wealth became especially alarming when they were coupled with disdain for the well-being of ordinary people. When a reporter in 1882 asked William Vanderbilt whether he considered the public good when running his railroads, he shot back, "The public be damned." The fear that America had become a society ruled by the rich gained credence from the fact that the wealthiest 1 percent of the population owned more than half the real and personal property in the country.

> ## QUICK REVIEW

What global trends were reflected in the growth of American cities in the late nineteenth century?

CHAPTER LOCATOR | Why did American cities grow so fast in the late nineteenth century?

516 CHAPTER 19 THE GROWTH OF AMERICA'S CITIES, 1870–1900

Sweatshop Worker Sweatshop workers endured crowded and often dangerous conditions. Young working girls earned low wages but prided themselves on their independence. Notice the young woman's stylish hairdo, white shirtwaist, and necklace. George Eastman House.

What kinds of work did people do in industrial America?

THE NUMBER OF INDUSTRIAL WAGEWORKERS in the United States exploded in the second half of the nineteenth century, more than tripling from 5.3 million in 1860 to 17.4 million in 1900. These workers toiled in a variety of settings. Many skilled workers and artisans still earned a living in small workshops. But with the rise of corporate capitalism, large factories, mills, and mines increasingly dotted the landscape. The best way to get a sense of the diversity of workers and work-places is to look at the industrial nation at work.

America's Diverse Workers

Common laborers formed the backbone of the American labor force. These "human machines" stood at the bottom of the country's economic ladder and generally came from the most recent immigrant groups. Initially, the Irish wielded the picks and shovels that built American cities, but by the turn of the twentieth century, as the Irish bettered their lot, Slavs and Italians took their place.

At the opposite end of labor's hierarchy stood skilled craftsmen like iron puddler James J. Davis, a Welsh immigrant who worked in the Pennsylvania mills. The job of iron puddler required intelligence and experience, and Davis drew good wages, up to $7 a day, when there was work. But most industry and manufacturing

| What kinds of work did people do in industrial America? | What steps did workers take to organize in the 1870s and 1880s? | How did industrialization transform home life and leisure? | How did cities respond to the challenges of growth? | Conclusion: Who built the cities? |

517

1860
- There are 5.3 million industrial workers in the United States.

1880s
- The number of foreign-born mill workers doubles.
- Mill workers in Fall River, Massachusetts, work twelve hours a day, six days a week, for about $1 a day.

1890
- Typical male worker earns $500 a year, equivalent to about $12,000 a year today.
- Twenty-five percent of married African American women work outside the home.
- Three percent of married white women work outside the home.

1900
- There are 17.4 million industrial workers in the United States.

work in the nineteenth century remained seasonal; few workers could count on year-round pay. In addition, two major depressions only twenty years apart, beginning in 1873 and 1893, spelled unemployment and hardship. In an era before unemployment insurance, workers' compensation, or old-age pensions, even the best worker could not guarantee security for his family. "The fear of ending in the poorhouse is one of the terrors that dog a man through life," Davis confessed.

Skilled workers like Davis wielded power on the shop floor. Employers attempted to limit workers' control by replacing people with machines, breaking down skilled work into ever-smaller tasks that could be performed by unskilled factory operatives. New England's textile mills provide a classic example of the effects of mechanized factory labor in the nineteenth century. Mary, a weaver at the mills in Fall River, Massachusetts, went to work in the 1880s at the age of twelve. By then, mechanization of the looms had reduced the job of the weaver to watching for breaks in the thread. "At first the noise is fierce, and you have to breathe the cotton all the time, but you get used to it," Mary told a reporter from the *Independent* magazine. "When the bobbin flies out and a girl gets hurt, you can't hear her shout—not if she just screams, you can't. She's got to wait, 'till you see her. . . . Lots of us is deaf."

During the 1880s, the number of foreign-born mill workers almost doubled. At Fall River, Mary and her Scots-Irish family resented the new immigrants. "The Polaks learn weavin' quick," she remarked. "They just as soon live on nothin' and work like that. But it won't do 'em much good for all they'll make out of it." Employers encouraged racial and ethnic antagonism because it inhibited labor organization.

The majority of factory operatives in the textile mills were young, unmarried women like Mary. They worked from six in the morning to six at night six days a week, and they took home about $1 a day. The seasonal nature of the work also drove wages down. "Like as not your mill will 'shut down' three months," and "some weeks you only get two or three days' work," Mary recounted.

Mechanization transformed the garment industry as well. With the introduction of the foot-pedaled sewing machine in the 1850s and the use of mechanical cloth-cutting knives in the 1870s, independent tailors were replaced with workers hired by contractors to sew pieces of cloth into suits and dresses. Working in sweatshops, small rooms hired for the season or even in the contractor's own tenement, women and children formed an important segment of garment workers. Discriminated against in the marketplace, where they earned less than men, women generally worked for wages only eight to ten years, until they married.

The Family Economy: Women and Children

In 1890, the typical male worker earned $500 a year, about $12,000 in today's dollars. Many working-class families, whether native-born or immigrant, lived in or near poverty, their economic survival dependent on the contributions of all family members, regardless of sex or age. The paid and unpaid work of women and children proved essential for family survival and economic advancement.

In the cities, boys as young as six years old plied their trades as bootblacks and newsboys. Often working under an adult contractor, these children earned as little as fifty cents a day. Many of them were homeless—orphaned or cast off by their families. "We wuz six, and we ain't got no father," a child of twelve told reporter Jacob Riis. "Some of us had to go."

CHAPTER LOCATOR | Why did American cities grow so fast in the late nineteenth century?

Bootblacks

The faces and hands of the two bootblacks shown here with a third boy on a New York City street in 1896 testify to their grimy trade. Boys as young as six worked on city streets as bootblacks and newsboys. For these child workers, education was a luxury they could not afford.
Alice Austin photo, Staten Island Historical Society.

Child labor increased decade by decade after 1870. The percentage of children under fifteen engaged in paid labor did not drop until after World War I. The number of women workers also rose sharply, with their most common occupation changing slowly from domestic service to factory work and then to office work. Between 1870 and 1890, the number of women working for wages in nonagricultural occupations more than doubled (**Figure 19.1**, page 520). Women's working patterns varied considerably according to race and ethnicity. White married women, even among the working class, rarely worked for wages outside the home. In 1890, only 3 percent were employed. Black women, married and unmarried, worked for wages in much greater numbers. The 1890 census showed that 25 percent of married African American women were employed, often as domestics in the houses of white families.

White-Collar Workers: Managers, "Typewriters," and Salesclerks

In the late nineteenth century, business expansion and consolidation led to a managerial revolution, creating a new class of white-collar workers who worked in offices and stores. As skilled workers saw their crafts replaced by mechanization, some moved into management positions. "The middle class is becoming a salaried class," a writer for the *Independent* magazine observed, "and is rapidly losing the economic and moral independence of former days." As large business organizations consolidated, corporate development separated management from

| What kinds of work did people do in industrial America? | What steps did workers take to organize in the 1870s and 1880s? | How did industrialization transform home life and leisure? | How did cities respond to the challenges of growth? | Conclusion: Who built the cities? |

519

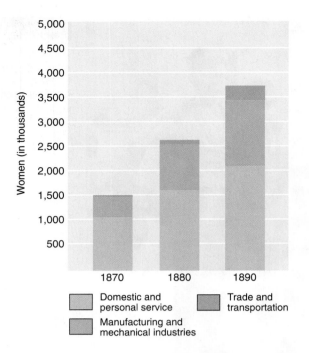

FIGURE 19.1 ■ Women and Work, 1870–1890

In 1870, close to 1.5 million women worked in nonagricultural occupations. By 1890, that number had more than doubled to 3.7 million. More and more women sought work in manufacturing and mechanical industries, although domestic service still constituted the largest employment arena for women.

ownership, and the job of directing the firm became the province of salaried executives and managers, the majority of whom were white men drawn from the 8 percent of Americans who held high school diplomas.

Until late in the century, when engineering schools began to supply recruits, many skilled workers moved from the shop floor to positions of considerable responsibility. William "Billy" Jones, the son of a Welsh immigrant, was one such worker. Beginning as an apprentice at the age of ten, Jones rose through the ranks to become plant superintendent at Andrew Carnegie's Pittsburgh steelworks in 1872.

The new white-collar workforce also included women "typewriters" and salesclerks. In the decades after the Civil War, as businesses became larger and more far-flung, the need for more elaborate and exact records, as well as the greater volume of correspondence, led to the hiring of more office workers. Mechanization transformed business as it had industry and manufacturing. The adding machine, the cash register, and the typewriter came into general use in the 1880s. Employers seeking literate workers soon turned to women. Educated men had many other career choices, but for middle-class white women, secretarial work constituted one of very few areas where they could put their literacy to use for wages.

Sylvie Thygeson was typical of the young women who went to work as secretaries. When her father died in 1884, Thygeson went to work as a country schoolteacher at the age of sixteen, after graduating high school. Realizing that teaching school did not pay a living wage, she mastered typing and stenography and found work as a secretary to help support her family. According to her account, she made "a fabulous sum of money." Nevertheless, she gave up her job after a few years when she met and married her husband.

By the 1890s, secretarial work was the overwhelming choice of native-born white women, who constituted more than 90 percent of the female clerical force. Not only considered more genteel than factory work or domestic labor, office work also meant more money for shorter hours. Boston's clerical workers made more than $6 a week in 1883, compared with less than $5 for women working in manufacturing.

As a new consumer culture came to dominate American urban life in the late nineteenth century, department stores offered another employment opportunity for women in the cities. Stores such as Macy's in New York, Wanamaker's in Philadelphia, and Marshall Field in Chicago stood as monuments to the material promise of the era. Within these palaces of consumption, cash girls, stock clerks, and wrappers earned as little as $3 a week, while at the top of the scale, buyers like Belle Cushman of the fancy goods department at Macy's earned $25 a week. Salesclerks counted themselves a cut above factory workers. Their work was neither dirty nor dangerous, and even when they earned less than factory workers, they felt a sense of superiority.

Clerical Worker

A stenographer takes dictation in an 1890s office. In the 1880s, with the invention of the typewriter, many women put their literacy skills to use in the nation's offices. Brown Brothers.

QUICK REVIEW <

How did business expansion and consolidation change workers' occupations in the late nineteenth century?

> What steps did workers take to organize in the 1870s and 1880s?

Destruction from the Great Railroad Strike of 1877

Pictures of the devastation caused in Pittsburgh during the strike shocked many Americans. When militiamen fired on striking workers, killing more than twenty strikers, the mob retaliated by destroying a two-mile area along the track. Carnegie Library of Pittsburgh.

BY THE LATE NINETEENTH CENTURY, industrial workers were losing ground in the workplace. In the fierce competition to reduce prices and cut costs, industrialists like Andrew Carnegie invested heavily in new machinery that enabled them to replace skilled workers with unskilled labor. The erosion of skills and the redefinition of labor as mere "machine tending" left the worker with a growing sense of individual helplessness that served as a spur to collective action. In the 1870s and 1880s, labor organizations grew, and the Knights of Labor and the American Federation of Labor attracted workers. Convinced of the inequity of the wage-labor system, labor organizers spoke eloquently of abolishing class privileges and monopoly.

The Great Railroad Strike of 1877

Economic depression following the panic of 1873 threw as many as three million people out of work. Those who were lucky enough to keep their jobs watched as pay cuts eroded their wages until they could no longer feed their families. In the summer of 1877, the Baltimore and Ohio (B&O) Railroad announced a 10 percent wage cut at the same time it declared a 10 percent dividend to its stockholders. Angry brakemen in West Virginia, whose wages had already fallen from $70 to $30 a month, walked out on strike.

The West Virginia brakemen's strike touched off the **Great Railroad Strike** of 1877, a nationwide uprising that spread rapidly to Pittsburgh and Chicago, St. Louis and San Francisco (**Map 19.3**). Within a few days, nearly 100,000 railroad workers walked off the job. An estimated 500,000 laborers soon joined the train workers. In Reading, Pennsylvania, militiamen refused to fire on the strikers,

Great Railroad Strike
▶ Strike that began in 1877 with a strike of West Virginia railroad brakemen and quickly spread to include roughly 600,000 workers. Responding to pressure from railroad owners and managers, President Rutherford B. Hayes used federal troops to break the strike. Despite the strike's failure, it led to a surge in union membership.

CHAPTER LOCATOR | Why did American cities grow so fast in the late nineteenth century?

MAP 19.3 ■ The Great Railroad Strike of 1877
Starting in West Virginia and Pennsylvania, the strike spread as far north as Albany, New York, and as far west as San Francisco, bringing rail traffic to a standstill. Called the Great Uprising, the strike heralded the beginning of a new era of working-class protest and trade union organization.

CHRONOLOGY

1869
- Knights of Labor is founded.

1873
- Panic on Wall Street touches off depression.

1877
- In Great Railroad Strike, more than 600,000 workers across the country go on strike.

1878
- Knights of Labor launches a campaign to organize all workers.

1886
- American Federation of Labor (AFL) is founded to represent skilled workers.
- Haymarket bombing in Chicago deals a death blow to the Knights of Labor.

saying, "We may be militiamen, but we are workmen first." Rail traffic ground to a halt; the nation lay paralyzed.

Violence erupted as the strike spread. In Pittsburgh, militia brought in from Philadelphia opened fire on a crowd, killing twenty people. Angry workers retaliated by reducing an area two miles long beside the tracks to rubble. Before the day ended, twenty more workers had been shot, and the railroad had sustained property damage totaling $2 million.

Within eight days, the governors of nine states, acting at the prompting of the railroad owners and managers, defined the strike as an "insurrection" and called for federal troops. President Rutherford B. Hayes, after hesitating briefly, called out the army. By the time the troops arrived, the violence had run its course. Federal troops did not shoot a single striker in 1877. But they struck a blow against labor by acting as strikebreakers—opening rail traffic, protecting nonstriking "scab" train crews, and maintaining peace along the line. In three weeks, the strike was over.

Although many middle-class Americans initially sympathized with the conditions that led to the strike, they condemned the strikers for the violence and property damage that occurred. The *Independent* magazine offered the following advice on how to deal with "rioters": "If the club of a policeman, knocking out the brains of the rioter, will answer then well and good; but if it does not promptly meet the exigency, then bullets and bayonets . . . constitutes [*sic*] the one remedy and one duty of the hour."

"The strikes have been put down by force," President Hayes noted in his diary on August 5. "But now for the real remedy. Can't something be done by education of the strikers, by judicious control of the capitalists, by wise general policy to end or diminish the evil? The railroad strikers, as a rule, are good men,

| What kinds of work did people do in industrial America? | **What steps did workers take to organize in the 1870s and 1880s?** | How did industrialization transform home life and leisure? | How did cities respond to the challenges of growth? | Conclusion: Who built the cities? |

sober, intelligent, and industrious." While Hayes acknowledged the workers' grievances, most businessmen and industrialists did not and fought the idea of labor unions. For their part, workers quickly recognized that they held little power individually and flocked to join unions. As labor leader Samuel Gompers noted, the strike served as an alarm bell to labor "that sounded a ringing message of hope to us all."

The Knights of Labor and the American Federation of Labor

The **Knights of Labor**, the first mass organization of America's working class, proved the chief beneficiary of labor's newfound consciousness. Founded in 1869, the Knights were a secret society that envisioned a "universal brotherhood" of all workers, from common laborers to master craftsmen. Secrecy and ritual served to bind Knights together at the same time that it discouraged company spies and protected members from reprisals.

Although the Knights played no active role in the 1877 railroad strike, membership swelled as a result of the growing interest in labor organizing that followed the strike. In 1878, the Knights abandoned secrecy and launched an ambitious campaign to organize workers regardless of skill, sex, race, or nationality. The Knights attempted to bridge the boundaries of ethnicity, gender, ideology, race, and occupation. Leonora Barry served as general investigator for women's work from 1886 to 1890, helping the Knights recruit teachers, waitresses, housewives, and domestics along with factory and sweatshop workers. Women comprised perhaps 20 percent of the membership. The Knights also included African Americans, organizing more than 95,000 black workers. That the Knights of Labor often fell short of its goals to unify the working class proved less surprising than the scope of its efforts.

Under the direction of Grand Master Workman **Terence V. Powderly**, the Knights became the dominant force in labor during the 1880s. The organization advocated a kind of workers' democracy that embraced reforms including public ownership of the railroads, an income tax, equal pay for women workers, and the abolition of child labor. The Knights called for one big union to create a cooperative commonwealth that would supplant the wage system and remove class distinctions. Only the "parasitic" members of society—gamblers, stockbrokers, lawyers, bankers, and liquor dealers—were denied membership.

In theory, the Knights of Labor opposed strikes. Powderly championed arbitration and preferred to use boycotts. But in practice, much of the organization's appeal came from a successful strike the Knights mounted in 1885 against railroads controlled by Jay Gould. Despite the reservations of its leadership, the Knights became a militant labor organization that won support from working people with the slogan "An injury to one is the concern of all."

The Knights of Labor was not without rivals. Many skilled workers belonged to craft unions organized by trade. Trade unionists spurned the broad reform goals of the Knights and focused on workplace issues such as higher pay and better working conditions. **Samuel Gompers** promoted what he called "pure and simple" unionism. Gompers founded the Organized Trades and Labor Unions in 1881 and reorganized it in 1886 into the **American Federation of Labor (AFL)**, which coordinated the activities of craft unions throughout the United States.

Knights of Labor

▶ The first mass organization of America's working class. Founded in 1869, the Knights of Labor attempted to bridge the boundaries of ethnicity, gender, ideology, race, and occupation to build a brotherhood of all workers. The 1886 Haymarket bombing contributed to the Knights' decline and the ascendancy of trade unionism.

Terence V. Powderly

▶ Leader of the Knights of Labor during the 1880s. Under his leadership, the Knights became the dominant force in labor during the decade. Powderly's Knights called for one big union to create a cooperative commonwealth that would supplant the wage system and remove class distinctions.

Samuel Gompers

▶ Labor organizer who founded the Organized Trades and Labor Unions in 1881 and reorganized it in 1886 into the American Federation of Labor (AFL). Gompers organized skilled workers and focused on workplace issues such as wages and working conditions.

American Federation of Labor (AFL)

▶ Organization created by Samuel Gompers in 1886 that coordinated the activities of craft unions throughout the United States. Under Gompers's leadership, the AFL worked to achieve immediate benefits for skilled workers. In its early days, the AFL attracted fewer members than the Knights of Labor, but in time its approach to unionism came to prevail.

CHAPTER LOCATOR | Why did American cities grow so fast in the late nineteenth century?

CHAPTER 19

524 THE GROWTH OF AMERICA'S CITIES, 1870–1900

Gompers at first drew few converts. The AFL had only 138,000 members in 1886, compared with 730,000 for the Knights of Labor. But events soon brought down the Knights, and Gompers's brand of unionism came to prevail.

Haymarket and the Specter of Labor Radicalism

While the AFL and the Knights of Labor competed for members, more-radical labor groups, including socialists and anarchists, believed that reform was futile and called instead for social revolution. Both groups, sensitive to criticism that they preferred revolution in theory to improvements here and now, rallied around the popular issue of the eight-hour day.

Since the 1840s, labor had sought to end the twelve-hour workday, which was standard in industry and manufacturing. By the mid-1880s, it seemed clear to many workers that labor shared too little in the new prosperity of the decade, and pressure mounted for the eight-hour day. Labor rallied to the popular issue and launched major rallies in cities across the nation. Supporters of the movement set May 1, 1886, as the date for a nationwide general strike in support of the eight-hour workday.

All factions of the labor movement came together in Chicago on May Day. A group of labor radicals led by anarchist Albert Parsons, a *Mayflower* descendant, and August Spies, a German socialist, spearheaded the eight-hour movement in Chicago. Chicago's Knights of Labor rallied to the cause even though Terence Powderly and the union's national leadership refused to endorse the movement for shorter hours. Samuel Gompers was on hand, too, to lead the city's trade unionists, although he privately urged the AFL assemblies not to participate in the general strike.

Gompers's skilled workers were labor's elite. Many still worked in small shops where negotiations between workers and employers took place in an environment tempered by personal relationships. The AFL's skilled workers stood in sharp contrast to the dispossessed workers out on strike across town at Chicago's McCormick reaper works. There strikers watched helplessly as the company brought in strikebreakers to take their jobs and marched the "scabs" to work under the protection of the Chicago police and private security guards.

During the May Day rally, 45,000 workers paraded peacefully down Michigan Avenue in support of the eight-hour day. Trouble came two days later, when strikers attacked strikebreakers outside the McCormick works and police opened fire, killing or wounding six men. Angry radicals called on workers to "arm yourselves and appear in full force" at a rally in Haymarket Square.

"The Chicago Riot"

Inflammatory pamphlets like this one published in the wake of the Haymarket bombing presented a one-sided view of the incident and stirred public passion. Chicago Historical Society.

▶ FOR MORE HELP ANALYZING THIS IMAGE, see the visual activity for this chapter in the Online Study Guide at bedfordstmartins.com/roarkunderstanding.

| What kinds of work did people do in industrial America? | **What steps did workers take to organize in the 1870s and 1880s?** | How did industrialization transform home life and leisure? | How did cities respond to the challenges of growth? | Conclusion: Who built the cities? |

On the evening of May 4, the turnout at Haymarket was disappointing. No more than two or three thousand gathered to hear Spies, Parsons, and the other speakers. Mayor Carter Harrison, known as a friend of labor, mingled conspicuously in the crowd, pronounced the meeting peaceable, and went home. A short time later, police captain John "Blackjack" Bonfield marched his men into the crowd, by now fewer than three hundred people, and demanded that it disperse. Suddenly, someone threw a bomb into the police ranks. After a moment of stunned silence, the police drew their revolvers. "Fire and kill all you can," shouted a police lieutenant. When the melee ended, seven policemen and an unknown number of other people lay dead. An additional sixty policemen and thirty or forty civilians suffered injuries.

News of the "Haymarket riot" provoked a nationwide convulsion of fear and rage directed at anarchists, labor unions, strikers, immigrants, and the working class in general. Eight men, including Parsons and Spies, went on trial in Chicago. "Convict these men," thundered the state's attorney, Julius S. Grinnell, "make examples of them, hang them, and you save our institutions." Although the state could not link any of the defendants to the **Haymarket bombing**, the jury nevertheless found them all guilty. Four were executed, one committed suicide, and three received prison sentences.

The bomb blast at Haymarket had lasting repercussions. To commemorate the death of the Haymarket martyrs, labor made May 1 an annual international celebration of the worker. But the Haymarket bomb, in the eyes of one observer, proved "a godsend to all enemies of the labor movement." It effectively scotched the eight-hour day movement and dealt a blow to the Knights of Labor, already wracked by internal divisions. With the labor movement under attack, many skilled workers turned to the American Federation of Labor. Gompers's narrow economic strategy made sense at the time and enabled one segment of the workforce—the skilled—to organize effectively and achieve tangible gains. But the nation's unskilled workers remained untouched by the AFL's brand of trade unionism.

Haymarket bombing

▶ May 4, 1886, conflict between labor protesters and police in which both workers and policemen were killed or wounded. The violence began when an unknown person threw a bomb into the ranks of the police assigned to the labor gathering. The incident created a powerful backlash against labor activism.

> **QUICK REVIEW**

What were the long-term effects of the Great Railroad Strike of 1877 and the Haymarket bombing in 1886?

CHAPTER LOCATOR | Why did American cities grow so fast in the late nineteenth century?

CHAPTER 19
526 THE GROWTH OF AMERICA'S CITIES, 1870–1900

Beach Scene at Coney Island Opened in the 1870s, Coney Island came into its own at the turn of the twentieth century with the development of elaborate amusement parks. It became a symbol of commercialized leisure and mechanical excitement. This fanciful rendering captures the frenetic goings-on. Weekend crowds on the island reportedly reached one million. Library of Congress.

How did industrialization transform home life and leisure?

THE GROWTH OF URBAN INDUSTRIALISM not only dramatically altered the workplace but also transformed home and family life and gave rise to new forms of commercialized leisure. Industrialization redefined the very concepts of work and home. Increasingly, men went out to work for wages, while most white married women stayed home, either working in the home without pay—cleaning, cooking, and rearing children—or supervising paid domestic servants who did the housework.

Domesticity and "Domestics"

The separation of the workplace and the home that marked the shift to industrial society led to a new ideology, one that sentimentalized the home and women's role in it. The cultural ideology that dictated woman's place in the home has been called the cult of domesticity, a phrase used to prescribe an ideal of middle-class, white womanhood that dominated the period from 1820 to the end of the nineteenth century (see chapter 11).

The cult of domesticity and the elaboration of the middle-class home led to a major change in patterns of hiring household help. The live-in servant, or domestic, became a fixture in the North, replacing the hired girl of the previous century. (The South continued to rely on black female labor, first slave and later free.) In American cities by 1870, 15 to 30 percent of all households included live-in domestic servants, more than 90 percent of them women. By the mid-nineteenth century, native-born women increasingly took up other work and left domestic service to immigrants.

Servants by all accounts resented the long hours and lack of privacy. "She is liable to be rung up at all hours," one study reported. "Her very meals are not secure from interruption, and even her sleep is not sacred." Domestic service

| What kinds of work did people do in industrial America? | What steps did workers take to organize in the 1870s and 1880s? | **How did industrialization transform home life and leisure?** | How did cities respond to the challenges of growth? | Conclusion: Who built the cities? |

527

1869
- Cincinnati Red Stockings becomes the first professional baseball team. By the 1870s, baseball is the "national pastime" for men.

1870
- Between 15 and 30 percent of urban households employ live-in domestic servants, some 90 percent of them women.

1890s
- Coney Island, New York, becomes one of the largest and most elaborate amusement parks in the country, attracting as many as one million visitors a weekend.

Coney Island

▶ Popular leisure destination for New York City's residents, particularly its working class. In the 1890s, Coney Island became the site of some of the largest and most elaborate amusement parks in the country. Coney Island embodied the commercialization of entertainment in the late nineteenth century.

became the occupation of last resort, a "hard and lonely life" in the words of one servant girl.

For women of the white middle class, domestics were a boon, freeing them from household drudgery and giving them more time to spend with their children or to pursue club work or reform. Thus, while domestic service supported the cult of domesticity, it created, for those women who could afford it, opportunities to expand their horizons outside the home in areas such as women's clubs and the temperance and suffrage movements.

Cheap Amusements

Growing class divisions manifested themselves in patterns of leisure as well as in work and home life. The poor and working class took their leisure, not in the crowded tenements that housed their families, but increasingly in the cities' new dance halls, music houses, ballparks, and amusement arcades, which by the 1890s formed a familiar part of the urban landscape.

The growing anonymity of urban industrial society posed a challenge to traditional rituals of courtship. Adolescent working girls no longer met prospective husbands only through their families. Fleeing crowded tenements, the young sought each other's company in dance halls and other commercial retreats. Young workingwomen, who rarely could afford more than trolley fare when they went out, counted on being "treated" by men, a transaction that often implied sexual payback. Young women's need to negotiate sexual encounters if they wished to participate in commercial amusements blurred the line between respectability and promiscuity and made the dance halls a favorite target of reformers who feared they lured girls into prostitution.

For men, baseball became a national pastime in the 1870s, one force in urban life capable of uniting a city across class lines. Cincinnati mounted the first entirely paid team, the Red Stockings, in 1869. Soon professional teams proliferated in cities across the nation, and Mark Twain hailed baseball as "the very symbol, the outward and visible expression, of the drive and push and rush and struggle of the raging, tearing, booming nineteenth century."

The increasing commercialization of entertainment in the late nineteenth century can best be seen at **Coney Island**, New York. Long a center for popular amusements, in the 1890s Coney Island was transformed into the site of some of the largest and most elaborate amusement parks in the country. Promoter George Tilyou built Steeplechase Park in 1897, advertising "10 hours of fun for 10 cents." With its mechanical thrills and fun-house laughs, the amusement park encouraged behavior that one schoolteacher aptly described as "everyone with the brakes off." By 1900, as many as a million New Yorkers flocked to Coney Island on any given weekend, making the amusement park the unofficial capital of a new mass culture.

> **QUICK REVIEW**

How did urban industrialism shape the world of leisure?

CHAPTER LOCATOR | Why did American cities grow so fast in the late nineteenth century?

Central Park Lake

Looking south across Central Park Lake, this photograph shows boaters and well-dressed New Yorkers taking their leisure on Bethesda Terrace. The bronze figure in the center of the photograph, *Angel of the Waters*, was the work of sculptor Emma Stebbins. Calvert Vaux, who along with Frederick Law Olmsted designed the landscaping, considered Bethesda Terrace the "drawing room of the park." People of all ages, from children floating toy sailboats (inset) to grandparents out for a stroll, found something to enjoy in the park.
Photo: Culver Pictures; Boat: Picture Research Consultants & Archives.

PRIVATE ENTERPRISE, not planners, built the cities of the United States. With a few notable exceptions, cities simply mushroomed, formed by the dictates of private enterprise and the exigencies of local politics. With the rise of the city came the need for public facilities, transportation, and services that would tax the imaginations of America's architects and engineers and set the scene for the rough-and-tumble of big-city government, politics, and politicians.

Building Cities of Stone and Steel

In the late nineteenth century, Americans rushed to embrace new technology of all kinds, making their cities the most modern in the world. Structural steel made enormous advances in building possible. The Brooklyn Bridge, a soaring monument to the New York City, opened in 1883. As the age of steel supplanted the age of stone and iron, skyscrapers and mighty bridges dominated the imagination and the urban landscape.

Chicago, not New York, gave birth to the modern skyscraper. Rising from the ashes of the Great Fire of 1871, which destroyed three square miles and left eighteen thousand people homeless, Chicago offered a generation of skilled architects and engineers the chance to experiment. A group of architects known as the "Chicago school," whose members included Louis Sullivan and John Wellborn Root, gave Chicago some of the world's finest commercial buildings. Employing the dictum "Form follows function," they built startlingly modern structures.

| What kinds of work did people do in industrial America? | What steps did workers take to organize in the 1870s and 1880s? | How did industrialization transform home life and leisure? | How did cities respond to the challenges of growth? | Conclusion: Who built the cities? |

529

1871
- Boss Tweed's rule in New York ends.
- Chicago's Great Fire destroys three square miles and leaves eighteen thousand people homeless.

1873
- New York's Central Park is completed.

1883
- Brooklyn Bridge opens.

1893
- World's Columbian Exposition is held in Chicago.
- Panic on Wall Street touches off major economic depression.

1895
- Boston Public Library opens.

Frederick Law Olmsted

▶ Landscape architect who designed numerous urban parks in the late nineteenth century. Olmsted is best known for New York's Central Park, completed in 1873. His parks were meant to provide city residents with a place where they could retreat from crowded, noisy city streets.

William Marcy "Boss" Tweed

▶ The most notorious city boss. In the mid-nineteenth century, Tweed was the leader of New York's Democratic machine, Tammany Hall. Through the use of bribery and graft, Tweed kept the Democratic Party in power and ran New York City. Tweed's excesses produced demands for reform and led to his fall from power in 1871.

Across the United States, municipal governments undertook public works on a scale never before seen. They paved streets, built sewers and water mains, installed electric lights, ran trolley tracks, and dug underground to build subways. Cities became more beautiful with the creation of urban public parks. Much of the credit for America's greatest parks goes to one man—landscape architect **Frederick Law Olmsted**. Olmsted designed parks for many cities, but he is best remembered for the creation of New York City's Central Park. Completed in 1873, it became the first landscaped public park in the United States. Olmsted's goal for the eight hundred acres between 59th and 110th streets was to create a place where people "may stroll for an hour, seeing, hearing, and feeling nothing of the bustle and jar of the streets."

American cities did not overlook the mind in their efforts at improvement. In the late nineteenth century, American cities created the most extensive free public library system in the world. In 1895, the Boston Public Library opened with more than 700,000 books available to the reading public. Cities also created a comprehensive free public school system that educated everyone from the children of the middle class to the sons and daughters of immigrant workers. The exploding urban population strained the system and led to crowded and inadequate facilities. In 1899, more than 544,000 pupils attended school in New York's five boroughs.

The parks, the libraries, and even the subways and sewers benefited some city dwellers more than others. Few library cards were held by Boston's laborers, who worked six days a week and found the library closed on Sunday. And in the 1890s, there was nothing central about New York's Central Park. It was a four-mile walk from the tenements of Hester Street to the park's entrance at 59th Street and Fifth Avenue.

Any story of the American city, it seems, must be a tale of two cities—or, given the cities' great diversity, a tale of many cities within each metropolis. At the turn of the twentieth century, a central paradox emerged: The enduring monuments of America's cities—the bridges, skyscrapers, parks, and libraries—stood as the undeniable achievements of the same system of municipal government that reformers dismissed as boss-ridden, criminal, and corrupt.

City Government and the "Bosses"

The physical growth of the cities required the expansion of public services and the creation of entirely new facilities: streets, subways, elevated trains, bridges, docks, sewers, and public utilities. With work to be done and money to be made, the professional politician—the colorful big-city boss—became a phenomenon of urban growth. Though corrupt and often criminal, the boss saw to the building of the city and provided needed social services for the new residents. Yet not even the big-city boss could be said to rule the city. The governing of America's cities resembled more a tug-of-war than boss rule.

The most notorious of all the city bosses was **William Marcy "Boss" Tweed** of New York. At midcentury, Boss Tweed's Democratic Party "machine" held sway. A machine was really no more than a political party organized at the grassroots level. Its purpose was to win elections and reward its followers, often with jobs on the city's payroll. New York's citywide Democratic machine, Tammany Hall, commanded an army of party functionaries. They formed a shadow government more powerful than the city's elected officials.

The only elected office Tweed ever held was alderman. But as chairman of the Tammany general committee, he wielded more power than the mayor. Through the use

CHAPTER LOCATOR | Why did American cities grow so fast in the late nineteenth century?

530 CHAPTER 19 THE GROWTH OF AMERICA'S CITIES, 1870–1900

of bribery and graft, he kept the Democratic Party together and ran the city. "As long as I count the votes," he shamelessly boasted, "what are you going to do about it?"

The excesses of the Tweed ring soon led to a clamor for reform. Cartoonist Thomas Nast pilloried Tweed in the pages of *Harper's Weekly*. His cartoons, easily understood even by those who could not read, did the boss more harm than hundreds of outraged editorials. Tweed's rule ended in 1871. Eventually, he was tried and convicted and later died in jail.

New York was not the only city to experience bossism and corruption. More than 80 percent of the nation's thirty largest cities experienced some form of boss rule in the decades around the turn of the twentieth century. However, infighting among powerful ward bosses often meant that no single boss enjoyed exclusive power in the big cities.

Urban reformers and proponents of good government (derisively called "goo goos" by their rivals) challenged machine rule and sometimes succeeded in electing reform mayors, but they rarely managed to stay in office for long. The bosses enjoyed continued success largely because the urban political machines helped the cities' immigrants and poor, who remained machine rule's staunchest allies. "What tells in holding your district," a Tammany ward boss observed, "is to go right down among the poor and help them in the different ways they need help. It's philanthropy, but it's politics, too—mighty good politics."

The big-city boss, through the skillful orchestration of rewards, exerted powerful leverage and lined up support for his party from a broad range of constituents, from the urban poor to wealthy industrialists. In 1902, when journalist Lincoln Steffens began "The Shame of the Cities," a series of articles exposing city corruption, he found that business leaders who refused to mingle socially with the bosses nevertheless struck deals with them. "He is a self-righteous fraud, this big businessman," Steffens concluded. "I found him buying boodlers [bribers] in St. Louis, defending grafters in Minneapolis, originating corruption in Pittsburgh, sharing with bosses in Philadelphia, deploring reform in Chicago, and beating good government with corruption funds in New York."

For all the color and flamboyance of the big-city boss, he was simply one of many players in municipal government. Old-stock aristocrats, new professionals, saloonkeepers, pushcart peddlers, and politicians all fought for their interests. They didn't much like each other, and they sometimes fought savagely. But they learned to live with one another. Compromise and accommodation—not boss rule—best characterized big-city government by the turn of the twentieth century, although the cities' reputation for corruption left an indelible mark on the consciousness of the American public.

Tammany Bank

This cast-iron bank, a campaign novelty, bears the name of the New York City Democratic machine. It conveys its political reform message graphically: When you put a penny in the politician's hand, he puts it in his pocket. Collection of Janice L. and David J. Frent.

What kinds of work did people do in industrial America?

What steps did workers take to organize in the 1870s and 1880s?

How did industrialization transform home life and leisure?

How did cities respond to the challenges of growth?

Conclusion: Who built the cities?

White City or City of Sin?

Americans have always been of two minds about the city. They like to boast of its skyscrapers and bridges, its culture and sophistication, and they pride themselves on its bigness and bustle. At the same time, they fear it as the city of sin, the home of immigrant slums, the center of vice and crime. Nowhere did the divided view of the American city take form more graphically than in Chicago in 1893.

In that year, Chicago hosted the **World's Columbian Exposition**, the grandest world's fair in the nation's history. The fairground, called the White City and built on the shores of Lake Michigan, offered a lesson in what Americans on the eve of the twentieth century imagined a city might be. Only five miles down the shore from downtown Chicago, the White City seemed light-years away. Its very name celebrated a harmony and pristine beauty unknown in Chicago, with its stockyards, slums, and bustling terminals. Frederick Law Olmsted and architect Daniel Burnham supervised the creation of a paradise of lagoons, fountains, wooded islands, gardens, and imposing buildings.

Visitors from home and abroad strolled the elaborate grounds and visited the exhibits—everything from a model of the Brooklyn Bridge carved in soap to the latest goods and inventions. Half carnival, half culture, the great fair offered something for everyone. On the Midway Plaisance, crowds thrilled to the massive wheel built by Mr. Ferris and watched agog as Little Egypt danced the hootchy-kootchy.

In October, the fair closed its doors in the midst of the worst depression the country had yet seen. During the winter of 1894, Chicago's unemployed and homeless took over the grounds, vandalized the buildings, and frightened the city's comfortable citizens. When reporters asked Daniel Burnham what should be done with the moldering remains of the White City, he responded, "It should be torched." And it was. In July 1894, in a clash between federal troops and striking railway workers, incendiaries set fires that leveled the fairgrounds.

In the end, the White City remained what it had always been, a dreamscape. Perhaps it was not so strange, after all, that the legacy of the White City could be found on Coney Island, where two new amusement parks, Luna and Dreamland, sought to combine, albeit in a more tawdry form, the beauty of the White City and the thrill of the Midway Plaisance. More enduring than the White City itself was what it represented: the emergent industrial might of the United States, at home and abroad, with its inventions, manufactured goods, and growing consumer culture.

World's Columbian Exposition
▶ World's fair held in Chicago in 1893. Millions of fairgoers visited the fabulous grounds that came to be known as the White City. The White City embodied the American urban ideal and offered a stark contrast to the realities of Chicago life.

> ## QUICK REVIEW

How did American cities change in the late nineteenth century?

CHAPTER LOCATOR | Why did American cities grow so fast in the late nineteenth century?

CHAPTER 19
532 THE GROWTH OF AMERICA'S CITIES, 1870–1900

Picture Research Consultants & Archives

AS MUCH AS THE GREAT INDUSTRIALISTS and financiers, common workers, most of them immigrants, built the nation's cities. The unprecedented growth of urban, industrial America resulted from the labor of millions of men, women, and children who toiled in workshops and factories, in sweatshops and mines, on railroads and construction sites across America.

America's cities in the late nineteenth century teemed with life. Americans from all walks of life lived in the cities and contributed to their growth. Town houses and tenements jostled for space with skyscrapers and great department stores, while parks, ball fields, amusement arcades, and public libraries provided the city masses with recreation and entertainment. Municipal governments, straining to build the new cities, experienced the rough-and-tumble of machine politics as bosses and their constituents looked to profit from city growth.

For America's workers, urban industrialism, along with the rise of big business and corporate consolidation, drastically changed the workplace. Industrialists replaced skilled workers with new machines that could be operated by cheaper unskilled labor. And during hard times, employers did not hesitate to cut workers' already meager wages. Organization held out the best hope for the workers; first the Knights of Labor and later the American Federation of Labor won converts among the nation's working class.

The rise of urban industrialism challenged the American promise, which for decades had been dominated by Jeffersonian agrarian ideals. Could such a promise exist in the changing world of cities, tenements, immigrants, and huge corporations? In the great depression that came in the 1890s, mounting anger and frustration would lead workers and farmers to join forces and create a grassroots movement to fight for change under the banner of a new People's Party.

SO NOW YOU KNOW

The late nineteenth century witnessed an influx of "new" immigrants into the United States, most of them from Southern and Eastern Europe. Ellis Island, the destination of many new immigrants to the East Coast, was just the first stop for the newcomers who would provide critical labor in building America's growing cities.

What kinds of work did people do in industrial America?	What steps did workers take to organize in the 1870s and 1880s?	How did industrialization transform home life and leisure?	How did cities respond to the challenges of growth?	**Conclusion: Who built the cities?**

CHAPTER 19 STUDY GUIDE

Online Study Guide
bedfordstmartins.com/roarkunderstanding

STEP 1 GETTING STARTED

Below are basic terms from this period in American history. Can you identify each term below and explain why it matters? To do this exercise online or to download this chart, visit bedfordstmartins.com/roarkunderstanding.

TERM	WHO OR WHAT & WHEN	WHY IT MATTERS
Ellis Island, p. 515		
Great Railroad Strike, p. 522		
Knights of Labor, p. 524		
Terrence V. Powderly, p. 524		
Samuel Gompers, p. 524		
American Federation of Labor, p. 524		
Haymarket bombing, p. 526		
Coney Island, p. 528		
Frederick Law Olmsted, p. 530		
William Marcy "Boss" Tweed, p. 530		
World's Columbian Exposition, p. 532		

STEP 2 MOVING BEYOND THE BASICS

The exercise below represents a more advanced understanding of the chapter material. Describe the key characteristics of American cities at the turn of the twentieth century and the impact that these characteristics had on city life. How did growth contribute to changes in work and social relationships? How did the influx of immigrants in the late nineteenth century shape city politics? How did the relationship among work, domestic life, and leisure activities change over the course of the late nineteenth and early twentieth centuries? To do this exercise online or to download this chart, visit bedfordstmartins.com/roarkunderstanding.

Characteristic	The American city, ca. 1900	Impact on city life
Population		
Diversity		
Social structure		
Work and labor relations		
Politics		
Domestic life		
Leisure		

Now that you have reviewed key elements of the chapter, take a step back and try to explain the big picture by answering these questions. Remember to use specific examples from the chapter in your answers. To do this exercise online, visit bedfordstmartins.com/roarkunderstanding.

URBANIZATION

▶ What factors led immigrants to American cities in the late nineteenth century? How did their arrival change the cities in which they settled?

▶ How and why did the social geography of the American city change in the late nineteenth century?

INDUSTRY AND LABOR

▶ What new social divisions accompanied business expansion and industrialization?

▶ What kinds of organizations did workers form in the late nineteenth century, and why did they start them? How successful were they?

CITY LIFE

▶ How did urban industrialism transform home and family life?

▶ What led to the rise of the big-city boss? Whose interests did late-nineteenth-century city governments serve?

LOOKING BACKWARD, LOOKING AHEAD

▶ How did early-twentieth-century American cities differ from their early-nineteenth-century counterparts?

▶ How did the rise of urban industrialism change Americans' sense of themselves as a people?

IN YOUR OWN WORDS

Imagine that you must explain chapter 19 to someone who hasn't read it. What would be the most important points to include and why?

20
A DECADE OF DISSENT, DEPRESSION, AND WAR

1890–1900

> This chapter explores the political and economic conflicts of the 1890s. It looks at the responses of a variety of Americans to the challenges of the 1880s and 1890s, concluding with an examination of the shift in American foreign policy at the end of the nineteenth century.

> What were the reasons behind the farmers' revolt?

> What led to the "labor wars" of the 1890s?

> How were women involved in late-nineteenth-century politics?

> How did economic problems shape American politics in the 1890s?

> Why did the United States move away from isolationism?

> Why did America go to war with Spain in 1898?

> Conclusion: What was the connection between domestic tensions and U.S. foreign policy?

DID YOU KNOW?

The first march on Washington took place in 1894 when thousands of unemployed Americans demanded that the government take action to find them work.

The Unemployed—Scene at Country Railway Station. *The Graphic*, Chicago, September 9, 1893.

What were the reasons behind the farmers' revolt?

Nebraska Farm Family

A Nebraska farm family posed in front of their sod hut in Custer County, Nebraska, in 1889. The house is formed of blocks of sod cut from the prairie. The photo testifies to the hard, lonely life of farmers on the Great Plains. Nebraska State Historical Society.

HARD TIMES in the 1880s and 1890s created a groundswell of agrarian revolt. A bitter farmer wrote from Minnesota, "I settled on this Land in good Faith Built House and Barn. Broken up Part of the Land. Spent years of hard Labor in grubbing fencing and Improving." About to lose his farm to foreclosure, he lamented, "Are they going to drive us out like trespassers . . . and give us away to the Corporations?"

Farm prices fell decade after decade, even as American farmers' share of the world market grew. In parts of Kansas, corn sold for as little as ten cents a bushel, and angry farmers burned it for fuel rather than market it at that price. At the same time, consumer prices soared. In Kansas alone, almost half the farms had fallen into the hands of the banks by 1894 because poor farmers could no longer afford to pay their mortgages (**Figure 20.1**).

At the heart of the problem stood a banking system dominated by eastern commercial banks committed to the gold standard, a railroad rate system that was capricious and unfair, and rampant speculation that drove up the price of land. In the West, farmers rankled under a system that allowed railroads to charge them exorbitant freight rates while granting rebates to large shippers like grain elevator companies (see chapter 18). In the South, lack of currency and credit drove farmers to the stopgap credit system of the crop lien. To pay for seed and supplies, farmers had to pledge their crops to local creditors, called "furnishing merchants," whose exorbitant prices meant chronic debt and destitution for southern farmers. Determined to do something, farmers banded together to fight for change.

The Farmers' Alliance

Farm protest was not new. In the 1870s, farmers had supported the Grange and the Greenback Labor Party. As the farmers' situation grew more desperate, they

CHAPTER LOCATOR | What were the reasons behind the farmers' revolt? | What led to the "labor wars" of the 1890s?

CHAPTER 20
538   A DECADE OF DISSENT, DEPRESSION, AND WAR , 1890–1900

organized, forming regional alliances. The first of the **Farmers' Alliances** came together in Lampasas County, Texas, to fight "landsharks and horse thieves." During the 1880s, the movement spread rapidly. Across the country, separate groups of farmers formed similar alliances for self-help.

As the movement grew, farmers' groups consolidated into two regional alliances. The Northwestern Farmers' Alliance was active in Kansas, Nebraska, and other midwestern Granger states. The more radical Southern Farmers' Alliance got its start in Texas and spread rapidly. In the 1880s, traveling lecturers preached the Alliance message. Overnight, scores of local alliances sprang up, each with its own lecturer, who in turn carried the word throughout the South. By 1887, the Southern Farmers' Alliance had grown to more than 200,000 members, and by 1890, it counted more than 3 million members.

Radical in its inclusiveness, the Southern Alliance reached out to African Americans, women, and industrial workers. Through cooperation with the Colored Farmers' Alliance, an African American group founded in Texas in the 1880s, blacks and whites attempted to make common cause. As Georgia's Tom Watson, a Southern Alliance stalwart, pointed out, "The colored tenant is in the same boat as the white tenant, . . . and . . . the accident of color can make no difference in the interests of farmers, croppers, and laborers." The political culture of the Alliance encouraged the inclusion of women and children and used the family as its defining symbol. Women rallied to the Alliance banner. "I am going to work for prohibition, the Alliance, and for Jesus as long as I live," swore one woman.

CHRONOLOGY

1876
– First Farmers' Alliance forms in Lampasas County, Texas.

1886
– Colored Farmers' Alliance is founded.

1890
– Southern Farmers' Alliance numbers three million members.

1892
– People's (Populist) Party is founded.

1894
– Almost half of Kansas farms are in the hands of banks.

Farmers' Alliance
▶ Movement to form local organizations to advance farmers' collective interests that gained popularity in the 1880s. Over time, farmers' groups consolidated into two regional alliances: the Northwestern Farmers' Alliance and the Southern Farmers' Alliance. In 1892, the Farmers' Alliance gave birth to the People's Party and launched the Populist movement.

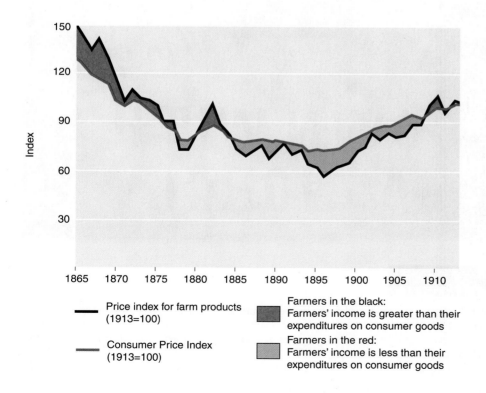

Price index for farm products (1913=100)

Consumer Price Index (1913=100)

Farmers in the black:
Farmers' income is greater than their expenditures on consumer goods

Farmers in the red:
Farmers' income is less than their expenditures on consumer goods

FIGURE 20.1 ■ Consumer Prices and Farm Income, 1865–1910
Around 1870, consumer prices and farm income were about equal. During the 1880s and 1890s, however, farmers suffered great hardships as prices for their crops steadily declined and the cost of consumer goods continued to rise.

| How were women involved in late-nineteenth-century politics? | How did economic problems shape American politics in the 1890s? | Why did the United States move away from isolationism? | Why did America go to war with Spain in 1898? | Conclusion: What was the connection between domestic tensions and U.S. foreign policy? |

At the heart of the Alliance movement stood a series of farmers' cooperatives. By selling their cotton together, farmers could negotiate a better price. And by setting up trade stores and exchanges, they sought to escape the grasp of the merchant/creditor. Through the cooperatives, the Farmers' Alliance promised to change the way farmers lived. "We are going to get out of debt and be free and independent people once more," exulted one Georgia farmer. But the Alliance faced insurmountable difficulties in running successful cooperatives. Opposition by merchants, bankers, wholesalers, and manufacturers made it impossible for the cooperatives to get credit. As the cooperative movement died, the Farmers' Alliance moved, often reluctantly, toward direct political action and the creation of a third political party.

Buffalo Banner from the 1892 Populist Convention

This flag graphically declares the frustration with the Democratic and Republican parties that led angry Americans, particularly farmers, to gather in St. Louis in 1892 to create a new People's Party. Featuring the buffalo (American bison) as a symbol, the flag urged the election of "honest men" and proclaimed as its motto "Down with Monopoly." Nebraska State Historical Society.

CHAPTER LOCATOR | What were the reasons behind the farmers' revolt? | What led to the "labor wars" of the 1890s?

CHAPTER 20
540   A DECADE OF DISSENT, DEPRESSION, AND WAR , 1890–1900

The Populist Movement

Although there was resistance to the farmers' move into politics, by 1892 they had formed a third party at a convention of laborers, farmers, and common folk in St. Louis. There, the Farmers' Alliance gave birth to the **People's Party** and launched the Populist movement. The same spirit of religious revival that animated the Farmers' Alliance infused the People's Party. Convinced that the money and banking systems worked to the advantage of the wealthy few, the Populists demanded economic democracy. To help farmers get the credit they needed at reasonable rates, southern farmers hit on the idea of a subtreasury—a plan that would allow farmers to store their nonperishable crops and receive commodity credit from the federal government. The subtreasury promised to get rid of the crop lien system once and for all. To the western farmer, the Populists promised land reform, championing a plan that would claim excessive land granted to railroads or sold to foreign investors. The Populists' boldest proposal called for government ownership of the railroads and the telegraph system to put an end to discriminatory rates.

The Populists also demanded currency reform, calling for free silver and greenbacks—attempts to increase the nation's tight money supply and thus make credit easier to obtain. And to empower the common people, the Populist platform called for the direct election of senators and for other electoral reforms, including the secret ballot and the right to initiate legislation, to recall elected officials, and to submit issues to the people by means of a referendum. Because the Populists shared common cause with labor against corporate interests, they also supported the eight-hour workday and an end to contract labor.

The sweeping array of Populist reforms enacted in the Populist platform changed the agenda of politics for decades to come. More than just a response to hard times, Populism presented an alternative vision of American economic democracy.

People's Party (Populist Party)

▶ Political party formed in 1892 by the Farmers' Alliance to advance the goals of the Populist movement. Populists sought economic democracy, promoting land, electoral, banking, and monetary reform. Republican victory in the presidential election of 1896 effectively destroyed the People's Party.

QUICK REVIEW <

Why did the Farmers' Alliance decide to form a third political party in 1892?

| How were women involved in late-nineteenth-century politics? | How did economic problems shape American politics in the 1890s? | Why did the United States move away from isolationism? | Why did America go to war with Spain in 1898? | Conclusion: What was the connection between domestic tensions and U.S. foreign policy? |

National Guard Occupying Pullman, Illinois

After President Grover Cleveland called out troops to put down the Pullman strike in 1894, the National Guard occupied the town of Pullman. The intervention enabled owner George M. Pullman to bring in strikebreakers and defeat the unions. Chicago Historical Society.

What led to the "labor wars" of the 1890s?

WHILE FARMERS UNITED to fight for change, industrial laborers fought their own battles in a series of bloody strikes so fiercely waged on both sides that historians have called them the "labor wars." Industrial workers felt increasingly threatened as businesses combined into huge corporations, and in the 1890s labor took a stand. At issue was the right of workers to organize and to speak through unions to bargain collectively for better working conditions, higher wages, shorter hours, and greater worker control in the face of increased mechanization. Three major conflicts of the period—the lockout of steelworkers in Homestead, Pennsylvania, in 1892; the miners' strike in Cripple Creek, Colorado, in 1894; and the Pullman strike in Illinois that same year—raised fundamental questions about the rights of labor and the sanctity of private property.

The Homestead Lockout

In 1892, steelworkers in Pennsylvania squared off against Andrew Carnegie in a decisive struggle over the right to organize in the Homestead steel mills. In 1892, Carnegie resolved to crush the Amalgamated Iron and Steel Workers, one of the largest and richest craft unions in the American Federation of Labor (AFL). When the Amalgamated attempted to renew its contract at Carnegie's Homestead mill, its leaders were told that since "the vast majority of our employees are Non union, the Firm has decided that the minority must give place to the majority." While it was true that only 800 skilled workers belonged to the elite Amalgamated, the union had long enjoyed the support of the plant's 3,000 nonunion workers. Slavs, who did much of the unskilled work, made common cause with the Welsh, Scots, and Irish skilled workers who belonged to the union.

CHAPTER LOCATOR | What were the reasons behind the farmers' revolt? | What led to the "labor wars" of the 1890s?

In anticipation of the coming conflict, Carnegie put Henry Clay Frick, the toughest antilabor man in the industry, in charge of the Homestead plant. By summer, a strike looked inevitable. Frick prepared by erecting a fifteen-foot fence around the plant and topping it with barbed wire. To defend the plant and protect strikebreakers, Frick hired 316 mercenaries from the Pinkerton National Detective Agency at the rate of $5 per day, more than double the wage of the average Homestead worker.

On June 28, the Homestead lockout began when Frick locked the workers out of the mills and prepared to bring in strikebreakers. Hugh O'Donnell, the young Irishman who led the union, vowed to prevent the "scabs" from entering the plant. On July 6 at four in the morning, a lookout spotted two barges moving up the Monongahela River. Frick was attempting to smuggle Pinkertons into Homestead.

Workers sounded the alarm, and within minutes a crowd of more than a thousand, hastily armed with rifles, hoes, and fence posts, rushed to the riverbank. For twelve hours, the workers, joined by their family members, threw everything they had at the barges, from fireworks to dynamite. Finally, the Pinkertons hoisted a white flag and arranged with O'Donnell to surrender. With three workers already dead and scores wounded, the crowd, numbering perhaps ten thousand, was in no mood for conciliation. As the hated "Pinks" came up the hill, they were forced to run a gantlet of screaming, cursing men, women, and children. When a young guard dropped to his knees, weeping for mercy, a woman used her umbrella to poke out his eye. One Pinkerton had been killed in the siege on the barges. In the grim rout that followed their surrender, not one avoided injury. In the aftermath of the battle, the workers took control of the plant and elected a council to run the community. At first, public opinion favored their cause. Newspapers urged Frick to negotiate or submit to arbitration. Populists, meeting in St. Louis, condemned the use of "hireling armies."

The action of the Homestead workers struck at the heart of the capitalist system, pitting the workers' right to their jobs against the rights of private property. The workers' insistence that "we are not destroying the property of the company—merely protecting our rights" did not prove as compelling to the courts and the state as the property rights of the mill owners. Four days after the confrontation, Pennsylvania's governor, who sympathized with the workers, nonetheless yielded to pressure from Frick and ordered eight thousand National Guard troops into Homestead. The strikers, thinking they had nothing to fear from the militia, welcomed the troops with a brass band. But the troops' occupation not only protected Carnegie's property but also enabled Frick to reopen the mills and bring in strikebreakers. "We have been deceived," one worker complained bitterly. "We have stood idly by and let the town be occupied by soldiers who come here, not as our protectors, but as the protectors of non-union men. . . . If we undertake to resist the seizure of our jobs, we will be shot down like dogs."

Then, in a misguided effort to ignite a general uprising, Alexander Berkman, a Russian immigrant and anarchist, attempted to assassinate Frick. Berkman bungled his attempt. Shot twice and stabbed with a dagger, Frick survived. "I do not think that I shall die," Frick remarked coolly, "but whether I do or not, the Company will pursue the same policy and it will win."

After the assassination attempt, public opinion turned against the workers. Berkman was quickly tried and sentenced to prison. Although the Amalgamated and the AFL denounced his action, the incident linked anarchism and unionism,

CHRONOLOGY

1890
- George Pullman establishes model company town outside of Chicago.

1892
- Unionized steelworkers in Homestead, Pennsylvania, are locked out by management.

1893
- Stock market crash touches off severe economic depression.

1894
- Miners' strike in Cripple Creek, Colorado.
- Federal troops and court injunction crush Pullman strike.

How were women involved in late-nineteenth-century politics?

How did economic problems shape American politics in the 1890s?

Why did the United States move away from isolationism?

Why did America go to war with Spain in 1898?

Conclusion: What was the connection between domestic tensions and U.S. foreign policy?

The nation's attention was riveted on labor strife at the Homestead steel mill in the summer of 1892. Frank Leslie's *Illustrated Weekly* ran a cover story on the violence that Pinkerton agents faced from a crowd of men, women, and children armed with clubs, guns, and ax handles. The workers were enraged that Henry Clay Frick had hired the Pinkertons to bring in strikebreakers. The illustration shows a boy with a gun in the foreground. Although the mob was armed, not one of the Pinkertons was shot as they ran the gantlet. All, however, were beaten. The New-York Society Library.

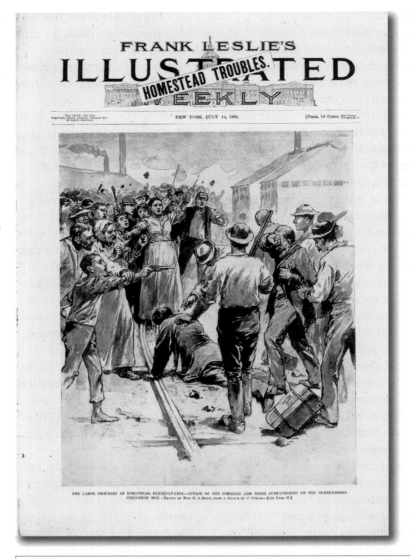

FRANK LESLIE'S
ILLUSTRATED
HOMESTEAD TROUBLES.
WEEKLY

NEW YORK, JULY 16, 1892.

THE LABOR TROUBLES AT HOMESTEAD, PENNSYLVANIA—ATTACK OF THE STRIKERS AND THEIR SYMPATHIZERS ON THE SURRENDERED PINKERTON MEN.

▶ FOR MORE HELP ANALYZING THIS IMAGE, see the visual activity for this chapter in the Online Study Guide at bedfordstmartins.com/roarkunderstanding.

already associated in the public mind as a result of the Haymarket bombing in 1886 (see chapter 19). In the end, the workers capitulated. The Homestead mill reopened in November, and the men returned to work, except for the union leaders, now blacklisted in every steel mill in the country. With the owners firmly in charge, the company slashed wages, reinstated the twelve-hour day, and eliminated five hundred jobs.

The workers at Homestead had been taught a significant lesson. They would never again, in the words of the National Guard commander, "believe the works are their's [*sic*] quite as much as Carnegie's." Another forty-five years would pass before steelworkers, unskilled as well as skilled, successfully unionized. In the meantime, Carnegie's production tripled, even in the midst of a depression.

CHAPTER LOCATOR | What were the reasons behind the farmers' revolt? | What led to the "labor wars" of the 1890s?

CHAPTER 20
544   A DECADE OF DISSENT, DEPRESSION, AND WAR , 1890–1900

"Ashamed to tell you profits these days," Carnegie wrote a friend in 1899. And no wonder: Carnegie's profits had grown from $4 million in 1892 to $40 million in 1900.

The Cripple Creek Miners' Strike of 1894

Less than a year after the Homestead lockout, a panic on Wall Street in the spring of 1893 touched off an economic depression. In the West, silver mines fell on hard times, touching off the Cripple Creek miners' strike of 1894. When mine owners moved to lengthen the workday from eight to ten hours, the newly formed Western Federation of Miners (WFM) vowed to hold the line in Cripple Creek, Colorado. In February 1894, the WFM threatened to strike all mines working more than eight-hour shifts. The mine owners divided: Some quickly settled with the WFM; others continued to demand ten-hour workdays, provoking a strike.

The striking miners received help from many quarters. Working miners paid $15 a month to a strike fund, and miners in neighboring districts sent substantial contributions. The miners enjoyed the support and assistance of local businesses and grocers, who provided credit to the strikers. With these advantages, the Cripple Creek strikers could afford to hold out for their demands.

Even more significant, Governor Davis H. Waite, a Populist elected in 1892, had strong ties to the miners and refused to use the power of the state against the strikers. Governor Waite asked the strikers to lay down their arms and demanded that the mine owners disperse their hired deputies. The miners agreed to arbitration and selected Waite as their sole arbitrator. By May, the recalcitrant mine owners capitulated, and the union won an eight-hour day.

Governor Waite's intervention demonstrated the pivotal power of the state in the nation's labor wars. A decade later, in 1904, with Waite out of office, mine owners relied on state troops to take back control of the mines, defeating the WFM and blacklisting all of its members. In retrospect, the Cripple Creek miners' strike of 1894 proved the exception to the rule of state intervention on the side of private property.

Eugene V. Debs and the Pullman Strike

The economic depression that began in 1893 swelled the ranks of the unemployed to three million, almost half of the working population. "A fearful crisis is upon us," wrote a labor publication. Nowhere were workers more demoralized than in the model town of Pullman, on the outskirts of Chicago.

In the wake of the Great Railroad Strike of 1877, George M. Pullman, who built Pullman railroad cars, moved his plant and workers nine miles south of Chicago to a model town boasting parks, fountains, playgrounds, an auditorium, a library, a hotel, shops, and markets, along with 1,800 units of housing. Noticeably absent was a saloon.

The housing in Pullman was superior to that in neighboring areas, but workers paid a high price to live there. Pullman's rents ran 10 to 20 percent higher than housing costs in nearby communities. In addition, George Pullman refused to "sell an acre under any circumstances." As long as he had the power of eviction over his employees, he could quickly get rid of "troublemakers." Although observers at

How were women involved in late-nineteenth-century politics?

How did economic problems shape American politics in the 1890s?

Why did the United States move away from isolationism?

Why did America go to war with Spain in 1898?

Conclusion: What was the connection between domestic tensions and U.S. foreign policy?

545

A Pullman Craftsworker

Pullman Palace cars were known for their luxurious details. Here, a painter working in the 1890s applies elaborate decoration to the exterior of a Pullman car. The Pullman workers' strike in 1894 stemmed in part from the company's efforts to undermine the status of craftsworkers by reducing them to low-paid piecework. *Chicago Historical Society.*

first praised the beauty and orderliness of the town, critics by the 1890s compared Pullman's model town to a "gilded cage" for workers.

The depression brought hard times to Pullman. Workers saw their wages slashed five times between May and December 1893, with cuts totaling at least 28 percent. At the same time, Pullman refused to lower the rents in his model town, insisting that "the renting of the dwellings and the employment of workmen at Pullman are in no way tied together." When workers went to the bank to cash their paychecks, they found the rent had been taken out. One worker discovered only forty-seven cents in his pay envelope for two weeks' work. At the same time, Pullman continued to pay his stockholders an 8 percent dividend, and the company accumulated a $25 million surplus.

At the heart of the labor problems at Pullman lay not only economic inequity but also the company's attempt to control the work process, substituting piecework for day wages and undermining skilled craftsworkers. During the spring of 1894, Pullman's desperate workers, seeking help, flocked to the ranks of the American Railway Union (ARU), led by the charismatic **Eugene V. Debs**. The ARU, unlike the skilled craft unions of the AFL, pledged to organize all railway workers—from engineers to engine wipers.

George Pullman responded to union organization at his plant by firing three of the union's leaders the day after they led a delegation to protest wage cuts. Angry men and women walked off the job in disgust. What began as a spontaneous protest in May 1894 quickly blossomed into a strike that involved more than 90 percent of Pullman's 3,300 workers. Pullman countered by shutting down the plant. In June, the Pullman strikers appealed to the ARU for aid. Debs hesitated and pleaded with the workers to find another solution. When George Pullman adamantly refused arbitration, the ARU membership voted to boycott all Pullman cars. Beginning on June 29, switchmen across the United States refused to handle any train that carried Pullman cars.

The conflict escalated quickly. The General Managers Association (GMA), an organization of managers from twenty-four different railroads, acted in concert to quash the Pullman boycott. They recruited strikebreakers and fired all the protesting switchmen. Their tactics set off a chain reaction. Entire train crews walked off the job in a show of solidarity with the Pullman workers. By July 2, rail lines from New York to California lay paralyzed. Even the GMA was forced to concede that the railroads had been "fought to a standstill."

The boycott remained surprisingly peaceful. In contrast to the Great Railroad Strike of 1877, no major riots broke out, and no serious property damage occurred.

CHAPTER LOCATOR | What were the reasons behind the farmers' revolt? | What led to the "labor wars" of the 1890s?

CHAPTER 20
546 A DECADE OF DISSENT, DEPRESSION, AND WAR , 1890–1900

Debs fired off telegrams to all parts of the country advising his followers to avoid violence and respect law and order. But the nation's newspapers, fed press releases by the GMA, distorted the issues and misrepresented the strike. Across the country, papers ran headlines like "Wild Riot in Chicago" and "Mob Is in Control."

In Washington, Attorney General Richard B. Olney, a lawyer with strong ties to the railroads, determined to put down the strike. In his way stood the governor of Illinois, John Peter Altgeld, who refused to call out troops. To get around Altgeld, Olney convinced President Grover Cleveland that federal troops had to intervene to protect the mails. To further cripple the boycott, two conservative Chicago judges issued an injunction so sweeping that it prohibited Debs from speaking in public. By issuing the injunction, the court made the boycott a crime punishable by a jail sentence for contempt of court, a civil process that did not require a jury trial. Even the conservative *Chicago Tribune* judged the injunction "a menace to liberty . . . a weapon ever ready for the capitalist."

Olney's strategy worked. With the strikers violating a federal injunction and with the mails in jeopardy (the GMA made sure that Pullman cars were put on every mail train), Cleveland called out the army. On July 5, nearly 8,000 troops marched into Chicago. Violence immediately erupted. In one day, troops killed 25 workers and wounded more than 60. Nonetheless, the strikers held firm. "Troops cannot move trains," Debs reminded his followers, a fact borne out as the railroads remained paralyzed despite the military intervention. But if the army could not put down the boycott, the injunction could and did. Debs was arrested and imprisoned for contempt of court. With its leader in jail, the ARU was defeated. Pullman reopened his factory, hiring new workers to replace many of the strikers and leaving 1,600 workers without jobs.

In the aftermath of the strike, a special commission investigated the events at Pullman, taking testimony from 107 witnesses, including Pullman himself. Stubborn and self-righteous, Pullman steadfastly affirmed the right of business to safeguard its interests through confederacies such as the GMA and at the same time denied labor's right to organize. "If we were to receive these men as representatives of the union," he stated, "they could probably force us to pay any wages which they saw fit."

With the courts and the government ready to side with industrialists in the interest of defending private property, Debs realized that labor had little recourse. Strikes seemed futile, and unions remained helpless; workers would have to take control of the state itself. Debs went into jail a trade unionist and came out six months later a socialist. At first, he turned to the People's Party, but after its demise, he formed the Socialist Party in 1900 and ran for president five times. Debs's dissatisfaction with the status quo was shared by another group even more alienated from the political process—women.

Eugene V. Debs

▶ Charismatic leader of the American Railroad Union (ARU). In 1894, Debs and the ARU came to the aid of striking Pullman workers by organizing a boycott of Pullman cars. Debs's skillful orchestration of the peaceful boycott was to no avail, as railroad and government officials collaborated, using propaganda, troops, and a dubious injunction to bring an end to the boycott and to imprison Debs.

QUICK REVIEW

Why were the labor conflicts of the 1890s so often marked by violence?

How were women involved in late-nineteenth-century politics?

Frances Willard

Frances Willard, the forward-thinking leader of the Woman's Christian Temperance Union, learned to ride a bicycle at age fifty-three. The bicycle became hugely popular in the 1890s, even though traditionalists fulminated that it was unladylike for women to straddle a bike and immodest for them to wear the divided skirts that allowed them to pedal. Willard, shown here in 1895, declared bicycling a "harmless pleasure" that encouraged "clear heads and steady hands." Courtesy of the Frances E. Willard Memorial Library and Archives (WCTU).

"DO EVERYTHING," Frances Willard urged her followers in 1881. The new president of the Woman's Christian Temperance Union (WCTU) meant what she said. The WCTU followed a trajectory that was common for women in the late nineteenth century. As women organized to deal with issues that touched their homes and families, they moved into politics, lending new urgency to the cause of woman suffrage. Like men, women sought political change and organized to promote issues central to their lives, campaigning for temperance and woman suffrage.

Frances Willard and the Woman's Christian Temperance Union

Frances Willard

▶ Visionary leader of the Woman's Christian Temperance Union (WCTU). When Willard became president of the WCTU in 1879, she radically changed the direction of the organization. Viewing alcoholism as a disease rather than a sin, the organization became involved in political and labor issues, urging the vote for women.

Frances Willard, the visionary leader of the WCTU, spoke for a group left almost entirely out of the U.S. electoral process—women. In 1890, only one state, Wyoming, allowed women to vote in national elections. But lack of the franchise did not mean that women were apolitical. The WCTU demonstrated the breadth of women's political activity in the late nineteenth century.

When Frances Willard became president of the WCTU in 1879, she radically changed the direction of the organization. Viewing alcoholism as a disease rather than a sin and poverty as a cause rather than a result of drink, the WCTU became involved in labor issues, joining with the Knights of Labor to press for better working conditions for women workers. Describing workers in a textile mill, a WCTU member wrote in the *Union Signal*, "It is dreadful to see these girls, stripped almost to the skin . . . and running like racehorses from the beginning to the end of the day." She concluded, "The hard slavish work is drawing the girls into the saloon."

CHAPTER LOCATOR | What were the reasons behind the farmers' revolt? | What led to the "labor wars" of the 1890s?

Willard capitalized on the cult of domesticity as a shrewd political tactic. Using "home protection" as her watchword, she argued as early as 1884 that women needed the vote to protect home and family. By the 1890s, the WCTU was a formidable group with more than 200,000 dues-paying members and a grassroots network of local unions that had spread to all but the most isolated rural areas of the country.

Willard worked to create a broad reform coalition in the 1890s, embracing the Knights of Labor, the People's Party, and the Prohibition Party. Until her death in 1898, she led the first organized mass movement of women united around a women's issue. By 1900, thanks largely to the WCTU, women could claim a generation of experience in political action. As Willard observed, "All this work has tended more toward the liberation of women than it has toward the extinction of the saloon."

Elizabeth Cady Stanton, Susan B. Anthony, and the Movement for Woman Suffrage

Unlike the WCTU, the organized movement for woman suffrage remained small and relatively weak in the late nineteenth century. In 1869, Elizabeth Cady Stanton and her ally, **Susan B. Anthony**, launched the National Woman Suffrage Association (NWSA), demanding the vote for women (see chapter 18). A more conservative group, the American Woman Suffrage Association (AWSA), formed the same year. Composed of men as well as women, the AWSA believed that women should vote in local but not national elections.

By 1890, the split had healed, and the new National American Woman Suffrage Association (NAWSA) launched campaigns on the state level to gain the vote for women. Twenty years had made a great change. Woman suffrage, though not yet generally supported, was no longer considered a crackpot idea, thanks in part to the WCTU's support of the "home protection" ballot. The NAWSA elected Elizabeth Cady Stanton as its first president, but Susan B. Anthony, who took the helm in 1892, emerged as the leading figure in the new united organization.

Stanton and Anthony, both in their seventies, were coming to the end of their public careers. Since the days of the Seneca Falls woman's rights convention, they had worked for reforms for their sex, including property rights, custody rights, and the right to education and gainful employment. But the prize of woman suffrage still eluded them. Never losing faith, Susan B. Anthony remarked in her last public appearance, in 1906, "Failure is impossible." Although it would take until 1920 for all women to gain the vote with the ratification of the Nineteenth Amendment, the unification of the woman suffrage movement in 1890 signaled a new era in women's fight for the vote.

CHRONOLOGY

1879
– Frances Willard becomes president of the Woman's Christian Temperance Union (WCTU).

1884
– The WCTU calls for woman suffrage.

1890
– National American Woman Suffrage Association is formed.

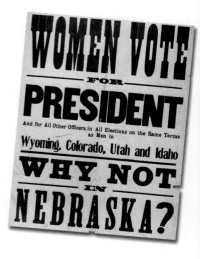

Susan B. Anthony
▶ Women's rights activist, who, along with Elizabeth Cady Stanton, spearheaded the movement in 1848. While in her seventies, Anthony emerged as the leader of the newly united National American Woman Suffrage Association, a move that began a new era in women's fight for voting rights.

QUICK REVIEW

How did the Woman's Christian Temperance Union contribute to the cause of woman suffrage?

| How were women involved in late-nineteenth-century politics? | How did economic problems shape American politics in the 1890s? | Why did the United States move away from isolationism? | Why did America go to war with Spain in 1898? | Conclusion: What was the connection between domestic tensions and U.S. foreign policy? |

How did economic problems shape American politics in the 1890s?

Coxey's Army A contingent of Coxey's army stops to rest on its way to Washington, D.C. A "petition in boots," Coxey's followers were well dressed, as evidenced by the men in this photo wearing white shirts, vests, neckties, and bowler hats. Music was an important component of the march; band members are pictured on the right with their instruments. Ohio Historical Society.

THE DEPRESSION that began in the spring of 1893 and lasted for more than four years put nearly half of the labor force out of work, a higher percentage than during the Great Depression of the 1930s. The human cost of the depression was staggering. "I Take my pen in hand to let you know that we are Starving to death," a Kansas farm woman wrote to the governor in 1894. "Last cent gone," wrote a young widow in her diary. "Children went to work without their breakfasts." Following the harsh dictates of social Darwinism and laissez-faire, the majority of America's elected officials believed that it was inappropriate for the government to intervene. But the scope of the depression made it impossible for local agencies to supply sufficient relief, and increasingly Americans called on the federal government to take action. Armies of the unemployed marched on Washington to demand relief, and the Populist Party experienced a surge of support as the election of 1896 approached.

Coxey's Army

Masses of unemployed Americans marched to Washington, D.C., in the spring of 1894 to call attention to their plight and to urge Congress to enact a public works

CHAPTER LOCATOR | What were the reasons behind the farmers' revolt? | What led to the "labor wars" of the 1890s?

program to end unemployment. Jacob S. Coxey of Massillon, Ohio, led the most publicized contingent. Convinced that men could be put to work building badly needed roads for the nation, Coxey proposed a scheme to finance public works through non-interest-bearing bonds. "What I am after," he maintained, "is to try to put this country in a condition so that no man who wants work shall be obliged to remain idle." His plan won support from the AFL and the Populists.

Starting out from Ohio with one hundred men, **Coxey's army**, as it was dubbed, swelled as it marched east. In Pennsylvania, Coxey recruited several hundred from the ranks of those left unemployed by the Homestead lockout. On May 1, Coxey's army arrived in Washington. When Coxey defiantly marched his men onto the Capitol grounds, police set upon the demonstrators with nightsticks, arresting Coxey and his lieutenants for walking on the grass. But other armies of the unemployed, totaling possibly as many as five thousand people, were still on their way. The more daring contingents commandeered entire trains, stirring fears of revolution. Journalists who covered the march did little to quiet the nation's fears. Describing themselves as "war correspondents," they gave the episode a tone of urgency and heightened the sense of a nation imperiled.

By August, the leaderless armies dissolved. Although the "On to Washington" movement proved ineffective in forcing federal relief legislation, Coxey's army dramatized the plight of the unemployed and acted, in the words of one participant, as a "living, moving object lesson." Like the Populists, Coxey's army called into question the underlying values of the new industrial order and demonstrated how ordinary citizens turned to means outside the regular party system to influence politics in the 1890s.

The People's Party and the Election of 1896

Even before the depression of 1893, the Populists had railed against the status quo. "We meet in the midst of a nation brought to the verge of moral, political, and material ruin," Ignatius Donnelly had declared in his keynote address at the creation of the People's Party in St. Louis in 1892. "The fruits of the toil of millions are boldly stolen to build up colossal fortunes for a few. . . . From the same prolific womb of governmental injustice we breed the two great classes—tramps and millionaires."

The fiery rhetoric frightened many who saw in the People's Party a call not to reform but to revolution. Throughout the country, the press denounced the Populists as "cranks, lunatics, and idiots." When one self-righteous editor dismissed them as "calamity howlers," Populist governor Lorenzo Lewelling of Kansas shot back, "If that is so I want to continue to howl until those conditions are improved."

The People's Party captured more than a million votes in the presidential election of 1892, a respectable showing for a new party (**Map 20.1**). But increasingly, sectional and racial animosities threatened its unity. Realizing that race prejudice obscured the common economic interests of black and white farmers, Populist Tom

CHRONOLOGY

1894
– Coxey's army marches to Washington, D.C.

1896
– Democrats and Populists support William Jennings Bryan for president.
– Republican William McKinley is elected president.

Coxey's army
▶ Unemployed men who marched to Washington, D.C., in 1894 to protest economic conditions in the wake of the panic of 1893. The leader of the march, Jacob S. Coxey, advocated public works programs to alleviate unemployment. Coxey's army inspired many other groups of unemployed Americans to head to Washington.

How were women involved in late-nineteenth-century politics?	How did economic problems shape American politics in the 1890s?	Why did the United States move away from isolationism?	Why did America go to war with Spain in 1898?	Conclusion: What was the connection between domestic tensions and U.S. foreign policy?

551

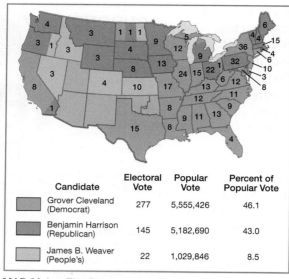

Candidate	Electoral Vote	Popular Vote	Percent of Popular Vote
Grover Cleveland (Democrat)	277	5,555,426	46.1
Benjamin Harrison (Republican)	145	5,182,690	43.0
James B. Weaver (People's)	22	1,029,846	8.5

MAP 20.1 ■ The Election of 1892

William Jennings Bryan

► Democratic candidate for president in 1896. Bryan was famed for his oratorical skills and his passionate support of free silver. He was nominated in 1896 by both the Democrats and the Populists but lost by a narrow margin to Republican William McKinley.

Watson of Georgia openly courted African Americans, appearing on platforms with black speakers and promising "to wipe out the color line." When angry Georgia whites threatened to lynch a black Populist preacher, Watson rallied two thousand gun-toting Populists to the man's defense. Although many Populists remained racist in their attitudes toward African Americans, the spectacle of white Georgians riding to protect a black man from lynching was symbolic of the enormous changes the Populist Party promised in the South.

As the presidential election of 1896 approached, the depression intensified cries for reform not only from the Populists but also throughout the electorate. Depression worsened the tight money problem caused by the deflationary pressures of the gold standard. Once again, proponents of free silver (the unlimited coinage of silver in addition to gold) stirred rebellion in the ranks of both the Democratic and the Republican parties. When the Republicans nominated Ohio governor William McKinley on a platform pledging the preservation of the gold standard, western advocates of free silver representing miners and farmers walked out of the convention. Open rebellion also split the Democratic Party as vast segments in the West and South repudiated President Grover Cleveland because of his support for gold.

At the 1896 Democratic National Convention in Chicago, thirty-six-year-old **William Jennings Bryan** of Nebraska whipped the convention into a frenzy with his passionate call for free silver, closing his dramatic keynote speech with a ringing exhortation: "Do not crucify mankind upon a cross of gold." Pandemonium broke loose as delegates stampeded to nominate Bryan, the youngest candidate ever to run for the presidency.

When the People's Party met in St. Louis, a week after the Democrats adjourned, many western Populists urged the party to ally with the Democrats and endorse Bryan. A major obstacle in the path of fusion, however, was Bryan's running mate, Arthur M. Sewall. A Maine railway director and bank president, Sewall, who had been placed on the ticket to appease conservative Democrats, embodied everything the Populists detested. Moreover, die-hard southern Populists wanted no part of fusion. Southern Democrats had resorted to fraud and violence to steal elections from the Populists in 1892 and 1894, and support for a Democratic ticket proved hard to swallow.

Populists struggled to work out a compromise. To show that they remained true to their principles, delegates first voted to support all the planks of the 1892 platform, adding to it a call for public works projects for the unemployed. To deal with the problem of fusion, the convention selected the vice presidential candidate first. The nomination of Tom Watson undercut opposition to Bryan's candidacy. And although Bryan quickly sent a telegram to protest that he would not drop Sewall as his running mate, mysteriously his message never reached the convention floor. Watson's vice presidential nomination paved the way for the selection of Bryan. The Populists did not know it, but their cheers for Bryan signaled the death knell of the People's Party.

Few contests in the nation's history have been as fiercely fought as the presidential election of 1896. On one side stood Republican William McKinley, backed

CHAPTER LOCATOR | What were the reasons behind the farmers' revolt? | What led to the "labor wars" of the 1890s?

552 CHAPTER 20
A DECADE OF DISSENT, DEPRESSION, AND WAR , 1890–1900

by the wealthy industrialist and party boss Mark Hanna. Hanna played on the business community's fears of Populism to raise a Republican war chest more than double the amount of any previous campaign. On the other side, William Jennings Bryan struggled to make up in energy and eloquence what his party lacked in campaign funds, crisscrossing the country in a whirlwind tour. According to his own reckoning, he visited twenty-seven states and spoke to more than five million Americans.

On election day, four out of five voters went to the polls in an unprecedented turnout. In the critical midwestern swing states, as many as 95 percent of the eligible voters cast their ballots. In the end, the election hinged on between 100 and 1,000 votes in several key states, including Wisconsin, Iowa, and Minnesota. Although McKinley won twenty-three states to Bryan's twenty-two, the electoral vote showed a lopsided 271 to 176 in McKinley's favor (**Map 20.2**).

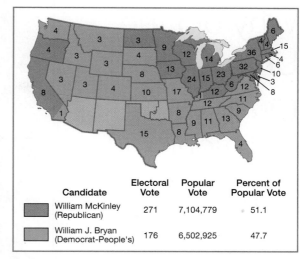

Candidate	Electoral Vote	Popular Vote	Percent of Popular Vote
William McKinley (Republican)	271	7,104,779	51.1
William J. Bryan (Democrat-People's)	176	6,502,925	47.7

MAP 20.2 ■ The Election of 1896

The biggest losers in 1896 turned out to be the Populists. On the national level, they polled fewer than 300,000 votes, a million less than in 1894. In the clamor to support Bryan, Populists in the South had drifted back to the Democratic Party. The People's Party was crushed, and with it the agrarian revolt.

But if Populism proved unsuccessful at the polls, it nevertheless set the domestic political agenda for the United States in the next decades, highlighting issues such as banking and currency reform, electoral reforms, and an enlarged role for the federal government in the economy. Meanwhile, as the decade ended, America's attention turned to foreign affairs. The struggle for social justice gave way to a war for empire as the United States asserted its power on the world stage.

QUICK REVIEW

Why was the People's Party unable to translate national support into victory in the 1896 election?

How were women involved in late-nineteenth-century politics?

How did economic problems shape American politics in the 1890s?

Why did the United States move away from isolationism?

Why did America go to war with Spain in 1898?

Conclusion: What was the connection between domestic tensions and U.S. foreign policy?

Why did the United States move away from isolationism?

The Open Door The trade advantage gained by the United States through the Open Door policy, enunciated by Secretary of State John Hay in 1900, is portrayed graphically in this political cartoon. Uncle Sam stands prominently in the "open door," while representatives of the other great powers seek admittance to the "Flowery Kingdom" of China. In fact, the Open Door policy promised equal access for all powers to the China trade, not U.S. preeminence as the cartoon implies. Culver Pictures.

▶ FOR MORE HELP ANALYZING THIS IMAGE, see the visual activity for this chapter in the Online Study Guide at bedfordstmartins.com/roarkunderstanding.

THROUGHOUT MUCH OF THE SECOND HALF of the nineteenth century, U.S. interest in foreign policy took a backseat to territorial expansion in the American West. The United States fought the Indian wars while European nations, along with the increasingly powerful Japan, competed for empires in Asia, Africa, Latin America, and the Pacific.

At the turn of the twentieth century, American foreign policy consisted of two currents—isolationism and expansionism. Although the determination to remain aloof from European politics had been a hallmark of U.S. foreign policy since the nation's founding, Americans simultaneously believed in manifest destiny—the "obvious" right to expand the nation from ocean to ocean. The United States' determination to protect its sphere of influence in the Western Hemisphere at the same time it expanded its trading in Asia moved the nation away from isolationism and toward a more active role on the world stage.

Markets and Missionaries

The depression of the 1890s provided a powerful impetus to American commercial expansion. As markets weakened at home, American businesses looked abroad for profits. As the depression deepened, one diplomat warned that

CHAPTER LOCATOR | What were the reasons behind the farmers' revolt? | What led to the "labor wars" of the 1890s?

Americans "must turn [their] eyes abroad, or they will soon look inward upon discontent."

Exports constituted a small but significant percentage of the profits of American business in the 1890s (**Figure 20.2**). And where American interests led, businessmen expected the government's power and influence to follow to protect their investments. Companies like Standard Oil actively sought to use the U.S. government as their agent, often putting foreign service employees on the payroll. "Our ambassadors and ministers and consuls," wrote John D. Rockefeller appreciatively, "have aided to push our way into new markets and to the utmost corners of the world." Whether "our" referred to the United States or to Standard Oil remained ambiguous.

America's foreign policy often appeared to be little more than a sidelight to business development. In Hawaii (first called the Sandwich Islands), American sugar interests toppled the increasingly independent Queen Liliuokalani in 1893. They pushed Congress to annex the islands, which would allow planters to avoid the high McKinley tariff on sugar. When President Cleveland learned that Hawaiians opposed annexation, he withdrew the proposal from Congress. But expansionists still coveted the islands and continued to look for an excuse to push through annexation.

Business interests alone, however, did not account for the new expansionism that seized the nation during the 1890s. As Captain Alfred Thayer Mahan, leader of a growing group of American expansionists, confessed, "Even when material interests are the original exciting cause, it is the sentiment to which they give rise, the moral tone which emotion takes that constitutes the greater force." Much

CHRONOLOGY

1893
- President Grover Cleveland rejects attempt to annex Hawaii.

1899–1900
- Secretary of State John Hay enunciates Open Door policy in China.
- Boxer uprising in China.

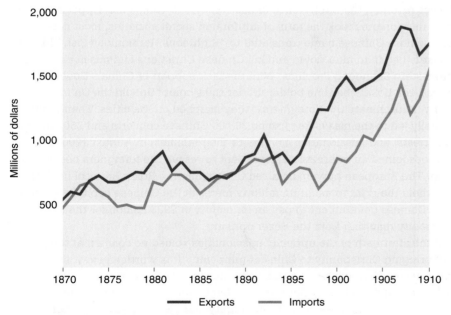

FIGURE 20.2 ■ Expansion in U.S. Trade, 1870–1910

Between 1870 and 1910, American exports more than tripled. Imports generally rose, but they were held in check by the high protective tariffs championed by Republican presidents from Ulysses S. Grant to William Howard Taft. A decline in imports is particularly noticeable after the passage of the prohibitive McKinley tariff in 1890.

How were women involved in late-nineteenth-century politics?	How did economic problems shape American politics in the 1890s?	**Why did the United States move away from isolationism?**	Why did America go to war with Spain in 1898?	Conclusion: What was the connection between domestic tensions and U.S. foreign policy?

Methodist women missionaries in China's Szechuan province relied on traditional means of transportation, in this case "back chairs." Women constituted 60 percent of America's foreign missionaries by 1890.
Special Collections, Yale Divinity School Library.

of that moral tone was set by American missionaries, many of whom set their sights on China.

The 1858 Tientsin treaty admitted foreign missionaries to China. Although Christians converted only 100,000 in a population of 400 million, the Chinese nevertheless resented the interference of missionaries in village life. Opposition to foreign missionaries took the form of antiforeign secret societies, most notably the Boxers, whose Chinese name translated to "Righteous Harmonious Fist." In 1899, the Boxers began to hunt down and kill Chinese Christians and missionaries in northwestern Shandong Province. With the tacit support of China's Dowager Empress, the Boxers became bolder. Under the slogan "Uphold the Ch'ing Dynasty, Exterminate the Foreigners," they marched on the cities. Their rampage eventually led to the massacre of some 30,000 Chinese converts and 250 foreign nuns, priests, and missionaries along with their families. In August 1900, 2,500 U.S. troops joined an international force sent to rescue the foreigners besieged in Beijing. The European powers imposed the humiliating Boxer Protocol in 1901, giving them the right to maintain military forces in the Chinese capital and requiring the Chinese government to pay an indemnity of $333 million for the loss of life and property resulting from the Boxer uprising.

In the aftermath of the uprising, missionaries voiced no concern at the paradox of bringing Christianity to China at gunpoint. "It is worth any cost in money, worth any cost in bloodshed," argued one bishop, "if we can make millions of Chinese true and intelligent Christians." Merchants and missionaries alike shared such reasoning. Indeed, trade and Christianity marched into Asia together. "Missionaries," admitted the American clergyman Charles Denby, "are the pioneers of trade and commerce. . . . The missionary, inspired by holy zeal, goes everywhere and by degrees foreign commerce and trade follow."

CHAPTER LOCATOR | What were the reasons behind the farmers' revolt? | What led to the "labor wars" of the 1890s?

CHAPTER 20
556 A DECADE OF DISSENT, DEPRESSION, AND WAR , 1890–1900

The Monroe Doctrine and the Open Door Policy

The emergence of the United States as a world power pitted the nation against other colonial powers, particularly Germany and Japan, which posed a threat to the twin pillars of America's expansionist foreign policy. The first, the Monroe Doctrine, came to be interpreted as establishing the Western Hemisphere as an American "sphere of influence" and warned European powers to stay away or risk war. The second, the Open Door, dealt with maintaining market access to China.

American diplomacy actively worked to buttress the Monroe Doctrine, with its assertion of American hegemony (domination) in the Western Hemisphere. In the 1880s, Republican secretary of state James G. Blaine promoted hemispheric peace and trade through Pan-American cooperation but at the same time used American troops to intervene in Latin American border disputes. In 1895, Americans risked war with Great Britain to enforce the Monroe Doctrine when a conflict developed between Venezuela and British Guiana.

In Central America, American business triumphed in a bloodless takeover that saw French and British interests routed. The United Fruit Company of Boston virtually dominated the Central American nations of Costa Rica and Guatemala, while an importer from New Orleans turned Honduras into a "banana republic" (a country run by U.S. business interests). Thus, by 1895, the United States, through business as well as diplomacy, had successfully achieved hegemony in Latin America and the Caribbean.

At the same time that American foreign policy warned European powers to stay out of the Western Hemisphere, the United States competed for trade in the Eastern Hemisphere. As American interests in China grew, the United States became more aggressive in defending its presence in Asia and the Pacific.

In the 1890s, China, weakened by years of internal warfare, was beginning to be partitioned into spheres of influence by Britain, Japan, Germany, France, and Russia. Concerned about the integrity of China and no less about American trade, Secretary of State John Hay in 1899–1900 wrote a series of notes calling for an "open door" policy that would ensure trade access to all and maintain Chinese sovereignty. The notes were greeted by the major powers with polite evasion. Nevertheless, Hay skillfully managed to maneuver the major powers into doing his bidding, and in 1900 he boldly announced the Open Door as international policy. The United States, by insisting on the **Open Door policy**, managed to secure access to Chinese markets, expanding its economic power while avoiding the problems of maintaining a far-flung colonial empire on the Asian mainland. But as the Spanish-American War soon demonstrated, Americans found it hard to resist the temptations of overseas empire.

Open Door policy
▶ Proposal first put forward by Secretary of State John Hay in 1899–1900 recommending that all major powers share access to trade with China and that Chinese sovereignty be maintained. The proposal was made against a backdrop of intensifying efforts by the other major powers to establish spheres of influence in China. Through skillful diplomacy, Hay was able to establish the Open Door as international policy.

QUICK REVIEW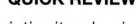

What roles did business and Christianity play in American foreign policy in the 1890s?

| How were women involved in late-nineteenth-century politics? | How did economic problems shape American politics in the 1890s? | **Why did the United States move away from isolationism?** | Why did America go to war with Spain in 1898? | Conclusion: What was the connection between domestic tensions and U.S. foreign policy? |

> Why did America go to war with Spain in 1898?

COLUMBIA'S EASTER BONNET.

Columbia's Easter Bonnet

The United States, symbolized by the female figure of Columbia, tries on "World Power" in this cartoon from *Puck* that appeared in 1901 after the Spanish-American War left the United States in control of Spain's former colonies in Guam, the Philippines, and Puerto Rico. "Expansion," spelled out in the smoke from the ship's smokestack, points to a new overseas direction for American foreign policy at the turn of the twentieth century. Library of Congress.

THE SPANISH-AMERICAN WAR began as an effort to free Cuba from Spain's colonial grasp and ended with the United States itself acquiring territory overseas and fighting a guerrilla war with Filipino nationalists, who, like the Cubans, sought independence. Behind the contradiction stood the twin pillars of American foreign policy: The Monroe Doctrine made Spain's presence in Cuba unacceptable, and U.S. determination to keep open the door to Asia made the Philippines attractive as a stepping-stone to China.

"A Splendid Little War"

Looking back on the **Spanish-American War** of 1898, Secretary of State John Hay judged it "a splendid little war; begun with the highest motives, carried on with magnificent intelligence and spirit, favored by that fortune which loves the brave." At the close of a decade marred by bitter depression, social unrest, and political upheaval, the war offered Americans a chance to wave the flag and march in unison. Few argued the merits of the conflict until it was over and the time came to divide the spoils.

Spanish-American War

▶ 1898 war between Spain and the United States that began as an effort to free Cuba from Spain's colonial rule. It ended with the United States acquiring control of Cuba and colonies in Puerto Rico, Guam, and the Philippines. The war itself was both popular and brief. When it was over, the United States stood as an imperial power.

CHAPTER LOCATOR | What were the reasons behind the farmers' revolt? | What led to the "labor wars" of the 1890s?

The war began with moral outrage over the treatment of Cuban revolutionaries, who had launched a fight for independence against the Spanish colonial regime in 1895. In an attempt to isolate the guerrillas, the Spanish general Valeriano Weyler herded Cubans into concentration camps, where thousands died of hunger, disease, and exposure. Starvation soon spread to the cities. Tens of thousands of Cubans died, and countless others were left without food, clothing, or shelter. By 1898, fully a quarter of the island's population had perished in the Cuban revolution.

As the Cuban rebellion dragged on, pressure for American intervention mounted. American newspapers fueled public outrage at Spain. A fierce circulation war raged in New York City between William Randolph Hearst's *Journal* and Joseph Pulitzer's *World*. Their competition provoked what came to be called **yellow journalism**. Practitioners of yellow journalism pandered to the public's appetite for sensationalism. The Cuban war provided a wealth of dramatic copy. Hearst sent artist Frederic Remington to document the horror, and when Remington wired home, "There is no trouble here. There will be no war," Hearst shot back, "You furnish the pictures and I'll furnish the war."

American interests in Cuba were, in the words of the U.S. minister to Spain, more than "merely theoretical or sentimental." American business had more than $50 million invested in Cuban sugar, and, as a result of the rebellion, American trade with Cuba had dropped to near zero. Nevertheless, the business community balked, wary of a war with Spain. When industrialist Mark Hanna, the Republican kingmaker and senator from Ohio, urged restraint, Theodore Roosevelt exploded, "We will have this war for the freedom of Cuba, Senator Hanna, in spite of the timidity of commercial interests."

To expansionists like Roosevelt, more than Cuban independence was at stake. Appointed assistant secretary of the navy in April 1897, Roosevelt took the helm in the absence of his boss and audaciously ordered the U.S. fleet to Manila in the Philippines. In the event of conflict with Spain, Roosevelt put the navy in a position to capture the islands and gain an entry point to China.

President McKinley slowly moved toward intervention. In a show of American force, he dispatched the battleship *Maine* to Cuba. On the night of February 15, 1898, a mysterious explosion destroyed the *Maine*, killing 267 crew members. The source of the explosion remained unclear, but inflammatory stories in the press enraged Americans, who immediately blamed the Spanish government. Rallying to the cry "Remember the *Maine*," Congress declared war on Spain in April. In a surge of patriotism, more than a million men rushed to enlist. War brought with it a unity of purpose and national harmony that ended a decade of political dissent and strife. "In April, everywhere over this good fair land, flags were flying," wrote Kansas editor William Allen White. "At the stations, crowds gathered to hurrah for the soldiers, and to throw hats into the air, and to unfurl flags."

Five days after McKinley signed the war resolution, a U.S. navy squadron commanded by Admiral George Dewey destroyed the Spanish fleet in Manila Bay (**Map 20.3**, page 560). Dewey's stunning victory caught the United States by surprise. Although naval strategists including Theodore Roosevelt had been orchestrating the move for some time, few Americans had ever heard of the Philippines. Even McKinley confessed that he could not immediately locate the archipelago on the map. Nevertheless, he dispatched U.S. troops to secure the islands.

CHRONOLOGY

1898
- U.S. battleship *Maine* explodes in Havana harbor.
- Congress declares war on Spain.
- Admiral George Dewey destroys Spanish fleet in Manila Bay, the Philippines.
- U.S. troops defeat Spanish forces in Cuba.
- Treaty of Paris ends war with Spain and cedes the Philippines, Puerto Rico, and Guam to the United States.
- United States annexes Hawaii.

yellow journalism
▶ Term given to sensationalistic newspaper reporting and cartoon images rendered in yellow to promote U.S. entry into war with Spain. A fierce circulation war between two New York City papers provoked the journalistic tactics that helped fuel popular support for the war.

How were women involved in late-nineteenth-century politics?   How did economic problems shape American politics in the 1890s?   Why did the United States move away from isolationism?   Why did America go to war with Spain in 1898?   Conclusion: What was the connection between domestic tensions and U.S. foreign policy?

559

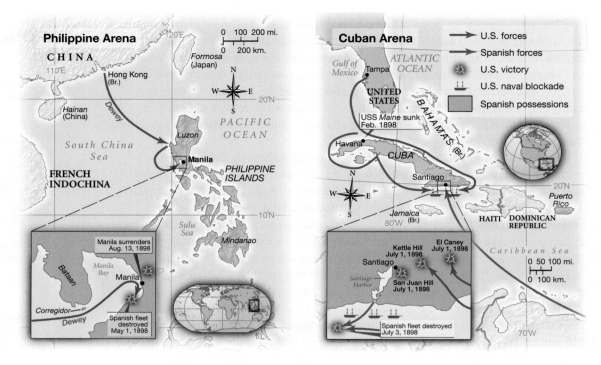

MAP 20.3 ■ The Spanish-American War, 1898

The Spanish-American War was fought in two theaters, the Philippine Islands and Cuba. Five days after President William McKinley called for a declaration of war, Admiral George Dewey captured Manila without the loss of a single American sailor. The war lasted only eight months. Troops landed in Cuba in mid-June and by mid-July had taken Santiago and Havana and had destroyed the Spanish fleet.

> ▶ FOR MORE HELP ANALYZING THIS MAP, see the map activity for this chapter in the Online Study Guide at bedfordstmartins.com/roarkunderstanding.

The war in Cuba ended almost as quickly as it began. The first U.S. troops landed on June 22, and after a handful of battles, the Spanish surrendered on July 17. The war lasted just long enough to elevate Theodore Roosevelt to the status of war hero. Roosevelt resigned his navy post and formed the Rough Riders, a regiment composed of Ivy League polo players and cowboys Roosevelt learned to respect during his stint as a cattle rancher in the Dakotas. The Rough Riders' charge up Kettle Hill and Roosevelt's role in the decisive battle of San Juan Hill made front-page news. Overnight, Roosevelt became the most famous man in America. By the time he sailed home from Cuba, a coalition of independent Republicans was already plotting his political future.

The Debate over American Imperialism

After a few brief campaigns in Cuba and Puerto Rico brought the Spanish-American War to an end, America gained possession of an empire that stretched halfway around the globe. As part of the spoils of war, the United States acquired Cuba, Puerto Rico, Guam, and the Philippines. Yielding to pressure from American sugar

CHAPTER LOCATOR | What were the reasons behind the farmers' revolt? | What led to the "labor wars" of the 1890s?

560 CHAPTER 20
A DECADE OF DISSENT, DEPRESSION, AND WAR , 1890–1900

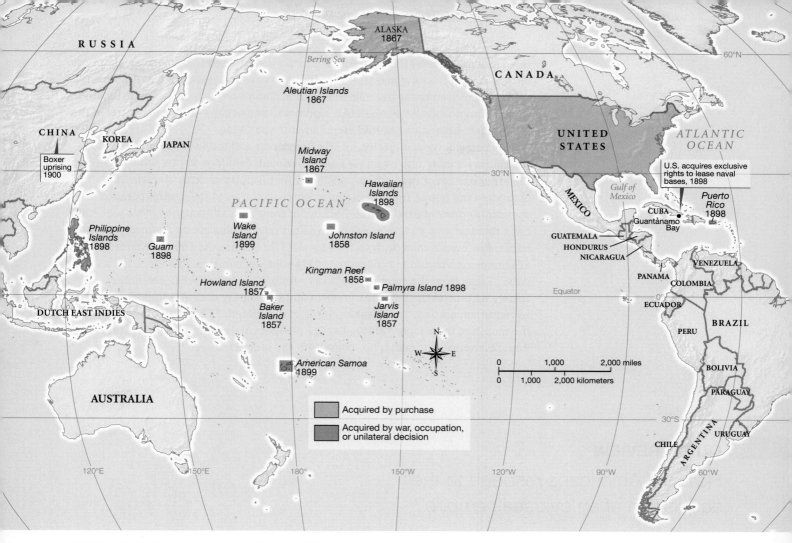

MAP 20.4 ■ **U.S. Overseas Expansion through 1900**
The United States extended its interests abroad with a series of territorial acquisitions. Although Cuba was granted independence, the Platt Amendment kept the new nation firmly under U.S. control. In the wake of the Spanish-American War, the United States woke up to find that it held an empire extending halfway around the globe.

planters, President McKinley expanded the empire further, annexing Hawaii in July 1898.

Contemptuous of the Cubans, the U.S. government dictated a Cuban constitution in 1898. It included the so-called Platt Amendment—a series of provisions that granted the United States the right to intervene to protect Cuba's "independence," as well as the power to oversee Cuban debt so that European creditors would not find an excuse for intervention. The United States also gave itself a ninety-nine-year lease on a naval base at Guantánamo. In return, McKinley promised to implement an extensive sanitation program to clean up the island, making it more attractive to American investors.

In the formal Treaty of Paris (1898), Spain ceded the Philippines to the United States along with its former colonies of Puerto Rico and Guam (**Map 20.4**). Filipino

| How were women involved in late-nineteenth-century politics? | How did economic problems shape American politics in the 1890s? | Why did the United States move away from isolationism? | Why did America go to war with Spain in 1898? | Conclusion: What was the connection between domestic tensions and U.S. foreign policy? |

revolutionaries under Emilio Aguinaldo, who had greeted U.S. troops as liberators, bitterly fought the new masters. It would take seven years and 4,000 American dead—almost ten times the number killed in Cuba—not to mention an estimated 20,000 Filipino casualties, to defeat Aguinaldo and secure American control of the Philippines, America's coveted stepping-stone to China.

At home, a vocal minority, mostly Democrats and former Populists, resisted the country's foray into overseas empire. William Jennings Bryan, who enlisted in the army but never saw action, concluded that American expansionism only distracted the nation from problems at home. Pointing to the central paradox of the war, Representative Bourke Cockran of New York admonished, "We who have been the destroyers of oppression are asked now to become its agents." The anti-imperialists were soon drowned out by cries for empire. As Senator Knute Nelson of Minnesota assured his colleagues, "We come as ministering angels, not as despots." Fresh from the conquest of Native Americans in the West, the nation largely embraced the mixture of racism and missionary zeal that fueled American adventurism abroad. The *Washington Post* trumpeted, "The taste of empire is in the mouth of the people," thrilled at the prospect of "an imperial policy, the Republic renascent, taking her place with the armed nations."

> **QUICK REVIEW**

How did Americans respond to their acquisition of an overseas empire?

Chicago History Museum.

Conclusion: What was the connection between domestic tensions and U.S. foreign policy?

A DECADE OF DOMESTIC STRIFE ended amid the blare of martial music and the waving of flags. The Spanish-American War drowned out the calls for social reform that had fueled the Populist politics of the 1890s. During that decade, angry farmers facing hard times looked to the Farmers' Alliance to fight for their vision of economic democracy, workers staged bloody strikes across the country to assert their rights, and women attacked drunkenness and the conditions that fostered it and mounted a suffrage movement to secure their basic political rights. In St. Louis in 1892, disaffected Americans formed a new People's Party to fight for change.

The bitter depression that began in 1893 led to increased labor strife. The Pullman boycott brutally dramatized the power of property and the conservatism of the laissez-faire state. But workers' willingness to confront capitalism on the streets of Chicago, Homestead, Cripple Creek, and a host of other sites across America eloquently testified to labor's growing determination, unity, and strength.

As the depression deepened, the sight of Coxey's army of unemployed men marching on Washington to demand federal intervention in the economy signaled a growing shift in the public mind against the stand-pat politics of laissez-faire. The call for the government to take action to better the lives of workers, farmers, and the dispossessed manifested itself in the fiercely fought presidential campaign of William Jennings Bryan in 1896. With the outbreak of the Spanish-American War in 1898, the decade ended on a harmonious note with patriotic Americans rallying around the flag. But even though Americans basked in patriotism and contemplated empire, old grievances had not been laid to rest. The People's Party had been beaten, but the Populists' call for greater government involvement in the economy, expanded opportunities for direct democracy, and a more equitable balance of profits and power between the people and the big corporations sounded the themes that would be taken up by a new generation of progressive reformers in the first decades of the twentieth century.

SO NOW YOU KNOW

The first march on Washington by Coxey's army in 1894 signified the frustration of America's working people with the economic collapse of the 1890s and the failure of political leaders to ameliorate the most basic hardships of American citizens.

How were women involved in late-nineteenth-century politics?

How did economic problems shape American politics in the 1890s?

Why did the United States move away from isolationism?

Why did America go to war with Spain in 1898?

Conclusion: What was the connection between domestic tensions and U.S. foreign policy?

STEP 1
GETTING STARTED

Below are basic terms from this period in American history. Can you identify each term below and explain why it matters? To do this exercise online or to download this chart, visit bedfordstmartins.com/roarkunderstanding.

TERM	WHO OR WHAT & WHEN	WHY IT MATTERS
Farmers' Alliance, p. 539		
People's Party, p. 541		
Eugene V. Debs, p. 547		
Frances Willard, p. 548		
Susan B. Anthony, p. 549		
Coxey's army, p. 551		
William Jennings Bryan, p. 552		
Open Door policy, p. 557		
Spanish-American War, p. 558		
yellow journalism, p. 559		

STEP 2
MOVING BEYOND THE BASICS

The exercise below represents a more advanced understanding of the chapter material. Begin by identifying the key issues in each of four major focal points of conflict: agriculture, labor, temperance, and women's rights. Then describe the goals and actions of activists and reformers in each area. When you are finished, look for connections among activists and reformers in all four areas. Then assess the success or failure of each movement. To do this exercise online or to download this chart, visit bedfordstmartins.com/roarkunderstanding.

Point of conflict	Key issues	Goals and actions of activists and reformers	How successful?
Agriculture			
Labor			
Temperance			
Women's rights			

STEP

3

PUTTING IT ALL TOGETHER

Now that you have reviewed key elements of the chapter, take a step back and try to explain the big picture by answering these questions. Remember to use specific examples from the chapter in your answers. To do this exercise online, visit bedfordstmartins.com/roarkunderstanding.

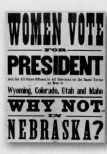

ECONOMICS

▶ What key issues fueled farm protest in the late nineteenth century? How did the Farmers' Alliance attempt to address these issues?

▶ What strategies and tactics did unions employ in the late nineteenth century? How did companies fight back?

POLITICS

▶ How did reform movements provide a vehicle for women's involvement in public political life?

▶ How did the depression of the mid-1890s shape the politics of the decade?

EMPIRE

▶ How did U.S. foreign policy reflect the tension between American tendencies toward isolationism and expansionism?

▶ How did the Spanish-American War change the place of the United States in global politics?

LOOKING BACKWARD, LOOKING AHEAD

▶ What were the United States' most important strengths and weaknesses in 1900? How had the nation's place in the world changed since 1800?

▶ Defend or refute the following statement: "With its victory in the Spanish-American War in 1898, the United States became an imperial power."

IN YOUR OWN WORDS

Imagine that you must explain chapter 20 to someone who hasn't read it. What would be the most important points to include and why?

21

PROGRESSIVISM FROM THE GRASS ROOTS UP

1890–1916

> This chapter examines the efforts of progressives to combat the ills of industrial America. It explores the grassroots initiatives of progressive activists, their core values and beliefs, and the impact of the progressive agenda on local, state, and national politics. Finally, it looks at the limits of progressive reform.

> How did grassroots progressives attack the problems of industrial America?

> What were the key tenets of progressive theory?

> How did Theodore Roosevelt advance the progressive agenda?

> How did progressivism fare during the Taft administration?

> What was Woodrow Wilson's progressive agenda and how did it change during his administration?

> What were the limits of progressive reform?

> Conclusion: How did the liberal state transform during the Progressive Era?

DID YOU KNOW?

The NAACP, an integrated organization, was founded more than 100 years ago.

Progressive social work. An Infant Welfare Society nurse instructs an immigrant mother on clean home care in 1910.

How did grassroots progressives attack the problems of industrial America?

Jane Addams Jane Addams's desire to live among the poor and her insistence that settlement house work benefited educated women such as herself as well as her immigrant neighbors separated her from the charity workers who had come before her and marked the distance from philanthropy to progressive reform. Her autobiographical *Twenty Years at Hull-House*, published in 1910, is shown in the inset. Photo: Jane Addams Memorial Collection (JAMC neg. 14) Special Collections, University of Illinois at Chicago, photographer: Max Platz; book: Newberry Library.

MUCH OF PROGRESSIVE REFORM began at the grassroots level and percolated upward into local, state, and eventually national politics as reformers attacked the social problems fostered by urban industrialism. Although reform flourished in many different settings across the country, urban problems inspired the progressives' greatest efforts. In their zeal to "civilize the city," reformers founded settlement houses, professed a new Christian social gospel, and campaigned against vice and crime in the name of "social purity."

Civilizing the City

Progressives attacked the problems of the city on many fronts. The **settlement house** movement attempted to bridge the distance between the classes. The movement began in England and came to the United States in 1886 with the opening of the University Settlement House in New York City. The needs of poor urban neighborhoods provided the impetus for these social settlements. In 1889, Jane Addams leased a house in an immigrant neighborhood in Chicago. Throwing open

settlement houses
▶ Settlements established in poor neighborhoods beginning in the 1880s by reformers attempting to bridge the distance between the classes. Reformers like Jane Addams and Lillian Wald believed that only by living among the poor could they help bridge the growing class divide. College-educated women formed the backbone of the settlement house movement.

CHAPTER LOCATOR | How did grassroots progressives attack the problems of industrial America? | What were the key tenets of progressive theory?

the doors of Hull House, she invited her neighbors to share their interests and problems. And she invited young college graduates like herself to come and offer their expertise. Within a decade, Hull House had expanded from one rented floor to some thirteen buildings housing a remarkable variety of activities, including public baths, a nursery and kindergarten, a labor museum, manual training workshops, and the first public playground in Chicago.

The Progressives and Urban Reform

Settlement house movement	Effort by reformers to bridge the social divide by living and working among the poor
Social gospel	Call for churches and their members to play an active role in social reformation
Social purity movement	Campaign to clean up vice, particularly prostitution

Women, particularly college-educated women, formed the backbone of the settlement house movement and stood in the vanguard of the progressive movement. Settlement houses gave college-educated women eager to use their knowledge a place to put their talents to work in the service of society and to champion progressive reform. Largely due to women's efforts, settlements like Jane Addams's Hull House in Chicago and Lillian Wald's Henry Street in New York City grew in number from six in 1891 to more than four hundred in 1911. In the process, settlement house women created a new profession—social work—and stimulated a new reform movement—progressivism.

For their part, churches confronted urban social problems by enunciating a new **social gospel**, one that saw its mission not simply to reform individuals but to reform society. The social gospel offered a powerful corrective to social Darwinism and the gospel of wealth, which fostered the belief that riches signaled divine favor. In place of the gospel of wealth, progressive clergy exhorted their congregations to put Christ's teachings to work in their daily lives. Charles M. Sheldon's popular book *In His Steps* (1898) called on men and women to Christianize capitalism by asking the question "What would Jesus do?"

Ministers also played an active role in the social purity movement, the campaign to attack vice. To end the "social evil," as reformers euphemistically called prostitution, the social purity movement brought together clergymen who wished to stamp out sin, doctors concerned about the spread of venereal disease, and women reformers determined to fight the double standard that tolerated male promiscuity but demanded chastity of women. Advanced progressive reformers linked prostitution to poverty and championed higher wages for women. "Is it any wonder," asked the Chicago vice commission, "that a tempted girl who receives only six dollars per week working with her hands sells her body for twenty-five dollars per week when she learns there is a demand for it and men are willing to pay the price?"

Attacks on alcohol went hand in hand with the push for social purity. Reformers pointed to links between drinking, prostitution, wife and child abuse, unemployment, and industrial accidents. The powerful liquor lobby fought back, spending liberally in election campaigns, fueling the charge that liquor corrupted the political process.

CHRONOLOGY

1889
– Jane Addams opens Hull House settlement in Chicago.

1903
– Women's Trade Union League, an alliance of women workers and middle-class "allies," is founded.

1908
– In *Muller v. Oregon*, U.S. Supreme Court upholds an Oregon law limiting the number of hours women can work.

1909
– Some 20,000 garment workers, most of them women, strike in New York City for better working conditions.

1911
– Triangle fire in New York City kills 146 workers.

social gospel

▶ A vision of Christianity that saw its mission not simply to reform individuals but to reform society. The social gospel offered a powerful corrective to social Darwinism and the gospel of wealth. In place of the gospel of wealth, progressive clergy exhorted their congregations to put Christ's teachings to work in their daily lives.

How did Theodore Roosevelt advance the progressive agenda?	How did progressivism fare during the Taft administration?	What was Woodrow Wilson's progressive agenda and how did it change during his administration?	What were the limits of progressive reform?	Conclusion: How did the liberal state transform during the Progressive Era?

An element of nativism (dislike of foreigners) ran through the movement for prohibition, as it did in a number of progressive reforms. The Irish, the Italians, and the Germans were among the groups stigmatized by temperance reformers for their drinking. To deny the working class access to alcohol, these progressives pushed for state legislation to outlaw the sale of liquor. By 1912, seven states were "dry."

Core Progressive Attitudes

A willingness to take action

The belief that environment, not heredity alone, determined human behavior

Optimism that reform could be achieved through government action without radically altering America's economy or institutions

Progressives and the Working Class

Day-to-day contact with their neighbors made settlement house workers particularly sympathetic to labor unions. When Mary Kenney O'Sullivan complained that her bookbinders' union met in a dirty, noisy saloon, Jane Addams invited the union to meet at Hull House. And during the Pullman strike in 1894, Hull House residents organized strike relief. "Hull-House has been so unionized," grumbled one Chicago businessman, "that it has lost its usefulness and become a detriment and harm to the community." But to the working class, the support of middle-class reformers marked a significant gain.

Attempts to forge a cross-class alliance became institutionalized in 1903 with the creation of the **Women's Trade Union League (WTUL)**. The WTUL brought together women workers and middle-class "allies." Its goal was to organize workingwomen into unions under the auspices of the American Federation of Labor (AFL).

Although the alliance between workingwomen, primarily immigrants and daughters of immigrants, and their middle-class allies was not without tension, the WTUL helped workingwomen achieve significant gains. Its most notable success came in 1909 in the "uprising of the twenty thousand," when women employees of the Triangle Shirtwaist Company in New York City went on strike to protest low wages, dangerous working conditions, and management's refusal to recognize their union, the International Ladies' Garment Workers Union (ILGWU). By the time the strike ended in February 1910, the workers had won important demands in many shops. The solidarity shown by the women workers proved to be the strike's greatest achievement. As Clara Lemlich, one of the strike's leaders, exclaimed, "They used to say that you couldn't even organize women. They wouldn't come to union meetings. They were 'temporary' workers. Well we showed them!"

The WTUL made enormous contributions to the strike. It provided volunteers for the picket lines, posted more than $29,000 in bail, protested police brutality, organized a parade of ten thousand strikers, took part in the arbitration conference, appealed for funds, and generated publicity for the strike. Under the leadership of the WTUL, women from every class of society, from J. P. Morgan's

Women's Trade Union League (WTUL)

▶ A cross-class alliance created in 1903 that brought together women workers and middle-class "allies." Its goal was to organize workingwomen into unions. The WTUL helped workingwomen achieve significant gains. Its most notable success came in 1909 in the "uprising of the twenty thousand," in New York City.

CHAPTER LOCATOR | How did grassroots progressives attack the problems of industrial America? | What were the key tenets of progressive theory?

CHAPTER 21

570 PROGRESSIVISM FROM THE GRASS ROOTS UP, 1890–1916

14. Viewing the unfortunates at the Morgue

Triangle Fire Morgue

After the Triangle fire on March 26, 1911, New York City set up a makeshift morgue where the remains of more than a hundred young women and two dozen young men were laid out in coffins for their friends and relatives to identify. Artist John Sloan created this striking illustration to commemorate those who died in the fire—a businessman weeps over his lost profits while a young woman worker lies burning on the pavement and a leering skeleton poses on the left. Photo: United Archives, Kheel Center, Cornell University, Ithaca, N.Y.; Illustration: Granger Collection.

▶ FOR MORE HELP ANALYZING THIS IMAGE, see the visual activity for this chapter in the Online Study Guide at bedfordstmartins.com/roarkunderstanding.

daughter Anne to socialists on New York's Lower East Side, joined the strikers in a dramatic display of cross-class alliance.

But for all its success, the uprising of the twenty thousand failed fundamentally to change conditions for women workers, as a tragic fire at the Triangle factory dramatized in 1911. A WTUL member described the scene on the street as the factory burned: "Two young girls whom I knew to be working in the vicinity came rushing toward me, tears were running from their eyes and they were white and shaking as they caught me by the arm. 'Oh,' shrieked one of them, 'they are jumping. Jumping from ten stories up! They are going through the air like bundles of clothes.'"

The terrified Triangle workers had little choice but to jump. Flames blocked one exit, and the other door had been locked to prevent workers from pilfering. The flimsy, rusted fire escape collapsed under the weight of fleeing workers, killing dozens. Trapped, 54 workers jumped to their deaths from the ninth-floor window. Of 500 workers, 146 died and scores of others were injured. The owners of the Triangle firm went to trial for negligence, but they avoided conviction when authorities determined that the fire had been started by a careless smoker. The Triangle Shirtwaist Company reopened in another firetrap within a matter of weeks.

| How did Theodore Roosevelt advance the progressive agenda? | How did progressivism fare during the Taft administration? | What was Woodrow Wilson's progressive agenda and how did it change during his administration? | What were the limits of progressive reform? | Conclusion: How did the liberal state transform during the Progressive Era? |

Outrage and frustration overwhelmed Rose Schneiderman, a leading WTUL organizer, who spoke at the memorial service for the dead Triangle workers. "I would be a traitor to those poor burned bodies if I came here to talk good fellowship," she told her audience. "We have tried you good people of the public and we have found you wanting. . . . I know from my experience it is up to the working people to save themselves . . . by a strong working class movement." The Triangle fire severely tested the bonds of the cross-class alliance. Along with Rose Schneiderman, WTUL leaders experienced a growing sense of futility. It seemed not enough to organize and to strike. Increasingly, the WTUL turned its efforts to lobbying for protective legislation—laws that would limit hours and regulate working conditions for women workers.

Advocates of protective legislation won a major victory in 1908 when the U.S. Supreme Court, in *Muller v. Oregon*, reversed its previous rulings and upheld an Oregon law that limited to ten the number of hours women could work in a day. A mass of sociological evidence put together by Florence Kelley of the National Consumers' League and Josephine Goldmark of the WTUL convinced the Court that long hours endangered women and therefore the entire human race. The Court's ruling set a precedent, but one that separated the well-being of women workers from that of men by arguing that women's reproductive role justified special treatment. Later generations of women fighting for equality would question the effectiveness of this strategy and argue that it ultimately closed good jobs to women.

The National Consumers' League, like the WTUL, fostered cross-class alliance. And, like the WTUL, the National Consumers' League increasingly promoted protective legislation to improve working conditions for working women. Frustrated by the reluctance of the private sector to respond to the need for reform, progressives turned to government at all levels.

Reform also fueled the fight for woman suffrage. For women like Jane Addams and Florence Kelley, involvement in social reform led inevitably to support for woman suffrage. Emphasizing the reforms that could be accomplished if women had the vote, these new suffragists argued that in an urban, industrial society, a good housekeeper could not protect her family unless she became involved in politics and wielded the ballot—and not just the broom—in the service of "municipal housekeeping."

> **QUICK REVIEW**

How did progressives work to "civilize" the city?

CHAPTER LOCATOR | How did grassroots progressives attack the problems of industrial America? | What were the key tenets of progressive theory?

What were the key tenets of progressive theory?

Tom Johnson

The reform mayor of Cleveland from 1901 to 1909, Tom Johnson is shown here campaigning in Cleveland's Wade Park in 1908. To get a three-cent streetcar fare and win the support of the working classes, Johnson instituted municipal ownership of the transit system. The Western Reserve Historical Society, Cleveland, Ohio.

THE PROGRESSIVES EMPHASIZED action and experimentation. Dismissing the view that humans should leave progress to the dictates of natural selection, progressive reform Darwinists argued that human intelligence could shape change and improve society. Progressive theory found practical application in state and local politics, where reformers challenged traditional laissez-faire government.

Reform Darwinism and Social Engineering

Without abandoning the evolutionary framework of Darwinism, a new group of sociologists argued that evolution could be advanced more rapidly if men and women used their intellects to alter the environment. Sociologist Lester Frank Ward put it clearly in his book *Dynamic Sociology* (1883). "I insist that the time must soon come," he wrote, "when control of blind natural forces in society must give way to human foresight." Dubbed **reform Darwinism**, the new sociological theory condemned the laissez-faire approach, insisting that the liberal state should play a more active role in solving social problems.

Efficiency and *expertise* became watchwords in the progressive vocabulary. In *Drift and Mastery* (1914), journalist and critic Walter Lippmann called for "technocrats" to use scientific techniques to control and direct social change. At its extreme, the application of expertise and social engineering took the form of scientific management. Frederick Winslow Taylor pioneered "systematized shop management." Obsessed with making humans and machines produce more and faster, Taylor carefully timed workers and attempted to break down their work into its simplest components. An advocate of piecework, quotas, and pay incentives for productivity, he insisted that unions were unnecessary. Taylor won many converts among corporate managers, but workers hated the monotony of

reform Darwinism

▶ Sociological theory developed in the 1880s that condemned the laissez-faire approach to government, insisting that the liberal state should play a more active role in solving social problems. Reform Darwinists believed that the human intellect could shape and speed up the process of human evolution. This belief was reflected in a variety of progressive initiatives.

How did Theodore Roosevelt advance the progressive agenda?	How did progressivism fare during the Taft administration?	What was Woodrow Wilson's progressive agenda and how did it change during his administration?	What were the limits of progressive reform?	Conclusion: How did the liberal state transform during the Progressive Era?

1901
- William McKinley is assassinated; Theodore Roosevelt becomes president.

1902
- Federal government files antitrust lawsuit against Northern Securities Company.
- Roosevelt mediates anthracite coal strike.

1903
- United States begins construction of Panama Canal.

1904
- Roosevelt Corollary to Monroe Doctrine.

1906
- Pure Food and Drug Act and Meat Inspection Act.

1907
- Panic on Wall Street.
- Roosevelt signs "Gentlemen's Agreement" with Japan, restricting immigration.

control the trusts." The Sherman Antitrust Act of 1890 had been badly weakened by a conservative Supreme Court and by attorneys general more willing to use it against labor unions than against monopolies. In one of his first acts as president, Roosevelt ordered his attorney general to begin a secret antitrust investigation of the Northern Securities Company that led to an antitrust suit filed by the government in February 1902. Northern Securities was a giant company that linked three competing railroads under one management and monopolized railroad traffic in the Northwest.

The news of the antitrust suit against Northern Securities rocked Wall Street. As one newspaper editor sarcastically observed, "Wall Street is paralyzed at the thought that a President of the United States would sink so low as to try to enforce the law." Roosevelt's thunderbolt put Wall Street on notice that the new president expected to be treated as an equal and was willing to use government as a weapon to curb business excesses. The Supreme Court, in a significant turnaround, upheld the Sherman Act and called for the dissolution of Northern Securities in 1904.

"Hurrah for Teddy the Trustbuster," cheered the papers. Roosevelt went on to use the Sherman Act against forty-three trusts, including such giants as American Tobacco, Du Pont, and Standard Oil. While willing to use the Sherman Act, he preferred regulation to antitrust suits. In 1903, he pressured Congress to pass the Elkins Act, outlawing railroad rebates. And he created the new cabinet-level Department of Commerce and Labor, with the subsidiary Bureau of Corporations to act as a corporate watchdog.

In his handling of the anthracite coal strike in 1902, Roosevelt again demonstrated his willingness to assert the authority of the presidency, this time to mediate between labor and management. In May, 147,000 coal miners in Pennsylvania went on strike. The United Mine Workers (UMW) demanded a reduction in the workday from twelve to ten hours, an equitable system of weighing each miner's output, and a 10 percent wage increase, along with recognition of the union.

The strike dragged on through the summer and into the fall. Hoarding and profiteering drove the price of coal from $2.50 to $6.00 a ton. As winter approached, coal shortages touched off near riots in the nation's big cities. At this juncture, Roosevelt stepped in to mediate, inviting representatives from both sides to meet in Washington in October. His unprecedented intervention served notice that government counted itself an independent force in business and labor disputes. At the same time, it gave unionism a boost by granting the UMW a place at the table.

At the meeting, the mine owners refused to talk with the union representative—a move that angered the attorney general and insulted the president. The meeting ended in an impasse. Beside himself with anger over the "wooden-headed obstinacy and stupidity" of management, Roosevelt threatened to seize the mines and run them with federal troops. It was a powerful bluff, one that called into question not only the supremacy of private property but also the rule of law. But it brought management around. In the end, the miners won a reduction in hours and a wage increase, but the owners succeeded in preventing formal recognition of the UMW.

Taken together, Roosevelt's actions in the Northern Securities case and the anthracite coal strike marked a dramatic departure from the passivity of Gilded

CHAPTER LOCATOR | How did grassroots progressives attack the problems of industrial America? | What were the key tenets of progressive theory?

576 CHAPTER 21 PROGRESSIVISM FROM THE GRASS ROOTS UP, 1890–1916

Age presidents. Roosevelt's actions demonstrated conclusively that government intended to act as a countervailing force to the power of the big corporations. Pleased with his role in the anthracite strike, he announced that all he had tried to do was give labor and capital a "square deal."

The phrase "Square Deal" became Roosevelt's campaign slogan in the 1904 election. Roosevelt easily defeated the Democrats, who abandoned their candidate, William Jennings Bryan, to support Judge Alton B. Parker, a "safe" candidate they hoped would lure business votes away from Roosevelt. In the months before the election, the president prudently toned down his criticism of big business. Roosevelt swept into office with the largest popular majority—57.9 percent—any candidate had polled up to that time.

Breaker Boys

Child labor in America's mines and mills was common at the turn of the twentieth century, despite state laws that tried to restrict it. Here, "breaker boys," some as young as seven years old, pick over coal in a Pennsylvania mine. Brown Brothers.

Roosevelt the Reformer

"Tomorrow I shall come into my office in my own right," Roosevelt is said to have remarked on the eve of his election. "Then watch out for me!" Roosevelt's stunning victory gave him a mandate for reform. The Senate, however, remained controlled by a conservative Republican "old guard," with many senators on the payrolls of the corporations Roosevelt sought to curb. Roosevelt's pet project remained railroad regulation. The Elkins Act prohibiting rebates had not worked. No one could stop big shippers like Standard Oil from wringing concessions from the railroads. Roosevelt determined that the only solution lay in giving the Interstate Commerce Commission (ICC) real power to set rates and prevent discriminatory practices.

The result of Roosevelt's efforts was the Hepburn Act, passed in May 1906, which gave the ICC the power to set rates subject to court review. The law left the courts too much power and failed to provide adequate means for the ICC to determine rates, but its passage proved a landmark in federal control of private industry. For the first time, a government commission had the power to investigate private business records and to set rates.

Passage of the Hepburn Act marked the high point of Roosevelt's presidency. In a serious political blunder, Roosevelt had announced on the eve of his election in 1904 that he would not run again. By 1906, he had become a "lame duck" at the very moment he enjoyed his greatest public popularity.

Always an apt reader of the public temper, Roosevelt witnessed a growing appetite for reform fed by newspaper and magazine revelations of corporate and political wrongdoing and social injustice. Roosevelt counted many of the new investigative journalists among his friends. But he warned them against going too far, citing the allegorical character in *Pilgrim's Progress* who was so busy raking muck that he took no notice of higher things. Roosevelt's criticism gave the American vocabulary a new word, *muckraker*, which journalists soon appropriated as a title of honor.

| How did Theodore Roosevelt advance the progressive agenda? | How did progressivism fare during the Taft administration? | What was Woodrow Wilson's progressive agenda and how did it change during his administration? | What were the limits of progressive reform? | Conclusion: How did the liberal state transform during the Progressive Era? |

The Jungle

Novelist Upton Sinclair, a lifelong socialist, wrote *The Jungle* to expose the evils of capitalism. But readers were more horrified by his descriptions of the unsanitary conditions in the meatpacking industry, where the novel's hapless hero sees rats, filth, and diseased animals processed into meat products. The public outcry surrounding *The Jungle* contributed to the enactment of pure food and drug legislation and a federal meat inspection law.

Picture Research Consultants, Inc.

Muckraking, as Roosevelt well knew, provided enormous help in securing progressive legislation. In the spring of 1906, publicity generated by the muckrakers about poisons in patent medicines goaded the Senate, with Roosevelt's backing, into passing a pure food and drug bill. Opponents in the House of Representatives hoped to keep the legislation locked up in committee. There it would have died, were it not for the publication of Upton Sinclair's novel *The Jungle* (1906), with its sensational account of filthy conditions in meatpacking plants. A massive public outcry led to the passage of the Pure Food and Drug Act and the Meat Inspection Act in 1906.

In the waning years of his administration, Roosevelt allied with the more progressive elements of the Republican Party. Styling himself a "radical," he claimed credit for leading the "ultra conservative" party of McKinley to a position of "progressive conservatism and conservative radicalism."

When an economic panic developed in the fall of 1907, business interests quickly blamed the president. Once again, J. P. Morgan stepped in to avert disaster, this time switching funds from one bank to another to prop up weak institutions. For his services, he claimed the Tennessee Coal and Iron Company, an independent steel business that had long been coveted by the U.S. Steel Corporation. Persuaded that the sale of the company would aid the economy "but little benefit" U.S. Steel, Roosevelt tacitly agreed not to institute antitrust proceedings against U.S. Steel over the acquisition. In fact, U.S. Steel acquired Tennessee Coal and Iron for a price well below market value, doing away with a competitor and undercutting the economy of the Southeast. Roosevelt's promise not to institute antitrust proceedings against U.S. Steel would give rise to the charge that he acted as a tool of the Morgan interests.

The charge of collusion between business and government underscored the extent to which corporate leaders like Morgan found federal regulation preferable to unbridled competition or harsher state measures. During the Progressive Era, enlightened business leaders cooperated with government in the hope of avoiding antitrust prosecution. Convinced that regulation and not trust-busting offered the best way to deal with big business, Roosevelt never acknowledged that his regulatory policies fostered an alliance between business and government that today is called corporate liberalism.

Roosevelt and Conservation

In the area of conservation, Roosevelt proved indisputably ahead of his time. When he took office, some 45 million acres of land remained as government reserves. By the time he left office, he had saved more than 230 million acres of wild America for posterity.

As the first president to have lived and worked in the West, Roosevelt came to the White House convinced of the need for better management of the nation's rivers and forests. During his presidency, he placed the nation's conservation

CHAPTER LOCATOR | How did grassroots progressives attack the problems of industrial America? | What were the key tenets of progressive theory?

policy in the hands of experts like his chief forester, Gifford Pinchot. Pinchot preached conservation—the efficient use of natural resources. Willing to permit grazing, lumbering, and the development of hydroelectric power, conservationists fought private interests only when they felt business acted irresponsibly or threatened to monopolize water and electric power. Preservationists like John Muir, founder of the Sierra Club, believed the wilderness needed to be protected. Roosevelt, ever the pragmatist, believed in both conservation and preservation and worked for both throughout his lifetime.

In 1907, Congress put the brakes on Roosevelt's conservation program by passing a law limiting his power to create forest reserves in six western states. In the days leading up to the law's enactment, Roosevelt created twenty-one new reserves and enlarged eleven more, saving sixteen million acres. "Opponents of the forest service turned handsprings in their wrath," he wrote, "but the threats . . . were really only a tribute to the efficiency of our action." Today, the six national parks, sixteen national monuments, and fifty-one wildlife refuges that he created bear witness to his substantial accomplishments as a conservationist (**Map 21.1**).

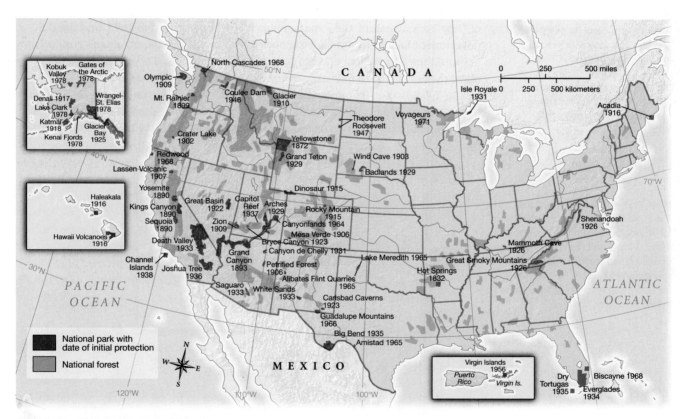

MAP 21.1 ■ **National Parks and Forests**

The national park system in the West began with Yellowstone in 1872. Grand Canyon, Yosemite, Kings Canyon, and Sequoia followed in the 1890s. During his presidency, Theodore Roosevelt added six parks—Crater Lake, Wind Cave, Petrified Forest, Lassen Volcanic, Mesa Verde, and Zion.

▶ FOR MORE HELP ANALYZING THIS MAP, see the map activity for this chapter in the Online Study Guide at bedfordstmartins.com/roarkunderstanding.

How did Theodore Roosevelt advance the progressive agenda?	How did progressivism fare during the Taft administration?	What was Woodrow Wilson's progressive agenda and how did it change during his administration?	What were the limits of progressive reform?	Conclusion: How did the liberal state transform during the Progressive Era?

The Big Stick

Roosevelt's activism extended to his foreign policy. A fierce proponent of America's interests abroad, he relied on executive power to pursue a vigorous foreign policy, sometimes stretching the powers of the presidency beyond legal limits. In his relations with the European powers, he relied on military strength and diplomacy, a combination he aptly described with the aphorism "Speak softly but carry a big stick."

A strong supporter of the Monroe Doctrine, Roosevelt's proprietary attitude toward the Western Hemisphere became evident in the case of the Panama Canal. Roosevelt had long advocated a canal linking the Caribbean and the Pacific. By enabling ships to move quickly from the Atlantic to the Pacific, a canal could effectively double the U.S. Navy's power. Having decided on a route across the Panamanian isthmus (a narrow strip of land connecting North and South America), then part of Colombia, Roosevelt in 1902 offered the Colombian government a one-time sum of $10 million and an annual rent of $250,000. When Colombia turned down the deal, Roosevelt became incensed at what he called the "homicidal corruptionists" in Colombia for trying to "blackmail" the United States. At the prompting of a group of New York investors, the Panamanians staged an uprising in 1903, and the U.S. government hastily recognized the new government. The Panamanians promptly accepted the $10 million, and the building got under way. The canal would take eleven years and $375 million to complete; it opened in 1914 (**Map 21.2**).

In 1904, Roosevelt announced what became known as the **Roosevelt Corollary** to the Monroe Doctrine. The corollary declared that the United States would not intervene in Latin America as long as nations there conducted their affairs with

Roosevelt Corollary

▶ Declaration that the United States would intervene in Latin America to protect its financial and strategic interests. Issued in 1904, the Roosevelt Corollary in effect made the United States the policeman of the Western Hemisphere and served notice to the European powers to keep out.

MAP 21.2 ■ The Panama Canal, 1914
The Panama Canal, completed in 1914, bisects the isthmus in a series of massive locks and dams. As Theodore Roosevelt had planned, the canal greatly strengthened the U.S. Navy by allowing ships to move from the Atlantic to the Pacific in a matter of days.

CHAPTER LOCATOR | How did grassroots progressives attack the problems of industrial America? | What were the key tenets of progressive theory?

580 CHAPTER 21
PROGRESSIVISM FROM THE GRASS ROOTS UP, 1890–1916

"decency." But the United States would step in if any Latin American nation proved guilty of "brutal wrongdoing." The Roosevelt Corollary in effect made the United States the policeman of the Western Hemisphere and served notice to the European powers to keep out.

In Asia, Roosevelt inherited the Open Door policy initiated by Secretary of State John Hay in 1899, designed to ensure U.S. commercial entry into China. As Britain, France, Russia, Japan, and Germany raced to secure Chinese trade and territory, Roosevelt was tempted to use force to enter the fray and gain economic or possibly territorial concessions. Realizing that Americans would not support an aggressive Asian policy, Roosevelt sensibly held back.

In his relations with Europe, Roosevelt sought to establish the United States as a rising force in world affairs. When tensions flared between France and Germany in Morocco in 1905, Roosevelt mediated at a conference in Algeciras, Spain, where he worked to maintain a balance of power that helped neutralize German ambitions. His skillful mediation gained him a reputation as an astute player on the world stage and demonstrated the nation's new presence in world affairs.

Roosevelt earned the Nobel Peace Prize in 1906 for his role in negotiating an end to the Russo-Japanese War, which had broken out when the Japanese invaded Chinese Manchuria, threatening Russia's sphere of influence. Once again, Roosevelt sought to maintain a balance of power, in this case working to curb Japanese expansionism. Roosevelt admired the Japanese, judging them "the most dashing fighters in the world," but he did not want Japan to become too strong in Asia.

When good relations with Japan were jeopardized by discriminatory legislation in California calling for segregated public schools for "Orientals," Roosevelt smoothed over the incident and negotiated the "Gentlemen's Agreement" in 1907, which allowed the Japanese to save face by voluntarily restricting immigration to the United States. To demonstrate America's naval power and counter Japan's growing bellicosity, Roosevelt dispatched the Great White Fleet, sixteen of the navy's most up-to-date battleships, on a "goodwill mission" around the world. U.S. relations with Japan improved, and in the 1908 Root-Takahira agreement, the two nations pledged to maintain the Open Door and support the status quo in the Pacific.

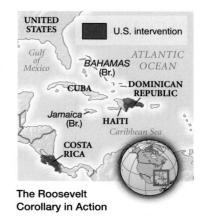

The Roosevelt Corollary in Action

QUICK REVIEW

How did Roosevelt change the relationship between big business and the federal government?

| How did Theodore Roosevelt advance the progressive agenda? | How did progressivism fare during the Taft administration? | What was Woodrow Wilson's progressive agenda and how did it change during his administration? | What were the limits of progressive reform? | Conclusion: How did the liberal state transform during the Progressive Era? |

How did progressivism fare during the Taft administration?

William Howard Taft

When President Theodore Roosevelt tapped William Howard Taft as his successor in 1908, Taft had never held an elected office. Taft had little aptitude for politics, and his actions angered progressives, leading Roosevelt to challenge him for the presidency in 1912. Library of Congress.

IN THE PRESIDENTIAL ELECTION OF 1908, Roosevelt's handpicked successor, William Howard Taft, a lawyer who had served as governor-general of the Philippines, soundly defeated the Democratic candidate, William Jennings Bryan. Any man would have found it difficult to follow in Roosevelt's footsteps, but Taft proved hopelessly ill suited to the task. A genial man with a talent for law, Taft had no experience in elective office, no feel for politics, and no nerve for controversy.

The Troubled Presidency of William Howard Taft

Once in office, Taft proved a perfect tool in the hands of Republicans who yearned for a return to the days of a less active executive. A lawyer by training and instinct, Taft believed that it was up to the courts, not the president, to arbitrate social issues. Wary of the progressive insurgents in Congress, Taft relied increasingly on conservatives in the Republican Party. As a progressive senator lamented, "Taft is a ponderous and amiable man completely surrounded by men who know exactly what they want."

Taft's troubles began on the eve of his inaugural, when he called a special session of Congress to deal with the tariff, which had grown inordinately high under Republican rule. Roosevelt had been too politically astute to tackle the troublesome tariff issue, even though he knew that rates needed to be lowered. Taft blundered into the fray. Shaped by the conservative Senate, the Payne-Aldrich bill that emerged from Congress actually raised the tariff, benefiting big business and

CHAPTER LOCATOR | How did grassroots progressives attack the problems of industrial America? | What were the key tenets of progressive theory?

the trusts at the expense of consumers. As if paralyzed, Taft neither fought for changes nor vetoed the measure. On a tour of the Midwest in 1909, he was greeted with jeers when he claimed, "I think the Payne bill is the best bill that the Republican Party ever passed." In the eyes of a growing number of Americans, Taft's praise of the tariff made him either a fool or a liar.

Taft's legalism soon got him into hot water in the area of conservation. He undid Roosevelt's work to preserve hydroelectric power sites when he learned that they had been improperly designated as ranger stations. And when Gifford Pinchot publicly denounced Taft's secretary of the interior as a tool of western land-grabbers, Taft fired Pinchot, touching off a storm of controversy that damaged Taft and alienated Roosevelt.

When Roosevelt returned to the United States from a safari in Africa in June 1910, he received a hero's welcome. Hurt, Taft kept his distance. By late summer, Roosevelt had taken sides with the progressive insurgents in his party. "Taft is utterly hopeless as a leader," Roosevelt confided to his son. Reading the mood of the country, Roosevelt began to sound more and more like a candidate.

With the Republican Party divided, the Democrats swept the congressional elections of 1910. Branding the Payne-Aldrich tariff "the mother of trusts," they captured a majority in the House of Representatives and won several key governorships. The revitalized Democratic Party could look to new leaders, among them the progressive governor of New Jersey, Woodrow Wilson.

The new Democratic majority in the House, working with progressive Republicans in the Senate, achieved a number of key reforms. Two significant constitutional amendments—the Sixteenth Amendment, which provided for a modest graduated income tax, and the Seventeenth Amendment, which called for the direct election of senators (formerly chosen by state legislatures)—went to the states, where they would win ratification in 1913. While Congress rode the high tide of progressive reform, Taft sat on the sidelines.

Achievements of the New Democratic Majority

Regulation of mine and railroad safety
Sixteenth and Seventeenth Amendments
The creation of the Children's Bureau in the Department of Labor
The establishment of an eight-hour day for federal workers

In foreign policy, Taft continued Roosevelt's policy of extending U.S. influence abroad, but here, too, Taft had a difficult time following in Roosevelt's footsteps. His policy of dollar diplomacy championed commercial goals rather than the strategic aims Roosevelt had pursued. Taft naively assumed he could substitute "dollars for bullets." In the Caribbean, he provoked anti-American feeling by attempting to force commercial treaties on Nicaragua and Honduras and by dispatching U.S. Marines to Nicaragua and the Dominican Republic in 1912. In Asia, he openly avowed his intent to promote in China "active intervention to secure for . . . our capitalists opportunity for profitable investment." Taft never recognized that an aggressive commercial policy could not exist without the willingness to use military might to back it up.

CHRONOLOGY

1908
- Republican William Howard Taft is elected president.

1909
- Payne-Aldrich tariff.

1910
- Democrats gain majority in the House of Representatives in midterm elections.
- Congress sends Sixteenth and Seventeenth Amendments to the states for ratification.

1911
- Taft launches antitrust suit against U.S. Steel.

1912
- Taft sends U.S. Marines to Nicaragua and the Dominican Republic.
- Roosevelt runs for president on Progressive Party ticket.

How did Theodore Roosevelt advance the progressive agenda?	How did progressivism fare during the Taft administration?	What was Woodrow Wilson's progressive agenda and how did it change during his administration?	What were the limits of progressive reform?	Conclusion: How did the liberal state transform during the Progressive Era?

Taft faced the limits of dollar diplomacy when revolution broke out in Mexico in 1911. Under pressure to protect American investments, he mobilized troops along the border. In the end, however, with no popular support for a war with Mexico, he had to fall back on diplomatic pressure to salvage American interests.

Taft hoped to encourage world peace through the use of a world court and arbitration. He unsuccessfully sponsored a series of arbitration treaties that Roosevelt vehemently opposed as weak and cowardly. By 1910, Roosevelt had become a vocal critic of Taft's foreign policy, which he dismissed as "maudlin folly."

Taft's "Dollar Diplomacy"

The final breach between Taft and Roosevelt came in 1911, when Taft's attorney general filed an antitrust suit against U.S. Steel. In its brief against the corporation, the government cited Roosevelt's agreement with the Morgan interests in the 1907 acquisition of Tennessee Coal and Iron. Thoroughly enraged, Roosevelt lambasted Taft's "archaic" antitrust policy and hinted that he might be persuaded to run for president again.

Progressive Insurgency and the Election of 1912

In February 1912, Roosevelt challenged Taft for the Republican nomination, announcing, "My hat is in the ring." Roosevelt took advantage of newly passed primary election laws and ran in thirteen states, winning 278 delegates to Taft's 48. But at the Chicago convention, Taft's party bosses refused to seat the Roosevelt delegates. Fistfights broke out on the convention floor as Taft won the nomination on the first ballot. Crying robbery, Roosevelt's supporters bolted the party.

Progressive Party Platform

Woman suffrage
Presidential primaries
Conservation of natural resources
An end to child labor
Workers' compensation
A minimum wage that would include women workers
Social security
A federal income tax

CHAPTER LOCATOR | How did grassroots progressives attack the problems of industrial America? | What were the key tenets of progressive theory?

Seven weeks later, the hastily organized Progressive Party met in Chicago to nominate Roosevelt. The delegates chose Roosevelt and Hiram Johnson to head the new party and approved the most ambitious platform since that of the Populists. Roosevelt arrived in Chicago to accept the nomination and announced that he felt "as strong as a bull moose," giving the new party a nickname and a mascot. But for all the excitement and the cheering, the new Progressive Party was doomed, and the candidate knew it. The people may have supported the party, but the politicians, even progressives like La Follette, stayed within the Republican fold. "I am under no illusion about it," Roosevelt confessed to a friend. "It is a forlorn hope."

The Democrats, delighted at the split in the Republican ranks, nominated Woodrow Wilson. Wilson's career in politics was nothing short of meteoric. He was elected governor of New Jersey in 1910, and after only eighteen months in office, the former professor of political science and president of Princeton University found himself running for president of the United States.

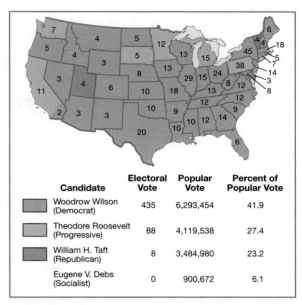

Candidate	Electoral Vote	Popular Vote	Percent of Popular Vote
Woodrow Wilson (Democrat)	435	6,293,454	41.9
Theodore Roosevelt (Progressive)	88	4,119,538	27.4
William H. Taft (Republican)	8	3,484,980	23.2
Eugene V. Debs (Socialist)	0	900,672	6.1

MAP 21.3 ■ The Election of 1912

Voters in 1912 could choose among four candidates who claimed to be progressives. Taft, Roosevelt, and Wilson each embraced the label, and even the Socialist Party candidate, Eugene V. Debs, styled himself a progressive. That the term progressive could stretch to cover these diverse candidates underscored major disagreements in progressive thinking about the relationship between business and government. Taft was generally viewed as the candidate of the old guard. The real contest for the presidency was between Roosevelt and Wilson and between the two political philosophies summed up in their respective campaign slogans: the New Nationalism and the New Freedom.

The New Nationalism expressed Roosevelt's belief in federal planning and regulation. He accepted the inevitability of big business but demanded that government act as "a steward of the people" to regulate the giant corporations. Wilson set a markedly different course with his New Freedom. Wilson promised to use antitrust legislation to get rid of big corporations and to give small businesses and farmers better opportunities in the marketplace.

In the end, the Republican vote split, while the Democrats remained united. No candidate claimed a majority of the popular vote. In the electoral college, however, Wilson won a decisive 435 votes, with 88 going to Roosevelt and only 8 to Taft (**Map 21.3**). The Progressive Party essentially collapsed after Roosevelt's defeat. It had always been, in the words of one astute observer, "a house divided against itself and already mortgaged."

QUICK REVIEW <

Why did the Republican Party split in 1912?

| How did Theodore Roosevelt advance the progressive agenda? | How did progressivism fare during the Taft administration? | What was Woodrow Wilson's progressive agenda and how did it change during his administration? | What were the limits of progressive reform? | Conclusion: How did the liberal state transform during the Progressive Era? |

What was Woodrow Wilson's progressive agenda and how did it change during his administration?

The Democrats turned to Woodrow Wilson to lead the party in 1912, nominating him on the forty-sixth ballot. The ribbon in this photograph belonged to a member of the Democratic National Committee, who traveled to Wilson's summer home in Sea Girt, New Jersey, to inform Wilson officially of his nomination. Collection of Janice L. and David J. Frent.

BORN IN VIRGINIA and raised in Georgia, Woodrow Wilson became the first southerner to be elected president since 1844 and only the second Democrat to occupy the White House since Reconstruction. Although he opposed big government in his campaign, Wilson was prepared to work on the base built by Roosevelt to strengthen presidential power, exerting leadership to achieve banking reform and working through his party in Congress to accomplish the Democratic agenda. Before he was finished, Wilson presided over progressivism at high tide and lent his support not only to the platform of the Democratic Party but also to many of the Progressive Party's social reforms.

Wilson's Reforms: Tariff, Banking, and the Trusts

With the Democratic Party firmly in control, Wilson called for tariff reform. "The object of the tariff," Wilson told Congress, "must be effective competition." The Democratic House of Representatives passed the Underwood tariff, which lowered rates by 15 percent. To compensate for lost revenue, the House approved a moderate federal income tax, made possible by ratification of the Sixteenth Amendment a month earlier. In the Senate, lobbyists for industries went to work to get the tariff raised, but Wilson rallied public opinion by attacking the "industrious and insidious lobby." In the harsh glare of publicity, the Senate passed the Underwood tariff, which earned praise as "the most honest tariff since the Civil War."

Wilson next turned his attention to banking. In 1913, a Senate committee investigated the "money trust," calling J. P. Morgan himself to testify. The committee uncovered an alarming concentration of banking power. J. P. Morgan and Company and its affiliates held 341 directorships in 112 corporations, controlling assets of more than $22 billion ($457 billion in today's dollars). The sensational findings created a mandate for banking reform.

The Federal Reserve Act of 1913 marked the most significant piece of domestic legislation of Wilson's presidency. It established a national banking system composed of twelve regional banks, privately controlled but regulated and supervised by the

CHAPTER LOCATOR | How did grassroots progressives attack the problems of industrial America? | What were the key tenets of progressive theory?

Federal Reserve Board, appointed by the president. It gave the United States its first efficient banking and currency system and, at the same time, provided for a greater degree of government control over banking. The new system made currency more elastic and credit adequate for the needs of business and agriculture.

Wilson tackled the trust issue next. When Congress reconvened in January 1914, he supported the introduction of the Clayton Antitrust Act to outlaw "unfair competition"—practices such as price discrimination and interlocking directorates (directors from one corporation sitting on the board of another). In the midst of the fight for the Clayton Act, Wilson changed course and threw his support behind the creation of the **Federal Trade Commission (FTC)**, precisely the kind of federal regulatory agency that Roosevelt had advocated in his New Nationalism platform. The FTC, created in 1914, had wide investigatory powers as well as the authority to prosecute corporations for "unfair trade practices" and to enforce its judgments by issuing "cease and desist" orders. Despite his campaign promises, Wilson's antitrust program worked to regulate rather than to break up big business.

Wilson, Reluctant Progressive

By the fall of 1914, Wilson declared that the progressive movement had fulfilled its mission and that the country needed "a time of healing." Progressives watched in dismay as Wilson repeatedly obstructed or refused to endorse further progressive reforms. He failed to support labor's demand for an end to court injunctions against labor unions. He threatened to veto legislation providing farm credits for nonperishable crops. He refused to support child labor legislation or woman suffrage. Wilson used the rhetoric of the New Freedom to justify his actions, claiming that his administration would condone "special privileges to none." But, in fact, his stance often reflected the interests of his small-business constituency.

In the face of Wilson's obstinacy, reform might have ended in 1913 had not politics intruded. In the congressional elections of 1914, the Republican Party, no longer split by Roosevelt's Bull Moose faction, won substantial gains. Democratic strategists, with their eyes on the 1916 presidential race, recognized that Wilson needed to pick up support in the Midwest and the West by capturing votes from former Bull Moose progressives. Wilson responded by lending his support to reform in the months leading up to the election of 1916, cultivating union labor, farmers, and social reformers. To please labor, he appointed progressive Louis Brandeis to the Supreme Court. To woo farmers, he threw his support behind legislation to obtain rural credits. And he won praise from labor by supporting workers' compensation and the Keating-Owen child labor law (1916), which outlawed the regular employment of children younger than sixteen. Wilson boasted that the Democrats had "opened their hearts to the demands of social justice" and had "come very near to carrying out the platform of the Progressive Party." Wilson's shift toward reform, along with his claim that he had kept the United States out of the war in Europe (see chapter 22), helped him win reelection in 1916.

(see chapter 22)

CHRONOLOGY

1912
- Democrat Woodrow Wilson is elected president.

1913
- Federal Reserve Act.

1914
- Federal Trade Commission is created.
- Clayton Antitrust Act passed.

1916
- Keating-Owen child labor law.

Federal Trade Commission (FTC)

▶ Federal regulatory agency created in 1914 that had wide investigatory powers, the authority to prosecute corporations for "unfair trade practices," and the power to enforce its judgments by issuing "cease and desist" orders. Woodrow Wilson supported the creation of the FTC, despite his campaign promises to break up big business rather than to regulate it.

QUICK REVIEW

How and why did Wilson's reform program evolve during his first term?

| How did Theodore Roosevelt advance the progressive agenda? | How did progressivism fare during the Taft administration? | What was Woodrow Wilson's progressive agenda and how did it change during his administration? | What were the limits of progressive reform? | Conclusion: How did the liberal state transform during the Progressive Era? |

> What were the limits of progressive reform?

Booker T. Washington and Theodore Roosevelt Dine at the White House

When Theodore Roosevelt invited Booker T. Washington to the White House in 1901, he stirred up a hornet's nest of controversy that continued into the election of 1904. This Republican campaign piece gives the meeting a positive slant, showing Roosevelt and a light-skinned Washington sitting under a portrait of Abraham Lincoln, a symbol of the party's historic commitment to African Americans. Democrats, in contrast, pictured Washington with darker skin and implied that Roosevelt favored "race mingling" and had "painted the White House black." Collection of Janice L. and David J. Frent.

WHILE PROGRESSIVISM CALLED for a more active role for the liberal state, at heart it was a movement that sought reforms designed to preserve American institutions and stem the tide of more radical change. Its basic conservatism can be seen by comparing it to the more radical movements of socialism, radical labor, and birth control—and by looking at the groups progressive reform left behind, including women and African Americans.

Radical Alternatives

The year 1900 marked the birth of the Social Democratic Party in America, later called simply the Socialist Party. Like the progressives, the socialists were middle-class and native-born. They had broken with the older, more militant Socialist Labor Party precisely because of its dogmatic approach and immigrant constituency.

The Socialist Party chose as its presidential standard-bearer Eugene V. Debs. Debs would run for president five times, in every election (except the one in 1916) from 1900 to 1920. The socialism Debs advocated preached cooperation over competition and urged men and women to liberate themselves from "the barbarism of private ownership and wage slavery." In the 1912 election, Debs indicted

CHAPTER LOCATOR | How did grassroots progressives attack the problems of industrial America? | What were the key tenets of progressive theory?

both old parties as "Tweedledee and Tweedledum," each dedicated to the preservation of capitalism and the continuation of the wage system. Only through socialism, he argued, could democracy exist. Debs's best showing came in 1912, when he polled 6 percent of the popular vote, capturing more than 900,000 votes.

Farther to the left of the socialists stood the Industrial Workers of the World (IWW), nicknamed the Wobblies. In 1905, Debs, along with Western Federation of Miners leader William Dudley "Big Bill" Haywood, created the IWW, "one big union" dedicated to organizing the most destitute segment of the workforce, the unskilled workers. Seeing workers on the lowest rung of the social ladder as the victims of violent repression, the IWW advocated direct action, sabotage, and the general strike—tactics designed to trigger a workers' uprising. The IWW never had more than 10,000 members at any one time. Nevertheless, the IWW's influence on the country extended far beyond its numbers.

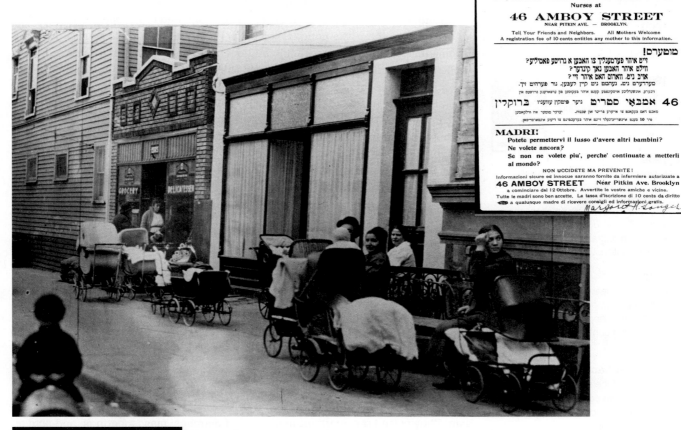

Margaret Sanger's Brownsville Birth Control Clinic

Margaret Sanger opened the first birth control clinic in the United States in the Brownsville section of Brooklyn in 1916. During the nine days it operated before police shut it down, more than four hundred women visited the clinic. Her clinic was located in the heart of an immigrant neighborhood, so Sanger published her fliers in English, Yiddish, and Italian. Sophia Smith Collection, Smith College.

▶ FOR MORE HELP ANALYZING THIS IMAGE, see the visual activity for this chapter in the Online Study Guide at bedfordstmartins.com/roarkunderstanding.

How did Theodore Roosevelt advance the progressive agenda?

How did progressivism fare during the Taft administration?

What was Woodrow Wilson's progressive agenda and how did it change during his administration?

What were the limits of progressive reform?

Conclusion: How did the liberal state transform during the Progressive Era?

Margaret Sanger
▶ Leader of the movement to promote birth control as a means for producing social change. A nurse who worked among New York City's poor, Sanger opened the nation's first birth control clinic in October 1916. Under her leadership, birth control gained legitimacy, if not legality.

In contrast to political radicals like Debs and Haywood, **Margaret Sanger** promoted birth control as a movement for social change. Sanger, a nurse who had worked among the poor on New York's Lower East Side, coined the term *birth control* in 1915 and launched a movement with broad social implications. Sanger and her followers saw birth control not only as a sexual and medical reform but also as a means to alter social and political power relationships and to alleviate human misery.

The desire for family limitation was widespread, and in this sense, birth control was nothing new. But the open advocacy of *contraception*, the use of artificial means to prevent pregnancy, struck many people as shocking. And it was illegal. Anthony Comstock, New York City's commissioner of vice, promoted laws in the 1870s making it a felony not only to sell contraceptive devices but also to publish information on how to prevent pregnancy.

When Margaret Sanger used her militant feminist newspaper, the *Woman Rebel*, to promote birth control, the Post Office confiscated Sanger's publication and brought charges against her. Facing arrest, she fled to Europe, only to return in 1916 as something of a national celebrity. In her absence, birth control had become linked with free speech and had been taken up as a liberal cause. Under public pressure, the government dropped the charges against Sanger, who undertook a nationwide tour to publicize the birth control cause.

Sanger then turned to direct action, opening the nation's first birth control clinic in October 1916. Located in the heart of a Jewish and Italian immigrant neighborhood in Brooklyn, the clinic attracted 464 clients. On the tenth day, police shut down the clinic and threw Sanger in jail. By then, she had become a national figure, and the cause she championed had gained legitimacy, if not legality.

Progressivism for White Men Only

The day before President Woodrow Wilson's inauguration in March 1913, the largest mass march to date in the nation's history took place as more than five thousand demonstrators took to the streets in Washington to demand the vote for women. A rowdy crowd on hand to celebrate the Democrats' triumph attacked the marchers. "If my wife were where you are," a burly cop told one suffragist, "I'd break her head." Wilson, who didn't believe that a "lady" should vote, pointedly ignored woman suffrage in his inaugural address the next day.

The march served as a reminder that the political gains of progressivism were not spread equally throughout the population. Increasingly, however, woman suffrage had become an international movement. In Great Britain, Emmeline Pankhurst and her daughters Cristabel and Sylvia promoted a new, militant suffragism. They seized the spotlight in a series of marches, mass meetings, and acts of civil disobedience that sometimes escalated into riots, violence, and arson.

Alice Paul, a Quaker social worker who had visited England and participated in suffrage activism there, returned to the United States in 1910 in time to plan the mass march on the eve of Wilson's inauguration. Paul's tactics alienated many in the National American Woman Suffrage Association. In 1916, Paul founded the militant National Woman's Party, which became the radical voice of the suffrage movement.

CHAPTER LOCATOR | How did grassroots progressives attack the problems of industrial America? | What were the key tenets of progressive theory?

Women weren't the only group left out in progressive reform. Progressivism, as it was practiced in the West and South, was tainted with racism and sought to limit the rights of African and Asian Americans. Anti-Asian bigotry in the West led to a renewal of the Chinese Exclusion Act in 1902. In 1913, California governor Hiram Johnson caved in to popular pressure and signed the Alien Land Law, which barred Japanese immigrants from purchasing land in California.

In the South, the progressives' racism targeted African Americans. Progressives preached the disfranchisement of black voters as a "reform." During the bitter electoral fights that had pitted Populists against Democrats in the 1890s, the Democratic Party held its power by votes purchased or coerced from African Americans. Southern progressives proposed to "reform" the electoral system by eliminating black voters. Beginning in 1890 with Mississippi, southern states curtailed the African American vote through devices such as poll taxes (fees required for voting) and literacy tests. The racist intent of southern voting legislation became especially clear after 1900, when states resorted to the grandfather clause, a legal provision that allowed men who failed a literacy test to vote if their grandfathers had cast a ballot. Grandfathering permitted southern white men to vote while excluding blacks.

The Progressive Era also witnessed the rise of Jim Crow laws to segregate public facilities. Soon, separate railcars, separate waiting rooms, separate bathrooms, and separate dining facilities for blacks sprang up across the South. In courtrooms in Mississippi, blacks were required to swear on a separate Bible.

In the face of this growing repression, **Booker T. Washington**, the preeminent black leader of the day, urged caution and restraint. A former slave, Washington had opened the Tuskegee Institute in Alabama in 1881 to teach vocational skills to African Americans. He emphasized education and economic progress for his race and urged African Americans to put aside issues of political and social equality. In an 1895 speech in Atlanta that came to be known as the Atlanta Compromise, he stated, "In all things that are purely social we can be as separate as the fingers, yet one as the hand in all things essential to mutual progress." Washington's accommodationist policy appealed to whites and elevated him to the role of national spokesman for African Americans.

The year after Washington proclaimed the Atlanta Compromise, the Supreme Court upheld the legality of racial segregation, affirming in *Plessy v. Ferguson* (1896) the constitutionality of the doctrine of "separate but equal." Blacks could be segregated in separate schools, restrooms, and other facilities as long as the facilities were "equal" to those provided for whites. Of course, facilities for blacks rarely proved equal.

Woodrow Wilson brought to the White House southern attitudes toward race and racial segregation. He instituted segregation in the federal workforce, especially the Post Office, and approved segregated drinking fountains and restrooms in the nation's capital. When critics attacked the policy, Wilson insisted that segregation was "in the interest of the Negro."

In 1906, a major race riot in Atlanta called into question Booker T. Washington's strategy of uplift and accommodation. For three days in September, angry white mobs chased and cornered any blacks they happened upon, pulling passengers from streetcars and invading black neighborhoods to kill and loot.

Booker T. Washington

▶ Preeminent black leader of the late nineteenth century. A former slave, Washington opened the Tuskegee Institute in Alabama in 1881 to teach vocational skills to African Americans. He emphasized education and economic progress for his race and urged African Americans to put aside issues of political and social equality.

Plessy v. Ferguson

▶ 1896 Supreme Court ruling that upheld the legality of racial segregation. According to the ruling, blacks could be segregated in separate schools, restrooms, and other facilities as long as the facilities were "equal" to those provided for whites. *Plessy v. Ferguson* gave official sanction to the proliferation of Jim Crow legislation.

How did Theodore Roosevelt advance the progressive agenda?

How did progressivism fare during the Taft administration?

What was Woodrow Wilson's progressive agenda and how did it change during his administration?

What were the limits of progressive reform?

Conclusion: How did the liberal state transform during the Progressive Era?

In 1895, W. E. B. Du Bois became the first African American to earn a doctorate from Harvard. Throughout his lifetime, he urged African Americans to work for political and racial equality. He wrote in *The Souls of Black Folk* in 1903 that he wished "to make it possible for a man to be both a Negro and an American, without being cursed and spit upon by his fellows." Special Collections Department, W. E. B. Du Bois Library, University of Massachusetts, Amherst.

W. E. B. Du Bois

▶ Black intellectual and opponent of Booker T. Washington's accommodationist position. Du Bois founded the Niagara movement in 1905, calling for universal male suffrage, civil rights, and leadership of a black intellectual elite. In 1909, the Niagara movement helped found the National Association for the Advancement of Colored People (NAACP).

An estimated 250 African Americans died in the riots—members of Atlanta's black middle class along with the poor and derelict. Professor William Crogman of Clark College noted the central irony of the riot: "Here we have worked and prayed and tried to make good men and women of our colored population," he observed, "and at our very doorstep the whites kill these good men." The riot caused many African Americans to question Washington's strategy of gradualism and accommodation.

Foremost among Washington's critics stood **W. E. B. Du Bois**, a Harvard graduate who urged African Americans to fight for civil rights and racial justice. In *The Souls of Black Folk* (1903), Du Bois attacked the "Tuskegee Machine," comparing Washington to a political boss who used his influence to silence his critics and reward his followers. Du Bois founded the Niagara movement in 1905, calling for universal male suffrage, civil rights, and leadership of a black intellectual elite. In 1909, the Niagara movement helped found the National Association for the Advancement of Colored People (NAACP), a coalition of blacks and whites that sought legal and political rights for African Americans through the courts.

> **QUICK REVIEW**

How did race, class, and gender shape the limits of progressive reform?

CHAPTER LOCATOR | How did grassroots progressives attack the problems of industrial America? | What were the key tenets of progressive theory?

CHAPTER 21
592 PROGRESSIVISM FROM THE GRASS ROOTS UP, 1890–1916

Chicago History Museum.

PROGRESSIVISM'S GOAL WAS TO REFORM the existing system—by government intervention if necessary, but without uprooting any of the traditional American political, economic, or social institutions. As Theodore Roosevelt, the bellwether of the movement, insisted, "The only true conservative is the man who resolutely sets his face toward the future." Roosevelt was such a man, and progressivism was such a movement. But although progressivism was never radical, progressives' willingness to use the power of government to regulate business and achieve a measure of social justice redefined liberalism in the twentieth century, tying it to the expanded power of the state.

Progressivism contained many paradoxes. A diverse coalition of individuals and interests, the progressive movement began at the grass roots but left as its legacy a stronger presidency and unprecedented federal involvement in the economy and social welfare. A movement that believed in social justice, progressivism often promoted social control. And while progressives called for greater democracy, they fostered elitism with their worship of experts and efficiency.

Whatever its inconsistencies and limitations, progressivism took action to deal with the problems posed by urban industrialism. Progressivism saw grassroots activists address social problems on the local and state levels and search for national solutions. By increasing the power of the presidency and expanding the power of the state, progressives worked to bring about greater social justice and to achieve a better balance between government and business. Jane Addams and Theodore Roosevelt could lay equal claim to the movement that redefined liberalism and launched the liberal state of the twentieth century. War on a global scale would provide progressivism with yet another challenge even before it had completed its ambitious agenda.

SO NOW YOU KNOW

Despite the advances of social and political reform and the increased regulation of business and industry during the Progressive Era, blacks and other minorities remained marginalized, workers continued to fight for union recognition, and women continued their struggle for suffrage.

> CHAPTER 21 STUDY GUIDE

Online Study Guide
bedfordstmartins.com/roarkunderstanding

STEP 1 GETTING STARTED

Below are basic terms from this period in American history. Can you identify each term below and explain why it matters? To do this exercise online or to download this chart, visit bedfordstmartins.com/roarkunderstanding.

TERM	WHO OR WHAT & WHEN	WHY IT MATTERS
settlement houses, p. 568		
social gospel, p. 569		
Women's Trade Union League (WTUL), p. 570		
reform Darwinism, p. 573		
Roosevelt Corollary, p. 580		
Federal Trade Commission (FTC), p. 587		
Margaret Sanger, p. 590		
Booker T. Washington, p. 591		
Plessy v. Ferguson, p. 591		
W. E. B. Du Bois, p. 592		

STEP 2 MOVING BEYOND THE BASICS

The exercise below represents a more advanced understanding of the chapter material. First, describe the actions and proposals of the progressives at the local, state, and national levels in the 1890s and during the administrations of three Progressive Era presidents. Then describe the progressive successes during each period. When you are finished, consider the following questions. How did progressive reforms at the grassroots level influence progressive politics at the state and national levels? In what areas and during what times were the progressives most successful? To do this exercise online or to download this chart, visit bedfordstmartins.com/roarkunderstanding.

Period	Actions and proposals at local, state, and national levels	Reforms implemented
1890s		
Theodore Roosevelt administration		
William H. Taft administration		
Woodrow Wilson administration		

Now that you've reviewed various parts of the chapter, take a step back and try to see the big picture by answering these questions. Remember to use specific examples from the chapter in your answers. To do this exercise online, visit bedfordstmartins.com/roarkunderstanding.

PROGRESSIVES AND PROGRESSIVISM

▶ What core principles underlay progressivism? How was progressivism different from earlier reform movements?

▶ Why was grassroots activism so important to the progressive movement?

THEODORE ROOSEVELT AND PROGRESSIVISM

▶ What progressive ideals were embodied in Roosevelt's Square Deal?

▶ What were the limits of Roosevelt's reform activities? Was he a true progressive? Why or why not?

WOODROW WILSON AND PROGRESSIVISM

▶ How did Wilson's progressivism differ from that of Roosevelt?

▶ How did Wilson's progressive agenda change during his presidency? What evidence can you produce to support your answer?

LOOKING BACKWARD, LOOKING AHEAD

▶ Defend or refute the following statement: "The progressive movement enacted the Populist platform."

▶ What progressive ideas and policies continue to influence American social and political life today?

IN YOUR OWN WORDS

Imagine that you must explain chapter 21 to someone who hasn't read it. What would be the most important points to include and why?

22

THE UNITED STATES IN WORLD WAR I

1914–1920

> This chapter explores the nature and impact of America's involvement in World War I. It examines Woodrow Wilson's role in taking the country to war and in shaping the peace that followed, the contribution of American armed forces to the Allied victory, the impact of the war on Americans at home, and the uneasy years that followed the return of peace.

> What was Woodrow Wilson's foreign policy agenda?

> What role did the United States play in World War I?

> What impact did the war have on the home front?

> What part did Woodrow Wilson play in the Paris peace conference?

> Why was America's transition from war to peace so turbulent?

> Conclusion: What was the domestic cost of foreign victory?

DID YOU KNOW?

During World War I, Americans across the nation changed the name of German toast to French toast.

Writing home. A Salvation Army worker writes a letter for a wounded American soldier, 1918.

What was Woodrow Wilson's foreign policy agenda?

"Enlist"

This poster depicting a young mother and her baby sinking beneath the cold waters of the Atlantic Ocean brought home the terrible cost of Germany's sinking of the British passenger liner *Lusitania* in 1915. Burned into American memory, the *Lusitania* remained a compelling reason to enlist in the armed forces after the United States entered the war in 1917.
Library of Congress.

▶ FOR MORE HELP ANALYZING THIS IMAGE, see the visual activity for this chapter in the Online Study Guide at bedfordstmartins.com/roarkunderstanding.

SHORTLY AFTER WINNING election to the presidency in 1912, Woodrow Wilson confided to a friend: "It would be an irony of fate if my administration had to deal with foreign affairs." Indeed, Wilson had focused his life and career on domestic concerns, seldom venturing far from home and traveling abroad only on brief vacations.

But Wilson could not avoid the world and its problems. Economic interests compelled the nation outward. Moreover, Wilson was drawn abroad by his own progressive political principles. He believed that the United States had a moral duty to champion national self-determination, peaceful free trade, and political democracy. "We have no selfish ends to serve," he proclaimed. "We desire no conquest, no dominion. . . . We are but one of the champions of the rights of mankind." Yet as president, Wilson revealed he was as ready as any American president to apply military solutions to problems of foreign policy.

Taming the Americas

When he took office, Wilson sought to distinguish his foreign policy from what he saw as the belligerent policies of his Republican predecessors, Roosevelt and Taft.

CHAPTER LOCATOR | What was Woodrow Wilson's foreign policy agenda?

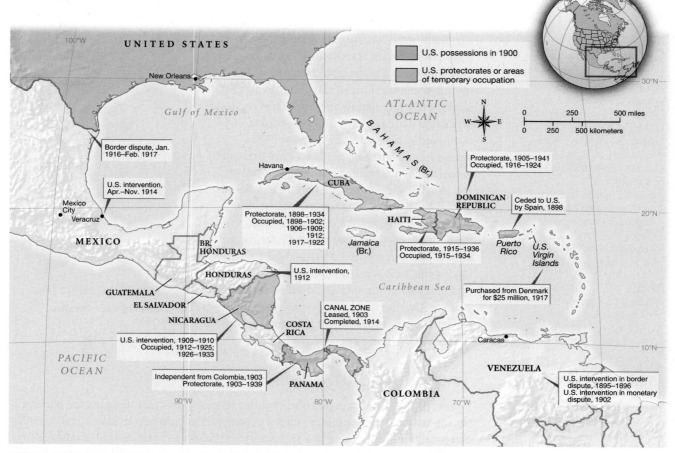

MAP 22.1 ■ U.S. Involvement in Latin America and the Caribbean, 1895–1941
Victory against Spain in 1898 made Puerto Rico an American possession and Cuba a protectorate. The United States later gained control of the Panama Canal Zone. The nation was quick to protect expanding economic interests with military force by propping up friendly, though not necessarily democratic, governments.

To signal a new direction, Wilson appointed William Jennings Bryan as secretary of state. A pacifist on religious grounds, Bryan immediately turned his attention to making agreements with thirty nations for the peaceful settlement of disputes.

But Wilson and Bryan, like Roosevelt and Taft, also believed that the Monroe Doctrine gave the United States special rights and responsibilities in the Western Hemisphere. Wilson thus authorized U.S. military intervention in Nicaragua, Haiti, and the Dominican Republic, paving the way for U.S. banks and corporations to take financial control. All the while, Wilson believed that U.S. actions were promoting order and democracy. "I am going to teach the South American Republics to elect good men!" he declared (**Map 22.1**).

Wilson's most serious involvement in Latin America came in Mexico. When General Victoriano Huerta seized power by violent means, most European nations promptly recognized Mexico's new government, but Wilson refused, declaring that he would not support a "government of butchers." In April 1914, Wilson sent 800 marines to seize the port of Veracruz to prevent the unloading of a large shipment of arms for Huerta, who was by then involved in a civil war of his own. Huerta fled to Spain, and the United States welcomed a more compliant government.

| What role did the United States play in World War I? | What impact did the war have on the home front? | What part did Woodrow Wilson play in the Paris peace conference? | Why was America's transition from war to peace so turbulent? | Conclusion: What was the domestic cost of foreign victory? |

599

1914
- **April.** U.S. Marines occupy Veracruz, Mexico, during the Mexican revolution.
- **June 28.** Archduke Franz Ferdinand of Austria is assassinated by a Bosnian Serb terrorist.
- **July 18.** Austria-Hungary declares war on Serbia.
- **August 3.** Germany attacks Russia and France.
- **August 4.** Great Britain declares war on Germany.

1915
- German U-boat sinks the British passenger liner *Lusitania*, killing 128 Americans.

1916
- Wilson is reelected.

1916–1917
- General John Pershing pursues Mexican revolutionary leader Pancho Villa.

1917
- **January.** Germany resumes unrestricted submarine warfare.
- **February.** Zimmermann telegram between Germany and Mexico is intercepted.
- **April.** United States declares war on Germany.

But a rebellion erupted among desperately poor farmers who believed that the new government of Venustiano Carranza, aided by U.S. business interests, had betrayed the revolution's promise to help the common people. In January 1916, the rebel army, commanded by Francisco "Pancho" Villa, seized a train carrying gold to Texas from an American-owned mine in Mexico and killed the 17 American engineers aboard. On March 9, another band of Villa's men crossed the border for a predawn raid on Columbus, New Mexico, where they killed 18 Americans. Wilson promptly dispatched 12,000 troops, led by General John J. Pershing. But Villa avoided capture, and in January 1917, Wilson recalled Pershing so that he might prepare the army for the possibility of fighting in the Great War.

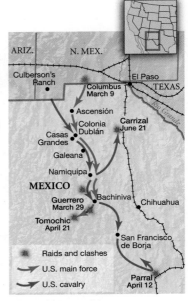

U.S. Intervention in Mexico, 1916–1917

The European Crisis

Before 1914, Europe had enjoyed decades of peace, but just beneath the surface lay the potentially destructive forces of nationalism and imperialism. The consolidation of the German and Italian states into unified nations and the similar ambition of Russia to create a Pan-Slavic union initiated new rivalries throughout Europe. As the conviction spread that colonial possessions were a mark of national greatness, competition expanded onto the world stage. Most ominously, Germany's efforts under Kaiser Wilhelm II to challenge Great Britain's world supremacy by creating industrial muscle at home, an empire abroad, and a mighty navy threatened the balance of power and thus the peace.

European nations sought to avoid an explosion with a complex web of military and diplomatic alliances. By 1914, Germany, Austria-Hungary, and Italy (the Triple Alliance) stood opposed to Great Britain, France, and Russia (the Triple Entente, also known as "the Allies"). But in their effort to prevent war through a balance of power, Europeans had actually magnified the possibility of large-scale conflict (**Map 22.2**). Treaties, some of them secret, obligated members of the alliances to come to the aid of another member if attacked.

The fatal sequence began on June 28, 1914, in the Bosnian city of Sarajevo, when a Bosnian-Serb terrorist assassinated Archduke Franz Ferdinand, heir to the Austro-Hungarian throne. On July 18, Austria-Hungary declared war on Serbia. The elaborate alliance system meant that the war could not remain local. Russia announced that it would back the Serbs. Compelled by treaty to support Austria-Hungary, Germany on August 3 attacked Russia and France. In response, on August 4, Great Britain, upholding its pact with France, declared war on Germany. Within weeks, Europe was engulfed in war. The conflict became a world war when Japan, seeing an opportunity to rid itself of European competition in China, joined the cause against Germany.

CHAPTER LOCATOR | What was Woodrow Wilson's foreign policy agenda?

600 CHAPTER 22 THE UNITED STATES IN WORLD WAR I, 1914–1920

MAP 22.2 ■ European Alliances after the Outbreak of World War I
With Germany and Austria-Hungary wedged between their Entente rivals and all parties fully armed, Europe was poised for war when Archduke Franz Ferdinand of Austria-Hungary was assassinated in Sarajevo in June 1914.

The Ordeal of American Neutrality

Woodrow Wilson promptly announced that because the war engaged no vital American interest and involved no significant principle, the United States would remain neutral. Neutrality entitled the United States to trade safely with all nations at war, he declared. Unfettered trade with Europe, Wilson believed, was not only a right under international law but also a necessity because the U.S. economy had in 1913 slipped into a recession, which wartime disruption of trade could drastically worsen.

Although Wilson proclaimed neutrality, his sympathies, like those of many Americans, lay with Great Britain and France. Americans gratefully remembered crucial French assistance in the American Revolution and shared with the British a language, a culture, and a commitment to liberty. Germany, in contrast, was a monarchy with strong militaristic traditions. Still, Wilson insisted on neutrality, in

| What role did the United States play in World War I? | What impact did the war have on the home front? | What part did Woodrow Wilson play in the Paris peace conference? | Why was America's transition from war to peace so turbulent? | Conclusion: What was the domestic cost of foreign victory? |

601

Sinking of the *Lusitania*, 1915

U-boats

▶ *Unterseebooten*, or German submarines. Germany used U-boats to try to halt international trade with Britain. In the process, they sank a number of ships with Americans on board, most famously the *Lusitania* in 1915. Germany's resumption of unrestricted submarine warfare in January 1917 directly contributed to America's entry into the war.

part because he feared the conflict's effects on the United States as a nation of immigrants. As he told the German ambassador, "We definitely have to be neutral, since otherwise our mixed populations would wage war on each other."

Britain's powerful fleet controlled the seas and quickly set up an economic blockade of Germany. The United States vigorously protested, but Britain refused to give up its naval advantage. The blockade actually had little economic impact on the United States. Between 1914 and the spring of 1917, while trade with Germany evaporated, war-related exports to Britain—food, clothing, steel, and munitions—escalated by some 400 percent. Although the British blockade violated American neutrality, the Wilson administration gradually acquiesced, thus beginning the fateful process of alienation from Germany.

Germany retaliated with a submarine blockade of British ports. German *Unterseebooten*, or **U-boats**, threatened traditional rules of war. Unlike surface warships that could harmlessly stop freighters and prevent them from entering a war zone, submarines relied on sinking their quarry. And once they sank a ship, the U-boats could not pick up survivors. Britain portrayed the submarine as an outlaw weapon that violated notions of "civilized" warfare. Nevertheless, in February 1915, Germany announced that it intended to sink on sight enemy ships en route to the British Isles. On May 7, 1915, a German U-boat torpedoed the British passenger liner *Lusitania*, killing 1,198 passengers, 128 of them U.S. citizens.

American newspapers featured drawings of drowning women and children, and some demanded war. Others pointed out that Germany had warned prospective passengers and that the *Lusitania* carried millions of rounds of ammunition and so was a legitimate target. Secretary of State Bryan resisted the hysteria and declared that a ship carrying war materiel "should not rely on passengers to protect her from attack—it would be like putting women and children in front of an army." He counseled Wilson to warn American citizens that they traveled on ships of belligerent countries at their own risk.

Wilson sought a middle course that would retain his commitment to peace and neutrality without condoning German attacks on passenger ships. On May 10, 1915, Wilson declared that any further destruction of ships would be regarded as "deliberately unfriendly" and might lead the United States to break diplomatic relations with Germany. Wilson essentially demanded that Germany abandon unrestricted submarine warfare. Bryan resigned, predicting that the president had placed the United States on a collision course with Germany. Wilson's replacement for Bryan, Robert Lansing, was far from neutral. He believed that Germany's antidemocratic character and goal of "world dominance" meant that it "must not be permitted to win this war or even to break even."

After Germany apologized for the civilian deaths on the *Lusitania*, tensions subsided. But in 1916, Germany went further, promising no more submarine attacks without warning and without provisions for the safety of civilians. Wilson's supporters celebrated the success of his middle-of-the-road strategy.

Wilson's diplomacy proved helpful in his bid for reelection in 1916. In the contest against Republican Charles Evans Hughes, the Democratic Party ran Wilson under the slogan "He kept us out of war." The Democrats' case for Wilson's neutrality appealed to enough of those in favor of peace to eke out a majority. Wilson won, but only by the razor-thin margins of 600,000 popular and 23 electoral votes.

CHAPTER LOCATOR | What was Woodrow Wilson's foreign policy agenda?

The United States Enters the War

Step-by-step, the United States backed away from "absolute neutrality." The consequence of protesting the German blockade of Great Britain but accepting the British blockade of Germany was that by 1916 the United States was supplying the Allies with 40 percent of their war materiel. When France and Britain ran short of money to pay for U.S. goods and asked for loans, Wilson argued that "loans by American bankers to any foreign government which is at war are inconsistent with the true spirit of neutrality." But rather than jeopardize America's wartime prosperity, Wilson relaxed his objections, and billions of dollars in loans kept American goods flowing to Britain and France.

In January 1917, Germany decided that it could no longer afford to allow neutral shipping to reach Great Britain and announced that it would resume unrestricted submarine warfare and sink without warning any ship, enemy or neutral, found in the waters off Great Britain. Germany understood that the decision would probably bring the United States into the war but gambled that the submarines would strangle the British economy and allow German armies to win a military victory in France before American troops arrived in Europe.

Resisting demands for war, Wilson continued to hope for a negotiated peace and only broke off diplomatic relations with Germany. Then on February 25, 1917, British authorities informed Wilson of a secret telegram sent by the German foreign secretary, Arthur Zimmermann, to the German minister in Mexico. It promised that in the event of war between Germany and the United States, Germany would see that Mexico regained its "lost provinces" of Texas, New Mexico, and Arizona if Mexico would declare war against the United States. Wilson angrily responded to the **Zimmermann telegram** by asking Congress to approve a policy of "armed neutrality" that would allow merchant ships to fight back against any attackers.

In March, German submarines sank five American vessels off Britain, killing 66 Americans. On April 2, the president asked Congress to issue a declaration of war. Wilson called for a "war without hate" and insisted that the destruction of Germany was not the goal of the United States. Rather, America fought to "vindicate the principles of peace and justice." He promised a world made "safe for democracy." On April 6, 1917, Congress voted to declare war.

Wilson feared what war would do at home. He said despairingly, "Once lead this people into war, and they'll forget there ever was such a thing as tolerance. To fight you must be brutal and ruthless, and the spirit of ruthless brutality will infect Congress, the courts, the policeman on the beat, the man in the street."

Zimmermann telegram

▶ February 1917 telegram sent by the German foreign secretary, Arthur Zimmermann, to the German minister in Mexico. The telegram suggested that in the event that Germany and the United States went to war, Mexico would regain "lost territories" in the Southwest if it declared war on the United States. The British intercepted the telegram and passed it on to the United States, leading to an escalation of tensions between the United States and Germany.

QUICK REVIEW <

How was the United States drawn into the conflict in Europe?

What role did the United States play in World War I?	What impact did the war have on the home front?	What part did Woodrow Wilson play in the Paris peace conference?	Why was America's transition from war to peace so turbulent?	Conclusion: What was the domestic cost of foreign victory?

What role did the United States play in World War I?

Life in the Trenches One U.S. soldier in a rat-infested trench tensely looks out for danger, another slumps in exhausted sleep, and a third lies flat on his stomach. Nothing could make living in such holes anything better than miserable. Photo: Imperial War Museum.

TWO MILLION AMERICAN TROOPS eventually reached Europe. Filled with a sense of democratic mission and trained to be morally upright as well as fiercely effective, some doughboys found the adventure exhilarating and maintained their idealism to the end. The majority, however, saw little that was gallant in rats, lice, and poison gas, and—despite the progressives' hopes—little to elevate the human soul in a landscape of utter destruction and death.

The Call to Arms

When America entered the war, Britain and France were nearly exhausted after almost three years of conflict. Another Allied power, Russia, was in turmoil. In March 1917, a revolution had forced Czar Nicholas II to abdicate, and eight months later, in a separate peace with Germany, the Bolshevik revolutionary government withdrew Russia from the war.

On May 18, 1917, Wilson signed a sweeping Selective Service Act, authorizing a draft of all young men into the armed forces. Conscription soon transformed a tiny volunteer armed force of 80,000 men into a vast army and navy. Draft boards eventually inducted 2.8 million men into the armed services, in addition to the 2 million who volunteered.

FOLLOW THE FLAG

ENLIST IN THE NAVY
U.S. NAVY RECRUITING STATION
34 East 23rd Street, New York

"Follow the Flag"

This heroic navy recruiting poster helped attract thousands of volunteers into the U.S. military, but President Wilson was unwilling to trust voluntary enlistments. He included in his war message to Congress an endorsement of "the principle of universal liability to service"—in other words, a draft. When the war ended, 2 million men had volunteered for military service, and 2.8 million had been drafted. Image by © Swim Ink 2, LLC/Corbis.

CHAPTER LOCATOR | What was Woodrow Wilson's foreign policy agenda?

Pershing Button

General John J. Pershing, surrounded by the flags of the Allied nations, stares out at the viewer. The words circling the button declare that the Allies are "united in the cause of liberty," echoing President Woodrow Wilson's insistence that American democratic ideals were universal and could be achieved internationally through U.S. participation in the war. Collection of Janice L. and David J. Frent.

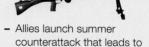
Among the 4.8 million men under arms, 370,000 were black Americans. Although African Americans remained understandably skeptical about President Wilson's war for democracy, most followed W. E. B. Du Bois's advice to "close ranks" and to temporarily "forget our special grievances" until the nation had won the war. During training, black recruits suffered the same prejudices that they encountered in civilian life. Rigidly segregated, they faced abuse and miserable conditions, and they were usually assigned to labor battalions, rather than combat units.

Training camps sought to transform white recruits into fighting men. Progressives in the government were also determined that the camps turn out soldiers with the highest moral and civic values. Secretary of War Newton D. Baker created the Commission on Training Camp Activities, staffed by YMCA workers and veterans of the settlement house and playground movements. Military training included games, singing, and college extension courses. The army asked soldiers to stop thinking about sex, explaining that a "man who is thinking below the belt is not efficient." The Military Draft Act of 1917 prohibited prostitution and alcohol near training camps. Wilson's choice to command the American Expeditionary Force (AEF), Major General **John "Black Jack" Pershing,** was as morally upright as he was militarily uncompromising. Described by one observer as "lean, clean, keen," he gave progressives perfect confidence.

The War in France

At the front, the AEF discovered a desperate situation. The war had degenerated into a stalemate of armies dug defensively into hundreds of miles of trenches across France. When ordered "over the top," troops raced desperately toward the enemy's trenches, only to be entangled in barbed wire, enveloped in poison gas, and mowed down by machine guns. The three-day battle of the Somme in 1916 cost the French and British forces 600,000 dead and wounded and the Germans 500,000. The deadliest battle of the war allowed the Allies to advance their trenches only a few meaningless miles.

Still, U.S. troops saw almost no combat in 1917. The only exception was the 92nd Division of black troops. When Pershing received an urgent call for troops from the French, he sent the 92nd to the front to be integrated into the French army because he did not want to lose command over the white troops he valued more. In the 191 days they spent in battle—longer than any other American outfit—the 369th Regiment of the 92nd Division won more medals than any other American combat unit. Black soldiers recognized the irony of having to serve with the French to gain respect.

John "Black Jack" Pershing

▶ Commander of the American Expeditionary Force. Pershing led the American forces that went to France in 1917 to fight in World War I. Known to be as morally upright as he was militarily uncompromising, Pershing expected his troops to conform to a high standard of behavior on and off the battlefield.

| What role did the United States play in World War I? | What impact did the war have on the home front? | What part did Woodrow Wilson play in the Paris peace conference? | Why was America's transition from war to peace so turbulent? | Conclusion: What was the domestic cost of foreign victory? |

605

MAP 22.3 ■ The American Expeditionary Force, 1918
In the last year of the war, the AEF joined the French army on the western front to respond to the final German offensive and pursue the retreating enemy until surrender.

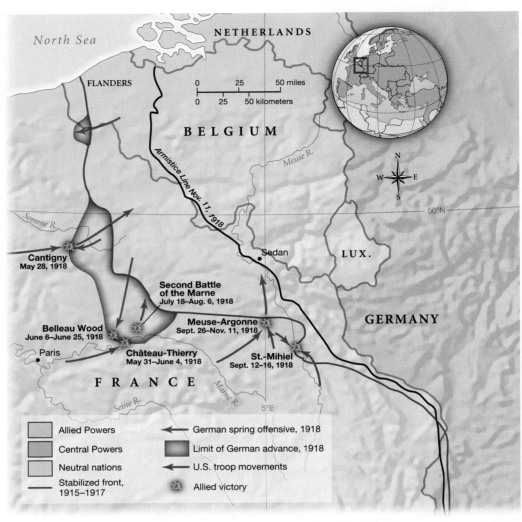

▶ FOR MORE HELP ANALYZING THIS MAP, see the map activity for this chapter in the Online Study Guide at bedfordstmartins.com/roarkunderstanding.

White troops continued to train and used their free time to explore places that most of them otherwise could never have hoped to see. The sightseeing ended abruptly in March 1918. The Brest-Litovsk treaty signed that month by Germany and the Bolsheviks officially took Russia out of the war, and the Germans launched a massive offensive aimed at French ports on the Atlantic. After a million German soldiers punched a hole in the Allied lines, Pershing decided that the right moment for U.S. action had finally come.

In May and June, at Cantigny and then at Château-Thierry, the Americans checked the German advance with a series of assaults (**Map 22.3**). Then they headed toward the forest stronghold of Belleau Wood, moving against streams of retreating Allied soldiers who cried defeat: "La guerre est finie!" (The war is over!). A French officer commanded American soldiers to retreat with them, but the American commander replied sharply, "Retreat, hell. We just got here." After charging through a wheat field against withering machine-gun fire, the marines plunged into hand-to-hand combat. Victory came hard, but a German report praised the enemy's spirit,

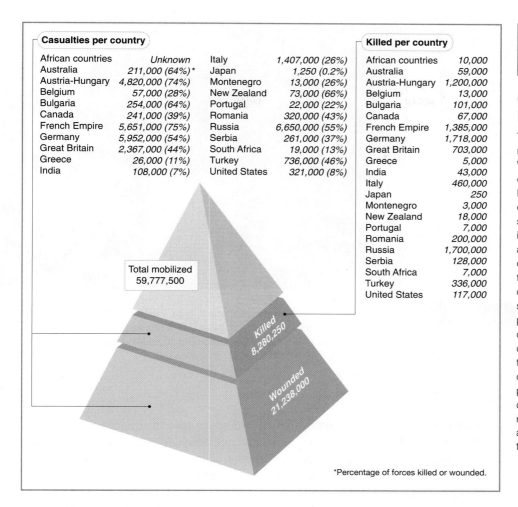

Casualties per country

Country	Casualties	Country	Casualties
African countries	Unknown	Italy	1,407,000 (26%)
Australia	211,000 (64%)*	Japan	1,250 (0.2%)
Austria-Hungary	4,820,000 (74%)	Montenegro	13,000 (26%)
Belgium	57,000 (28%)	New Zealand	73,000 (66%)
Bulgaria	254,000 (64%)	Portugal	22,000 (22%)
Canada	241,000 (39%)	Romania	320,000 (43%)
French Empire	5,651,000 (75%)	Russia	6,650,000 (55%)
Germany	5,952,000 (54%)	Serbia	261,000 (37%)
Great Britain	2,367,000 (44%)	South Africa	19,000 (13%)
Greece	26,000 (11%)	Turkey	736,000 (46%)
India	108,000 (7%)	United States	321,000 (8%)

Killed per country

African countries	10,000
Australia	59,000
Austria-Hungary	1,200,000
Belgium	13,000
Bulgaria	101,000
Canada	67,000
French Empire	1,385,000
Germany	1,718,000
Great Britain	703,000
Greece	5,000
India	43,000
Italy	460,000
Japan	250
Montenegro	3,000
New Zealand	18,000
Portugal	7,000
Romania	200,000
Russia	1,700,000
Serbia	128,000
South Africa	7,000
Turkey	336,000
United States	117,000

Total mobilized
59,777,500

Killed
8,280,250

Wounded
21,238,000

*Percentage of forces killed or wounded.

GLOBAL COMPARISON

Casualties of the First World War

There is no agreement about the number of casualties in World War I. Record keeping in many countries was only rudimentary. Moreover, the destructive nature of the war meant that countless soldiers were wholly obliterated or instantly buried. However approximate, these figures make clear that the conflict that raged from 1914 to 1918 was a truly catastrophic world war. Although soldiers came from almost every part of the globe, the human devastation was not evenly distributed. Which country suffered the most casualties? Which country lost the greatest percentage of its soldiers? What do you think was the principal reason that the United States lost a smaller percentage of its soldiers than most other nations lost?

noting that "the Americans' nerves are not yet worn out." Indeed, it was German morale that was on the verge of cracking.

In the summer of 1918, the Allies launched a massive counteroffensive that would end the war. A quarter of a million U.S. troops joined in the rout of German forces along the Marne River. In September, more than a million Americans took part in the assault that threw the Germans back from positions along the Meuse River. In November, a revolt against the German government sent Kaiser Wilhelm II fleeing to Holland. On November 11, 1918, a delegation from the newly established German republic met with the French high command to sign an armistice that brought the fighting to an end.

By the end, 112,000 AEF soldiers perished from wounds and disease, while another 230,000 Americans suffered casualties but survived. European nations, however, suffered much greater losses. (See "Global Comparison.") Where they had fought, the landscape was as blasted and barren as the moon.

QUICK REVIEW <

How did the American Expeditionary Force contribute to the defeat of Germany?

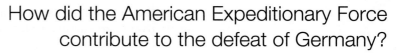

| What role did the United States play in World War I? | What impact did the war have on the home front? | What part did Woodrow Wilson play in the Paris peace conference? | Why was America's transition from war to peace so turbulent? | Conclusion: What was the domestic cost of foreign victory? |

> What impact did the war have on the home front?

Women's Liberty Bell Suffragists in Pennsylvania made great efforts to get their message out to rural people. This life-size replica of the Liberty Bell in Philadelphia, which suffragists called the Women's Liberty Bell or the Justice Bell, toured country roads on a specially reinforced truck. Historical Society of Pennsylvania.

MANY PROGRESSIVES HOPED that war would improve the quality of American life as well as free Europe from tyranny and militarism. Mobilization helped propel the crusades for woman suffrage and prohibition to success. Progressives enthusiastically channeled industrial and agricultural production into the war effort. Labor shortages caused by workers' entering the military provided new opportunities for women in the booming wartime economy. With labor at a premium, unionized workers gained higher pay and shorter hours. To instill loyalty in Americans whose ancestry was rooted in the belligerent nations, Wilson launched a campaign to foster patriotism. But boosting patriotism led to suppressing dissent. When the government launched a harsh assault on civil liberties, mobs gained license to attack those whom they considered disloyal. Democracy took a beating at home when the nation undertook its foreign crusade for democracy.

The Progressive Stake in the War

The idea of the war as an agent of national improvement fanned the zeal of the progressive movement. The Wilson administration, realizing that the federal government would have to assert greater control to mobilize the nation's human and physical resources, created new agencies charged with managing the war effort. Bernard Baruch headed the War Industries Board, created to stimulate and direct industrial production. Baruch brought industrial management and labor together into a team that produced everything from boots to bullets and made U.S. troops the best-equipped soldiers in the world.

Herbert Hoover headed the Food Administration. He led remarkably successful "Hooverizing" campaigns for "meatless" Mondays and "wheatless"

CHAPTER LOCATOR | What was Woodrow Wilson's foreign policy agenda?

Wednesdays and other ways of conserving resources. Guaranteed high prices, the American heartland not only supplied the needs of U.S. citizens and armed forces but also became the breadbasket of America's allies. As the war went on, wartime agencies multiplied.

Wartime Agencies

Railroad Administration	Directed railroad traffic
Fuel Administration	Coordinated the coal industry and other fuel suppliers
Shipping Board	Organized the merchant marine
National War Labor Policies Board	Resolved labor disputes

Some progressives, however, refused to accept the argument that war and reform marched together. Wisconsin senator Robert La Follette attacked the war unrelentingly, claiming that Wilson's promises of peace and democracy were a case of "the blind leading the blind" at home and abroad.

Industrial leaders found that wartime agencies enforced efficiency and helped corporate profits triple. Some working people also had cause to celebrate. Mobilization meant high prices for farmers and plentiful jobs at high wages in the new war industries. Because increased industrial production required peaceful labor relations, the National War Labor Policies Board enacted the eight-hour day, a living minimum wage, and collective bargaining rights in some industries. Wages rose sharply during the war (as did prices), and the American Federation of Labor (AFL) saw its membership soar from 2.7 million to more than 5 million.

The war also provided a huge boost to the crusade to ban alcohol. By 1917, prohibitionists had convinced nineteen states to go dry. Liquor's opponents now argued that banning alcohol would make the cause of democracy powerful and pure. At the same time, shutting down the distilleries would save millions of bushels of grain that could feed the United States and its allies. "Shall the many have food or the few drink?" the drys asked. In December 1917, Congress passed the **Eighteenth Amendment**, which banned the manufacture, transportation, and sale of alcohol. After swift ratification by the states, the amendment went into effect on January 1, 1920.

Women, War, and the Battle for Suffrage

Women had made real strides during the Progressive Era, but war presented new opportunities. More than 25,000 women served in France. About half were nurses. The others drove ambulances; ran canteens for the Salvation Army, Red Cross, and YMCA; worked with French civilians in devastated areas; and acted as telephone operators and war correspondents. Like men who joined the war effort, they believed that they were taking part in a great national venture. "I am more than willing to live as a soldier and know of the hardships I would have to undergo," one canteen worker declared when applying to go overseas, "but I want to help my country. . . . I want . . . to do the *real* work." And like men, women struggled against disillusionment in France. One woman explained: "Over in America, we thought we knew something about the war . . . but when you get

CHRONOLOGY

1915
– Women's Peace Party is formed.

1917
– War Industries Board is formed.
– Committee on Public Information is created.
– Congress passes Eighteenth Amendment, banning the manufacture and sale of alcohol in the United States.

1917–1918
– The Espionage Act, the Trading with the Enemy Act, and the Sedition Act give the government sweeping powers to suppress opposition to the war.

1918
– Republicans gain majority in House and Senate.

1919
– Congress passes Nineteenth Amendment, extending suffrage to women.

1920
– **January 1.** Prohibition begins.
– **August.** Nineteenth Amendment is ratified.

Eighteenth Amendment
▶ Amendment banning the manufacture, transportation, and sale of alcohol. Congress passed the amendment in December 1917, and it was ratified in January 1920. The war provided a huge boost to the crusade to ban alcohol and was key to the passage of the amendment.

| What role did the United States play in World War I? | What impact did the war have on the home front? | What part did Woodrow Wilson play in the Paris peace conference? | Why was America's transition from war to peace so turbulent? | Conclusion: What was the domestic cost of foreign victory? |

609

here the difference is [like the one between] studying the laws of electricity and being struck by lightning."

At home, long-standing barriers against hiring women fell when millions of workingmen became soldiers and few new immigrant workers crossed the Atlantic. Tens of thousands of women found work in defense plants as welders, metalworkers, and heavy machine operators and with the railroads. A black woman, a domestic before the war, celebrated her job as a laborer in a railroad yard: "We are making more money at this than any work we can get, and we do not have to work as hard as at housework which requires us to be on duty from six o'clock in the morning until nine or ten at night, with might[y] little time off and at very poor wages." Other women found white-collar work. Between 1910 and 1920, the number of women clerks doubled. Before the war ended, more than a million women had found work in war industries.

The most dramatic advance for women came in the political arena. Adopting a state-by-state approach, suffragists had achieved some success, but before 1910 only four small western states had adopted woman suffrage (**Map 22.4**). Elsewhere, voting rights for women met strong hostility and defeat. After 1910, suffrage leaders added a federal campaign to amend the Constitution, targeting Congress and the president, to the traditional state-by-state strategy for suffrage.

The radical wing of the suffragists, led by Alice Paul, picketed the White House, where the marchers unfurled banners that proclaimed "America Is Not a Democracy. Twenty Million Women Are Denied the Right to Vote." They chained themselves to fences and went to jail, where many engaged in hunger strikes. "They seem bent on making their cause as obnoxious as possible," Woodrow Wilson declared. But membership in the mainstream organization, the National American Woman Suffrage Association (NAWSA), led by Carrie Chapman Catt, soared to some two million members. The NAWSA even accepted African American

Full voting with effective date	Partial voting rights for women (presidential vote in all; local, county vote in some)	No voting rights for women

MAP 22.4 ■ Women's Voting Rights before the Nineteenth Amendment
The long campaign for women's voting rights reversed the pioneer epic that moved from east to west. From its first successes in the new democratic West, suffrage rolled eastward toward the entrenched, male-dominated public life of the Northeast and South.

CHAPTER LOCATOR | What was Woodrow Wilson's foreign policy agenda?

CHAPTER 22
610 THE UNITED STATES IN WORLD WAR I, 1914–1920

women into its ranks, though not on an equal basis. Seeing the handwriting on the wall, the Republican and Progressive parties endorsed woman suffrage in 1916.

In 1918, Wilson gave his support to suffrage, calling the amendment "vital to the winning of the war." He conceded that it would be wrong not to reward the wartime "partnership of suffering and sacrifice" with a "partnership of privilege and right." By linking their cause to the wartime emphasis on national unity, the advocates of woman suffrage finally triumphed. In 1919, Congress passed the **Nineteenth Amendment**, granting women the vote, and by August 1920, the required two-thirds of the states had ratified it.

Rally around the Flag—or Else

When Congress committed the nation to war, most peace advocates rallied around the flag. The Carnegie Endowment for International Peace adopted new stationery with the heading "Peace through Victory" and issued a resolution saying that "the most effectual means of promoting peace is to prosecute the war against the Imperial German Government."

Only a handful of reformers resisted the tide of patriotism. A group of professional women, led by settlement house leader Jane Addams and economics professor Emily Greene Balch, denounced what Addams described as "the pathetic belief in the regenerative results of war." The Women's Peace Party that emerged in 1915 and its foreign affiliates in the Women's International League for Peace and Freedom led the struggle to persuade governments to negotiate peace and spare dissenters from harsh punishment. After America entered the conflict, advocates for peace were routinely labeled cowards and traitors.

To suppress criticism of the war, Wilson stirred up patriotic fervor. In 1917, the president created the Committee on Public Information under the direction of George Creel. Creel sent "Four-Minute Men," a squad of 75,000 volunteers, around the country to give brief pep talks that celebrated successes on the battlefields and in the factories. Posters, pamphlets, and cartoons depicted brave American soldiers and sailors defending freedom and democracy against the evil "Huns," the derogatory nickname applied to German soldiers. America rallied around Creel's campaign. The film industry produced pro-war movies and taught audiences to hiss at the German kaiser. A musical, *The Kaiser: The Beast of Berlin*, opened on Broadway in 1918. Colleges and universities generated war propaganda in the guise of scholarship. When Professor James McKeen Cattell of Columbia University urged that America seek peace with Germany short of victory, university president Nicholas Murray Butler fired him on the grounds that "what had been folly is now treason."

Across the nation, "100% American" campaigns enlisted ordinary people to sniff out disloyalty. German, the most widely taught foreign language in 1914, practically disappeared from the nation's schools. Targeting German-born Americans, the *Saturday Evening Post* declared that it was time to rid the country of

Nineteenth Amendment

▶ Amendment granting women the vote. Congress passed the amendment in 1919, and it was ratified in August 1920. Like proponents of prohibition, the advocates of woman suffrage triumphed by linking their cause to the war.

D. W. Griffith's *Hearts of the World*

Hollywood joined the government's efforts to stir up rage against the Germans. In a 1918 film made by D. W. Griffith for the British and French governments, a hulking German is about to whip a defenseless farm woman. Library of Congress.

| What role did the United States play in World War I? | **What impact did the war have on the home front?** | What part did Woodrow Wilson play in the Paris peace conference? | Why was America's transition from war to peace so turbulent? | Conclusion: What was the domestic cost of foreign victory? |

"the scum of the melting pot." Anti-German action reached its extreme with the lynching of Robert Prager, a German-born baker with socialist leanings. Persuaded by the defense lawyer who praised what he called a "patriotic murder," the jury at the trial of the killers took only twenty-five minutes to acquit.

As hysteria increased, the campaign reached absurd levels. In Montana, a school board barred a history text that had good things to say about medieval Germany. Menus across the nation changed German toast to French toast and sauerkraut to liberty cabbage. In Milwaukee, vigilantes mounted a machine gun outside the Pabst Theater to prevent the staging of Schiller's *Wilhelm Tell*, a powerful protest against tyranny.

The Wilson administration's zeal in suppressing dissent contrasted sharply with its war aims of defending democracy. In the name of self-defense, the Espionage Act (June 1917), the Trading with the Enemy Act (October 1917), and the Sedition Act (May 1918) gave the government sweeping powers to punish any opinion or activity it considered "disloyal, profane, scurrilous, or abusive." When Postmaster General Albert Burleson blocked mailing privileges for dissenting publications, dozens of journals were forced to close down. Of the fifteen hundred individuals eventually charged with sedition, all but a dozen had merely spoken words the government found objectionable. One of them was Eugene V. Debs, the leader of the Socialist Party, who was convicted under the Espionage Act for speeches condemning the war as a capitalist plot and was sent to the Atlanta penitentiary.

The president hoped that national commitment to the war would silence partisan politics, but his Republican rivals used the war as a weapon against the Democrats. Republicans outshouted Wilson on the nation's need to mobilize for war but then complained that Wilson's War Industries Board crushed free enterprise. Such attacks appealed to widely diverse business, labor, and patriotic groups. As the war progressed, Republicans gathered power against the Democrats, who had narrowly reelected Wilson in 1916.

In 1918, Republicans gained a narrow majority in both the House and Senate. The end of Democratic control of Congress not only halted further domestic reform but also meant that the United States would advance toward military victory in Europe with political power divided between a Democratic president and a Republican Congress likely to challenge Wilson's plans for international cooperation.

> **QUICK REVIEW**

How did progressive ideals fare during wartime?

CHAPTER LOCATOR | What was Woodrow Wilson's foreign policy agenda?

CHAPTER 22

612 THE UNITED STATES IN WORLD WAR I, 1914–1920

Leaders of the Paris Peace Conference

The three leaders in charge of putting the world back together after the Great War—from left to right, David Lloyd George, prime minister of Great Britain; Georges Clemenceau, premier of France; and U.S. president Woodrow Wilson—amiably and confidently stride toward the peace conference at the Versailles palace. Gamma Liaison.

What part did Woodrow Wilson play in the Paris peace conference?

WILSON DECIDED TO REAFFIRM his noble war ideals by announcing his peace aims before the end of hostilities. He hoped the victorious Allies would adopt his plan for international democracy, but he was sorely disappointed. America's allies understood that Wilson's principles jeopardized their own postwar plans for the acquisition of enemy territory, new colonial empires, and reparations. Wilson also faced strong opposition at home from those who feared that his enthusiasm for international cooperation would undermine American sovereignty.

Wilson's Fourteen Points

On January 8, 1918, President Wilson revealed to Congress his **Fourteen Points**, his blueprint for a new democratic world order. The first five points affirmed basic liberal ideals: an end to secret treaties; freedom of the seas; removal of economic barriers to free trade; reduction of weapons of war; and recognition of the rights of colonized peoples. The next eight points supported the right to self-determination of European peoples who had been dominated by Germany or its allies. Wilson's fourteenth point called for a "general association of nations"—a **League of Nations**—to provide "mutual guarantees of political independence and territorial integrity to great and small states alike." Only such an organization of "peace-loving nations," he believed, could justify the war and secure a lasting peace. During the final year of the war, he pressured the Allies to accept the Fourteen Points as the basis of the postwar settlement.

Fourteen Points
▶ Woodrow Wilson's plan, first put forward in January 1918, for achieving a lasting postwar peace. Wilson's plan affirmed basic liberal ideals, supported the right to self-determination, and called for the creation of a League of Nations. Wilson was forced to compromise on his plan at the 1919 Paris peace conference, and the U.S. Senate refused to ratify the resulting treaty.

League of Nations
▶ Woodrow Wilson's vision of an international association of nations that would support democracy around the world and maintain the peace. The League of Nations was the key element in Wilson's Fourteen Points, put forward in 1918. Wilson, however, was unable to overcome opposition to the league in the Senate, and the United States never became a member.

| What role did the United States play in World War I? | What impact did the war have on the home front? | **What part did Woodrow Wilson play in the Paris peace conference?** | Why was America's transition from war to peace so turbulent? | Conclusion: What was the domestic cost of foreign victory? |

The Paris Peace Conference

From January 18 to June 28, 1919, the eyes of the world focused on the Paris peace conference. Wilson, inspired by his mission, decided to head the U.S. delegation. He said he owed it to the American soldiers. "It is now my duty," he announced, "to play my full part in making good what they gave their life's blood to obtain." A dubious British diplomat retorted that Wilson was drawn to Paris "as a debutante is entranced by the prospect of her first ball." The decision to leave the country at a time when his political opponents were challenging his leadership was risky enough, but his refusal to include prominent Republicans in the delegation proved foolhardy and eventually cost him his dream of a new world order.

After four terrible years of war, the common people of Europe almost worshipped Wilson, believing that he would create a safer, more decent world. When the peace conference convened at Louis XIV's magnificent palace at Versailles, however, Wilson encountered a different reception. To the Allied leaders, Wilson appeared a naive and impractical moralist. His desire to gather former enemies within a new international democratic order showed how little he understood European realities. Georges Clemenceau, premier of France, claimed that Wilson "believed you could do everything by formulas" and "empty theory." Disparaging the Fourteen Points, he added, "God himself was content with ten commandments."

Allied Leaders at the Paris Peace Conference

United States	Woodrow Wilson
Great Britain	David Lloyd George
France	Georges Clemenceau
Italy	Vittorio Orlando

The Allies wanted to fasten blame for the war on Germany, totally disarm it, and make it pay so dearly that it would never threaten its neighbors again. The French demanded retribution in the form of territory containing Germany's richest mineral resources. The British made it clear that they were not about to give up the powerful weapon of naval blockade for the vague principle of freedom of the seas.

The Allies forced Wilson to make drastic compromises. In return for France's moderating its territorial claims, he agreed to support Article 231 of the peace treaty, assigning war guilt to Germany. Though saved from permanently losing Rhineland territory to the French, Germany was outraged at being singled out as the instigator of the war and saddled with more than $33 billion in damages. Many Germans felt that their nation had been betrayed. After agreeing to an armistice in the belief that peace terms would be based on Wilson's Fourteen Points, they faced hardship and humiliation instead.

Wilson had better success in establishing the principle of self-determination. But from the beginning, Secretary of State Robert Lansing knew that the president's concept of self-determination was "simply loaded with dynamite." Lansing wondered, "What unit has he in mind? Does he mean a race, a territorial area, or a community?" Even Wilson was vague about what self-determination actually meant. "When I gave utterance to those words," he admitted, "I said them without the knowledge that nationalities existed, which are coming to us day after day."

Lansing suspected that the notion "will raise hopes which can never be realized. It will, I fear, cost thousands of lives. In the end it is bound to be discredited, to be called the dream of an idealist who failed to realize the danger until it was too late."

Yet partly on the basis of self-determination, the conference redrew the map of Europe and parts of the rest of the world. Portions of Austria-Hungary were ceded to Italy, Poland, and Romania, and the remainder was reassembled into Austria, Hungary, Czechoslovakia, and Yugoslavia—independent republics whose boundaries were drawn with attention to concentrations of major ethnic groups. More arbitrarily, the Ottoman empire was carved up into small mandates (including Palestine) run by local leaders but under the control of France and Great Britain. The conference reserved the mandate system for those regions it deemed insufficiently "civilized" to have full independence. Thus, the reconstructed nations—each beset with ethnic and nationalist rivalries—faced the challenge of making a new democratic government work (**Map 22.5**). Many of today's bitterest disputes—in the Balkans and Iraq, between Greece and Turkey, between Arabs and Jews—have roots in the decisions made in Paris in 1919.

Wilson hoped that self-determination would also dictate the fate of Germany's colonies in Asia and Africa. But the Allies, which had taken over the colonies during the war, only allowed the League of Nations a mandate to administer them.

MAP 22.5 ■ Europe after World War I
The post–World War I settlement redrew boundaries to create new nations based on ethnic groupings. This outcome left within defeated Germany and Russia bitter peoples who resolved to recover the territory taken from them.

What role did the United States play in World War I?

What impact did the war have on the home front?

What part did Woodrow Wilson play in the Paris peace conference?

Why was America's transition from war to peace so turbulent?

Conclusion: What was the domestic cost of foreign victory?

Technically, the mandate system rejected imperialism, but in reality it allowed the Allies to maintain control. Thus, while denying Germany its colonies, the Allies retained and added to their own empires.

The cause of democratic equality suffered another setback when the peace conference rejected Japan's call for a statement of racial equality in the treaty. Wilson's belief in the superiority of whites, as well as his apprehension about how white Americans would respond to such a declaration, led him to oppose the clause. To soothe hurt feelings, Wilson agreed to grant Japan a mandate over the Shantung Peninsula in northern China, which had formerly been controlled by Germany. The gesture mollified Japan's moderate leaders, but the military faction preparing to take over the country used bitterness toward racist Western colonialism to build support for expanding Japanese power throughout Asia.

Closest to Wilson's heart was finding a new way to manage international relations. In Wilson's view, war had discredited the old strategy of balance of power. Instead, he proposed a League of Nations that would provide collective security. The league would establish rules of international conduct and resolve conflicts between nations through rational and peaceful means. When the Allies agreed to the league, Wilson was overjoyed. He believed that the league would rectify the errors his colleagues had forced on him in Paris.

To some Europeans and Americans, the **Versailles treaty** came as a bitter disappointment. Wilson's admirers were shocked that the president dealt in compromise like any other politician. But without Wilson's presence, the treaty that was signed on June 28, 1919, surely would have been more vindictive. Wilson returned home in July 1919 consoled that, despite his frustrations, he had gained what he most wanted—a League of Nations.

The Fight for the Treaty

The tumultuous reception Wilson received when he arrived home persuaded him, probably correctly, that the American people supported the treaty. When the president submitted the treaty to the Senate in July 1919, he warned that failure to ratify it would "break the heart of the world." By then, however, criticism of the treaty was mounting, especially from Americans convinced that their countries of ethnic origin had not been given fair treatment. Irish Americans, Italian Americans, and German Americans launched especially sharp attacks. Others worried that the president's concessions at Versailles had jeopardized the treaty's capacity to provide a generous plan for rebuilding Europe and to guarantee world peace.

In the Senate, a group of Republican "irreconcilables" condemned the treaty for entangling the United States in world affairs. A larger group of Republicans did not object to American participation in world politics but feared that membership in the League of Nations would jeopardize the nation's ability to act independently. No Republican, in any case, was eager to hand Wilson and the Democrats a foreign policy victory.

At the center of Republican opposition was Wilson's archenemy, Senator **Henry Cabot Lodge** of Massachusetts. Lodge was no isolationist, but he thought that much of the Fourteen Points was a "general bleat about virtue being better than vice." Lodge expected the United States' economic and military power to propel the nation into a major role in world affairs. But he insisted that membership in the League of Nations, which would require collective action to maintain

Versailles treaty
▶ Treaty signed on June 28, 1919, that brought World War I to a formal conclusion. The treaty assigned Germany sole responsibility for the war and saddled it with a debt of $33 billion in war damages. Most Germans felt the terms of the treaty were unduly harsh, and resentment of the treaty laid the foundation for future conflict between Germany and the Allied nations of France and England.

Henry Cabot Lodge
▶ Senator from Massachusetts who in 1919 and 1920 led the opposition to America's membership in the League of Nations. Lodge had a strong personal dislike of Wilson, but he also thought the league would compromise American independence. When Wilson refused to go along with Lodge's amendments to the Versailles treaty, the treaty was doomed to go down to defeat.

CHAPTER LOCATOR | What was Woodrow Wilson's foreign policy agenda?

CHAPTER 22
616 THE UNITED STATES IN WORLD WAR I, 1914–1920

peace, threatened the nation's independence in foreign relations.

With Lodge as its chairman, the Senate Foreign Relations Committee crafted several amendments, or "reservations," that sought to limit the consequences of American membership in the league. For example, several reservations required approval of both the House and Senate before the United States could participate in league-sponsored economic sanctions or military action.

It gradually became clear that ratification of the treaty depended on acceptance of the Lodge reservations. Democratic senators, who overwhelmingly supported the treaty, urged Wilson to accept Lodge's terms, arguing that they left the essentials of the treaty intact. Wilson, however, insisted that the reservations cut "the very heart out of the treaty."

Wilson decided to take his case directly to the people. On September 3, 1919, he set out by train on the most ambitious speaking tour ever undertaken by a president. On September 25 in Pueblo, Colorado, Wilson collapsed and had to return to Washington. There, he suffered a massive stroke that partially paralyzed him. From his bedroom, Wilson sent messages instructing Democrats in the Senate to hold firm against any and all reservations. Wilson commanded enough loyalty to ensure a vote against the Lodge reservations. But when the treaty without reservations came before the Senate in March 1920, the combined opposition of the Republican irreconcilables and reservationists left Wilson six votes short of the two-thirds majority needed for passage.

The nations of Europe organized the League of Nations at Geneva, Switzerland, but the United States never became a member. Whether American membership could have prevented the world war that would begin in Europe in 1939 is highly unlikely, but the United States' failure to join certainly weakened the league from the start. In refusing to accept relatively minor compromises with Senate moderates, Wilson lost his treaty and American membership in the league.

"Refusing to Give the Lady a Seat"

When stiff opposition to American membership in the League of Nations developed in the United States, friends of the league mounted a counterattack. This cartoon skewers the three leading Republican opponents of the league—Senators William Borah of Idaho, Henry Cabot Lodge of Massachusetts, and Hiram Johnson of California—who stubbornly refuse to budge an inch for the angel of peace. Picture Research Consultants & Archives.

QUICK REVIEW ‹

Why did the Senate fail to ratify the Versailles treaty?

What role did the United States play in World War I?

What impact did the war have on the home front?

What part did Woodrow Wilson play in the Paris peace conference?

Why was America's transition from war to peace so turbulent?

Conclusion: What was the domestic cost of foreign victory?

Why was America's transition from war to peace so turbulent?

African Americans Migrate North

This southern family arrived in a new home in an unnamed northern city in 1912. Wearing their Sunday best, family members carried the rest of what they owned in two suitcases. In Chicago, the League on Urban Conditions among Negroes, which eventually became the Urban League, sought to ease the transition of southern blacks to life in the North. Photographs and Prints Division, Schomburg Center for Research in Black Culture, New York Public Library, Astor, Lenox, and Tilden Foundations.

▶ FOR MORE HELP ANALYZING THIS IMAGE, see the visual activity for this chapter in the Online Study Guide at bedfordstmartins.com/roarkunderstanding.

THE DEFEAT OF WILSON'S plan for international democracy proved the crowning blow to progressives who had hoped that the war would boost reform at home. When the war ended, Americans wanted to demobilize swiftly. In the process, servicemen, defense workers, and farmers lost their war-related jobs. The volatile combination—of unemployed veterans returning home, a stalled economy, and leftover wartime patriotism looking for a new cause—threatened to explode.

Economic Hardship and Labor Upheaval

Americans greeted peace with a demand that the United States return to a peacetime economy. The government abruptly abandoned its wartime economic controls and canceled war contracts worth millions of dollars. In a matter of months, more than three million soldiers were mustered out of the military and flooded the job market just as war production ceased. Unemployment soared. At the same time, consumers went on a postwar spending spree that drove inflation skyward. In 1919, prices rose 75 percent over prewar levels, and in 1920 prices rose another 28 percent.

Most of the gains workers had made during the war evaporated. Freed from wartime controls, business turned against the eight-hour day and attacked labor unions. With inflation eating up their paychecks, workers fought back. The year 1919 witnessed nearly 3,600 strikes involving 4 million workers. The most spectacular strike occurred in February 1919 in Seattle, where shipyard workers had been put out of work by demobilization. When a coalition of the radical Industrial Workers of the World (IWW, known as Wobblies) and the moderate American Federation of Labor called a general strike, the largest work stoppage in American history shut down the city. Newspapers claimed that the walkout was "a Bolshevik effort to start a revolution." The suppression of the Seattle general strike by officials cost the AFL many of its wartime gains and contributed to the destruction of the IWW soon afterward.

A strike by Boston policemen in the fall of 1919 underscored postwar hostility toward labor militancy. Although the police were paid less than pick-and-shovel laborers, they won little sympathy. Once the officers stopped walking their beats, looters sacked the city. Massachusetts governor Calvin Coolidge called in the National Guard to restore order. The public, yearning for peace and security in the wake of war, welcomed Coolidge's anti-union assurance that "there is no right to strike against the public safety by anybody, anywhere, any time."

Labor strife climaxed in the steel strike of 1919. Faced with the industry's plan to revert to seven-day weeks, twelve-hour days, and weekly wages of about $20, Samuel Gompers, head of the AFL, called for a strike. In response, 350,000 workers in fifteen states walked out in September 1919. The steel industry hired 30,000 strikebreakers (many of them African Americans) and convinced the public that the strikers were radicals and subversives. In January 1920, after eighteen striking workers were killed, the strike collapsed. That defeat initiated a sharp decline in the fortunes of the labor movement, a trend that would continue for almost twenty years.

The Red Scare

Suppression of labor strikes was one response to the widespread fear of internal subversion that swept the nation in 1919. The **Red scare** ("Red" referred to the color of the Bolshevik flag) had homegrown causes: the postwar recession, labor unrest, and the difficulties of reintegrating millions of returning veterans. But unsettling events abroad also added to Americans' anxieties.

Russian bolshevism became even more menacing in March 1919, when the new Soviet leaders created the Comintern, a worldwide association of Communist leaders intent on fomenting revolution in capitalist countries. A Communist revolution in the United States was extremely unlikely, but edgy Americans faced with a flurry of terrorist acts, most notably thirty-eight bombs mailed to prominent individuals, believed otherwise. Attorney General A. Mitchell Palmer launched a hunt to find terrorists. Targeting men and women who harbored ideas that Palmer believed could lead to violence, even though the individuals may not have done anything illegal, the Justice Department sought to purge the supposed enemies of America.

In January 1920, Palmer ordered a series of raids that netted 6,000 alleged subversives. Finding no revolutionary conspiracies, Palmer nevertheless ordered 500 noncitizen suspects deported. His action came in the wake of a campaign against the most notorious radical alien, Russian-born Emma Goldman. Before the war, Goldman's support of labor strikes, women's rights, and birth control had made her a symbol of radicalism. Finally, after a stay in prison for attacking military conscription, she was ordered deported by J. Edgar Hoover, the director of

CHRONOLOGY

1910–1920
- Mexican-born population in the United States more than doubles.

1915–1920
- Ten percent of the South's black population migrates north.

1919
- Prices rise 75 percent over prewar levels.
- Wave of labor strikes sweeps the country.
- The Red scare—fear of internal subversion and Russian bolshevism—engulfs the country.
- *Schenck v. United States* establishes a "clear and present danger" test for war resisters.

1920
- **November.** Republican Warren G. Harding is elected president.

Red scare

► The widespread fear of internal subversion that swept the nation in 1919. The Red scare had many domestic causes: the postwar recession, labor unrest, and the difficulties of reintegrating millions of returning veterans. It was also stimulated by the creation of the Comintern by Soviet leaders in March 1919. The Red scare resulted in widespread suppression of dissent, carried out by both private citizens and government officials.

| What role did the United States play in World War I? | What impact did the war have on the home front? | What part did Woodrow Wilson play in the Paris peace conference? | **Why was America's transition from war to peace so turbulent?** | Conclusion: What was the domestic cost of foreign victory? |

Emma Goldman Is Deported

In the fall of 1919, federal agents arrested hundreds of "Bolsheviks" whom they considered a "menace to law and order." In December 1919, anarchist Emma Goldman and some 250 others were deported to Soviet Russia.
© Bettmann/Corbis.

the Justice Department's Radical Division. In December 1919, Goldman and some 250 others boarded a ship for exile in Russia.

The effort to rid the country of alien radicals was matched by efforts to crush troublesome citizens. Law enforcement officials and vigilante groups joined hands against so-called Reds. In November 1919 in the lumber town of Centralia, Washington, a menacing crowd gathered in front of the IWW hall. Nervous Wobblies inside opened fire, killing three people. Three IWW members were arrested and later convicted of murder, but another, ex-soldier Wesley Everett, was carried off by the mob, which castrated him, hung him from a bridge, and then riddled his body with bullets. His death was officially ruled a suicide.

Public institutions joined the attack on civil liberties. Local libraries removed dissenting books. Schools fired unorthodox teachers. Police shut down radical newspapers. State legislatures refused to seat elected representatives who professed socialist ideas. And in 1919, Congress removed its lone socialist representative, Victor Berger, on the pretext that he was a threat to national safety.

That same year, the Supreme Court provided a formula for restricting free speech. In upholding the conviction of socialist Charles Schenck for publishing a pamphlet urging resistance to the draft during wartime (*Schenck v. United States*), the Court established a "clear and present danger" test. Such utterances as Schenck's during a time of national peril, Justice Oliver Wendell Holmes wrote, were equivalent to shouting "Fire!" in a crowded theater.

In time, the Red scare lost credibility, especially after Attorney General Palmer warned in 1920 that radicals were planning to celebrate the Bolshevik Revolution with a nationwide wave of violence. Officials called out state militias, mobilized bomb squads, and even placed machine-gun nests at major city intersections. When May 1 came and went without a single disturbance, the public mood turned from fear to scorn. The Red scare collapsed as a result of its excesses.

The Great Migrations of African Americans and Mexicans

Before the Red scare lost steam, the government raised alarms about the loyalty of African Americans. A Justice Department investigation concluded that Reds were fomenting racial unrest among blacks. Although the report was wrong about Bolshevik influence, it was correct in noticing a new assertiveness among African Americans.

In 1900, nine of every ten blacks still lived in the South, where poverty, disfranchisement, segregation, and violence dominated their lives. Whites remained committed to keeping blacks down. "If we own a good farm or horse, or cow, or bird-dog, or yoke of oxen," a black sharecropper in Mississippi observed in 1913, "we are harassed until we are bound to sell, give away, or run away, before we can have any peace in our lives."

The First World War provided African Americans with new opportunities. War channeled almost five million American workers into military service and all but ended European immigration. Deprived of their traditional sources of laborers just as production demands were increasing, northern industrialists turned to black labor. From 1915 to 1920, half a million blacks (approximately 10 percent of the South's black population) boarded trains bound for Philadelphia, Detroit, Cleveland, Chicago, St. Louis, and other industrial cities.

Thousands of migrants wrote home to tell family and friends about their experiences in the North. One man announced proudly that he had recently been promoted to "first assistant to the head carpenter." He added, "I should have been here twenty years ago. I just begin to feel like a man. . . . My children are going to the same school with the whites and I don't have to [h]umble to no one. I have registered—will vote the next election and there ain't any 'yes sir'—it's all yes and no and Sam and Bill."

But the North was not the promised land. Black men stood on the lowest rungs of the labor ladder. Jobs of any kind proved scarce for black women, and most worked as domestic servants as they did in the South. The existing black middle class sometimes shunned the less educated, less sophisticated rural southerners crowding into northern cities. Many whites, fearful of losing jobs and status, lashed out against the new migrants. Savage race riots ripped through two dozen northern cities. In 1918, the nation witnessed ninety-six lynchings of blacks, some of them returning war veterans still in uniform.

Still, most black migrants stayed in the North and encouraged friends and family to follow. By 1940, more than one million blacks had left the South, profoundly changing their own lives and the course of the nation's history. Black enclaves such as Harlem in New York and the South Side of Chicago emerged in the North. These assertive communities provided a foundation for black protest and political organization in the years ahead.

At nearly the same time, another migration was under way in the American Southwest. Between 1910 and 1920, the Mexican-born population in the United States soared from 222,000 to 478,000. Mexican immigration resulted from developments on both sides of the border. When Mexicans revolted against dictator Porfirio Díaz in 1910, initiating a ten-year civil war, migrants flooded northward. In the United States, the Chinese Exclusion Act of 1882 and later the disruption of World War I cut off the supply of cheap foreign labor and caused western employers in the expanding rail, mining, construction, and agricultural industries to look south to Mexico for workers. By 1920, ethnic Mexicans made up about three-fourths of California's farm laborers. They were also crucial to the Texas economy, accounting for three-fourths of laborers in the cotton fields and in construction there.

Like immigrants from Europe and black migrants from the South, Mexicans in the American Southwest dreamed of a better life. And like the others, they found both opportunity and disappointment. Wages were better than in Mexico, but life in the fields, mines, and factories was hard, and living conditions often were dismal. Signs warning "No Mexicans Allowed" increased rather than declined. Among Mexican Americans, some of whom had lived in the Southwest for a

Mexican Women Arriving in El Paso, 1911

These Mexican women, carrying bundles and wearing traditional shawls, try to get their bearings upon arriving in El Paso, Texas—the Ellis Island for Mexican immigrants. Women like them found work in the cotton and sugar beet fields, canneries, and restaurants of the Southwest, as well as at home taking in sewing, laundry, and boarders. Courtesy of the Rio Grande Historical Collections, New Mexico State University, Las Cruces, New Mexico.

| What role did the United States play in World War I? | What impact did the war have on the home front? | What part did Woodrow Wilson play in the Paris peace conference? | **Why was America's transition from war to peace so turbulent?** | Conclusion: What was the domestic cost of foreign victory? |

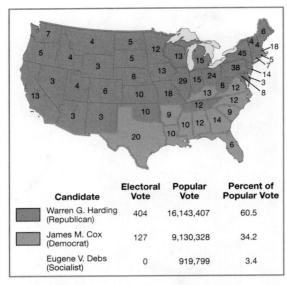

Candidate	Electoral Vote	Popular Vote	Percent of Popular Vote
Warren G. Harding (Republican)	404	16,143,407	60.5
James M. Cox (Democrat)	127	9,130,328	34.2
Eugene V. Debs (Socialist)	0	919,799	3.4

MAP 22.6 ■ The Election of 1920

century or more, *los recien llegados* (the recent arrivals) encountered mixed reactions. One Mexican American expressed this ambivalence: "We are all Mexicans anyway because the *gueros* [Anglos] treat us all alike." But he also called for immigration quotas because the recent arrivals drove down wages and incited white prejudice that affected all ethnic Mexicans.

Despite friction, large-scale immigration into the Southwest meant a resurgence of the Mexican cultural presence, which became the basis for greater solidarity and political action for the ethnic Mexican population. In 1929, Mexican Americans formed the League of United Latin American Citizens in Texas.

Postwar Politics and the Election of 1920

A thousand miles away in Washington, D.C., President Woodrow Wilson, bedridden and paralyzed, ignored the country's many domestic troubles and insisted that the 1920 election would be a "solemn referendum" on the League of Nations. Dutifully, the Democratic nominees for president, James M. Cox of Ohio, and for vice president, Franklin Delano Roosevelt of New York, campaigned on Wilson's international ideals. The Republican Party chose the handsome, gregarious Warren Gamaliel Harding, senator from Ohio. Harding's rise in Ohio politics was a tribute to his amiability, not his mastery of the issues.

Harding found the winning formula when he declared that "America's present need is not heroics, but healing; not nostrums [questionable remedies] but normalcy." But what was "normalcy"? Harding explained: "By 'normalcy' I don't mean the old order but a regular steady order of things. I mean normal procedure, the natural way, without excess." Eager to put wartime crusades and postwar strife behind them, voters responded by giving Harding the largest presidential victory ever: 60.5 percent of the popular vote and 404 out of 531 electoral votes (**MAP 22.6**). Once in office, Harding and his wife, Florence, threw open the White House gates, which had been closed since the declaration of war in 1917. Their welcome brought throngs of visitors and lifted the national pall, signaling a new, more easygoing era.

> **QUICK REVIEW**

How did the Red scare contribute to the erosion of civil liberties after the war?

CHAPTER LOCATOR | What was Woodrow Wilson's foreign policy agenda?

CHAPTER 22
622 THE UNITED STATES IN WORLD WAR I, 1914–1920

National Archives.

Conclusion: What was the domestic cost of foreign victory?

AMERICA'S EXPERIENCE IN WORLD WAR I was exceptional. For much of the world, the Great War produced great destruction, acres of blackened fields, ruined factories, and millions of casualties. But in the United States, war and prosperity marched hand in hand. America emerged from the war with the strongest economy in the world and a position of international preeminence.

Still, the nation paid a heavy price both at home and abroad. American soldiers and sailors encountered unprecedented horrors—submarines, poison gas, machine guns— and more than 100,000 died. On Memorial Day 1919, at the Argonne Cemetery, where 14,200 Americans lie, General John J. Pershing said: "It is not for us to proclaim what they did, their silence speaks more eloquently than words, but it is for us to uphold the conception of duty, honor and country for which they fought and for which they died. It is for the living to carry forward their purpose and make fruitful their sacrifice." Rather than redeeming their sacrifice, however, as Wilson promised, the peace that followed the armistice tarnished it. At home, rather than permanently improving working conditions, advancing public health, and spreading educational opportunity, as progressives had hoped, the war threatened to undermine the achievements of the previous two decades. Moreover, rather than promoting democracy in the United States, the war bred fear, intolerance, and repression that led to a crackdown on dissent and a demand for conformity. Reformers could count only woman suffrage as a permanent victory.

Woodrow Wilson had promised more than anyone could deliver. Progressive hopes of extending democracy and liberal reform nationally and internationally were dashed. In 1920, a bruised and disillusioned society stumbled into a new decade. The era coming to an end had called on Americans to crusade and to sacrifice. The new era promised peace, prosperity, and a good time.

Beat back the HUN *with* LIBERTY BONDS

SO NOW YOU KNOW

Not only did menus across the United States change the name of German toast to French toast, but some people also expressed their anger toward Germany and political dissidents in ways that at times included violence. Rather than promoting democracy and freedom at home, World War I bred fear, intolerance, and repression and justified demands for conformity and the erosion of civil liberties.

> CHAPTER 22 STUDY GUIDE

Online Study Guide
bedfordstmartins.com/roarkunderstanding

STEP 1 GETTING STARTED

Below are basic terms from this period in American history. Can you identify each term below and explain why it matters? To do this exercise online or to download this chart, visit bedfordstmartins.com/roarkunderstanding.

TERM	WHO OR WHAT & WHEN	WHY IT MATTERS
U-boats, p. 602		
Zimmermann telegram, p. 603		
John "Black Jack" Pershing, p. 605		
Eighteenth Amendment, p. 609		
Nineteenth Amendment, p. 611		
Fourteen Points, p. 613		
League of Nations, p. 613		
Versailles treaty, p. 616		
Henry Cabot Lodge, p. 616		
Red scare, p. 619		

STEP 2 MOVING BEYOND THE BASICS

The exercise below represents a more advanced understanding of the chapter material. Use the following chart to describe the United States' entry into the war and to list government initiatives in three areas: wartime agencies, legislation, and propaganda. When you are finished, assess the overall effects of the government's efforts. Was the government able to harness the economy to the war effort? Did the public come to support the war? How did the various tools at the government's disposal contribute to the war effort? Finally, reflect on the costs of the government's domestic war policies. How much damage was done to civil liberties? To do this exercise online or to download this chart, visit bedfordstmartins.com/roarkunderstanding.

	Description or list	Reasons for	Effects of
U.S. entry into World War I			
Wartime agencies			
Legislation			
Propaganda			

Now that you have reviewed key elements of the chapter, take a step back and try to explain the big picture. Remember to use specific examples from the chapter in your answers. To do this exercise online, visit bedfordstmartins.com/roarkunderstanding.

STEP 3

PUTTING IT ALL TOGETHER

THE PATH TO WAR

▶ Describe Woodrow Wilson's foreign policy during his first term in office. How did Wilson see the relationship between the United States and the rest of the world?

▶ Is it fair to describe the American people as "isolationist" prior to America's entry into World War I? Why or why not?

THE HOME FRONT

▶ How did the war affect the progressive agenda? How did progressives use the war to achieve their goals?

▶ To what extent did U.S. participation in World War I involve the domestic efforts of the American people?

A TROUBLED PEACE

▶ What vision did Wilson have of the postwar world? Why did the Senate refuse to endorse his vision, as embodied in the Treaty of Versailles?

▶ What led to the Red scare, and why did it eventually subside?

LOOKING BACKWARD, LOOKING AHEAD

▶ Why did a majority of Americans initially oppose the country's entry into World War I? What events and experiences in the country's past helped shape prewar public opinion?

▶ How did World War I change the place of the United States in the world? What role in world affairs was America poised to take as it entered the 1920s?

IN YOUR OWN WORDS

Imagine that you must explain chapter 22 to someone who hasn't read it. What would be the most important points to include and why?

23
FROM NEW ERA TO GREAT DEPRESSION

1920–1932

> This chapter examines the central place of business in 1920s society, the policies of the Republican administrations, the key cultural trends and conflicts of the decade, and the events that led to the collapse of the American economy. Finally, this chapter addresses the failure of government to adequately respond to the human toll of economic catastrophe.

> How did big business shape the New Era of the 1920s?

> In what ways did the Roaring Twenties challenge traditional values?

> Why did the divide between rural and urban America grow in the 1920s?

> What caused the crash of 1929?

> What was life like in the early years of the depression?

> Conclusion: Why did the hope of the 1920s turn to despair?

DID YOU KNOW?

By 1929, more than 80 million people went to the movies every week, as many as lived in the entire United States.

"Sheik with Sheba." Cover of *Judge* magazine, by A. John Held, Jr.

> How did big business shape the New Era of the 1920s?

Henry and Edsel Ford

In this 1924 photograph, Henry Ford looks fondly at his first car while his son, Edsel, stands next to the ten millionth Model T. Henry Ford Museum and Greenfield Village.

ONCE WOODROW WILSON left the White House, energy flowed away from civic reform and toward private economic endeavor. The rise of a freewheeling economy and a heightened sense of individualism caused Secretary of Commerce Herbert Hoover to declare that America had entered a "New Era," one of many labels used to describe the complex 1920s.

America in the twenties was many things, but President Calvin Coolidge got at an essential truth when he declared, "The business of America is business." Politicians and diplomats proclaimed business the heart of American civilization. Average men and women bought into the idea that business and its products were what made America great, as they snatched up the flood of new consumer items American factories sent forth.

A Business Government

Republicans controlled the White House from 1921 to 1933. The first of the three Republican presidents was Warren Gamaliel Harding, the Ohio senator who in his 1920 campaign called for a "return to normalcy," by which he meant the end of public crusades and a return to private pursuits. Harding promised a government run by the best minds, and he appointed a few men of real stature to his cabinet, including Herbert Hoover, who became secretary of commerce. But wealth and friendship also counted. Andrew Mellon, one of the richest men in

CHAPTER LOCATOR | How did big business shape the New Era of the 1920s?

America, became secretary of the treasury, and Harding handed out jobs to members of his old "Ohio gang," whose only qualification was their friendship. This curious combination of merit and cronyism made for a disjointed administration.

When Harding was elected in 1920 (see chapter 22, Map 22.6), the unemployment rate hit 20 percent, the highest ever up to that point. Farmers fared the worst; their bankruptcy rate increased tenfold. Harding pushed measures to regain national prosperity—high tariffs to protect American businesses, price supports for agriculture, and the dismantling of wartime government control over industry in favor of unregulated private business. "Never before, here or anywhere else," the U.S. Chamber of Commerce said proudly, "has a government been so completely fused with business."

Harding's policies to boost American enterprise made him very popular, but ultimately his small-town congeniality and trusting ways did him in. Some of his friends in the Ohio gang were up to their necks in lawbreaking. Three of Harding's appointees would go to jail. Interior Secretary Albert Fall was convicted of accepting bribes of more than $400,000 for leasing oil reserves on public land in Teapot Dome, Wyoming, and "Teapot Dome" became a synonym for political corruption.

On August 2, 1923, when the fifty-eight-year-old Harding died from a heart attack, Vice President Calvin Coolidge became president. Coolidge once expressed his belief that "the man who builds a factory builds a temple, the man who works there worships there." Reverence for free enterprise meant that Coolidge continued and extended Harding's policies of promoting business and limiting government. Secretary of the Treasury Andrew Mellon reduced the government's control over the economy and cut taxes for corporations and wealthy individuals. New rules for the Federal Trade Commission severely limited its power to regulate business. Secretary of Commerce Herbert Hoover limited government authority by encouraging trade associations that ideally would keep business honest and efficient through voluntary cooperation.

Coolidge found an ally in the Supreme Court. The Court ruled against closed shops—businesses where only union members could be employed—while confirming the right of owners to form exclusive trade associations. In 1923, the Court declared unconstitutional the District of Columbia's minimum-wage law for women, asserting that the law interfered with the freedom of employer and employee to make labor contracts. The Court and the president attacked government intrusion in the free market, even when the prohibition of government regulation threatened the welfare of workers.

The election of 1924 confirmed the defeat of the progressive principle that the state should take a leading role in ensuring the general welfare. To oppose Coolidge, the Democrats nominated John W. Davis, a corporate lawyer whose conservative views differed little from Republican principles. Only the Progressive Party and its presidential nominee, Senator Robert La Follette of Wisconsin, offered a genuine alternative. When La Follette championed labor unions, regulation of business, and protection of civil liberties, Republicans coined the slogan "Coolidge or Chaos." Turning their backs on what they considered labor radicalism and reckless reform, voters chose Coolidge in a landslide. Coolidge was right when he declared, "This is a business country, and it wants a business

CHRONOLOGY

1920
- Republican Warren G. Harding is elected president.

1922
- Teapot Dome scandal shakes Harding's administration.
- Five-Power Naval Treaty reduces the naval forces of Britain, France, Japan, Italy, and the United States.

1923
- Harding dies; Vice President Calvin Coolidge becomes president.

1924
- Coolidge is elected president.
- Dawes Plan lowers reparation payments and provides for loans for Germany.

1928
- In the Kellogg-Briand pact, nearly fifty nations pledge to renounce war.

1929
- One in four American jobs is linked to the automobile industry.

| In what ways did the Roaring Twenties challenge traditional values? | Why did the divide between rural and urban America grow in the 1920s? | What caused the crash of 1929? | What was life like in the early years of the depression? | Conclusion: Why did the hope of the 1920s turn to despair? |

government." What was true of the government's relationship to business at home was also true abroad.

Promoting Prosperity and Peace Abroad

After orchestrating the Senate's successful effort to block U.S. membership in the League of Nations, Henry Cabot Lodge boasted, "We have torn Wilsonism up by the roots." But repudiation of Wilsonian internationalism and rejection of collective security through the League of Nations did not mean that the United States retreated into isolationism. The United States emerged from World War I with its economy intact and enjoyed a decade of stunning growth. Economic involvement in the world and the continuing chaos in Europe made an American retreat into isolationism impossible. New York replaced London as the center of world finance, and the United States became the world's chief creditor.

One of the Republicans' most ambitious foreign policy initiatives was the Washington Disarmament Conference, which convened to establish a global balance of naval power. Secretary of State Charles Evans Hughes shaped the Five-Power Naval Treaty of 1922 committing Britain, France, Japan, Italy, and the United States to a proportional reduction of naval forces. The treaty led to the scrapping of more than two million tons of warships, by far the world's greatest success in disarmament. By fostering international peace, Harding helped make the world a safer place for American trade.

A second major effort on behalf of world peace came in 1928, when Secretary of State Frank Kellogg joined French foreign minister Aristide Briand to produce the Kellogg-Briand pact. Nearly fifty nations signed the solemn pledge to renounce war and settle international disputes peacefully.

But Republican administrations preferred private sector diplomacy to state action. With the blessing of the White House, a team of American financiers led by Chicago banker Charles Dawes swung into action when Germany suspended its war reparation payments in 1923. Impoverished, Germany was staggering under the massive bill of $33 billion presented by the victorious Allies in the Versailles treaty. When Germany failed to meet its annual payment, France occupied Germany's industrial Ruhr Valley, creating the worst international crisis since the war. In 1924, American corporate leaders produced the Dawes Plan, which halved Germany's annual reparation payments, initiated fresh American loans to Germany, and caused the French to retreat from the Ruhr. Although the United States failed to join the League of Nations, it continued to exercise significant economic and diplomatic influence abroad. These Republican successes overseas helped fuel prosperity at home.

Automobiles, Mass Production, and Assembly-Line Progress

Henry Ford
▶ Founder of the Ford Motor Company and pioneer of the mass production of automobiles. Affordable cars like those Ford produced transformed America.

The automobile industry emerged as the largest single manufacturing industry in the nation. **Henry Ford**, pioneer of the mass production of automobiles, shrewdly located his company in Detroit, knowing that key materials for his automobiles were manufactured in nearby states (**Map 23.1**). Keystone of the American

CHAPTER LOCATOR | How did big business shape the New Era of the 1920s?

CHAPTER 23
630 FROM NEW ERA TO GREAT DEPRESSION, 1920–1932

economy, the automobile industry not only employed hundreds of thousands of workers directly but also brought whole industries into being—filling stations, garages, fast-food restaurants, and "guest cottages" (motels). The need for tires, glass, steel, highways, oil, and refined gasoline for automobiles provided millions of related jobs. By 1929, one American in four found employment directly or indirectly in the automobile industry. "Give us our daily bread" was no longer addressed to the Almighty, one commentator quipped, but to Detroit.

The Ford Motor Company in the 1920s

1920–1927	Nine million cars are sold.
1920–1925	Speed of production increases sixfold.
1920–1928	Cost of a Ford car falls from $845 to less than $300.

Cars changed where people lived, what work they did, how they spent their leisure, even how they thought. Hundreds of small towns decayed because the automobile enabled rural people to bypass them in favor of more distant cities and towns. In cities, streetcars began to disappear as workers moved to the suburbs and commuted to work along crowded highways. Nothing shaped modern America more than the automobile, and efficient mass production made the automobile revolution possible.

Mass production by the assembly-line technique had become standard in almost every factory, from automobiles to meatpacking to cigarettes. To improve efficiency, corporations reduced assembly-line work to the simplest, most repetitive tasks. They also established specialized divisions—procurement,

mass production

▶ The production of large quantities of a given product through efficient production methods. During the 1920s, mass production by the assembly-line technique became standard in almost every American factory. Mass production resulted in greater productivity and profits for American businesses but also removed skilled jobs from the economy.

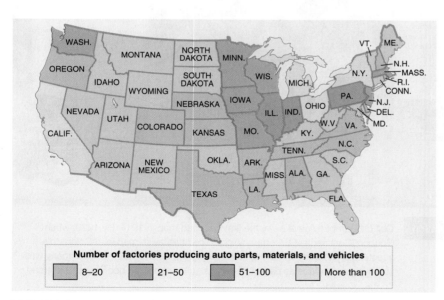

Number of factories producing auto parts, materials, and vehicles

| 8–20 | 21–50 | 51–100 | More than 100 |

MAP 23.1 ■ Auto Manufacturing
By the mid-1920s, the massive coal and steel industries of the Midwest had made that region the center of the new automobile industry. A major road-building program by the federal government carried the thousands of new cars produced each day to every corner of the country.

In what ways did the Roaring Twenties challenge traditional values?	Why did the divide between rural and urban America grow in the 1920s?	What caused the crash of 1929?	What was life like in the early years of the depression?	Conclusion: Why did the hope of the 1920s turn to despair?

Detroit and the Automobile Industry in the 1920s

production, marketing, and employee relations—each with its own team of professionally trained managers. Changes on the assembly line and in management, along with technological advances, significantly boosted overall efficiency. Between 1922 and 1929, productivity in manufacturing increased 32 percent. Average wages, however, increased only 8 percent.

Industries also developed programs for workers that came to be called welfare capitalism. Some businesses improved safety and sanitation inside factories and instituted paid vacations and pension plans. Welfare capitalism encouraged loyalty to the company and discouraged traditional labor unions. One labor organizer in the steel industry bemoaned the success of welfare capitalism. "So many workmen here had been lulled to sleep by the company union, the welfare plans, the social organizations fostered by the employer," he declared, "that they had come to look upon the employer as their protector, and had believed vigorous trade union organization unnecessary for their welfare."

Colorado Filling Station Gulf Oil Company gave away the first free road map in 1914. By 1929, when Conoco (Continental Oil Company) produced this lavish map with Colorado's spectacular mountains looming in the background, nearly every oil company was supplying road maps as part of its campaign to attract the booming tourist trade. Courtesy, Colorado Historical Society.

▶ FOR MORE HELP ANALYZING THIS IMAGE, see the visual activity for this chapter in the Online Study Guide at bedfordstmartins.com/roarkunderstanding.

CHAPTER LOCATOR | How did big business shape the New Era of the 1920s?

Consumer Culture

Mass production fueled corporate profits and national economic prosperity. During the 1920s, per capita income increased by a third, the cost of living stayed the same, and unemployment remained low. But the rewards of the economic boom were not evenly distributed. Americans who labored with their hands inched ahead, while white-collar workers enjoyed significantly more spending money and more leisure time to spend it. Mass production of a broad range of new products—automobiles, radios, refrigerators, electric irons, washing machines—produced a consumer-goods revolution.

In this new era of abundance, more people than ever conceived of the American dream in terms of the things they could acquire. *Middletown* (1929), a study of the lives of the inhabitants of Muncie, Indiana, revealed that Muncie had become, above all, "a culture in which everything hinges on money." Moreover, faced with technological and organizational change beyond their comprehension, many citizens had lost confidence in their ability to play an effective role in civic affairs. More and more they became passive consumers, deferring to leaders in politics and economics.

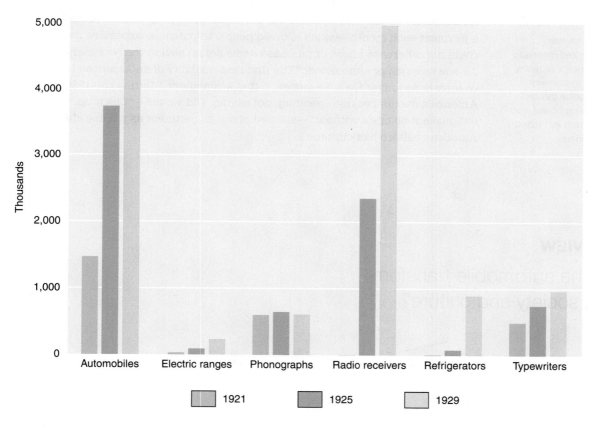

FIGURE 23.1 ■ Production of Consumer Goods, 1920–1930
Transportation, communications, and entertainment changed the lives of consumers in the 1920s. Laborsaving devices for the home were popular, but the vastly greater sales of automobiles and radios showed that consumerism was powerful in moving people's attention beyond their homes.

| In what ways did the Roaring Twenties challenge traditional values? | Why did the divide between rural and urban America grow in the 1920s? | What caused the crash of 1929? | What was life like in the early years of the depression? | Conclusion: Why did the hope of the 1920s turn to despair? |

The rapidly expanding business of advertising stimulated the desire for new products and undermined the traditional values of thrift and saving. Advertising linked material goods to the fulfillment of every spiritual and emotional need. Americans increasingly defined and measured their social status, and indeed their personal worth, on the yardstick of material possessions. Happiness itself rode on owning a car and choosing the right cigarettes and toothpaste.

By the 1920s, the United States had achieved the physical capacity to satisfy Americans' material wants (**Figure 23.1**, page 633). The economic problem shifted from production to consumption: Who would buy the goods flying off American assembly lines? One solution was to expand America's markets in foreign countries, and government and business joined in that effort. Another solution to the problem of consumption was to expand the market at home.

Henry Ford realized early on that "mass production requires mass consumption." He understood that automobile workers not only produced cars but would also buy them if they made enough money. "One's own employees ought to be one's own best customers," Ford said. In 1914, he raised wages in his factories to $5 a day, more than twice the going rate. High wages made for workers who were more loyal and more exploitable, and high wages returned as profits when workers bought Fords.

Many people's incomes, however, were too puny to satisfy the growing desire for consumer goods. The solution was **installment buying**—a little money down, a payment each month—which allowed people to purchase expensive items they could not otherwise afford or purchase items before saving the necessary money. As one newspaper announced, "The first responsibility of an American to his country is no longer that of a citizen, but of a consumer." During the 1920s, America's maxim became spending, not saving. Old values—"Use it up, wear it out, make it do or do without"—seemed about as pertinent as a horse and buggy. American culture had shifted.

installment buying

▶ Purchasing on credit with little money down and monthly payments. In the 1920s, installment buying allowed consumers with limited means to participate in America's growing consumer culture. Installment buying helped disguise the fact that consumer buying power was not keeping pace with increased American production.

> **QUICK REVIEW**

How did the automobile transform American society and culture?

CHAPTER LOCATOR | How did big business shape the New Era of the 1920s?

634 CHAPTER 23 FROM NEW ERA TO GREAT DEPRESSION, 1920–1932

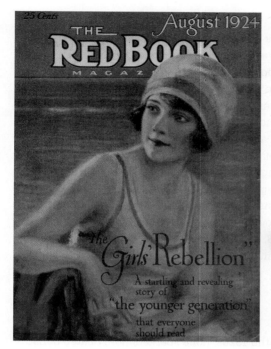

In what ways did the Roaring Twenties challenge traditional values?

A NEW ETHIC OF PERSONAL FREEDOM excited many Americans to seek pleasure without guilt in a whirl of activity that earned the decade the name "Roaring Twenties." Prohibition made lawbreakers of millions of otherwise decent folk. Flappers and "new women" challenged traditional gender boundaries. Other Americans enjoyed the Roaring Twenties through the words and images of vastly expanded mass communication. In America's big cities, particularly New York, a burst of creativity produced the "New Negro," who confounded and disturbed white Americans. The "Lost Generation" of writers, profoundly disillusioned with mainstream America's cultural direction, fled the country.

Prohibition

Republicans generally sought to curb the powers of government, but the twenties witnessed a great exception to this rule when the federal government implemented one of the last reforms of the Progressive Era: the Eighteenth Amendment, which banned the manufacture and sale of alcohol and took effect in January 1920 (see chapter 22) and made the United States the world's only society ever to outlaw alcohol. Supporters of **prohibition** believed that stopping consumption would boost productivity, eliminate crime, and lift the nation's morality.

The Treasury Department agents charged with enforcing prohibition faced a staggering task. In 1929, an agent in Indiana reported, "Conditions in most important cities very bad. Lax and corrupt public officials great handicap . . . prevalence of drinking among minor boys and the . . . middle or better class of adults." The "speakeasy," a place where men (and, increasingly, women) drank publicly, became a common feature of the urban landscape. One dealer, trading on common knowledge that whiskey still flowed in the White House, distributed cards advertising himself as the "President's Bootlegger."

prohibition
▶ The ban on the manufacture and sale of alcohol that went into effect in January 1920. Enforcement of prohibition proved almost impossible. By the end of the 1920s, most Americans had concluded that the social and political costs of prohibition outweighed the benefits. In 1933, the Eighteenth Amendment, which had created prohibition, was repealed.

In what ways did the Roaring Twenties challenge traditional values?	Why did the divide between rural and urban America grow in the 1920s?	What caused the crash of 1929?	What was life like in the early years of the depression?	Conclusion: Why did the hope of the 1920s turn to despair?

new woman

▶ Alternative image of womanhood that came into the American mainstream in the 1920s. After the ratification of the Nineteenth Amendment, which granted women the right to vote, the mass media frequently portrayed young, college-educated women who drank cocktails, smoked cigarettes, bobbed their hair, and wore makeup and skimpy dresses. New women defied old notions about acceptable appearances for women, and they also challenged American convictions about separate spheres for women and men and the sexual double standard.

Eventually, serious criminals took over the liquor trade. During the first four years of prohibition, Chicago witnessed more than two hundred gang-related killings as rival mobs struggled for control of the lucrative liquor trade. The most notorious event came on St. Valentine's Day 1929, when Al Capone's Italian-dominated mob machine-gunned seven members of a rival Irish gang. Federal authorities finally sent Capone to prison for income tax evasion. "I give the public what the public wants," Capone told a reporter, "and all I get is abuse."

Gang-war slayings prompted demands for the repeal of the Eighteenth Amendment. In 1931, a panel of distinguished experts reported that prohibition, which supporters had defended as "a great social and economic experiment," had failed. The social and political costs of prohibition outweighed the benefits. Prohibition caused ordinary citizens to disrespect the law, corrupted the police, and demoralized the judiciary. In 1933, after thirteen years, the nation ended prohibition, making the Eighteenth Amendment the only constitutional amendment to be repealed.

The New Woman

Of all the changes in American life in the 1920s, none sparked more heated debate than the alternatives offered to the traditional roles of women. Increasing numbers of women worked and went to college, defying older gender hierarchies and norms. Even mainstream magazines such as the *Saturday Evening Post* began publishing stories about young, college-educated women who drank gin cocktails, smoked cigarettes, and wore skimpy dresses and dangly necklaces. Before the Great War, the **new woman** dwelt in New York City's bohemian Greenwich Village, but afterward the mass media brought her into middle-class America's living rooms.

When the Nineteenth Amendment, ratified in 1920, granted women the vote, feminists felt liberated and expected women to reshape the political landscape. A Kansas woman declared, "I went to bed last night a *slave*[;] I awoke this morning a *free woman*." Women began pressuring Congress to pass laws that especially concerned women, including measures to protect women in factories and grant federal aid to schools. Black women lobbied particularly for federal courts to assume jurisdiction over the crime of lynching. But women's only significant legislative success came in 1921 when Congress enacted the Sheppard-Towner Act, which extended federal assistance to states seeking to reduce high infant mortality rates.

A number of factors helped thwart women's political influence. Male domination of both political parties, the rarity of female candidates, and lack of experience in voting, especially among recent immigrants, kept many women away from the polls. In the South, poll taxes, literacy tests, and outright terrorism continued to decimate the vote of African Americans, men and women alike.

Most important, rather than forming a solid voting bloc, feminists divided. Some argued for women's right to special protection; others demanded equal protection. The radical National Woman's Party fought for an Equal Rights Amendment that stated flatly: "Men and women shall have equal rights throughout the United States." The more moderate League of Women Voters feared that the amendment's wording threatened state laws that provided women special protection, such as preventing them from working on certain machines. Put before Congress in 1923, the Equal Rights Amendment went down to defeat,

CHAPTER LOCATOR | How did big business shape the New Era of the 1920s?

and radical women were forced to work for the causes of birth control, legal equality for minorities, and the end of child labor through other means.

Economically, more women worked for pay—approximately one in four by 1930—but they clustered in "women's jobs." The proportion of women working as secretaries, stenographers, and typists skyrocketed. Women almost monopolized the occupations of librarian, nurse, elementary school teacher, and telephone operator. Women also represented 40 percent of salesclerks by 1930. More female white-collar workers meant that fewer women were interested in protective legislation for women; new women wanted salaries and opportunities equal to men's.

Increased earnings gave working women more buying power in the new consumer culture. A stereotype soon emerged of the flapper, so called because of the short-lived fad of wearing unbuckled galoshes. The flapper had short "bobbed" hair and wore lipstick and rouge. She dressed in the latest styles—short skirts, drop waists, bare arms, and no petticoats—and she danced all night to wild jazz.

The new woman both reflected and propelled the modern birth control movement. Margaret Sanger, the crusading pioneer for contraception during the Progressive Era, restated her principal conviction in 1920: "No woman can call herself free until she can choose consciously whether she will or will not be a mother." By shifting strategy in the twenties, Sanger courted the conservative American Medical Association; linked birth control with the eugenics movement, which advocated limiting reproduction among "undesirable" groups; and thus made contraception a respectable subject for discussion.

New women challenged American convictions about separate spheres for women and men, the double standard of sexual conduct, and Victorian ideas of proper female appearance and behavior. Although only a minority of American women became flappers, all women, even those who remained at home, felt the great changes of the era.

The New Negro

The 1920s witnessed the emergence not only of the new woman but also of the New Negro. African Americans who challenged the caste system that confined dark-skinned Americans to the lowest levels of society confronted whites who insisted that race relations would not change.

The prominent African American intellectual W. E. B. Du Bois and the National Association for the Advancement of Colored People (NAACP) aggressively pursued the passage of a federal antilynching law to counter mob violence against blacks in the South. At the same time, the Jamaican-born visionary Marcus Garvey urged African Americans to rediscover the heritage of Africa, take pride in their own achievements, and maintain racial purity by avoiding miscegenation. In 1917, Garvey launched the Universal Negro Improvement Association to help African Americans gain economic and political independence entirely outside white society. In 1927 the federal government pinned charges of illegal practices on Garvey and deported him to Jamaica. Nevertheless, the issues Garvey raised about racial pride, black identity, and the search for equality persisted, and his legacy remains at the center of black nationalist thought.

Still, most African Americans maintained hope in the American promise. In New York City, hope and talent came together. Black artists, sculptors, novelists, musicians, and poets poured into Harlem in uptown Manhattan, where they set

| In what ways did the Roaring Twenties challenge traditional values? | Why did the divide between rural and urban America grow in the 1920s? | What caused the crash of 1929? | What was life like in the early years of the depression? | Conclusion: Why did the hope of the 1920s turn to despair? |

Noah's Ark

Kansas-born painter Aaron Douglas expressed the Harlem Renaissance visually. Douglas sought ways of integrating the African cultural heritage with American experience. This depiction of an African Noah commanding the loading of the ark displays a technique that became closely associated with African American art: strong silhouetted figures awash in misty color, indicating a connection between Christian faith and the vital, colorful origins of black Americans in a distant, mythologized African past.
Fisk University Art Galleries.

Harlem Renaissance

▶ African American cultural flowering that took place in Harlem in the 1920s. The Harlem Renaissance produced dazzling literary, musical, and artistic talent. The vigor of the Harlem Renaissance left a powerful legacy for black Americans, but the creative burst did little in the short run to dissolve the prejudice of white society.

out to create a distinctive African American culture that drew on their identities as Americans and Africans. As scholar Alain Locke put it in 1925, they introduced to the world the "New Negro," who rose from the ashes of slavery and segregation to proclaim African Americans' creative genius.

The emergence of the New Negro came to be known as the **Harlem Renaissance**. "We younger Negro artists . . . intend to express our individual dark-skinned selves without fear or shame," poet Langston Hughes said of the Harlem Renaissance. "If white people are pleased, we are glad. If they are not, it doesn't matter. We know we are beautiful. And ugly, too."

The Harlem Renaissance produced dazzling literary, musical, and artistic talent. Despite such vibrancy, Harlem for most whites remained a separate black ghetto known only for its lively nightlife. Fashionable whites crowded into Harlem's nightclubs, where they believed they could hear "real" jazz, a relatively new musical form, in its "natural" surroundings. The vigor of the Harlem Renaissance left a powerful legacy for black Americans, but the creative burst did little in the short run to dissolve the prejudice of white society.

Leaders of the Harlem Renaissance

James Weldon Johnson	writer, civil rights leader
Langston Hughes, Claude McKay, Countee Cullen	poets
Zora Neale Hurston	novelist
Aaron Douglas	artist

Mass Culture

In the twenties, popular culture, like consumer goods, was mass-produced and mass-consumed. The proliferation of movies, radios, music, and sports meant that Americans found plenty to do, and in doing the same things, they helped create a national culture.

Nothing offered escapist delights like the movies (**Figure 23.2**). Hollywood, California, discovered the successful formula of combining opulence, sex, and adventure. By 1929, the movies were drawing more than 80 million people in a single week, as many as lived in the entire country. Rudolph Valentino, described as "catnip to women," and Clara Bow, the "It Girl" (everyone knew what *it* was), became household names. Most loved of all was the comic Charlie Chaplin, whose famous character, the Little Tramp, showed an endearing inability to cope with the rules and complexities of modern life.

Americans also found heroes in sports. Baseball solidified its place as the national pastime in the 1920s. It remained essentially a game played by and for the working class. In George Herman "Babe" Ruth, baseball had the most cherished free spirit of the time. The rowdy escapades of the "Sultan of Swat" demonstrated to fans that sports offered a way to break out of the ordinariness of everyday life. By "his sheer exuberance," one sportswriter declared, Ruth "has lightened the cares of the world."

CHAPTER LOCATOR | How did big business shape the New Era of the 1920s?

The public also fell in love with a young boxer from the grim mining districts of Colorado, Jack Dempsey. When he took the heavyweight crown just after World War I, he was revered as the people's champ, a stand-in for the average American who felt increasingly confined by bureaucracy and machine-made culture.

Football, essentially a college sport, held greater sway with the upper classes. But in keeping with the times, football moved toward a more commercial spectacle. Harold "Red" Grange, "the Galloping Ghost," led the way by going from stardom at the University of Illinois to the Chicago Bears in the new professional football league.

The decade's hero worship reached its zenith in the celebration of Charles Lindbergh, a young pilot who set out on May 20, 1927, to become the first person to fly nonstop across the Atlantic. Lindbergh was the perfect hero for an age that celebrated individual accomplishment. "Charles Lindbergh," one journalist proclaimed, "is the stuff out of which have been made the pioneers that opened up the wilderness. His are the qualities which we, as a people, must nourish." Lindbergh realized, however, that technical and organizational complexity was fast reducing chances for solitary achievement. Consequently, he titled his book about the flight *We* (1927) to include the machine that had made it all possible.

Another machine—the radio—became important to mass culture in the 1920s. The nation's first licensed radio station, KDKA in Pittsburgh, began broadcasting in 1920, and soon American airwaves buzzed with news, sermons, soap operas, sports, comedy, and music. Because they could now reach prospective customers in their own homes, advertisers bank-rolled radio's rapid growth. Between 1922 and 1929, the number of radio stations in the United States increased from 30 to 606. In just seven years, homes with radios jumped from 60,000 to a staggering 10.25 million.

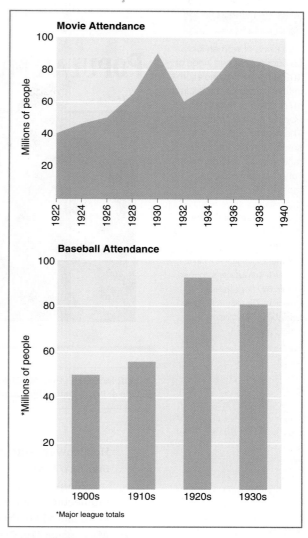

FIGURE 23.2 ■ **Movie and Baseball Attendance**
America's favorite pastimes, movies and baseball, tracked the economy. The rise and fall of weekly movie attendance and seasonal baseball attendance shown here mirrored the rise and fall of prosperity.

The Lost Generation

Some writers and artists felt alienated from America's mass-culture society, which they found shallow, anti-intellectual, and materialistic. Young, white, and mostly college educated, these expatriates, as they came to be called, felt embittered by the war and renounced the progressives who had promoted it as a crusade. For them, Europe—not Hollywood or Harlem—seemed the place to seek their renaissance.

The American-born writer Gertrude Stein, long established in Paris, remarked famously as the young exiles gathered around her, "They are the lost generation." Most of the expatriates, however, believed to the contrary that they had finally found themselves. The **Lost Generation** helped launch the most creative period in American art and literature in the twentieth century. The novelist whose spare, clean style best exemplified the expatriate efforts to make art mirror basic reality was Ernest

Lost Generation
▶ Generation of young Americans who were disillusioned with American society and sought inspiration in Europe. Young, white, and mostly college educated, the Lost Generation felt alienated from America's mass-culture society, which they found shallow, anti-intellectual, and materialistic. The Lost Generation helped launch the most creative period in American art and literature in the twentieth century.

| In what ways did the Roaring Twenties challenge traditional values? | Why did the divide between rural and urban America grow in the 1920s? | What caused the crash of 1929? | What was life like in the early years of the depression? | Conclusion: Why did the hope of the 1920s turn to despair? |

Two kinds of women look up adoringly at two kinds of 1920s heroes. A wholesome image is seen on the left in a 1927 cover of *People's Popular Monthly* magazine. The healthy outdoor girl, smartly turned out in her raccoon coat and pennant, flatters a naive college football hero. On the right, the pale, sensitive Vilma Banky kneels before the gaze of the movies' greatest heartthrob, Rudolph Valentino. Magazine: Picture Research Consultants & Archives; Poster: Billy Rose Theatre Collection, The New York Public Library at Lincoln Center.

▶ FOR MORE HELP ANALYZING THIS IMAGE, see the visual activity for this chapter in the Online Study Guide at bedfordstmartins.com/roarkunderstanding.

Hemingway. Admirers found the terse language and hard lessons of his novel *The Sun Also Rises* (1926) to be perfect expressions of a world stripped of illusions.

Many writers who remained in America were exiles in spirit. Before the war, intellectuals had eagerly joined progressive reform movements. Afterward, they were more likely critics of American cultural vulgarity. Novelist Sinclair Lewis in *Main Street* (1920) and *Babbitt* (1922) satirized his native Midwest as a cultural wasteland. Humorists such as James Thurber created outlandish characters to poke fun at American stupidity and inhibitions. And southern writers, led by William Faulkner, explored the South's grim class and race heritage. Worries about alienation surfaced as well. F. Scott Fitzgerald spoke sadly in *This Side of Paradise* (1920) of a disillusioned generation "grown up to find all Gods dead, all wars fought, all faiths in man shaken."

> ## QUICK REVIEW

How did the cultural change in the 1920s affect older conceptions of gender and race?

CHAPTER LOCATOR | How did big business shape the New Era of the 1920s?

Why did the divide between rural and urban America grow in the 1920s?

WKKK Badge

Some half a million women were members of the Women of the Ku Klux Klan (WKKK). Klanswomen fit perfectly within the KKK because the organization proclaimed itself the defender of the traditional virtues of pure womanhood and decent homes. This badge from Harrisburg, Pennsylvania, advertises the local WKKK's support for a home for "orphan and dependent children." Klanswomen also joined in boycotts of businesses owned by Jews and others whom they did not consider "100% American." Collection of Janice L. and David J. Frent.

LARGE AREAS OF THE COUNTRY did not share in the wealth of the 1920s and had little confidence that they would anytime soon. By the end of the decade, 40 percent of the nation's farmers were landless, and 90 percent of rural homes had no indoor plumbing, gas, or electricity. By the 1920s, the census reported that the majority of the population had shifted from the country to the city (**Map 23.2**, page 642).

Cities seemed to stand for everything rural areas stood against. Rural America imagined itself as solidly Anglo-Saxon (despite the presence of millions of African Americans in the South and Mexican Americans, Native Americans, and Asian Americans in the West), and the cities seemed to be filled with undesirable immigrants. Rural America was the home of old-time Protestant religion, and the cities teemed with Catholics, Jews, liberal Protestants, and atheists. Rural America championed old-fashioned moral standards—abstinence and self-denial—while the cities spawned every imaginable vice. Once the "backbone of the Republic," rural Americans had become poor country cousins. Urban domination over the nation's political and cultural life and sharply rising economic disparity drove rural Americans in often ugly, reactionary directions.

Rejecting the Undesirables

Before the war, when about a million immigrants arrived each year, some Americans warned that unassimilable foreigners were smothering the nation. War

| In what ways did the Roaring Twenties challenge traditional values? | **Why did the divide between rural and urban America grow in the 1920s?** | What caused the crash of 1929? | What was life like in the early years of the depression? | Conclusion: Why did the hope of the 1920s turn to despair? |

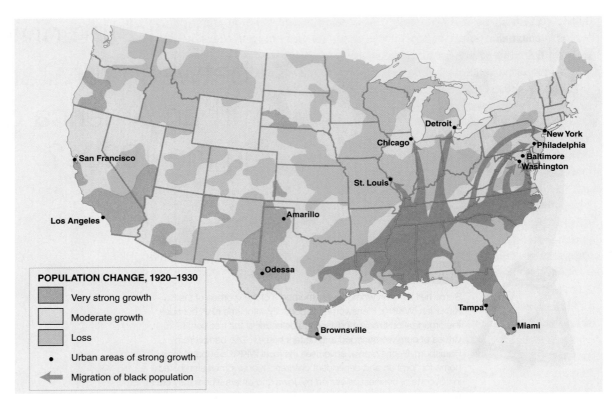

POPULATION CHANGE, 1920–1930

Very strong growth

Moderate growth

Loss

● Urban areas of strong growth

← Migration of black population

MAP 23.2 ■ The Shift from Rural to Urban Population, 1920–1930
The movement of whites and Hispanics toward urban and agricultural opportunity made Florida, the West, and the Southwest the regions of fastest population growth. In contrast, large numbers of blacks left the rural South to find a better life in the North. Because almost all migrating blacks went from the countryside to cities in distant parts of the nation, while white and Hispanic migrants tended to move shorter distances toward familiar places, the population shift brought more drastic overall change to blacks than to whites and Hispanics.

▶ FOR MORE HELP ANALYZING THIS MAP, see the map activity for this chapter in the Online Study Guide at bedfordstmartins.com/roarkunderstanding.

Johnson-Reid Act

▶ 1924 law that severely restricted immigration to the United States. The law limited the number of immigrants to no more than 161,000 a year and established quotas for each European nation. Racist by design, the new restrictions were intended to staunch the flow of immigrants from southern and eastern Europe and Asia.

against Germany and its allies expanded nativist and antiradical sentiment. After the war, large-scale immigration resumed (another 800,000 immigrants arrived in 1921) at a moment when industrialists no longer needed new factory laborers. African American and Mexican migration had relieved labor shortages. Moreover, union leaders feared that millions of poor immigrants would undercut their efforts to organize American workers. Rural American Protestants were particularly alarmed that most of the immigrants were Catholic or Jewish. In 1921, Congress responded by severely restricting immigration.

In 1924, Congress went further. The **Johnson-Reid Act** limited the number of immigrants to no more than 161,000 a year and established quotas for each European nation. The act revealed the fear and bigotry that fueled anti-immigration legislation. While it cut immigration by more than 80 percent, it squeezed some nationalities far more than others. Backers of Johnson-Reid openly declared that America had become the "garbage can and the dumping ground of the world," and they manipulated quotas to ensure entry only to "good" immigrants from western Europe. The law effectively reversed the trend toward immigration from southern and eastern Europe, which by 1914 had amounted to 75 percent of the yearly total.

The 1924 law reaffirmed the 1880s legislation barring Chinese immigrants and added Japanese and other Asians to the list of the excluded. But it left open immigration from the Western Hemisphere, and during the 1920s, some 500,000 Mexicans crossed the border. Farm interests preserved Mexican immigration because of Mexicans' value in southwestern agriculture. Rural Americans strongly supported the law, as did industrialists and labor leaders.

Antiforeign hysteria climaxed in the trial of two anarchist immigrants from Italy, Nicola Sacco and Bartolomeo Vanzetti. Arrested in 1920 for robbery and murder in South Braintree, Massachusetts, the men were sentenced to death by a judge who openly referred to them as "anarchist bastards." In response to doubts about the fairness of the verdict, a review committee found the trial judge guilty of a "grave breach of official decorum" but refused to recommend a motion for retrial. When Massachusetts executed Sacco and Vanzetti on August 23, 1927, fifty thousand mourners followed their caskets, convinced that the men had died because they were immigrants and radicals, not because they were murderers.

The Rebirth of the Ku Klux Klan

The nation's antiforeign mood struck a responsive chord in members of the **Ku Klux Klan**. The Klan first appeared in the South during Reconstruction to thwart black freedom and expired with the reestablishment of white supremacy. In 1915, the Klan was reborn at Stone Mountain, Georgia, but when the new Klan extended its targets beyond black Americans, it quickly spread beyond the South. Under a banner proclaiming "100 percent Americanism," the Klan promised to defend family, morality, and traditional American values against the threats posed by blacks, immigrants, radicals, feminists, Catholics, and Jews.

Building on the frustrations of rural America, the Klan attracted three million to four million members—women as well as men. By the mid-1920s, the Klan had spread throughout the nation, almost controlling Indiana and influencing politics in Illinois, California, Oregon, Texas, Louisiana, Oklahoma, and Kansas. In 1926, Klan imperial wizard Hiram Wesley Evans described the assault of modernity: "One by one all our traditional moral standards went by the boards or were so disregarded that they ceased to be binding," he explained. "The sacredness of our Sabbath, of our homes, of chastity, and finally even of our right to teach our own children in schools [were] fundamental facts and truth torn away from us."

Eventually, social changes, along with lawless excess, crippled the Klan. Immigration restrictions eased the worry about invading foreigners, and sensational wrongdoing by Klan leaders cost it the support of traditional moralists. Grand Dragon David Stephenson of Indiana, for example, went to jail for the kidnapping and rape of a woman who subsequently committed suicide. Yet the social grievances, economic problems, and religious anxieties of the countryside and small towns remained unresolved.

CHRONOLOGY

1915
- Ku Klux Klan is reborn at Stone Mountain, Georgia.

1921
- Congress restricts immigration.

1924
- Johnson-Reid Act restricts immigration further.

1925
- Scopes trial challenges the right to prohibit teaching evolution in public schools.

1927
- Nicola Sacco and Bartolomeo Vanzetti are executed amid the Red scare.

1928
- Republican Herbert Hoover is elected president.

Ku Klux Klan
▶ Racist organization that, in the 1920s, fought against perceived threats posed by blacks, immigrants, radicals, feminists, Catholics, and Jews. The Klan first emerged after the Civil War to thwart black freedom but was reborn in 1915 with a broader agenda. The new Klan spread well beyond the South, attracting some three million to four million members in the 1920s.

| In what ways did the Roaring Twenties challenge traditional values? | **Why did the divide between rural and urban America grow in the 1920s?** | What caused the crash of 1929? | What was life like in the early years of the depression? | Conclusion: Why did the hope of the 1920s turn to despair? |

The Scopes Trial

In 1925 in a Tennessee courtroom, old-time religion and the new spirit of science went head-to-head. The confrontation occurred after several southern states passed legislation barring the teaching of Charles Darwin's theory of evolution in the public schools. At the urging of scientists and civil liberties organizations, John Scopes, a young biology teacher in Dayton, Tennessee, offered to test his state's ban on teaching evolution. When Scopes came to trial, Clarence Darrow, a brilliant defense lawyer from Chicago, volunteered to defend him. Darrow, an avowed agnostic, took on the prosecution's William Jennings Bryan, three-time Democratic nominee for president, symbol of rural America, and fervent fundamentalist.

Scopes trial

▶ 1925 trial of John Scopes, a biology teacher in Dayton, Tennessee, for violating his state's ban on teaching evolution. The first trial to be covered live on radio, it attracted a nationwide audience and came to be seen as a showdown between urban and rural values.

The **Scopes trial** quickly degenerated into a media circus. The first trial to be covered live on radio, it attracted a nationwide audience. Most of the reporters from big-city newspapers were hostile to Bryan. When, under relentless questioning by Darrow, Bryan declared on the witness stand that he did indeed believe that the world had been created in six days and that Jonah had lived in the belly of a whale, his humiliation in the eyes of most urban observers was complete. Nevertheless, the Tennessee court upheld the law and punished Scopes with a $100 fine. Although fundamentalism won the battle, it lost the war. The journalist H. L. Mencken had the last word in a merciless obituary for Bryan, who died just a week after the trial ended. Portraying the "monkey trial" as a battle between the country and the city, Mencken flayed Bryan as a "charlatan, a mountebank, a zany without shame or dignity," motivated solely by "hatred of the city men who had laughed at him for so long."

As Mencken's acid prose indicated, Bryan's humiliation was not purely a victory of reason and science. It also revealed the disdain urban people felt for country people and the values they clung to. The Ku Klux Klan revival and the Scopes trial dramatized and inflamed divisions between city and country, intellectuals and the uneducated, the privileged and the poor, the scoffers and the faithful.

Al Smith and the Election of 1928

The presidential election of 1928 brought many of the developments of the 1920s—prohibition, immigration, religion, and the clash of rural and urban values—into sharp focus. Republicans emphasized the economic success of their party's pro-business government and turned to Herbert Hoover, the energetic secretary of commerce and leading public symbol of 1920s prosperity. But because both parties generally agreed that the American economy was basically sound, the campaign turned on social issues that divided Americans.

The Democrats nominated four-time governor of New York Alfred E. Smith. Smith seemed to represent all that rural Americans feared and resented. A child of immigrants, Smith got his start in politics with the help of New York's Tammany Hall political machine, to many the epitome of big-city corruption. He denounced immigration quotas, signed New York State's anti-Klan bill, and opposed prohibition, believing that it was a nativist attack on immigrant customs.

CHAPTER LOCATOR | How did big business shape the New Era of the 1920s?

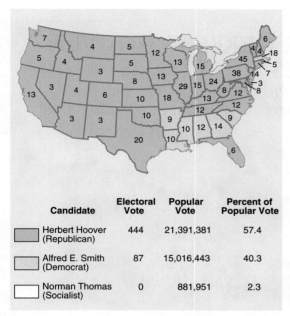

Candidate	Electoral Vote	Popular Vote	Percent of Popular Vote
Herbert Hoover (Republican)	444	21,391,381	57.4
Alfred E. Smith (Democrat)	87	15,016,443	40.3
Norman Thomas (Socialist)	0	881,951	2.3

MAP 23.3 ■ The Election of 1928

Prohibition forces dubbed him "Alcohol Al." Smith's greatest vulnerability in the heartland, however, was his religion. He was the first Catholic to run for president. A Methodist bishop in Virginia denounced Roman Catholicism as "the Mother of ignorance, superstition, intolerance and sin" and begged Protestants not to vote for a candidate who represented "the kind of dirty people that you find today on the sidewalks of New York."

Hoover, who neatly combined the images of morality, efficiency, service, and prosperity, won the election by a landslide (**Map 23.3**). He received nearly 58 percent of the vote and gained 444 electoral votes to Smith's 87. The only bright spot for Democrats was the nation's cities, which voted Democratic, indicating the rising strength of ethnic minorities, including Smith's fellow Catholics.

QUICK REVIEW <

Why did rural Americans increasingly fear and mistrust urban America?

| In what ways did the Roaring Twenties challenge traditional values? | Why did the divide between rural and urban America grow in the 1920s? | What caused the crash of 1929? | What was life like in the early years of the depression? | Conclusion: Why did the hope of the 1920s turn to despair? |

> What caused the crash of 1929?

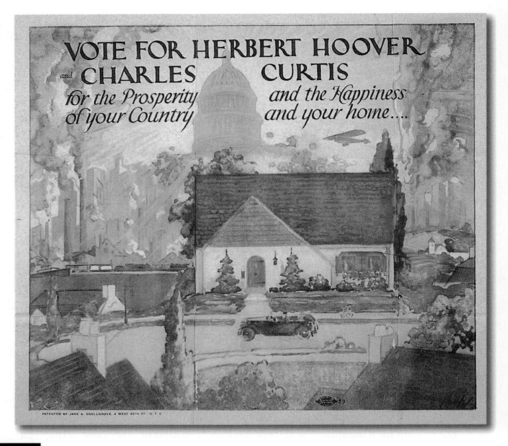

Hoover Campaign Poster

This poster effectively illustrates Herbert Hoover's 1928 campaign message: Republican administrations in the 1920s had produced middle-class prosperity, complete with a house in the suburbs and the latest automobile. To remind voters that Hoover as secretary of commerce had promoted industry that made the suburban dream possible, the poster portrays smoking chimneys at a discreet distance. Collection of Janice L. and David J. Frent.

Herbert Hoover

▶ Engineer and progressive Republican who made his name as secretary of commerce in the Harding and Coolidge administrations and won the presidential election in 1928. As president after the stock market crash in 1929, Hoover relied primarily on private enterprise as the solution to the economic crisis; his decision to limit government intervention in the economy contributed to the downward spiral that created the Great Depression.

AT HIS INAUGURATION in 1929, Herbert Hoover told the American people, "Given a chance to go forward with the policies of the last eight years, we shall soon with the help of God be in sight of the day when poverty will be banished from this nation." Within eight months, the prosperity Hoover touted collapsed with the stock market, and the nation ended nearly three decades of barely interrupted economic growth. Like much of the world, the United States fell into the most serious economic depression of all time.

Herbert Hoover: The Great Engineer

When **Herbert Hoover** became president in 1929, he seemed the perfect choice to lead a prosperous business nation. His rise from poverty to become one of the world's most celebrated mining engineers personified America's rags-to-riches

CHAPTER LOCATOR | How did big business shape the New Era of the 1920s?

ideal. His success in managing efforts to feed civilian victims of the fighting during World War I won him acclaim as the "Great Humanitarian" and led Woodrow Wilson to name him head of the Food Administration once the United States entered the war. Hoover's reputation soared even higher as secretary of commerce in the Harding and Coolidge administrations.

Hoover belonged to the progressive wing of his party, and as early as 1909, he declared, "The time when the employer could ride roughshod over his labor is disappearing with the doctrine of 'laissez-faire' on which it is founded." He urged a limited business-government partnership that would manage the sweeping changes Americans were experiencing. When Hoover entered the White House, he brought a reform agenda: "We want to see a nation built of home owners and farm owners. We want to see their savings protected. We want to see them in steady jobs. We want to see more and more of them insured against death and accident, unemployment and old age. We want them all secure."

But Hoover also had ideological and political liabilities. Principles that appeared strengths in the prosperous 1920s—individual self-reliance, industrial self-management, and a limited federal government—became straitjackets when economic catastrophe struck. Moreover, Hoover had never held an elected public office, had a poor political touch, and was too thin-skinned to be an effective politician. Prophetically, he confided to a friend his fear that "if some unprecedented calamity should come upon the nation . . . I would be sacrificed to the unreasoning disappointment of a people who expected too much." The distorted national economy set the stage for the calamity Hoover so feared.

The Distorted Economy

In the spring of 1929, the United States enjoyed a fragile prosperity. Although America had become the world's leading economy, it had done little to help rebuild Europe's shattered economy after World War I. Instead, the Republican administrations demanded that Allied nations repay their war loans, creating a tangled web of debts and reparations that sapped Europe's economic vitality. Moreover, to boost American business, the United States enacted tariffs that prevented other nations from selling their goods to Americans. Fewer sales meant that foreign nations had less money to buy American goods. American banks propped up the nation's export trade by extending credit to foreign customers, deepening their debt.

The domestic economy was also in trouble. Wealth was badly distributed. Farmers continued to suffer from low prices and chronic indebtedness; the average income of families working the land amounted to only $240 per year. The wages of industrial workers, though rising during the decade, failed to keep up with productivity and corporate profits. Overall, nearly two-thirds of all American families lived on less than the $2,000 per year that economists estimated would "supply only basic necessities." In sharp contrast, the top 1 percent received 15 percent of the nation's income, an amount equal to that received by the bottom 42 percent of the population. The Coolidge administration worsened the deepening inequality by cutting taxes on the wealthy.

By 1929, the inequality of wealth produced a serious problem in consumption. The rich spent lavishly, but they could absorb only a tiny fraction of the nation's output. For a time, the new device of installment buying—buying on credit—kept

CHRONOLOGY

1929
- Farm Board is created to buy up surplus agricultural products and keep food prices from falling.
- **October.** Stock market collapses.

1930
- Congress authorizes $420 million for public works projects.
- Hawley-Smoot tariff establishes the highest rates in history.

1932
- Reconstruction Finance Corporation is established to lend government funds to banks and corporations.

In what ways did the Roaring Twenties challenge traditional values?	Why did the divide between rural and urban America grow in the 1920s?	What caused the crash of 1929?	What was life like in the early years of the depression?	Conclusion: Why did the hope of the 1920s turn to despair?

consumer demand up. By the end of the decade, four out of five cars and two out of three radios were bought on credit.

Signs of economic trouble began to appear at mid-decade. New construction slowed down. Automobile sales faltered. Companies began cutting back production and laying off workers. Between 1921 and 1928, as investment and loan opportunities faded, five thousand banks failed, wiping out the life savings of thousands.

The Crash of 1929

Even as the economy faltered, America's faith in it remained unshaken. Hoping for even bigger slices of the economic pie, Americans speculated wildly in the stock market on Wall Street. Between 1924 and 1929, the values of stocks listed on the New York Stock Exchange increased by more than 400 percent. Buying stocks on margin—that is, putting up only part of the money at the time of purchase—accelerated. Many people got rich this way, but those who bought on credit could finance their loans only if their stocks increased in value.

Finally, in the autumn of 1929, the market hesitated. Investors nervously began to sell their overvalued stocks. The dip quickly became a panic on October 24, the day that came to be known as Black Thursday. More panic selling came on Black Tuesday, October 29, the day the market suffered a greater fall than ever before. In the next six months, the stock market lost six-sevenths of its total value.

It was once thought that the crash alone caused the Great Depression. It did not. In 1929, the national and international economies were already riddled with severe problems. But the dramatic losses in the stock market crash and the fear of risking what was left acted as a great brake on economic activity. The collapse on Wall Street shattered the New Era's confidence that America would enjoy perpetually expanding prosperity.

Hoover and the Limits of Individualism

In November 1929, to keep the stock market collapse from ravaging the entire economy, Herbert Hoover called a White House conference of business and labor leaders and urged them to join in a voluntary plan for recovery: Businesses would maintain production and keep their workers on the job; labor would accept existing wages, hours, and conditions. Within a few months, however, the bargain fell apart. As demand for their products declined, industrialists cut production, sliced wages, and laid off workers. Poorly paid or unemployed workers could not buy much, and their decreased spending led to further cuts in production and further loss of jobs. Thus began the terrible spiral of economic decline.

To deal with the problems of rural America, Hoover got Congress to pass the Agricultural Marketing Act in 1929. The act created the Farm Board, which used its budget of $500 million to buy up agricultural surpluses and thus, it was hoped, raise prices. But prices declined. To help end the decline, Hoover joined conservatives in urging protective tariffs on agricultural goods, and the Hawley-Smoot tariff of 1930 established the highest rates in history. The same year, Congress also authorized $420 million for public works projects to give the unemployed jobs and

CHAPTER LOCATOR | How did big business shape the New Era of the 1920s?

648 CHAPTER 23 FROM NEW ERA TO GREAT DEPRESSION, 1920–1932

create more purchasing power. In three years, the Hoover administration nearly doubled federal public works expenditures.

But with each year of Hoover's term, the economy weakened. Tariffs did not end the suffering of farmers because foreign nations retaliated with increased tariffs of their own that crippled American farmers' ability to sell abroad. In 1932, Hoover hoped to help hard-pressed industry with the Reconstruction Finance Corporation (RFC), a federal agency empowered to lend government funds to endangered banks and corporations. The theory was trickle-down economics: Pump money into the economy at the top, and in the long run, the people at the bottom would benefit. In the end, very little of what critics of the RFC called a "millionaires' dole" trickled down to the poor.

Meanwhile, hundreds of thousands of workers lost their jobs each month. By 1932, an astounding one-quarter of the American workforce—more than twelve million people—were unemployed. There was no direct federal assistance, and state services and private charities were swamped. The depression that began in 1929 devastated much of the world, but no other modern nation provided such feeble support to the jobless. Cries grew louder for the federal government to give hurting people relief.

In responding, Hoover revealed the limits of his conception of government's proper role. He compared direct federal aid to the needy to the "dole" in Britain, which he thought destroyed the moral fiber of the chronically unemployed. In 1931, he allowed the Red Cross to distribute government-owned agricultural surpluses to the hungry. In 1932, he relaxed his principles further to offer small federal loans, not gifts, to the states to help them in their relief efforts. But Hoover's circumscribed notions of legitimate government action proved vastly inadequate to address the problems of restarting the economy and ending human suffering.

QUICK REVIEW <

Why and how did the American
economy collapse in 1929?

| In what ways did the Roaring Twenties challenge traditional values? | Why did the divide between rural and urban America grow in the 1920s? | What caused the crash of 1929? | What was life like in the early years of the depression? | Conclusion: Why did the hope of the 1920s turn to despair? |

> What was life
like in the early
years of the
depression?

An Unemployed Youth Joblessness was frightening and humiliating. Brought up to believe that if you worked hard, you got ahead, the unemployed had difficulty seeing failure to find work as anything other than personal failure. Many slipped into despair and depression. Library of Congress.

IN 1930, SUFFERING on a massive scale set in as unemployment increased and poverty spread and deepened. The gap between the American people and leaders who failed to resolve these contradictions widened as the depression deepened. By 1932, America's economic problems had created a dangerous social and political crisis.

The Human Toll

Statistics only hint at the human tragedy of the Great Depression. When Herbert Hoover took office in 1929, the American economy stood at its peak. When he left in 1933, it had reached its twentieth-century low (**FIGURE 23.3**). In 1929, national income was $88 billion. By 1933, it had declined to $40 billion. In 1929, unemployment was 3.1 percent, or 1.5 million workers. By 1933, unemployment stood at 25 percent, or 12.5 million workers. By 1932, more than 9,000 banks had shut their doors, and depositors had lost more than $2.5 billion.

Jobless, homeless victims wandered in search of work, and the tramp, or hobo, became one of the most visible figures of the 1930s. Riding the rails or hitchhiking, a million vagabonds moved southward and westward looking for seasonal agricultural work. Other unemployed men and women, sick or less hopeful, huddled in doorways, overcome, one man remembered, by "helpless despair and submission." Scavengers haunted alleys behind restaurants in search

CHAPTER LOCATOR | How did big business shape the New Era of the 1920s?

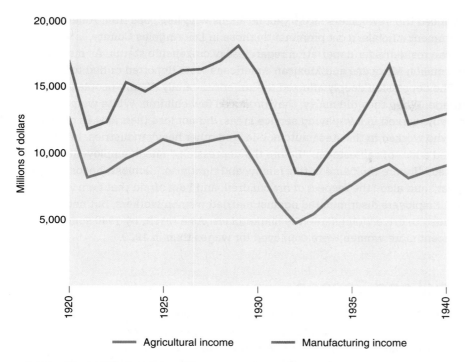

FIGURE 23.3 ■ Manufacturing and Agricultural Income, 1920–1940
After economic collapse, recovery in the 1930s began under New Deal auspices. The sharp declines in 1937–1938, when federal spending was reduced, indicated that New Deal stimuli were still needed to restore manufacturing and agricultural income.

CHRONOLOGY

1931
- Scottsboro Boys, nine young black men in Alabama, are arrested on trumped-up rape charges.
- The American Communist Party supports the Harlan County, Kentucky, coal strike.

1932
- Unemployed workers demonstrate at Henry Ford's River Rouge factory in Dearborn, Michigan.
- Farmers form the National Farmers' Holiday Association to take a "holiday" from shipping crops to market.

of food. "I don't want to steal," a Pennsylvania man wrote to the governor in 1931, "but I won't let my wife and boy cry for something to eat. . . . How long is this going to keep up? I cannot stand it any longer."

Rural poverty was most acute. Tenant farmers and sharecroppers, mainly in the South, came to symbolize how poverty crushed the human spirit. Eight and a half million people, three million of them black, crowded into cabins without plumbing, electricity, or running water. They subsisted—just barely—on salt pork, cornmeal, molasses, beans, peas, and whatever they could hunt or fish. When economist John Maynard Keynes was asked whether anything like this degradation had existed before, he replied, "Yes, it was called the Dark Ages and it lasted four hundred years."

There was no federal assistance to meet this human catastrophe, only a patchwork of charities and destitute state and local agencies. For a family of four without any income, the best the city of Philadelphia could do was provide $5.50 per week. That was not enough to live on but was still comparatively generous. New York City provided only $2.39 per week; and Detroit, devastated by the auto industry's failure, allotted 60 cents a week before the city ran out of money altogether.

The deepening crisis roused old fears and caused some Americans to look for scapegoats. Among the most thoroughly scapegoated were Mexican Americans. During the 1920s, cheap agricultural labor from Mexico flowed legally across the U.S. border, welcomed by the large farmers. In the 1930s, however, the public

| In what ways did the Roaring Twenties challenge traditional values? | Why did the divide between rural and urban America grow in the 1920s? | What caused the crash of 1929? | **What was life like in the early years of the depression?** | Conclusion: Why did the hope of the 1920s turn to despair? |

denounced the newcomers as dangerous aliens who took jobs from Americans. Government officials, most prominently those in Los Angeles County, targeted Mexican residents for deportation regardless of citizenship status. As many as half a million Mexicans and Mexican Americans were deported or fled to Mexico.

The depression deeply affected the American family. Young people postponed marriage. When they did marry, they produced few children. White women, who generally worked in low-paying service areas, did not lose their jobs as often as men who worked in the steel, automobile, and other heavy industries. Idle men suffered a loss of self-esteem. "Before the depression," one unemployed father reported, "I wore the pants in this family, and rightly so." Jobless, he lost "self-respect" and also "the respect of my children, and I am afraid that I am losing my wife." Employers discriminated against married women workers, but necessity continued to drive women into the marketplace. As a result, by 1940 some 25 percent more women were employed for wages than in 1930.

Denial and Escape

President Hoover assured the American people that economic recovery was on its way. Contradicting the president's optimism were makeshift shantytowns, called "Hoovervilles," that sprang up on the edges of America's cities. Bitter jokes circulated about the increasingly unpopular president. One told of Hoover asking for a nickel to telephone a friend. Flipping him a dime, an aide said, "Here, call them both."

While Hoover practiced denial, other Americans sought refuge from reality at the movies. Throughout the depression, between 60 million and 75 million people (nearly two-thirds of the nation) scraped together enough change to fill the movie palaces every week. Box office hits such as *Forty-second Street* and *Gold Diggers of 1933* capitalized on the hope that prosperity lay just around the corner. But a few filmmakers grappled with hard realities rather than escape them. *The Public Enemy* (1931) taught hard lessons about gangsters' ill-gotten gains. Indeed, under the new production code of 1930, designed to protect public morals, all movies had to find some way to show that crime did not pay.

Despite Hollywood's efforts to keep Americans on the right side of the law, crime increased. Out in the countryside, the plight of people who had lost their farms to bank foreclosures led to the romantic idea that bank robbers were only getting back what banks had stolen from the poor. Woody Guthrie, the populist folksinger from Oklahoma, captured the public's tolerance for outlaws in his tribute to a murderous bank robber with a choirboy face, "The Ballad of Pretty Boy Floyd":

> Yes, as through this world I ramble,
> I see lots of funny men,
> Some will rob you with a six-gun,
> Some will rob you with a pen.
> But as through your life you'll travel,
> Wherever you may roam,
> You won't never see an outlaw drive
> A family from their home.

CHAPTER LOCATOR | How did big business shape the New Era of the 1920s?

Working-Class Militancy

Members of the nation's working class bore the brunt of the economic collapse. By 1931, William Green, head of the American Federation of Labor (AFL), had turned militant. "I warn the people who are exploiting the workers," he shouted, "that they can drive them only so far before they will turn on them and destroy them. They are taking no account of the history of nations in which governments have been overturned. Revolutions grow out of the depths of hunger."

The American people were slow to anger, but on March 7, 1932, several thousand unemployed autoworkers massed at the gates of Henry Ford's River Rouge factory in Dearborn, Michigan, to demand work. Pelted with rocks, Ford's private security forces responded with gunfire, killing four demonstrators. Forty thousand outraged citizens turned out for the unemployed men's funerals.

Farmers mounted uprisings of their own. When Congress refused to guarantee farm prices, several thousand farmers created the National Farmers' Holiday

"Scottsboro Boys" Nine black youths stand in front of rifle-bearing National Guard troops called up by Alabama governor B. M. Miller, who feared a mob lynching after two white women accused the nine of rape in March 1931. Despite a lack of evidence, an all-white jury convicted the nine of rape and sentenced them to death. Although none was executed, all nine spent years in jail. Eventually, the state dropped the charges against the youngest four and granted paroles to the others. The last "Scottsboro Boy" left jail in 1950. © Bettmann/Corbis.

| In what ways did the Roaring Twenties challenge traditional values? | Why did the divide between rural and urban America grow in the 1920s? | What caused the crash of 1929? | What was life like in the early years of the depression? | Conclusion: Why did the hope of the 1920s turn to despair? |

Harlan County Coal Strike, 1931

Association in 1932, so named because its members planned to take a "holiday" from shipping crops to market. Farm militants also resorted to what they called "penny sales." When banks foreclosed and put farms up for auction, neighbors warned others not to bid, bought the foreclosed property for a few pennies, and returned it to the bankrupt owners. Militancy won farmers little in the way of long-term solutions, but one individual observed that "the biggest and finest crop of revolutions you ever saw is sprouting all over the country right now."

In 1932, thousands of unemployed World War I veterans traveled to Washington, D.C., to petition Congress for the immediate payment of the pension (known as a "bonus") that Congress had promised in 1924. Hoover feared that the veterans would spark a riot and ordered the U.S. Army to evict the Bonus Marchers from the city. The spectacle of the army driving peaceful, petitioning veterans from the nation's capital further undermined public support for the beleaguered Hoover.

The Great Depression—the massive failure of capitalism—catapulted the Communist Party to its greatest size and influence in American history. Some 100,000 Americans—workers, intellectuals, college students—joined the Communist Party in the belief that only an overthrow of the capitalist system could save the victims of the depression. In 1931, the party, through its National Miners Union, moved into Harlan County, Kentucky, to support a strike by brutalized coal miners. The mine owners unleashed thugs against the strikers and eventually beat the miners down. But the Communist Party gained a reputation as the most dedicated and fearless champion of the union cause.

The left also led the fight against racism. While both major parties refused to challenge segregation in the South, the Socialist Party, led by Norman Thomas, attacked the system of sharecropping that left many African Americans in near servitude. The Communist Party also took action. When nine young black men in Scottsboro, Alabama (the **Scottsboro Boys**), were arrested on trumped-up rape charges in 1931, a team of lawyers sent by the party saved the defendants from the electric chair.

Radicals on the left often sparked action, but protests by moderate workers and farmers occurred on a far greater scale. Breadlines, soup kitchens, foreclosures, unemployment, and cold despair drove patriotic men and women to question American capitalism. "I am as conservative as any man could be," a Wisconsin farmer explained, "but any economic system that has in its power to set me and my wife in the streets, at my age—what can I see but red?"

Scottsboro Boys

▶ Nine African American youths, ranging in age from thirteen to twenty-one, who were arrested for the alleged rape of two white women in Scottsboro, Alabama, in 1931. After an all-white jury sentenced the young men to death, the Communist Party took action that saved them from the electric chair.

> **QUICK REVIEW**

How did the depression reshape American life and politics?

CHAPTER LOCATOR | How did big business shape the New Era of the 1920s?

The Granger Collection, New York.

Conclusion: Why did the hope of the 1920s turn to despair?

IN THE AFTERMATH of World War I, America turned its back on progressive crusades and embraced conservative Republican politics, the growing influence of corporate leaders, and business values. Changes in the nation's economy propelled fundamental change throughout society. Living standards rose, economic opportunity increased, and Americans threw themselves into private pleasures. At home in Harlem and abroad in Paris, American literature, art, and music flourished.

For many Americans, however, none of the glamour and vitality had much meaning. The vast majority struggled to earn a decent living. Blue-collar America did not participate fully in white-collar prosperity. Country folk, deeply suspicious and profoundly discontented, championed prohibition, revived the Klan, attacked immigration, and defended old-time Protestant religion.

The crash of 1929 and the depression that followed starkly revealed the economy's crises of international trade and consumption. The depression hurt everyone, but the poor were hurt most. As farmers and workers sank into aching hardship, businessmen rallied around Herbert Hoover to proclaim that private enterprise would get the country moving again. But things fell apart, and Hoover faced increasingly more radical opposition. Membership in the Socialist and Communist parties surged, and more and more Americans contemplated desperate measures. By 1932, the depression had nearly brought the nation to its knees. America faced its greatest crisis since the Civil War, and citizens demanded new leaders who would save them from the "Hoover Depression."

SO NOW YOU KNOW

The economic changes of the 1920s led to higher incomes and better standards of living for many Americans, who eagerly consumed new products and amusements such as automobiles, washing machines, baseball games, and movies.

In what ways did the Roaring Twenties challenge traditional values?	Why did the divide between rural and urban America grow in the 1920s?	What caused the crash of 1929?	What was life like in the early years of the depression?	**Conclusion: Why did the hope of the 1920s turn to despair?**

STEP 1

GETTING STARTED

Below are basic terms from this period in American history. Can you identify each term below and explain why it matters? To do this exercise online or to download this chart, visit bedfordstmartins.com/roarkunderstanding.

TERM	WHO OR WHAT & WHEN	WHY IT MATTERS
Henry Ford, p. 630		
mass production, p. 631		
installment buying, p. 634		
prohibition, p. 635		
new woman, p. 636		
Harlem Renaissance, p. 638		
Lost Generation, p. 639		
Johnson-Reid Act, p. 642		
Ku Klux Klan, p. 643		
Scopes trial, p. 644		
Herbert Hoover, p. 646		
Scottsboro Boys, p. 654		

STEP 2

MOVING BEYOND THE BASICS

The exercise below represents a more advanced understanding of the chapter material. Examine the social, cultural, and economic trends that marked the 1920s as a "New Era" and the changes that occurred as the nation entered the Great Depression. Fill in the chart below by providing details of each development. When you are finished, ask yourself how change in each area affected the others. How, for example, did changes in manufacturing lead to new patterns of consumer behavior? What role did consumption play in changing gender roles? To do this exercise online or to download this chart, visit bedfordstmartins.com/roarkunderstanding.

	Characteristics/developments in the 1920s	Changes from 1929 to 1932
Business and manufacturing/urban life		
Agriculture/rural life		
Society: consumerism, religion, mass culture		
Population: gender, race relations, immigrants		
Government and politics		
The economy		

Now that you have reviewed key elements of the chapter, take a step back and try to explain the big picture by answering these questions. Remember to use specific examples from the chapter in your answers. To do this exercise online, visit bedfordstmartins.com/roarkunderstanding.

POSTWAR DEVELOPMENTS

▶ What place did big business hold in the politics and culture of the 1920s?

▶ How did the economic changes of the 1920s contribute to challenges to social, cultural, and ethical norms?

RESISTANCE TO CHANGE

▶ What explains the rising anti-immigrant mood of America in the 1920s?

▶ What cultural divisions between rural and urban America were highlighted by the election of 1928?

LOOKING BACKWARD, LOOKING AHEAD

▶ In your opinion, were the 1920s truly a New Era? Why or why not?

▶ How were American life and culture challenged by the economic collapse of 1929? How did economic disaster make political change possible?

THE CRASH AND THE GREAT DEPRESSION

▶ What underlying weaknesses in the American and world economies led to the Great Depression?

▶ How did Herbert Hoover respond to the economic crisis that engulfed his presidency? Why were his efforts unsuccessful?

▶ What was the "human toll" of the Great Depression?

IN YOUR OWN WORDS

Imagine that you must explain chapter 23 to someone who hasn't read it. What would the most important points to include and why?

24
FORGING THE NEW DEAL

1932–1939

> This chapter traces the efforts of President Franklin D. Roosevelt's administration to respond to the Great Depression. It also explores the principles and political factors that shaped the development and implementation of New Deal policies and examines the impact of those policies on 1930s America.

> How did Franklin D. Roosevelt and the Democrats win the 1932 election?

> What were the goals and achievements of the first New Deal?

> Who opposed the New Deal and why?

> How did the second phase of the New Deal differ from the first?

> Why did support for the New Deal decline in the late 1930s?

> Conclusion: What were the achievements and limitations of the New Deal?

DID YOU KNOW?

Congress established Social Security as part of the New Deal.

"Work Pays America!" Poster from the New Deal's Works Progress Administration.

How did Franklin D. Roosevelt and the Democrats win the 1932 election?

Roosevelt's Common Touch

Sensing that his presentation of himself as a good neighbor was responsible for much of his popularity, Roosevelt arranged to have a friendly chat outside the polls in his hometown of Hyde Park with working-class voter Ruben Appel. In this photograph, Appel seems unaware that Roosevelt's standing was itself a feat of stagecraft. Franklin D. Roosevelt Library.

▶ FOR MORE HELP ANALYZING THIS IMAGE, see the visual activity for this chapter in the Online Study Guide at bedfordstmartins.com/roarkunderstanding.

UNLIKE MILLIONS of impoverished Americans, Franklin Roosevelt came from a wealthy and privileged background that contributed to his optimism, self-confidence, and vitality. He drew on these personal qualities in his political career to bridge the chasm that separated him from the struggles of ordinary people. During the twelve years he served as president (1933–1945), many elites came to hate him as a traitor to his class, while millions more Americans, especially the hardworking poor and dispossessed, revered him because he cared about them and their problems.

The Making of a Politician

Born in 1882, **Franklin Delano Roosevelt** was steeped at home and school in high-minded doctrines of public service and Christian duty to help the poor and

Franklin Delano Roosevelt

▶ The thirty-second president of the United States. Roosevelt was elected in 1932 and reelected three times. He proposed a set of policies and legislation during the Great Depression that he called the "New Deal." He died in office shortly after beginning his fourth term.

CHAPTER LOCATOR

How did Franklin D. Roosevelt and the Democrats win the 1932 election?

weak. He prepared for a career in politics, hoping to follow in the footsteps of his fifth cousin, Theodore Roosevelt. Unlike Teddy, Franklin Roosevelt sought his political fortune in the Democratic Party. In 1920, he catapulted to the second spot on the national Democratic ticket as the vice presidential candidate of presidential nominee James M. Cox. Although Cox lost the election (see chapter 22), Roosevelt's performance convinced Democratic leaders that he had a future in national politics.

In the summer of 1921, Roosevelt became infected with polio. For the rest of his life, he wore heavy steel braces, and he could only walk a few steps by leaning on another person. Tireless physical therapy helped him regain his vitality and intense desire for high political office. After his polio attack, Roosevelt frequented a polio therapy facility at Warm Springs, Georgia. There, he made overtures to southern Democrats, forging relationships that would prove valuable for the rest of his political career.

By 1928, Roosevelt had recovered sufficiently to campaign successfully for governor of New York. His activist policies as governor foreshadowed his presidency. Governor Roosevelt believed that government should intervene to protect citizens from the economic hardships that came with the **Great Depression**. In contrast, many conservatives believed that government help for the needy sapped individual initiative and impeded the self-correcting forces of the market by rewarding people for losing the economic struggle to survive. Roosevelt lacked a full-fledged counterargument to these conservative claims, but he sympathized with the plight of poor people. "To these unfortunate citizens," he proclaimed, "aid must be extended by governments. . . . [No one should go] unfed, unclothed, or unsheltered." His many supporters appreciated his energy, activism, and conviction that government should do something to help Americans climb out of the economic abyss.

The Election of 1932

Democrats knew that President Herbert Hoover's unpopularity gave them a historic opportunity to recapture the White House in 1932. To do so, however, Democrats had to overcome warring factions within their party. Southern Democrats chaired powerful committees in Congress thanks to their continual reelection in the one-party South devoted to white supremacy. This southern, native-born, white, rural, Protestant, conservative wing of the Democratic Party found little common ground with the northern, immigrant, urban, disproportionately Catholic, liberal wing. Eastern-establishment Democrats shared few goals with angry farmers and factory workers. Still, this unruly coalition managed to agree to nominate Franklin Roosevelt as their presidential candidate.

In his acceptance speech, Roosevelt vowed to help "the forgotten man at the bottom of the pyramid" with "bold, persistent experimentation." Highlighting his differences with Hoover and the Republicans, he pledged "a new deal for the American people." Although few details about what Roosevelt meant by "a new deal" emerged during the presidential campaign, voters decided that whatever his new deal might be, it was better than reelecting Hoover.

Roosevelt won the 1932 presidential election in a historic landslide (**Map 24.1,** page 662). He received 57 percent of the nation's votes, the first time a Democrat

CHRONOLOGY

1882
– Franklin D. Roosevelt is born.

1920
– Roosevelt campaigns for vice president with Democratic presidential nominee James M. Cox.

1921
– Roosevelt contracts polio.

1928
– Roosevelt is elected governor of New York.

1932
– Roosevelt is elected president of the United States.

Great Depression
▶ Massive economic crisis that began in the late 1920s and continued until the United States entered World War II in 1941. The depression was a worldwide phenomenon, affecting not only the United States but most other nations as well.

| What were the goals and achievements of the first New Deal? | Who opposed the New Deal and why? | How did the second phase of the New Deal differ from the first? | Why did support for the New Deal decline in the late 1930s? | Conclusion: What were the achievements and limitations of the New Deal? |

Candidate	Electoral Vote	Popular Vote	Percent of Popular Vote
Franklin D. Roosevelt (Democrat)	472	22,821,857	57.4
Herbert C. Hoover (Republican)	59	15,761,841	39.7
Norman Thomas (Socialist)	0	881,951	2.2
William Z. Foster (Communist)	0	102,991	0.3

MAP 24.1 ■ The Election of 1932

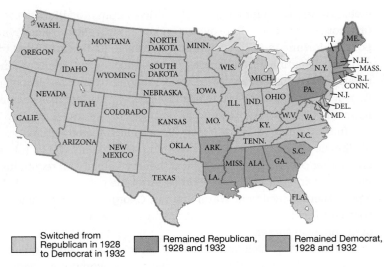

Switched from Republican in 1928 to Democrat in 1932	Remained Republican, 1928 and 1932	Remained Democrat, 1928 and 1932

MAP 24.2 ■ Electoral Shift, 1928–1932
The Democratic victory in 1932 signaled the rise of a New Deal coalition within which women and minorities, many of them new voters, made the Democrats the majority party for the first time in the twentieth century.

had won a majority of the popular vote since 1852 (**Map 24.2**). Roosevelt's coattails swept Democrats into control of Congress by large margins.

Roosevelt's victory represented the emergence of what came to be known as the New Deal coalition. Attracting support from farmers, factory workers, immigrants, city folk, African Americans, women, progressive intellectuals, and traditional Democratic strongholds in the South, Roosevelt launched a realignment of the nation's political loyalties. The New Deal coalition dominated American politics throughout Roosevelt's presidency and remained powerful long after his death in 1945. United less by ideology or support for specific policies, voters in the New Deal coalition instead expressed faith in Roosevelt's promise of a government that would, somehow, change things for the better.

> **QUICK REVIEW**

Why did Franklin D. Roosevelt win the 1932 presidential election by such a large margin?

CHAPTER LOCATOR | How did Franklin D. Roosevelt and the Democrats win the 1932 election?

A tireless ambassador of the New Deal, Eleanor Roosevelt used her status as First Lady to highlight New Dealers' sympathy for the plight of poor, unemployed, and neglected working people. Said one North Carolina woman about her, "One of my great pleasures was meeting Mrs. Roosevelt . . . she was so free of prejudice . . . she was always willing to take a stand."
© Bettmann/Corbis.

What were the goals and achievements of the first New Deal?

AT NOON ON MARCH 4, 1933, Americans gathered around their radios to hear the inaugural address of the newly elected president. Roosevelt began by asserting his "firm belief that the only thing we have to fear is fear itself—nameless, unreasoning, unjustified terror which paralyzes needed efforts to convert retreat into advance." He promised "direct, vigorous action," and the first months of his administration, termed "the Hundred Days," fulfilled that promise in a whirlwind of government initiatives that launched the **New Deal**.

Roosevelt and his advisers had three interrelated objectives: relief, recovery, and reform. The New Deal never fully achieved these goals, but by aiming for them, Roosevelt's experimental programs enormously expanded government's role in the nation's economy and society.

New Deal

▶ The legislation, policies, and initiatives launched during Franklin Roosevelt's presidency that were aimed at easing the crisis of the Great Depression. Although the New Deal never fully achieved its goals, Roosevelt and his advisers had three interrelated objectives: relief, recovery, and reform.

| What were the goals and achievements of the first New Deal? | Who opposed the New Deal and why? | How did the second phase of the New Deal differ from the first? | What were the varieties of domestic insurrections in 1774–1775? | Conclusion: What changes did Americans want in 1775? |

CHRONOLOGY

1933
March
- In his inaugural address, Roosevelt promises government action.
- Emergency Banking Act and the Glass-Steagall Banking Act
- Roosevelt gives first fireside chat.
- Civilian Conservation Corps is established.

May
- Federal Emergency Relief Administration is established.
- Agricultural Adjustment Act
- Tennessee Valley Authority is created.

June
- National Relief Administration is established.

1934
June
- Securities and Exchange Commission is established.

Eleanor Roosevelt

▶ Wife of Franklin Roosevelt and First Lady of the United States from 1933 to 1945. Eleanor Roosevelt was a champion of her husband's New Deal policies. She traveled throughout the United States to meet with ordinary Americans and hear their concerns.

Goals of the New Deal

Relief	Provide help to the millions of poor and unemployed Americans victimized by the depression.
Recovery	Foster economic recovery of farms and businesses, thereby creating jobs and reducing the need for relief.
Reform	Reshape government and the economy to protect citizens against future economic downturns.

The New Dealers

To design and implement the New Deal, Roosevelt convened a "Brains Trust" of economists and other leaders to offer suggestions and advise him about the problems facing the nation. Among the most important reformers to join the Roosevelt administration were two veterans of Roosevelt's New York governorship: Harry Hopkins and Frances Perkins. Hopkins, a social worker, administered New Deal relief efforts and served as one of the president's loyal confidants. Perkins, who had extensive experience trying to improve working conditions in shops and factories, served as secretary of labor, making her the first woman cabinet member in American history.

No New Dealers were more important than the president and his wife, Eleanor. The gregarious president radiated charm and good cheer, giving the New Deal a benevolent human face. **Eleanor Roosevelt** became the New Deal's unofficial ambassador, traveling throughout the nation meeting Americans of all colors and creeds in church basements, town halls, and front parlors.

As Roosevelt and his advisers developed plans to meet the economic emergency, their watchwords were *action*, *experiment*, and *improvise*. Without a sharply defined template for how to provide relief, recovery, and reform, they moved from ideas to policies as quickly as possible, hoping to identify ways to help people and to boost the economy. Four guiding ideas shaped their policies.

First, Roosevelt and his advisers sought capitalist solutions to the economic crisis. They believed that the depression had resulted from basic imbalances in the nation's capitalist economy—imbalances they wanted to correct. They had no desire to end capitalism. Instead, they hoped to save the capitalist economy by remedying its flaws.

Second, they believed that underconsumption was the root cause of the current economic paralysis. Factories and farms produced more than they could sell to consumers, causing factories to lay off workers and farmers to lose money on bumper crops. Workers without wages and farmers without profits shrank consumption and choked the economy. Somehow, the balance between consumption and production needed to be restored.

Third, New Dealers believed that the immense size and economic power of American corporations needed to be counterbalanced by government and by organization among workers and small producers. Unlike progressive trustbusters, New Dealers did not seek to splinter big businesses. Instead, Roosevelt and his advisers hoped to counterbalance big economic institutions with government programs focused on protecting individuals and the public interest.

CHAPTER LOCATOR

How did Franklin D. Roosevelt and the Democrats win the 1932 election?

Fourth, New Dealers felt that government must somehow moderate the imbalance of wealth created by American capitalism. Wealth concentrated in a few hands reduced consumption by most Americans and thereby contributed to the current economic gridlock. In the long run, government needed to find a way to permit ordinary working people to share more fully in the fruits of the economy. In the short term, New Dealers sought to lend a helping hand to poor people who suffered from the maldistribution of wealth.

Banking and Finance Reform

As Roosevelt took the oath of office on March 4, 1933, the nation's banking system was on the brink of collapse (**Figure 24.1**). New Dealers rushed to draft the Emergency Banking Act, which gave the secretary of the treasury the power to decide which banks could be safely reopened and to release funds from the Reconstruction Finance Corporation to bolster banks' assets. To secure the confidence of depositors, Congress passed the Glass-Steagall Banking Act, setting up the Federal Deposit Insurance Corporation (FDIC), which guaranteed bank customers that the federal government would reimburse them for deposits if their banks failed.

On Sunday night, March 12, while the banks were still closed, Roosevelt broadcast the first of a series of "fireside chats." Speaking in a friendly, informal manner, he explained the new banking legislation. This and subsequent fireside chats forged a direct connection between Roosevelt and millions of Americans, a connection felt by a man from Paris, Texas, who wrote to Roosevelt, "You are the one & only President that ever helped a Working Class of People. . . . Please help us some way[.] I Pray to God for relief." The banking legislation and fireside chat

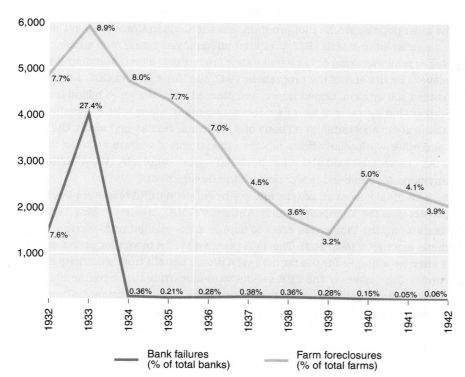

FIGURE 24.1 ■ Bank Failures and Farm Foreclosures, 1932–1942
New Deal legislation to stabilize the economy had its most immediate and striking effect in preventing banks, along with their depositors, from failing and farmers from losing their land.

What were the goals and achievements of the first New Deal?

Who opposed the New Deal and why?

How did the second phase of the New Deal differ from the first?

Why did support for the New Deal decline in the late 1930s?

Conclusion: What were the achievements and limitations of the New Deal?

worked. Within a few days, most of the nation's major banks reopened, and they remained solvent as reassured depositors returned funds to their bank accounts.

To prevent the fraud, corruption, and insider trading that had tainted Wall Street and contributed to the crash of 1929, Roosevelt pressed Congress to regulate the stock market. Legislation in 1934 created the Securities and Exchange Commission (SEC) to oversee financial markets by licensing investment dealers, monitoring all stock transactions, and requiring corporate officers to make full disclosures about their companies.

Relief and Conservation Programs

Patching the nation's financial structure provided little relief for the hungry and unemployed. A poor man from Nebraska asked Eleanor Roosevelt, "if the folk who was borned here in America . . . are this Forgotten Man, the President had in mind, [and] if we are this Forgotten Man[,] then we are still Forgotten." Since its founding, the federal government had never assumed responsibility for needy people, except in moments of natural disaster or emergencies such as the Civil War. Instead, churches, private charities, county and municipal governments, and occasionally states provided poor relief, usually with meager payments. The depression necessitated unprecedented federal relief efforts, according to Harry Hopkins and other New Dealers. As one New Yorker who still had a job wrote the government, "We work, ten hours a day for six days. In the grime and dirt of a nation [for] . . . low pay [making us] . . . slaves—slaves of the depression!"

Hopkins galvanized support for the Federal Emergency Relief Administration (FERA), which supported four million to five million households with $20 or $30 a month. FERA also created jobs for the unemployed on thousands of public works projects, organized by Hopkins into the Civil Works Administration (CWA), which put paychecks worth more than $800 million into the hands of previously jobless workers. CWA laborers renovated schools, dug sewers, and rebuilt roads and bridges.

The most popular work relief program was the Civilian Conservation Corps (CCC), established in March 1933. It offered unemployed young men a chance to earn wages while working to conserve natural resources, a long-standing interest of Roosevelt. By the end of the program in 1942, the three million CCC workers had checked soil erosion, tamed rivers, and planted more than two billion trees. CCC workers left a legacy of vast new recreation areas, along with roads that made those areas accessible to millions of Americans. Just as important, the CCC, CWA, and other work relief efforts replaced the stigma of welfare with the dignity of jobs. As one woman said about her husband's work relief job, "We aren't on relief anymore. My husband is working for the Government."

The New Deal's most ambitious and controversial natural resources development project was the Tennessee Valley Authority (TVA), created in May 1933 to build dams along the Tennessee River to supply impoverished rural communities with cheap electricity (**Map 24.3**). The TVA planned model towns for power station workers and new homes for the farmers who would benefit from electricity and flood control. Supporters of the TVA set out to demonstrate that a partnership between the federal government and local residents could overcome the barriers of state governments and private enterprises to make efficient use of abundant natural resources and break the ancient cycle of poverty. The TVA never fully realized these utopian ends, but it improved the lives of millions in the region with electric power, flood protection, soil reclamation, and jobs.

CHAPTER LOCATOR

How did Franklin D. Roosevelt and the Democrats win the 1932 election?

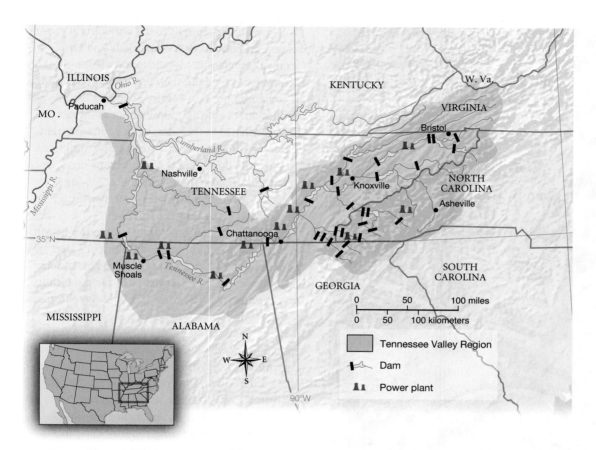

MAP 24.3 ■ **The Tennessee Valley Authority**
The New Deal created the Tennessee Valley Authority to modernize a vast impoverished region with hydroelectric power dams and, at the same time, to reclaim eroded land and preserve old folkways.

> ► FOR MORE HELP ANALYZING THIS MAP, see the map activity for this chapter in the Online Study Guide at bedfordstmartins.com/roarkunderstanding.

Other New Deal programs also addressed the needs of rural America. When Roosevelt became president, 90 percent of rural Americans lacked electricity. Beginning in 1935, the Rural Electrification Administration (REA) made low-cost loans available to local cooperatives for power plants and transmission lines to serve rural communities. Within ten years, the REA delivered electricity to nine out of ten farms, giving rural Americans access for the first time to modern electric conveniences.

Agricultural Initiatives

Farmers had been mired in a depression since the end of World War I. Farmers tried to compensate for low crop prices by growing more crops, hoping to boost their earnings by selling larger quantities. Instead, producing more crops pushed prices lower still. Income among farm families plunged to $167 a year, barely one-tenth of the national average.

| What were the goals and achievements of the first New Deal? | Who opposed the New Deal and why? | How did the second phase of the New Deal differ from the first? | Why did support for the New Deal decline in the late 1930s? | Conclusion: What were the achievements and limitations of the New Deal? |

1936 Campaign Poster

This campaign poster calls Roosevelt "A Real Depression Buster" and highlights his alphabet soup of New Deal agencies.

Collection of Janice L. and David J. Frent.

New Dealers sought to cut agricultural production, thereby raising crop prices and farmers' income. Farm families—who made up one-third of all Americans—would then buy more goods and lift consumption in the entire economy. To reduce production, the Agricultural Adjustment Act (AAA) authorized the "domestic allotment plan," which paid farmers *not* to grow crops. Individual farmers who agreed not to plant crops on a portion of their fields (their "allotment") would receive a government payment compensating them for the crops they did not plant.

With the formation of the Commodity Credit Corporation, the federal government allowed farmers to hold their harvested crops off the market and wait for a higher price. In the meantime, the government stored the crop and gave farmers a "commodity loan" based on a favorable price. In effect, commodity loans addressed the problem of underconsumption by making the federal government a major consumer of agricultural goods and reducing farmers' vulnerability to low prices. New Dealers also sponsored the Farm Credit Act (FCA) to provide long-term credit on mortgaged farm property, allowing debt-ridden farmers to avoid foreclosures that were driving thousands off their land.

Crop allotments, commodity loans, and mortgage credit made farmers major beneficiaries of the New Deal. Crop prices rose impressively, farm income jumped 50 percent by 1936, and FCA loans financed 40 percent of farm mortgage debt by the end of the decade. These gains were distributed fairly equally among farmers in the corn, hog, and wheat region of the Midwest. In the South's cotton belt, however, landlords controlled the distribution of New Deal agricultural benefits and shamelessly rewarded themselves while denying benefits to many sharecroppers and tenant farmers—blacks and whites—by taking the land they had worked out of production and assigning it to the allotment program. The president of the Oklahoma Tenant Farmers' Union explained that large farmers who got "Triple-A" payments often used the money to buy tractors and then "forced their tenants and [share] croppers off the land," causing these "Americans to be starved and dispossessed of their homes in our land of plenty."

Industrial Recovery

Unlike farmers, industrialists cut production with the onset of the depression. But falling industrial production meant that millions of working people lost their jobs. Mass unemployment reduced consumer demand for industrial products, contributing to a downward spiral in both production and jobs, with no end in sight.

CHAPTER LOCATOR

How did Franklin D. Roosevelt and the Democrats win the 1932 election?

Industries responded by reducing wages for employees who still had jobs, further reducing demand—a trend made worse by competition among industrial producers. New Dealers struggled to find a way to break this cycle of unemployment and underconsumption—a way consistent with corporate profits and capitalism.

The New Deal's National Industrial Recovery Act (NIRA) opted for a government-sponsored form of industrial self-government through the National Recovery Administration (NRA), established in June 1933. The NRA encouraged industrialists in every part of the economy to agree on rules, known as codes, to define fair working conditions, to set prices, and to minimize competition. The idea behind these codes was to stabilize existing industries and maintain their workforces while avoiding what both industrialists and New Dealers termed "destructive competition," which forced employers to cut wages and jobs. Industry after industry wrote elaborate codes addressing production, pricing, and competition. In exchange for relaxing federal antitrust regulations that prohibited such business agreements, the participating businesses promised to recognize the right of working people to organize and engage in collective bargaining. To encourage consumers to patronize businesses participating in NRA codes, the New Deal mounted a public relations campaign that displayed the NRA's Blue Eagle in shop windows and on billboards throughout the nation.

New Dealers hoped that NRA codes would ensure fair treatment of workers and consumers and promotion of the general economic welfare. Instead, NRA codes tended to strengthen conventional business practices. Large corporations wrote codes that served primarily their own interests rather than the needs of workers or the welfare of the national economy. The failure of codes to cover agricultural or domestic workers led one woman to complain to Roosevelt that the NRA "never mentioned the robbery of the Housewives" by the privations caused by the depression. In the end, the NRA did little to reduce unemployment, raise consumption, or relieve the depression.

QUICK REVIEW <

How effective was the first New Deal in bringing about relief, recovery, and reform?

| What were the goals and achievements of the first New Deal? | Who opposed the New Deal and why? | How did the second phase of the New Deal differ from the first? | Why did support for the New Deal decline in the late 1930s? | Conclusion: What were the achievements and limitations of the New Deal? |

> Who opposed the New Deal and why?

THE FIRST NEW DEAL INITIATIVES engendered fierce criticism and political opposition. From the right, Republicans and business people charged that New Deal programs were too radical, undermining private property, economic stability, and democracy. Critics on the left faulted the New Deal for its failure to allay the human suffering caused by the depression and for its timidity in attacking corporate power and greed.

Resistance to Business Reform

Business leaders lambasted Roosevelt, even though their economic prospects improved more than those of most other Americans during the depression. Although concentrated corporate power avoided reform, business leaders still conducted stridently anti–New Deal campaigns that expressed their resentment and fear of regulations, taxes, and unions. One opponent called the president "Stalin Delano Roosevelt" and insisted that the New Deal was really a "Raw Deal."

CHAPTER LOCATOR

How did Franklin D. Roosevelt and the Democrats win the 1932 election?

By 1935, two major business organizations, the National Association of Manufacturers and the Chamber of Commerce, had become openly anti–New Deal. Their critiques were amplified by the American Liberty League, founded in 1934. To League members, the AAA was a "trend toward fascist control of agriculture," relief programs marked "the end of democracy," and the NRA was a plunge into the "quicksand of visionary experimentation."

Economists who favored rational planning in the public interest and labor leaders who sought to influence wages and working conditions by organizing unions attacked the New Deal from the left. In their view, the NRA stifled enterprise by permitting monopolistic practices. Labor leaders especially resented the NRA's willingness to allow businesses to form company-controlled unions while blocking workers from organizing genuine grassroots unions to bargain for themselves.

The Supreme Court stepped into this cross fire of criticisms in May 1935 and declared that the NRA unconstitutionally conferred powers reserved to Congress on an administrative agency staffed by government appointees. The NRA codes soon lost the little authority they had. The failure of the NRA demonstrated the depth of many Americans' resistance to economic planning and the stubborn refusal of business leaders to yield to government regulations or reforms.

Casualties in the Countryside

The AAA fared better in the face of criticism than the NRA. Allotment checks for keeping land fallow and crop prices high created loyalty among farmers with enough acreage to participate. Agricultural processors and distributors, however, criticized the AAA. They objected that the program reduced the volume of crop production—the only source of their profits—while they paid a tax on processed crops that funded the very program that disadvantaged them. In 1936, the Supreme Court agreed with their contention that they were victims of an illegal tax. The AAA rebounded from the Supreme Court ruling by eliminating the offending tax and funding allotment payments from general government revenues.

Protests stirred, however, among those who did not qualify for allotments. The Southern Farm Tenants Union argued passionately that the AAA enriched large farmers and impoverished small farmers who rented rather than owned their land. One black sharecropper explained why so little New Deal money trickled down to her: "De landlord is landlord, de politicians is landlord, de judge is landlord, de shurf [sheriff] is landlord, ever'body is landlord, en we [sharecroppers] ain' got nothin'!" Such testimony showed that the AAA, like the NRA, tended to help most those who least needed help.

Displaced tenants often joined the army of migrant workers who straggled across rural America during the 1930s. Hundreds of thousands of "Okies" streamed out of the Dust Bowl of Oklahoma, Kansas, Texas, and Colorado, where chronic drought and harmful agricultural practices blasted crops and hopes. Many migrated to the lush fields and orchards of California, but few found steady or secure work. As one Okie said, "When they need us they call us migrants, and when we've picked their crop, we're bums and we got to get out."

CHRONOLOGY

1932
- Huey Long of Louisiana is elected to U.S. Senate.

1934
- Pro-business, anti–New Deal American Liberty League is founded.
- Upton Sinclair runs for governor of California.
- Dr. Francis Townsend proposes Old Age Revolving Pension plan.

1935
- Supreme Court declares the NRA unconstitutional.
- Father Charles Coughlin founds the National Union for Social Justice.
- Huey Long is assassinated.

1936
- U.S. Supreme Court strikes down parts of the AAA.

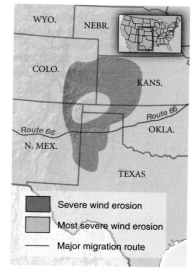

Severe wind erosion

Most severe wind erosion

—— Major migration route

The Dust Bowl

| What were the goals and achievements of the first New Deal? | Who opposed the New Deal and why? | How did the second phase of the New Deal differ from the first? | Why did support for the New Deal decline in the late 1930s? | Conclusion: What were the achievements and limitations of the New Deal? |

What specific solutions to the crisis of the depression did critics of the New Deal propose?

| What were the goals and achievements of the first New Deal? | Who opposed the New Deal and why? | How did the second phase of the New Deal differ from the first? | Why did support for the New Deal decline in the late 1930s? | Conclusion: What were the achievements and limitations of the New Deal? |

> How did the second phase of the New Deal differ from the first?

California Farmworkers Mural

During the 1930s, artists—many of them employed by New Deal agencies—painted thousands of murals depicting the variety and vigor of American life. California-born Maxine Albro, one of the first woman muralists commissions by the WPA, painted this mural depicting farmworkers harvesting the bounty of California's fields.
© Corbis. All Rights Reserved.

THE POPULAR MANDATE for the New Deal revealed by the congressional elections persuaded Roosevelt to press ahead with bold new efforts to achieve relief, recovery, and reform. Despite the initiatives of the Hundred Days, the depression still strangled the economy. Rumbles of discontent from Father Coughlin, Huey Long, and their supporters showed that New Deal programs had fallen far short of their goals. In 1935, Roosevelt capitalized on his congressional majorities to enact major new programs that signaled the emergence of an American welfare state.

Although many citizens remained unprotected, New Deal programs provided a safety net that helped millions with jobs, relief, and government support. Underlying these programs was the idea that when people suffered because of forces beyond their control, the federal government bore responsibility to support and protect individual Americans. The safety net of welfare programs tied the political loyalty of working people to the New Deal and the Democratic Party. As a North Carolina mill worker said, "Mr. Roosevelt is the only man we ever had in the White House who would understand that my boss is a sonofabitch."

CHAPTER LOCATOR | How did Franklin D. Roosevelt and the Democrats win the 1932 election?

Relief for the Unemployed

First and foremost, millions of Americans still needed jobs. In response, Roosevelt and his advisers launched a massive work relief program. Roosevelt believed that direct government handouts crippled recipients with "spiritual and moral disintegration . . . destructive to the human spirit." Jobs, in contrast, bolstered individuals' "self-respect, . . . self-confidence, . . . courage, and determination." With a congressional appropriation of nearly $5 billion—more than all government revenues in 1934—the New Deal created the **Works Progress Administration (WPA)** to give unemployed Americans government-funded jobs on public works projects. The WPA put millions of jobless citizens to work on roads, bridges, parks, public buildings, and more. By 1936, the WPA provided jobs for 7 percent of the nation's labor force. In effect, the WPA made the federal government the employer of last resort, creating useful jobs when the private sector failed to do so. Overall, WPA jobs put 13 million Americans to work and gave them paychecks worth $10 billion.

About three out of four WPA jobs involved construction and renovation of the nation's physical infrastructure. In addition, the WPA gave jobs to thousands of artists, musicians, actors, journalists, poets, and novelists. Throughout the nation, WPA projects displayed tangible evidence of the New Deal's commitment to public welfare.

Empowering Labor

During the Great Depression, factory workers who managed to keep their jobs worried constantly about being laid off while their wages and working hours were cut. When workers tried to organize labor unions to protect themselves, municipal and state governments usually sided with employers. The New Deal dramatically reversed the federal government's stance toward unions, lending the government's support to an unprecedented wave of union organizing among the nation's working people. When the head of the United Mine Workers, John L. Lewis, told coal miners that "the President wants you to join a union," he exaggerated only a little. New Dealers believed that unions would counterbalance the power of big corporations by defending working people, maintaining wages, and replacing the violence that often accompanied strikes with economic peace and commercial stability.

Violent battles across the nation showed the determination of militant labor leaders to organize unions. In 1934, striking workers in Toledo, Minneapolis, San Francisco, and elsewhere were beaten and shot by police and the National Guard. In Congress, labor leaders lobbied for the National Labor Relations Act (NLRA), a bill sponsored by Senator Robert Wagner of New York that authorized the federal government to intervene in labor disputes and supervise the organization of labor unions. Signed into law in July 1935, the **Wagner Act**, as it came to be called, guaranteed industrial workers the right to organize unions, putting the might of federal law behind the appeals of labor leaders. The Wagner Act created the National Labor Relations Board (NLRB) to sponsor and oversee elections for union representation. If the majority of workers at a company voted for a union, then the union became the sole bargaining agent for the entire workplace, and the employer was required to negotiate with the elected union leaders.

CHRONOLOGY

1934
- In a historic shift, African American voters switch from the Republican to the Democratic Party in midterm elections.
- Indian Reorganization Act.

1935
- Works Progress Administration is created.
- National Labor Relations Act (Wagner Act).
- Committee for Industrial Organization is founded.
- Social Security Act.

1937
- Sit-down strike by United Auto Workers against General Motors.

1941
- Ford Motor Company capitulates to United Auto Workers, leaving the entire auto industry unionized.

Works Progress Administration (WPA)
▶ Federal New Deal program that provided government jobs to millions of Americans during the depression, in areas ranging from construction to the arts.

Wagner Act
▶ 1935 law that guaranteed industrial workers the right to organize into unions; also known as the National Labor Relations Act. The Wagner Act also created the National Labor Relations Board to oversee elections for union representation.

What were the goals and achievements of the first New Deal?	Who opposed the New Deal and why?	**How did the second phase of the New Deal differ from the first?**	Why did support for the New Deal decline in the late 1930s?	Conclusion: What were the achievements and limitations of the New Deal?

The Wagner Act and renewed labor militancy resulted in impressive increases in union membership (**Figure 24.2**) Most of the new union members were factory workers and unskilled laborers, many of them immigrants, women, and African Americans. For decades, established AFL unions had no desire to organize factory and unskilled workers, who struggled along without unions. In 1935, under the aggressive leadership of the mine workers' John L. Lewis and the head of the Amalgamated Clothing Workers, Sidney Hillman, a coalition of unskilled workers formed the Committee for Industrial Organization (CIO; later the Congress of Industrial Organizations). The CIO, helped by the Wagner Act, mobilized organizing drives in major industries, including the bitterly anti-union automobile and steel industries.

The bloody struggle by the CIO-affiliated United Auto Workers (UAW) to organize workers at General Motors climaxed in January 1937. Striking workers occupied the main assembly plant in Flint, Michigan, in a **"sit-down"** strike that slashed the plant's production of 15,000 cars a week to a mere 150. General Motors eventually surrendered and agreed to make the UAW the sole bargaining agent for all the company's workers and to refrain from interfering with union activity. Having subdued the auto industry's leading producer, the UAW expanded its campaign until, after much violence, the entire industry was unionized when the Ford Motor Company capitulated in 1941.

The CIO hoped to achieve similar success in the steel industry. But after unionizing the industry giant U.S. Steel, the CIO ran up against ruthless opposition from smaller steel firms. Following a police attack that killed ten strikers at Republic Steel outside Chicago in May 1937, the battered steelworkers halted their organizing campaign. In steel and other major industries, organizing efforts stalled until after 1941, when military mobilization created labor shortages that gave workers greater bargaining power.

"sit-down" strike

▶ A strike in which workers stop working but remain at their workplace. A sit-down strike at the General Motors Company in Flint, Michigan, in 1937 forced the company to recognize the United Auto Workers union as the bargaining agent for the workers.

FIGURE 24.2 ■ Labor Union Membership, 1930–1939

U.S. Department of Commerce, *Historical Statistics of the United States: Colonial Times to 1970* (Washington, D.C.: U.S. Government Printing Office, 1975), 178.

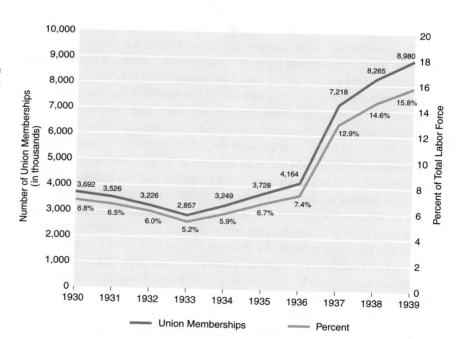

CHAPTER LOCATOR

How did Franklin D. Roosevelt and the Democrats win the 1932 election?

Social Security and Tax Reform

The single most important feature of the New Deal's emerging welfare state was **Social Security**. An ambitious, far-reaching, and permanent reform, Social Security was designed to provide a modest income to relieve the poverty of elderly people. Prompted by the popular but impractical panaceas of Dr. Townsend, Father Coughlin, and Huey Long, Roosevelt became the first president to advocate protection for the elderly. He told Congress that "it is our plain duty to provide for that security upon which welfare depends . . . and undertake the great task of furthering the security of the citizen and his family through social insurance."

The political struggle for Social Security highlighted class differences among Americans. Support for the measure came from a coalition of advocacy groups for the elderly and the poor, traditional progressives, leftists, social workers, and labor unions. Arrayed against them were economic conservatives, including the Republican Party, the American Liberty League, the National Association of Manufacturers, the Chamber of Commerce, and the American Medical Association. Despite such opposition, the large New Deal majority in Congress passed the Social Security Act in August 1935.

Social Security

▶ A federal program designed to provide a modest income for elderly people. Social Security became the longest-lasting and most far-reaching of all the New Deal programs.

Key Provisions of Social Security

Used tax contributions from workers and their employers to fund pensions for the elderly.
Stipulated that, upon reaching retirement age, workers would earn benefits based on their contributions and years of work.
Placed no means test on eligibility for benefits.
Created unemployment insurance that provided modest benefits for workers who lost their jobs.

Not all workers benefited from the Social Security Act. It excluded domestic and agricultural workers, thereby making ineligible about half of all African Americans and more than half of all employed women—about five million people in all. In addition, the law excluded workers employed by religious and nonprofit organizations, such as schools and hospitals, rendering ineligible even more working women and minorities.

In a bow to traditional beliefs about local governments' responsibility for public assistance, Social Security issued multimillion-dollar grants to the states to help support dependent children, public health services, and the blind. After the Supreme Court in 1937 upheld Social Security, the program was expanded to include benefits for dependent survivors of deceased recipients. The system gave millions of working people the assurance that, when they became too old to work, they would receive a modest income from the federal government.

Roosevelt saw in tax reform a way to redistribute wealth that would weaken conservative opposition, advance the cause of social equity, and defuse political challenges from Huey Long and Father Coughlin. In June 1935, as the Social Security Act was being debated, Roosevelt delivered a message to Congress outlining comprehensive reform. Charging that large fortunes put "great and undesirable concentration of control in [the hands of] relatively few individuals," Roosevelt urged a graduated tax on corporations, an inheritance tax, and an increase in

| What were the goals and achievements of the first New Deal? | Who opposed the New Deal and why? | How did the second phase of the New Deal differ from the first? | Why did support for the New Deal decline in the late 1930s? | Conclusion: What were the achievements and limitations of the New Deal? |

At the urging of Eleanor Roosevelt, Mary McLeod Bethune, a southern educational and civil rights leader, became director of the National Youth Administration's Division of Negro Affairs. The first black woman to head a federal agency, Bethune used her position to promote social change. Moorland-Spingarn Research Center, Howard University.

Mary McLeod Bethune

▶ Activist who was the highest-ranking black official in Franklin Roosevelt's administration. She was a strong advocate for the hiring of African Americans to federal New Deal jobs.

maximum personal income taxes. Congress endorsed Roosevelt's basic principle by taxing those with higher incomes at a somewhat higher rate.

Neglected Americans and the New Deal

The patchwork of New Deal reforms erected a two-tier welfare state. In the top tier, organized workers in major industries were the greatest beneficiaries of New Deal initiatives. In the bottom tier, millions of neglected Americans—women, children, and old folks, along with the unorganized, unskilled, uneducated, and unemployed—often fell through the New Deal safety net. Many working people remained more or less untouched by New Deal benefits. The average unemployment rate for the 1930s stayed high—17 percent. Workers in industries that resisted unions received little help from the Wagner Act or the WPA. Domestic workers—almost all of them women—and agricultural workers— many of them African, Hispanic, or Asian Americans—were neither unionized nor eligible for Social Security.

The New Deal neglected few citizens more than African Americans. About half of black Americans in cities were jobless. In the rural South, where the vast majority of African Americans lived, conditions were worse. New Deal agricultural policies such as the AAA favored landowners and often resulted in black sharecroppers and tenants being pushed off the land they farmed. Disfranchisement by intimidation and legal subterfuge prevented southern blacks from protesting their plight at the ballot box. Protesters risked vicious retaliation from local whites. After years of decline, lynching increased during the 1930s. In 1935, a riot in Harlem focused on white-owned businesses, dramatizing blacks' resentment and despair. Bitter critics charged that the New Deal's NRA stood for "Negro Run Around" or "Negroes Ruined Again."

Roosevelt responded to such criticisms with great caution, since New Deal reforms required the political support of powerful conservative, segregationist, southern white Democrats, who would be alienated by programs that aided blacks. Nonetheless, New Dealers still tried to attract political support from black leaders. Roosevelt's overtures to African Americans prompted northern black voters in the 1934 congressional elections to shift from the Republican to the Democratic Party, helping elect New Deal Democrats.

Eleanor Roosevelt sponsored the appointment of **Mary McLeod Bethune**—the energetic cofounder of the National Council of Negro Women—as head of the Division of Negro Affairs in the National Youth Administration. The highest-ranking black official in Roosevelt's administration, Bethune used her position to guide a small number of black professionals and civil rights activists to posts within New Deal agencies. Nicknamed the "Black Cabinet," these men and women composed the first sizable representation of African Americans in white-collar posts in the federal government, and they ultimately helped about one in four African Americans get access to New Deal relief programs.

CHAPTER LOCATOR | How did Franklin D. Roosevelt and the Democrats win the 1932 election?

Despite these gains, by 1940 African Americans still suffered severe handicaps. Most of the thirteen million black workers toiled at low-paying menial jobs, unprotected by the New Deal safety net. Making a mockery of the "separate but equal" doctrine, segregated black schools had less money and worse facilities than white schools, and only 1 percent of black students earned college degrees. In southern states, there were no black police officers or judges and hardly any black lawyers, and vigilante violence against blacks went unpunished.

Hispanic Americans fared no better. About a million Mexican Americans lived in the United States in the 1930s, most of them first- or second-generation immigrants who worked crops throughout the West. To preserve scarce jobs for U.S. citizens, the federal government choked off immigration from Mexico, while state and local officials prohibited the employment of aliens on work relief projects and deported tens of thousands of Mexican Americans, many with their American-born children. Local white administrators of many New Deal programs throughout the West discriminated against Hispanics and other people of color. A New Deal study concluded that "the Mexican is . . . segregated from the rest of the community as effectively as the Negro . . . [by] poverty and low wages."

Asian Americans had similar experiences. Asian immigrants were still excluded from U.S. citizenship and in many states were not permitted to own land. By 1930, more than half of Japanese Americans had been born in the United States, but they were still liable to discrimination. One young Asian American expressed the frustration felt by many others: "I am a fruit-stand worker. I would much rather it were doctor or lawyer . . . but my aspirations [were] frustrated long ago by circumstances [and] I am only what I am, a professional carrot washer."

Native Americans also suffered neglect from New Deal agencies. As a group, they remained the poorest of the poor. Since the Dawes Act of 1887 (see chapter 17), the federal government had encouraged Native Americans to assimilate—to abandon their Indian identities and adopt the cultural norms of the majority society. Under the leadership of the New Deal's commissioner of Indian affairs, John Collier, the New Deal's Indian Reorganization Act (IRA) of 1934 largely reversed that policy. The IRA brought little immediate benefit to Native Americans and remained a divisive issue for decades, but it provided an important foundation for Indians' economic, cultural, and political resurgence a generation later.

Singer and songwriter Woody Guthrie, the troubadour of working people, traveled the nation for eight years during the 1930s and heard other rambling men tell him "the story of their life," giving voice to experiences common among Americans neglected by the New Deal: "how the home went to pieces, how . . . the crops got to where they wouldn't bring nothing, work in factories would kill a dog . . . and—always, always [you] have to fight and argue and cuss and swear . . . to try to get a nickel more out of the rich bosses."

QUICK REVIEW <

What features of a welfare state did the New Deal create and why?

| What were the goals and achievements of the first New Deal? | Who opposed the New Deal and why? | **How did the second phase of the New Deal differ from the first?** | Why did support for the New Deal decline in the late 1930s? | Conclusion: What were the achievements and limitations of the New Deal? |

Why did support for the New Deal decline in the late 1930s?

Distributing Surplus Food to the Needy When bountiful harvests produced surplus crops that would depress prices if they were sent to market, the New Deal arranged to distribute some of them to needy Americans. Here, farmworkers near the New Mexico border in east-central Arizona line up to receive a ration of potatoes authorized by the New Deal agent checking the box of index cards. Library of Congress.

TO ACCELERATE the sputtering economic recovery, Roosevelt shifted the emphasis of the New Deal in the mid-1930s. Instead of seeking cooperation from conservative business leaders, he decided to rely on the growing New Deal coalition to enact reforms over the strident opposition of the Supreme Court, Republicans, and corporate interests.

The Election of 1936

Roosevelt believed that the presidential election of 1936 would test his leadership and progressive ideals. The depression still had a stranglehold on the economy. Conservative leaders believed that the New Deal's failure to lift the nation out of the depression indicated that Americans were ready for a change. Left-wing critics insisted that the New Deal had missed the opportunity to displace capitalism with a socialist economy and that voters would embrace candidates who recommended more radical remedies.

Republicans chose Governor Alfred (Alf) Landon of Kansas as their presidential nominee. A moderate who had supported some New Deal measures, Landon stressed mainstream Republican proposals to achieve a balanced federal budget

CHAPTER LOCATOR

How did Franklin D. Roosevelt and the Democrats win the 1932 election?

and to ease the perils of illness and old age with old-fashioned neighborliness instead of new government bureaucracies.

Roosevelt won 60.8 percent of the popular vote, making it the widest margin of victory in a presidential election to date. Third parties—including the Socialist and Communists parties—fell pitifully short of the support they expected and never again mounted a significant challenge to the New Deal. Congressional results were equally lopsided, with Democrats outnumbering Republicans more than three to one in both houses.

In his inaugural address, Roosevelt pledged to use his mandate to help all citizens achieve a decent standard of living. He announced, "I see one third of a nation ill-housed, ill-clad, [and] ill-nourished," and he promised to devote his second term to alleviating their hardship.

Court Packing

In the afterglow of his reelection triumph, Roosevelt targeted the Supreme Court as the largest remaining obstacle to New Deal reforms. Laden with conservative justices appointed by Republican presidents, the Court had invalidated eleven New Deal measures as unconstitutional interferences with free enterprise. Now, Social Security, the Wagner Act, the Securities and Exchange Commission, and other New Deal innovations were about to be considered by justices.

To ensure that the Supreme Court's "horse and buggy" notions did not dismantle the New Deal, Roosevelt proposed a "court-packing" plan that added one new justice for each existing judge who had served for ten years and was over the age of seventy. In effect, the proposed law would give Roosevelt the power to pack the Court with up to six new justices.

But the president had not reckoned with Americans' deeply rooted deference to the independent authority of the Supreme Court. More than two-thirds of Americans believed that the Court should be free from political interference. The suggestion that individuals over age seventy had diminished mental capacity offended many elderly members of Congress, which defeated the bill in 1937.

Although Roosevelt's court-packing plan failed, Supreme Court justices got the message. After the furor abated, Chief Justice Charles Evans Hughes and fellow moderate Owen Roberts changed their views enough to keep the Court from invalidating the Wagner Act and Social Security. Then the most conservative of the elderly justices retired. Roosevelt eventually named eight justices to the Court—more than any other president, ultimately giving New Deal laws safe passage through the Court.

Reaction and Recession

Emboldened by their defeat of the court-packing plan, Republicans and southern Democrats rallied around their common conservatism to obstruct additional reforms. Democrats' arguments over whether the New Deal needed to be expanded—and if so, how—undermined the consensus among reformers and sparked antagonism between Congress and the White House. The ominous rise of belligerent regimes in Germany, Italy, Japan, and elsewhere slowed reform as some Americans began to worry more about defending the nation than changing it.

CHRONOLOGY

1936
- Roosevelt is elected to a second term in a landslide.

1937
- Congress defeats Roosevelt's "court-packing" plan.
- Farm Security Administration is created.
- National Housing Act.

1937–1938
- Roosevelt's reduction in government spending leads to a sharp economic downturn.

1938
- Fair Labor Standards Act.

| What were the goals and achievements of the first New Deal? | Who opposed the New Deal and why? | How did the second phase of the New Deal differ from the first? | Why did support for the New Deal decline in the late 1930s? | Conclusion: What were the achievements and limitations of the New Deal? |

Roosevelt himself favored slowing the pace of the New Deal. He believed that existing New Deal measures had steadily boosted the economy and largely eliminated the depression crisis. Roosevelt's unwarranted optimism about the economic recovery persuaded him that additional deficit spending by the federal government was no longer necessary.

Roosevelt failed to consider the stubborn realities of unemployment and poverty, and the reduction in deficit spending reversed the improving economy. Even at the high-water mark of recovery in the summer of 1937, seven million people lacked jobs. In the next few months, national income and production slipped so steeply that almost two-thirds of the economic gains since 1933 were lost by June 1938. Farm prices dropped 20 percent, and unemployment rose by more than two million. This economic reversal hurt the New Deal politically. Conservatives argued that this recession proved that New Deal measures produced only an illusion of progress. Many New Dealers insisted instead that the continuing depression demanded that Roosevelt revive federal spending and redouble efforts to stimulate the economy. In 1938, Congress heeded such pleas and enacted a massive new program of federal spending.

The recession scare of 1937–1938 taught the president the lesson that economic growth had to be carefully nurtured. The English economist John Maynard Keynes argued in his influential work *The General Theory of Employment, Interest, and Money* (1936) that only government intervention could pump enough money into the economy to restore prosperity. Roosevelt never had the inclination or time to master Keynesian theory, but he understood that escape from the depression required a plan for large-scale spending to alleviate distress and stimulate economic growth. (See "Global Comparison.")

The Last of the New Deal Reforms

From the moment he was sworn in, Roosevelt sought to expand the powers of the presidency. He believed that the president needed more authority to meet emergencies such as the depression and to administer the sprawling federal bureaucracy. In September 1938, Congress passed the Administrative Reorganization Act, which gave Roosevelt (and future presidents) new influence over the bureaucracy. Combined with a Democratic majority in Congress, a now-friendly Supreme Court, and the revival of deficit spending, the newly empowered White House seemed to be in a good position to move ahead with a revitalized New Deal.

Resistance to further reform was also on the rise, however. Conservatives argued that the New Deal had pressed government centralization too far. Even the New Deal's friends became weary of one emergency program after another while economic woes continued to shadow New Deal achievements. By the midpoint of Roosevelt's second term, restive members of Congress balked at new initiatives. Clearly, the New Deal was losing momentum, but enough support remained for one last burst of reform.

Agriculture still had strong claims on New Deal attention in the face of drought, declining crop prices, and impoverished sharecroppers and tenants. In 1937, the Agriculture Department created the Farm Security Administration (FSA) to provide housing and loans to help tenant farmers become independent. A black tenant farmer in North Carolina who received an FSA loan told a New Deal inter-

CHAPTER LOCATOR

How did Franklin D. Roosevelt and the Democrats win the 1932 election?

682 CHAPTER 24
FORGING THE NEW DEAL, 1932–1939

viewer, "I wake up in the night sometimes and think I must be half-dead and gone to heaven." But relatively few tenants received loans because the FSA was starved for funds and ran up against the major farm organizations intent on serving their own interests. For those who owned farms, the New Deal offered renewed prosperity with a second Agricultural Adjustment Act (AAA) in 1938. To moderate price swings by regulating supply, the plan combined production quotas on five staple crops—cotton, tobacco, wheat, corn, and rice—with storage loans through its Commodity Credit Corporation. The most prosperous farmers benefited most, but the act's Federal Surplus Commodities Corporation added an element of charity by issuing food stamps so that the poor could obtain surplus food. The AAA of 1938 brought stability to American agriculture and ample food to most—but not all—tables.

	Population (millions)	Gross Domestic Product (millions of dollars)
United States		
Britain		
British Colonies		
France		
French Colonies		
Italy		
Italian Colonies		
Netherlands		
Dutch Colonies		
USSR		
Japan		
Japanese Colonies		
Germany		
Austria		
Czechoslovakia		
Poland		
Hungary		
Yugoslavia		
Romania		

⍟ = 10 million people
$ = 10 million dollars

GLOBAL COMPARISON

National Populations and Economies, circa 1938

Throughout the Great Depression, the United States remained more productive than any other nation in the world. Despite the lingering effects of the depression, by 1938 the United States produced more than twice as much as Germany and the Soviet Union, nearly three times as much as Britain, more than four times as much as France and Japan, and more than five times as much as Italy. From the viewpoint of Germany, if the European nations listed here could be brought under German control, its economy would be greater than that of the United States and the mightiest in the world. Economically, how important were colonies to the major powers? In general, what do these data suggest about the relationship between population and gross domestic product?

What were the goals and achievements of the first New Deal?

Who opposed the New Deal and why?

How did the second phase of the New Deal differ from the first?

Why did support for the New Deal decline in the late 1930s?

Conclusion: What were the achievements and limitations of the New Deal?

Advocates for the urban poor also made modest gains after decades of neglect. New York senator Robert Wagner convinced Congress to pass the National Housing Act in 1937. By 1941, some 160,000 residences had been made available to poor people at affordable rents. The program did not come close to meeting the need for affordable housing, but for the first time, the federal government took an active role in providing decent urban housing.

The last major piece of New Deal labor legislation, the Fair Labor Standards Act of June 1938, reiterated the New Deal pledge to provide workers with a decent standard of living. After lengthy debate that revealed the waning strength of the New Deal, Congress finally agreed to intervene in the long-sacrosanct realm of worker contracts. The new law set wage and hours standards and at long last curbed the use of child labor. The minimum-wage level was modest—twenty-five cents an hour for a maximum of forty-four hours a week. And, in order to attract enough conservative votes, the act exempted merchant seamen, fishermen, domestic help, and farm laborers—relegating most women and African Americans to lower wages. Enforcement of the minimum-wage standards was weak and haphazard. Nevertheless, the Fair Labor Standards Act slowly advanced Roosevelt's inaugural promise to improve the living standards of the poorest Americans.

The final New Deal reform effort failed to make much headway against entrenched racial injustice. Although Roosevelt denounced lynching as murder, he would not jeopardize his vital base of white southern political support by demanding anti-lynching legislation, and Congress voted down attempts to make lynching a federal crime. Laws to eliminate the poll tax—used to deny blacks the opportunity to vote—encountered the same overwhelming resistance. The New Deal refused to confront racial injustice with the same vigor it brought to bear on economic hardship.

By the end of 1938, the New Deal had lost steam and encountered stiff opposition. In the congressional elections of 1938, Republicans made gains that gave them more congressional influence than they had enjoyed since 1932. New Dealers could claim unprecedented achievements since 1933, but nobody needed reminding that those achievements had not ended the depression. In his annual message to Congress in January 1939, Roosevelt signaled a halt to New Deal reforms by speaking about preserving the progress already achieved rather than extending it. Roosevelt pointed to the ominous threats posed by fascist aggressors in Germany and Japan, and he proposed defense expenditures that surpassed New Deal appropriations for relief and economic recovery.

> **QUICK REVIEW**

How and why did political support for New Deal reforms decline?

Library of Congress.

Conclusion: What were the achievements and limitations of the New Deal?

THE NEW DEAL reflected Roosevelt's confidence, optimism, and energetic pragmatism. A growing majority of Americans agreed with Roosevelt that the federal government should help those in need, thereby strengthening the political coalition that propelled the New Deal. In the process of seeking relief for victims of the depression, recovery of the general economy, and basic reform of major economic institutions, the New Deal vastly expanded the size and influence of the federal government and changed the way the American people viewed Washington. New Dealers achieved significant victories, such as Social Security, labor's right to organize, and guarantees that farm prices would be maintained through controls on production and marketing. New Deal measures marked the emergence of a welfare state, but the New Deal's limited, two-tier character left many needy Americans with little aid.

Full-scale relief, recovery, and reform eluded New Deal programs, and in 1940 the depression still plagued the economy. The most durable New Deal achievements were reforms that stabilized agriculture, encouraged the organization of labor unions, and created the safety net of Social Security and fair labor standards. Perhaps the most impressive achievement of the New Deal was what did not happen. Although authoritarian governments and anticapitalist policies were common outside the United States during the 1930s, they were shunned by the New Deal coalition. Republicans and other conservatives claimed that the New Deal amounted to a form of socialism that threatened democracy and capitalism. But rather than attack capitalism and democracy, Franklin Roosevelt sought to save them, and he succeeded.

New Dealers repeatedly described their programs as a kind of warfare against the economic adversities of the 1930s. In the next decade, with the depression only partly vanquished, the Roosevelt administration had to turn from the New Deal's war against economic crisis at home to participate in a worldwide conflagration to defeat the enemies of democracy abroad.

SO NOW YOU KNOW

At the beginning of this chapter, you were asked if you knew that Social Security originated in the New Deal. Today, Social Security payments to elderly and dependent Americans account for over a third of federal government expenditures, all paid for by contributions from workers and their employers. Now that you've read the chapter, what have you learned about this program? What other New Deal programs had a long-term impact on American life?

| What were the goals and achievements of the first New Deal? | Who opposed the New Deal and why? | How did the second phase of the New Deal differ from the first? | Why did support for the New Deal decline in the late 1930s? | **Conclusion: What were the achievements and limitations of the New Deal?** |

STEP 1

GETTING STARTED

Below are basic terms from this period in U.S. history. Can you identify each term below and explain why it matters? To do this exercise online or to download this chart, visit bedfordstmartins.com/roarkunderstanding.

TERM	WHO OR WHAT & WHEN	WHY IT MATTERS
Franklin D. Roosevelt, p. 660		
Great Depression, p. 661		
New Deal, p. 663		
Eleanor Roosevelt, p. 664		
Huey Long, p. 673		
Works Progress Administration, p. 675		
Wagner Act, p. 675		
"sit-down" strike, p. 676		
Social Security, p. 677		
Mary McLeod Bethune, p. 678		

STEP 2

MOVING BEYOND THE BASICS

The exercise below represents a more advanced understanding of the chapter material. Identify the following programs and legislation and decide if they were enacted to pursue the New Deal goal of relief, recovery, or reform. Describe each program and explain your reasoning for putting it into the appropriate category. Then determine the extent to which the program/legislation could be considered a success and why. To do this exercise online or to download this chart, visit bedfordstmartins.com/roarkunderstanding.

Program/legislation	Description	Relief, recovery, or reform?	How successful or unsuccessful was it?
Agricultural Adjustment Act			
Civilian Conservation Corps			
Emergency Banking Act			
Fair Labor Standards Act			
Federal Emergency Relief Administration			
Indian Reorganization Act			
National Recovery Administration			
National Youth Administration			
Public Works Administration			
Social Security Act			
Tennessee Valley Authority			
Works Progress Administration			

Now that you've reviewed various parts of the chapter, take a step back and try to see the big picture by answering these questions. Remember to use specific examples from the chapter in your answers. To do this exercise online, visit bedfordstmartins.com/roarkunderstanding.

FRANKLIN D. ROOSEVELT

▶ Why was Franklin Roosevelt so popular? Why did he win the elections of 1932 and 1936?

▶ How was Eleanor Roosevelt a part of her husband's political career?

THE NEW DEAL

▶ What were the greatest achievements of the New Deal, both generally and specifically?

▶ What were the differences between the first phase of the New Deal and the second?

THE OPPOSITION

▶ Who initially opposed the New Deal and why?

▶ Why did general support for the New Deal decline?

LOOKING BACKWARD, LOOKING AHEAD

▶ What was distinctive about the New Deal compared with previous government reforms in the twentieth century?

▶ What was the long-term significance of the New Deal?

IN YOUR OWN WORDS

Imagine that you must explain chapter 24 to someone who hasn't read it. What would be the most important points to include and why?

25
THE UNITED STATES AND THE SECOND WORLD WAR

1939–1945

> This chapter examines the involvement of the United States in World War II. It explores the events leading up to American entry into the war, the course of the war, the impact of the war on the home front, and the events that led to Allied victory.

DID YOU KNOW?

During World War II, military production in the United States was more than twice than that of Germany, Japan, and Italy combined.

> How did America respond to international developments in the 1930s?

> What led to the outbreak of war in Europe and the Pacific?

> How did the United States prepare for war?

> How did the Allies turn the tide in Europe and the Pacific?

> How did the war change life for Americans on the home front?

> How did the Allies achieve victory in World War II?

> Conclusion: Why did America emerge as a superpower at the end of the war?

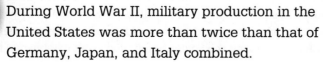

Antiaircraft in Action. Noted American illustrator Dean Cornwell painted this scene for the U.S. Army.

How did America respond to international developments in the 1930s?

Good Neighbor Button

This button encourages support for aiding the British by declaring that the United States and Britain are neighbors. Collection of Stuart S. Corning, Jr./Picture Research Consultants, Inc.

THE FIRST WORLD WAR left a dangerous and ultimately deadly legacy. The victors—especially Britain, France, and the United States—sought to avoid future wars at almost any cost. The defeated nations, as well as those that felt humiliated by the Versailles peace settlement—particularly Germany, Italy, and Japan—aspired to reassert their power and avenge their losses by means of renewed warfare. The aggressive, militaristic, antidemocratic regimes in Germany, Italy, and Japan seemed to most people in the United States during the 1930s a smaller threat than the economic crisis at home. Americans hoped to avoid entanglement in foreign woes and to concentrate on climbing out of the nation's economic abyss.

Roosevelt and Reluctant Isolation

Like most Americans during the 1930s, Franklin Roosevelt believed that the nation's highest priority was to attack the domestic causes and consequences of the depression. But Roosevelt had also long advocated an active role for the United States in international affairs. After World War I, Roosevelt embraced Woodrow Wilson's vision that the United States should take the lead in making the world "safe for democracy," and he continued to advocate American membership in the League of Nations during the isolationist 1920s.

The depression forced Roosevelt to retreat from his previous internationalism. During his 1932 presidential campaign, he pulled back from his endorsement of the League of Nations and reversed his previous support for forgiving European war debts. Once in office, Roosevelt sought to combine domestic economic recovery with a low-profile foreign policy that encouraged free trade and disarmament.

Roosevelt's pursuit of international amity was limited by economic circumstances and American popular opinion. After an opinion poll demonstrated popular support for recognizing the Soviet Union, Roosevelt established formal diplomatic

CHAPTER LOCATOR | How did America respond to international developments in the 1930s? | What led to the outbreak of war in Europe and the Pacific?

CHAPTER 25

690 THE UNITED STATES AND THE SECOND WORLD WAR , 1939–1945

relations in 1933. But when the League of Nations condemned Japanese and German aggression, Roosevelt did not support the league's attempts to keep the peace because he feared jeopardizing isolationists' support for New Deal measures in Congress. America did nothing when Japan withdrew from the league and ignored the limitations on its navy imposed after World War I. The United States also looked the other way when Hitler rearmed Germany and recalled its representative to the league in 1933.

The Good Neighbor Policy

Under Franklin Roosevelt, the United States pursued "the policy of the good neighbor" in Latin America, where U.S. military forces had often intervened in local affairs. Reversing previous American policy, the Roosevelt administration asserted that no nation had the right to intervene in the internal or external affairs of another.

The good neighbor policy did not indicate a U.S. retreat from empire in Latin America. Instead, it declared that the United States would not depend on military force to exercise its influence in the region. Military nonintervention did not prevent the United States from exerting its economic influence in Latin America. In 1934, Congress passed the Reciprocal Trade Agreements Act, which gave the president the power to reduce tariffs on goods imported into the United States from nations that agreed to lower their own tariffs on U.S. exports. By 1940, twenty-two nations had agreed to reciprocal tariff reductions, helping to double U.S. exports to Latin America and contributing to the New Deal's goal of boosting the domestic economy through free trade. Although the economic power of the United States continued to overshadow that of its neighbors, the nonintervention policy planted seeds of friendship and hemispheric solidarity.

The Price of Noninvolvement

In Europe, **Adolf Hitler** rebuilt Germany's military strength, defying the terms of the Versailles peace treaty. Britain and France only made verbal protests. Emboldened, Hitler plotted to avenge defeat in World War I by recapturing territories with German inhabitants, all the while accusing Jews of polluting German purity. The venomous anti-Semitism of Hitler and his Nazi Party unified non-Jewish Germans and attracted sympathizers among many other Europeans, even in France and Britain, thereby weakening support for opposing Hitler or defending the Jews.

Across the Pacific, Japan invaded Manchuria in 1931 and planned to follow up with conquests extending throughout Southeast Asia. The Manchurian invasion bogged down in a long and vicious war when Chinese Nationalists rallied around their leader, Chiang Kai-shek, to fight against the Japanese. Preparations for new Japanese conquests continued, however. In 1936, Japan further violated naval limitation treaties by building a fleet designed to achieve naval superiority in the Pacific.

In the United States, the hostilities in Asia and Europe reinforced isolationist sentiments. Popular disillusionment with the failure of Woodrow Wilson's idealistic goals caused many Americans to question the nation's participation in World War I. In 1933, Gerald Nye, a Republican from North Dakota, chaired a Senate committee that investigated why the United States had gone to war in 1917. The Nye

CHRONOLOGY

1931
- Japan invades Manchuria.

1934
- Reciprocal Trade Agreements Act.

1935–1937
- Congress passes neutrality acts.

1936
- Nazi Germany occupies Rhineland.
- Italy conquers Ethiopia.
- Spanish civil war begins.
- Japan begins to expand naval power.

1937
- Japanese troops capture Nanking.
- Roosevelt introduces his quarantine policy.

Adolf Hitler
▶ Nazi dictator who led Germany during World War II. Hitler's territorial ambitions and racial theories led him to remilitarize Germany during the 1930s and start a general war in Europe in 1939. Hitler's forces were defeated by the Allies in 1945.

How did the United States prepare for war? | How did the Allies turn the tide in Europe and the Pacific? | How did the war change life for Americans on the home front? | How did the Allies achieve victory in World War II? | Conclusion: Why did America emerge as a superpower at the end of the war?

691

committee concluded that war profiteers had pushed America into war, and the committee's findings persuaded many Americans that it could happen again. International tensions and the Nye committee report prompted Congress to pass a series of neutrality acts between 1935 and 1937 designed to avoid entanglement in foreign wars. The neutrality acts prohibited making loans and selling arms to nations at war.

The Neutrality Act of 1937 attempted to reconcile the nation's desire for both peace and foreign trade with a "cash-and-carry" policy that required warring nations to pay cash for nonmilitary goods and to transport them in their own ships. This policy supported foreign trade and thereby benefited the nation's economy, but it also helped foreign aggressors by supplying them with goods and thereby undermining peace.

The desire for peace in France, Britain, and the United States led Germany, Italy, and Japan to launch military offensives on the assumption that the Western democracies lacked the will to oppose them. In March 1936, Nazi troops marched into the industry-rich Rhineland on Germany's western border, in blatant violation of the Treaty of Versailles. One month later, Italian armies completed their conquest of Ethiopia. In December 1937, Japanese invaders captured Nanking and celebrated their triumph in the "Rape of Nanking," a deadly rampage of murder, rape, and plunder that killed 200,000 Chinese civilians.

In Spain, a bitter civil war broke out in July 1936 when fascist rebels led by General Francisco Franco attacked the democratically elected Republican government. Both Germany and Italy reinforced Franco with soldiers, weapons, and aircraft, while the Soviet Union provided much less aid to the Republican Loyalists. Although individual Americans fought for the Loyalists in the Spanish civil war, neither the European democracies nor the U.S. government came to the Loyalists' aid, despite sympathizing with their cause. Abandoned by the Western nations, the Loyalists and their allies were defeated in 1939, and Franco built a fascist bulwark in southwestern Europe.

Hostilities in Europe, Africa, and Asia alarmed Roosevelt and other Americans. The president sought to persuade most Americans to moderate their isolationism (the desire to retreat from the world's conflicts) and find a way to support the victims of fascist aggression. Speaking in Chicago in October 1937, Roosevelt declared that the "epidemic of world lawlessness is spreading" and warned that "mere isolation or neutrality" offered no remedy for the "contagion" of war. Instead, he proposed that the United States "quarantine" aggressor nations and stop the spread of war's contagion.

Roosevelt's speech ignited a storm of protest from isolationists. The *Chicago Tribune* accused the president of seeking to replace "Americanism" with "internationalism." The strength of isolationism and the absence of congressional support for his quarantine policy disappointed Roosevelt, who remarked, "It's a terrible thing to look over your shoulder when you are trying to lead and find no one there." The popularity of isolationist sentiment convinced Roosevelt that he needed to maneuver carefully if the United States were to help prevent fascist aggressors from conquering Europe and Asia.

> **QUICK REVIEW**

How did isolationist sentiment constrain Roosevelt's foreign policy in the 1930s?

CHAPTER LOCATOR | How did America respond to international developments in the 1930s? | What led to the outbreak of war in Europe and the Pacific?

CHAPTER 25
692 THE UNITED STATES AND THE SECOND WORLD WAR , 1939–1945

German Invasion of Poland

In 1940, German infantry reserves marched to the eastern front led by two officers on horseback. Although the German blitzkrieg massed thousands of tanks and aircraft at the front, German forces lacked sufficient trucks and other motorized vehicles to move soldiers and military supplies. The Germans' dependence on horse and foot travel limited the mobility of their troops compared with the more thoroughly motorized Allied armies. © Bettmann/Corbis.

BETWEEN 1939 AND 1941, fascist victories overseas eventually eroded American isolationism. Continuing German and Japanese aggression caused more and more Americans to believe that it was time for the nation to take a stand.

Nazi Aggression and War in Europe

Under the spell of isolationism, Americans passively watched Hitler's relentless campaign to dominate Europe. Hitler bullied Austria in 1938 into accepting incorporation—*Anschluss*—into the Nazi Third Reich. Next, Hitler turned his attention to Czechoslovakia's German-speaking Sudetenland. Hoping to avoid war, British prime minister Neville Chamberlain went to Munich, Germany, in September 1938 and offered Hitler terms of **appeasement** that would give the Sudetenland to Germany if Hitler agreed to leave the rest of Czechoslovakia alone. Hitler accepted Chamberlain's offer and promised that he would make no more territorial claims in Europe. But Hitler never intended to honor his promise. In March 1939, the German army conquered Czechoslovakia without firing a shot (**Map 25.1**).

In April 1939, Hitler demanded that Poland return the German territory it had been awarded after World War I. Recognizing that appeasement had failed, Britain and France assured Poland that they would go to war with Germany if Hitler launched an attack. In turn, Hitler negotiated with Soviet premier **Joseph Stalin**, offering him concessions in order to prevent the Soviet Union from joining Britain and France in opposing a German attack on Poland. Despite the enduring hatred between fascist Germany and the Communist Soviet Union, the two powers signed the Nazi-Soviet treaty of nonaggression in August 1939.

At dawn on September 1, 1939, Hitler unleashed his *blitzkrieg* (literally, "lightning war") on Poland. The attack triggered Soviet attacks on eastern Poland

appeasement
► British strategy aimed at avoiding a war with Germany in the late 1930s. British prime minister Neville Chamberlain believed that if concessions were offered to Hitler, peace in Europe could be maintained. The German conquest of Czechoslovakia and Poland proved Chamberlain wrong.

Joseph Stalin
► Soviet premier from 1922 to 1953. Despite a neutrality agreement that had allowed Germany and the Soviet Union to divide Poland in 1939, Germany invaded the Soviet Union in 1941. Under Stalin's leadership, Soviet forces stopped and then reversed Germany's advance, a defeat that played a crucial role in the ultimate Allied victory.

| How did the United States prepare for war? | How did the Allies turn the tide in Europe and the Pacific? | How did the war change life for Americans on the home front? | How did the Allies achieve victory in World War II? | Conclusion: Why did America emerge as a superpower at the end of the war? |

and declarations of war from France and Britain two days later. After the Nazis overran Poland, Hitler paused for a few months before launching a westward blitzkrieg. In April 1940, German forces smashed through Denmark and Norway. In May, Germany invaded the Netherlands, Belgium, Luxembourg, and France.

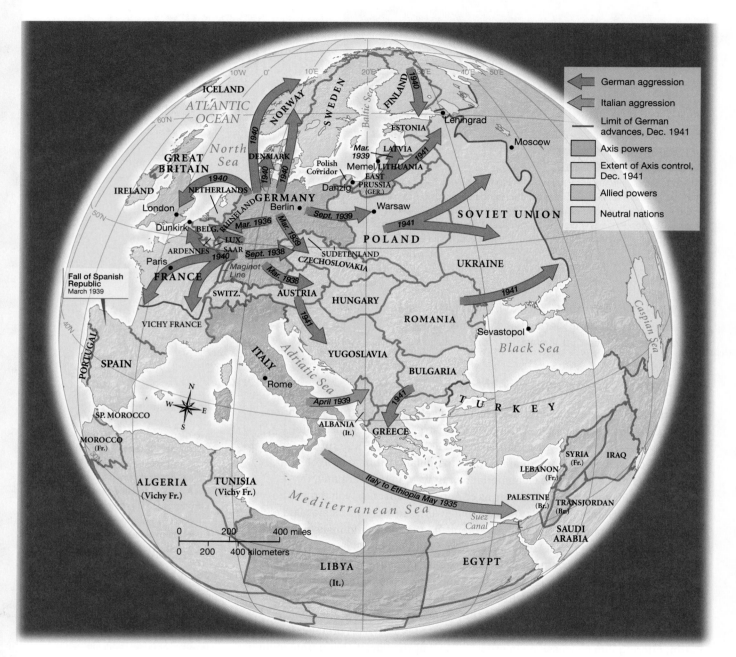

MAP 25.1 ■ Axis Aggression through 1941

For different reasons, Adolf Hitler and Benito Mussolini launched a series of surprise military strikes before 1942. Mussolini sought to re-create the Roman empire in the Mediterranean. Hitler struck to reclaim German territories occupied by France after World War I and to annex Austria. When the German dictator began his campaign to rule "inferior" peoples beyond Germany's border by attacking Poland, World War II broke out.

CHAPTER LOCATOR | How did America respond to international developments in the 1930s? | What led to the outbreak of war in Europe and the Pacific?

The French believed that their Maginot Line, a concrete fortification built after World War I, would halt the German attack (see Map 25.1). But the Maginot Line did little to slow down Hitler's mechanized divisions, which wheeled around it and raced toward Paris.

The speed of the German attack trapped more than 300,000 British and French soldiers, who retreated to the French port of Dunkirk, where an improvised armada of British vessels hurriedly ferried them to safety across the English Channel. By mid-June 1940, France had signed an armistice that gave Germany control of the entire French coastline and nearly two-thirds of the countryside. A collaborationist French government was installed at Vichy in southern France. With an empire that stretched across Europe from Poland to France, Hitler seemed invincible as he poised to attack Britain.

The new British prime minister, **Winston Churchill**, vowed that Britain, unlike France, would never surrender to Hitler. "We shall fight on the seas and oceans [and] . . . in the air," he proclaimed, "whatever the cost may be, we shall fight on the beaches, . . . and in the fields and in the streets." Beginning in mid-June 1940, wave after wave of German bombers targeted British military installations and cities, killing tens of thousands of civilians. The undermanned and outgunned Royal Air Force fought as doggedly as Churchill had predicted and finally won the **Battle of Britain** by November, handing Hitler his first defeat. Victorious in the air, Britain was battered and exhausted and could not hold out for long without American help, as Churchill repeatedly wrote Roosevelt in private.

From Neutrality to the Arsenal of Democracy

When the Nazi attack on Poland ignited the war in Europe, Roosevelt issued an official proclamation of American neutrality. Most Americans condemned German aggression and favored Britain and France, but isolationism remained powerful. Roosevelt feared that if Congress did not repeal the arms embargo mandated by the Neutrality Act of 1937, France and Britain would soon succumb to the Nazis. After heated debate, Congress voted in November 1939 to revise the neutrality legislation and allow belligerent nations to buy arms, as well as nonmilitary supplies, on a cash-and-carry basis.

In practice, the revised neutrality law permitted Britain and France to purchase American war materiel and carry it across the Atlantic in their own ships, thereby shielding American vessels from attack. Roosevelt wrote a friend, "What worries me is that public opinion . . . is patting itself on the back every morning and thanking God for the Atlantic Ocean (and the Pacific Ocean)" and underestimating "the serious implications" of the European war "for our own future." Roosevelt searched for a way to aid Britain short of entering a formal alliance or declaring war against Germany. By late summer in 1940, Roosevelt concocted a scheme to deliver fifty old destroyers to Britain in exchange for American access to British bases in the Western Hemisphere. With this swap, Roosevelt took the first steps toward building a firm Anglo-American alliance against Hitler.

Roosevelt decided to run for an unprecedented third term as president in 1940. He hoped to woo voters away from their complacent isolationism to back the nation's international interests as well as New Deal reforms. But the presidential election, which Roosevelt won handily over Republican Wendell Willkie, provided no clear mandate for American involvement in the European war. Once reelected,

CHRONOLOGY

1938
- Germany annexes Austria.

1939
- German troops occupy Czechoslovakia.
- Nazi-Soviet nonaggression pact.
- **September 1.** Germany's attack on Poland begins World War II.

1940
- Germany invades Denmark, Norway, France, Belgium, Luxembourg, and the Netherlands.
- British and French evacuation from Dunkirk.
- Vichy government is installed in France.
- Battle of Britain.
- Japan, Germany, and Italy sign Tripartite Pact.

1941 Lend-Lease Act
- **June.** Germany invades Soviet Union.
- **August.** Roosevelt and Churchill issue Atlantic Charter.
- **December 7.** Japanese attack Pearl Harbor.

Winston Churchill
▶ British prime minister from 1940 to 1945, and again from 1951 to 1955. A bitter opponent of Neville Chamberlain's policy of appeasement before the war, Churchill led the British resistance to Nazi domination of Europe. As one of the "Big Three," along with Roosevelt and Stalin, Churchill participated in negotiations that shaped the postwar world.

Battle of Britain
▶ Battle for air supremacy over Britain. Starting in June 1940, in preparation for an invasion, the German air force bombed British military installations and cities, killing tens of thousands of civilians. British victory in the Battle of Britain stalled Hitler's invasion plans.

How did the United States prepare for war?	How did the Allies turn the tide in Europe and the Pacific?	How did the war change life for Americans on the home front?	How did the Allies achieve victory in World War II?	Conclusion: Why did America emerge as a superpower at the end of the war?

Roosevelt maneuvered to support Britain in every way short of war. In a fireside chat shortly after Christmas 1940, he proclaimed that it was incumbent on the United States to become "the great arsenal of democracy" and send "every ounce and every ton of munitions and supplies that we can possibly spare to help the defenders who are in the front lines."

In January 1941, Roosevelt proposed the Lend-Lease Act, which allowed the British to obtain arms from the United States without paying cash but with the promise to reimburse the United States when the war ended. The purpose of Lend-Lease, Roosevelt proclaimed, was to defend democracy and human rights throughout the world, specifically the Four Freedoms: "freedom of speech and expression . . . freedom of every person to worship God in his own way . . . freedom from want . . . [and] freedom from fear." Congress passed the Lend-Lease Act in March 1941 and started a flood of supplies to Britain that persisted throughout the war.

Stymied in his plans for an invasion of England, Hitler turned his army eastward and on June 22, 1941, launched a surprise attack on the Soviet Union. Neither Roosevelt nor Churchill had any love for Joseph Stalin or communism, but they both welcomed the Soviet Union to the anti-Nazi cause. Both Western leaders understood that Hitler's attack on Russia would provide relief for the hard-pressed British. Roosevelt quickly persuaded Congress to extend Lend-Lease to the Soviet Union, beginning the shipment of millions of tons of trucks, jeeps, and other equipment that, in all, supplied about 10 percent of Russian war materiel.

As Hitler's Wehrmacht (army) raced across the Russian plains and Nazi U-boats tried to choke off supplies to Britain and the Soviet Union, Roosevelt met with Churchill aboard a ship near Newfoundland to cement the Anglo-American alliance. In August 1941, the two leaders issued the Atlantic Charter, pledging the two nations to freedom of the seas and free trade as well as the right of national self-determination.

Japan Attacks America

Hitler exercised a measure of restraint by not provoking America directly. In contrast, Japanese ambitions in Asia clashed more openly with American interests and commitments, especially in China and the Philippines. And unlike Hitler, the Japanese high command planned to attack the United States if necessary to pursue Japan's aspirations to rule an Asian empire it termed the Greater East Asia Co-Prosperity Sphere. Appealing to widespread Asian bitterness toward such white colonial powers as the British in India and Burma, the French in Indochina (now Vietnam), and the Dutch in the East Indies (now Indonesia), the Japanese campaigned to preserve "Asia for the Asians." Japan's invasion of China—which had lasted for ten years by 1941—proved that its true goal was Asia for the Japanese (**Map 25.2**). Japan coveted the raw materials available from China and Southeast Asia and ignored American demands to stop its campaign of aggression.

In 1940, Japan signaled a new phase of its imperial designs by entering a defensive alliance with Germany and Italy—the Tripartite Pact. In 1941, U.S. naval intelligence learned that Tokyo also planned to invade the resource-rich Dutch East Indies. To thwart these plans, in July 1941 Roosevelt announced a trade embargo that denied Japan access to oil, scrap iron, and other goods essential for its war machines.

CHAPTER LOCATOR | How did America respond to international developments in the 1930s?

What led to the outbreak of war in Europe and the Pacific?

CHAPTER 25
696 THE UNITED STATES AND THE SECOND WORLD WAR , 1939–1945

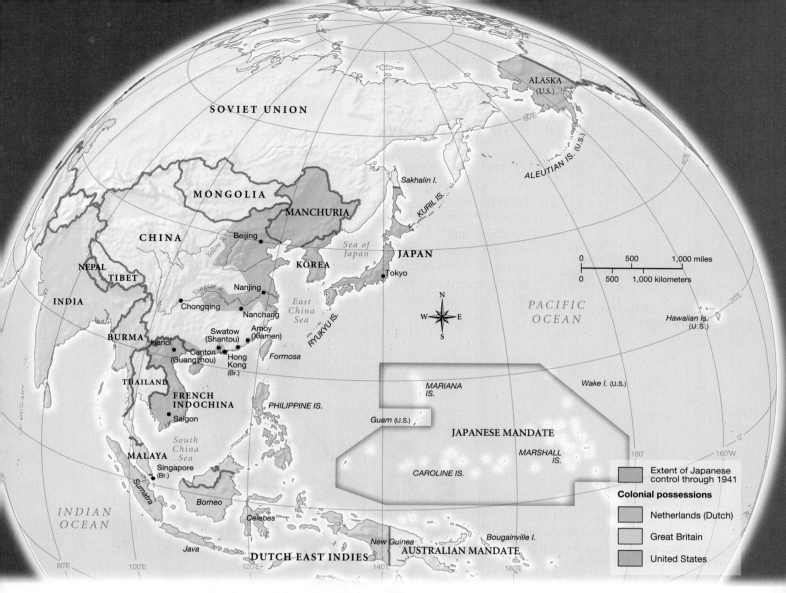

MAP 25.2 ■ Japanese Aggression through 1941

Beginning with the invasion of Manchuria in 1931, Japan sought to extend its imperialist control over most of East Asia. Japanese aggression was driven by the need for raw materials for the country's expanding industries and by the military government's devotion to martial honor.

The American embargo played into the hands of Japanese militarists headed by General Hideki Tojo, who seized control of the government in October 1941 and persuaded other leaders, including Emperor Hirohito, that swift destruction of American naval bases in the Pacific would leave Japan free to expand its empire. On December 7, 1941, Japanese aircraft attacked the U.S. Pacific Fleet at **Pearl Harbor** on the Hawaiian island of Oahu. The devastating attack almost crippled U.S. war-making capacity in the Pacific. Luckily for the United States, Japanese pilots failed to destroy the vital machine shops and oil storage facilities at Pearl Harbor, and none of the nation's aircraft carriers happened to be in port at the time of the attack.

Pearl Harbor

▶ Surprise attack by the Japanese on the U.S. fleet based in Hawaii on December 7, 1941. The attack brought America into the war against both Japan and Germany. The Japanese scored a tactical victory at Pearl Harbor, but in the long run, the attack proved a colossal blunder.

How did the United States prepare for war?	How did the Allies turn the tide in Europe and the Pacific?	How did the war change life for Americans on the home front?	How did the Allies achieve victory in World War II?	Conclusion: Why did America emerge as a superpower at the end of the war?

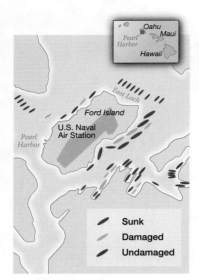

Bombing of Pearl Harbor,
December 7, 1941

Sunk
Damaged
Undamaged

American Losses at Pearl Harbor

Eighteen ships sunk or disabled, including all of the fleet's battleships.

2,400 Americans killed.

1,000 Americans wounded.

The Japanese scored a tactical victory at Pearl Harbor, but in the long run, the attack proved a colossal blunder. The victory made many Japanese commanders overconfident about their military power. Worse for the Japanese, Americans instantly united in their desire to avenge the attack, which Roosevelt termed "dastardly and unprovoked." On December 8, Congress endorsed the president's call for a declaration of war. Neither Hitler nor Benito Mussolini, Italy's fascist leader, knew about the Japanese attack in advance, but they both declared war against America on December 11, bringing the United States into all-out war with the Axis powers—Germany, Italy, and Japan—in both Europe and Asia.

Pearl Harbor Attack

Brothers Wesley and Edward Heidt from Los Angeles were one of thirty-four pairs of brothers killed when Japanese warplanes sank the battleship *Arizona* at Pearl Harbor. This pennant was salvaged from the ship's wreckage. Also included here is the official telegram informing the Heidt brothers' mother that her sons "lost their life in the service of their country." U.S.S. *Arizona* Memorial, Hawaii, National Park Service/photos by Douglas Peebles.

▶ FOR MORE HELP ANALYZING THIS IMAGE, see the visual activity for this chapter in the Online Study Guide at bedfordstmartins.com/roarkunderstanding.

> **QUICK REVIEW**

How did Roosevelt respond to the outbreak of war in Europe?

CHAPTER LOCATOR | How did America respond to international developments in the 1930s? | What led to the outbreak of war in Europe and the Pacific?

CHAPTER 25

698 THE UNITED STATES AND THE SECOND WORLD WAR , 1939–1945

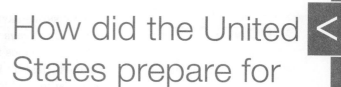

African American Machine Gunners These African American soldiers prepare their machine gun for action on the side of a road near Pisa, Italy, in September 1944. They and other black soldiers who served in combat in segregated units repeatedly earned praise from their commanders for gallantry and courage under fire. As a Mississippi-born African American veteran of the Pacific theater recalled, "We had two wars to fight: prejudice . . . and those Japs." © Bettmann/Corbis.

THE TIME HAD COME, Roosevelt announced, for the prescriptions of "Dr. New Deal" to be replaced by the stronger medicines of "Dr. Win-the-War." Under Roosevelt's direction, military and civilian leaders rushed to secure the nation against possible attacks, to enlist millions of Americans in the armed forces, and to transform the American economy into the world's greatest military machine.

Home-Front Security

Shortly after declaring war against the United States, Hitler dispatched German submarines to hunt American ships along the Atlantic coast. The U-boats had devastating success for about eight months, sinking hundreds of U.S. ships and threatening to disrupt the Lend-Lease lifeline to Britain and the Soviet Union. But by mid-1942, the U.S. Navy had chased German submarines away from the East Coast and into the mid-Atlantic, reducing the direct threat to the nation.

Within the continental United States, Americans remained sheltered from the chaos and destruction the war was bringing to hundreds of millions in Europe and Asia. Nevertheless, the government worried constantly about espionage and

CHRONOLOGY

1940
- Congress passes the Selective Service Act to register men of military age for the draft.

1942
- U.S. economy rebounds as a result of defense spending.
- President Roosevelt orders the internment of Japanese Americans living in the West.

internal subversion. Billboards and posters warned Americans that "Enemy agents are always near; if you don't talk, they won't hear." The campaign for patriotic vigilance focused on German and Japanese foes, but Americans of Japanese descent became targets of official and popular persecution because of Pearl Harbor and long-standing racial prejudice against people of Asian descent.

About 320,000 people of Japanese descent lived in U.S. territory in 1941, two-thirds of them in Hawaii, where they largely escaped wartime persecution because they were essential and valued members of society. On the mainland, however, Japanese Americans were a tiny minority subject to frenzied wartime suspicions and persecution. Although an official military survey concluded that Japanese Americans posed no danger, popular hostility fueled a campaign to round up all mainland Japanese Americans—two-thirds of them U.S. citizens. "A Jap's a Jap. . . . It makes no difference whether he is an American citizen or not," one official declared.

On February 19, 1942, Roosevelt issued Executive Order 9066, which authorized sending all Americans of Japanese descent to ten makeshift internment camps located in remote areas of the West (**Map 25.3**). Allowed little time to secure or sell their property, Japanese Americans lost homes and businesses worth about $400 million and lived out the war penned in by barbed wire and armed guards. Although several thousand Japanese Americans served with distinction in the U.S. armed forces and no case of subversion by a Japanese American was ever uncovered, the Supreme Court, in its 1944 *Korematsu* decision, declared that Executive Order 9066's violation of constitutional rights was justified by "military necessity."

Building a Citizen Army

In 1940, Congress passed the Selective Service Act to register men of military age for a draft. In all, more than 16 million men and women served in uniform during the war, two-thirds of them draftees, mostly young men. Women were barred from combat duty, but they worked at nearly every noncombatant task, eroding traditional barriers to women's military service.

MAP 25.3 ■ **Western Relocation Authority Centers**
Responding to prejudice and fear of sabotage, President Roosevelt authorized the roundup and relocation of all Americans of Japanese descent in 1942. Taken from their homes in the cities and fertile farmland of the far West, Japanese Americans were confined in desolate camps scattered as far east as the Mississippi River.

▲ WRA relocation camp

☐ More than 1,000 Japanese Americans sent to relocation centers

CHAPTER LOCATOR | How did America respond to international developments in the 1930s? | What led to the outbreak of war in Europe and the Pacific?

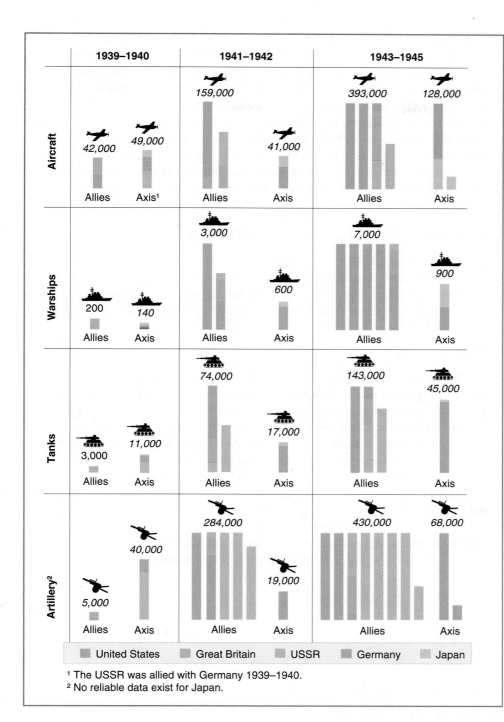

Weapons Production by the Axis and Allied Powers during World War II

This chart demonstrates the massive contribution of the United States to Allied weapons production during World War II. In the air and on the sea, U.S. weapons predominated, after 1940 accounting for more aircraft and many more warships than Britain and the Soviet Union combined. Together, the three Allied powers produced about three times as many aircraft and five to eight times as many warships as the two Axis powers. On the ground, the Soviet Union led the other Allies in the production of tanks and artillery, an outgrowth of the colossal battles on the eastern front. Overall, the Allies produced almost three times as many tanks as the Axis powers and more than seven times as many artillery pieces as Germany (no figures are available for Japan). What do these data suggest about the significance of America's entry into the war in December 1941? What do they suggest about the kind of warfare emphasized by each of the belligerents? What do they suggest about the chronology of weapons production during the war?

1939–1940 | **1941–1942** | **1943–1945**

Aircraft
Allies 42,000 | Axis¹ 49,000 | Allies 159,000 | Axis 41,000 | Allies 393,000 | Axis 128,000

Warships
Allies 200 | Axis 140 | Allies 3,000 | Axis 600 | Allies 7,000 | Axis 900

Tanks
Allies 3,000 | Axis 11,000 | Allies 74,000 | Axis 17,000 | Allies 143,000 | Axis 45,000

Artillery²
Allies 5,000 | Axis 40,000 | Allies 284,000 | Axis 19,000 | Allies 430,000 | Axis 68,000

■ United States   ■ Great Britain   ■ USSR   ■ Germany   ■ Japan

¹ The USSR was allied with Germany 1939–1940.
² No reliable data exist for Japan.

The Selective Service Act prohibited discrimination "on account of race or color," and almost a million African Americans donned uniforms, as did half a million Mexican Americans, 25,000 Native Americans, and 13,000 Chinese Americans. The abuse and discrimination suffered by all people of color made some soldiers ask, as a Mexican American GI did on his way to the European front, "Why fight for America when you have not been treated as an American?" Only black Americans were trained in segregated camps, confined in segregated barracks,

How did the United States prepare for war?	How did the Allies turn the tide in Europe and the Pacific?	How did the war change life for Americans on the home front?	How did the Allies achieve victory in World War II?	Conclusion: Why did America emerge as a superpower at the end of the war?

and assigned to segregated units. Most black Americans were consigned to manual labor, and relatively few served in combat until late in 1944, when the need for
military manpower in Europe intensified. Then, as General George Patton told
black soldiers in a tank unit in Normandy, "I don't care what color you are, so long
as you go up there and kill those Kraut sonsabitches."

Homosexuals also served in the armed forces, although in much smaller numbers than black Americans. Allowed to serve as long as their sexual preferences
remained covert, gay Americans, like other minorities, sought to demonstrate
their worth under fire. As a gay GI remarked, "Who in the hell is going to worry
about [homosexuality]" in the midst of the life-or-death realities of war?

Conversion to a War Economy

In 1940, the American economy remained mired in the depression. Shortly after
the attack on Pearl Harbor, Roosevelt announced the goal of converting the
economy to produce "overwhelming . . . , crushing superiority of equipment in any
theater of the world war." Factories were converted from making passenger cars
to assembling tanks and airplanes, and production soared to record levels. By the
end of the war, jobs exceeded workers, plants operated at full capacity, and the
federal budget had increased tenfold to $100 billion.

To organize and oversee military production, Roosevelt called upon business
leaders to come to Washington and head new government agencies such as the
War Production Board, which, among other things, set production priorities and
pushed for maximum output. Contracts flowed to large corporations, often on a
basis that guaranteed their profits. During the first half of 1942, the government
issued contracts worth more than the entire gross national product in 1941.

Overall, conversion to war production achieved Roosevelt's ambitious goal of
"crushing superiority" in military goods. At a total cost of $304 billion during the
war, the nation produced more than double the combined military output of
Germany, Japan, and Italy. (See "Global Comparison," page 701.) This outpouring
of military goods supplied not only U.S. forces but also America's allies, making
good on Roosevelt's pledge to make America the "arsenal of democracy."

> **QUICK REVIEW**

How did the Roosevelt administration mobilize
the human and industrial resources necessary
to fight a two-front war?

CHAPTER LOCATOR | How did America
respond to international
developments in the
1930s? | What led to the outbreak
of war in Europe and the
Pacific?

CHAPTER 25
702 THE UNITED STATES AND THE SECOND WORLD WAR , 1939–1945

Marine Pinned Down on Saipan Over 100,000 American GIs assaulted the Japanese garrison on Saipan in the Mariana Islands in June 1944. The battle lasted nearly a month and inflicted 14,000 casualties on American troops. The intensity of the fighting is visible on the face of the marine shown here. The suicidal defenses of the Japanese in Saipan persuaded American military planners that the final assault on the Japanese homeland would cause hundreds of thousands of American casualties. Marine Corps Photo, National Archives.

THE UNITED STATES CONFRONTED a daunting military challenge in December 1941. The attack on Pearl Harbor destroyed much of its Pacific Fleet, crippling the nation's ability to defend against Japan's offensive throughout the southern Pacific. In the Atlantic, Hitler's U-boats sank American ships, while German armies occupied most of western Europe and relentlessly advanced eastward into the Soviet Union. To fight back effectively against Germany and Japan, the United States had to coordinate military and political strategy with its allies and muster all its human and economic assets. But in 1941, nobody knew whether that would be enough.

Turning the Tide in the Pacific

In the Pacific theater, Japan's leading military strategist, Admiral Isoroku Yamamoto, believed that if his forces did not quickly conquer and secure the territories they targeted, Japan would eventually lose the war as a result of America's far greater resources. Swiftly, the Japanese assaulted American airfields in the Philippines and captured U.S. outposts on Guam and Wake Island. Singapore, the British naval base in Malaya, surrendered to the Japanese in February 1942, and most of Burma had fallen by March. All that stood in the way of Japan's domination of the southern Pacific was the American stronghold in the Philippines.

The Japanese unleashed an assault against the Philippines in January 1942 (see Map 25.5, page 715). American defenders surrendered to the Japanese in May, and the Japanese marched captured American and Filipino soldiers to a concentration camp. Thousands died during the Bataan Death March, and 16,000 more perished in the camp. By the summer of 1942, the Japanese had conquered the oil-rich Dutch East Indies and were poised to strike Australia and New Zealand.

| How did the United States prepare for war? | **How did the Allies turn the tide in Europe and the Pacific?** | How did the war change life for Americans on the home front? | How did the Allies achieve victory in World War II? | Conclusion: Why did America emerge as a superpower at the end of the war? |

In November, an American army under General Dwight D. Eisenhower landed far to the west, in French Morocco. By May 1943, the Allied armies had defeated the Germans in North Africa.

The Impact of the North Africa Campaign

350,000 Axis soldiers were killed or captured.

The Germans were pushed out of Africa.

The Mediterranean was made safe for Allied shipping.

The door was opened for an Allied invasion of Italy.

In January 1943, Roosevelt traveled to the Moroccan city of Casablanca to confer with Churchill and other Allied leaders. Stalin did not attend but urged his allies to keep their promise of opening a major second front in western Europe. Roosevelt and Churchill announced that they would accept nothing less than the "unconditional surrender" of the Axis powers, ruling out peace negotiations. But Churchill and Roosevelt concluded that they needed more time to amass sufficient forces for the cross-Channel invasion of France that Stalin demanded. In the meantime, they planned to capitalize on their success in North Africa and strike against Italy.

On July 10, 1943, combined American and British amphibious forces landed 160,000 troops in Sicily. Soon afterward, Mussolini was deposed in Italy, ending the reign of Italian fascism. Quickly, the Allies invaded the mainland, and the Italian government surrendered unconditionally. The Germans responded by rushing reinforcements to Italy and seizing control of Rome, turning the Allies' Italian campaign into a series of battles to liberate Italy from German occupation.

German troops dug into strong fortifications and fought to defend every inch of Italian territory. Only after a long, deadly, and frustrating campaign up the Italian peninsula did the Allies finally liberate Rome in June 1944. Allied forces continued to push into northern Italy against stubborn German defenses for the remainder of the war, making the Italian campaign the war's deadliest for American infantrymen. One soldier wrote that his buddies "died like butchered swine."

Stalin denounced the Allies' Italian campaign because it left "the Soviet Army, which is fighting not only for its country, but also for its Allies, to do the job alone, almost single-handed." The Italian campaign exacted a high cost from the Americans and the British, bringing the Nazis no closer to surrender and consuming men and materiel that might have been reserved for a second front in France.

> ## QUICK REVIEW

How did the United States seek to counter the Japanese in the Pacific and the Germans in Europe?

CHAPTER LOCATOR | How did America respond to international developments in the 1930s? | What led to the outbreak of war in Europe and the Pacific?

CHAPTER 25

706 THE UNITED STATES AND THE SECOND WORLD WAR , 1939–1945

How did the war change life for Americans on the home front?

This poster encourages women and children to contribute to the war effort by collecting scrap metal for recycling into weaponry. The poster highlights the middle-class prosperity of the war years, a sharp contrast to the hard times of the 1930s. Chicago Historical Society.

▶ FOR MORE HELP ANALYZING THIS IMAGE, see the visual activity for this chapter in the Online Study Guide at bedfordstmartins.com/roarkunderstanding.

THE WAR EFFORT MOBILIZED Americans as never before. Ever-increasing wartime production drew workers, both men and women, from small towns and farms to America's cities. Despite rationing and shortages, unprecedented government expenditures for war production brought prosperity to many Americans after years of depression-era poverty. The wartime ideology of human rights provided justification for the many sacrifices Americans were required to make in support of the military effort. It also established a standard of basic human equality that became a potent weapon in the campaign for equal rights at home and against the atrocities of the Holocaust perpetrated by the Nazis.

How did the United States prepare for war?	How did the Allies turn the tide in Europe and the Pacific?	**How did the war change life for Americans on the home front?**	How did the Allies achieve victory in World War II?	Conclusion: Why did America emerge as a superpower at the end of the war?

Women and Families, Guns and Butter

Millions of American women took their places on assembly lines in defense industries. At the start of the war, about a quarter of adult women worked outside the home, most as teachers, nurses, social workers, and domestic servants. But wartime mobilization of the economy and the siphoning of millions of men into the armed forces left factories begging for women workers.

Government advertisements urged women to take industrial jobs by assuring them they were capable of work on the "Victory Line." One billboard proclaimed, "If you've sewed on buttons, or made buttonholes, on a [sewing] machine, you can learn to do spot welding on airplane parts." Millions of women responded, and by the end of the war, 18 million women worked outside the home, 50 percent more than in 1939 (**Figure 25.1**). Contributing to the war effort also paid off in wages. A Kentucky woman remembered her job at a munitions plant, where she earned "the fabulous sum of $32 a week. To us it was an absolute miracle."

The majority of married women remained at home. But they, too, supported the war effort, planting Victory Gardens to provide homegrown vegetables, saving tin cans and newspapers for recycling into war materiel, and hoarding pennies and nickels to buy war bonds. Many families scrimped to cope with the 30 percent inflation during the war, but families supported by men and women in manufacturing industries enjoyed wages that grew twice as fast as inflation.

The wartime prosperity and abundance enjoyed by most Americans contrasted with the experiences of their hard-pressed allies. Personal consumption fell by 22 percent in Britain, and food output plummeted to just one-third of prewar levels in the Soviet Union, creating widespread hunger and even starvation. Few went hungry in the United States. New Deal restraints on agricultural production were lifted, and farm output grew by 25 percent each year during the war, providing food for export to the Allies.

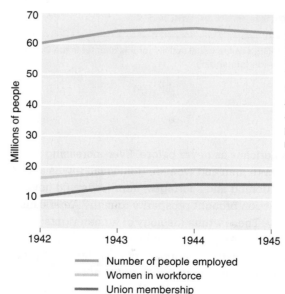

FIGURE 25.1 ■ **World War II and the Economy, 1942–1945**
War mobilization sent employment and union membership soaring. Women found employment in all sectors of the economy, including heavy industry. Although they lost many jobs in industry after the war, they continued to participate in the workforce in increased numbers.

Legend:
- Number of people employed
- Women in workforce
- Union membership

Y-axis: Millions of people (10–70)
X-axis: 1942, 1943, 1944, 1945

CHAPTER LOCATOR | How did America respond to international developments in the 1930s? | What led to the outbreak of war in Europe and the Pacific?

The Double V Campaign

Fighting against the Nazis and their ideology of Aryan racial supremacy, Americans were confronted with the racial prejudice in their own country. The *Pittsburgh Courier*, a leading black newspaper, asserted that the wartime emergency called for a **Double V campaign** seeking "victory over our enemies at home and victory over our enemies on the battlefields abroad." It was time, the *Courier* proclaimed, "to persuade, embarrass, compel and shame our government and our nation . . . into a more enlightened attitude."

In 1941, African American organizations demanded that the federal government require companies receiving defense contracts to integrate their workforces. A. Philip Randolph, head of the Brotherhood of Sleeping Car Porters, promised that 100,000 African American marchers would descend on Washington if the president did not eliminate discrimination in defense industries. Roosevelt decided to risk offending his white allies in the South and in unions and issued Executive Order 8802 in mid-1941. It authorized the Committee on Fair Employment Practices to investigate and prevent racial discrimination in employment. Civil rights champions hailed the act, and Randolph called off the march.

Progress came slowly, however. In 1940, nine out of ten black Americans lived below the federal poverty line, and those who worked earned an average of just 39 percent of whites' wages. In search of better jobs and living conditions, 5.5 million black Americans migrated from the South to centers of industrial production in the North and West. Many discovered that unskilled jobs were available but that unions and employers often barred blacks from skilled trades. Severe labor shortages and government fair employment standards opened assembly-line jobs in defense plants to African Americans, causing black unemployment to drop by 80 percent during the war. But more jobs did not mean equal pay for blacks. The average income of black families rose during the war, but by the end of the conflict, it still stood at only half of what white families earned.

Blacks' migration to defense jobs intensified racial antagonisms. In 1943, 242 race riots erupted in 47 cities. In the "zoot suit riots" in Los Angeles, hundreds of white servicemen, claiming they were punishing draft dodgers, chased and beat young Mexican American men who dressed in distinctive broad-shouldered, peg-legged zoot suits. The worst mayhem occurred in Detroit, where tensions between whites and blacks over racially segregated housing ignited into a race war. Whites with clubs smashed through black neighborhoods, and blacks retaliated by destroying and looting white-owned businesses. In two days of violence, twenty-five blacks and nine whites were killed, and scores more were injured.

Racial violence created the impetus for the Double V campaign, officially supported by the National Association for the Advancement of Colored People (NAACP), which asserted black Americans' demands for the rights and privileges enjoyed by all other Americans—demands reinforced by the Allies' wartime ideology of freedom and democracy. While the NAACP focused on court challenges to segregation, a new organization founded in 1942, the Congress of Racial Equality (CORE), organized picketing and sit-ins against Jim Crow restaurants and theaters. The Double V campaign greatly expanded membership in the NAACP but achieved only limited success against racial discrimination during the war.

Double V campaign

▶ Wartime campaign in America to attack racism at home and abroad. Drawing on the wartime ideology of freedom and democracy, leading African American organizations argued that the struggle against fascism overseas had to coincide with a struggle against discrimination at home. The campaign greatly increased membership in the National Association for the Advancement of Colored People, which focused on legal challenges to segregation and discrimination.

How did the United States prepare for war? | How did the Allies turn the tide in Europe and the Pacific? | **How did the war change life for Americans on the home front?** | How did the Allies achieve victory in World War II? | Conclusion: Why did America emerge as a superpower at the end of the war?

709

Wartime Politics and the 1944 Election

Americans rallied around the war effort in unprecedented unity. Roosevelt, however, found it difficult to maintain the unity of his political coalition. Whites often resented blacks who migrated to northern cities. Many Americans complained about government price controls and the rationing of scarce goods while the war dragged on. Republicans seized the opportunity to roll back New Deal reforms. A conservative coalition of Republicans and southern Democrats succeeded in abolishing several New Deal agencies in 1942 and 1943, including the Work Projects Administration and the Civilian Conservation Corps.

In June 1944, Congress recognized the sacrifices made by millions of veterans, unanimously passing the GI Bill of Rights, which gave veterans funds for education, housing, and health care and provided loans to help them start businesses and buy homes. The GI Bill put the financial resources of the federal government behind the abstract goals of freedom and democracy for which veterans were fighting, and it empowered millions of GIs to better themselves and their families after the war.

After twelve years in the White House, Roosevelt was exhausted and gravely ill with heart disease. His poor health made the selection of a vice presidential candidate unusually important. Convinced that many Americans had soured on liberal reform, Roosevelt chose Senator Harry S. Truman of Missouri as his running mate. A reliable party man from a southern border state, Truman satisfied urban Democratic leaders while not worrying white southerners who were nervous about challenges to racial segregation.

Mass Execution of Jewish Women and Children

On October 14, 1942, Jewish women and children from the village of Mizocz in present-day Ukraine were herded into a ravine, forced to undress and lie facedown, and then shot at point-blank range by German police. This rare photograph, taken by one of the authorities at the scene, shows Germans killing the women who survived the initial gunfire. United States Holocaust Memorial Museum.

CHAPTER LOCATOR | How did America respond to international developments in the 1930s? | What led to the outbreak of war in Europe and the Pacific?

CHAPTER 25
710 THE UNITED STATES AND THE SECOND WORLD WAR , 1939–1945

The Republicans nominated as their presidential candidate the governor of New York, Thomas E. Dewey, who had made his reputation as a tough crime fighter. In the 1944 presidential campaign, Roosevelt's failing health alarmed many observers, but his frailty was outweighed by Americans' unwillingness to change presidents in the midst of the war and by Dewey's failure to persuade most voters that the New Deal was a creeping socialist menace. Voters gave Roosevelt a 53.5 percent majority, his narrowest presidential victory.

Reaction to the Holocaust

Since the 1930s, the Nazis had persecuted Jews in Germany and every German-occupied territory, causing many Jews to seek asylum beyond Hitler's reach. Roosevelt sympathized with the refugees' pleas for help, but he did not want to jeopardize his foreign policy or offend American voters. After Hitler's Anschluss in 1938, thousands of Austrian Jews sought to immigrate to the United States, but 82 percent of Americans opposed admitting them, and they were turned away. Roosevelt tried to persuade countries in Latin America and Africa to accept Jewish refugees, but none would do so.

In 1942, numerous reports that Hitler was implementing a "final solution" filtered out of German-occupied Europe. Jews and other "undesirables"—such as Gypsies, religious and political dissenters, and homosexuals—were being sent to concentration camps. Old people, children, and others deemed too weak to work were systematically slaughtered and cremated, while the able-bodied were put to work at slave labor until they died of starvation and abuse. Despite such reports, skeptical U.S. State Department officials refused to grant asylum to Jewish refugees. Most Americans, including top officials, believed that reports of the killing camps were exaggerated.

Desperate to stem the killing, the World Jewish Congress appealed to the Allies to bomb the death camps and the railroad tracks leading to them in order to hamper the killing and block further shipments of victims. Intent on achieving military victory as soon as possible, the Allies repeatedly turned down such bombing requests, arguing that the air forces could not divert resources from their military missions.

The nightmare of the **Holocaust** was all too real. When Russian troops arrived at the Auschwitz concentration camp in Poland in February 1945, they found emaciated prisoners, skeletal corpses, gas chambers, pits filled with human ashes, and loot the Nazis had stripped from the dead, including hair, gold dental fillings, and false teeth. At last, the truth about the Holocaust began to be known beyond the Germans who had perpetrated and tolerated these atrocities and the men, women, and children who had succumbed to the genocide. By then, it was too late for the 9 million victims—mostly Jews—of the Nazis' crimes against humanity.

The Holocaust, 1933–1945

Holocaust
▶ German effort to murder Europe's Jews, along with other groups the Nazis deemed "undesirable." Despite reports of the ongoing genocide, the Allies did almost nothing to interfere with Hitler's "final solution." In all, some 9 million people were killed in the Holocaust, most of them Jews.

QUICK REVIEW <

How did the Second World War influence American society?

| How did the United States prepare for war? | How did the Allies turn the tide in Europe and the Pacific? | **How did the war change life for Americans on the home front?** | How did the Allies achieve victory in World War II? | Conclusion: Why did America emerge as a superpower at the end of the war? |

> How did the Allies achieve victory in World War II?

D Day Invasion

"Taxi to Hell—and Back" is what Robert Sargent called his photograph of the D Day invasion of Normandy on June 6, 1944. Amid a dense fleet of landing craft, men lucky enough to have made it through rough seas and enemy fire struggle onto the beach to open a second front in Europe. Library of Congress.

BY FEBRUARY 1943, Soviet defenders defeated the German offensive against Stalingrad, turning the tide of the war in Europe. After fighting that had lasted for eighteen months, the Red Army forced Hitler's Wehrmacht to turn back toward the west. Now the Soviets and their Western allies faced the task of driving the Nazis out of eastern and western Europe. In the Pacific, the Allies had halted the expansion of the Japanese empire but now had the task of forcing the entrenched Japanese from their outposts.

From Bombing Raids to Berlin

While the Allied campaigns in North Africa and Italy were under way, British and American pilots flew bombing missions from England to German territories as a substitute for the delayed second front on the ground. During night raids, British bombers targeted general areas, hoping to hit civilians, create terror, and under-mine morale. Beginning in August 1942, American pilots carried out daytime raids on industrial targets vital for the German war machine, especially oil refineries and ball bearing factories.

CHAPTER LOCATOR | How did America respond to international developments in the 1930s? | What led to the outbreak of war in Europe and the Pacific?

German air defenses took a fearsome toll on Allied pilots and aircraft. In 1943, two-thirds of American airmen did not survive to complete their twenty-five-mission tours of duty. In all, 85,000 American airmen were killed. Many others were shot down and held as prisoners of war. In February 1944, the arrival of the P-51 Mustang fighter gave Allied bombers superior protection, allowing bombers to penetrate deep into Germany and pound civilian and military targets around the clock. In April 1944, the Allies began to target bridges and railroads in northwestern Europe in preparation for their cross-Channel invasion.

In November 1943, Churchill, Roosevelt, and Stalin met in Teheran to discuss wartime strategy and the second front. Roosevelt conceded to Stalin that the Soviet Union would exercise de facto control of the eastern European countries that the Red Army occupied as it pushed back the Germans. Stalin agreed to enter the war against Japan once Germany finally surrendered. Roosevelt and Churchill promised that they would at last launch a massive second-front assault in northern France in May 1944.

After frustrating delays caused by stormy weather, General Eisenhower launched the largest amphibious assault in world history on **D Day**, June 6, 1944. Rough seas and deadly fire from German machine guns slowed the assault, but Allied soldiers finally succeeded in securing the beachhead. As naval officer Tracy Sugarman recalled, "What I thought were piles of cordwood [on the beach] I later learned were the bodies of 2,500 men killed by withering fire from the Nazi gun emplacements." Sugarman reported that he and the other GIs who made the landing "were exhausted and we were exultant. We had survived D Day!"

Within a week, a flood of soldiers, tanks, and other military equipment swamped the Normandy beaches and propelled Allied forces toward Germany. On August 25, the Allies liberated Paris from four years of Nazi occupation. As Allied and Soviet armies closed on Germany in December 1944, Hitler ordered a counterattack to capture the Allies' essential supply port at Antwerp, Belgium. In the Battle of the Bulge (December 16, 1944, to January 31, 1945), German forces drove fifty-five miles into Allied lines before being stopped at Bastogne. More than 70,000 Allied soldiers were killed, including more Americans than in any other battle of the war. The Nazis lost more than 100,000 men and hundreds of tanks, fatally depleting Hitler's reserves.

In February 1945, Churchill, Stalin, and Roosevelt met secretly at the **Yalta Conference** (named for the Russian resort town where it was held) to discuss their plans for the postwar world. Seriously ill and noticeably frail, Roosevelt managed to secure Stalin's promise to permit votes of self-determination in the eastern European countries occupied by the Red Army. The Allies pledged to support Chiang Kai-shek as the leader of China. The Soviet Union obtained a role in the postwar governments of Korea and Manchuria in exchange for entering the war against Japan after the defeat of Germany.

The "Big Three" also agreed on the creation of a new international peacekeeping organization, the United Nations (UN). All nations would have a place in the UN General Assembly, but the Security Council would wield decisive power, and its permanent representatives from the Allied powers—China, France, Great Britain, the Soviet Union, and the United States—would possess a veto over UN actions. The Senate ratified the United Nations Charter in July 1945 by a vote of 89 to 2, reflecting the triumph of internationalism during the nation's mobilization for war.

CHRONOLOGY

1942
- Roosevelt authorizes Manhattan Project.

1944
- **June 6.** D Day.

1945
- **February.** Yalta Conference.
- **April 12.** Roosevelt dies; Vice President Harry Truman becomes president.
- **April 30.** Hitler commits suicide.
- **May 7.** Germany surrenders.
- **July.** United States joins United Nations.
- **August 6.** United States drops atomic bomb on Hiroshima.
- **August 9.** United States drops atomic bomb on Nagasaki.
- **August 14.** Japan surrenders, ending World War II.

D Day
▶ June 6, 1944, the date of the Allied invasion of northern France. D Day was the largest amphibious assault in world history. The invasion opened a second front against the Germans and moved the Allies closer to victory in Europe.

Yalta Conference
▶ February 1945 meeting at Yalta, a Russian resort town, during which Churchill, Stalin, and Roosevelt discussed their plans for the postwar world. Among the important decisions the Allied leaders made at the conference was the agreement to create the United Nations.

How did the United States prepare for war?	How did the Allies turn the tide in Europe and the Pacific?	How did the war change life for Americans on the home front?	**How did the Allies achieve victory in World War II?**	Conclusion: Why did America emerge as a superpower at the end of the war?

By April 11, Allied armies sweeping in from the west reached the banks of the Elbe River, the agreed-upon rendezvous with the Red Army, and paused while the Soviets smashed into Berlin, capturing it on May 2. Hitler had committed suicide on April 30, and the provisional German government surrendered unconditionally on May 7. The war in Europe was finally over, with the sacrifice of 135,576 American soldiers, nearly 250,000 British troops, and 9 million Russian combatants.

Roosevelt did not live to witness the end of the war. On April 12, while resting in Warm Springs, Georgia, he suffered a fatal stroke. Americans grieved for the man who had led them through years of depression and world war, and they worried aloud about his successor, Vice President Harry Truman, who would have to steer the nation to victory over Japan and protect American interests in the postwar world.

The Defeat of Japan

In 1943, British and American forces, along with Indian and Chinese allies, launched an offensive against Japanese outposts in southern Asia, pushing through Burma and into China, where the armies of Chiang Kai-shek continued to resist conquest. In the Pacific, Americans and their allies attacked Japanese strongholds by sea, air, and land, moving island by island toward the Japanese homeland (**Map 25.5**).

The island-hopping campaign began in August 1942, when American marines landed on Guadalcanal in the southern Pacific. For the next six months, a savage battle raged for control of the strategic area. Finally, during the night of February 8, 1943, Japanese forces withdrew. The terrible losses on both sides indicated to the marines how costly it would be to defeat Japan. After the battle, Joseph Steinbacher, a twenty-one-year-old from Alabama, sailed from San Francisco to New Guinea, where, he recalled, "all the cannon fodder waited to be assigned" to replace the killed and wounded.

As the Allies attacked island after island, Japanese soldiers were ordered to refuse to surrender no matter how hopeless their plight. The fierce Japanese resistance spurred remorseless Allied bombing attacks on Japanese-occupied islands, followed by amphibious landings by marines and grinding, inch-by-inch combat to root Japanese fighters out of bunkers and caves.

While the island-hopping campaign kept pressure on Japanese forces, the Allies invaded the Philippines in the fall of 1944. In the four-day Battle of Leyte Gulf, the American fleet crushed the Japanese armada, clearing the way for Allied victory in the Philippines. While the Philippine campaign was under way, American forces captured two crucial islands—Iwo Jima and Okinawa—from which they planned to launch an attack on the Japanese homeland. In desperation, Japanese leaders ordered thousands of suicide pilots, known as *kamikaze*, to crash their bomb-laden planes into Allied ships. But instead of destroying the American fleet, they demolished the last vestige of the Japanese air force. By June 1945, the Japanese were nearly defenseless on the sea and in the air. Still, their leaders prepared to fight to the death for their homeland.

Joseph Steinbacher and other GIs who had suffered "horrendous" casualties in the Philippines were now told by their commanding officer, "Men, in a few short months we are going to invade [Japan]. . . . We will be going in on the first

CHAPTER LOCATOR | How did America respond to international developments in the 1930s? | What led to the outbreak of war in Europe and the Pacific?

CHAPTER 25
714   THE UNITED STATES AND THE SECOND WORLD WAR , 1939–1945

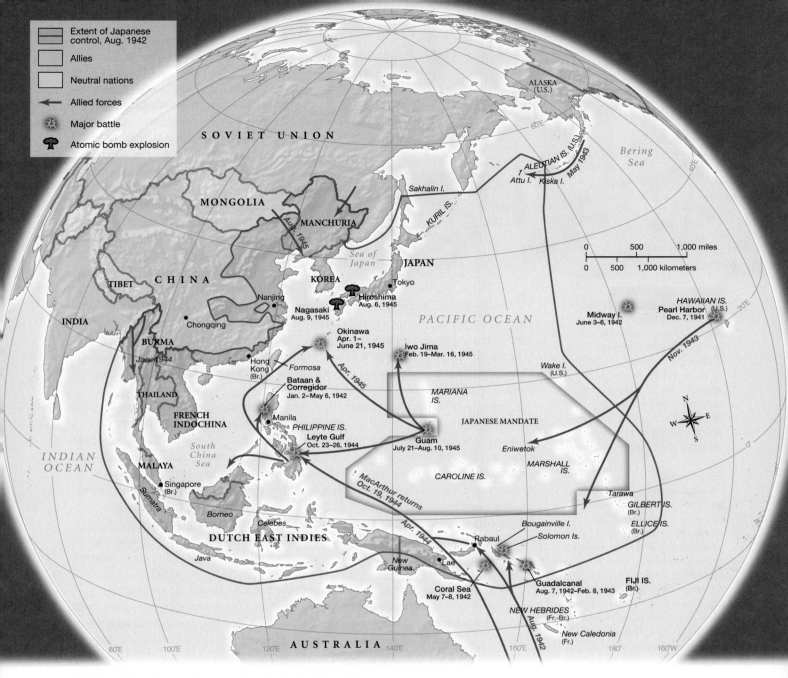

MAP 25.5 ■ The Pacific Theater of World War II, 1941–1945

To drive the Japanese from their far-flung empire, the Allies launched two combined naval and military offensives—one to recapture the Philippines and then attack Japanese forces in China, the other to hop from island to island in the Central Pacific toward the Japanese mainland.

wave and are expecting ninety percent casualties the first day. . . . For the few of us left alive the war will be over." Steinbacher later recalled his mental attitude at that moment: "I know that I am now a walking dead man and will not have a snowball's chance in hell of making it through the last great battle to conquer the home islands of Japan."

| How did the United States prepare for war? | How did the Allies turn the tide in Europe and the Pacific? | How did the war change life for Americans on the home front? | **How did the Allies achieve victory in World War II?** | Conclusion: Why did America emerge as a superpower at the end of the war? |

This rare shot taken by a news photographer in Hiroshima immediately after the atomic bomb exploded on August 6, 1945, suggests the shock and incomprehension that survivors later described as their first reactions. On August 9, another atomic bomb created similar devastation in Nagasaki. UN photo.

Hiroshima

▶ Japanese city devastated by an American-launched atomic bomb in August 1945. The bomb, developed in secret by scientists and engineers working at the government-funded Manhattan Project, killed 78,000 Japanese civilians. A second bomb was dropped on Nagasaki three days later, killing more than 100,000 people. The Japanese government surrendered on August 14, 1945, five days after the second attack.

Atomic Warfare

In mid-July 1945, as Allied forces prepared for the final assault on Japan, American scientists tested a secret weapon at a desert site near Los Alamos, New Mexico. In 1942, Roosevelt had authorized the top-secret Manhattan Project to find a way to convert nuclear energy into a super-bomb before the Germans added such a weapon to their arsenal. More than 100,000 Americans, led by scientists, engineers, and military officers at Los Alamos, worked frantically to win the race for an atomic bomb, conducting a successful test explosion on July 16, 1945.

A delegation of scientists and officials, troubled by the bomb's destructive force, secretly proposed that the United States give a public demonstration of the bomb's power, hoping to persuade Japan's leaders to surrender. But U.S. government officials quickly rejected such a demonstration. Despite Japan's numerous defeats, U.S. military advisers estimated that the invasion of Japan would cost the lives of at least 250,000 Americans.

President Truman heard about the successful bomb test when he was in Potsdam, Germany, negotiating with Stalin about postwar issues. Truman saw no reason not to use the atomic bomb against Japan if doing so would save American lives. But first he issued an ultimatum: Japan must surrender unconditionally or face utter ruin. When the Japanese failed to respond by the deadline, Truman ordered that a bomb be dropped on a Japanese city not already heavily damaged by American raids. On August 6, Colonel Paul Tibbets piloted the *Enola Gay* over **Hiroshima** and released an atomic bomb, leveling the city and incinerating 78,000 people. Three days later, after the Japanese government still refused to surrender, the United States dropped a second atomic bomb on Nagasaki, killing more than 100,000 civilians.

With American assurance that the emperor could retain his throne after the Allies took over, Japan surrendered on August 14. On a troop ship departing from Europe for what would have been the final assault on Japan, an American soldier spoke for millions of others when he heard the wonderful news that the killing was over: "We are going to grow to adulthood after all."

> **QUICK REVIEW**

Why did Truman elect to use the atomic bomb against Japan?

CHAPTER LOCATOR

How did America respond to international developments in the 1930s?

What led to the outbreak of war in Europe and the Pacific?

716 CHAPTER 25
THE UNITED STATES AND THE SECOND WORLD WAR , 1939–1945

U.S. Army Center of Military History.

Conclusion: Why did America emerge as a superpower at the end of the war?

SHORTLY AFTER PEARL HARBOR, Hitler pronounced America "a decayed country" without "much future"; a country "half Judaized, and the other half Negrified"; a country "where everything is built on the dollar" and bound to fall apart. American mobilization for World War II disproved Hitler's arrogant prophecy. At a cost of 405,399 American lives, the nation united with its allies to defeat Axis aggressors in Europe and Asia.

Wartime production lifted the nation out of the Great Depression. The gross national product soared to four times what it had been when Roosevelt became president in 1933. Jobs in defense industries eliminated chronic unemployment, provided wages for millions of women workers and African American migrants from southern farms, and boosted Americans' prosperity.

By the end of the war, the United States had emerged as a global superpower, buttressed by the military clout of the nation's nuclear monopoly. Although the war left much of the world a rubble-strewn wasteland, the American mainland had enjoyed immunity from attack. The Japanese occupation of China had left 50 million people without homes and millions more dead, maimed, and orphaned. The German offensive against the Soviet Union had killed more than 20 million Russian soldiers and civilians. Germany and Japan lay in ruins, their economies as shattered as their military forces. The Allies had killed more than 4 million Nazi soldiers and more than 1.2 million Japanese combatants, as well as hundreds of thousands of civilians.

As the dominant Western nation in the postwar world, the United States asserted its leadership in the reconstruction of Europe while occupying Japan and overseeing its economic and political recovery. America soon confronted new challenges in the tense aftermath of the war, as the Soviets seized political control of eastern Europe, a Communist revolution swept China, and national liberation movements emerged in the colonial empires of Britain and France. The surrender of the Axis powers ended the battles of World War II, but the forces unleashed by the war would shape the United States and the rest of the world for decades to come.

SO NOW YOU KNOW

During World War II, the United States' military production was more than double that of Germany, Japan, and Italy combined. This amazing level of wartime production supported the Allied victory over the Axis powers, lifted the nation out of the Great Depression, and established the United States as the dominant Western nation in the postwar world.

> CHAPTER 25 STUDY GUIDE

Online Study Guide
bedfordstmartins.com/roarkunderstanding

STEP 1 GETTING STARTED

Below are basic terms from this period in American history. Can you identify each term below and explain why it matters? To do this exercise online or to download this chart, visit bedfordstmartins.com/roarkunderstanding.

TERM	WHO OR WHAT & WHEN	WHY IT MATTERS
Adolf Hitler, p. 691		
appeasement, p. 693		
Joseph Stalin, p. 693		
Winston Churchill, p. 695		
Battle of Britain, p. 695		
Pearl Harbor, p. 697		
Battle of Midway, p. 704		
Double V campaign, p. 709		
Holocaust, p. 711		
D Day, p. 713		
Yalta Conference, p. 713		
Hiroshima, p. 716		

STEP 2 MOVING BEYOND THE BASICS

The exercise below represents a more advanced understanding of the chapter material. Fill in the chart by describing important developments in the United States and their impact during World War II in the following key areas: economic activity, employment, government, politics and the New Deal, race relations, and women's roles. When you are finished, consider these questions: How did the shift to a wartime economy affect women and racial minorities? What impact did the return to full employment have on the New Deal and the political balance of power? How did the war change the size and nature of the federal government? To do this exercise online or to download this chart, visit bedfordstmartins.com/roarkunderstanding.

	Developments	Impact
Economic activity		
Employment		
Government		
Politics and the New Deal		
Race relations		
Women's roles		

STEP

3

PUTTING
IT ALL
TOGETHER

Now that you've reviewed various parts of the chapter, take a step back and try to see the big picture by answering these questions. Remember to use specific examples from the chapter in your answers. To do this exercise online, visit bedfordstmartins.com/roarkunderstanding.

THE ONSET OF WORLD WAR II

► Why were the American people, as a whole, reluctant to become involved in World War II?

► How did Roosevelt use the economic power of the United States to aid Britain and the Soviet Union?

THE HOME FRONT

► How did the conversion to a war economy end the Great Depression? Who benefited most? What groups still struggled?

► What were the most important social consequences of America's involvement in World War II?

VICTORY

► How did the Allies achieve victory? What tensions among the Allies emerged in the final years of the war?

► What led to the decision to drop atomic bombs on Japan? In your opinion, was it a purely military decision, or were nonmilitary considerations important as well?

LOOKING BACKWARD, LOOKING AHEAD

► How did America's experience of World War I shape public opinion in 1939 and 1940 about U.S. involvement in World War II?

► How did World War II help set the stage for the social, economic, and political developments of the 1950s?

IN YOUR OWN WORDS

Imagine that you must explain chapter 25 to someone who hasn't read it. What would be the most important points to include and why?

26
COLD WAR POLITICS IN THE TRUMAN YEARS

1945–1953

> This chapter examines American politics in the years immediately following World War II. It explores the origins and impact of the Cold War, President Truman's domestic and foreign policy agendas, and the effects of the Korean War on American domestic politics.

> What factors contributed to the Cold War?

> What obstructed Truman's domestic agenda?

> How did America's Cold War policy lead to the Korean War?

> Conclusion: What were the costs and consequences of the Cold War?

DID YOU KNOW?

The U.S. armed forces were not desegregated until after World War II.

Statement on world peace. By Pulitzer Prize–winning cartoonist Rube Goldberg, 1948.

What factors contributed to the Cold War?

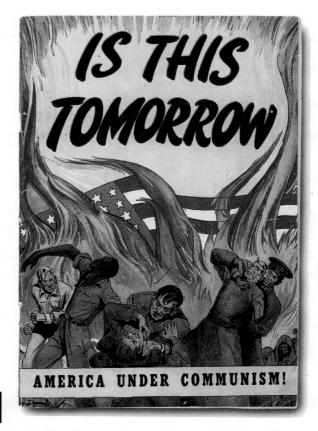

"Is This Tomorrow" Comic Book Cover

Fear of communism dominated much of postwar American life and politics, even invading popular culture. Four million copies of this comic book, published by a religious organization in 1947, painted a terrifying picture of what would happen to Americans if the Soviets took over the country. Such takeover stories appeared in movies, cartoons, and magazines as well as in other comic books. Collection of Charles H. Christensen.

> ▶ FOR MORE HELP ANALYZING THIS IMAGE, see the visual activity for this chapter in the Online Study Guide at bedfordstmartins.com/roarkunderstanding.

Harry S. Truman

▶ Democratic president who assumed office in 1945 upon Franklin Roosevelt's death and won another term in 1948. Although he had an ambitious domestic agenda in the areas of civil rights and social welfare, Truman succeeded in implementing only small portions of it. Instead, he focused on foreign policy and helped make containment a major component of post–World War II American foreign policy.

WITH JAPAN'S SURRENDER in August 1945, Americans besieged the government for the return of their loved ones. Baby booties arrived at the White House with a note, "Please send my daddy home." Americans wanted to dismantle the large military establishment and expected the Allies, led by the United States and working within the United Nations, to cooperate in the management of international peace. Postwar realities quickly dashed these hopes. New threats arose as the wartime alliance forged by the United States, Great Britain, and the Soviet Union crumbled, and the United States began to develop the means to contain the spread of Soviet power around the globe.

The Cold War Begins

"The guys who came out of World War II were idealistic," reported Harold Russell, a young paratrooper who had lost both hands in a training accident.

"We felt the day had come when the wars were all over." But political leaders were less optimistic. Once the Allies had overcome a common enemy, the prewar mistrust and antagonism between the Soviet Union and the West resurfaced over their very different visions of the postwar world.

The Western Allies' delay in opening a second front in Western Europe aroused Soviet suspicions during the war. The Soviet Union had lost more than twenty million citizens and vast portions of its agricultural and industrial capacity. Soviet leader Joseph Stalin wanted to make Germany pay for Soviet economic reconstruction and to expand Soviet influence in the world. Above all, he wanted friendly governments on the Soviet Union's borders in Eastern Europe. A ruthless dictator, he also wanted to maintain his own power.

In contrast to the Soviet devastation, enemy fire had never touched the mainland of the United States, and its 405,000 dead amounted to just 2 percent of the Soviet loss. With a vastly expanded economy and a monopoly on atomic weapons, the United States was the most powerful nation on earth. That sheer power, along with U.S. economic interests, policymakers' views about how the recent war might have been avoided, and a belief in the superiority of American institutions and intentions, all affected how American leaders approached the Soviet Union.

Fearing a return of the depression, U.S. officials believed that a healthy economy depended on opportunities abroad. American companies needed access to raw materials, markets for their goods, and security for their investments overseas. These needs could be met best in countries with similar economic and political systems. As Truman put it in 1947, "The American system can survive in America only if it becomes a world system." Yet both leaders and citizens regarded their foreign policy not as a self-interested campaign to guarantee economic interests, but as the means to preserve national security and bring freedom, democracy, and capitalism to the rest of the world. Laura Briggs spoke for many Americans who believed that "it was our destiny to prove that we were the children of God and that our way was right for the world."

Recent history also shaped postwar foreign policy. Americans believed that World War II might have been avoided had Britain and France resisted rather than appeased Hitler's initial aggression. Navy Secretary James V. Forrestal argued against trying to "buy [the Soviets'] understanding and sympathy. We tried that once with Hitler." This "appeasement" analogy would be invoked repeatedly when the United States faced challenges to the international status quo.

The man with ultimate responsibility for U.S. policy came to the White House with little international experience. **Harry S. Truman** envisioned Soviet-American cooperation, as long as the Soviet Union conformed to U.S. plans for the postwar world and restrained its expansionist impulses. Proud of his ability to make quick decisions, Truman determined to be firm with the Soviets, knowing well that America's nuclear monopoly gave him the upper hand.

Soviet and American interests clashed first in Eastern Europe. Stalin insisted that the Allies' wartime agreements gave him a free hand in the countries defeated or liberated by the Red Army, just as the United States was unilaterally reconstructing governments in Italy and Japan. The Soviet dictator used harsh methods to install Communist governments in neighboring Poland and Bulgaria. Elsewhere, the Soviets initially tolerated non-Communist governments in Hungary and Czechoslovakia. In the spring of 1946, Stalin responded to pressure from the

CHRONOLOGY

1945
- Soviet and U.S. interests clash first in Eastern Europe.

1946
- George F. Kennan drafts a call for the containment of communism.
- United States grants independence to the Philippines.

1947
- National Security Act creates the National Security Council and Central Intelligence Agency.
- Truman asks for aid to Greece and Turkey and announces Truman Doctrine.

WESTMINSTER COLLEGE
Harry Truman · Winston Churchill
FULTON, MO. 1946

1948
- Congress approves the Marshall Plan for European recovery.

1948–1949
- Berlin blockade and airlift.

1949
- Communists take over mainland China; Nationalists retreat to Taiwan.
- North Atlantic Treaty Organization is formed.
- Soviet Union detonates its first atomic bomb.

1950
- Truman approves development of hydrogen bomb.

1951
- United States ends occupation of Japan and signs peace treaty and mutual security pact.

CHAPTER LOCATOR | **What factors contributed to the Cold War?** | What obstructed Truman's domestic agenda? | How did America's Cold War policy lead to the Korean War? | Conclusion: What were the costs and consequences of the Cold War?

723

West and removed troops from Iran on the Soviet Union's southwest border, allowing U.S. access to the rich oil fields there.

Stalin considered U.S. officials hypocritical in demanding democratic elections in Eastern Europe while supporting dictatorships friendly to U.S. interests in Latin America. The United States clung to its sphere of influence while opposing Soviet efforts to create its own. But the Western Allies were unwilling to use military force against the Soviets. They issued sharp protests but failed to prevent the Soviet Union from establishing satellite countries throughout Eastern Europe.

In 1946, the wartime Allies contended over Germany's future. Both sides wanted to demilitarize Germany, but American policymakers sought rapid industrial revival there to foster European economic recovery and thus America's own long-term prosperity. By contrast, the Soviet Union wanted Germany weak militarily and economically, and Stalin demanded heavy reparations to help rebuild the dev-

MAP 26.1 ■ The Division of Europe after World War II

The "iron curtain," a term coined by Winston Churchill to refer to the Soviet grip on Eastern and central Europe, divided the continent for nearly fifty years. Communist governments controlled the countries along the Soviet Union's western border. The only exception was Finland, which remained neutral.

astated Soviet economy. Unable to settle their differences, the Allies divided Germany. The Soviet Union installed a Communist government in the eastern section, and in December 1946, Britain, France, and the United States unified their occupation zones, beginning the process that established the Federal Republic of Germany—West Germany—in 1949 (**Map 26.1**).

The war of words escalated early in 1946. Stalin told a Moscow audience in February that capitalism inevitably produced war. One month later, Truman accompanied Winston Churchill to Fulton, Missouri, where the former prime minister denounced Soviet interference in Eastern and central Europe. "From Stettin in the Baltic to Trieste in the Adriatic, an **iron curtain** has descended across the Continent," Churchill said. Stalin saw Churchill's proposal for joint British-American action to combat Soviet aggression as "a call to war against the USSR [the Soviet Union]."

In February 1946, George F. Kennan, a career diplomat and expert on Russia, wrote a comprehensive rationale for hard-line foreign policy. Downplaying the influence of Communist ideology in Soviet policy, he instead stressed the Soviets' insecurity and Stalin's need to maintain authority at home, which he believed prompted Stalin to exaggerate threats from abroad and to expand Soviet power. Kennan believed that the Soviet Union would retreat from its expansionist efforts "in the face of superior force," recommending that the United States respond with "unalterable counterforce." He predicted that this approach, which came to be called **containment**, would eventually end in "either the breakup or the gradual mellowing of Soviet power."

Not all public figures agreed. In September 1946, Secretary of Commerce Henry A. Wallace urged greater understanding of the Soviets' concerns about their nation's security, insisting that "we have no more business in the political affairs of Eastern Europe than Russia has in the political affairs of Latin America." State Department officials were furious, and Truman fired Wallace.

The Truman Doctrine and the Marshall Plan

In 1947, the United States began to implement the doctrine of containment. It was not an easy transition; Americans approved taking a hard line against the Soviet Union, but they wanted to keep their soldiers and tax dollars at home. In addition to selling containment to the public, Truman had to gain the support of a Republican-controlled Congress, which included a forceful bloc opposed to a strong U.S. presence in Europe.

Crises in two Mediterranean countries triggered the implementation of containment. In February 1947, Britain informed the United States that its crippled economy could no longer sustain military assistance either to Greece, where the autocratic government faced a leftist uprising, or to Turkey, which was trying to resist Soviet pressures. Truman promptly sought congressional authority to send the two countries military and economic aid. Meeting with congressional leaders, Undersecretary of State Dean Acheson predicted that if Greece and Turkey fell, communism would soon consume three-fourths of the world. After a stunned silence, Michigan senator Arthur Vandenberg, the Republican foreign policy leader, warned that to get approval, Truman would have to "scare hell out of the country."

Truman did just that. Outlining what would later be called the domino theory, he warned that if Greece fell to the rebels, "confusion and disorder might well

iron curtain
▶ Metaphor first introduced in 1946 by Winston Churchill. The term refers to the line that separated Soviet-controlled Eastern Europe from the democratic nations in the rest of Europe following World War II.

containment
▶ The American commitment to resisting Soviet expansion. President Truman initiated and implemented the containment policy during the crises in Turkey and Greece in 1947. The strategy of containment shaped American foreign policy throughout the Cold War.

CHAPTER LOCATOR | What factors contributed to the Cold War? | What obstructed Truman's domestic agenda? | How did America's Cold War policy lead to the Korean War? | Conclusion: What were the costs and consequences of the Cold War?

725

Truman Doctrine

▶ First articulated by President Truman in 1947 to gain support for U.S. intervention in Greece and Turkey, the Truman Doctrine committed the nation to "support free peoples who are resisting attempted subjugation by armed minorities or by outside pressures." The doctrine was subsequently used to support American aid to any kind of government if the only alternative appeared to be communism.

Marshall Plan (European Recovery Program)

▶ Program approved by Congress in 1948 to aid European economic recovery. Between 1948 and 1953, the United States spent $13 billion to restore the economies of sixteen Western European nations. The Marshall Plan marked the first step toward the European Union and yielded economic benefits for both the United States and Europe.

spread throughout the entire Middle East" and then create instability in Europe. According to what came to be called the **Truman Doctrine,** the United States needed to "support free peoples who are resisting attempted subjugation by armed minorities or by outside pressures." Despite some congressional opposition, the administration won the day, setting a precedent for forty years of Cold War interventions that would aid any kind of government if the only alternative appeared to be communism.

A much larger assistance program for Europe followed aid to Greece and Turkey. In May 1947, Acheson described a war-ravaged Western Europe, with "factories destroyed, fields impoverished, transportation systems wrecked, populations scattered and on the borderline of starvation." American citizens were sending generous amounts of private aid, but Europe needed large-scale assistance. European economic recovery, Acheson argued, was essential to halt the growth of socialist and Communist parties in France and Italy.

In March 1948, Congress approved the European Recovery Program—known as the **Marshall Plan**, after Secretary of State George C. Marshall, who proposed the plan. Over the next five years, the United States spent $13 billion to restore the economies of sixteen Western European nations. Marshall invited all European nations and the Soviet Union to cooperate in a request for aid, but the Soviets objected to the American terms of free trade and financial disclosure and ordered their Eastern European satellites likewise to reject the offer.

Marshall Plan Bread for Greek Children Greece was one of sixteen European nations that participated in the European Recovery Program. In this photograph taken in 1949, Greek children receive loaves of bread made from the first shipment of Marshall Plan flour from the United States. © Bettmann/Corbis.

The Marshall Plan marked the first step toward the European Union. Humanitarian impulses as well as the goal of keeping Western Europe free of communism drove the adoption of this enormous aid program. But the Marshall Plan also helped boost the U.S. economy because the European nations spent most of the dollars to buy American products and Europe's economic recovery created new markets and opportunities for American investment.

In February 1948, the Soviets staged a coup and installed a Communist regime in Czechoslovakia, the last democracy left in Eastern Europe. Next, Stalin threatened Western access to Berlin. That former capital of Germany lay within Soviet-controlled East Germany, but all four Allies jointly occupied Berlin, dividing it into separate administrative units. As the Western Allies moved to organize West Germany as a separate nation, the Soviets retaliated by blocking roads and rail lines between West Germany and the Western-held sections of Berlin, cutting off food, fuel, and other essentials to two million inhabitants.

"We stay in Berlin, period," Truman vowed. To avoid a confrontation with Soviet troops, for nearly a year U.S. and British pilots airlifted 2.3 million tons of goods to sustain West Berliners. Stalin hesitated to shoot down these cargo planes, and in 1949 he lifted the blockade. The city was then divided into East Berlin, under Soviet control, and West Berlin, which became part of West Germany. For many Americans, the Berlin airlift confirmed the wisdom of containment: When challenged, the Russians backed down.

Berlin Divided, 1948

Building a National Security State

In September 1949, the United States lost its nuclear monopoly when the Soviet Union detonated its own atomic bomb. To keep the United States ahead, in January 1950 Truman approved the development of a hydrogen bomb, equivalent to five hundred atomic bombs, rejecting the arguments of several scientists who had worked on the atomic bomb and of George Kennan, who warned of an endless arms race. The "super bomb" was ready by 1954, but the U.S. advantage was brief. In November 1955, the Soviets exploded their own hydrogen bomb.

The Six-Pronged Containment Strategy

1. Atomic weapons

2. Stronger traditional military forces

3. Military alliances with other nations

4. Military and economic aid to friendly nations

5. An espionage network and secret means to subvert Communist expansion

6. A propaganda offensive to win popular admiration for the United States around the world

From the 1950s through the 1980s, deterrence formed the basis of American nuclear strategy. To deter a Soviet Union attack, the United States strove to maintain a nuclear force more powerful than the Soviets'. Because the Russians pursued a similar policy, the superpowers became locked in a nuclear weapons race. Albert Einstein, whose mathematical discoveries had laid the foundations for

CHAPTER LOCATOR | What factors contributed to the Cold War? | What obstructed Truman's domestic agenda? | How did America's Cold War policy lead to the Korean War? | Conclusion: What were the costs and consequences of the Cold War?

727

nuclear weapons, warned that the war that came after World War III would "be fought with sticks and stones."

Implementing the second component of its containment strategy, the United States beefed up its conventional military power to deter Soviet threats that might not warrant nuclear retaliation. The National Security Act of 1947 united the military branches under a single secretary of defense and created the National Security Council (NSC) to advise the president. During the Berlin crisis in 1948, Congress hiked military appropriations and enacted a peacetime draft. In addition, Congress granted permanent status to the women's military branches, though it limited their numbers and rank and banned them from combat. With 1.5 million men and women in uniform in 1950, the military strength of the United States had quadrupled since the 1930s, and defense expenditures claimed one-third of the federal budget.

Collective security, the third prong of containment strategy, marked a sharp reversal of the nation's traditional foreign policy. In 1949, the United States joined Canada and Western European nations in its first peacetime military alliance, the **North Atlantic Treaty Organization (NATO)**, designed to counter a Soviet threat to Western Europe (see Map 26.1, page 724). For the first time in its history, the United States pledged to go to war if one of its allies was attacked.

The fourth element of defense strategy involved foreign assistance programs to strengthen friendly countries, such as aid to Greece and Turkey and the Marshall Plan. In addition, in 1949 Congress approved $1 billion of military aid to its NATO allies, and the government began economic assistance to nations in other parts of the world.

The fifth ingredient of containment improved the government's espionage capacities and ability to thwart communism through covert activities. The National Security Act of 1947 created the **Central Intelligence Agency (CIA)** not only to gather information but also to perform any activities "related to intelligence affecting the national security" that the NSC might authorize. Such functions included propaganda, sabotage, economic warfare, and support for "anti-communist elements in threatened countries of the free world." In 1948, secret CIA operations helped defeat Italy's Communist Party. Subsequently, CIA agents would intervene even more actively, helping to topple legitimate foreign governments and violating the rights of U.S. citizens.

Finally, the U.S. government organized cultural exchanges and spread propaganda throughout the world. The government expanded the Voice of America, created during World War II to broadcast U.S. propaganda abroad. In addition, the State Department sent books, exhibits, jazz musicians, and other performers to foreign countries as "cultural ambassadors."

By 1950, the United States had abandoned age-old tenets of foreign policy. Isolationism and neutrality had given way to a peacetime military alliance and efforts to control events far beyond U.S. borders. The United States aggressively and successfully promoted economic recovery and a military shield for those parts of Europe not behind the iron curtain.

Superpower Rivalry around the Globe

Efforts to implement containment moved beyond Europe. In Africa, Asia, and the Middle East, World War II accelerated a tide of national liberation movements

North Atlantic Treaty Organization (NATO)

▶ Military alliance formed in 1949 among the United States, Canada, and Western European nations to counter a Soviet threat to Western Europe. For the first time in its history, the United States pledged to go to war if one of its allies was attacked.

Central Intelligence Agency (CIA)

▶ Agency created by the National Security Act of 1947 to expand the government's espionage capacities and ability to thwart communism through covert activities. CIA functions came to include propaganda, sabotage, economic warfare, and support for anti-Communist forces around the world.

against war-weakened imperial powers. By 1960, forty countries, with more than a quarter of the world's people, had won their independence. These nations, along with Latin America, came to be referred to collectively as the third world, a term denoting countries outside the Western (first world) and Soviet (second world) orbits that had not yet developed industrial economies.

Like Woodrow Wilson during World War I, Roosevelt and Truman promoted the ideal of self-determination. The United States granted independence to the Philippines in 1946 and applauded the British withdrawal from India. At the same time, both the United States and the Soviet Union cultivated governments in emerging nations that were friendly to the superpowers' own interests.

Leaders of many liberation movements, impressed with Russia's rapid economic growth, adopted socialist or Communist ideas. Although few had formal ties with the Soviet Union, American leaders saw these movements as a threatening extension of Soviet power. Seeking to hold communism at bay by fostering economic development and political stability, the Truman administration initiated the Point IV Program in 1949, providing technical aid to developing nations.

In Asia, civil war raged in China, where the Communists, led by **Mao Zedong** (Mao Tse-tung), fought the official Nationalist government under Chiang Kai-shek. While the Communists gained support among the peasants for their land reforms and valiant stand against the Japanese, Chiang's corrupt and incompetent government alienated much of the population. Siding with Chiang, the United States provided almost $3 billion in aid to the Nationalists during the civil war. Yet, recognizing the ineptness of Chiang's government, Truman and his advisers refused to divert further resources from Europe to China.

In October 1949, Mao established the People's Republic of China (PRC), and the Nationalists fled to the island of Taiwan. Fearing a U.S.-supported invasion to recapture China for the Nationalists, Mao signed a mutual defense treaty with the Soviet Union in which each nation pledged to defend the other in case of attack. The United States refused to recognize the PRC, blocked its admission to the United Nations, and supported the Nationalist government in Taiwan. Only a massive U.S. military commitment could have stopped the Chinese Communists, yet some Republicans cried that Truman and "the pro-Communists in the State Department" had "lost" China.

With China in turmoil, the administration reconsidered its plans for postwar Japan. U.S. policy shifted to helping Japan rapidly reindustrialize and secure access to natural resources and markets in Asia. In a short time, the Japanese economy was flourishing, and the official military occupation ended when the two nations signed a peace treaty and a mutual security pact in September 1951. Like West Germany, Japan now sat squarely within the American orbit.

The one place where Cold War considerations did not control American policy was Palestine. In 1943, then-Senator Harry Truman spoke passionately about Nazi Germany's annihilation of the Jews, asserting, "This is not a Jewish problem, it is an American problem—and we must . . . face it squarely and honorably." As president, he made good on his words. Jews had been migrating to Palestine, their biblical homeland, since the nineteenth century, resulting in tension and hostilities with the Palestinian Arabs. After World War II, as hundreds of thousands of European Jews sought refuge and the creation of a national homeland in Palestine, fighting escalated into terrorism on both sides.

Mao Zedong

▶ Leader of the Communists in China who toppled the Nationalist government of Chiang Kai-shek and in October 1949 established the People's Republic of China. Fearing a U.S.-supported invasion to recapture China for the Nationalists, Mao signed a mutual defense treaty with the Soviet Union.

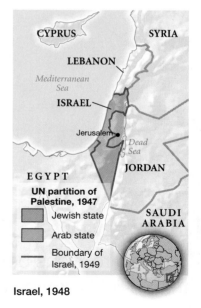

Israel, 1948

CHAPTER LOCATOR | What factors contributed to the Cold War? | What obstructed Truman's domestic agenda? | How did America's Cold War policy lead to the Korean War? | Conclusion: What were the costs and consequences of the Cold War?

729

Haganah Troops Mobilize in Palestine

Haganah originated in the 1910s as a paramilitary group to defend Jewish settlers in Palestine against Arabs who opposed the Zionists' expressed desire to build a Jewish state there. After Israel declared itself a nation in 1948, Haganah became the core of the Israel Defense Forces, Israel's main military organization. In this photo, Haganah troops are mobilizing in July 1948 to defend the new state from the armies of the surrounding nations of Syria, Jordan, Egypt, Lebanon, and Iraq. © Bettmann/Corbis.

Truman's foreign policy experts sought American-Arab friendship as a barrier against Soviet influence in the Middle East and as a means to secure access to Arabian oil. Uncharacteristically defying his advisers, the president responded instead to pleas from Jewish organizations, which coincided with his moral commitment to Holocaust survivors and his interest in the American Jewish vote for the 1948 election. When Jews in Palestine declared the state of Israel in May 1948, Truman quickly recognized the new country and made its defense the cornerstone of U.S. policy in the Middle East.

> ## QUICK REVIEW

Why did relations between the United States and the Soviet Union deteriorate after World War II?

Truman's Whistle-Stop Campaign Harry Truman rallies a crowd from his campaign train at a stop in Bridgeport, Pennsylvania, in October 1948. Truman Library.

What obstructed Truman's domestic agenda?

REFERRING TO THE CIVIL WAR GENERAL who coined the phrase "War is hell," Truman said in December 1945, "Sherman was wrong. I'm telling you I find peace is hell." Challenged by crises abroad, Truman also faced shortages, strikes, inflation, and other problems as the economy shifted to peacetime production. At the same time, he tried to expand New Deal reform with his own **Fair Deal** agenda of initiatives in civil rights, housing, education, and health care—efforts hindered by the wave of anti-Communist hysteria sweeping the country.

Fair Deal

▶ The package of initiatives proposed by President Truman in 1945. Truman hoped to follow up the accomplishments of the New Deal with initiatives in civil rights, housing, education, and health care. Republicans and southern Democrats blocked most of Truman's agenda.

Reconverting to a Peacetime Economy

Despite scarcities and deprivations during World War II, most Americans enjoyed a higher standard of living than ever before. Economic experts as well as ordinary citizens worried about sustaining that standard and providing jobs for millions of returning soldiers. Truman wasted no time unveiling his plan, asking Congress to enact a twenty-one-point program of social and economic reforms. He wanted to maintain the government's power to regulate the economy while it adjusted to peacetime production, and he sought government programs to provide basic essentials such as housing and health care to those in need. "Not even President Roosevelt ever asked for as much at one sitting," exploded Republican leader Joseph W. Martin Jr.

Congress approved one of Truman's key proposals—full-employment legislation—but even that was watered down. The Employment Act of 1946 called

CHAPTER LOCATOR | What factors contributed to the Cold War? | **What obstructed Truman's domestic agenda?** | How did America's Cold War policy lead to the Korean War? | Conclusion: What were the costs and consequences of the Cold War?

731

1944
- The Servicemen's Readjustment Act (GI Bill).

1946
- United States experiences postwar labor unrest triggered by inflation.
- Truman creates President's Committee on Civil Rights.
- Employment Act.
- Republicans gain control of Congress.

1947
- Jackie Robinson becomes the first African American to play major league baseball.
- Truman establishes loyalty program.
- Congress passes the antilabor Taft-Hartley Act over Truman's veto.

1948
- Truman orders desegregation of armed services.
- Truman wins a full presidential term in a close election.

1949
- The Housing Act establishes a federal housing program for the poor.

1950
- Senator Joseph McCarthy accuses the U.S. government of harboring Communists.

upon the federal government "to promote maximum employment, production, and purchasing power," thereby formalizing government's responsibility for maintaining a healthy economy. The law created the Council of Economic Advisors to assist the president, but it authorized no new powers to translate the government's obligation into effective action.

Inflation, not unemployment, turned out to be the most severe problem in the early postwar years. Consumers had $30 billion in wartime savings to spend, but shortages of meat, automobiles, housing, and other items persisted. Until industry could convert fully to civilian production and make more goods available, consumer demand would continue to drive up prices. Nonetheless, Truman's efforts to maintain price and rent controls fell to pressures from business groups and others determined to trim government powers.

Labor relations were another thorn in Truman's side. Organized labor survived the war stronger than ever, its 14.5 million members making up 35 percent of the civilian workforce. Yet union members feared the erosion of wartime gains and launched an intense struggle to preserve them. Five million workers went out on strike in 1946, affecting nearly every major industry. Workers saw corporate executives profiting at their expense. Shortly before voting to strike, a former marine and his coworkers calculated that a lavish party given by a company executive had cost more than they would earn in a whole year at the steel mill. "That sort of stuff made us realize, hell we had to bite the bullet . . . the bosses sure didn't give a damn for us." Although most Americans approved of unions in principle, they became fed up with strikes, blamed unions for shortages and rising prices, and called for government restrictions on organized labor. When the wave of strikes subsided, workers had won wage increases of about 20 percent, but the

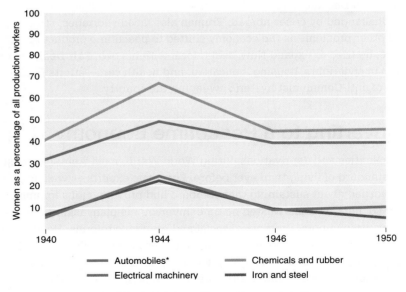

FIGURE 26.1 ■ Women Workers in Selected Industries, 1940–1950
Women demolished the idea that some jobs were "men's work" during World War II, but they failed to maintain their gains in the manufacturing sector after the war.

loss of overtime pay along with rising prices left their purchasing power only slightly higher than in 1942.

Women workers fared even less well. Polls indicated that as many as 68 to 85 percent wanted to keep their wartime jobs, but most who remained in the workforce had to settle for relatively low-paying jobs in light industry or the service sector. Displaced from her shipyard work, Marie Schreiber took a cashier's job, lamenting, "You were back to women's wages, you know . . . practically in half." Women's organizations and labor union women pushed for legislation to require equal pay for equal work, to provide child care for employed mothers, and to create a government commission to study the status of women. But at a time when women were viewed primarily as wives and mothers and a strong current of opinion resisted further expansion of federal powers, these initiatives got nowhere (Figure 26.1).

By 1947, the economy had stabilized, avoiding the postwar depression that so many had feared. Wartime profits enabled businesses to expand. Consumers could now spend their wartime savings on houses, cars, and appliances that had lain beyond their reach during the depression and the war. Defense spending and foreign aid that enabled war-stricken countries to purchase American products also stimulated the economy. A soaring birthrate further sustained consumer demand. Although prosperity was far from universal, the United States entered into a remarkable economic boom that lasted through the 1960s (see chapter 27).

Another economic boost came from the only large welfare measure passed after the New Deal. **The Servicemen's Readjustment Act (GI Bill)**, enacted in 1944, offered 16 million veterans job training and education; unemployment compensation while they looked for jobs; and low-interest loans to purchase homes, farms, and small businesses. By 1948, some 1.3 million veterans had bought houses with government loans. Helping 2.2 million ex-soldiers attend college, the subsidies sparked a boom in higher education. A drugstore clerk before his military service, Don Condren was able to get an engineering degree and buy his first house. "I think the GI Bill gave the whole country an upward boost economically," he said.

Condren overlooked the disparate ways in which the GI Bill operated. Like key New Deal programs such as unemployment insurance and aid to mothers with dependent children, GI programs were administered at the state and local levels, which especially in the South routinely discriminated against African Americans. Black veterans who sought jobs for which the military had trained them were shuttled into menial labor. One decorated veteran said that the GI Bill "draws no color line," yet "my color bars me from most decent jobs, and if, instead of

The Servicemen's Readjustment Act (GI Bill)

▶ Law passed in 1944 offering America's 16 million veterans job training and education; unemployment compensation while they looked for jobs; and low-interest loans to purchase homes, farms, and small businesses. Millions of Americans benefited from the GI Bill, but its impact was uneven as minorities were denied full access to the programs it created.

TRYING TO CATCH UP WITH YOUR DEMANDS...THOUSANDS OF NEW PROCTOR IRONS AND TOASTERS

Here they come!

PROCTOR
AUTOMATIC ELECTRIC APPLIANCES

Proctor Iron and Toaster

Like many manufacturers forced to convert to war production during World War II, Proctor Electric Company hoped to profit after the war from pent-up consumer demand. Even before the company had fully reconverted its plants, ads tempted consumers with products soon to come and asked them to be patient until Proctor could meet their needs, as this 1946 ad indicates.
Picture Research Consultants & Archives.

▶ FOR MORE HELP ANALYZING THIS IMAGE, see the visual activity for this chapter in the Online Study Guide at bedfordstmartins.com/roarkunderstanding.

CHAPTER LOCATOR | What factors contributed to the Cold War? | What obstructed Truman's domestic agenda? | How did America's Cold War policy lead to the Korean War? | Conclusion: What were the costs and consequences of the Cold War?

733

accepting menial work, I collect my $20 a week readjustment allowance, I am classified as a 'lazy nigger.'" Thousands of black veterans did benefit from the GI Bill, but it did not help all ex-soldiers equally.

Blacks and Mexican Americans Push for Their Civil Rights

"I spent four years in the army to free a bunch of Frenchmen and Dutchmen," an African American corporal declared, "and I'm hanged if I'm going to let the Alabama version of the Germans kick me around when I get home." Black veterans as well as civilians resolved that the return to peace would not be a return to the racial injustices of prewar America. Their political clout had grown with the migration of two million African Americans to northern and western cities, where they could vote. Pursuing civil rights through the courts and Congress, the National Association for the Advancement of Colored People (NAACP) counted half a million members.

In the postwar years, individual African Americans broke through the color barrier, achieving several "firsts." Jackie Robinson integrated major league baseball, playing for the Brooklyn Dodgers and braving abuse from fans and players to win the Rookie of the Year Award in 1947. In 1950, Ralph J. Bunche received the Nobel Peace Prize for his United Nations work, and Gwendolyn Brooks won the Pulitzer Prize for poetry.

Segregation The segregation visible on this bus was a feature of life in the South from the late nineteenth century until the 1960s. African Americans could not use white hospitals, cemeteries, schools, libraries, swimming pools, restrooms, or drinking fountains. They were relegated to balconies in movie theaters and kept apart from whites in all public meetings.
Stan Wayman/Time Life Pictures/Getty Images.

Still, for most African Americans, little had changed, especially in the South, where violence greeted their attempts to assert their rights. Armed white men turned back Medgar Evers (who would become a key civil rights leader in the 1960s) and four other veterans trying to vote in Mississippi. A mob lynched Isaac Nixon for voting in Georgia, and an all-white jury acquitted the men accused of his murder. In the South, political leaders and local vigilantes routinely intimidated potential black voters with threats of economic retaliation and violence.

The Cold War heightened American leaders' sensitivity to racial issues, as the superpowers vied for the allegiance of newly independent nations with nonwhite populations. Soviet propaganda repeatedly highlighted racial injustice in the United States. Republican senator Henry Cabot Lodge called race relations "our Achilles' heel before the world," while Secretary of State Dean Acheson noted that systematic segregation and discrimination endangered "our moral leadership of the free and democratic nations of the world."

"My very stomach turned over when I learned that Negro soldiers just back from overseas were being dumped out of army trucks in Mississippi and beaten," wrote Truman. Wrestling with the Democrats' need for northern black and liberal votes as well as southern white votes, Truman spoke more boldly on civil rights than any previous president. In 1946, he created the President's Committee on Civil Rights, and in February 1948 he asked Congress to enact the committee's recommendations. The first president to address the NAACP, Truman asserted that all Americans should have equal rights to housing, education, employment, and the ballot.

As with much of his domestic program, the president failed to act aggressively on his bold words. Congress rebuffed Truman's proposals for civil rights legislation, but some northern and western states passed laws against discrimination in employment and public accommodations. Running for reelection in 1948, Truman issued an executive order to desegregate the armed services, but it lay unimplemented until the Korean War. Despite the gap between Truman's words and what his administration actually accomplished, desegregation of the military and the administration's support of civil rights cases in the Supreme Court contributed to far-reaching changes, while his Committee on Civil Rights set an agenda for years to come.

Although discussion of race and civil rights usually focused on African Americans, Mexican Americans endured similar injustices. In 1929, they had formed the League of United Latin American Citizens (LULAC) to combat discrimination and segregation in the Southwest. Like black soldiers after World War II, Mexican American veterans believed, as one of them insisted, that "we had earned our credentials as American citizens. We had paid our dues." Problems with getting their veterans' benefits spurred a group in Corpus Christi, Texas, led by Dr. Héctor Peréz García, a combat surgeon who had earned the Bronze Star, to form the American GI Forum in 1948. It went on to become a key national organization battling discrimination against Latinos and electing sympathetic officials.

"Education is our freedom," read the GI Forum's motto, yet Mexican American children were routinely segregated in public schools. Parents filed a class action suit in Orange County, California, winning a federal court decision in 1947 that outlawed the practice of separating Mexican American and white children. In 1948, LULAC and the GI Forum achieved a similar victory over

CHAPTER LOCATOR | What factors contributed to the Cold War? | What obstructed Truman's domestic agenda? | How did America's Cold War policy lead to the Korean War? | Conclusion: What were the costs and consequences of the Cold War?

735

segregation in Texas schools. Such projects paralleled the efforts of the NAACP on behalf of African Americans that would culminate in the *Brown* decision in 1954 (see chapter 27). These efforts, along with challenges to discrimination in employment and efforts for political representation, demonstrated a growing mobilization of Mexican Americans in the Southwest.

The Fair Deal Flounders

Republicans capitalized on public frustrations with economic reconversion in the 1946 congressional election to capture control of Congress for the first time in fourteen years. Many had campaigned against New Deal "bureaucracy" and "radicalism" in 1946, and the new Congress was able to weaken some reform programs and enact tax cuts favoring higher-income groups.

Organized labor took the most severe blow when Congress passed the Taft-Hartley Act over Truman's veto in 1947. The law reduced the power of organized labor and made it more difficult to organize workers. For example, states could now pass "right-to-work" laws, which banned the practice of requiring all workers to join a union once a majority had voted for it. Many states, especially in the South and West, rushed to enact such laws, encouraging industries to relocate there. Taft-Hartley maintained the New Deal principle of government protection for collective bargaining, but it put the government more squarely between labor and management.

As the 1948 elections approached, Truman faced not only a resurgent Republican Party headed by its nominee, Thomas E. Dewey, but also two revolts within his own party. On the left, Henry A. Wallace, whose foreign policy views had cost him his cabinet seat, led the new Progressive Party. On the right, South Carolina governor J. Strom Thurmond headed the States' Rights Party—the Dixiecrats—formed by southern Democrats who had walked out of the 1948 Democratic Party convention when it passed a liberal civil rights plank.

Almost alone in believing he could win, Truman crisscrossed the country by train, answering supporters' cries of "Give 'em hell, Harry." So bleak were Truman's prospects that on election night, the *Chicago Daily Tribune* printed its next day's issue with the headline "DEWEY DEFEATS TRUMAN." But Truman took 303 electoral votes to Dewey's 189, and his party regained control of Congress (**Map 26.2**). His unexpected victory attested to the broad support for his foreign policy and the enduring popularity of New Deal reform.

Truman failed to turn his victory into success for his Fair Deal agenda. Congress made modest improvements in Social Security and raised the minimum wage, but it passed only one significant reform measure. The Housing Act of 1949 authorized 810,000 units of government-constructed housing over the next six years and represented a landmark commitment by the government to address the housing needs of the poor. Yet it fell far short of actual need, and slum clearance frequently displaced the poor without providing alternatives.

With southern Democrats often joining the Republicans, Congress rejected Truman's proposals for civil rights, a uni-

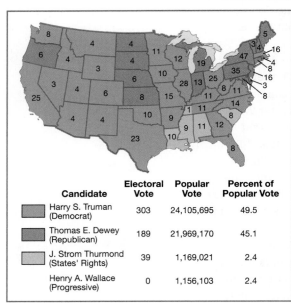

Candidate	Electoral Vote	Popular Vote	Percent of Popular Vote
Harry S. Truman (Democrat)	303	24,105,695	49.5
Thomas E. Dewey (Republican)	189	21,969,170	45.1
J. Strom Thurmond (States' Rights)	39	1,169,021	2.4
Henry A. Wallace (Progressive)	0	1,156,103	2.4

MAP 26.2 ■ The Election of 1948

versal health care program, and federal aid to education. His efforts to revise immigration policy were mixed. The McCarran-Walter Act of 1952 ended the outright ban on immigration and citizenship for Japanese and other Asians, but it also authorized the government to bar suspected Communists and homosexuals and maintained the discriminatory quota system established in the 1920s. Truman denounced that provision as "unworthy of our traditions and our ideals," but Congress overrode his veto.

By late 1950, the Korean War embroiled the president in controversy and depleted his power as a legislative leader. Truman's failure to make good on his domestic proposals set the United States apart from most European nations, which by the 1950s had in place comprehensive health, housing, and employment security programs to underwrite the material well-being of their populations.

The Domestic Chill: McCarthyism

Truman's domestic program also suffered from a wave of anticommunism that weakened liberal and leftist forces. "Red-baiting" (attempts to discredit individuals or ideas by associating them with communism) and official retaliation against leftist critics of the government had flourished during the Red scare at the end of World War I (see chapter 22). A second Red scare followed World War II, born of partisan political maneuvering, the collapse of the Soviet-American alliance, setbacks in U.S. foreign policy, and disclosures of Soviet espionage.

Republicans who had attacked the New Deal as a plot of radicals now jumped on such Cold War events as the Soviet takeover of Eastern Europe and the Communist triumph in China to accuse Democrats of fostering internal subversion. Wisconsin senator **Joseph R. McCarthy** avowed that "the Communists within our borders have been more responsible for the success of Communism abroad than Soviet Russia." McCarthy's charges—such as the allegation that retired general George C. Marshall belonged to a Communist conspiracy—were reckless and often ludicrous, but the press covered him avidly, and McCarthyism became a term synonymous with the anti-Communist crusade.

Joseph R. McCarthy

▶ Wisconsin senator who, beginning in 1950, led Senate investigations into alleged internal subversion of the United States. McCarthy's charges were reckless and often ludicrous, but the press covered him avidly, and McCarthyism became a term synonymous with the anti-Communist crusade.

Revelations of Soviet espionage gave some credibility to fears of internal communism. For example, a number of ex-Communists, including Whittaker Chambers and Elizabeth Bentley, testified that they and others had provided secret documents to the Soviets. Most alarming of all, in 1950 a British physicist working on the atomic bomb project confessed that he was a spy and implicated several Americans, including Ethel and Julius Rosenberg. The Rosenbergs pleaded innocent but were convicted of conspiracy to commit espionage and electrocuted in 1953.

Records opened in the 1990s showed that the Soviet Union did receive secret documents from Americans that probably hastened its development of nuclear weapons by a year or two. Yet the vast majority of individuals hunted down in the Red scare had done nothing more than at one time joining the Communist Party, associating with Communists, or supporting radical causes. And most of those activities had taken place long before the Cold War had made the Soviet Union an enemy.

The hunt for subversives was conducted by both Congress and the executive branch. Stung by charges of communism in the 1946 midterm elections, Truman

CHAPTER LOCATOR | What factors contributed to the Cold War? | What obstructed Truman's domestic agenda? | How did America's Cold War policy lead to the Korean War? | Conclusion: What were the costs and consequences of the Cold War?

737

issued Executive Order 9835 in March 1947, establishing loyalty review boards to investigate every federal employee. "A nightmare from which there [was] no awakening" was how State Department employee Esther Brunauer described it when she and her husband, a chemist in the navy, both lost their jobs because he had joined a Communist youth organization in the 1920s and associated with suspected radicals. Government investigators routinely violated the Bill of Rights by allowing anonymous informers to make charges and by placing the burden of proof on the accused. More than two thousand civil service employees lost their jobs, and another ten thousand resigned as Truman's loyalty program continued into the mid-1950s.

Congressional committees, such as the House Un-American Activities Committee (HUAC), also investigated individuals' past and present political associations. When those under scrutiny refused to name names, investigators charged that silence was tantamount to confession, and these "unfriendly witnesses" lost their jobs and suffered public ostracism. In 1947, HUAC investigated radical activity in Hollywood. Frank Sinatra protested, wondering if someone called for "a square deal for the underdog, will they call you a Commie? . . . Are they going to scare us into silence?" Some actors and directors cooperated, but ten refused, citing their First Amendment rights. The "Hollywood Ten" served jail sentences for contempt of Congress and then found themselves blacklisted in the movie industry.

The domestic Cold War spread beyond the nation's capital. State and local governments investigated citizens, demanded loyalty oaths, fired employees suspected of disloyalty, banned books from public libraries, and more. College professors and public school teachers lost their jobs in New York, California, and elsewhere. Because the Communist Party had helped organize unions and championed racial justice, labor and civil rights activists fell prey to McCarthyism as well. African American activist Jack O'Dell remembered that segregationists pinned the tag of Communist on "anybody who supported the right of blacks to have civil rights." McCarthyism caused untold harm to individuals innocent of breaking any law. Thousands of people were humiliated and discredited, hounded from their jobs, and in some cases even imprisoned. The anti-Communist crusade violated fundamental constitutional rights of freedom of speech and association, stifled expression of dissenting ideas, and removed unpopular causes from public contemplation.

> **QUICK REVIEW**

What was the impact of the Cold War on Truman's domestic agenda?

POWs in Korea

These demoralized U.S. soldiers reflect the grim situation for U.S. forces during the early months of the Korean War. Their North Korean captors forced them to march through Seoul in July 1950 carrying a banner proclaiming the righteousness of the Communist cause and attacking U.S. intervention. Wide World Photos, Inc.

How did America's Cold War policy lead to the Korean War?

THE COLD WAR ERUPTED into a shooting war in June 1950 when troops from Communist North Korea invaded South Korea. For the first time, Americans went into battle to implement containment. Confirming the global reach of the Truman Doctrine, U.S. involvement in Korea also marked the militarization of American foreign policy. The United States, in concert with the United Nations, ultimately held the line in Korea, but at a great cost in lives, dollars, and domestic unity.

Korea and the Military Implementation of Containment

The war grew out of the artificial division of Korea after World War II. Having expelled the Japanese, who had controlled Korea since 1904, the United States and the Soviet Union created two occupation zones separated by the thirty-eighth parallel (**Map 26.3,** page 740). With Moscow and Washington unable to agree on a unification plan, the United Nations sponsored elections in South Korea in July 1948. The American-favored candidate, Syngman Rhee, was elected president, and the United States withdrew most of its troops. In the fall of 1948, the Soviets established the People's Republic of North Korea under Kim Il-sung and also withdrew. Although doubting that Rhee's repressive government could sustain popular support, U.S. officials appreciated his staunch anticommunism and provided small amounts of economic and military aid to South Korea.

North and South Korean troops at the thirty-eighth parallel had engaged in skirmishes since 1948, but in June 1950, 90,000 North Koreans swept into South Korea. Assuming that the Soviet Union or China had instigated the attack (scholars learned later that they had not), Truman decided to intervene, viewing Korea as "the Greece of the Far East." With the Soviet Union boycotting the UN Security Council to protest its refusal to seat a representative from the People's Republic of

CHAPTER LOCATOR | What factors contributed to the Cold War? | What obstructed Truman's domestic agenda? | **How did America's Cold War policy lead to the Korean War?** | Conclusion: What were the costs and consequences of the Cold War?

739

China, the United States obtained UN sponsorship of a collective effort to repel the attack. Authorized to appoint a commander for the UN force, Truman named General Douglas MacArthur, World War II hero and head of the postwar occupation of Japan.

Sixteen nations, including many NATO allies, sent troops to Korea, but the United States furnished most of the personnel and weapons, deploying almost 1.8 million troops and dictating military strategy. By failing to ask Congress for a declaration of war, Truman violated the spirit if not the letter of the Constitution. Moreover, although Congress appropriated funds to fight the war, the president's political opponents called it "Truman's war" when the military situation worsened.

The first American soldiers rushed to Korea unprepared and ill equipped, enduring severe defeats early in the war. The North Koreans took the capital of Seoul and drove deep into South Korea, forcing UN troops to retreat to Pusan. General MacArthur then launched a bold counteroffensive at Inchon, 180 miles behind North Korean lines. By mid-October, UN forces had pushed the North Koreans back to the thirty-eighth parallel. Then came the momentous decision of whether to invade North Korea and seek to unify the country.

From Containment to Rollback to Containment

"Troops could not be expected . . . to march up to a surveyor's line and stop," remarked Secretary of State Dean Acheson, reflecting popular and official support for transforming the military objective from containment to elimination of the enemy and unification of Korea. Thus, for the only time during the Cold War, the United States tried to roll back communism by force. With UN approval, Truman authorized MacArthur to cross the thirty-eighth parallel. Concerned about possible intervention by China or the Soviet Union, the president directed him to keep his troops away from the Korean-Chinese border. Disregarding the order, MacArthur sent UN forces to within forty miles of China, whereupon 300,000 Chinese soldiers crossed the Yalu River into Korea. With Chinese help, the North Koreans recaptured Seoul.

After three months of grueling battle, UN forces fought their way back to the thirty-eighth parallel. At that point, Truman decided to seek a negotiated settlement. MacArthur was furious when the goal of the war reverted to containment, which to him represented defeat. Taking his case to the public challenged both the president's authority to conduct foreign policy and the principle of civilian control of the military. Truman fired him in April 1951. Many Americans, however, sided with MacArthur. "Quite an explosion. . . . Letters of abuse by the dozens," Truman recorded in his diary. The adulation for MacArthur reflected American frustrations with containment. Why should Americans die simply to preserve the status quo? Why not destroy the enemy once and for all? In siding with MacArthur, Americans

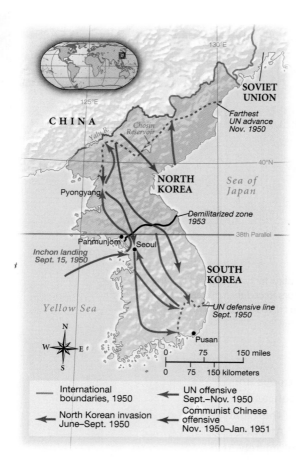

MAP 26.3 ■ The Korean War, 1950–1953
Although each side had plunged deep into enemy territory, the war ended in 1953 with the dividing line between North and South Korea nearly where it had been before the fighting began.

► FOR MORE HELP ANALYZING THIS MAP, see the map activity for this chapter in the Online Study Guide at bedfordstmartins.com/roarkunderstanding.

poor housing, and the loss of their traditional culture. "I wish we had never left home," said one woman whose husband was out of work. "It's dirty and noisy, and people all around, crowded. . . . It seems like I never see the sky or trees."

Reflecting long-standing disagreements among Indians themselves, some who overcame these obstacles applauded the program. But most urban Indians remained in or near poverty, and even many who had welcomed relocation began to worry that "we would lose our identity as Indian people, lose our culture and our [way] of living." Within two decades, a national pan-Indian movement, a by-product of urbanization, emerged to resist assimilation and demand much more for Indians (see chapter 28).

The 1956 Election and the Second Term

Eisenhower easily defeated Adlai Stevenson in 1956, doubling his margin of 1952. Yet Democrats kept control of Congress, and in the midterm elections two years later, they all but wiped out the Republican Party, gaining a 64–34 majority in the Senate and a 282–135 advantage in the House. Although Ike captured voters' hearts, a majority of Americans remained wedded to the programs and policies of the Democrats.

Eisenhower faced more serious leadership challenges in his second term. When the economy plunged into a recession in late 1957, Eisenhower fought with Congress over the budget and vetoed bills to expand housing, urban develop-ment, and public works projects. In the end, the first Republican administration after the New Deal left the size and functions of the federal government intact, though it tipped policy somewhat more in favor of corporate interests. Unparal-leled prosperity graced the 1950s, and Eisenhower celebrated what he called the "wide diffusion of wealth and incomes" across the United States. Yet neglected amid the remarkable abundance were some forty million Americans who lived below the poverty level. Rural deprivation was particularly pronounced, as was poverty among African Americans and other minorities.

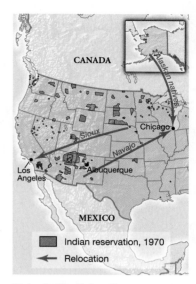

Major Indian Relocations, 1950–1970

QUICK REVIEW <

How did Eisenhower's domestic policies reflect his moderate political vision?

| How did Eisenhower's foreign policy differ from Truman's? | What fueled the prosperity of the 1950s? | How did prosperity affect American society and culture? | How did African Americans fight for their rights in the 1950s? | Conclusion: What unmet challenges did peace and prosperity mask? |

How did Eisenhower's foreign policy differ from Truman's?

The Nuclear Arms Race

Soviet Premier Nikita Khrushchev speaks at his arrival at Andrews Air Force Base in September 1959 for talks with President Eisenhower that both hoped would defuse the nuclear threat. Behind the two leaders are the Soviet ambassador, Mikhail Menshikov, and the U.S. Secretary of State, Christian Herter. At the close of their summit Eisenhower and Khrushchev issued a statement declaring that "the question of general disarmament is the most important one facing the world today." © Bettmann/Corbis.

AT HIS 1953 INAUGURATION, Eisenhower warned that "forces of good and evil are massed and armed and opposed as rarely before in history." Like Truman, he saw communism as a threat to the nation's security and economic interests. Eisenhower's foreign policy differed from Truman's, however, in three areas: its rhetoric, its means, and—after Stalin's death in 1953—its movement toward accommodation with the Soviet Union. Republican rhetoric, voiced most prominently by Secretary of State John Foster Dulles, deplored containment as "negative, futile, and immoral" because it accepted the existing Soviet sphere of control. Yet despite promises to roll back Soviet power, the Eisenhower administration continued the containment policy.

The "New Look" in Foreign Policy

To meet his goals of balancing the budget and cutting taxes, Eisenhower was determined to control military expenditures. Moreover, he feared that massive defense spending would threaten the nation's economic strength. Reflecting Americans' confidence in technology and opposition to a large peacetime army, Eisenhower's defense strategy concentrated U.S. military strength in nuclear

CHAPTER LOCATOR | What was Eisenhower's "middle way" on domestic issues?

weapons and the planes and missiles to deliver them. Instead of maintaining large ground forces of its own, the United States would give friendly nations American weapons and back them up with a nuclear arsenal. This was Eisenhower's "New Look" in foreign policy. Secretary of State Dulles believed that America's willingness to "go to the brink" of war—a strategy called brinkmanship—would block any Soviet efforts to expand.

Nuclear weapons could not stop a Soviet nuclear attack, but in response to one, they could inflict enormous destruction. This certainty of "massive retaliation" was meant to deter the Soviets from launching an attack. Because the Soviet Union could respond similarly to an American first strike, this nuclear standoff became known as **mutually assured destruction**, or **MAD**. Yet leaders of each nation sought not just balance but nuclear superiority, and they pursued an ever-escalating arms race.

Nuclear weapons, however, could not roll back the iron curtain. When a revolt against the Soviet-controlled government began in Hungary in 1956, Dulles's liberation rhetoric proved to be empty. A radio plea from Hungarian freedom fighters cried, "SOS! They just brought us a rumor that the American troops will be here within one or two hours." But help did not come. Eisenhower was unwilling to risk U.S. soldiers and possible nuclear war, and Soviet troops soon suppressed the insurrection, killing thousands of Hungarians.

Applying Containment to Vietnam

A major challenge to the containment policy came in Southeast Asia. During World War II, Ho Chi Minh, a Vietnamese nationalist, had founded a coalition called the Vietminh to fight both the occupying Japanese forces and the French colonial rulers. In 1945, the Vietminh declared Vietnam's independence from France, and when France fought to maintain its colony, the area plunged into war (see Map 29.2, page 808). Because Ho declared himself a Communist, the Truman administration quietly began to provide aid to the French.

Eisenhower viewed communism in Vietnam much as Truman had regarded it in Greece and Turkey, a view that became known as the domino theory. "You have a row of dominoes," Eisenhower explained, and "you knock over the first one, and what will happen to the last one is the certainty that it will go over very quickly." A Communist victory in Southeast Asia, he warned, could trigger the fall of Japan, Taiwan, and the Philippines. By 1954, the United States was contributing 75 percent of the cost of France's war, but Eisenhower resisted a larger role. When the French asked for troops and airplanes from the United States to avert almost certain defeat at Dien Bien Phu, Eisenhower, conscious of U.S. losses in the Korean War, said no.

Dien Bien Phu fell in May 1954 and with it the French colony of Vietnam. Two months later in Geneva, France signed a truce. The Geneva accords temporarily partitioned Vietnam at the seventeenth parallel, separating the Vietminh in the north from the puppet government established by the French in the south. Within two years, the Vietnamese people were to vote in elections for a unified government. Eisenhower began to send weapons and military advisers to South Vietnam and put the CIA to work infiltrating and destabilizing North Vietnam. Fearing a Communist victory in the elections mandated by the Geneva accords, the United States supported South Vietnamese prime minister Ngo Dinh Diem's refusal to hold the vote.

CHRONOLOGY

1953
- CIA engineers coup against government of Iran.

1954
- CIA stages coup against government of Guatemala.
- France signs Geneva accords, withdrawing from Vietnam.
- Eisenhower begins to send weapons and military advisers to South Vietnam.

1955
- Eisenhower and Khrushchev meet in Geneva.

1956
- Eisenhower pressures Britain and France to end the Suez crisis.

1957
- Soviets launch *Sputnik*.

1958
- National Aeronautics and Space Administration is established.

1960
- Soviets shoot down U.S. U-2 spy plane.

1961
- Eisenhower warns of military-industrial complex in farewell address.

mutually assured destruction (MAD)
▶ The proposition that the vast nuclear arsenals of the United States and the Soviet Union assured that both would be destroyed if either launched an attack on the other. This probability of mutually assured destruction led both superpowers to show restraint. It did not, however, prevent them from attempting to achieve nuclear superiority.

| How did Eisenhower's foreign policy differ from Truman's? | What fueled the prosperity of the 1950s? | How did prosperity affect American society and culture? | How did African Americans fight for their rights in the 1950s? | Conclusion: What unmet challenges did peace and prosperity mask? |

753

Geneva Accords, 1954

Despite massive American aid, South Vietnam's army proved unprepared for the guerrilla warfare that began in the late 1950s. With military assistance from Ho Chi Minh's government in Hanoi, Vietminh rebels in the south stepped up their guerrilla attacks on the Diem government. The insurgents gained support from the largely Buddhist peasants who were outraged by the repressive regime of the Catholic, Westernized Diem. Unwilling to abandon containment, Eisenhower left office with a deteriorating situation and a firm commitment to defend South Vietnam against communism.

Interventions in Latin America and the Middle East

While supporting friendly governments in Asia, the Eisenhower administration worked secretly to topple unfriendly ones in Latin America and the Middle East. Officials saw internal civil wars in terms of the Cold War conflict between the superpowers and tended to view nationalist uprisings as Communist threats to democracy. They also acted against governments that threatened U.S. economic interests. The Eisenhower administration took this course of action out of sight of Congress and the public, making the CIA an important arm of foreign policy.

The government of Guatemala, under the popularly elected reformist president Jacobo Arbenz, was not Soviet controlled, but it accepted support from the local Communist Party (see Map 29.1, page 805). In 1953, Arbenz moved to nationalize land owned but not cultivated by the United Fruit Company, a U.S. corporation whose annual profits were twice the size of the Guatemalan government's budget. United Fruit refused Arbenz's offer to compensate it at the value of the land the company had declared for tax purposes. Then, in response to the nationalization program, the CIA organized and supported an opposition army that overthrew the elected government and installed a military dictatorship in 1954. United Fruit kept its land, and Guatemala succumbed to a series of destructive civil wars that lasted through the 1990s.

When Cubans' desire for political and economic autonomy erupted in 1959, a CIA agent promised "to take care of Castro just like we took care of Arbenz." American companies had long controlled major Cuban resources, and decisions made in Washington directly influenced the lives of the Cuban people. An uprising in 1959 led by **Fidel Castro** drove out the U.S.-supported dictator Fulgencio Batista and led the CIA to warn Eisenhower that "Communists and other extreme radicals appear to have penetrated the Castro movement." When the United States denied Castro's requests for loans, he turned to the Soviet Union. And when U.S. companies refused Castro's offer to purchase them at their assessed value, he began to nationalize their property. Many anti-Castro Cubans fled to the United States and reported his atrocities, including the execution of hundreds of Batista's supporters. Before leaving office, Eisenhower broke off diplomatic relations with Cuba and authorized the CIA to train Cuban exiles for an invasion.

In the Middle East, the CIA intervened to oust an elected government, support an unpopular dictatorship, and maintain Western access to Iranian oil (see Map 30.3, page 841). Mohammed Mossadegh, the left-leaning democratic prime minister of Iran, accepted support from the Iranian Communist Party and

Fidel Castro

▶ Leader of the 1959 uprising against Fulgencio Batista, the Cuban dictator backed by the United States. Castro's policies, including the nationalization of American-owned industries in Cuba and the acquisition of loans from the Soviet Union, made him an enemy of the United States.

challenged the power of Shah Mohammad Reza Pahlavi, Iran's hereditary leader, who favored foreign oil interests and the Iranian wealthy classes. In 1951, the Iranian parliament nationalized the oil fields and refineries, then held mostly by the British.

Advisers convinced Eisenhower that Mossadegh's government left Iran vulnerable to communism, and the president wanted to keep oil-rich areas "under the control of people who are friendly." With his authorization, CIA agents instigated a coup. In August 1953, Iranian army officers captured Mossadegh and reestablished the shah's power, whereupon Iran renegotiated its oil concessions, giving U.S. companies a 40 percent share. Resentment over this use of force would poison U.S.-Iranian relations into the twenty-first century.

Elsewhere in the Middle East, the Eisenhower administration continued Truman's support of Israel but also sought to foster friendships with Arab nations to secure access to oil and to build a bulwark against communism. Yet U.S. officials demanded that smaller nations take the American side in the Cold War, even when those nations preferred neutrality. In 1955, as part of the U.S. effort to win Arab allies, Secretary of State Dulles began talks with Egypt about American support to build the Aswan Dam on the Nile River. The following year, Egypt's leader, Gamal Abdel Nasser, sought arms from Communist Czechoslovakia, formed a military alliance with other Arab nations, and recognized the People's Republic of China. In retaliation, Dulles called off the deal for the dam.

On July 26, 1956, Nasser responded by seizing the Suez Canal, then owned by Britain and France but scheduled to revert to Egypt within seven years. In response to the seizure, Israel, whose forces had been skirmishing with Egyptian troops along their common border since 1948, attacked Egypt with military help from Britain and France. Eisenhower opposed the intervention, recognizing that the Egyptians had claimed their own territory and that Nasser "embodie[d] the emotional demands of the people . . . for independence." He put economic pressure on Britain and France while calling on the United Nations to arrange a truce. The French and British soon pulled back, forcing Israel to retreat.

Despite staying out of the Suez crisis, Eisenhower made it clear that the United States would actively combat communism in the Middle East. In March 1957, Congress passed a joint resolution approving aid to any Middle Eastern nation "requesting assistance against armed aggression from any country controlled by international communism." The president invoked this Eisenhower Doctrine to send aid to Jordan in 1957 and troops to Lebanon in 1958 to counter anti-Western pressures on those governments.

The Nuclear Arms Race

While Eisenhower moved against perceived Communist inroads abroad, he also sought to reduce superpower tensions. After Stalin's death in 1953, a more moderate leadership under **Nikita Khrushchev** emerged. Like Eisenhower, who remarked

The CIA Helps Restore the Shah of Iran

In 1952, *Time* magazine called Iranian premier Mohammed Mossadegh, who was passionately committed to nationalism and democracy, "the Iranian George Washington." But Secretary of State John Foster Dulles believed that restoration of the shah's power would produce a more stable ally in an oil-rich region and he persuaded Eisenhower to approve a coup against Mossadegh. © Bettmann/Corbis.

Nikita Khrushchev

▶ More moderate Soviet leader who came to power after the death of Joseph Stalin in 1953. Khrushchev wanted to reduce defense spending and the threat of nuclear devastation. The change in leadership led to talks between Khrushchev and Eisenhower; the talks, however, failed to produce any agreements.

| How did Eisenhower's foreign policy differ from Truman's? | What fueled the prosperity of the 1950s? | How did prosperity affect American society and culture? | How did African Americans fight for their rights in the 1950s? | Conclusion: What unmet challenges did peace and prosperity mask? |

755

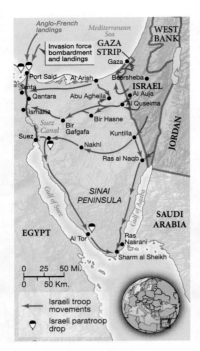

The Suez Crisis, 1956

military-industrial complex

▶ The name Eisenhower gave in his farewell address in 1961 to the combined effort of big business and the military to press for an ever-increasing share of national resources for the development of new weapons.

privately that the arms race would lead "at worst to atomic warfare, at best to robbing every people and nation on earth of the fruits of their own toil," Khrushchev wanted to reduce defense spending and the threat of nuclear devastation. Eisenhower and Khrushchev met in Geneva in 1955 at the first summit conference since the end of World War II. Although the meeting produced no new agreements, it symbolized what Eisenhower called "a new spirit of conciliation and cooperation."

In August 1957, the Soviets test-fired their first intercontinental ballistic missile and two months later beat the United States into space by launching *Sputnik*, the first artificial satellite to circle the earth. The United States launched a successful satellite of its own in January 1958, but *Sputnik* raised fears that the United States lagged behind the Soviet Union not only in missile development and space exploration but also in science and education. In response, Eisenhower established the National Aeronautics and Space Administration (NASA) and signed the National Defense Education Act, providing support for students in math, foreign languages, and science.

Eisenhower assured the public that the United States possessed nuclear superiority. In fact, during his presidency, the stockpile of nuclear weapons more than quadrupled. Yet these weapons could not guarantee security, because both superpowers possessed sufficient nuclear capacity to devastate each other. Most Americans did not follow Civil Defense Administration recommendations to construct home bomb shelters, but they did realize how precarious nuclear weapons had made their lives.

In the midst of the arms race, the superpowers continued to talk. In 1959, Khrushchev visited the United States, and Nixon went to the Soviet Union. By 1960, the two sides were close to a ban on nuclear testing. But just before a summit in Paris, a Soviet missile shot down a U-2 spy plane over Soviet territory. The State Department first denied that U.S. planes had been violating Soviet airspace, but the Soviets produced the pilot and the photos taken on his flight. Eisenhower and Khrushchev met briefly in Paris, but the U-2 incident dashed all prospects for a nuclear arms agreement.

As Eisenhower left office, he warned about the growing influence of the **military-industrial complex** in American government and life. Eisenhower had struggled against persistent pressures from defense contractors, who, in tandem with the military, sought more dollars for newer, more powerful weapons systems. In his farewell address, he warned that the "conjunction of an immense military establishment and a large arms industry . . . exercised a total influence . . . in every city, every state house, every office of the federal government." The Cold War had created a warfare state.

> **QUICK REVIEW**

Where and how did Eisenhower practice containment?

What was Eisenhower's "middle way" on domestic issues?

> ► FOR MORE HELP ANALYZING THIS IMAGE, see the visual activity for this chapter in the Online Study Guide at bedfordstmartins.com/roarkunderstanding.

STIMULATED IN PART by American military spending, economic productivity increased enormously in the 1950s. A multitude of new items came on the market, and consumption became the order of the day. Millions of Americans enjoyed new homes in the suburbs, and higher education enrollments skyrocketed. Although every section of the nation enjoyed the new abundance, the West and Southwest especially boomed in production, commerce, and population. And work itself changed. Fewer people labored on farms, service sector employment overtook manufacturing jobs, and women's employment grew. These economic shifts disadvantaged some Americans, and they did little to help the forty million who lived in poverty. Most Americans, however, enjoyed a higher standard of living, leading economist John Kenneth Galbraith to call the United States "the affluent society."

Technology Transforms Agriculture and Industry

Between 1940 and 1960, agricultural output mushroomed while the number of farmworkers declined by almost one-third. Farmers achieved unprecedented productivity through greater crop specialization, intensive use of fertilizers, and, above all, mechanization. The decline of family farms and the growth of large commercial farming, or agribusiness, were both causes and consequences of

| How did Eisenhower's foreign policy differ from Truman's? | **What fueled the prosperity of the 1950s?** | How did prosperity affect American society and culture? | How did African Americans fight for their rights in the 1950s? | Conclusion: What unmet challenges did peace and prosperity mask? |

757

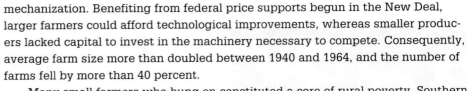

mechanization. Benefiting from federal price supports begun in the New Deal, larger farmers could afford technological improvements, whereas smaller producers lacked capital to invest in the machinery necessary to compete. Consequently, average farm size more than doubled between 1940 and 1964, and the number of farms fell by more than 40 percent.

Many small farmers who hung on constituted a core of rural poverty. Southern landowners replaced sharecroppers with machines, forcing them off the land. Hundreds of thousands of African Americans joined an exodus to cities, where racial discrimination and a lack of jobs mired many in urban poverty. A Mississippi mother realized that "it was going to be machines now that harvest the crops." Considering moving to Chicago, she worried that "it might be worse up there" for her children. "I'm afraid to leave and I'm afraid to stay."

Industrial production also benefited from new technologies. Technology transformed industries such as electronics, chemicals, and air transportation and promoted the growth of television, plastics, computers, and other newer industries. American businesses enjoyed access to cheap oil, ample markets abroad, and little foreign competition. Moreover, even with Eisenhower's conservative fiscal policies, government spending reached $80 billion annually and created new jobs.

Labor unions enjoyed their greatest success during the 1950s, and real earnings for production workers rose 40 percent. The merger in 1955 of the American Federation of Labor (AFL) and the Congress of Industrial Organizations (CIO) improved labor's bargaining position. As one worker put it, "We saw continual improvement in wages, fringe benefits like holidays, vacation, medical plans . . . all sorts of things that provided more security for people." In most industrial nations, government programs underwrote their citizens' security, but in the United States company-funded programs won by unions through collective bargaining played a much larger role in providing for retirement, health care, and the like. This system resulted in wide disparities among workers, severely disadvantaging those not represented by unions and those with irregular employment.

While the absolute number of organized workers continued to grow, union membership peaked at 27.1 percent of the labor force in 1957. Technological advances eliminated jobs in heavy industry, reducing the number of workers in the steel, copper, and aluminum industries by 17 percent. "You are going to have trouble collecting union dues from all of these machines," commented a Ford manager to union leader Walter Reuther. Moreover, the economy as a whole was shifting from production to service as more workers distributed goods, performed services, provided education, and carried out government work. Unions made some headway in these fields, especially among government employees, but most service industries resisted unionization.

The growing clerical and service occupations swelled the demand for female workers. By the end of the 1950s, women held nearly one-third of all jobs. The vast majority of them worked in offices, light manufacturing, domestic service, teaching, and nursing; because these were female occupations, wages were relatively low. In 1960, the average full-time female worker earned just 60 percent of the average male worker's wages. At the bottom of the employment ladder, black women took home only 42 percent of what white men earned.

CHAPTER LOCATOR | What was Eisenhower's "middle way" on domestic issues?

758 CHAPTER 27
THE POLITICS AND CULTURE OF ABUNDANCE, 1952–1960

Burgeoning Suburbs and Declining Cities

Although suburbs had existed since the nineteenth century, nothing symbolized the affluent society more than their tremendous expansion in the 1950s. Eleven million new homes went up in the suburbs, and by 1960 one in four Americans lived there. Builder William J. Levitt adapted the factory assembly-line process when he began construction of **Levittown** in 1947, planning nearly identical units so that individual construction workers could move from house to house and perform the same single operation in each one. By 1949, families could purchase mass-produced houses in his 17,000-home development on Long Island, New York, for just under $8,000 each. Developments similar to Levittown quickly went up throughout the country. The government underwrote home ownership with low-interest mortgage guarantees through the Federal Housing Administration and the Veterans Administration and by making interest on mortgages tax deductible. Thousands of miles of interstate highway running through urban areas indirectly subsidized suburban development.

The growing suburbs helped polarize society, especially along racial lines. Each Levittown homeowner signed a contract pledging not to rent or sell to a non-Caucasian. The Supreme Court declared such covenants unenforceable in 1948, but suburban America remained dramatically segregated. Levitt commented, "We can solve a housing problem, or we can try and solve a racial problem, but we cannot combine the two."

Although some African Americans joined the suburban migration, most moved to cities in search of economic opportunity, increasing their numbers in most cities by 50 percent during the 1950s. These migrants, however, came to cities that were already in decline, losing not only population but also commerce and industry to the suburbs or to southern and western states.

Levittown

▶ Housing development on Long Island, New York, made up of low-cost, mass-produced houses. Begun in 1947, Levittown had 17,000 homes by 1949 and became a prime example of the suburbanization of the United States.

The Rise of the Sun Belt

No regions experienced the postwar economic and population booms more intensely than the West and Southwest. Architect Frank Lloyd Wright quipped, "Everything loose will land in Los Angeles." California overtook New York as the most populous state.

A pleasant natural environment drew new residents to the West and Southwest, but no magnet proved stronger than the promise of economic opportunity (**Map 27.2, page 760**). As railroads had fueled western growth in the nineteenth century, so the automobile and airplane spurred the post–World War II surge. The technology of air-conditioning facilitated industrial development and by 1960 cooled nearly eight million homes in the so-called Sun Belt, which stretched from Florida to California.

So important was the defense industry to the South and West that the area was later referred to as the "Gun Belt." The aerospace industry boomed in Seattle-Tacoma, Los Angeles, and Dallas–Fort Worth, and military bases helped underwrite prosperity in cities such as San Diego and San Antonio. By the 1960s, nearly one of every three California workers held a defense-related job.

The surging populations and industries soon threatened the environment. Providing sufficient water and power to cities and to agribusiness meant building dams and reservoirs on free-flowing rivers. Native Americans lost fishing sites on

| How did Eisenhower's foreign policy differ from Truman's? | **What fueled the prosperity of the 1950s?** | How did prosperity affect American society and culture? | How did African Americans fight for their rights in the 1950s? | Conclusion: What unmet challenges did peace and prosperity mask? |

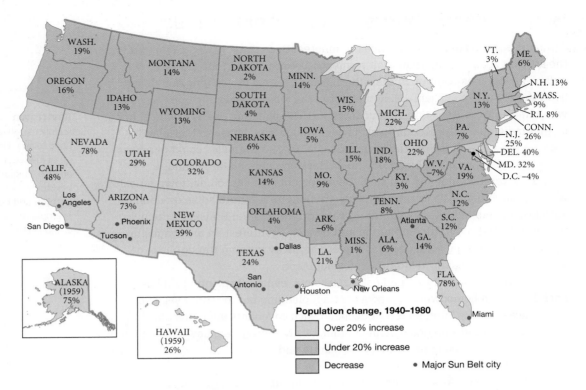

Population change, 1940–1980

Over 20% increase

Under 20% increase

Decrease ● Major Sun Belt city

MAP 27.2 ■ **The Rise of the Sun Belt, 1940–1980**

The growth of defense industries, a non-unionized labor force, and the spread of air-conditioning all helped spur economic development and population growth, which made the Sun Belt the fastest-growing region of the country between 1940 and 1980.

▶ FOR MORE HELP ANALYZING THIS MAP, see the map activity for this chapter in the Online Study Guide at bedfordstmartins.com/roarkunderstanding.

the Columbia River, and dams on the Upper Missouri displaced nine hundred Indian families. Sprawling urban and suburban settlement without efficient public transportation contributed to blankets of smog over Los Angeles and other cities.

The high-technology basis of postwar economic development drew well-educated, highly skilled workers to the West, but the economic promise also attracted the poor. "We see opportunity all around us here. . . . We smell freedom here, and maybe soon we can taste it," commented a black mother in California. Between 1945 and 1960, more than one-third of the African Americans who left the South moved west.

The Mexican American population also grew, especially in California and Texas. To supply California's vast agribusiness industry, the government continued the *bracero* program begun during World War II. Until the program ended in 1964, more than 100,000 Mexicans entered the United States each year to labor in the fields—and many of them stayed, legally or illegally. But permanent Mexican immigration was not as welcome as Mexicans' low-wage labor. In 1954, the government launched a series of raids called "Operation Wetback," resulting in deportation of more than one million Mexicans. Even Mexicans with legal status felt unwelcome and vulnerable to incidents of mistaken identity.

CHAPTER LOCATOR | What was Eisenhower's "middle way" on domestic issues?

At the same time, Mexican American citizens gained a small victory in their ongoing struggle for civil rights in *Hernandez v. Texas*. When a Texas jury convicted Pete Hernandez of murder, lawyers from the American GI Forum and the League of United Latin American Citizens (see chapter 26) appealed on the grounds that persons of Mexican origin had been routinely excluded from jury service. In 1954, the Supreme Court ruled unanimously that Mexican Americans constituted a distinct group and that their systematic exclusion from juries violated the constitutional guarantee of equal protection.

Free of the discrimination faced by minorities, white Americans enjoyed the fullest prosperity in the West. In April 1950, when California developers opened Lakewood, a large housing development in Los Angeles County, thirty thousand people lined up to buy houses at prices ranging from $68,000 to $85,000 in 2007 dollars. Many of the new homeowners were veterans, blue-collar and lower-level white-collar workers whose defense-based jobs at aerospace corporations enabled them to fulfill the American dream of the 1950s. A huge shopping mall, Lakewood Center, offered myriad products of the consumer culture, and the workers' children lived at commuting distance from community colleges and six state universities.

Rounding Up Undocumented Migrants

Not all Mexican Americans who wanted to work in the United States were accommodated by the *bracero* program. In 1953, Los Angeles police arrested these men, who did not have legal documents and were hiding in a freight train. © Bettmann/Corbis.

The Democratization of Higher Education

California's university system exemplified a spectacular transformation of higher education. Between 1940 and 1960, college enrollments in the United States more than doubled. Prosperity enabled more families to keep their children in school longer, and the federal government subsidized the education of more than two million veterans. The Cold War also sent millions of federal dollars to universities for defense-related research. And state governments vastly expanded the number of public colleges and universities, while municipalities began to build two-year community colleges.

Not all Americans benefited equally from the democratization of higher education. Although their college enrollments surged from 37,000 in 1941 to 90,000 in 1961, African Americans constituted only about 5 percent of all college students. For a time, the educational gap between white men and women grew. In 1940, women had earned 40 percent of undergraduate degrees, but as veterans flocked to college campuses, women's proportion fell to 25 percent in 1950 and rebounded to only 33 percent by 1960. The large veteran enrollments led colleges to relax rules that had forbidden students to marry. Unlike men, however, women tended to drop out of college after marriage and to take jobs so that their husbands could stay in school. Reflecting gender norms of the 1950s, most college women agreed that "it is natural for a woman to be satisfied with her husband's success and not crave personal achievement."

QUICK REVIEW <

What factors were most important
in the prosperity of the 1950s?

| How did Eisenhower's foreign policy differ from Truman's? | What fueled the prosperity of the 1950s? | How did prosperity affect American society and culture? | How did African Americans fight for their rights in the 1950s? | Conclusion: What unmet challenges did peace and prosperity mask? |

How did prosperity affect American society and culture?

TV with Scene from Ozzie and Harriet

The Adventures of Ozzie and Harriet began as a radio program in the 1940s and ran on television from 1952 to 1966. Along with other family sitcoms, it idealized white family life, in which no one got divorced or became gravely ill, no one took drugs or seriously misbehaved, fathers held white-collar jobs, mothers did not work outside the home, and husbands and wives slept in twin beds. Picture Research Consultants & Archives.

PROSPERITY IN THE 1950s intensified the transformation of the nation into a consumer society, changing the way Americans lived and converting the traditional work ethic into an ethic of consumption. People married at earlier ages, the birthrate soared, and dominant values celebrated family life and traditional gender roles. Undercurrents of rebellion, especially among young people, and women's increasing employment defied some of the dominant norms but did not greatly disrupt the complacency of the 1950s.

Consumption Rules the Day

Although the purchase and display of consumer goods was not new (see chapter 23), by the 1950s, consumption had become a reigning value, vital for economic prosperity and essential to individuals' identity and status. In place of the traditional emphasis on work and savings, the consumer culture encouraged satisfaction and happiness through the purchase and use of new products.

The consumer culture rested on a firm material base. Between 1950 and 1960, both the gross national product (the value of all goods and services produced) and median family income grew by 25 percent in constant dollars (**Figure 27.1**). Economists claimed that 60 percent of Americans enjoyed middle-class incomes in 1960. Referring to the popular ranch-style houses in the new suburbs, *House Beautiful* magazine boasted, "Our houses are all on one level, like our class structure." Though ignoring the one in five Americans who still lived in poverty, the statement reflected the increasing ability of people to consume products that made class differences less visible. By 1960, almost nine of every ten families owned a television set, nearly all had a refrigerator, and most owned at least one car. The number of shopping centers quadrupled between 1957 and 1963.

CHAPTER LOCATOR | What was Eisenhower's "middle way" on domestic issues?

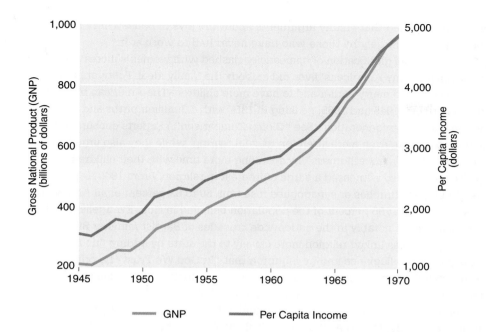

FIGURE 27.1 ■ The Postwar Economic Boom: GNP and Per Capita Income, 1945–1970
American dominance of the worldwide market, innovative technologies that led to new industries such as computers and plastics, population growth, and increases in worker productivity all contributed to the enormous economic growth of the United States after World War II.

Several forces spurred this unparalleled abundance. A population surge—from 152 million in 1950 to 180 million in 1960—expanded the demand for products and boosted industries ranging from housing to baby goods. Consumer borrowing also fueled the economic boom, as people increasingly made purchases on installment plans and began to use credit cards. In what *Life* magazine referred to as a "revolution in consumer purchasing," Americans now enjoyed their possessions while they paid for them instead of saving their money for future purchases.

Although the sheer need to support themselves and their families explained most women's employment, a desire to secure some of the new abundance sent growing numbers of women to work. In fact, married women's employment rose more than that of any other group in the 1950s. As one remarked, "My Joe can't put five kids through college . . . and the washer had to be replaced, and Ann was ashamed to bring friends home because the living room furniture was such a mess, so I went to work." The standards for family happiness imposed by the consumer culture increasingly required a second income.

The Revival of Domesticity and Religion

Despite married women's growing employment, a dominant ideology celebrated traditional family life and conventional gender roles. Both popular culture and public figures defined the ideal family as a male breadwinner, a full-time home-maker, and three or four children. Writer and feminist **Betty Friedan** gave a name to the idealization of women's domestic roles in her 1963 book *The Feminine Mystique.* Friedan criticized scholars, advertisers, and public officials for assuming that biological differences dictated different roles for men and women. According to the feminine mystique that they promulgated, women should find fulfillment in devotion to their homes, families, and serving others. Not many women directly challenged these ideas, but Edith Stern, a college-educated

Betty Friedan
▶ Writer and feminist who wrote *The Feminine Mystique* (1963), which criticized scholars, advertisers, and public officials for assuming that biological differences dictated different roles for men and women. According to the feminine mystique that they promulgated, women should find fulfillment in devotion to their homes, families, and serving others.

| How did Eisenhower's foreign policy differ from Truman's? | What fueled the prosperity of the 1950s? | How did prosperity affect American society and culture? | How did African Americans fight for their rights in the 1950s? | Conclusion: What unmet challenges did peace and prosperity mask? |

763

writer, maintained that "many arguments about the joys of housewifery have been advanced, largely by those who have never had to work at it."

Although the glorification of domesticity clashed with women's increasing employment, many Americans' lives did embody the family ideal. Postwar prosperity enabled people to marry earlier and to have more children. The American birthrate soared between 1945 and 1965, peaking in 1957 with 4.3 million births and producing the **baby boom** generation. (See "Global Comparison".) Experts encouraged mothers to devote even more attention to child rearing, while they also urged fathers to cultivate family "togetherness" by spending more time with their children.

The 1950s also witnessed a surge of interest in religion. From 1940 to 1960, membership in churches or synagogues rose from 50 to 63 percent of all Americans. Polls reported that 95 percent of the population believed in God. Evangelism took on new life, most notably in the nationwide crusades of Baptist minister Billy Graham. Congress linked religion more closely to the state by adding "under God" to the pledge of allegiance and by requiring that "In God We Trust" be printed on all currency. Religion helped to calm anxieties in the nuclear age, while ministers such as Graham made the Cold War a holy war, labeling communism "a great sinister anti-Christian movement masterminded by Satan." Some critics, however, questioned the depth of the religious revival, attributing the growth in church membership to a desire for conformity and a need for social outlets.

Television Transforms Culture and Politics

Just as family life and religion offered a respite from Cold War anxieties, so too did the new medium of television. By 1960, close to 90 percent of American homes

baby boom

▶ The surge in the United States' population that followed World War II. The American birthrate soared between 1945 and 1965, peaking in 1957 with 4.3 million births. The baby boom played an important role in shaping cultural, social, and economic developments in the 1950s and 1960s.

GLOBAL COMPARISON

The Baby Boom in International Perspective

The United States was not alone in welcoming bumper crops of babies in the 1950s. High fertility continued in nonindustrialized countries, while in Europe, as in the United States, birthrates rebounded from low levels during the Great Depression and World War II. Which countries had birthrates comparable to those of the United States? What might explain why countries such as Brazil, China, Iran, and Mexico had birthrates so much higher than those in the United States? What might explain why birthrates in Europe were lower than those in the United States?

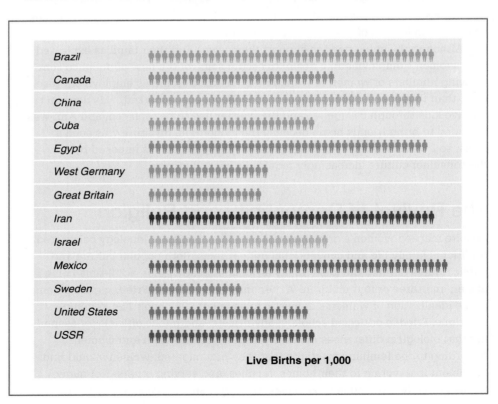

Brazil
Canada
China
Cuba
Egypt
West Germany
Great Britain
Iran
Israel
Mexico
Sweden
United States
USSR

Live Births per 1,000

boasted a television set, and the average viewer spent more than five hours each day in front of the screen. Audiences were especially attracted to situation comedies, which projected the family ideal and the feminine mystique into millions of homes. On TV, married women did not have paying jobs, and they deferred to their husbands, though they often got the upper hand through subtle manipulation.

Television also began to affect politics. Eisenhower's 1952 presidential campaign used TV ads for the first time, although he was not happy that "an old soldier should come to this." By 1960, television played a key role in election campaigns. Reflecting on his narrow victory in 1960, president-elect John F. Kennedy remarked, "We wouldn't have had a prayer without that gadget."

Television transformed politics in other ways. Money played a much larger role in elections because candidates needed to pay for expensive TV spots. The ability to appeal directly to voters in their living rooms put a premium on personal attractiveness and encouraged candidates to build their own campaign organizations, relying less on political parties. The declining strength of parties and the growing power of money in elections were not new trends, but TV helped accelerate them.

Unlike government-financed television in Europe, American TV was paid for by private enterprise. What NBC called a "selling machine in every living room" became the major vehicle for creating a consumer culture. In the mid-1950s, advertisers spent $10 billion to push their goods on TV. In 1961, Newton Minow, chairman of the Federal Communications Commission, called television a "vast wasteland." While acknowledging some of TV's great achievements, particularly documentaries and drama, Minow depicted it as "a procession of game shows, . . . formula comedies about totally unbelievable families, blood and thunder, mayhem, violence, sadism, murder . . . and cartoons." But viewers kept tuning in. In little more than a decade, television came to dominate Americans' leisure time, influence their consumption patterns, and shape their perceptions of the nation's leadership.

Countercurrents

Pockets of dissent underlay the complacency of the 1950s. Some intellectuals took exception to the materialism and conformity of the era. In *The Lonely Crowd* (1950), sociologist David Riesman lamented a shift from the "inner-directed" to the "other-directed" individual, as Americans replaced independent thinking with an eagerness to adapt to external standards of behavior and belief. Sharing that distaste for the importance of "belonging," William H. Whyte Jr., in his popular book *The Organization Man* (1956), blamed the modern corporation for making employees tailor themselves to the group. Vance Packard's 1959 best seller, *The Status Seekers*, decried "the vigorous merchandising of goods as status-symbols" and argued that "class lines . . . appear to be hardening."

Implicit in much of the critique of consumer culture was concern about the loss of traditional masculinity. Consumption itself was associated with women and their presumed greater susceptibility to manipulation. Men, required to conform in order to get ahead, moved further away from the nineteenth-century masculine ideals of individualism and aggressiveness. Moreover, the increase in married women's employment compromised the male ideal of breadwinner.

Into this gender confusion came *Playboy*, which began publication in 1953 and quickly gained a circulation of one million. The new magazine idealized masculine independence in the form of bachelorhood and assaulted the reigning middle-class

CHRONOLOGY

1953
– *Playboy* begins publication.
– Alfred Kinsey publishes *Sexual Behavior in the Human Female.*

1957
– Jack Kerouac publishes *On the Road*, a novel heralding the Beat generation.
– The baby boom, a term given to the high American birthrate, peaks with 4.3 million births.

1960
– Almost ninety percent of American families own a television set.
– The population of the United States reaches 180 million.

1963
– Betty Friedan publishes *The Feminine Mystique*, criticizing women's gender roles.

How did Eisenhower's foreign policy differ from Truman's? | What fueled the prosperity of the 1950s? | **How did prosperity affect American society and culture?** | How did African Americans fight for their rights in the 1950s? | Conclusion: What unmet challenges did peace and prosperity mask?

765

norms of domesticity and respectability. By associating the sophisticated bachelor with good wine, music, furnishings, and the like, the magazine made consumption more masculine while promoting sexual freedom, at least for men.

In fact, new research on Americans' sexual behavior disclosed that it often departed from the postwar family ideal. Two books published by Alfred Kinsey and other researchers at Indiana University—*Sexual Behavior in the Human Male* (1948) and *Sexual Behavior in the Human Female* (1953)—uncovered a surprising range of sexual conduct. In a large survey, Kinsey found that 85 percent of the men and 50 percent of the women had had sex before marriage, half of the husbands and a quarter of the wives had engaged in adultery, and significant numbers of men and women reported homosexual experiences. Although Kinsey's sampling procedures later cast doubt on his ability to generalize across the population, the books became best sellers.

Less direct challenges to mainstream standards appeared in the everyday behavior of young Americans. "Roll over Beethoven and tell Tchaikovsky the news!" belted out Chuck Berry in his 1956 hit record celebrating a new form of music that combined country sounds and black rhythm and blues—rock and roll. White teenagers lionized Elvis Presley, who shocked their parents with his tight pants, hip-rolling gestures, and sensuous rock-and-roll music. "Before there was Elvis . . . I started going crazy for 'race music,'" recalled a white man of his teenage years. "That got me into trouble with my parents and the schools." His recollection underscored African Americans' contributions to rock and roll, as well as the rebellion expressed by white youths' attraction to black music.

The most blatant revolt against conventionality came from the self-proclaimed Beat generation, a small group of primarily male literary figures based in New York City and San Francisco. Rejecting nearly everything in mainstream culture—patriotism, consumerism, technology, conventional family life, discipline—the Beats celebrated spontaneity and absolute personal freedom, including drug consumption and freewheeling sex. Jack Kerouac, who gave the Beat generation its name, published the best-selling novel *On the Road* (1957), recounting the impetuous cross-country travels of two young men. The Beats' lifestyles shocked "square" Americans, but they would provide a model for a much larger movement of youthful dissidents in the 1960s.

Bold new styles in the visual arts also showed the 1950s to be more than a decade of bland conventionality. In New York City, an artistic revolution known as "action painting" or "abstract expressionism" flowered, rejecting the idea that painting should represent recognizable forms. Jackson Pollock and other abstract expressionists, emphasizing spontaneity, poured, dripped, and threw paint on canvases or substituted sticks and other implements for brushes. The new form of painting so captivated and redirected the Western art world that New York replaced Paris as its center.

> **QUICK REVIEW**

Why did American consumption expand so dramatically in the 1950s, and what aspects of society and culture did it influence?

CHAPTER LOCATOR | What was Eisenhower's "middle way" on domestic issues?

766 CHAPTER 27 THE POLITICS AND CULTURE OF ABUNDANCE, 1952–1960

Montgomery Civil Rights Leaders

During the Montgomery bus boycott, local white officials sought to intimidate African Americans with arrests and lawsuits. Here Rosa Parks, one of ninety-two defendants, enters the Montgomery County courthouse. Parks later said of her actions, "People always say that I didn't give up my seat because I was tired, but that isn't true," Parks recalled. "I was not tired physically. . . . I was not old. . . . I was forty-two. No, the only tired I was, was tired of giving in." Wide World Photos.

BUILDING ON THE civil rights initiatives begun during World War II, African Americans posed the most dramatic challenge to the status quo of the 1950s as they sought to overcome discrimination and segregation. Although black protest was as old as American racism, in the 1950s a grassroots movement arose that attracted national attention and the support of white liberals. Pressed by civil rights groups, the Supreme Court delivered significant institutional reforms, but the most important changes of all occurred among blacks themselves. Ordinary African Americans in substantial numbers sought their own liberation, building a movement that would transform race relations in the United States.

African Americans Challenge the Supreme Court and the President

Several factors spurred black protest in the 1950s. Between 1940 and 1960, more than three million African Americans moved from the South into areas where they had a political voice. Black leaders made sure that foreign policy officials realized how racist practices at home handicapped the United States in its competition with the Soviet Union. In the South, the very system of segregation meant that African Americans controlled certain organizational resources, such as churches and colleges, where leadership skills could be honed and networks developed.

| How did Eisenhower's foreign policy differ from Truman's? | What fueled the prosperity of the 1950s? | How did prosperity affect American society and culture? | How did African Americans fight for their rights in the 1950s | Conclusion: What unmet challenges did peace and prosperity mask? |

Brown v. Board of Education

▶ 1954 Supreme Court ruling that overturned the "separate but equal" precedent established in *Plessy v. Ferguson* in 1896. The Court declared that separate educational facilities were inherently unequal and thus violated the Fourteenth Amendment. The ruling laid the foundation for the end of legal segregation in the United States.

The legal strategy of the major civil rights organization, the National Association for the Advancement of Colored People (NAACP), reached its crowning achievement with the Supreme Court decision in *Brown v. Board of Education* in 1954. *Brown* consolidated five separate suits that reflected the growing determination of black Americans to fight for their rights. Oliver Brown, a World War II veteran in Topeka, Kansas, filed suit because his daughter had to pass by a white school just seven blocks from their home to attend a black school more than a mile away. In Virginia, sixteen-year-old Barbara Johns initiated a student strike over conditions in her black high school, leading to another of the suits joined in *Brown*. The NAACP's lead lawyer, future Supreme Court justice Thurgood Marshall, urged the Court to overturn the "separate but equal" precedent established in *Plessy v. Ferguson* in 1896 (see chapter 21). A unanimous Court, headed by Chief Justice Earl Warren, declared, "Separate educational facilities are inherently unequal" and thus violated the Fourteenth Amendment.

School Integration in Little Rock, Arkansas

The nine African American teenagers who integrated Central High School in Little Rock, Arkansas, endured nearly three weeks of threats and hateful taunts before they even got through the doors. Here Elizabeth Eckford tries to ignore angry students and adults as she approaches the entrance to the school, only to be blocked by Arkansas National Guardsmen. Francis Miller/TimePix/Getty.

▶ FOR MORE HELP ANALYZING THIS IMAGE, see the visual activity for this chapter in the Online Study Guide at bedfordstmartins.com/roarkunderstanding.

Ultimate responsibility for enforcement of the decision lay with President Eisenhower, but he refused to endorse *Brown*. He also kept silent in 1955 when whites murdered Emmett Till, a fourteen-year-old black boy, for allegedly whistling at a white woman in Mississippi. Reflecting his own prejudice, his preference for limited federal intervention in the states, and a leadership style that favored consensus and gradual progress, Eisenhower kept his distance from civil rights issues. Such inaction fortified southern resistance to school desegregation and contributed to the gravest constitutional crisis since the Civil War.

The crisis came in Little Rock, Arkansas, in September 1957, when Governor Orval Faubus sent Arkansas National Guard troops to block the enrollment of nine black students in Little Rock's Central High School. Later, he allowed them to enter but withdrew the National Guard, leaving the students to face an angry white mob. "During those years when we desperately needed approval from our peers," Melba Patillo Beals remembered, "we were victims of the most harsh rejection imaginable." As television cameras transmitted the ugly scene, Eisenhower was forced to send regular army troops to Little Rock, the first federal military intervention in the South since Reconstruction. Paratroopers escorted the "Little Rock Nine" into the school.

Eisenhower did order the integration of public facilities in Washington, D.C., and on military bases, and he supported the first federal civil rights legislation since Reconstruction. Yet southern Democrats made sure that the Civil Rights Acts of 1957 and 1960 were little more than symbolic. Baseball star Jackie Robinson spoke for many African Americans when he wired Eisenhower in 1957, "We disagree that half a loaf is better than none. Have waited this long for a bill with meaning—can wait a little longer." Eisenhower appointed the first black professional to the White House staff, E. Frederick Morrow, but Morrow confided in his diary, "I feel ridiculous . . . trying to defend the administration's record on civil rights."

Montgomery and Mass Protest

What set the civil rights movement of the 1950s and 1960s apart from earlier acts of black protest was the large number of people involved, their willingness to confront white institutions directly, and the use of nonviolent protest and civil disobedience to bring about change. The Congress of Racial Equality (CORE) and other groups had experimented with these tactics in the 1940s, and African Americans had boycotted the segregated bus system in Baton Rouge, Louisiana, in 1953, but the first sustained protest to claim national attention began in Montgomery, Alabama, on December 1, 1955.

That day, police arrested **Rosa Parks** for violating a local segregation ordinance that required her to give up her seat so that a white man could sit down. The bus driver called the police, who promptly arrested her. Parks had long been active in the local NAACP, headed by E. D. Nixon. They had already talked about challenging bus segregation. So had the Women's Political Council (WPC), composed of black professional women and led by Jo Ann Robinson, an English professor at Alabama State College. Such local individuals and organizations, long committed to improving conditions for African Americans, laid critical foundations for the black freedom struggle throughout the South.

When word came that Parks would fight her arrest, WPC leaders mobilized teachers and students to distribute fliers calling for blacks to stay off the buses.

CHRONOLOGY

1954
– Supreme Court in *Brown v. Board of Education* rules that segregated schools are unconstitutional.

1955
– **December 1.** Rosa Parks is arrested in Montgomery, Alabama, for challenging segregation on city buses.

1955–1956
– Montgomery, Alabama, bus boycott.

1957
– Southern Christian Leadership Conference, headed by Martin Luther King Jr., is founded.
– President Eisenhower sends federal troops to enforce school integration in Little Rock, Arkansas.

Rosa Parks

▶ African American woman who was arrested on December 1, 1955, in Montgomery, Alabama, for refusing to give up her bus seat to a white man. Parks had long been active in the civil rights movement, and her decision to fight her arrest sparked the Montgomery bus boycott.

| How did Eisenhower's foreign policy differ from Truman's? | What fueled the prosperity of the 1950s? | How did prosperity affect American society and culture? | How did African Americans fight for their rights in the 1950s? | Conclusion: What unmet challenges did peace and prosperity mask? |

769

E. D. Nixon called a mass meeting at the Holt Street Baptist Church, where those assembled founded the Montgomery Improvement Association (MIA) to organize a bus boycott. The MIA arranged volunteer car pools and marshaled more than 90 percent of the black community to sustain the yearlong **Montgomery bus boycott**. Elected to head the MIA was twenty-six-year-old Martin Luther King Jr., a young Baptist pastor with a doctorate in theology from Boston University. King addressed mass meetings at churches throughout the boycott, inspiring blacks' courage and commitment by linking racial justice to Christianity. He promised, "If you will protest courageously and yet with dignity and Christian love . . . historians will have to pause and say, 'There lived a great people—a black people—who injected a new meaning and dignity into the veins of civilization.'"

Montgomery blacks summoned their courage and determination in abundance. They walked miles to get to work, contributed their meager financial resources, and stood up to intimidation and police harassment. An older woman insisted, "I'm not walking for myself, I'm walking for my children and my grandchildren." Authorities arrested several leaders, and whites firebombed King's house. Yet the movement persisted until November 1956, when the Supreme Court declared unconstitutional Alabama's laws requiring segregated buses.

King's face on the cover of *Time* magazine in February 1957 marked his rapid rise to national and international fame. In January, black clergy from across the South had chosen King to head the **Southern Christian Leadership Conference (SCLC)**, newly established to coordinate local protests against segregation and disfranchisement. The prominence of King and other ministers obscured the substantial numbers and critical importance of black women in the movement. In fact, the SCLC owed much of its success to Ella Baker, a seasoned activist who came from New York to manage its office in Atlanta.

Montgomery bus boycott

▶ Yearlong boycott of Montgomery's bus system in 1955–1956 by the city's African American population aimed at ending segregation on the buses. The bus boycott brought Martin Luther King Jr. to national prominence and ended in victory when the Supreme Court declared unconstitutional Alabama's laws requiring segregated transportation.

Southern Christian Leadership Conference (SCLC)

▶ Civil rights organization made up mostly of black clergy, established in 1957 to coordinate local protests against segregation and disfranchisement. Martin Luther King Jr. became its head and Ella Baker its key organizer.

> **QUICK REVIEW**

What were the goals and strategies of civil rights activists in the 1950s?

CHAPTER LOCATOR | What was Eisenhower's "middle way" on domestic issues?

CHAPTER 27
770 THE POLITICS AND CULTURE OF ABUNDANCE, 1952–1960

Leslie Gill.

Conclusion: What unmet challenges did peace and prosperity mask?

AFFLUENCE CHANGED THE very landscape of the United States. Suburban housing developments sprang up, interstate highways began to divide cities and connect the country, farms declined in number but grew in size, and population and industry moved south and west. Daily habits and even the values of ordinary people shifted as the economy became more service oriented and the appearance of a host of new products intensified the growth of a consumer culture.

The prosperity, however, masked a number of developments and problems that Americans would face head-on in later years: rising resistance to racial injustice, a 20 percent poverty rate, married women's movement into the labor force, and the emergence of a self-conscious youth generation. In general Eisenhower tried to curb domestic programs and let private enterprise have its way. His administration maintained the welfare state inherited from the Democrats but resisted substantial further reforms.

In global affairs, Eisenhower exercised restraint on large issues, recognizing the limits of U.S. power. In the name of deterrence, he promoted the development of more destructive atomic weapons, but he withstood pressures for even larger defense budgets. Still, Eisenhower took from Truman the assumption that the United States must fight communism everywhere, and when movements in Iran, Guatemala, Cuba, and Vietnam seemed too radical, too friendly to communism, or too inimical to American economic interests, he tried to undermine them, often with secret operations and severe consequences for native populations.

Although Eisenhower presided over eight years of peace and prosperity, his foreign policy inspired anti-Americanism, established dangerous precedents for the expansion of executive power, and forged commitments and interventions that future generations would deem unwise. As Eisenhower's successors took on the struggle against communism and grappled with the domestic challenges of race, poverty, and urban decay that he had avoided, the tranquility and consensus of the 1950s would give way to the turbulence and conflict of the 1960s.

SO NOW YOU KNOW

Not only did the CIA help engineer the overthrow of a democratically elected government in Iran, but it also conducted operations in Vietnam, Latin America, and elsewhere in the Middle East and set in place Cold War policies that would have long-term repercussions for the United States.

CHAPTER 27 STUDY GUIDE

Online Study Guide
bedfordstmartins.com/roarkunderstanding

STEP 1 GETTING STARTED

Below are basic terms from this period in American history. Can you identify each term below and explain why it matters? To do this exercise online or to download this chart, visit bedfordstmartins.com/roarkunderstanding.

TERM	WHO OR WHAT & WHEN	WHY IT MATTERS
Interstate Highway and Defense System Act of 1956, p. 749		
mutually assured destruction (MAD), p. 753		
Fidel Castro, p. 754		
Nikita Khrushchev, p. 755		
military-industrial complex, p. 756		
Levittown, p. 759		
Betty Friedan, p. 763		
baby boom, p. 764		
Brown v. Board of Education, p. 768		
Rosa Parks, p. 769		
Montgomery bus boycott, p. 770		
Southern Christian Leadership Conference (SCLC), p. 770		

STEP 2 MOVING BEYOND THE BASICS

The exercise below represents a more advanced understanding of the chapter material. Start by describing the developments that took place in each of the areas listed in the following chart. Then describe the impact of those changes on middle-class white society and culture. When you are finished, consider the society you have described as a whole. Is it fair to call it "the affluent society"? Who did not participate in the developments you described? What adjectives would you use to describe the society and culture you have depicted? To do this exercise online or to download this chart, visit bedfordstmartins.com/roarkunderstanding.

	Developments	Impact
Economic growth and consumerism		
Suburban growth/domesticity		
Culture/values		
The Cold War		

Now that you've reviewed various parts of the chapter, take a step back and try to see the big picture by answering these questions. Remember to use specific examples from the chapter in your answers. To do this exercise online, visit bedfordstmartins.com/roarkunderstanding.

THE COLD WAR IN THE 1950s

▶ What was the "New Look" in American foreign policy? In what ways, if any, did Eisenhower depart from the policies of Truman, and why did these changes occur?

▶ How did the United States use military intervention or CIA covert activities as a tool of foreign policy in the 1950s?

DOMESTIC DEVELOPMENTS

▶ What factors combined to produce enormous increases in American economic productivity in the 1950s? Who benefited the most from increased productivity? Who did not benefit? Why?

▶ How did consumption shape the culture of the 1950s?

THE CIVIL RIGHTS MOVEMENT

▶ Why was *Brown v. Board of Education* such a pivotal case in the history of the civil rights movement?

▶ What light does the Montgomery bus boycott shed on the goals and strategies of the 1950s civil rights movement?

LOOKING BACKWARD,
LOOKING AHEAD

▶ Compare and contrast the culture and society of 1920s and 1950s America. What were the most important similarities? What were the most important differences?

▶ What tensions within 1950s society suggest defining aspects of 1960s America?

IN YOUR OWN WORDS

Imagine that you must explain chapter 27 to someone who hasn't read it. What would be the most important points to include and why?

28
REFORM, REBELLION, AND REACTION

1960–1974

> This chapter examines efforts to reform and transform American society and politics in the 1960s and early 1970s. It explores the domestic agenda of the Johnson administration, the role of the Supreme Court, the evolution of the black freedom movement, the movements inspired by the struggle for civil rights, the backlash against reform, and the transformation of the liberal reform agenda under President Nixon.

> What liberal reforms were advanced during the Kennedy and Johnson administrations?

> How did the civil rights movement evolve in the 1960s?

> What other rights movements emerged in the 1960s?

> What were the goals of the new wave of feminism?

> How did liberal reform fare under President Nixon?

> Conclusion: What were the achievements and limitations of liberalism?

DID YOU KNOW?

The Environmental Protection Agency (EPA) was created by Republican president Richard Nixon.

Birmingham, Alabama. Police officers attack civil rights demonstrators with fire hoses at Kelley Ingram Park in 1963.

What liberal reforms were advanced during the Kennedy and Johnson administrations?

A Tribute to Johnson for Medicare

George Niedermeyer, who lived in Hollywood, Florida, and received a Social Security pension, painted pieces of wood and glued them together to create this thank-you to President Johnson for establishing Medicare. LBJ Library, photo by Henry Groskinsky.

AT THE 1960 DEMOCRATIC National Convention, John F. Kennedy announced "a New Frontier" that would confront "unsolved problems of peace and war, unconquered pockets of ignorance and prejudice, unanswered questions of poverty and surplus." Four years later, Lyndon B. Johnson invoked the ideal of a "Great Society, [which] rests on abundance and liberty for all [and] demands an end to poverty and racial injustice." Acting under the liberal faith that government should use its power to solve social and economic problems, end injustice, and promote the welfare of all citizens, the Democratic administrations of the 1960s won legislation on civil rights, poverty, education, medical care, housing, consumer protection, and environmental protection.

The Unrealized Promise of Kennedy's New Frontier

John F. Kennedy grew up in privilege, the child of an Irish Catholic businessman and diplomat. Helped by a distinguished World War II navy record, Kennedy won election to the House of Representatives in 1946 and the Senate in 1952. With a powerful political machine, his family's fortune, and a dynamic personality, Kennedy won the Democratic presidential nomination in 1960. He then stunned many Democrats by choosing as his running mate Lyndon B. Johnson of Texas, whom liberals disparaged as a typical southern conservative. In the general election, Kennedy narrowly defeated Vice President Richard M. Nixon. African American voters contributed to his victory, helping to offset the 52 percent of the white vote cast for Nixon and contributing to Kennedy's 118,550-vote margin

CHAPTER LOCATOR | What liberal reforms were advanced during the Kennedy and Johnson administrations?

776 CHAPTER 28
REFORM, REBELLION, AND REACTION, 1960–1974

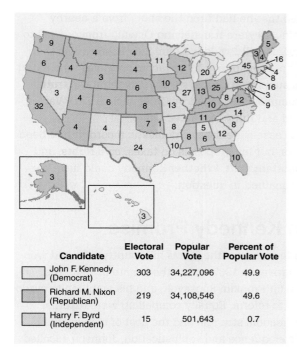

Candidate	Electoral Vote	Popular Vote	Percent of Popular Vote
John F. Kennedy (Democrat)	303	34,227,096	49.9
Richard M. Nixon (Republican)	219	34,108,546	49.6
Harry F. Byrd (Independent)	15	501,643	0.7

MAP 28.1 ▪ The Election of 1960

(**Map 28.1**). Kennedy benefited from the nation's first televised presidential debates, during which he appeared cool and confident beside a nervous and pale Nixon.

The Kennedy administration projected energy, idealism, youth, and glamour, although Kennedy was in most ways a cautious, pragmatic politician. At his inauguration, he called on Americans to serve the common good. "Ask not what your country can do for you," he implored, "ask what you can do for your country." Although Kennedy's idealism inspired many, he failed to redeem campaign promises to expand the welfare state with federal education and health care programs. Moreover, he resisted leadership on behalf of racial justice until civil rights activists gave him no choice.

Moved by the desperate conditions he observed while campaigning in Appalachia, Kennedy pushed poverty onto the national agenda. In 1962, he read Michael Harrington's *The Other America*, which described the poverty that left more than one in five Americans "maimed in body and spirit, existing at levels beneath those necessary for human decency." By 1962, Kennedy had won support for a $2 billion urban renewal program, providing incentives to businesses to locate in economically depressed areas and a training program for the unemployed. In the summer of 1963, Kennedy directed aides to plan a full-scale attack on poverty and called for a comprehensive civil rights bill, marking a turning point in his domestic agenda.

Kennedy had promised to make economic growth a key objective, and he asked Congress to pass an enormous tax cut in 1963, arguing that reducing taxes would infuse money into the economy and thus increase demand and create jobs. Enacted in February 1964, the law contributed to an economic boom, as unemployment dropped to 4.1 percent, and the gross national product grew by 7 to 9 percent annually between 1964 and 1966. Some liberal critics of the tax cut, however, pointed out that it favored the well-off and that economic growth alone would not eliminate poverty. They argued instead for increased spending on social programs.

Kennedy's economic efforts were in their infancy when he fell victim to an assassin's bullet on November 22, 1963. Within minutes of the shooting—which occurred as Kennedy's motorcade passed through Dallas, Texas—radio and television broadcast the unfolding horror to the nation. Stunned Americans struggled to understand what had happened. Soon after the assassination, police arrested

CHRONOLOGY

1960
– Democrat John F. Kennedy is elected president.

1962
– Michael Harrington's *The Other America*, detailing endemic poverty in America, is published.

1963
– Supreme Court decision in *Gideon v. Wainwright* guarantees defendants the right to an attorney.
– Supreme Court decision in *Abington School District v. Schempp* bans official prayer in public schools.
– **November 22.** President Kennedy is assassinated; Lyndon B. Johnson becomes president.

1964
– Civil Rights Act, the strongest measure since Reconstruction, is passed by Congress.
– Economic Opportunity Act, part of President Johnson's War on Poverty, is passed.

1965
– Federal funding for antipoverty programs doubles.
– Immigration and Nationality Act reforms immigration policy.
– Medicare and Medicaid health care programs are passed.

1965–1966
– Congress passes most of Johnson's Great Society domestic programs.

1967
– Supreme Court decision in *Loving v. Virginia* strikes down state laws against interracial marriage.

| How did the civil rights movement evolve in the 1960s? | What other rights movements emerged in the 1960s? | What were the goals of the new wave of feminism? | How did liberal reform fare under President Nixon? | Conclusion: What were the achievements and limitations of liberalism? |

Civil Rights Act of 1964

▶ Law that responded to demands of the civil rights movement by making discrimination in employment, education, and public accommodations illegal. Passage of the Civil Rights Act of 1964 required all of President Johnson's political skill. It was the strongest such measure since Reconstruction.

Lee Harvey Oswald and concluded that he had fired the shots from a nearby building. Two days later, while officers were transferring Oswald from one jail to another, a local nightclub operator, Jack Ruby, killed him. Suspicions arose that Ruby murdered Oswald to cover up a conspiracy by ultraconservatives who hated Kennedy, or by Communists who supported Castro's Cuba. To get at the truth, President Johnson appointed a commission headed by Chief Justice Earl Warren, which concluded that both Oswald and Ruby had acted alone.

Debate continued over how to assess Kennedy's domestic record. It had been unremarkable in his first two years, but his proposals on taxes, civil rights, and poverty in 1963 suggested an important shift. Whether Kennedy could have persuaded Congress to enact them remained in question.

Johnson Fulfills the Kennedy Promise

Lyndon B. Johnson was a self-made man from the Texas hill country who had won election to the House of Representatives in 1937 and to the Senate in 1948. His modest upbringing, his admiration for Franklin Roosevelt, and his ambition to outdo Roosevelt spurred his commitment to reform. Equally compelling were external pressures generated by the black freedom struggle and the host of movements it helped inspire. Lacking Kennedy's eloquence and sophistication, Johnson excelled behind the scenes, where he could entice, maneuver, or threaten legislators to support his objectives. The famous "Johnson treatment" became legendary. In his ability to achieve consensus around his goals, he had few peers in American history.

Johnson entreated Congress to act so that "John Fitzgerald Kennedy did not live or die in vain." He signed Kennedy's tax cut bill in February 1964. More remarkable was passage of the Civil Rights Act of 1964, which Kennedy had proposed in response to black protest. The strongest such measure since Reconstruction, the law required all of Johnson's political skill to pry sufficient votes from Republicans to balance the "nays" of southern Democrats. Senate Republican leader Everett Dirksen's aide reported that Johnson "never left him alone for thirty minutes."

Antipoverty legislation followed the Civil Rights Act. Johnson announced "an unconditional war on poverty" in his January 1964 State of the Union message, and Congress passed the Economic Opportunity Act of 1964 in August. The act authorized ten new programs, allocating $800 million—about 1 percent of the federal budget—for the first year. Many provisions targeted children and youths, including Head Start for preschoolers, work-study grants for college students, and the Job Corps for unemployed young people.

The "Johnson Treatment"

Abe Fortas, a distinguished lawyer who had argued a major criminal rights case, *Gideon v. Wainwright* (1963), before the Supreme Court, was a close friend of and adviser to President Johnson. This photograph of the president and Fortas taken in July 1965 illustrates how Johnson used his body as well as his voice to bend people to his will. Yoichi R. Okamoto/LBJ Library Collection.

CHAPTER LOCATOR | What liberal reforms were advanced during the Kennedy and Johnson administrations?

The Volunteers in Service to America (VISTA) program paid modest wages to volunteers working with the disadvantaged, and a legal services program provided lawyers for the poor.

The most controversial part of the law, the Community Action Program (CAP), required "maximum feasible participation" of the poor themselves in antipoverty projects. Poor people began to organize to take control of their neighborhoods and to make welfare agencies, school boards, police departments, and housing authorities more accountable to the people they served. Even though Johnson backed off from pushing thorough representation for the poor, CAP gave people usually excluded from government an opportunity to act on their own behalf and develop leadership skills.

Policymaking for a Great Society

As the 1964 election approached, Johnson projected stability and security in the midst of a booming economy. Few voters wanted to take a chance on his Republican opponent, Arizona senator Barry M. Goldwater, who attacked the welfare state and suggested using nuclear weapons if necessary to crush communism in Vietnam. Johnson achieved a record-breaking landslide of 61 percent of the popular vote, and Democrats won resounding majorities in the House (295–140) and Senate (68–32). Still, Goldwater's considerable grassroots support marked a growing movement on the right alongside the more noticeable left and liberal movements (see chapter 30).

"I want to see a whole bunch of coonskins on the wall," Johnson told his aides, using a hunting analogy to stress his ambitious legislative goals for what he called the **"Great Society."** The large Democratic majorities in Congress, his own political skills, and pressure from the black freedom struggle enabled Johnson to succeed. He persuaded Congress to act on discrimination, poverty, education, medical care, housing, consumer and environmental protection, and more.

The Economic Opportunity Act of 1964 was the opening shot in the **War on Poverty**. Congress doubled the program's funding in 1965, enacted new economic development measures for depressed regions, and authorized more than $1 billion to improve the nation's slums. Direct aid included a new food stamp program and rent supplements that provided alternatives to public housing projects for some poor families. Moreover, a movement of welfare mothers, the National Welfare Rights Organization, pushed administrators to ease restrictions on welfare recipients. The number of families receiving assistance jumped from less than one million in 1960 to three million by 1972, benefiting 90 percent of those eligible.

Central to Johnson's War on Poverty were efforts to equip the poor with the skills necessary to find jobs. His Elementary and Secondary Education Act of 1965 marked a turning point by involving the federal government in K–12 education. The measure sent federal dollars to local school districts with high poverty populations and provided equipment and supplies to private and parochial schools serving the poor. That same year, Congress passed the Higher Education Act, vastly expanding federal assistance to colleges and universities for buildings, programs, scholarships, and loans.

The federal government's responsibility for health care marked an even more significant watershed. Faced with a powerful medical lobby that opposed national

Great Society
▶ Term for President Johnson's domestic legislative agenda. Between 1964 and 1968, Johnson won passage of Great Society legislation dealing with discrimination, poverty, education, medical care, housing, consumer and environmental protection, and more. While critics pointed out shortcomings in Johnson's legislative record, the Great Society had a lasting impact on American life.

War on Poverty
▶ President Johnson's legislative effort to combat poverty in America. Key elements of the War on Poverty were included in the Economic Opportunity Act of 1964. While Johnson's efforts included substantial increases in direct aid, central to the War on Poverty were efforts to equip the poor with the skills necessary to find jobs.

| How did the civil rights movement evolve in the 1960s? | What other rights movements emerged in the 1960s? | What were the goals of the new wave of feminism? | How did liberal reform fare under President Nixon? | Conclusion: What were the achievements and limitations of liberalism? |

health insurance as "socialized medicine," Johnson focused on the elderly, who constituted a large portion of the nation's poor. Congress responded with the Medicare program, providing the elderly with universal compulsory medical insurance financed through Social Security taxes. A separate program, Medicaid, authorized federal grants to supplement state-funded medical care for poor people.

Whereas programs such as Medicare fulfilled New Deal and Fair Deal promises, the Great Society's civil rights legislation represented a break with tradition and an expansion of liberalism. The Civil Rights Act of 1964 made discrimination in employment, education, and public accommodations illegal. The **Voting Rights Act of 1965** banned literacy tests and authorized federal intervention to ensure access to the voting booth. Another form of bias fell with the Immigration and Nationality Act of 1965, which abolished quotas based on national origins that discriminated against immigrants from areas outside northern and western Europe. The law maintained caps on the total number of immigrants and for the first time limited those from the Western Hemisphere. The measure's unanticipated consequences would trigger a surge of immigration near the end of the century.

Great Society benefits reached well beyond victims of discrimination and the poor. Medicare, for example, covered the elderly, regardless of income. A groundswell of consumer activism won legislation making cars safer and raising standards for the food, drug, and cosmetics industries. Johnson insisted that the Great Society meet "not just the needs of the body but the desire for beauty and hunger for community." In 1965, he sent Congress the first presidential message on the environment, obtaining measures to control water and air pollution and to preserve the natural beauty of the American landscape. In addition, the National Arts and Humanities Act of 1965 funded artists, musicians, writers, and scholars and brought their work to public audiences.

The flood of reform legislation dwindled after 1966, when Democratic majorities in Congress diminished and a backlash against government programs arose. The Vietnam War dealt the largest blow to Johnson's ambitions, diverting his attention, spawning an antiwar movement that crippled his leadership, and devouring tax dollars that might have been used for reform (see chapter 29).

In 1968, Johnson pried out of Congress one more civil rights law, which banned discrimination in housing and jury service. He also signed the National Housing Act of 1968, which authorized an enormous increase in low-income housing—1.7 million units over three years—and left construction and ownership in private hands.

Assessing the Great Society

The reduction in poverty in the 1960s was considerable. The number of poor Americans fell from more than 20 percent of the population in 1959 to around 13 percent in 1968. Those who Johnson had said "lived on the outskirts of hope" saw new opportunities. To Rosemary Bray, what turned her family of longtime welfare recipients into taxpaying workers "was the promise of the civil rights movement and the war on poverty." A Mexican American who became a sheet metal worker through a jobs program reported that his children "will finish high school and maybe go to college. . . . I see my family and I know the chains are broken."

Certain groups, especially the aged, fared better than others. Many male-headed families rose out of poverty, but impoverishment among female-headed

Voting Rights Act of 1965

► Law empowering the federal government to intervene directly to enable African Americans to register to vote. As a result of the act, black voting and officeholding in the South shot up, initiating a major transformation in southern politics.

CHAPTER LOCATOR | What liberal reforms were advanced during the Kennedy and Johnson administrations?

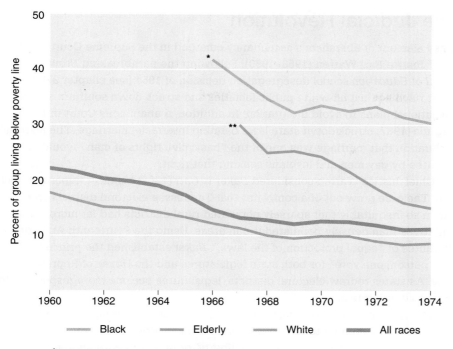

*Statistics on blacks for years 1960–1965 not available.
**Statistics on the elderly for years 1960–1966 not available.

FIGURE 28.1 ■ **Poverty in the United States, 1960–1974**
The short-term effects of economic growth and the Great Society's attack on poverty are seen here. Which groups experienced the sharpest decline in poverty, and what might account for the differences?

families actually increased. Whites escaped poverty faster than racial and ethnic minorities. Great Society programs contributed to a burgeoning black middle class, and the proportion of African Americans who were poor fell by 10 percentage points between 1966 and 1974. Still, one out of three remained poverty-stricken (**Figure 28.1**).

Conservative critics charged that Great Society programs discouraged initiative by giving the poor "handouts." Liberal critics claimed that focusing on training and education unjustly blamed the poor themselves for their poverty rather than an economic system that could not provide enough adequately paying jobs. Most government training programs prepared graduates for low-skilled labor and could not guarantee employment. In contrast to the New Deal, the Great Society avoided structural reform of the economy and spurned public works projects as a means of providing jobs for the disadvantaged.

Some critics argued that ending poverty required raising taxes in order to create jobs, overhaul welfare systems, and rebuild slums. Great Society programs did invest more heavily in the public sector, but they were funded from economic growth rather than from new taxes. There was no significant redistribution of income, despite large increases in subsidies for food stamps, housing, medical care, and Aid to Families with Dependent Children (AFDC). Economic prosperity allowed spending for the poor to rise and improved the lives of millions, but that spending never approached the amounts necessary to claim victory in the War on Poverty.

How did the civil rights movement evolve in the 1960s?

What other rights movements emerged in the 1960s?

What were the goals of the new wave of feminism?

How did liberal reform fare under President Nixon?

Conclusion: What were the achievements and limitations of liberalism?

The Judicial Revolution

A key element of liberalism's ascendancy emerged in the Supreme Court under Chief Justice Earl Warren (1953–1969). Following the pathbreaking *Brown v. Board of Education* school desegregation decision of 1954 (see chapter 27), the Court ruled against all-white public facilities and struck down southern states' educational plans to avoid integration. In addition, a unanimous Court in *Loving v. Virginia* (1967) struck down state laws banning interracial marriage. The justices' declaration that marriage was one of the "basic civil rights of man" would later be repeated by gay men and lesbians seeking that right.

Chief Justice Warren considered *Baker v. Carr* (1963) his most important decision. The case grew out of a complaint that Tennessee electoral districts were drawn so inequitably that sparsely populated rural districts had far more representatives than densely populated urban areas. Using the Fourteenth Amendment guarantee of "equal protection of the laws," *Baker* established the principle of "one person, one vote" for both state legislatures and the House of Representatives. As states redrew electoral districts, legislatures became more responsive to metropolitan interests.

The Warren Court also reformed the criminal justice system, using the Fourteenth Amendment to overturn a series of convictions on the grounds that the accused had been deprived of "life, liberty, or property, without due process of law." In decisions that dramatically altered law enforcement practices and the treatment of individuals accused of crimes, the Court declared that states, as well as the federal government, were subject to the Bill of Rights. *Gideon v. Wainwright* (1963) ruled that when an accused criminal could not afford to hire a lawyer, the state had to provide one. In 1966, *Miranda v. Arizona* required police officers to inform suspects of their rights upon arrest. The Court also overturned convictions based on evidence obtained by unlawful arrest, by electronic surveillance, or without a search warrant. Critics accused the justices of obstructing law enforcement and letting criminals go free; liberals argued that these rulings promoted equal treatment in the criminal justice system.

The Court's decisions on religion provoked even greater outrage. *Abington School District v. Schempp* (1963) ruled that requiring Bible reading and prayer in the schools violated the First Amendment principle of separation of church and state. Later decisions ruled against official prayer in public schools even if students were not required to participate. These decisions left students free to pray on their own but infuriated many Christians. The Court's supporters, however, declared that the religion cases protected the rights of non-Christians and atheists. Billboards demanding "Impeach Earl Warren" spoke for critics of the Court who joined a larger backlash mounting against Great Society liberalism. Nonetheless, the Court's major decisions withstood the test of time.

> **QUICK REVIEW**

How did the Kennedy and Johnson administrations exemplify a liberal vision of the federal government?

CHAPTER LOCATOR | What liberal reforms were advanced during the Kennedy and Johnson administrations?

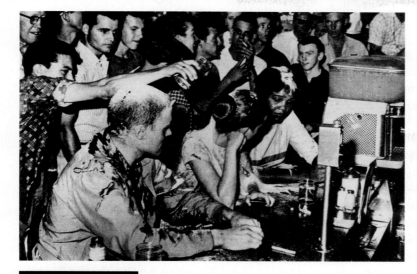

Lunch Counter Sit-in John Salter Jr., a professor at Tougaloo College, and students Joan Trumpauer and Anne Moody take part in a 1963 sit-in at the Woolworth's lunch counter in Jackson, Mississippi. Shortly before this photograph was taken, whites had thrown two students to the floor, and police had arrested one student. Salter was spattered with mustard and ketchup. State Historical Society of Wisconsin.

> ► FOR MORE HELP ANALYZING THIS IMAGE, see the visual activity for this chapter in the Online Study Guide at bedfordstmartins.com/roarkunderstanding.

BEFORE THE GREAT SOCIETY reforms—and, in fact, contributing to them—African Americans had mobilized a movement that struck down legal separation and discrimination in the South. Whereas the first Reconstruction reflected the power of northern Republicans in the aftermath of the Civil War, the second Reconstruction depended heavily on the courage and determination of black people themselves. The early black freedom struggle focused on legal rights in the South and won widespread acceptance. But when African Americans intensified their efforts for racial justice in the rest of the country and challenged the economic deprivation that equal rights left untouched, a strong backlash developed as the movement itself lost cohesion.

The Flowering of the Black Freedom Struggle

The Montgomery bus boycott of 1955–1956 gave racial issues national visibility and produced a leader in **Martin Luther King Jr.** In the 1960s, protest expanded dramatically, as blacks directly confronted the people and institutions that segregated and discriminated against them: retail establishments, public parks and libraries, buses and depots, voting registrars, and police forces.

Massive direct action began in February 1960, when four African American college students in Greensboro, North Carolina, requested service at the whites-only Woolworth's lunch counter. Within days, hundreds of young people joined them, and others launched sit-ins in thirty-one southern cities. From Southern Christian Leadership Conference (SCLC) headquarters, Ella Baker telephoned her young contacts at various colleges: "What are you going to do? It's time to move."

Martin Luther King Jr.

► Civil rights leader who first rose to national attention during the Montgomery bus boycott. His principles of civil disobedience and nonviolence shaped the civil rights movement from the mid-1950s through the mid-1960s. King was murdered in Memphis, Tennessee, in April 1968.

How did the civil rights movement evolve in the 1960s?	What other rights movements emerged in the 1960s?	What were the goals of the new wave of feminism?	How did liberal reform fare under President Nixon?	Conclusion: What were the achievements and limitations of liberalism?

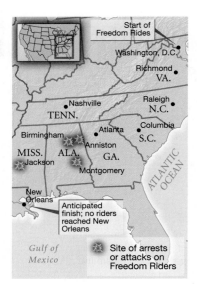

Civil Rights Freedom Rides,
May 1961

March on Washington for Jobs and Freedom

▶ The largest demonstration of the civil rights movement. Inspired by the strategy of A. Philip Randolph in 1941, the 1963 March on Washington drew 250,000 people to the nation's capital. Martin Luther King Jr.'s famous "I have a dream" speech capped the day's events.

In April, Baker helped student activists form a new organization, the Student Nonviolent Coordinating Committee (SNCC). Embracing civil disobedience and the nonviolence principles of Martin Luther King Jr., activists would confront their oppressors and stand up for their rights, but they would not respond if attacked. In the words of SNCC leader James Lawson, "Nonviolence nurtures the atmosphere in which reconciliation and justice become actual possibilities." SNCC, however, rejected the top-down leadership of King and the established civil rights organizations; instead, it adopted a structure that fostered decision making and the development of leadership at the grassroots level. Although some cities quietly met student demands, more typically activists encountered violence. Hostile whites poured food over demonstrators, burned them with cigarettes, called them "niggers," and pelted them with rocks. Local police attacked protesters with dogs, clubs, fire hoses, and tear gas and arrested thousands of demonstrators.

Another wave of protest occurred in May 1961, when the Congress of Racial Equality (CORE) organized Freedom Rides to integrate interstate transportation in the South. When a group of six whites and seven blacks reached Alabama, whites bombed their bus and beat them with baseball bats so fiercely that an observer "couldn't see their faces through the blood." After a huge mob attacked the riders in Montgomery, Alabama, Attorney General Robert Kennedy dispatched federal marshals to restore order. Freedom Riders arriving in Jackson, Mississippi, were promptly arrested, and several hundred spent part of the summer in jail. All told, more than four hundred blacks and whites participated in the Freedom Rides.

In the summer of 1961, SNCC and other groups began the Voter Education Project. They, too, met violence. Whites bombed black churches, threw tenant farmers out of their homes, and beat and jailed activists. In June 1963, Mississippi NAACP leader Medgar Evers was gunned down in front of his house in Jackson. Similar violence met King's 1963 campaign in Birmingham, Alabama, to integrate public facilities and open jobs to blacks. The police attacked demonstrators with dogs, cattle prods, and fire hoses—brutalities that television broadcast around the world.

The largest demonstration drew 250,000 blacks and whites to the nation's capital in August 1963 in the **March on Washington for Jobs and Freedom**. Speaking from the Lincoln Memorial, King put his indelible stamp on the day. "I have a dream," he repeated again and again, imagining the day "when all of God's children . . . will be able to join hands and sing . . . 'Free at last, free at last; thank God Almighty, we are free at last.'"

The euphoria of the March on Washington faded as activists returned to continued violence in the South. In 1964, the Mississippi Freedom Summer Project mobilized more than a thousand northern black and white college students to conduct voter registration drives. Resistance was fierce, and by the end of the summer, southern whites had killed several activists, beaten eighty, arrested more than a thousand, and burned thirty-five black churches. Hidden resistance came from the federal government itself, as the FBI spied on King and other leaders and expanded its activities to "expose, disrupt, misdirect, discredit, or otherwise neutralize" black protest.

In March 1965, Alabama state troopers used such force to turn back a voting rights march from Selma to the state capitol in Montgomery that the incident earned the name "Bloody Sunday" and compelled President Johnson to call up the Alabama National Guard to protect the marchers. Battered and hospitalized on

CHAPTER LOCATOR | What liberal reforms were advanced during the Kennedy and Johnson administrations?

The Selma March for Voting Rights

In 1963, the Student Nonviolent Coordinating Committee (SNCC) began a campaign for voting rights in Selma, Alabama, where white officials had registered only 335 of the 15,000 African Americans of voting age. In this photo, young African Americans take part in the fifty-four-mile march from Selma to Montgomery, the state capital, with nuns, priests, and other supporters. During the march, Juanita Williams wore out her shoes (shown here), which are now displayed at the National Museum of History in Washington, D.C. Photo: Steve Shapiro/TimePix/Getty; Shoes: Smithsonian Institution, Washington, D.C.

CHRONOLOGY

1960
- Lunch counter sit-ins aimed at ending legal segregation begin in Greensboro, North Carolina, and spread to thirty-one other cities.
- Student Nonviolent Coordinating Committee (SNCC) is established.

1961
- Congress of Racial Equality organizes Freedom Rides to challenge segregation on buses.

1963
- **August.** March on Washington draws 250,000 civil rights supporters.

1964
- Congress passes Civil Rights Act.
- Mississippi Freedom Summer Project is launched to register black voters.

1965
- Selma-to-Montgomery march pushes passage of the Voting Rights Act.

1965–1968
- Urban riots erupt in Los Angeles, Newark, Detroit, Washington, D.C., and dozens of other cities across the nation.

1966
- **June.** SNCC chair Stokely Carmichael calls for "black power."

1968
- **April.** Martin Luther King Jr. is assassinated.

Bloody Sunday, John Lewis, chairman of SNCC (and later a congressman), managed to make the final stretch of the Selma march to the capitol, which he counted as one of his most meaningful experiences: "[T]hat year the Voting Rights bill was passed and we all felt we'd had a part in it."

The Response in Washington

In June 1963, President Kennedy finally made good on his promise to seek strong antidiscrimination legislation. Pointing to the injustice suffered by blacks, Kennedy asked white Americans, "Who among us would then be content with the counsels of patience and delay?" Johnson took up Kennedy's commitment with passion, as scenes of violence against peaceful demonstrators appalled many television viewers across the nation. The resulting public support, the "Johnson treatment," and the president's appeal to memories of Kennedy all produced the most important civil rights law since Reconstruction.

The Civil Rights Act of 1964 guaranteed access for all Americans to public accommodations, public education, employment, and voting, and it extended constitutional protections to Indians on reservations. Title VII of the measure, banning discrimination in employment, not only attacked racial discrimination but also outlawed job discrimination against women. Because Title VII applied to every aspect of employment, including wages, hiring, and promotion, it represented a giant step for white women as well as for racial minorities.

Responding to black voter registration drives in the South, Johnson demanded legislation to remove "every remaining obstacle to the right and the opportunity to vote." In August 1965, he signed the Voting Rights Act, authorizing direct federal intervention to enable African Americans to register and vote, thereby launching a major transformation in southern politics. Black voting rates shot up dramatically (**Map 28.2**). In turn, the number of African Americans holding political office in the South increased from a handful in 1964 to more than a thousand by 1972. Such

| How did the civil rights movement evolve in the 1960s? | What other rights movements emerged in the 1960s? | What were the goals of the new wave of feminism? | How did liberal reform fare under President Nixon? | Conclusion: What were the achievements and limitations of liberalism? |

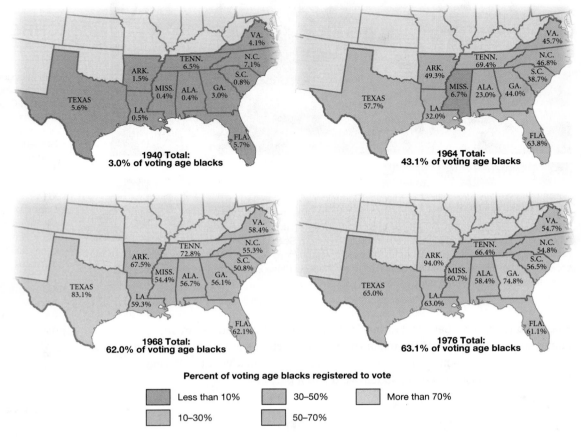

1940 Total:
3.0% of voting age blacks

VA. 4.1%
TENN. 6.5%
N.C. 7.1%
ARK. 1.5%
S.C. 0.8%
MISS. 0.4%
ALA. 0.4%
GA. 3.0%
TEXAS 5.6%
LA. 0.5%
FLA. 5.7%

1964 Total:
43.1% of voting age blacks

VA. 45.7%
TENN. 69.4%
N.C. 46.8%
ARK. 49.3%
S.C. 38.7%
MISS. 6.7%
ALA. 23.0%
GA. 44.0%
TEXAS 57.7%
LA. 32.0%
FLA. 63.8%

1968 Total:
62.0% of voting age blacks

VA. 58.4%
TENN. 72.8%
N.C. 55.3%
ARK. 67.5%
S.C. 50.8%
MISS. 54.4%
ALA. 56.7%
GA. 56.1%
TEXAS 83.1%
LA. 59.3%
FLA. 62.1%

1976 Total:
63.1% of voting age blacks

VA. 54.7%
TENN. 66.4%
N.C. 54.8%
ARK. 94.0%
S.C. 56.5%
MISS. 60.7%
ALA. 58.4%
GA. 74.8%
TEXAS 65.0%
LA. 63.0%
FLA. 61.1%

Percent of voting age blacks registered to vote

Less than 10%   30–50%   More than 70%

10–30%   50–70%

MAP 28.2 ■ **The Rise of the African American Vote, 1940–1976**
Voting rates of southern blacks increased gradually in the 1940s and 1950s but shot up dramatically in the deep South after the Voting Rights Act of 1965 provided for federal agents to enforce African Americans' right to vote.

▶ FOR MORE HELP ANALYZING THIS MAP, see the map activity for this chapter in the Online Study Guide at bedfordstmartins.com/roarkunderstanding.

gains translated into tangible benefits as black officials upgraded public facilities, police protection, and other basic services for their constituents.

Johnson also declared the need to realize "not just equality as a right and theory, but equality as fact and result." To this end, he issued an executive order in 1965 to require employers holding government contracts (affecting about one-third of the labor force) to take affirmative action to ensure equal opportunity. Extended to cover women in 1967, the affirmative action program required employers to counter the effects of centuries of oppression by acting forcefully to align their labor force with the available pool of qualified candidates. Most corporations came to see affirmative action as a good employment practice.

Johnson pried one final bill from a Congress increasingly resistant to reform. The Civil Rights Act of 1968 banned racial discrimination in housing and jury selection and authorized federal intervention when states failed to protect civil rights workers from violence.

CHAPTER LOCATOR | What liberal reforms were advanced during the Kennedy and Johnson administrations?

Black Power and Urban Rebellions

By 1966, black protest engulfed the entire nation, demanding not just legal equality but also economic justice and abandoning nonviolence as its basic principle. These developments were not entirely new. African Americans had waged campaigns for decent jobs and housing outside the South since the 1930s. Some African Americans had always armed themselves in self-defense, and many activists doubted that their passive suffering would change the hearts of racists. Still, the black freedom struggle began to appear more threatening to the white majority. The new emphases resulted from a combination of heightened activism and unrealized promise. Legal equality could not quickly improve the material conditions of blacks, and black rage at oppressive conditions erupted in waves of urban uprisings from 1965 to 1968.

In the North, Malcolm X posed a powerful challenge to the ethos of nonviolence. Calling for black pride and autonomy, separation from the "corrupt [white] society," and self-defense against white violence, Malcolm X attracted a large following, especially in urban ghettos. At a June 1966 rally in Greenwood, Mississippi, SNCC chairman Stokely Carmichael gave the ideas espoused by Malcolm X a new name when he shouted, "We want black power." Carmichael rejected integration and assimilation because that implied white superiority. African Americans were encouraged to develop independent businesses and control their own schools, communities, and political organizations. "Black is beautiful" emphasized pride in African American culture and connections to dark-skinned people around the world. Black power quickly became the rallying cry in SNCC and CORE as well as such organizations as the Black Panther Party for Self-Defense, organized in California to combat police brutality.

The press paid inordinate attention to black radicals, and the civil rights movement encountered a severe white backlash. Although the urban riots of the mid-1960s erupted spontaneously, triggered by specific incidents of alleged police mistreatment, whites blamed black power militants. By 1966, 85 percent of the white population—up from 34 percent two years earlier—thought that African Americans were pressing for too much too quickly.

Martin Luther King Jr. agreed with black power advocates about the need for "a radical reconstruction of society," yet he clung to nonviolence and integration as the means to this end. In April 1968, the thirty-nine-year-old leader went to Memphis to support striking municipal sanitation workers. There, on April 4, he was murdered by an escaped white convict.

Although black power organizations captured the headlines, they failed to gain the massive support from African Americans that King and other leaders had attracted. Nor could they alleviate the poverty and racism entrenched in the urban North and West. Yet black power's emphasis on racial pride and its critique of American institutions resonated loudly and helped shape the protest activities of other groups.

QUICK REVIEW <

How and why did the struggle for black freedom change over the course of the 1960s?

What other rights movements emerged in the 1960s?

Cesar Chavez and Dolores Huerta

Chavez and Huerta confer in Delano, California, in early 1968 during the United Farm Workers' five-year struggle with grape growers for better wages and working conditions and union recognition. The symbols surrounding them reflect the UFW's origins and connections. Arthur Schatz/TimePix/Getty Images.

▶ FOR MORE HELP ANALYZING THIS IMAGE, see the map activity for this chapter in the Online Study Guide at bedfordstmartins.com/roarkunderstanding.

THE CIVIL RIGHTS MOVEMENT's undeniable moral claims helped make protest more respectable, while its successes encouraged other groups with grievances. Native Americans, Latinos, college students, women, gay men and lesbians, environmentalists, and others drew on the black freedom struggle for inspiration and models of activism. Many of these groups engaged in direct-action protests, expressed their own cultural nationalism, and challenged dominant institutions and values. As a result, their grievances gained attention in the political arena, and they expanded justice and opportunity for many of their constituents.

Native American Protest

The cry "red power" reflected the influence of black radicalism on Native Americans, whose activism took on fresh militancy and goals in the 1960s. The assimilationist programs of the 1940s and 1950s, contrary to their intent, stirred a sense of Indian identity across tribal lines and a determination to preserve traditional culture. Native Americans demonstrated and occupied land and public buildings, claiming rights to natural resources and territory they had owned collectively before European settlement.

In 1969, Native American militants captured world attention when several dozen seized Alcatraz Island, an abandoned federal prison in San Francisco Bay, claiming their right of "first discovery" of this land. For nineteen months, they used the occupation to publicize injustices against Indians, promote pan-Indian cooperation, and celebrate traditional cultures. One of the organizers, Dr. LaNada Boyer, said of Alcatraz, "We were able to reestablish our identity as Indian people, as a culture, as political entities."

CHAPTER LOCATOR | What liberal reforms were advanced during the Kennedy and Johnson administrations?

In Minneapolis in 1968, two Chippewa Indians, Dennis Banks and George Mitchell, founded the **American Indian Movement (AIM)** to attack problems in cities, where about 300,000 Indians lived. AIM sought to protect Indians from police harassment, secure antipoverty funds, and establish "survival schools" to teach Indian history and values. The new movement filled many Indians with a new sense of purpose. AIM members did not have "that hangdog reservation look I was used to," Lakota activist Mary Crow Dog wrote; their visit to her South Dakota reservation "loosened a sort of earthquake inside me." AIM leaders helped organize the "Trail of Broken Treaties" caravan to the nation's capital in 1972, when activists occupied the Bureau of Indian Affairs to protest the bureau's policies and bureaucratic interference in Indians' lives.

Although these occupations failed to achieve their specific goals, Indians won the end of relocation and termination policies, greater tribal sovereignty and control over community services, protection of Indian religious practices, and a measure of respect and pride. A number of laws and court decisions restored rights to ancestral lands and compensated tribes for land seized in violation of treaties.

Latino Struggles for Justice

The fastest-growing minority group in the 1960s was Latino, or Hispanic American, an extraordinarily varied population encompassing people of Mexican, Puerto Rican, Caribbean, and other Latin American origins. (The term *Latino* stresses their common bonds as a minority group in the United States. The older, less political term *Hispanic* also includes people with origins in Spain.) People of Puerto Rican and Caribbean descent flocked to East Coast cities, but more than half of the nation's Latino population—including some six million Mexican Americans—lived in the Southwest. In addition, thousands illegally crossed the two-thousand-mile border between Mexico and the United States yearly in search of economic opportunity.

Political organization of Mexican Americans dated back to the League of United Latin American Citizens (LULAC), founded in 1929, which fought segregation and discrimination through litigation (see chapter 26). In the 1960s, however, young Mexican Americans increasingly rejected traditional politics in favor of direct action. One symbol of this generational challenge was young activists' adoption of the term *Chicano* (from *mejicano*, the Spanish word for "Mexican").

Chicano protest drew national attention to California, where **Cesar Chavez** and **Dolores Huerta** organized a movement to improve the conditions of migrant agricultural workers. As the child of migrant farmworkers, Chavez changed schools frequently and encountered indifference and discrimination. One teacher, he recalled, "hung a sign on me that said, 'I am a clown, I speak Spanish.'" After serving in World War II, Chavez began to organize voter registration drives among Mexican Americans.

In contrast to Chavez, Dolores Huerta grew up in an integrated urban neighborhood but still witnessed subtle forms of discrimination. Once, a high school teacher challenged her authorship of an essay because it was so well written. Believing that a labor union was the key to progress, she and Chavez founded the United Farm Workers (UFW) in 1962. To gain leverage for striking workers, the UFW mounted a nationwide boycott of California grapes, which drew support from millions of Americans and helped win a wage increase for the workers in

American Indian Movement (AIM)

▶ Organization established by Dennis Banks and George Mitchell in 1968 to address the problems Indians faced in American cities, including poverty and police harassment. The organization drew a large following that participated in public demonstrations and acts of civil disobedience. It contributed to Indians' successful efforts to end relocation and termination policies and to win greater control over their cultures and communities.

Cesar Chavez/ Dolores Huerta

▶ Organizers of a movement to improve the conditions of migrant agricultural workers. Huerta and Chavez founded the United Farm Workers (UFW) in 1962. The UFW's greatest success was the 1970 boycott of California grapes. Although the UFW struggled and lost membership during the 1970s, it helped politicize Mexican Americans and improve farmworkers' lives.

| How did the civil rights movement evolve in the 1960s? | What other rights movements emerged in the 1960s? | What were the goals of the new wave of feminism? | How did liberal reform fare under President Nixon? | Conclusion: What were the achievements and limitations of liberalism? |

1970. Although the UFW struggled and lost membership during the 1970s, it helped politicize Mexican Americans and improve farmworkers' lives.

Other Chicanos pressed the Equal Employment Opportunity Commission (EEOC), the enforcement agency of Title VII of the Civil Rights Act of 1964, to act against job discrimination against Mexican Americans. LULAC, the American GI Forum (see chapter 26), and other groups picketed government offices. President Johnson responded in 1967 by appointing Vicente T. Ximenes as the first Mexican American EEOC commissioner and by creating a special committee on Mexican American affairs.

Claiming "brown power," Chicanos organized to end discrimination in education, gain political power, and combat police brutality. In Denver, Rodolfo "Corky" Gonzales set up "freedom schools" where Chicano children learned Spanish and studied Mexican American history. The nationalist strains of Chicano protest were evident in La Raza Unida (the United Race), a political party founded in 1970 in Texas and based on cultural pride and brotherhood. Along with blacks and Native Americans, Chicanos continued to be disproportionately represented among the poor, but they gradually won more political offices, better enforcement of antidiscrimination legislation, and greater respect for their culture.

Student Rebellion, the New Left, and the Counterculture

Although materially and legally more secure than their African American, Indian, and Latino counterparts, white youths also expressed dissent, supporting the black freedom struggle and launching student protests, the antiwar movement, and the new feminist and environmental movements. They were part of a larger international phenomenon, as student movements arose around the globe.

The central organization of white student protest was Students for a Democratic Society (SDS), formed in 1960. In 1962, the organizers wrote in their statement of purpose, "We are people of this generation, bred in at least modest comfort, housed now in universities, looking uncomfortably at the world we inherit." The idealistic students criticized the complacency of their elders, the remoteness of decision makers, and the powerlessness and alienation generated by a bureaucratic society. SDS aimed to mobilize a "New Left" around the goals of civil rights, peace, and universal economic security. Other forms of student activism soon followed.

The first large-scale white student protest arose at the University of California, Berkeley, in 1964, when university officials banned students from setting up tables to recruit support for various causes. Led by whites back from civil rights work in the South, the "free speech" movement occupied the administration building, and more than seven hundred students were arrested before the California Board of Regents overturned the new restrictions.

Hundreds of student rallies and building occupations followed on campuses across the country, especially after 1965, when opposition to the Vietnam War mounted and students protested against universities' links to the military (see chapter 29). Students also changed the collegiate environment. Women at the University of Chicago, for example, charged in 1969 that all universities "discriminate against women, impede their full intellectual development, deny them places on the faculty, exploit talented women and mistreat women students." At Howard University, African American students called for a "Black Awareness Research

CHAPTER LOCATOR | What liberal reforms were advanced during the Kennedy and Johnson administrations?

CHAPTER 28

790 REFORM, REBELLION, AND REACTION, 1960–1974

Institute" and demanded that academic departments "place more emphasis on how these disciplines may be used to effect the liberation of black people."

Accomplishments of the Student Movement

Curricular reforms, such as the introduction of black studies, Latino studies, and women's studies programs

Increased financial aid for minority and poor students

Independence from paternalistic rules

A larger voice in campus decision making

Student protest bewildered and angered older Americans, even more so when it blended into a cultural revolution against nearly every conventional standard of behavior. Drawing on the ideas of the Beats of the 1950s, the "hippies," as they were called, rejected mainstream values such as materialism, order, and sexual control. Seeking personal rather than political change, they advocated "Do your own thing" and drew attention with their long hair, wildly colorful clothing, and use of illegal drugs. Across the country, thousands of radicals established communes in cities or on farms.

Rock and folk music defined both the counterculture and the political left. Music during the 1960s often carried insurgent political and social messages that reflected radical youth culture. The 1969 Woodstock Music Festival, attended by 400,000 young people, epitomized the centrality of music to the youth rebellion.

The hippies faded away in the 1970s, but many elements of the counterculture—rock music, jeans, and long hair, as well as new social attitudes—filtered into the mainstream. More tolerant approaches to sexual behaviors spawned what came to be called the "sexual revolution," with help from the birth control pill, which became available in the 1960s. Self-fulfillment became a dominant concern of many Americans, and questioning of authority became more widespread.

Gay Men and Lesbians Organize

More permissive sexual norms did not stretch easily to include tolerance of homosexuality. Gay men and lesbians avoided discrimination and ridicule only by concealing their sexual identities. Those who couldn't or wouldn't found themselves fired from jobs, arrested for their sexual activities, deprived of their children, or tagged as "perverted." Some of the first gay activism challenged the government's efforts to keep homosexuals out of the civil service. In October 1965, protesters gathered outside the White House with signs calling discrimination against homosexuals "as immoral as discrimination against Negroes and Jews." Not until ten years later, however, did the Civil Service Commission formally end its antigay policy.

A turning point in gay activism occurred in 1969 when police raided a gay bar, the Stonewall Inn, in New York City's Greenwich Village, and gay men and lesbians fought back. "Suddenly, they were not submissive anymore," a police officer remarked. Energized by the defiance shown at the Stonewall riots, gay

"Country Joe" McDonald's Guitar

The 1969 Woodstock Music Festival featured a wide variety of well-known and lesser-known artists, including the San Francisco–based Country Joe and the Fish, who inspired the crowd of 400,000 with the anti–Vietnam War song "Feel Like I'm Fixin' to Die" rag. The Oakland Museum of California.

| How did the civil rights movement evolve in the 1960s? | What other rights movements emerged in the 1960s? | What were the goals of the new wave of feminism? | How did liberal reform fare under President Nixon? | Conclusion: What were the achievements and limitations of liberalism? |

men and lesbians founded a host of new groups in the years that followed, such as the Gay Liberation Front and the National Gay and Lesbian Task Force.

In 1972, Ann Arbor, Michigan, passed the first antidiscrimination ordinance, and two years later, Elaine Noble's election to the Massachusetts legislature marked the first time an openly gay candidate won state office. In 1973, gay activists persuaded the American Psychiatric Association to remove its designation of homosexuality as a mental disease. By the mid-1970s, gay men and lesbians had established a movement through which they could claim equal rights and express pride in their identities.

A New Movement to Save the Environment

Unlike other social movements, environmentalism was organized around a cause rather than around the identity of its members. The movement that emerged in the 1950s and 1960s resembled the conservation movement born in the Progressive Era (see chapter 21). Especially in the West, post–World War II economic and population growth created increased demands for electricity and water. Environmental groups began mobilizing in the 1950s to stop the construction of dams that would disrupt national parks and wilderness areas.

The new environmentalists, however, went beyond conservationism. Polluted air and water and the use of deadly chemicals threatened the sustainability of human life itself. Biologist Rachel Carson drew national attention to the harmful effects of toxic chemicals such as the pesticide DDT in 1962 with her best seller *Silent Spring*. To the leaders of a new organization, Friends of the Earth, unlimited economic growth was "no longer healthy, but a cancer." The Sierra Club and other older conservation organizations expanded their agendas, and a host of new groups arose.

Responding to these concerns, the federal government staked out a new role in environmental regulation. Lyndon Johnson sent Congress the first presidential message on the environment and signed laws controlling air and water pollution. Richard Nixon's 1970 State of the Union message called "clean air, clean water, open spaces . . . the birthright of every American," and that year he created the **Environmental Protection Agency (EPA)** to enforce clean air and water policies and to regulate pesticides. Congress also passed the Occupational Safety and Health Act (OSHA), protecting workers against workplace accidents and disease, and the Clean Air Act of 1970, setting national standards for air quality and restricting factory and automobile emissions of carbon dioxide and other pollutants.

Nevertheless, the desire for economic growth often trumped environmental concerns. Corporations resisted restrictions. "If you're hungry and out of work, eat an environmentalist," read a union bumper sticker reflecting fears that regulations threatened jobs. Many Americans who wanted to protect the environment also valued economic expansion, personal acquisition, and convenience. Despite these conflicts, the environmental movement achieved cleaner air and water, a reduction in toxic wastes, and some preservation of endangered species and wilderness.

Environmental Protection Agency (EPA)
▶ Federal agency charged with enforcing environmental regulations. Created by President Nixon in 1970, the EPA played a key role in the push toward cleaner air, cleaner water, and a less toxic environment.

> ## QUICK REVIEW

What were the goals and achievements of the other reform movements of the 1960s and 1970s?

CHAPTER LOCATOR | What liberal reforms were advanced during the Kennedy and Johnson administrations?

Cover of the First Issue of *Ms.* Magazine

In 1972, Gloria Steinem and other journalists and writers published the premier issue of the first mass-circulation magazine for and controlled by women. *Ms.: The New Magazine for Women* ignored the recipes and fashion tips of typical women's magazines. It featured literature by women writers and articles on a broad range of feminist issues. Courtesy, Lang Communications.

BECOMING VISIBLE by the late 1960s, a multifaceted women's movement reached its high tide in the 1970s and persisted into the twenty-first century. By that time, despite a powerful countermovement, women had experienced tremendous transformations in their legal status, public opportunities, and personal and sexual relationships, and popular expectations about appropriate gender roles had shifted dramatically.

A Multifaceted Movement Emerges

Beginning in the 1940s, large demographic changes laid the preconditions for a resurgence of feminism. As more women took jobs, the importance of their paid work to the economy and their families challenged traditional views of women and awakened many women workers, especially labor union women, to the inferior conditions of their employment. The democratization of higher education brought more women to college campuses, where their aspirations exceeded the confines of domesticity and of routine, subordinate jobs.

Policy initiatives in the early 1960s reflected both these larger transformations and the efforts of women's rights activists. In 1961, Assistant Secretary of Labor Esther Peterson persuaded President Kennedy to create the President's Commission on the Status of Women (PCSW). In 1963, the commission reported widespread discrimination against women and recommended remedies. One of the PCSW's concerns was addressed even before it issued its report, when Congress passed the Equal Pay Act of 1963, making it illegal to pay women less than men for the same work.

| How did the civil rights movement evolve in the 1960s? | What other rights movements emerged in the 1960s? | **What were the goals of the new wave of feminism?** | How did liberal reform fare under President Nixon? | Conclusion: What were the achievements and limitations of liberalism? |

businesses. Congress took the initiative in other areas. In 1970, it extended the Voting Rights Act of 1965, and in 1972, it strengthened the Civil Rights Act of 1964 by enlarging the powers of the Equal Employment Opportunity Commission.

Several measures of the Nixon administration also specifically attacked sex discrimination. Although the president privately expressed patronizing attitudes about women, he confronted a growing feminist movement that included Republican women. Nixon vetoed a child care bill and publicly opposed abortion, but he signed the pathbreaking Title IX, guaranteeing equality in all aspects of education, and allowed his Labor Department to push affirmative action.

President Nixon gave more public support for justice to Native Americans than to any other group. While not bowing to radical demands, the administration dealt cautiously with extreme protests, such as the occupation of the Bureau of Indian Affairs in Washington, D.C. Nixon signed measures recognizing claims of Alaskan and New Mexican Indians and set in motion legislation restoring tribal lands and granting Indians more control over their schools and other institutions.

> ## QUICK REVIEW

Why and how did Republican president Richard Nixon expand the liberal reforms of previous administrations?

SO NOW YOU KNOW

Republican president Richard Nixon created the Environmental Protection Agency in 1970 in response to the demands of a new environmental movement that sought to limit the spread of toxic pollutants and to conserve nature.

CHAPTER LOCATOR | What liberal reforms were advanced during the Kennedy and Johnson administrations?

© Bob Adelman.

Con
Wh
ach
and
of li

CHAPTER

STEP

THE GREAT SOCIETY expanded the New Deal's focus on economic security and refashioned liberalism to embrace individual rights. Yet opposition to Johnson's leadership grew so strong by 1968 that he abandoned hopes for reelection. Some Americans resented the millions of federal dollars going to the poor and minorities. Others charged that many antipoverty programs benefited industry and professionals more than they did the poor and focused more on fixing individual shortcomings than on economic reforms that would ensure adequately paying jobs for all.

When the civil rights movement attacked racial barriers and sought equality in fact as in law, it faced a powerful backlash. By the end of the 1960s, the revolution in the legal status of African Americans was complete and significant numbers began to enter the middle class, but African Americans remained, with Native Americans and Chicanos, at the bottom of the economic ladder.

The Great Society did contain successful and lasting elements. Medicare and Medicaid provided access to health care for the elderly and the poor and contributed to a sharp decline in poverty among the elderly. Federal aid for education and housing became permanent elements of national policy. Moreover, the Nixon administration implemented school desegregation in the South and affirmative action, expanded environmental regulations, and secured new rights for Native Americans and women.

Yet the perceived shortcomings of government programs contributed to social turmoil and fueled the resurgence of conservative politics. Young radicals launched direct confrontations with the government and universities that, together with racial conflict, escalated into political discord and social disorder. The war in Vietnam polarized American society as much as did racial issues or the behavior of young people, and it devoured resources that might have been used for social reform and undermined faith in presidential leadership.

Below are basic terms from this period in American history. Can you identify each term below and explain why it matters? To do this exercise online or to download this chart, visit bedfordstmartins.com/roarkunderstanding.

1 GETTING STARTED

TERM	WHO OR WHAT & WHEN	WHY IT MATTERS
Civil Rights Act of 1964, p. 778		
Great Society, p. 779		
War on Poverty, p. 779		
Voting Rights Act of 1965, p. 780		
Martin Luther King Jr., p. 783		
March on Washington for Jobs and Freedom, p. 784		
American Indian Movement (AIM), p. 789		
Cesar Chavez/Dolores Huerta, p. 789		
Environmental Protection Agency (EPA), p. 792		
National Organization for Women (NOW), p. 794		
Equal Rights Amendment (ERA), p. 795		
Roe v. Wade, p. 795		

STEP 2 MOVING BEYOND THE BASICS

The exercise below represents a more advanced understanding of the chapter material. Fill in the chart by describing the goals, strategy and tactics, and achievements of the major rights movements of the 1960s. If significant disagreement existed within a group over goals, strategies, or tactics, make sure to include a description of those divisions. When you are finished, ask yourself the following questions: What did the various rights movements of the 1960s have in common? Which movements were most successful and why? To do this exercise online or to download this chart, visit bedfordstmartins.com/roarkunderstanding.

Rights movement	Goals	Strategy and tactics	Achievements
African Americans			
Latinos			
Native Americans			
Students			
Feminists			
Gays and lesbians			
Environmentalists			

Now that you've reviewed various parts of the chapter, take a step back and try to see the big picture by answering these questions. Remember to use specific examples from the chapter in your answers. To do this exercise online, visit bedfordstmartins.com/roarkunderstanding.

LYNDON JOHNSON AND THE GREAT SOCIETY

▶ What were the most important domestic achievements of the Johnson administration? What were its most important failures?

▶ What assumptions about the relationship between government and society underlay Johnson's Great Society programs?

PROTEST AND REBELLION

▶ What role did students play in the civil rights struggles of the 1960s? How did the civil rights movement change toward the end of the decade?

▶ What were the key achievements of 1960s feminism? What goals did it fail to fulfill?

LIBERAL REFORM IN THE NIXON ADMINISTRATION

▶ What liberal initiatives did the Nixon administration embrace, and what explains these actions?

▶ Should Richard Nixon be considered an environmentalist? Why or why not?

LOOKING BACKWARD, LOOKING AHEAD

▶ How did the African American civil rights movement of the 1960s differ from the movement of the 1950s?

▶ What kinds of opposition emerged in the late 1960s to liberal reforms and radical protest? How might that trend influence politics in the decades after the 1960s?

IN YOUR OWN WORDS

Imagine that you must explain chapter 28 to someone who hasn't read it. What would be the most important points to include and why?

29
VIETNAM AND THE LIMITS OF POWER

1961–1975

> This chapter explores U.S. foreign policy from 1961 to 1975, placing American involvement in the Vietnam War in the larger context of American politics and relations with the Soviet Union, China, and developing nations. It examines the escalation of U.S. involvement in Vietnam under Presidents Kennedy and Johnson, the polarizing effect of the war on American society and politics, and the gradual American withdrawal from Vietnam under President Nixon.

> How did American foreign policy change under Kennedy?

> Why did Johnson escalate American involvement in Vietnam?

> How did the war in Vietnam polarize the nation?

> How did American foreign policy change under Nixon?

> Conclusion: Was Vietnam an unwinnable war?

DID YOU KNOW?

The average age of a U.S. soldier in Vietnam was nineteen.

Vietnam. Marines patrol near the demilitarized zone in Vietnam during Operation Prairie, 1966.

Early in his presidency, Kennedy determined to show Khrushchev "that we can be as tough as he is." But when the two met in June 1961 in Vienna, Austria, Khrushchev was belligerent and shook the president's confidence. Khrushchev demanded an agreement recognizing the existence of two Germanys and made veiled threats about America's occupation rights in and access to West Berlin. Khrushchev was concerned about the massive exodus of East Germans into West Berlin, a major embarrassment for the Communists. To stop these escapees, in August 1961 East Germany shocked the world by erecting a wall between East and West Berlin. With the Berlin Wall stemming the tide of migration and Kennedy insisting that West Berlin was "the great testing place of Western courage and will," Khrushchev backed off from his threats.

Kennedy used the Berlin crisis to add $3.2 billion to the defense budget. He increased draft calls and mobilized the reserves and National Guard, adding 300,000 troops to the military. This buildup of conventional forces provided for a "flexible response," offering "a wider choice than humiliation or all-out nuclear action." Still, Kennedy also pushed for the development of new nuclear weapons and delivery systems, more than doubling the nation's nuclear force within three years.

New Approaches to the Third World

Complementing Kennedy's hard-line policy toward the Soviet Union were fresh approaches to the independence movements that had arisen since the end of World War II. Much more than his predecessors, Kennedy publicly supported third world aspirations, believing that the United States could win the hearts and minds of people in developing nations by helping to fulfill hopes for autonomy and democracy. To that end, in 1961 Kennedy created the Alliance for Progress, pledging $20 billion in aid for Latin America over the next decade. Yet, by 1969, the United States had provided only half of the promised $20 billion, much of which went to military projects or corrupt ruling elites.

Kennedy launched his most dramatic third world initiative in 1961 with an idea borrowed from Senator Hubert H. Humphrey: the Peace Corps. The program recruited young people to work in developing countries, attracting many who had been moved by Kennedy's appeal for idealism and sacrifice in his inaugural address. One volunteer's service eased his guilt at having been "born between clean sheets when others were issued into the dust with a birthright of hunger." By the mid-1970s, more than 60,000 volunteers had served in Latin America, Africa, and Asia. Peace Corps projects were generally welcomed, but they did not address the receiving countries' larger economic and political structures.

Kennedy also used direct military means to bring political stability to the third world. He rapidly expanded the elite special forces corps established under Eisenhower to aid groups sympathetic to the United States and fighting against Communist-leaning movements. These counterinsurgency forces, including the army's Green Berets and the navy's SEALs, were trained to wage guerrilla warfare and equipped with the latest technology. They would get their first test in Vietnam.

The Arms Race and the Nuclear Brink

The final piece of Kennedy's defense strategy was to strengthen American nuclear dominance. He upped the number of nuclear weapons based in Europe from 2,500 to 7,200 and multiplied fivefold the supply of intercontinental ballistic missiles (ICBMs).

CHAPTER LOCATOR | How did American foreign policy change under Kennedy?

CHAPTER 29

806 VIETNAM AND THE LIMITS OF POWER, 1961–1975

Concerned that this buildup would enable the United States to launch a first strike and wipe out Soviet missile sites before they could respond, the Soviet Union stepped up its own ICBM program. Thus began the most intense arms race in history.

The **Cuban missile crisis** of 1962 brought the superpowers perilously close to using their weapons when Khrushchev decided to install nuclear missiles in Cuba, while insisting to Kennedy that he had no intention of doing so. Khrushchev wanted to protect Cuba from further U.S. attempts at intervention and to balance the U.S. missiles aimed at the Soviet Union from Britain, Italy, and Turkey. On October 16, the CIA showed Kennedy aerial photographs of missile launching sites under construction in Cuba. On October 22, Kennedy announced that the military was on full alert and that the navy would turn back any Soviet vessel suspected of carrying offensive missiles to Cuba. Kennedy warned that any attack launched from Cuba would trigger a full nuclear assault against the Soviet Union.

With the superpowers on the brink of nuclear war, Kennedy and Khrushchev negotiated an agreement. The Soviets removed the missiles and pledged not to introduce new offensive weapons into Cuba. The United States promised not to invade the island. Secretly, Kennedy also agreed to remove the U.S. missiles from Turkey. The Cuban crisis led to Khrushchev's fall from power two years later, and Kennedy emerged triumphant. The image of an inexperienced president fumbling the Bay of Pigs invasion gave way to that of a strong leader bringing the United States through its "hour of maximum danger."

Having proved his toughness, Kennedy worked with Khrushchev to prevent future confrontations by installing a special "hot line" to speed top-level communication. In a major speech at American University in June 1963, Kennedy called for a reexamination of Cold War assumptions, asking Americans "not to see conflict as inevitable." Acknowledging the superpowers' differences, Kennedy stressed what they had in common: "We all breathe the same air. We all cherish our children's future and we are all mortal." In August 1963, the United States, the Soviet Union, and Great Britain signed a limited nuclear test ban treaty, reducing the threat of radioactive fallout from nuclear testing and raising hopes for further superpower accord.

A Growing War in Vietnam

In his American University speech, Kennedy criticized the idea of "a Pax Americana enforced on the world by American weapons of war," but in 1961 he began to increase the flow of those weapons into South Vietnam. Kennedy's strong anticommunism and attachment to a vigorous foreign policy prepared him to expand the commitment in Vietnam that he had inherited from Eisenhower. By the time Kennedy took office, more than $1 billion in aid and 700 U.S. military advisers had failed to stabilize South Vietnam. Two major obstacles stood in the way. First, the South Vietnamese insurgents—whom Americans called Vietcong, short for *Vietnam Cong-san* ("Vietnamese Communists")—were an indigenous force whose initiative came from within, not from the Soviet Union or China as many American officials supposed. Because the Saigon government refused to hold elections, the rebels saw no choice but to take up arms. Increasingly, Ho Chi Minh's Communist government in North Vietnam supplied them with weapons and soldiers.

Second, the South Vietnamese government and army (ARVN) refused to satisfy the demands of the insurgents but could not defeat them militarily. Ngo Dinh Diem, South Vietnamese premier from 1954 to 1963, chose self-serving military

Cuban missile crisis

▶ Urgent situation provoked by the Soviet decision in 1962 to deploy nuclear missiles in Cuba. When the Americans discovered evidence of the construction of missile launching sites in Cuba, the ensuing confrontation brought the superpowers to the brink of nuclear war. The two sides reached a negotiated settlement, with the Soviet Union agreeing to remove its missiles from Cuba and the United States agreeing to remove its missiles from Turkey.

U.S. blockade zone
Range of Soviet missiles
Soviet missile and jet bomber base

Cuban Missile Crisis, 1962

Why did Johnson escalate American involvement in Vietnam?

How did the war in Vietnam polarize the nation?

How did American foreign policy change under Nixon?

Conclusion: Was Vietnam an unwinnable war?

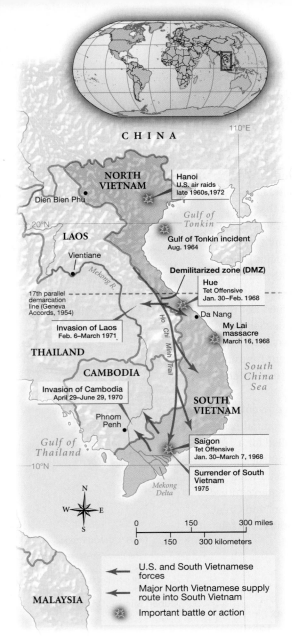

MAP 29.2 ■ The Vietnam War, 1964–1975
The United States sent 2.6 million soldiers to Vietnam and spent more than $150 billion on the longest war in American history, but it was unable to prevent the unification of Vietnam under a Communist government.

▶ FOR MORE HELP ANALYZING THIS MAP, see the map activity for this chapter in the Online Study Guide at bedfordstmartins.com/roarkunderstanding.

leaders for their personal loyalty rather than for their effectiveness. Many South Vietnamese saw Diem as a corrupt and brutal tool of the West. Even Secretary of State Dean Rusk called him "an oriental despot."

The growing intervention by North Vietnam made matters worse. In 1960, the Hanoi government established the National Liberation Front, composed of South Vietnamese rebels but directed by the northern army. In addition, Hanoi constructed a network of infiltration routes, called the Ho Chi Minh Trail, in neighboring Laos and Cambodia, through which it sent people and supplies to help liberate the South (**Map 29.2**). Violence escalated between 1960 and 1963, bringing the Saigon government close to collapse.

Kennedy responded to the deteriorating situation with measured steps, gradually escalating the U.S. commitment. By the spring of 1963, military aid had doubled, and the 9,000 Americans serving in Vietnam as military advisers occasionally participated in actual combat. The South Vietnamese government promised reform but never made good on its promises.

Reflecting racist attitudes of American superiority over nonwhite populations, officials assumed that U.S. technology and sheer power could win in Vietnam. Yet advanced weapons were ill suited to the guerrilla warfare practiced by the enemy, whose surprise attacks were designed to weaken support for the South Vietnamese government. In addition, U.S. weapons and strategy harmed the very people they were intended to save. Thousands of peasants were uprooted and resettled in "strategic hamlets," supposedly secure from the Communists. Those left in the countryside fell victim to bombs—containing the highly flammable substance napalm—dropped by the South Vietnamese air force to quell the Vietcong. In January 1962, U.S. planes began to spray herbicides such as Agent Orange to destroy the Vietcong's jungle hideouts and food supply.

With tacit permission from Washington, South Vietnamese military leaders executed a coup against Diem and his brother, who headed the secret police, on November 2, 1963. Kennedy expressed shock that the two had been murdered but indicated no change in policy. In a speech to be given on the day he was assassinated, he referred specifically to Southeast Asia and warned, "We dare not weary of the task." At his death, 16,700 Americans were stationed in Vietnam, and 100 had died there.

> ## QUICK REVIEW

Why did Kennedy believe that engagement in Vietnam was crucial to American foreign policy?

CHAPTER LOCATOR | How did American foreign policy change under Kennedy?

CHAPTER 29
808 VIETNAM AND THE LIMITS OF POWER, 1961–1975

Why did Johnson escalate American involvement in Vietnam?

American Soldiers Confront the South Vietnamese

The unconventional nature of the Vietnam War often resulted in U.S. soldiers harming the very people they were sent to save. In this photo, a trooper of the U.S. First Cavalry stands guard while a medic treats South Vietnamese civilians who had been wounded during a search-and-destroy mission that destroyed their hamlet near Da Nang in October 1967. © Bettmann/Corbis.

THE COLD WAR ASSUMPTIONS that had shaped Kennedy's foreign policy underlay his successor's approach to Southeast Asia and Latin America. Retaining Kennedy's key advisers—Secretary of State Dean Rusk, Secretary of Defense Robert McNamara, and National Security Adviser McGeorge Bundy—**Lyndon B. Johnson** continued the massive buildup of nuclear weapons and conventional and counterinsurgency forces. Then in 1965, Johnson made the fateful decisions to order U.S. troops into combat and to initiate sustained bombing of the North.

An All-Out Commitment in Vietnam

The president who wanted to make his mark on domestic policy was compelled to deal with the commitments his predecessors had made to stopping communism in Vietnam. Early in Johnson's administration, the public paid little attention to Vietnam and seemed willing to follow the administration's lead. Yet some advisers, politicians, and international leaders raised questions about the wisdom of a greater commitment in Vietnam. Senate majority leader Mike Mansfield wondered whether Vietnam could be won with a "limited expenditure of American lives and resources somewhere commensurate with our national interests." Senate Armed Services Committee member Richard Russell warned, "It'd take a half million men. They'd be bogged down there for ten years."

Johnson disregarded the opportunity for disengagement that these critics saw in 1964 and expanded the United States' military involvement. Along with most of his advisers, he believed that American credibility was on the line.

Lyndon B. Johnson

▶ Texas Democrat who served as U.S. president from 1963 to 1969. Johnson continued President Kennedy's buildup of nuclear weapons and conventional forces. In 1965, Johnson sent U.S. forces to prop up the South Vietnamese government, bringing the United States directly into the Vietnam War. The difficult, costly, and unpopular war in Vietnam undermined Johnson's presidency.

| Why did Johnson escalate American involvement in Vietnam? | How did the war in Vietnam polarize the nation? | How did American foreign policy change under Nixon? | Conclusion: Was Vietnam an unwinnable war? |

CHRONOLOGY

1963
– President Kennedy is assassinated; Lyndon B. Johnson becomes president.

1964
– Anti-American rioting in Panama Canal Zone.
– Congress grants the president broad powers to wage war in Vietnam with the Gulf of Tonkin Resolution.

1965
– Operation Rolling Thunder, the gradual intensification of the bombing of North Vietnam, begins.
– Johnson orders the first combat troops to Vietnam.
– U.S. troops invade the Dominican Republic.

Gulf of Tonkin Resolution

► 1964 congressional resolution granting President Johnson the authority to widen the war in Vietnam. The resolution came in the wake of a confrontation between U.S. naval forces and the North Vietnamese in the Gulf of Tonkin. Although there was much uncertainty about the precise nature of the events involved, Johnson used the confrontation as a justification for increasing American military pressure on North Vietnam.

Moreover, the president's own credibility also came into play. Like Kennedy, he feared the domestic political repercussions of disengagement without victory. His own insecurities and fear of being compared unfavorably with Kennedy precluded a course that might make him appear soft or cowardly.

Johnson understood the ineffectiveness of his South Vietnamese allies and agonized over sending young men into combat. Yet he continued to dispatch more military advisers, weapons, and economic aid and, in August 1964, seized an opportunity to increase the pressure on North Vietnam. During a routine espionage mission in the Gulf of Tonkin, off the coast of North Vietnam, two U.S. destroyers reported that North Vietnamese gunboats had fired on them (see Map 29.2, page 808). Johnson quickly ordered air strikes on North Vietnamese torpedo bases and oil storage facilities. Concealing the uncertainty about whether the second attack had even occurred and the provocative U.S. operations along the North Vietnamese coast, he won from Congress the **Gulf of Tonkin Resolution,** granting him authority to take "all necessary measures to repel any armed attacks against the forces of the United States and to prevent further aggression."

Soon after winning the election in 1964, Johnson widened the war. He rejected peace overtures from North Vietnam, which insisted on American withdrawal and a coalition government in South Vietnam as steps toward ultimate unification of the country. Instead, in February 1965, Johnson authorized Operation Rolling Thunder, a strategy of gradually intensified bombing of North Vietnam. Less than a month later, Johnson ordered the first U.S. combat troops to South Vietnam, and in July he shifted U.S. troops from defensive to offensive operations, dispatching 50,000 more soldiers (**Figure 29.1**). Although the administration downplayed the import of these decisions, they marked a critical turning point. Now it was genuinely America's war.

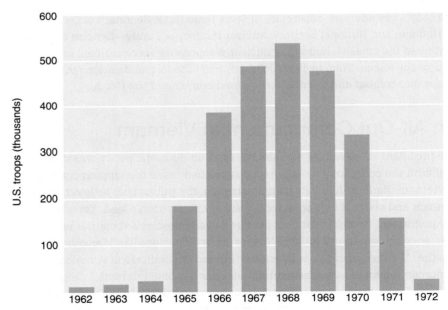

FIGURE 29.1 ■ U.S. Troops in Vietnam, 1962–1972
The steepest increases in the American military presence in Vietnam came in 1965 and 1966. Although troop levels declined significantly in 1971 and 1972, the United States continued massive bombing attacks.

CHAPTER LOCATOR | How did American foreign policy change under Kennedy?

Preventing Another Castro in Latin America

Closer to home, Johnson faced persistent problems in Latin America. Thirteen times during the 1960s, military coups toppled Latin American governments, and local insurgencies grew apace. The administration's response varied from case to case but centered on the determination to prevent any more Castro-type revolutions.

In 1964, riots erupted in the Panama Canal Zone, which the United States had seized and made a U.S. territory early in the twentieth century (see chapter 21). Instigated by Panamanians who viewed the United States as a colonial power, the riots left four U.S. soldiers and more than twenty Panamanians dead. Johnson sent troops to quell the disturbance, but he also initiated negotiations that eventually returned the canal to Panamanian authority in 2000.

Elsewhere, Johnson's Latin American policy generated new cries of "Yankee imperialism." In 1961, voters in the Dominican Republic ousted a longtime dictator and elected a constitutional government headed by reformist Juan Bosch, who was overthrown by a military coup two years later. In 1965, when Bosch supporters launched an uprising against the military government, Johnson sent more than 20,000 soldiers to quell what he perceived to be a leftist revolt and to take control of the island. A truce was arranged, and in 1966 Dominicans voted in a constitutional government under a moderate rightist.

This first outright show of force in Latin America in four decades damaged the administration at home and abroad. Although the administration had justified intervention on the grounds that Communists were among the rebels, it quickly became clear that they had played no significant role, and U.S. actions kept the reform-oriented Boschists from returning to power. Moreover, the president had not consulted the Dominicans or the Organization of American States (OAS), to which the United States had pledged that it would respect national sovereignty in Latin America.

The Americanized War

The military success in the Dominican Republic no doubt encouraged the president to press on in Vietnam. From 1965 to early 1968, the United States gradually escalated attacks against the North Vietnamese and their Vietcong allies. Over the course of the war, U.S. pilots dropped 3.2 million tons of explosives, more than the United States had dropped in all of World War II. Claiming monthly death tolls of more than 2,000 North Vietnamese, the intensive bombing nonetheless failed to dampen the Hanoi government's commitment.

On the ground, General William Westmoreland's strategy of attrition was designed to seek out and kill the Vietcong and soldiers in the North Vietnamese regular army. The military used helicopters extensively to conduct offensives all over South Vietnam. Because there was no battlefront as in previous wars, officials calculated progress not in territory seized but in "body counts" and

U.S. Troops in the Dominican Republic

These U.S. paratroopers were among the 20,000 troops sent to the Dominican Republic in April and May 1965. The American invasion helped restore peace but kept the popularly elected government of Juan Bosch from regaining office. Outraged Dominicans painted anti-American slogans throughout the capital, Santo Domingo, and Bosch himself said, "This was a democratic revolution smashed by the leading democracy in the world." © Bettmann/Corbis.

| Why did Johnson escalate American involvement in Vietnam? | How did the war in Vietnam polarize the nation? | How did American foreign policy change under Nixon? | Conclusion: Was Vietnam an unwinnable war? |

"kill ratios"—the number of enemies killed relative to the cost in American and ARVN lives.

Teenagers fought the Vietnam War. In contrast to World War II, in which the average soldier was twenty-six years old, the average soldier in Vietnam was nineteen. Men of all classes had fought in World War II, but in Vietnam, the poor and working class constituted about 80 percent of the troops. More-privileged youths avoided the draft by using college deferments or family connections to get into the National Guard. Sent from Plainville, Kansas, to Vietnam in 1965, Mike Clodfelter could not recall "a single middle-class son of the town's businessmen, lawyers, doctors, or ranchers from my high school graduating class who experienced the Armageddon of our generation."

Much more than World War II, Vietnam was a men's war. Because the United States did not undergo full mobilization for Vietnam, officials did not seek women's sacrifices for the war effort. Still, between 7,500 and 10,000 women served in Vietnam, the vast majority of them nurses.

Early in the war, African Americans constituted 31 percent of combat troops, often choosing the military over the meager opportunities in the civilian economy. Special forces ranger Arthur E. Woodley Jr. recalled, "I was just what my country needed. A black patriot. . . . The only way I could possibly make it out of the ghetto was to be the best soldier I possibly could." Death rates among black soldiers were disproportionately high until 1966, when the military adjusted personnel assignments to achieve a better racial balance.

The young troops faced extremely difficult conditions. Soldiers fought in thick jungles and swamps filled with leeches, in rain and oppressive heat. Lieutenant Philip Caputo remembered "conducting vicious manhunts through jungles and swamps where snipers harassed us constantly and booby traps cut us down one by one." The U.S. military inflicted great losses on the enemy, yet the war remained a stalemate.

The South Vietnamese government was an enormous obstacle to victory, even though in 1965 it settled into a period of stability headed by two military leaders. Graft and corruption continued to flourish in the government. In the intensified fighting and inability to distinguish friend from foe, ARVN and American troops killed and wounded thousands of South Vietnamese civilians and destroyed their villages. By 1968, nearly 30 percent of the population had become refugees. The failure to stabilize South Vietnam even as the U.S. military presence expanded enormously created grave challenges for the administration at home.

> ## QUICK REVIEW

How did the experiences of American troops serving in Vietnam differ from those who served in World War II?

CHAPTER LOCATOR | How did American foreign policy change under Kennedy?

CHAPTER 29
812 VIETNAM AND THE LIMITS OF POWER, 1961–1975

How did the war in Vietnam polarize the nation?

Protest in Chicago The worst violence surrounding the 1968 Democratic National Convention in Chicago came on August 28 when protesters assembled in Grant Park preparing to march to the convention site. Near the Hilton Hotel, where most of the delegates stayed, some 3,000 protesters came up against a line of police. The police attacked not only the demonstrators but also reporters, hotel guests, and bystanders with nightsticks and mace. AP Images/Michael Boyer.

SOON PRESIDENT JOHNSON was fighting a war on two fronts. Domestic opposition to the war swelled after 1965 as daily television broadcasts made it the first "living-room war." In March 1968, torn between his domestic critics and the military's clamor for more troops, Johnson announced restrictions on the bombing, a new effort at negotiations, and his decision not to pursue reelection. Throughout 1968, demonstrations, violence, and assassinations convulsed the increasingly polarized nation.

The Widening War at Home

Johnson's authorization of Operation Rolling Thunder expanded the previously quiet doubts and criticism into a mass movement against the war. In April 1965, Students for a Democratic Society (SDS) recruited 20,000 people for the first major demonstration against the war in Washington, D.C. Thousands of students protested against the presence of Reserve Officers Training Corps (ROTC) programs, CIA recruiters, and defense industry research and recruiters on their campuses. Martin Luther King Jr. deployed his moral authority, rebuking the U.S. government in 1967 as "the greatest purveyor of violence in the world today." Environmentalists attacked the use of chemical weapons, such as the deadly Agent Orange. In the spring of 1968, as many as one million students participated in a nationwide strike.

Antiwar sentiment entered society's mainstream. The *New York Times* began questioning the war in 1965, and by 1968 there were many more media critics. Clergy, business people, scientists, and physicians formed their own groups to pressure Johnson to stop the bombing and start negotiations. Prominent

CHRONOLOGY

1965
– First major demonstration against Vietnam War.

1967
– U.S. troop strength in Vietnam nears half a million, and total military deaths approach 20,000.

1968
– Demonstrations against Vietnam War increase.
– Tet Offensive, a series of attacks by North Vietnam on cities and U.S. bases in South Vietnam, begins.
– Johnson decides not to seek a second term.
– Peace negotiations between the United States and North Vietnam begin in Paris.
– Martin Luther King Jr. and Senator Robert F. Kennedy are assassinated.
– Police and protesters clash near the Democratic convention in Chicago.

Democratic senators urged Johnson to substitute negotiation for force. Although the peace movement never claimed a majority of the population, it focused media attention on the war and severely limited the administration's options. The twenty-year-old consensus around Cold War foreign policy had broken down.

Many would not fight in the war. More than 170,000 men who opposed the war on moral or religious grounds gained conscientious objector status and performed nonmilitary duties at home or in Vietnam. About 60,000 fled the country to escape the draft, and more than 200,000 were accused of failing to register or of committing other draft offenses.

Opponents of the war held diverse views. Those who saw the conflict in moral terms wanted total withdrawal, insisting that their country had no right to interfere in a civil war and stressing the suffering of the Vietnamese people. A larger segment of antiwar sentiment reflected practical considerations—the belief that the war could not be won at a bearable cost. Those activists wanted Johnson to stop bombing North Vietnam and seek negotiations. Working-class people were no more antiwar than other groups, but they recognized the class dimensions of the war and the antiwar movement. A firefighter whose son had died in Vietnam said bitterly, "It's people like us who give up our sons for the country."

The antiwar movement outraged millions of Americans who supported the war. Some members of the generation who had fought against Hitler could not understand younger men's refusal to support their government. They expressed their anger at war protesters with bumper stickers that read "America: Love It or Leave It."

By 1967, the administration realized that "discontent with the war is now wide and deep." President Johnson used various means to silence critics. His administration deceived the public by making optimistic statements and concealing officials' doubts about the possibility of victory. Johnson ordered the CIA to spy on peace advocates, and without the president's specific authorization, the FBI infiltrated the peace movement, disrupted its work, and spread false information about activists.

Pro-War Demonstrators

Advocates as well as opponents of the war in Vietnam took to the streets, as these New Yorkers did in support of the U.S. invasion of Cambodia in May 1970. Construction workers—called "hard hats"—and other union members marched with American flags and posters championing President Nixon's policies and blasting New York mayor John Lindsay for his antiwar position. Paul Fusco/Magnum Photos, Inc.

▶ FOR MORE HELP ANALYZING THIS IMAGE, see the visual activity for this chapter in the Online Study Guide at bedfordstmartins.com/roarkunderstanding.

CHAPTER LOCATOR | How did American foreign policy change under Kennedy?

1968: Year of Upheaval

The year 1968 was marked by violent confrontations around the world. Protests against governments erupted from Mexico City to Paris to Tokyo, usually led by students in collaboration with workers. American society also became increasingly polarized. On one side, the so-called hawks charged that the United States was fighting with one hand tied behind its back and called for intensification of the war. The doves wanted de-escalation or withdrawal. As U.S. troop strength neared half a million and military deaths approached 20,000 by the end of 1967, most people were torn between weariness with the war and a desire to fulfill the U.S. commitment. As one woman said, "I want to get out but I don't want to give up."

Grave doubts penetrated the administration itself in 1967. Secretary of Defense Robert McNamara, a principal architect of U.S. involvement, now believed that the North Vietnamese "won't quit no matter how much bombing we do." He feared for the image of the United States, "the world's greatest superpower, killing or seriously injuring 1,000 noncombatants a week, while trying to pound a tiny, backward nation into submission on an issue whose merits are hotly disputed." McNamara did not publicly oppose the war, but in early 1968 he left the administration.

A critical turning point came with the **Tet Offensive.** On January 30, 1968, the North Vietnamese and Vietcong launched attacks on key cities and every major American base in South Vietnam. Militarily, the Communists suffered a defeat, losing ten times as many soldiers as ARVN and U.S. forces. Psychologically, however, Tet was devastating to the United States.

The Tet Offensive underscored the credibility gap between official statements and the war's actual progress. TV anchorman Walter Cronkite wondered, "What the hell is going on? I thought we were winning the war." The attacks created a million more South Vietnamese refugees as well as widespread destruction. Explaining how he had defended a village, a U.S. Army official said, "We had to destroy the town to save it." The statement epitomized for more and more Americans the brutality and senselessness of the war. Public approval of Johnson's handling of the war dropped to 26 percent.

In the aftermath of Tet, Johnson conferred with advisers in the Defense Department and an unofficial group of foreign policy experts who had been key architects of Cold War policies for two decades. Dean Acheson, Truman's secretary of state, summarized their conclusion: "We can no longer do the job we set out to do in the time we have left and we must begin to take steps to disengage."

On March 31, 1968, Lyndon Johnson announced in a televised speech that the United States would reduce its bombing of North Vietnam and pursue peace negotiations. He added the stunning declaration that he would not run for reelection. The gradual escalation of the war was over, and military strategy shifted from "Americanization" to "Vietnamization" of the war. The goal remained a non-Communist South Vietnam; the United States would simply rely more heavily on the South Vietnamese to achieve it.

Negotiations began in Paris in May 1968. The United States would not agree to recognition of the Hanoi government's National Liberation Front, to a coalition government, or to American withdrawal. The North Vietnamese would agree to nothing less. Although the talks continued, so did the fighting.

Meanwhile, violence escalated at home. Protests occurred on two hundred college campuses in the spring of 1968. In the bloodiest action, students occupied buildings at Columbia University in New York City. When negotiations failed,

Tet Offensive

▶ January 30, 1968, attack by North Vietnamese and Vietcong forces on key cities and every major American base in South Vietnam. Militarily, the Communists suffered a defeat, losing ten times as many soldiers as ARVN and U.S. forces, but the attacks cast doubts on the optimistic statements of U.S. leaders about the war.

| Why did Johnson escalate American involvement in Vietnam? | How did the war in Vietnam polarize the nation? | How did American foreign policy change under Nixon? | Conclusion: Was Vietnam an unwinnable war? |

university officials called in the city police, who cleared the buildings, injuring scores of demonstrators and arresting hundreds. An ensuing student strike prematurely ended the academic year.

In June, two months after the murder of Martin Luther King Jr. and the riots that followed, another assassination shook the nation. Antiwar candidate Senator Robert F. Kennedy, campaigning in California for the Democratic Party's presidential nomination, was shot by a Palestinian Arab refugee who was outraged by Kennedy's support for Israel.

In August, protesters battled the police in Chicago, where the Democratic Party had convened to nominate its presidential ticket. Several thousand demonstrators came to the city, some to support the peace candidate Senator Eugene McCarthy, others to cause disruption. On August 25, when demonstrators jeered at orders to disperse, police attacked them with tear gas and clubs. Street battles continued for three days, culminating in a police riot on the night of August 28. Taunted by the crowd, the police used mace and nightsticks, clubbing not only those who had come to provoke violence but also reporters, peaceful demonstrators, and convention delegates. Although the bloodshed in Chicago horrified those who saw it on television, it had little effect on the convention's outcome. Vice President Hubert H. Humphrey trounced the remaining antiwar candidate, McCarthy, by nearly three to one for the Democratic nomination.

In contrast to the turmoil around the **1968 Democratic convention,** the Republican convention met peacefully and nominated former vice president Richard Nixon on the first ballot. A strong third candidate entered the electoral scene when the American Independent Party nominated former Alabama governor and staunch segregationist George C. Wallace. Wallace appealed to those Americans who were dissatisfied with the reforms and rebellions of the 1960s and outraged at the assaults on traditional values. Nixon guardedly played on the resentments that fueled the Wallace campaign, calling for "law and order."

Nixon and Humphrey differed little on the central issue of Vietnam. Nixon promised "an honorable end" to the war but did not indicate how he would achieve it. Humphrey had strong reservations about U.S. policy in Vietnam, yet as vice president he was tied to Johnson's policies. With nearly 13 percent of the total popular vote, the American Independent Party produced the strongest third-party finish since 1924. Nixon edged out Humphrey by just half a million popular votes but garnered 301 electoral college votes to Humphrey's 191 and Wallace's 46. The Democrats maintained control of Congress.

The 1968 election revealed deep cracks in the coalition that had kept the Democrats in power for most of the previous thirty years. Johnson's liberal policies on race shattered a century of Democratic Party dominance in the South, which delivered all its electoral votes to Wallace and Nixon. Elsewhere, large numbers of blue-collar workers broke union ranks to vote for Wallace or Nixon, as did other groups that associated the Democrats with racial turmoil, poverty programs, changing sexual mores, and failure to turn the tide in Vietnam. These resentments would soon be mobilized into a resurging right in American politics (see chapter 30).

1968 Democratic convention

▶ Site of violent confrontations between antiwar demonstrators and Chicago police that took place in late August of that year. After taunting by some in the crowd, the police responded with mace and nightsticks, clubbing both disruptive and peaceful protesters as well as reporters and convention delegates. The bloodshed horrified those who witnessed it but had little effect on the convention's outcome.

> **QUICK REVIEW**

How did the Vietnam War affect the election of 1968?

CHAPTER LOCATOR | How did American foreign policy change under Kennedy?

How did American foreign policy change under Nixon?

Nixon in China

Nixon's trip to China was meticulously planned to dramatize the event on television and, aside from criticism from some conservatives, won overwhelming support from Americans. The Great Wall of China forms the setting for this photograph of Nixon and his wife, Pat. Nixon Presidential Materials Project, National Archives and Record Administration.

RICHARD M. NIXON took office with ambitious foreign policy goals, hoping to make his mark on history by applying his broad understanding of international relations to a changing world. Diverging from Republican orthodoxy, he made dramatic overtures to the Soviet Union and China. Yet anticommunism remained central to U.S. policy. Nixon backed repressive regimes around the world and aggressively pursued the war in Vietnam, expanding the conflict into Cambodia and Laos and ordering ferocious bombing of North Vietnam. Yet in the end, he was forced to settle for peace without victory.

Moving toward Détente with the Soviet Union and China

Well aware of the increasing conflict between the Soviet Union and China, Nixon worked with National Security Adviser **Henry A. Kissinger,** his key foreign policy adviser, to exploit the situation. Following two years of secret negotiations, in February 1972 Nixon became the nation's first president to set foot on Chinese soil. Although his visit was largely symbolic, cultural and scientific exchanges followed, and American manufacturers began to find markets in China—small steps in the process of globalization that would take giant strides in the 1990s (see chapter 31).

As Nixon and Kissinger had hoped, the warming of U.S.-Chinese relations furthered their strategy of détente, their term for easing conflict with the Soviet Union. Détente did not mean abandoning containment; instead, it involved focusing on issues of common concern, such as arms control and trade. Containment would be achieved not only by military threat but also by ensuring that the Soviets and Chinese had stakes in a stable international order. Nixon's goal was "a stronger healthy United States, Europe, Soviet Union, China, Japan, each balancing the other."

Richard M. Nixon

▶ Republican president who narrowly won the 1968 election and held office until his resignation in 1974. He made dramatic overtures in pursuit of détente with both the Soviet Union and China and oversaw the eventual withdrawal of American troops from Vietnam.

Henry A. Kissinger

▶ Key foreign policy adviser to President Nixon. Kissinger and Nixon pursued a policy of détente, their term for easing conflict with the Soviet Union. To this end, they pursued closer relationships with both China and the Soviet Union, not abandoning containment, but instead focusing on issues of common concern, such as arms control and trade.

Why did Johnson escalate American involvement in Vietnam? | How did the war in Vietnam polarize the nation? | How did American foreign policy change under Nixon? | Conclusion: Was Vietnam an unwinnable war?

817

1967
- Arab-Israeli Six-Day War.

1968
- Republican Richard Nixon is elected president.

1969
- Nixon orders secret bombing of Cambodia.

1970
- Students are killed during protests at Kent State University and Jackson State College.

1971
- *New York Times* publishes the *Pentagon Papers*.

1972
- Nixon visits China and the Soviet Union.

1973
- Paris Peace Accords.
- CIA-backed military coup in Chile.
- Yom Kippur War leads to Arab oil embargo.

1975
- North Vietnam takes over South Vietnam, ending the war.

Strategic Arms Limitation Talks (SALT)

▶ 1972 treaty between the United States and the Soviet Union in which the superpowers agreed to limit antiballistic missiles (ABMs) to two each. Limiting the capacity to mount a defense against nuclear attacks was significant because it prevented either nation from building so secure an ABM defense against a nuclear attack that it would risk a first strike.

Arms control, trade, and stability in Europe were three areas where the United States and the Soviet Union had common interests. In May 1972, Nixon visited Moscow, signing several agreements on trade and cooperation in science and space. Most significantly, Soviet and U.S. leaders concluded arms limitation treaties that had grown out of the **Strategic Arms Limitation Talks (SALT)** begun in 1969, agreeing to limit antiballistic missiles (ABMs) to two each. Giving up pursuit of a defense against nuclear weapons was a crucial move, because it prevented either nation from building so secure an ABM defense against a nuclear attack that it would risk a first strike against the other.

Although the policy of détente made little progress after 1974, U.S., Soviet, and European leaders signed a historic agreement in 1975 in Helsinki, Finland, that formally recognized the post–World War II boundaries in Europe. The Helsinki accords were controversial because they acknowledged Soviet domination over Eastern Europe—a condition that had triggered the Cold War thirty years earlier. Yet they also contained a clause committing the signing countries to recognize "the universal significance of human rights and fundamental freedoms." Dissidents in the Soviet Union and its Eastern European satellites used this official promise of rights to challenge the Soviet dictatorship.

Shoring Up Anticommunism in the Third World

Nixon promised in 1973 that "[t]he time has passed when America will make every other nation's conflict our own . . . or presume to tell the people of other nations how to manage their own affairs." Yet in Vietnam and elsewhere, Nixon and Kissinger continued to view left-wing movements as threats to U.S. interests and actively resisted social revolutions that might lead to communism.

Consequently, the Nixon administration helped to overthrow Salvador Allende, a self-proclaimed Marxist who was elected president of Chile in 1970.

Chile

Since 1964, the Central Intelligence Agency (CIA) and U.S. corporations concerned about nationalization of their Chilean properties had assisted Allende's opponents. After Allende became president, Nixon ordered the CIA director to destabilize his government. In 1973, the CIA helped the Chilean military engineer a coup, killing Allende and establishing a brutal dictatorship under General Augusto Pinochet.

In other parts of the world, too, the Nixon administration stood by repressive regimes. In southern Africa, it eased pressures on white minority governments that tyrannized blacks. In the Middle East, the United States sent massive arms shipments to support the shah of Iran's harsh regime because Iran had enormous petroleum reserves and seemed a stable anti-Communist ally.

Like his predecessors, Nixon pursued a delicate balance between defending Israel's

CHAPTER LOCATOR | How did American foreign policy change under Kennedy?

818 CHAPTER 29 VIETNAM AND THE LIMITS OF POWER, 1961–1975

security and seeking the goodwill of Arab nations strategically and economically important to the United States. Conflict between Israel and the Arab nations had escalated into the **Six-Day War** in 1967, when Israel attacked Egypt after that nation had massed troops on its border and cut off the sea passage to Israel's southern port. Although Syria and Jordan joined the war on Egypt's side, Israel won a stunning victory, seizing territory that amounted to twice its original size.

That decisive victory did not quell Middle Eastern turmoil. In October 1973, on the Jewish holiday Yom Kippur, Egypt and Syria surprised Israel with a full-scale attack. When the Nixon administration sided with Israel in the Yom Kippur War, Arab nations retaliated with an oil embargo that created severe shortages in the United States. After Israel repulsed the attack, Kissinger attempted to mediate between Israel and the Arab nations, but with very limited success. The Arab countries refused to recognize Israel's right to exist, Israel began to settle its citizens in territories occupied during the Six-Day War, and no solution could be found for the Palestinian refugees who had been displaced by the creation of Israel in the late 1940s. The simmering conflict contributed to anti-American sentiment among Arabs who viewed the United States as Israel's supporter.

Vietnam Becomes Nixon's War

"I'm going to stop that war. Fast," Nixon asserted. He withdrew U.S. ground troops, but he was unwilling to be the president who allowed South Vietnam to fall to the Communists. That goal was tied to the larger objective of maintaining American credibility. Regardless of the wisdom of the initial intervention, Kissinger asserted, "the commitment of 500,000 Americans has settled the importance of Vietnam. For what is involved now is confidence in American promises."

From 1969 to 1972, Nixon and Kissinger pursued a four-pronged approach. First, they tried to strengthen the South Vietnamese military and government. Second, to disarm the antiwar movement at home, Nixon gradually replaced U.S. forces with South Vietnamese soldiers and American technology and bombs. Third, the United States negotiated with both North Vietnam and the Soviet Union. Fourth, the military applied intensive bombing to persuade Hanoi to accept American terms at the bargaining table.

As part of the Vietnamization of the war, ARVN forces grew to more than a million, and the South Vietnamese air force became the fourth largest in the world. The United States also promoted land reform, village elections, and the building of schools, hospitals, and transportation facilities. Meanwhile, U.S. forces withdrew, decreasing from 543,000 in 1968 to 140,000 by the end of 1971.

In the spring of 1969, Nixon began a ferocious air war in Cambodia, carefully hiding it from Congress and the public for more than a year. Seeking to knock out North Vietnamese sanctuaries in Cambodia, Americans dropped more than 100,000 tons of bombs but succeeded only in sending the North Vietnamese to other hiding places. Echoing Johnson, Kissinger believed that a "fourth-rate power like North Vietnam" had to have a "breaking point," but the massive bombing failed to find it.

To support a new, pro-Western Cambodian government installed through a military coup in 1970 and "to show the enemy that we were still serious about our commitment in Vietnam," Nixon ordered a joint U.S.-ARVN invasion of Cambodia in April 1970. That order made Vietnam "Nixon's war" and provoked outrage at

Israeli Territorial Gains in the Six-Day War, 1967

Six-Day War

▶ 1967 conflict between Israel and the Arab nations of Egypt, Syria, and Jordan. Israel attacked Egypt after that nation had massed troops on its border and cut off the sea passage to Israel's southern port. Although Syria and Jordan joined the war on Egypt's side, Israel won a stunning victory, seizing territory that amounted to twice its original size.

U.S. Invasion of Cambodia, 1970

**Kent State University/
Jackson State College**

▶ College campuses that were the sites of violent confrontations between demonstrating students and those sent to disperse them. On May 4, 1970, at Ohio's Kent State, nervous National Guard troops fired at students who were protesting the war in Vietnam, killing four and wounding ten others. On May 14, 1970, police called to Jackson State College shot into a dormitory and killed two black students.

Pentagon Papers

▶ Secret government documents published by the *New York Times* in 1971 consisting mostly of an internal study of the war begun in 1967. The documents undermined public trust in government by revealing that officials harbored considerable pessimism even as they made rosy public pronouncements about the progress of the war. Government efforts to stop publication of the documents were blocked by the Supreme Court.

home. Nixon made a belligerent speech defending his move and emphasizing the importance of U.S. credibility: "If when the chips are down, the world's most powerful nation acts like a pitiful helpless giant, the forces of totalitarianism and anarchy will threaten free nations" everywhere.

In response, more than 100,000 people protested in Washington, D.C., and students boycotted classes on hundreds of campuses. At **Kent State University** in Ohio, National Guard troops were dispatched after protesting students burned an old ROTC building. Then, at a rally there on May 4, when some students threw rocks at the troops, guardsmen fired at the students, killing four and wounding ten others. "They're starting to treat their own children like they treat us," commented a black woman in Harlem. In a confrontation at **Jackson State College** in Mississippi on May 14, police shot into a dormitory, killing two black students.

In their determination to win the war in Vietnam, Johnson and Nixon had taken extreme measures to deceive the public and silence their critics. The bombing and invasion of Cambodia infuriated enough legislators that the Senate voted to terminate the Gulf of Tonkin Resolution, which had given the president virtually a blank check in Vietnam, and to cut off funds for the Cambodian operation. The House refused to go along, but by the end of June, Nixon had pulled all U.S. troops out of Cambodia.

In 1971, Vietnam veterans became a visible part of the peace movement, the first men in U.S. history to protest a war in which they had fought. Veterans held a public investigation of "war crimes" in Vietnam, rallied in front of the Capitol, and cast away their war medals. In May 1971, veterans numbered among the 40,000 protesters who engaged in civil disobedience in an effort to shut down Washington. Officials made more than 12,000 arrests, which courts later ruled violations of protesters' rights.

After the spring of 1971, there were fewer massive antiwar demonstrations, but protest continued. Public attention focused on the court-martial of Lieutenant William Calley, which began in November 1970. During the trial, Americans learned that in March 1968, Calley's company had systematically killed every inhabitant of the hamlet of My Lai, even though they had encountered no enemy forces there. These four hundred villagers were nearly all old men, women, and children. The military covered up the atrocity for more than a year before a journalist exposed it. Eventually, twelve officers and enlisted men faced charges ranging from murder to dereliction of duty for covering up the massacre, but only Calley was convicted—of premeditated murder.

Administration policy suffered another blow in June 1971 when the *New York Times* published the **Pentagon Papers**, an internal government study of the war begun in 1967. Even though the study did not cover the Nixon administration, government lawyers went to court to stop further publication. The Supreme Court, however, ruled that the attempt to stop publication was a violation of the First Amendment. Subsequent circulation of the *Pentagon Papers*, which revealed considerable pessimism among officials even as they made rosy promises, heightened disillusionment with the war by casting doubts on the government's credibility. More than 60 percent of Americans polled in 1971 considered it a mistake to have sent American troops to Vietnam; 58 percent believed the war to be immoral.

Military morale sank in the last years of the war. Having been exposed to the antiwar movement at home, many of the remaining soldiers had less faith in the war than their predecessors had had. Racial tensions among soldiers mounted,

CHAPTER LOCATOR | How did American foreign policy change under Kennedy?

820 CHAPTER 29 VIETNAM AND THE LIMITS OF POWER, 1961–1975

Kent State Shootings

On May 4, 1970, John Filo, a photojournalism student at Kent State University in Ohio, decided to take pictures of students demonstrating against President Nixon's recently announced decision to invade Cambodia. He observed several hundred protesters, some of whom threw rocks at National Guardsmen, who in turn sprayed tear gas toward the students. Suddenly, some guardsmen opened fire, killing four students and wounding ten. Filo took this photograph of fourteen-year-old runaway Mary Ann Vecchio sobbing over the dead body of Kent State student Jeffrey Miller. John Filo.

▶ FOR MORE HELP ANALYZING THIS IMAGE, see the visual activity for this chapter in the Online Study Guide at bedfordstmartins.com/roarkunderstanding.

many soldiers sought escape in illegal drugs, and enlisted men committed hundreds of "fraggings," attacks on officers. In a 1971 report, a retired Marine Corps colonel described the lack of discipline: "Our army that now remains in Vietnam [is] near mutinous."

The Peace Accords and the Legacy of Defeat

Nixon and Kissinger continued to believe that intensive firepower could bring the North Vietnamese to their knees. In March 1972, responding to a strong North Vietnamese offensive, the United States resumed sustained bombing of the North, mined Haiphong and other harbors for the first time, and announced a naval blockade. With peace talks stalled, in December Nixon ordered the most devastating bombing of North Vietnam yet.

The intense bombing was costly to both sides, but it brought renewed negotiations. On January 27, 1973, representatives of the United States, North Vietnam,

| Why did Johnson escalate American involvement in Vietnam? | How did the war in Vietnam polarize the nation? | How did American foreign policy change under Nixon? | Conclusion: Was Vietnam an unwinnable war? |

821

Evacuating South Vietnam

As Communist troops rolled south toward Saigon in the spring of 1975, desperate South Vietnamese attempted to flee along with the departing Americans. These South Vietnamese, carrying little or nothing, attempt to scale the wall of the U.S. Embassy to reach evacuation helicopters. Thousands of Vietnamese who wanted to be evacuated were left behind.
AP Images.

South Vietnam, and the Vietcong signed a formal peace accord in Paris. The agreement required removal of all U.S. troops and military advisers but allowed North Vietnamese forces to remain. Both sides agreed to return prisoners of war. Nixon called the agreement "peace with honor," but in fact it allowed only a face-saving withdrawal for the United States.

Fighting resumed immediately among the Vietnamese. Nixon's efforts to support the South Vietnamese government were hampered by what came to be known as the Watergate scandal (see chapter 30). Nixon was forced to resign in 1974, and in 1975 North Vietnam launched a new offensive. On April 30, it occupied Saigon and renamed it Ho Chi Minh City to honor the Communist leader. The Americans hastily evacuated, along with 150,000 of their South Vietnamese allies.

Confusion, humiliation, and tragedy marked the rushed departure. The United States lacked sufficient transportation capabilities and time to evacuate all the South Vietnamese who had supported the South Vietnamese government and were desperate to leave. One journalist reported that his departing helicopter "took some ground fire from South Vietnamese soldiers who probably felt that the Americans had betrayed them."

During the four years it took Nixon to end the war, he had expanded the conflict into Cambodia and Laos and had launched massive bombing campaigns. Although increasing numbers of legislators criticized the war, Congress never denied the president the funds to fight it. Only after the peace accords did the legislative branch stiffen its constitutional authority in the making of war, passing the War Powers Act in November 1973. The law required the president to report to Congress within forty-eight hours of deploying military forces abroad. If Congress failed to endorse the president's action within sixty days, the troops would have to be withdrawn. The new law, however, did little to dispel the distrust of and disillusionment with the government that resulted from Americans' realization that their leaders had not told the truth about Vietnam.

The disorder that had accompanied antiwar protests and bitter divisions among Americans were other legacies of the war. Vietnam created federal budget deficits and triggered inflation that contributed to ongoing economic crises throughout the 1970s (see chapter 30).

Four presidents had declared that the survival of South Vietnam was essential for U.S. containment policy, but their dire predictions that a Communist victory in South Vietnam would set the dominoes cascading did not materialize. Although Vietnam, Laos, and Cambodia all fell within the Communist camp in the spring of 1975, Thailand, Burma, Malaysia, and the rest of Southeast Asia did not. When China and Vietnam reverted to their historically hostile relationship, the myth of a monolithic Communist power overrunning Asia evaporated.

CHAPTER LOCATOR | How did American foreign policy change under Kennedy?

The cruelest legacy of Vietnam fell on those who had served. The failure of the United States to win the war, the war's unpopularity at home, and its character as a guerrilla war denied veterans the traditional soldiers' homecoming. Many believed in the war's purposes and felt betrayed by the government for not letting them win it. Other veterans blamed the government for sacrificing the nation's youth in an immoral or unnecessary war, expressing their sense of the war's futility by referring to their dead comrades as having been "wasted." Some veterans belonging to minority groups had more reason to doubt the nobility of their purpose. A Native American soldier assigned to resettle Vietnamese civilians saw that as "just like when they moved us to the rez [reservation]. We shouldn't have done that."

Because the Vietnam War was a civil war involving guerrilla tactics, combat was especially brutal (**Table 29.1**). The terrors of conventional warfare were multiplied, and so were the motivations to commit atrocities. To demonstrate the immorality of the war, peace advocates stressed the atrocities, contributing to a distorted image of the Vietnam veteran as dehumanized and violent. Most veterans came home to public neglect; some faced harassment from antiwar activists who failed to distinguish the war from the warriors. Yet two-thirds of Vietnam veterans said that they would serve again, and most veterans readjusted well to civilian life.

Nonetheless, some suffered long after the war ended. The Veterans Administration (VA) estimated that nearly one-sixth of the veterans suffered from post-traumatic stress disorder, with its symptoms of recurring nightmares, feelings of guilt and shame, violence, drug and alcohol abuse, and suicidal tendencies. Thirty years after performing army intelligence work in Saigon, Doris Allen "still hit the floor sometimes when [she heard] loud bangs." Many of those who had served in Vietnam began to produce deformed children and fell ill themselves with cancer and other ailments. Veterans claimed a link between those illnesses and Agent Orange, a poisonous herbicide that the military had sprayed over Vietnam. Not until 1991 did Congress provide assistance to veterans with diseases linked to the poison.

By then, the climate had changed. The war began to enter the realm of popular culture, with novels, TV shows, and hit movies depicting a broad range of military experience—from soldiers reduced to brutality to men and women serving with courage and integrity. The incorporation of the Vietnam War into the collective experience was symbolized most dramatically in the Vietnam Veterans Memorial unveiled in Washington, D.C., in November 1982. Designed by Yale architecture student Maya Lin, the black, V-shaped wall inscribed with the names of 58,200 men and women lost in the war became one of the most popular sites in the nation's capital. In an article describing the memorial's dedication, a Vietnam combat veteran spoke to and for his former comrades: "Welcome home. The war is over."

TABLE 29.1 ■ Vietnam War Casualties

United States	
Battle deaths	47,434
Other deaths	10,786
Wounded	153,303
South Vietnam	
Killed in action	110,357
Military wounded	499,026
Civilians killed	415,000
Civilians wounded	913,000
Communist Regulars and Guerrillas	
Killed in action	66,000

Source: U.S. Department of Defense.

QUICK REVIEW

What were the lasting legacies of American involvement in Vietnam?

Why did Johnson escalate American involvement in Vietnam?

How did the war in Vietnam polarize the nation?

How did American foreign policy change under Nixon?

Conclusion: Was Vietnam an unwinnable war?

Conclusion: Was Vietnam an unwinnable war?

Larry Burrows.

VIETNAM WAS AMERICA's longest war. The United States spent more than $150 billion (nearly $600 billion in 2010 dollars) and sent 2.6 million young men and women to Vietnam. Of those, 58,200 never returned, and 150,000 suffered serious injury. The war shattered consensus at home, increased presidential power at the expense of congressional authority and public accountability, weakened the economy, and contributed to the downfall of two presidents.

Even as Nixon and Kissinger took steps to ease Cold War tensions with the major Communist powers—the Soviet Union and China, which were also the main suppliers of the North Vietnamese—they also acted vigorously throughout the third world to install or prop up anti-Communist governments. They embraced their predecessors' commitment to South Vietnam as a necessary Cold War engagement: To do otherwise would threaten American credibility and make the United States appear weak. Defeat in Vietnam did not make the United States the "pitiful helpless giant" predicted by Nixon, but it did mark a relative decline of U.S. power and the impossibility of containment on a global scale.

One of the constraints on U.S. power was the tenacity of revolutionary movements determined to achieve national independence. Overestimating the effectiveness of American technological superiority, U.S. officials badly underestimated

CHAPTER LOCATOR | How did American foreign policy change under Kennedy?

the sacrifices that the enemy was willing to make and failed to realize how easily the United States could be perceived as a colonial intruder.

A second constraint on Eisenhower, Kennedy, Johnson, and Nixon was their resolve to avoid a major confrontation with the Soviet Union or China. For Johnson, who conducted the largest escalation of the war, caution was especially critical so as not to provoke direct intervention by the Communist superpowers. After China exploded its first atomic bomb in 1964, the potential heightened for the Vietnam conflict to escalate into worldwide disaster.

Third, in Vietnam the United States sought to prop up an extremely weak ally engaged in a civil war. The South Vietnamese government failed to win the support of its people, and short of taking over the South Vietnamese government and military, the United States could do little to strengthen South Vietnam's ability to resist communism.

Finally, domestic opposition to the war, which by 1968 had spread to mainstream America, constrained the options of Johnson and Nixon. As the war dragged on, with increasing American casualties and growing evidence of the damage being inflicted on innocent Vietnamese, more and more civilians wearied of the conflict. In 1973, Nixon and Kissinger bowed to the resoluteness of the enemy and the limitations of U.S. power. As the war wound down, passions surrounding it contributed to a rising conservative movement that would substantially alter the post–World War II political order.

SO NOW YOU KNOW

The Vietnam War was fought primarily by young men who faced extremely grim conditions during their one-year tours of duty and who came home to public neglect. Young men and women also organized the first major antiwar protests in 1965 and spurred an antiwar movement that broke down the consensus about Cold War foreign policy and divided the American public.

STEP 1

GETTING STARTED

Below are basic terms from this period in American history. Can you identify each term below and explain why it matters? To do this exercise online or to download this chart, visit bedfordstmartins.com/roarkunderstanding.

TERM	WHO OR WHAT & WHEN	WHY IT MATTERS
John F. Kennedy, p. 804		
Cuban missile crisis, p. 807		
Lyndon B. Johnson, p. 809		
Gulf of Tonkin Resolution, p. 810		
Tet Offensive, p. 815		
1968 Democratic convention, p. 816		
Richard M. Nixon, p. 817		
Henry A. Kissinger, p. 817		
Strategic Arms Limitation Talks (SALT), p. 818		
Six-Day War, p. 819		
Kent State University/Jackson State College, p. 820		
Pentagon Papers, p. 820		

STEP 2

MOVING BEYOND THE BASICS

The exercise below represents a more advanced understanding of the chapter material. In the chart, list the key American policy decisions regarding Vietnam between 1961 and 1974. Then explain the rationale and impact of each decision. When you are done, consider the following questions: Why was the United States drawn ever deeper into the Vietnam conflict? At what points, if any, could policymakers have reversed course? How was U.S. involvement in Vietnam shaped by policymakers' larger vision of global politics? To do this exercise online or to download this chart, visit bedfordstmartins.com/roarkunderstanding.

	Policy Decision	Rationale	Impact
Kennedy administration			
Johnson administration			
Nixon administration			

Now that you've reviewed various parts of the chapter, take a step back and try to see the big picture by answering these questions. Remember to use specific examples from the chapter in your answers. To do this exercise online, visit bedfordstmartins.com/roarkunderstanding.

KENNEDY'S FOREIGN POLICY

► How did Kennedy's view of America's place in the world affect his foreign policy decisions in 1961 and 1962?

► How were Kennedy's decisions with respect to Vietnam shaped by the Cold War?

JOHNSON AND VIETNAM

► Why did Lyndon Johnson disregard some of his advisers who urged him to disengage from Vietnam?

► How did the divisions over Vietnam contribute to Nixon's election in 1968?

NIXON'S FOREIGN POLICY

► What impact did Nixon's strategies in Vietnam have on the United States?

► How did Nixon's approach to foreign policy differ from that of his predecessors?

LOOKING BACKWARD, LOOKING AHEAD

► How did American foreign policy in the 1950s set the stage for the escalation of U.S. involvement in Vietnam in the 1960s?

► How did American foreign policy change between 1961 and 1975? What impact did the Vietnam conflict have on these changes?

IN YOUR OWN WORDS

Imagine that you must explain chapter 29 to someone who hasn't read it. What would be the most important points to include and why?

30
THE CONSERVATIVE TURN

1969–1989

> This chapter explores the rise of conservatism as a major force in late-twentieth-century American politics. It examines the emergence of new strands of conservatism in the 1960s, the evolution of conservatism in the post-Watergate years, and its full expression in the politics and policies of Ronald Reagan.

DID YOU KNOW?

The United States' original involvement in Afghanistan occurred as part of U.S. efforts to contain the Soviet Union during the Cold War.

> How did the Nixon presidency reflect the rise of postwar conservatism?

> Why was the Watergate scandal significant?

> Why did the "outsider" presidency of Jimmy Carter fail to gain broad support?

> What conservative goals were realized in the Reagan administration?

> What strategies did liberals use to fight the conservative turn?

> How did Ronald Reagan's foreign policy affect the Cold War?

> Conclusion: What was the long-term impact of the conservative turn?

Inauguration of Ronald Reagan, 1981. Chief Justice Warren Burger administers the oath of office to President Ronald Reagan.

How did the Nixon presidency reflect the rise of postwar conservatism?

School Busing Controversy over busing as a means to integrate public schools erupted in Boston when the 1974–1975 school year started. Clashes between blacks and whites in Boston, such as this one in February 1975 outside Boston's Hyde Park High School, prompted authorities to dispatch police to protect black students. AP/Wide World.

AS WE SAW IN CHAPTER 28, Nixon acquiesced in the continuation of most Great Society programs and even approved pathbreaking environmental and minority and women's rights measures. Yet his public rhetoric and some of his actions signaled the country's rightward move in both politics and sentiment. Whereas Kennedy had appealed to Americans to contribute to the common good, Nixon invited Americans to "let each of us ask—not just what will government do for me, but what can I do for myself?" His words invoked individualism and reliance on the market and private enterprise rather than on government.

During Nixon's presidency, a new strand of conservatism, focused on "traditional values," joined the older movement that focused on anticommunism, a strong national defense, and a limited federal role in domestic affairs.

Emergence of a Grassroots Movement

Hidden beneath Lyndon Johnson's landslide victory over Arizona senator Barry Goldwater in 1964 lay a rising conservative movement. Defining his purpose as "enlarging freedom at home and safeguarding it from the forces of tyranny abroad," Goldwater argued that government intrusions into economic life hindered prosperity, stifled personal responsibility, and interfered with individuals' rights to determine their own values. Conservatives assailed big government in domestic affairs but demanded a strong military to eradicate "Godless communism."

Behind Goldwater's nomination was a growing grassroots movement. Grassroots conservatism was not limited to the West and South, but a number of Sun Belt characteristics made it especially strong in places such as Orange

CHAPTER LOCATOR | How did the Nixon presidency reflect the rise of postwar conservatism? | Why was the Watergate scandal significant?

830 CHAPTER 30 THE CONSERVATIVE TURN, 1969–1989

County, California; Dallas, Texas; and Scottsdale, Arizona. Such predominantly white areas contained relatively homogeneous, skilled, and economically comfortable populations, as well as military bases and defense production facilities. The West harbored a long-standing tradition of Protestant morality, individualism, and opposition to interference by a remote federal government. That tradition continued with the emergence of the New Right, even though it was hardly consistent with the Sun Belt's economic dependence on defense spending and on huge federal projects providing water and power for the burgeoning region. The South, which also benefited from military bases and the space program, shared the West's antipathy toward the federal government. Hostility to racial change, however, was much more central to the South's conservatism. After signing the Civil Rights Act of 1964, President Lyndon Johnson remarked privately, "I think we just delivered the South to the Republican Party." Indeed, Barry Goldwater carried five southern states in 1964.

Grassroots movements proliferated around what conservatives believed marked the "moral decline" of their nation. For example, in 1962, Mel and Norma Gabler succeeded in getting the Texas board of education to drop books that they found not in conformity with "the Christian-Judeo morals, values, and standards as given to us by God through . . . the Bible." Sex education roused the ire of Eleanor Howe in Anaheim, California, who felt that "nothing [in the sex education curriculum] depicted my values. . . . It wasn't so much the information. It was the shift in values." The Supreme Court's liberal decisions on issues such as school prayer, obscenity, and birth control also galvanized conservatives to restore "traditional values."

In the 1970s, grassroots protests against taxes grew alongside concerns about morality. As Americans struggled with inflation and unemployment, many also found themselves paying higher taxes, especially higher property taxes as the value of their homes increased. In 1978, Californians passed a popular referendum, reducing property taxes by more than one-half and limiting the state legislature's ability to raise taxes. Similar antitax crusades soon appeared in other states.

Nixon Courts the Right

In his 1968 presidential campaign, Richard Nixon exploited hostility to black protest and new civil rights policies, wooing white southerners and a considerable number of northern voters away from the Democratic Party. As president, he used this "southern strategy" to make further inroads into traditional Democratic strongholds in the 1972 election.

The Nixon administration reluctantly enforced court orders to achieve high degrees of integration in southern schools, but it resisted efforts to deal with segregation outside the South. In northern and western cities, where segregation resulted from discrimination in housing and in the drawing of school district boundaries, half of all African American children attended nearly all-black schools. After courts began to order the transfer of students between schools in white and black neighborhoods to achieve desegregation, busing became an incendiary political issue.

Violence erupted in Boston in 1974 when a district judge found that school officials had maintained what amounted to a dual system based on race and ordered busing "if necessary to achieve a unitary school system." When black

CHRONOLOGY

1964
– Barry Goldwater's nomination for president reflects growing conservative movement.

1968
– Republican Richard Nixon is elected president.

1969
– Warren E. Burger is appointed chief justice of U.S. Supreme Court.

1971
– Nixon vetoes comprehensive child care bill.

1974
– Violence erupts in Boston over school busing.

1978
– Supreme Court ruling in *Regents of University of California v. Bakke* limits affirmative action.

Percent of black students statewide attending schools more than 50% white

	60% or more		30–40%
	50–60%		20–30%
	40–50%		20% or less

Integration of Public Schools, 1968

| Why did the "outsider" presidency of Jimmy Carter fail to gain broad support? | What conservative goals were realized in the Reagan administration? | What strategies did liberals use to fight the conservative turn? | How did Ronald Reagan's foreign policy affect the Cold War? | Conclusion: What was the long-term impact of the conservative turn? |

students began to attend the formerly all-white South Boston High School, white students boycotted classes, and angry whites threw rocks at black students disembarking from buses.

White parents and students eventually became more accepting of integration, especially after the creation of magnet schools and other new mechanisms for desegregation offered more choice. Nonetheless, integration propelled white flight to the suburbs. By 1987, the number of white students in Boston public schools was just one-third of what it had been in 1974.

Nixon's judicial appointments also reflected the southern strategy. He criticized the Supreme Court under Chief Justice Earl Warren for being "unprecedentedly politically active . . . using their interpretation of the law to remake American society according to their own social, political, and ideological precepts." When Warren resigned in 1969, Nixon replaced him with Warren E. Burger, a federal appeals court judge who was a strict constructionist—someone inclined to interpret the Constitution narrowly and to limit government intervention on behalf of individual rights. The Burger Court proved more sympathetic than the Warren Court to the president's agenda, but it continued to uphold many of the liberal programs of the 1960s. For example, the Court limited the range of affirmative action in *Regents of the University of California v. Bakke* (1978), but it allowed affirmative action programs to attack the results of past discrimination if they avoided strict quotas or racial classifications.

Nixon's southern strategy and other repercussions of the civil rights revolution of the 1960s ended the Democratic hold on the "solid South." A number of conservative southern Democrats changed their party affiliation in the 1960s and 1970s, and by 2005, Republicans held the majority of southern seats in Congress and governorships in seven southern states.

In addition to exploiting racial fears, Nixon aligned himself with those anxious about women's changing roles and new demands. In 1971, he vetoed a bill providing federal funds for day care centers with a message that combined the old and new conservatism. Parents should purchase child care services "in the private, open market," he insisted, not through government programs. He appealed to social conservatives by warning about the measure's "family-weakening implications." In response to the movement to liberalize abortion laws, Nixon sided with "defenders of the right to life of the unborn," anticipating the Republican Party's eventual embrace of the issue.

> QUICK REVIEW

How did Nixon's policies reflect conservatives' increasing influence on the Republican Party?

CHAPTER LOCATOR | How did the Nixon presidency reflect the rise of postwar conservatism? | Why was the Watergate scandal significant?

CHAPTER 30
832 THE CONSERVATIVE TURN, 1969–1989

Why was the Watergate scandal significant?

NIXON WON A RESOUNDING VICTORY in the 1972 election. Two years later, however, the so-called Watergate scandal caused him to abandon his office. His successor, Gerald Ford, helped restore confidence in the presidency, but the aftermath of Watergate and severe economic problems returned the White House to the Democrats in 1976. Nonetheless, the rising conservative tide not only survived the temporary setback when Nixon resigned the presidency but also quickly challenged the Democratic administration that followed.

The Election of 1972

Nixon's ability to appeal to concerns about Vietnam, race, law and order, and traditional morality heightened his prospects for reelection in 1972. Although the war in Vietnam continued, antiwar protests diminished with the end of the draft and the decrease in American ground forces and casualties. Nixon's economic initiatives had temporarily checked inflation and unemployment (see chapter 28), and his attacks on busing and antiwar protesters had appealed to the right, positioning him favorably for the 1972 election.

A large field of contenders vied for the Democratic nomination, including New York representative Shirley Chisholm, the first African American to make a serious bid for the presidency. South Dakota senator George S. McGovern came to the Democratic convention as the clear leader and was easily nominated. Nonetheless, McGovern struggled against Nixon from the outset. Republicans portrayed him as a leftist extremist, and his support for busing, a generous welfare program, and immediate withdrawal from Vietnam alienated conservative Democrats.

Why did the "outsider" presidency of Jimmy Carter fail to gain broad support?	What conservative goals were realized in the Reagan administration?	What strategies did liberals use to fight the conservative turn?	How did Ronald Reagan's foreign policy affect the Cold War?	Conclusion: What was the long-term impact of the conservative turn?

Watergate

▶ The 1972 break-in at Democratic Party headquarters in the Watergate complex by men working for President Nixon's re-election, along with Nixon's efforts to cover it up. The Watergate scandal led to President Nixon's resignation.

Nixon achieved a landslide victory, winning 60.7 percent of the popular vote and every state except Massachusetts. Although the Democrats maintained control of Congress, Nixon won majorities among traditional Democrats—southerners, Catholics, urbanites, and blue-collar workers. Shortly after the election, however, revelations began to emerge about crimes committed to ensure the victory.

Watergate

During the early-morning hours of June 17, 1972, five men working for Nixon's reelection campaign crept into Democratic Party headquarters in the Watergate complex in Washington, D.C. Intending to repair a bugging device installed in an earlier break-in, they were discovered and arrested. Nixon and his aides then tried to cover up the intruders' connection to administration officials, setting the stage for the scandal reporters dubbed **Watergate**.

Nixon was not the first president to lie to the public or to misuse power. Every president since Franklin D. Roosevelt had enlarged the powers of his office, justifying his actions as necessary to protect national security. This expansion of executive powers weakened the traditional checks and balances on the executive branch and opened the door to abuses. No president, however, had dared go as far as Nixon, who saw opposition to his policies as a personal attack and was willing to violate the Constitution to stop it. Upon learning of the Watergate arrests, Nixon plotted to conceal links between the burglars and the White House while publicly denying any connection. In April 1973, after investigations by a grand jury and the Senate suggested that White House aides had been involved, Nixon accepted official responsibility for Watergate but denied any knowledge of the break-in or cover-up. He also announced the resignations of three White House aides and the attorney general. In May, he authorized the appointment of an independent special prosecutor, Archibald Cox, to conduct an investigation.

Meanwhile, speaking before a Senate investigating committee headed by Democrat Samuel J. Ervin of North Carolina, White House counsel John Dean described projects to harass "enemies" through tax audits and other illegal means and implicated the president in efforts to cover up the Watergate break-in. A White House aide struck the most damaging blow when he disclosed that all conversations in the Oval Office were taped. Both Cox and the Ervin committee immediately asked for the tapes related to Watergate. When Nixon refused, citing executive privilege and separation of powers, Cox and Ervin took their case to court.

Additional disclosures exposed Nixon's misuse of federal funds and tax evasion. In August 1973, Vice President Spiro Agnew resigned after an investigation revealed that he had taken bribes while governor of Maryland. Nixon's choice of House minority leader Gerald Ford of Michigan to succeed Agnew won widespread approval, but Agnew's resignation further tarnished the administration, and Nixon's popular support plummeted to 27 percent.

In February 1974, the House of Representatives voted to begin an impeachment investigation. In April, Nixon began to release edited transcripts of the tapes. The transcripts revealed Nixon's orders to aides in March 1973: "I don't give a shit what happens. I want you all to stonewall it, let them plead the Fifth Amendment, cover up or anything else, if it'll save it—save the plan."

CHAPTER LOCATOR | How did the Nixon presidency reflect the rise of postwar conservatism? | Why was the Watergate scandal significant?

CHAPTER 30
834 THE CONSERVATIVE TURN, 1969–1989

In July 1974, the House Judiciary Committee voted to present articles of impeachment against the president to the House. Ordered by a unanimous Supreme Court to hand over the remaining tapes, Nixon released transcripts on August 5 that contained his conversations about how to hinder the FBI's investigation of the break-in. This was sufficient evidence to seal his fate.

In July 1974, the House Judiciary Committee considered specific charges for impeachment: (1) obstruction of justice, (2) abuse of power, (3) contempt of Congress, (4) unconstitutional waging of war by the secret bombing of Cambodia, and (5) tax evasion and the selling of political favors. The committee voted to take the first three charges to the House, where a vote of impeachment seemed certain. Ordered by a unanimous Supreme Court to hand over the remaining tapes, Nixon released transcripts on August 5 that contained his conversations about how to hinder the FBI's investigation of the break-in. This was sufficient evidence to seal his fate.

Nixon announced his resignation to a national television audience on August 8, 1974. Acknowledging some incorrect judgments, he insisted that he had always tried to do what was best for the nation. The next morning, Nixon ended an emotional farewell to his staff with some advice: "Always remember, others may hate you, but those who hate you don't win unless you hate them, and then you destroy yourself."

The Ford Presidency and the 1976 Election

Upon taking office, **Gerald R. Ford** announced, "Our long nightmare is over." But he shocked many Americans one month later when he granted Nixon a pardon "for all offenses against the United States which he . . . has committed or may have committed or taken part in" during his presidency. This sweeping pardon saved Nixon from nearly certain indictment and trial, and it provoked a tremendous outcry from Congress and the public.

Congress's efforts to guard against the types of abuses revealed in the Watergate investigations had only limited effects. The Federal Election

Gerald R. Ford

▶ House minority leader from Michigan who became Nixon's vice president in 1973 and president in 1974, when Nixon resigned. Ford was popular for his integrity and humility, but his decision to pardon Nixon provoked widespread outrage and strengthened the Democratic Party.

Why did the "outsider" presidency of Jimmy Carter fail to gain broad support?	What conservative goals were realized in the Reagan administration?	What strategies did liberals use to fight the conservative turn?	How did Ronald Reagan's foreign policy affect the Cold War?	Conclusion: What was the long-term impact of the conservative turn?

James Earl "Jimmy" Carter Jr.

▶ Democratic president who served from 1977 until 1981 and moved the party away from the liberalism of the 1960s. Carter's modest lifestyle, religious commitment, and status as a Washington outsider appealed to a nation reeling from the scandals of the Nixon administration. Nevertheless, his performance in office in the face of domestic and foreign crises did not inspire confidence, and he lost his bid for reelection.

Campaign Act of 1974 established public financing of presidential campaigns and imposed some restrictions on contributions to help prevent the selling of political favors. Yet politicians found other ways of raising money, such as through political action committees (PACs). Moreover, in *Buckley v. Valeo* (1976), the Supreme Court struck down limitations on campaign spending as violations of freedom of speech. Ever-larger campaign donations flowed to candidates from interest groups, corporations, labor unions, and wealthy individuals.

Special investigating committees in Congress discovered a host of illegal FBI and CIA activities stretching back to the 1950s, including harassment of political dissenters and plots to assassinate Fidel Castro and other foreign leaders. In response to these revelations, President Ford established new controls on covert operations, and Congress created permanent committees to oversee the intelligence agencies. Yet these measures did little to diminish the public's cynicism about their government.

Disillusionment grew as the Ford administration struggled with serious economic problems. Ford carried these burdens into the election campaign of 1976, while contending with a major challenge from the Republican right. Blasting Nixon's and Ford's foreign policy of détente for causing the "loss of U.S. military supremacy," California governor Ronald Reagan came close to capturing the nomination.

The Democrats nominated **James Earl "Jimmy" Carter Jr.**, former governor of Georgia. Carefully prepared on policy issues, Carter appealed to the rise of evangelical religion and alienation from government by stressing his faith as a "born-again Christian" and his distance from the government in Washington. Although he selected liberal senator Walter F. Mondale of Minnesota as his running mate, Carter's nomination nonetheless marked a rightward turn in the party.

Carter had considerable appeal as a candidate who carried his own bags, lived modestly, and taught a Bible class at his Baptist church. He also benefited from Ford's failure to solve the country's economic problems, which helped him win the traditional Democratic coalition of blacks, organized labor, and ethnic groups, and even recapture some of the white southerners who had voted for Nixon in 1972. Nonetheless, Carter received just 50 percent of the popular vote to Ford's 48 percent (**Map 30.1**).

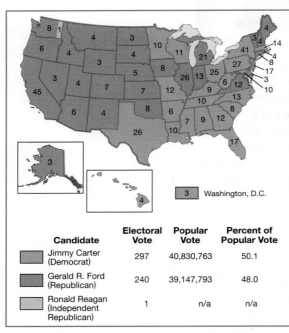

Candidate	Electoral Vote	Popular Vote	Percent of Popular Vote
Jimmy Carter (Democrat)	297	40,830,763	50.1
Gerald R. Ford (Republican)	240	39,147,793	48.0
Ronald Reagan (Independent Republican)	1	n/a	n/a

MAP 30.1 ■ The Election of 1976

> **QUICK REVIEW**

What impact, if any, did Watergate have on the political fortunes of the conservative movement?

CHAPTER LOCATOR | How did the Nixon presidency reflect the rise of postwar conservatism? | Why was the Watergate scandal significant?

Why did the "outsider" presidency of Jimmy Carter fail to gain broad support?

Jimmy Carter's Inauguration

After his inauguration in January 1977, Jimmy Carter shunned the customary presidential limousine and instead walked with his wife, daughter, and two sons and their wives down Pennsylvania Avenue from the Capitol to the White House. Carter wanted to emphasize his opposition to some of the trappings of office that separated government from the people. Jimmy Carter Presidential Library.

JIMMY CARTER PROMISED a government that was "competent" as well as "decent, open, fair, and compassionate." He also warned Americans "that even our great Nation has its recognized limits, and that we can neither answer all questions nor solve all problems." Carter's humility and personal integrity helped revive trust in the presidency, but he lost support as he struggled with domestic and foreign crises.

Retreat from Liberalism

Jimmy Carter vowed "to help the poor and aged, to improve education, and to provide jobs," but at the same time "not to waste money." When these goals conflicted, reform took second place to budget balancing. Increasing numbers of Americans unhappy about their tax dollars being used to benefit the disadvantaged while a poor economy eroded their own material status welcomed Carter's approach. But his fiscal stringency frustrated liberal Democrats, who accused him of deserting the Democratic reform tradition stretching back to Franklin D. Roosevelt.

A number of factors hindered Carter's ability to lead. His outsider status contributed to his election but left him without strong ties to party leaders in Congress. Democrats complained of inadequate consultation and Carter's tendency to flood them with comprehensive proposals when they were more accustomed to incremental reforms. In addition, Carter refused to offer simple solutions to the American people, who were impatient for quick action to fix the economy. But the economic problems Carter inherited—unemployment, inflation, and sluggish economic growth—confounded economic doctrine. Usually, rising prices accompanied a growing economy with a strong demand for labor. Now, however, the nation faced steep inflation and high unemployment at the same time, a combination called stagflation.

Why did the "outsider" presidency of Jimmy Carter fail to gain broad support?	What conservative goals were realized in the Reagan administration?	What strategies did liberals use to fight the conservative turn?	How did Ronald Reagan's foreign policy affect the Cold War?	Conclusion: What was the long-term impact of the conservative turn?

1976
- Democrat Jimmy Carter is elected president.

1977
- Carter signs Panama Canal treaty.

1978
- Congress deregulates the airlines.
- Congress passes National Energy Act of 1978.

1979
- Iranian revolution overthrows the shah of Iran and institutes a fundamentalist Islamic government.
- In the Camp David accords, Egypt is the first Arab state to recognize Israel.
- Carter establishes formal diplomatic relations with China.
- Accident occurs at Three Mile Island nuclear facility.
- Hostage crisis in Iran begins.
- Soviet Union invades Afghanistan.

1980
- Congress deregulates the banking, trucking, and railroad industries.
- Inflation surpasses 13 percent.

Carter first targeted unemployment, signing bills that pumped $14 billion into the economy through public works and public service jobs programs and cut taxes by $34 billion. Unemployment receded, but then inflation surged. Working people, wrote one journalist, "winced and ached" as their paychecks bought less and less. To curb inflation, Carter curtailed federal spending, and the Federal Reserve Board tightened the money supply. Not only did these measures fail to halt inflation, which surpassed 13 percent in 1980, but they also contributed to rising unemployment, reversing the gains made in Carter's first two years.

Carter's commitment to holding down the federal budget frustrated Democrats pushing for comprehensive welfare reform, national health insurance, and a substantial jobs program that would make government the employer of last resort. Carter did sign legislation to ensure solvency in the Social Security system, but the measure increased both employer and employee contributions, thereby increasing the tax burden on lower- and middle-income Americans.

By contrast, corporations and wealthy individuals gained from new legislation, such as a sharp cut in the capital gains tax. When the Chrysler Corporation approached bankruptcy in 1979, Congress provided $1.5 billion in loan guarantees to bail out the tenth-largest corporation in the country. Congress also acted on Carter's proposals to deregulate the airlines in 1978 and the banking, trucking, and railroad industries in 1980. Carter's successor would move much further, implementing conservatives' attachment to a free market and unfettered private enterprise.

Energy and Environmental Reform

Complicating the government's efforts to deal with stagflation were the nation's enormous consumption of energy and its dependence on foreign nations to fill one-third of its energy demands. Consequently, Carter proposed a comprehensive program to conserve energy, and he elevated its importance by establishing the Department of Energy. Responding to Carter's proposal, Congress passed the National Energy Act of 1978, which penalized manufacturers of gas-guzzling automobiles and provided other incentives for conservation and development of alternative fuels, but the act fell far short of a long-term, comprehensive program.

In 1979, a new upheaval in the Middle East, the Iranian revolution, created the most severe energy crisis yet. In midsummer, shortages caused 60 percent of gasoline stations to close down, resulting in long lines and high prices. "We are struggling with a profound transition from a time of abundance to a time of

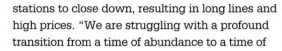

The 1980 Fuel Shortage

This billboard was sponsored by the Outdoor Advertising Association of America in 1980, while Iran held Americans hostage in Teheran and gasoline shortages and rising gas prices vexed motorists all over the country. John W. Hartman Center/Duke University Special Collections Library.

▶ FOR MORE HELP ANALYZING THIS IMAGE, see the visual activity for this chapter in the Online Study Guide at bedfordstmartins.com/roarkunderstanding.

CHAPTER LOCATOR | How did the Nixon presidency reflect the rise of postwar conservatism? | Why was the Watergate scandal significant?

growing scarcity in energy," Carter told the nation, asking Congress for additional measures to address the shortages. Congress reduced controls on the oil and gas industries to stimulate American production and imposed a windfall profits tax on producers to redistribute some of the profits they would reap from deregulation.

Carter's energy measures failed to reduce American dependence on foreign oil. European nations shared that dependence but more successfully controlled consumption. They levied high taxes on gasoline, causing people to rely more on public transportation and prompting manufacturers to produce more energy-efficient cars. In the automobile-dependent United States, however, politicians dismissed that approach. By the end of the century, the United States, with 6 percent of the world's population, would consume more than 25 percent of global oil production. (See "Global Comparison," page 840, and **Map 30.2.**)

One alternative fuel, nuclear energy, aroused opposition from a vigorous environmental movement. The perils of nuclear energy claimed international attention in March 1979, when a meltdown of the reactor core was narrowly averted at the Three Mile Island nuclear facility near Harrisburg, Pennsylvania. Popular opposition and the great expense of building nuclear power plants stalled further development of the industry. The explosion of a nuclear reactor in Chernobyl, Ukraine, in 1986 further solidified antinuclear concerns as part of the environmental movement.

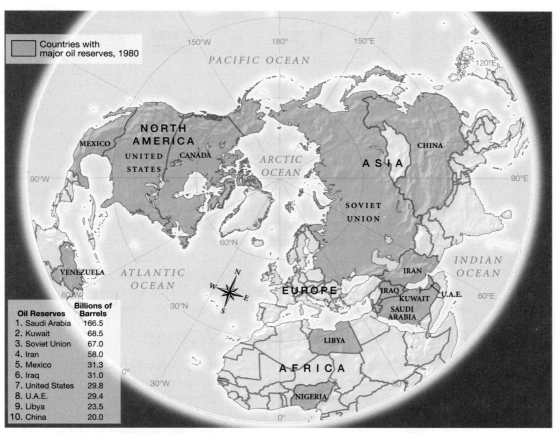

MAP 30.2 ■ Worldwide Oil Reserves, 1980

Data produced by geologists and engineers enable experts to estimate the size of "proved oil reserves," quantities that are recoverable with existing technology and costs. In 1980, the total worldwide reserves were estimated at 645 billion barrels.

Why did the "outsider" presidency of Jimmy Carter fail to gain broad support?	What conservative goals were realized in the Reagan administration?	What strategies did liberals use to fight the conservative turn?	How did Ronald Reagan's foreign policy affect the Cold War?	Conclusion: What was the long-term impact of the conservative turn?

Energy Consumption per Capita, 1980

Relative to most other industrialized nations, the United States consumed energy voraciously, with a per capita rate of consumption in 1980 that was more than twice as high as that of Great Britain, France, or Japan and nearly twice as high as that of the Soviet Union. A number of factors influence a nation's energy consumption (shown here in British thermal units, or Btus), including standard of living, climate, size of landmass and dispersal of population, availability and price of energy, and government policies such as support for public transportation. What country had a per capita rate of consumption even higher than that of the United States?

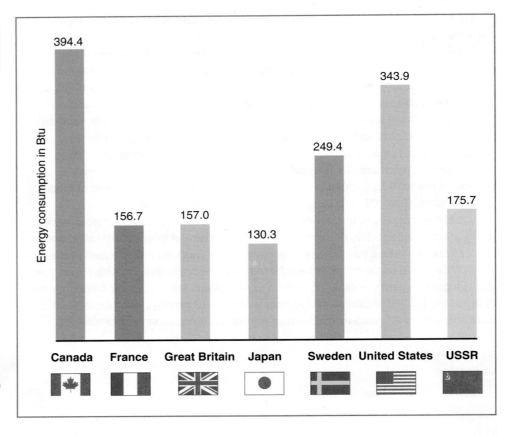

A disaster at Love Canal in Niagara Falls, New York, advanced other environmental goals by underscoring the human costs of unregulated development. Residents suffering high rates of serious illness noted that their homes sat amid highly toxic waste products from a nearby chemical company. Finally responding to the residents' claims in 1978, the State of New York agreed to help families relocate, and the Carter administration sponsored legislation in 1980 that created the so-called Superfund, $1.6 billion for cleanup of hazardous wastes left by the chemical industry.

Carter also signed bills to improve clean air and water programs; to expand the Arctic National Wildlife Refuge preserve in Alaska; and to control stripmining, which left destructive scars on the land. During the 1979 gasoline crisis, Carter attempted to balance the development of domestic fuel sources with environmental concerns, winning legislation to conserve energy and to provide incentives for the development of solar energy and alternative fuels.

Promoting Human Rights Abroad

As president, Jimmy Carter promised to reverse U.S. support of dictators, secret diplomacy, interference in the internal affairs of other countries, and excessive reliance on military solutions. Instead, human rights formed the cornerstone of his approach. The Carter administration applied economic pressure on governments that denied their citizens basic rights, denying aid or trading privileges to nations such as Chile and El Salvador, as well as to the white minority governments of Rhodesia and South Africa. Yet in other instances, Carter sacrificed human rights ideals to strategic and security considerations. He invoked no sanctions against repressive

CHAPTER LOCATOR | How did the Nixon presidency reflect the rise of postwar conservatism? | Why was the Watergate scandal significant?

840 CHAPTER 30 THE CONSERVATIVE TURN, 1969–1989

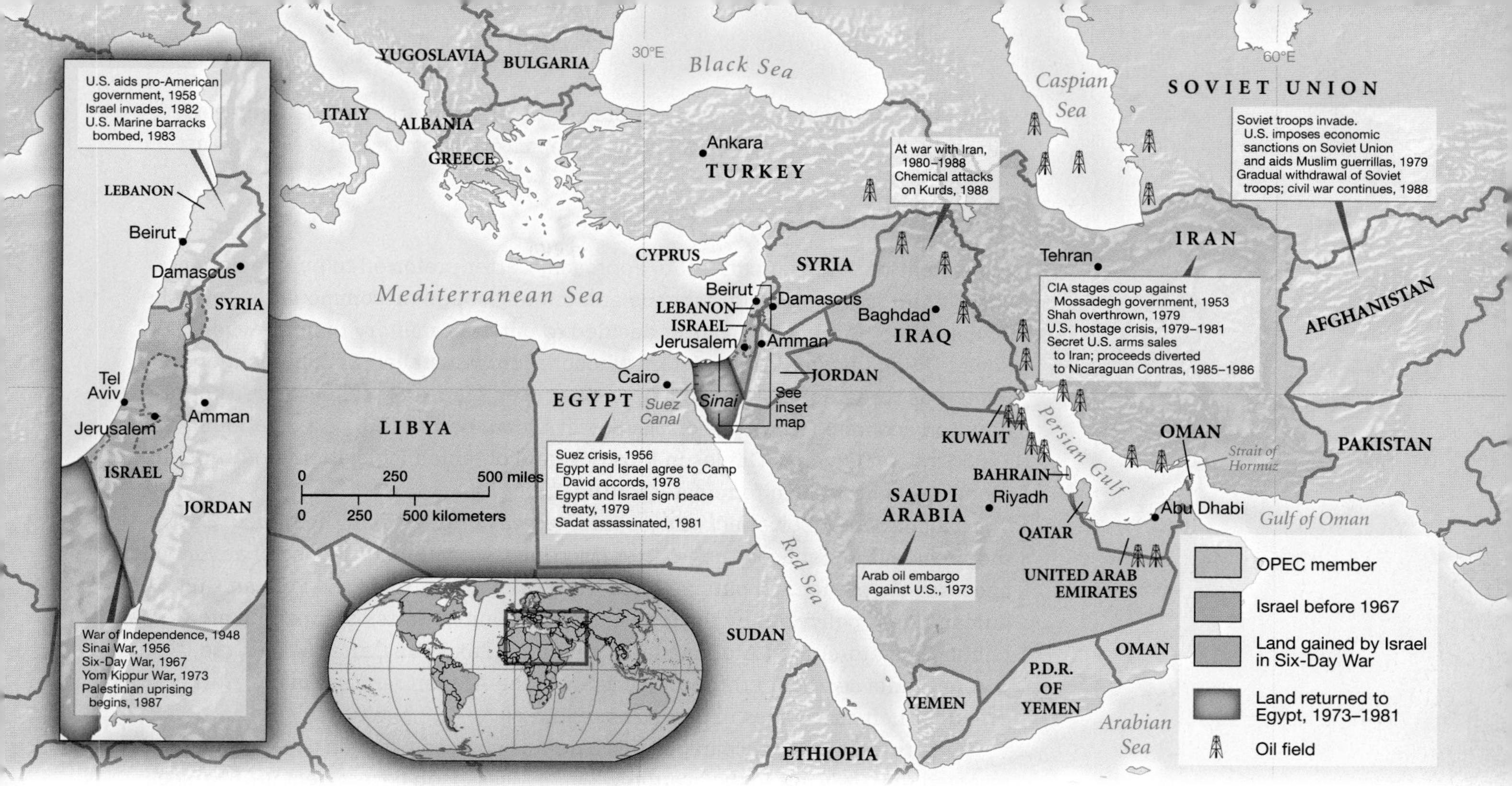

YUGOSLAVIA
BULGARIA
30°E
Black Sea
Caspian Sea
60°E
SOVIET UNION
U.S. aids pro-American government, 1958
Israel invades, 1982
U.S. Marine barracks bombed, 1983
ITALY
ALBANIA
GREECE
Ankara
TURKEY
At war with Iran, 1980–1988
Chemical attacks on Kurds, 1988
Soviet troops invade.
U.S. imposes economic sanctions on Soviet Union and aids Muslim guerrillas, 1979
Gradual withdrawal of Soviet troops; civil war continues, 1988
LEBANON
Beirut
Damascus
SYRIA
CYPRUS
SYRIA
IRAN
Tehran
Mediterranean Sea
Beirut
Damascus
LEBANON
ISRAEL
Jerusalem
Amman
Baghdad
IRAQ
CIA stages coup against Mossadegh government, 1953
Shah overthrown, 1979
U.S. hostage crisis, 1979–1981
Secret U.S. arms sales to Iran; proceeds diverted to Nicaraguan Contras, 1985–1986
AFGHANISTAN
Tel Aviv
Jerusalem
Amman
ISRAEL
JORDAN
Cairo
EGYPT
Suez Canal
Sinai
See inset map
JORDAN
LIBYA
KUWAIT
Persian Gulf
OMAN
Strait of Hormuz
PAKISTAN
0 250 500 miles
0 250 500 kilometers
Suez crisis, 1956
Egypt and Israel agree to Camp David accords, 1978
Egypt and Israel sign peace treaty, 1979
Sadat assassinated, 1981
BAHRAIN
SAUDI ARABIA
Riyadh
QATAR
Abu Dhabi
Gulf of Oman
Red Sea
Arab oil embargo against U.S., 1973
UNITED ARAB EMIRATES
OPEC member
Israel before 1967
Land gained by Israel in Six-Day War
Land returned to Egypt, 1973–1981
Oil field
War of Independence, 1948
Sinai War, 1956
Six-Day War, 1967
Yom Kippur War, 1973
Palestinian uprising begins, 1987
SUDAN
OMAN
P.D.R. OF YEMEN
YEMEN
Arabian Sea
ETHIOPIA

▸ FOR MORE HELP ANALYZING THIS MAP, see the map activity for this chapter in the Online Study Guide at bedfordstmartins.com/roarkunderstanding.

MAP 30.3 ▪ The Middle East, 1948–1989
Determination to preserve access to the rich oil reserves of the Middle East and commitment to the security of Israel were the fundamental—and often conflicting—principles of U.S. foreign policy in that region.

governments in Iran, South Korea, and the Philippines, for example, and he established formal diplomatic relations with the People's Republic of China in 1979.

Carter's human rights principles faced another test when a popular movement overthrew an oppressive dictatorship in Nicaragua. U.S. officials were uneasy about the leftist Sandinistas who led the rebellion and had ties to Cuba. Once they assumed power in 1979, however, Carter recognized the new government and sent economic aid, signaling that the way a government treated its citizens was as important as how anti-Communist and friendly to American interests it was.

Applying moral principles to relations with Panama, Carter sped up negotiations over control of the Panama Canal and in 1977 signed a treaty providing for Panama's takeover of the canal in 2000. Supporters viewed the treaty as recompense for the use of U.S. power to obtain the canal in 1903. Opponents insisted on retaining the vital waterway. "We bought it, we paid for it, it's ours," claimed Ronald Reagan during the presidential primaries of 1976. It took a massive effort by the administration to get Senate ratification of the Panama Canal treaty.

Seeking to promote peace in the Middle East, Carter seized on the courage of Egyptian president Anwar Sadat, the first Arab leader to risk his political career by talking directly with Israeli officials. In 1979, Carter invited Sadat and Israeli prime minister Menachem Begin to the presidential retreat at Camp David, Maryland. These talks led to the **Camp David accords**, whereby Egypt became the first Arab state to recognize Israel, and Israel agreed to gradual withdrawal from the Sinai Peninsula, which it had seized in the 1967 Six-Day War (**Map 30.3**). Although the issues of Palestinian self-determination in other Israeli-occupied territories (the

Camp David accords
▸ Agreements between Egypt and Israel reached at the 1979 talks held at Camp David. In the accords, Egypt became the first Arab state to recognize Israel, and Israel agreed to gradual withdrawal from the Sinai Peninsula, which it had seized in the 1967 Six-Day War. President Carter played a key role in bringing the two parties together and ensuring that the talks were a success.

West Bank and Gaza) and the plight of Palestinian refugees remained unresolved, Carter had nurtured the first meaningful steps toward peace in the Middle East.

The Cold War Intensifies

Consistent with his human rights approach, Carter preferred to pursue national security through nonmilitary means and initially sought accommodation with the Soviet Union. But in 1979, Carter decided to pursue a military buildup when the Soviet Union invaded Afghanistan, whose recently installed Communist government was threatened by Muslim opposition (see Map 30.3, page 841). Carter also imposed economic sanctions on the Soviet Union, barred U.S. participation in the 1980 Summer Olympic Games in Moscow, and obtained legislation requiring all nineteen-year-old men to register for the draft.

Claiming that Soviet actions jeopardized oil supplies from the Middle East, the president announced the "Carter Doctrine," threatening the use of any means necessary to prevent an outside force from gaining control of the Persian Gulf. His human rights policy fell by the wayside as the United States stepped up aid to the military dictatorship in Afghanistan's neighbor, Pakistan. Carter authorized the CIA to funnel secret aid through Pakistan to the Afghan rebels. Finally, Carter called for hefty increases in defense spending.

Events in Iran also encouraged this hard-line approach. Iranian dissidents resented the CIA's role in the overthrow of the Mossadegh government in 1953 (see chapter 27), condemned the shah's savage attempts to silence opposition, and detested his adoption of Western culture and values. These grievances erupted into a revolution in 1979 that forced the shah out of Iran and brought to power Shiite Islamic fundamentalists led by Ayatollah Ruholla Khomeini, whom the shah had exiled in 1964.

Carter's decision to allow the shah into the United States for medical treatment enraged Iranians, who believed that the United States would put the shah back in power as it had done in 1953. On November 4, 1979, a crowd broke into the U.S. Embassy in Iran's capital, Teheran, and seized sixty-six U.S. diplomats, CIA officers, citizens, and military attachés. Refusing the captors' demands that the shah be returned to Iran for trial, Carter froze Iranian assets in U.S. banks and placed an embargo on Iranian oil. In April 1980, he sent a small military operation into Iran, but the rescue mission failed.

Iran hostage crisis

▶ Crisis that began in 1979 after the Iranian revolution against the shah. Iranians broke into the U.S. Embassy in Teheran and took sixty-six Americans hostage. The hostage crisis undermined the Carter presidency and damaged his chances at reelection.

The disastrous rescue attempt and scenes of blindfolded U.S. citizens paraded before TV cameras fed Americans' feelings of impotence, simmering since the defeat in Vietnam. These frustrations in turn increased support for a more militaristic foreign policy. Opposition to Soviet-American détente, combined with the Soviet invasion of Afghanistan, nullified the thaw in superpower relations that had begun in the 1960s. The **Iran hostage crisis** dominated the news during the 1980 presidential campaign and contributed to Carter's defeat. Iran freed the hostages the day he left office, but relations with the United States remained tense.

> ## QUICK REVIEW

Why were so many Americans uninspired by Carter's leadership?

CHAPTER LOCATOR | How did the Nixon presidency reflect the rise of postwar conservatism? | Why was the Watergate scandal significant?

842 CHAPTER 30 THE CONSERVATIVE TURN, 1969–1989

Ronald Reagan Nominated for President

Nancy and Ronald Reagan respond to cheers at the 1980 Republican National Convention, where he was nominated for president. Reagan became one of the most popular presidents of the twentieth century. Lester Sloan/Woodfin Camp & Associates.

What conservative goals were realized in the Reagan administration?

RONALD REAGAN'S ELECTION in 1980 marked the most important turning point in politics since Franklin D. Roosevelt won the presidency in 1932. Reagan's victory established conservatism's dominance in the Republican Party, while Democrats searched for voter support by moving toward the right. The United States was not alone in this political shift. Conservatives rose to power in Britain with Prime Minister Margaret Thatcher, and they led governments in Germany, Canada, and Sweden, while socialist and social democratic governments elsewhere trimmed their welfare states.

Appealing to the New Right and Beyond

Sixty-nine-year-old **Ronald Reagan** was the oldest candidate ever nominated for the presidency. Coming first to national attention as a movie actor, he initially shared the politics of his staunchly Democratic father but moved to the right in the 1940s and 1950s and campaigned for Barry Goldwater in 1964.

Reagan's political career took off when he was elected governor of California in 1966. He ran as a conservative, but in office he displayed considerable flexibility, approving a major tax increase, a strong water pollution bill, and a liberal abortion law. Displaying similar agility in the 1980 presidential campaign, he softened earlier attacks on programs such as Social Security and chose the moderate George H. W. Bush as his running mate.

Reagan's campaign capitalized on the economic recession and the international challenges symbolized by the Americans held hostage in Iran. Repeatedly, Reagan asked voters, "Are you better off now than you were four years ago?" He promised to "take government off the backs of the people" and to restore Americans' morale and other nations' respect. Reagan won the 1980 election, and Republicans took control of the Senate for the first time since the 1950s.

Ronald Reagan

▶ Republican president who held office from 1981 until 1989. The enormously popular former actor and governor of California implemented a wide-ranging conservative agenda that rolled back taxes, industry regulations, environmental protections, and social welfare programs. Reagan also oversaw a dramatic thawing in U.S.-Soviet relations.

| Why did the "outsider" presidency of Jimmy Carter fail to gain broad support? | **What conservative goals were realized in the Reagan administration?** | What strategies did liberals use to fight the conservative turn? | How did Ronald Reagan's foreign policy affect the Cold War? | Conclusion: What was the long-term impact of the conservative turn? |

1966
- Republican Ronald Reagan is elected governor of California.

1979
- Jerry Falwell founds Moral Majority.

1980
- Republican Ronald Reagan is elected president.

1981
- Economic Recovery Tax Act is enacted.
- Reagan fires striking members of the Professional Air Traffic Controllers Organization.

1984
- Reagan wins second term as president.

1989
- Pat Robertson founds Christian Coalition.
- Congress bails out savings and loan industry.

Christian Right
▶ Term for new conservatives who attacked what they saw as immorality in public life and who called for a return to traditional or "family" values. Jerry Falwell and Pat Robertson were key leaders of the Christian Right.

supply-side economics
▶ Economic theory that held that cutting taxes would lead to economic growth by increasing productivity and thereby increasing demand for goods and services. Despite proponents' promises to the contrary, under Ronald Reagan supply-side economics led to large increases in the federal budget deficit.

The Reagan Coalition

Free-market advocates
Militant anti-Communists
Fundamentalist Christians
White southerners
Reagan Democrats: white working-class Democrats who were disenchanted with the policies of the Democratic Party

While the economy and Iran sealed Reagan's victory, he also benefited from the burgeoning grassroots conservative movements. Reagan's support from religious conservatives, predominantly Protestants, constituted a relatively new phenomenon in politics known as the New Right or New **Christian Right.** During the 1970s, evangelical and fundamentalist Christianity claimed thousands of new adherents. Evangelical ministers such as Pat Robertson preached to huge television audiences, attacking feminism, abortion, and homosexuality and calling for the restoration of old-fashioned "family values."

Conservatives created political organizations such as the Moral Majority, founded by minister Jerry Falwell in 1979 to fight "left-wing, social-welfare bills, . . . pornography, homosexuality, [and] the advocacy of immorality in school textbooks." The Christian Coalition, founded by Pat Robertson in 1989, claimed 1.6 million members and control of the Republican Party in more than a dozen states. The organizations and publications of more traditional conservatives, who stressed limited government at home and militant anticommunism abroad, likewise flourished.

Reagan spoke for the New Right on such issues as abortion and school prayer, but he did not push hard for so-called moral or social policies. Instead, his major achievements fulfilled goals of the older right—strengthening the nation's anti-Communist posture and reducing taxes and government restraints on free enterprise. "In the present crisis," Reagan declared, "government is not the solution to our problem, government is the problem."

Reagan was extraordinarily popular, appealing even to Americans who opposed his policies but warmed to his optimism, confidence, and easygoing humor. Ignoring the darker moments of the American past, he presented a version of history that Americans could feel good about.

Unleashing Free Enterprise

Reagan's first domestic objective was a massive tax cut. In support of this objective, Reagan relied on a new theory called **supply-side economics**, which held that cutting taxes would actually increase revenue. According to this theory, tax cuts would enable businesses to expand, encourage individuals to work harder because they could keep more of their earnings, and increase the production of goods and services—the supply—which in turn would boost demand. Reagan promised that the economy would grow so much that the government would recoup the lost taxes, but instead it incurred a galloping deficit.

In the summer of 1981, Congress passed the Economic Recovery Tax Act, the largest tax reduction in U.S. history. A second measure, the Tax Reform Act of 1986, cut taxes still further. Although the 1986 law narrowed loopholes used primarily by

CHAPTER LOCATOR | How did the Nixon presidency reflect the rise of postwar conservatism? | Why was the Watergate scandal significant?

the wealthy, affluent Americans saved far more on their tax bills than did average taxpayers, and the distribution of wealth tipped further in favor of the rich.

Carter had confined deregulation to particular industries, such as air transportation and banking, while increasing health, safety, and environmental regulations. The Reagan administration, by contrast, pursued across-the-board deregulation. It declined to enforce the Sherman Antitrust Act's limits on monopolies (see chapter 18) against an unprecedented number of business mergers and takeovers. Reagan also loosened regulations protecting employee health and safety, and he weakened labor unions. When members of the Professional Air Traffic Controllers Organization struck in 1981, Reagan fired them, destroying their union and intimidating organized labor.

Ronald Reagan blamed environmental laws for the nation's sluggish economic growth and targeted them for deregulation. His first secretary of the interior, James Watt, declared, "We will mine more, drill more, cut more timber," releasing federal lands to private exploitation. Meanwhile, the head of the Environmental Protection Agency relaxed enforcement of air and water pollution standards. Of environmentalists, Reagan wisecracked, "I don't think they'll be happy until the White House looks like a bird's nest," but their numbers grew in opposition to his policies. Popular support for environmental protection forced several officials to resign and blocked full realization of Reagan's deregulatory goals.

Deregulation of the banking industry, begun under Carter with bipartisan support, created a crisis in the savings and loan industry. Some of the newly deregulated savings and loan institutions (S&Ls) extended enormous loans to real estate developers and invested in other high-yield but risky ventures. When real estate values began to plunge, hundreds of S&Ls went bankrupt. After Congress voted to bail out the S&L industry in 1989, American taxpayers bore the burden of the largest financial scandal in U.S. history, estimated at more than $100 billion.

The S&L crisis deepened the federal deficit. The administration cut funds for food stamps, job training, student aid, and other social welfare programs, and hundreds of thousands of people lost benefits. Yet increases in defense spending far exceeded the budget cuts. Under Reagan, the nation's debt tripled to $2.3 trillion, and interest on the debt consumed one-seventh of all federal expenditures. Despite Reagan's antigovernment rhetoric, the number of federal employees increased from 2.9 million to 3.1 million during his presidency.

It took the severest recession since the 1930s to squeeze inflation out of the U.S. economy. Unemployment approached 11 percent late in 1982, and record numbers of banks and businesses closed. The threat of unemployment further undermined organized labor, forcing unions to make concessions that management insisted were necessary for industry's survival. In 1983, the economy recovered and entered a period of unprecedented growth.

That economic upswing and Reagan's own popularity posed a formidable challenge to the Democrats in the 1984 election. They nominated Carter's vice president, Walter F. Mondale, to head the ticket, but even his precedent-breaking move in choosing a woman as his running mate—New York representative Geraldine A. Ferraro—did not save the Democrats from defeat. Reagan charged his opponents with concentrating on America's failures, while he emphasized success and possibility. Democrats, he claimed, "see an America where every day is April 15th [the due date for income tax returns] . . . we see an America where every day is the Fourth of July." Reagan was reelected in a landslide victory, winning 59 percent of the popular vote and every state but Minnesota.

Why did the "outsider" presidency of Jimmy Carter fail to gain broad support?

What conservative goals were realized in the Reagan administration?

What strategies did liberals use to fight the conservative turn?

How did Ronald Reagan's foreign policy affect the Cold War?

Conclusion: What was the long-term impact of the conservative turn?

Winners and Losers in a Flourishing Economy

After the economy took off in 1983, some Americans won great fortunes. Popular culture celebrated making money and displaying wealth. Participating conspicuously in the new affluence were some members of the baby boom generation, known popularly as "yuppies," short for "young urban professionals." Though definitely a minority, these mostly white, well-educated young men and women established consumption standards that many tried to emulate. Many of the newly wealthy got rich from moving assets around rather than from producing goods, making money by manipulating debt and restructuring corporations through mergers and takeovers. Most financial wizards operated within the law, but greed sometimes led to criminal convictions.

Older industries faced increasing international pressures. German and Japanese corporations overtook U.S. manufacturing in steel, automobiles, and electronics. International competition forced the collapse of some older companies. Others moved factories and jobs abroad to be closer to foreign markets or to benefit from the low wages in countries such as Mexico and Korea. Service industries expanded and created new jobs at home, but these jobs paid substantially lower wages. The number of full-time workers earning wages below the poverty level ($12,195 for a family of four in 1990) rose from 12 percent to 18 percent of all workers in the 1980s.

The weakening of organized labor combined with the decline in manufacturing to erode the position of blue-collar workers. Chicago steelworker Ike Mazo, who contemplated the $6-an-hour jobs available to him, fumed, "It's an attack on the living standards of workers." Increasingly, a second income was needed to stave off economic decline. By 1990, nearly 60 percent of married women with young children worked outside the home. Yet even with two incomes, families struggled. Speaking of her children, Mazo's wife confessed, "I worry about their future every day. Will we be able to put them through college?" The average $10,000 gap between men's and women's annual earnings made things even harder for the nearly 20 percent of families headed by women.

In keeping with conservative philosophy, Reagan adhered to supply-side economics, insisting that a booming economy would benefit everyone. Average personal income did rise during his tenure, but the trend toward greater economic inequality that had begun in the 1970s intensified in the 1980s, encouraged in part by his tax policies. Social Security and Medicare helped to stave off destitution among the elderly. Less fortunate were other groups that the economic boom had bypassed: racial minorities, families headed by women, and children. One child in five lived in poverty.

Inequality under Reagan (1979–1987)

Personal income rose sharply for the wealthiest 20 percent of Americans.

Personal income of the poorest Americans fell by 9.8 percent.

The percentage of Americans living in poverty increased from 11.7 to 13.5, the highest poverty rate in the industrialized world.

> ## QUICK REVIEW

Why did economic inequality increase during the Reagan administration?

CHAPTER LOCATOR | How did the Nixon presidency reflect the rise of postwar conservatism? | Why was the Watergate scandal significant?

CHAPTER 30
846   THE CONSERVATIVE TURN, 1969–1989

What strategies did liberals use to fight the conservative turn?

| "Parents & Friends of Lesbians & Gays" |

In June 1970, gays and lesbians marched in New York City to commemorate the first anniversary of the Stonewall riot (see chapter 28). Since then, gay pride parades have taken place throughout the United States and in other countries every year in June. Increasingly, friends, supporters, and families of homosexuals participate in the parades, as this sign from a parade in Los Angeles indicates. © Bettmann/Corbis.

▶ FOR MORE HELP ANALYZING THIS IMAGE, see the visual activity for this chapter in the Online Study Guide at bedfordstmartins.com/roarkunderstanding.

THE RISE OF CONSERVATISM put liberal social movements on the defensive, as the Reagan administration moved away from the national commitment to equal opportunity undertaken in the 1960s. Feminists and minority groups fought to keep protections they had recently won, and they achieved some modest gains.

Battles in the Courts and Congress

Ronald Reagan agreed with conservatives that the nation had moved too far in guaranteeing rights to minority groups. Crying "reverse discrimination," conservatives maintained that affirmative action unfairly hurt whites. Instead they called for "color-blind" policies, ignoring statistics showing that minorities and white women still lagged far behind white men in opportunities and income. Intense mobilization by civil rights groups, educational leaders, and even corporate America prevented the administration from abandoning affirmative action, and the Supreme Court upheld important antidiscrimination policies. Moreover, against Reagan's wishes, Congress voted to extend the Voting Rights Act with veto-proof majorities. The administration did, however, limit civil rights

| Why did the "outsider" presidency of Jimmy Carter fail to gain broad support? | What conservative goals were realized in the Reagan administration? | **What strategies did liberals use to fight the conservative turn?** | How did Ronald Reagan's foreign policy affect the Cold War? | Conclusion: What was the long-term impact of the conservative turn? |

1981
- Researchers discover AIDS virus.
- Sandra Day O'Connor becomes the first woman justice on the Supreme Court.

1982
- Time limit for ratification of the Equal Rights Amendment runs out.

1984
- Supreme Court decision in *Grove City v. Bell* weakens antidiscrimination provisions of the Education Amendments Act of 1972.

Equal Rights Amendment (ERA)

► Constitutional amendment intended to guarantee women equality of rights under the law. Time ran out for ratification of the ERA in 1982.

enforcement by appointing conservatives to the Justice Department, the Civil Rights Commission, and other agencies and by slashing their budgets.

Congress stepped in to defend antidiscrimination programs after the Justice Department, in the case of *Grove City v. Bell* (1984), persuaded the Supreme Court to severely weaken Title IX of the Education Amendments Act of 1972, a key law promoting equal opportunity in education. In 1988, Congress passed the Civil Rights Restoration Act, which reversed the administration's victory in *Grove City* and banned any organization that practiced discrimination on the basis of race, color, national origin, sex, disability, or age from receiving government funds.

The *Grove City* decision reflected a rightward movement in the federal judiciary. With the opportunity to appoint half of the 761 federal court judges and three new Supreme Court justices, President Reagan encouraged this trend by carefully selecting conservative candidates. Thus, he turned the tide back toward strict construction—the literal interpretation of the Constitution that narrowly adheres to the words of its authors, thereby limiting judicial power to protect individual rights.

Feminism on the Defensive

Ratified the ERA

Did not ratify the ERA

Ratified and then voted to rescind ratification

The Fight for the Equal Rights Amendment

A signal achievement of the New Right was capturing the Republican Party's position on women's rights. For the first time in its history, the Republican Party took an explicitly antifeminist tone, opposing both the **Equal Rights Amendment (ERA)** and a woman's right to abortion, key goals of women's rights activists. When the time limit for ratification of the ERA ran out in 1982, feminists suffered defeat on a key goal (see chapter 28).

Cast on the defensive, feminists focused more on women's economic and family problems, where they found some common ground with the Reagan administration. The Child Support Enforcement Amendments Act helped single and divorced mothers collect court-ordered child support payments from absent fathers. The Retirement Equity Act of 1984 benefited divorced and older women by strengthening their claims to their husbands' pensions and enabling women to qualify more easily for private retirement pensions.

Reagan eventually appointed three women to cabinet posts and, in 1981, selected the first woman, Sandra Day O'Connor, a moderate, for the Supreme Court, despite the Christian Right's objection to her support of abortion. But these actions accompanied a general decline in the number of women and minorities in high-level government positions. And with higher poverty rates than men, women suffered most from Reagan's cuts in social programs.

Although court decisions placed restrictions on women's ability to obtain abortions, feminists fought successfully to retain the basic principles of *Roe v. Wade*. Moreover, they won a key decision from the Supreme Court ruling that

CHAPTER LOCATOR | How did the Nixon presidency reflect the rise of postwar conservatism? | Why was the Watergate scandal significant?

CHAPTER 30
848 THE CONSERVATIVE TURN, 1969–1989

sexual harassment in the workplace constituted sex discrimination. Feminists also made some gains at the state level in such areas as pay equity, rape, and domestic violence.

The Gay and Lesbian Rights Movement

States with antidiscrimination laws

Antidiscrimination Laws for Gays and Lesbians, 1982–2000

In contrast to feminism and other social movements, gay and lesbian rights activism grew during the 1980s, galvanized in part by the discovery in 1981 of a devastating disease, **acquired immune deficiency syndrome (AIDS).** Because initially the disease disproportionately affected male homosexuals in the United States, activists mobilized to promote public funding for AIDS education, prevention, and treatment.

The gay and lesbian rights movement helped closeted homosexuals "come out," and their visibility increased awareness, if not always acceptance, of homosexuality among the larger population. Beginning with the election of Elaine Noble to the Massachusetts legislature in 1974, several openly gay politicians won offices ranging from mayor to member of Congress, and the Democrats began to include gay rights in their party platforms. Activists organized gay rights marches throughout the country.

Popular attitudes about homosexuality moved toward greater tolerance but remained complex, leading to uneven changes in policies. Dozens of cities banned job discrimination against homosexuals, and beginning with Wisconsin in 1982, eleven states made sexual orientation a protected category under civil rights laws. Local governments and large corporations began to offer health insurance and other benefits to same-sex domestic partners.

Yet a strong countermovement challenged the drive for recognition of gay rights. The Christian Right targeted gays and lesbians as symbols of national immorality and succeeded in overturning some homosexual rights measures. Many states removed antisodomy laws from the books, but in 1986 the Supreme Court upheld the constitutionality of such laws. Until the Court reversed that opinion in 2003, more than a dozen states retained statutes that left homosexuals vulnerable to criminal charges for private consensual behavior.

acquired immune deficiency syndrome (AIDS)

▶ Deadly disease discovered in 1981. Because the disease at first disproportionately affected male homosexuals in the United States, AIDS education, prevention, and treatment became central concerns of gay rights activists.

QUICK REVIEW <

What gains and setbacks did minorities, feminists, and gays and lesbians experience during the Reagan years?

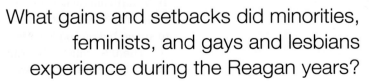

Why did the "outsider" presidency of Jimmy Carter fail to gain broad support? | What conservative goals were realized in the Reagan administration? | What strategies did liberals use to fight the conservative turn? | How did Ronald Reagan's foreign policy affect the Cold War? | Conclusion: What was the long-term impact of the conservative turn?

How did Ronald Reagan's foreign policy affect the Cold War?

The Cold War Thaws U.S. president Ronald Reagan and Soviet premier Mikhail Gorbachev shake hands as they meet in June 1988 for a round of Strategic Arms Reduction Talks (START). Moving beyond the Strategic Arms Limitation Talks (SALT) of the 1970s, these negotiations aimed to reduce rather than limit nuclear warheads and the bombers that carried them. The talks culminated with a comprehensive treaty signed by Reagan's successor, George H. W. Bush, and Gorbachev in July 1991. Kenneth Jarecke/Contact Press Images.

REAGAN ACCELERATED THE ARMS BUILDUP that began under Carter and harshly censured the Soviet Union, calling it "an evil empire." Yet despite the new aggressiveness—or, as some argued, because of it—Reagan presided over the most impressive thaw in superpower conflict since the Cold War had begun. On the periphery of the Cold War, however, Reagan practiced militant anticommunism, assisting antileftist movements in Asia, Africa, and Central America and dispatching troops to the Middle East and the Caribbean.

Militarization and Interventions Abroad

Reagan expanded the military with new bombers and missiles, an enhanced nuclear force in Europe, a larger navy, and a rapid-deployment force. Throughout Reagan's presidency, defense spending averaged $216 billion a year, up from $158 billion in the Carter years and higher even than in the Vietnam era.

Reagan startled many of his own advisers in March 1983 by announcing plans for research on the Strategic Defense Initiative (SDI). Immediately dubbed "Star Wars" by critics who doubted its feasibility, the project would deploy lasers in space to destroy enemy missiles before they could reach their targets. Such a defense would upset the nuclear balance by allowing the United States to strike first and not fear retaliation. The Soviets reacted angrily because SDI violated the 1972 antiballistic missile treaty and because they would require huge investments to develop their own Star Wars technology. Subsequent administrations continued to spend billions on SDI research without producing a working system.

The U.S. military buildup could not extinguish the growing threat of terrorism by nonstate organizations that sought political objectives by attacking civilian populations. Terrorism had a long history throughout the world, but in the

1970s and 1980s, Americans saw it escalate in the Middle East, where terrorist tactics were used by Palestinians after the Israeli occupation of the West Bank and by other groups hostile to Western policies. The terrorist organization Hezbollah, composed of Shiite Muslims and backed by Iran and Syria, arose in Lebanon in 1982 after Israeli forces invaded that country to stop the Palestine Liberation Organization (PLO) from using sanctuaries in Lebanon to launch attacks on Israel.

Reagan's effort to stabilize Lebanon by sending 2,000 marines to join an international peacekeeping mission failed. In April 1983, a suicide attack on the U.S. Embassy in Beirut killed 63 people, and in October a Hezbollah fighter drove a bomb-filled truck into a U.S. barracks there, killing 241 marines (see Map 30.3, page 841). The attack prompted the withdrawal of U.S. troops, and Lebanon remained in chaos, while incidents of murder, kidnapping, and hijacking by various Middle Eastern extremist groups continued.

Following a Cold War pattern begun under Eisenhower, the Reagan administration sought to contain leftist movements across the globe. In October 1983, 5,000 U.S. troops invaded Grenada, a small island nation in the Caribbean that had succumbed to a Marxist coup. In Asia, the United States moved more quietly, aiding the Afghan rebels' war against Afghanistan's Soviet-backed government. In the African nation of Angola, the United States armed rebel forces against the government supported by the Soviet Union and Cuba. Reagan also sided with the South African government, which was brutally suppressing black protest against apartheid, forcing Congress to override his veto in order to impose economic sanctions against South Africa.

Administration officials were most fearful of left-wing movements in Central America, which Reagan claimed could "destabilize the entire region from the Panama Canal to Mexico." When a leftist uprising occurred in El Salvador in 1981, the United States sent money and military advisers to prop up the authoritarian government. In neighboring Nicaragua, the administration aided the Contras (literally, "opposers"), an armed coalition seeking to unseat the left-wing Sandinistas, who had toppled a long-standing dictatorship.

El Salvador and Nicaragua

The Iran-Contra Scandal

Fearing another Vietnam, many Americans opposed aligning the United States with reactionary forces not supported by the majority of Nicaraguans. Congress repeatedly instructed the president to stop aiding the Contras, but the administration continued to secretly provide them with weapons and training and helped wreck the Nicaraguan economy. With support for his government undermined, Nicaragua's president, Daniel Ortega, agreed to a political settlement, and when he was defeated by a coalition of all the opposition groups, he stepped aside.

Secret aid to the Contras was part of a larger project that came to be known as the Iran-Contra scandal. It began in 1985 when officials of the National Security Council and CIA arranged to sell arms to Iran, then in the midst of an eight-year war with neighboring Iraq, even while the United States supplied Iraq with funds and weapons. The purpose was to get Iran to pressure Hezbollah to release seven American hostages being held in Lebanon (see Map 30.3, page 841). Funds from the arms sales were then channeled to the Nicaraguan Contras. Over the objections of his secretary of state and secretary of defense, Reagan approved the

Iran-Contra scandal
▶ Reagan administration scandal that involved the sale of arms to Iran in exchange for the release of hostages held by Middle Eastern extremist groups, and the redirection of the proceeds of those sales to the Nicaraguan Contras. The Iran-Contra scandal was the most serious case of executive branch misconduct since Watergate.

| Why did the "outsider" presidency of Jimmy Carter fail to gain broad support? | What conservative goals were realized in the Reagan administration? | What strategies did liberals use to fight the conservative turn? | **How did Ronald Reagan's foreign policy affect the Cold War?** | Conclusion: What was the long-term impact of the conservative turn? |

CHRONOLOGY

1982
– Reagan sends 2,000 marines to Lebanon to join an international peacekeeping force.

1983
– Terrorist bomb kills 241 U.S. Marines in Beirut, Lebanon.
– Reagan announces plans for Strategic Defense Initiative ("Star Wars").
– United States invades Grenada.

1985
– Mikhail Gorbachev assumes power in the Soviet Union.

1986
– Iran-Contra scandal.

1987
– INF agreement eliminates all short- and medium-range missiles from Europe.

intermediate-range nuclear forces (INF) agreement

▶ Nuclear disarmament agreement reached between the United States and the Soviet Union in 1987, signifying a major thaw in the Cold War. The treaty eliminated all short- and medium-range missiles from Europe and provided for on-site inspection for the first time.

arms sales, but the three subsequently denied knowing that the proceeds were diverted to the Contras.

When news of the affair surfaced in November 1986, the Reagan administration faced serious charges. Investigations by an independent prosecutor appointed by Reagan led to a trial in which seven individuals pleaded guilty or were convicted of lying to Congress and destroying evidence. One felony conviction was later overturned on a technicality, and President George H. W. Bush pardoned the other six officials in December 1992. The independent prosecutor's final report found no evidence that Reagan had broken the law, but it concluded that he had known about the diversion of funds to the Contras and had "knowingly participated or at least acquiesced" in covering up the scandal—the most serious case of executive branch misconduct since Watergate.

A Thaw in Soviet-American Relations

A momentous reduction in Cold War tensions soon overshadowed the Iran-Contra scandal. The new Soviet-American accord depended both on Reagan's flexibility and on an innovative Soviet head of state who recognized that his country's domestic problems demanded an easing of Cold War antagonism. Mikhail Gorbachev assumed power in 1985 determined to revitalize an inefficient Soviet economy incapable of delivering basic consumer goods. Gorbachev introduced some elements of free enterprise and proclaimed a new era of *glasnost* (greater freedom of expression), eventually allowing contested elections and challenges to Communist rule.

Concerns about immense defense budgets moved both Reagan and Gorbachev to the negotiating table. With growing popular support for arms reductions, Reagan made disarmament a major goal in his last years in office and readily responded when Gorbachev took the initiative. Reagan and Gorbachev met four times between 1985 and 1988. Although Reagan's insistence on proceeding with SDI nearly killed the talks, by December 1987 the superpowers had completed an **intermediate-range nuclear forces (INF) agreement**. The INF treaty eliminated all short- and medium-range missiles from Europe and provided for on-site inspection for the first time. This was also the first time either nation had pledged to eliminate weapons already in place.

In 1988, Gorbachev further reduced tensions by announcing a gradual withdrawal from Afghanistan, which had become the Soviet equivalent of America's Vietnam. In addition, the Soviet Union, the United States, and Cuba agreed on a political settlement of the civil war in the African nation of Angola. In the Middle East, both superpowers supported a cease-fire and peace talks in the eight-year war between Iran and Iraq. Within three years, the Cold War that had defined the world for nearly half a century would be history.

> QUICK REVIEW

How did anticommunism shape Reagan's foreign policy?

CHAPTER LOCATOR | How did the Nixon presidency reflect the rise of postwar conservatism? | Why was the Watergate scandal significant?

852 CHAPTER 30 THE CONSERVATIVE TURN, 1969–1989

Dirck Halstead/Getty Images.

Conclusion: What was the long-term impact of the conservative turn?

"OURS WAS THE FIRST REVOLUTION in the history of mankind that truly reversed the course of government," boasted Ronald Reagan in his farewell address in 1989. The word *revolution* exaggerated the change, but his administration did mark the slowdown or reversal of expanding federal budgets, programs, and regulations that had taken off in the 1930s.

Antigovernment sentiment grew along with the backlash against the reforms of the 1960s and the conduct of the Vietnam War. Watergate and other misdeeds of the Nixon administration further disillusioned Americans. Presidents Ford and Carter restored morality to the White House, but neither could solve the problems of slow economic growth, stagflation, and an increasing trade deficit. Even the Democrat Carter gave higher priority to fiscal austerity than to social reform, and he began the government's retreat from regulation of key industries.

A new conservative movement helped Reagan win the presidency and flourished during his administration. Reagan's tax cuts, combined with hefty increases in defense spending, created a federal deficit crisis that justified cuts in social welfare spending and made new federal initiatives unthinkable. Many Americans continued to support specific federal programs, but public sentiment about the government in general had taken a U-turn from the Roosevelt era. Instead of seeing the government as a helpful and problem-solving institution, many believed that not only was it ineffective at solving national problems, but it also often made things worse. As Reagan appointed new justices, the Supreme Court retreated from liberalism, curbing the government's authority to protect individual rights and regulate the economy.

With the economic recovery that set in after 1982 and his optimistic rhetoric, Reagan lifted the confidence of Americans about their nation and its promise—confidence that had eroded with the economic and foreign policy blows of the 1970s. Beginning his presidency with harsh rhetoric against the Soviet Union and a huge military buildup, Reagan helped move the two superpowers to the highest level of cooperation since the Cold War began. That cooperation signaled developments that would transform U.S.-Soviet relations—and the world—in the next decade.

SO NOW YOU KNOW

The United States began a military buildup in Afghanistan in 1979 to support Muslims who were fighting the Soviet troops sent to protect the country's newly elected Communist government. These rebels succeeded in ousting the pro-Soviet government, but the government they helped install harbored the Islamic fundamentalists who would attack the United States in 2001.

CHAPTER 30 STUDY GUIDE

Online Study Guide
bedfordstmartins.com/roarkunderstanding

STEP 1 GETTING STARTED

Below are terms that every college graduate should know about this period in American history. Can you identify each term below and explain why it matters? To do this exercise online or to download this chart, visit bedfordstmartins.com/roarkunderstanding.

TERM	WHO OR WHAT & WHEN	WHY IT MATTERS
Watergate, p. 834		
Gerald R. Ford, p. 835		
James Earl "Jimmy" Carter Jr., p. 836		
Camp David accords, p. 841		
Iran hostage crisis, p. 842		
Ronald Reagan, p. 843		
Christian Right, p. 844		
supply-side economics, p. 844		
Equal Rights Amendment (ERA), p. 848		
acquired immune deficiency syndrome (AIDS), p. 849		
Iran-Contra scandal, p. 851		
intermediate-range nuclear forces (INF) agreement, p. 852		

STEP 2 MOVING BEYOND THE BASICS

The exercise below represents a more advanced understanding of the chapter material. Using the chart, describe the major concerns of the groups that made up the Reagan coalition. Then describe each group's expectations of the Reagan administration. Finally, list the Reagan administration policies that addressed the major concerns of each group. When you are done, consider the following questions: What concerns and expectations, if any, did the various groups have in common? What tensions might there have been between component groups of the Reagan coalition? To do this exercise online or to download this chart, visit bedfordstmartins.com/roarkunderstanding.

Reagan coalition group	Major concerns	Expectations	Administration policies
Free-market advocates			
Militant anti-Communists			
Fundamentalist Christians			
White southerners			
Reagan Democrats			

Now that you've reviewed various parts of the chapter, take a step back and try to see the big picture by answering these questions. Remember to use specific examples from the chapter in your answers. To do this exercise online, visit bedfordstmartins.com/roarkunderstanding.

NIXON AND WATERGATE

▶ How did the Nixon administration appeal to the conservative movement?

▶ What were Nixon's biggest mistakes in the Watergate scandal?

THE CARTER ADMINISTRATION

▶ Should Jimmy Carter be considered a liberal? Why or why not?

▶ Is it fair to describe the Carter administration as a "failed presidency"? Why or why not?

LOOKING BACKWARD, LOOKING AHEAD

▶ How did Reagan's experience of the Cold War during the 1950s and 1960s influence his foreign policy?

▶ In what ways does Ronald Reagan's presidency continue to shape the American political landscape?

RONALD REAGAN AND THE CONSERVATIVE TURN

▶ What did voters find appealing about Ronald Reagan in 1980? What groups were most attracted to his message?

▶ What specific policies of the Reagan administration satisfied conservative goals? What did conservatives fail to win?

IN YOUR OWN WORDS

Imagine that you must explain chapter 30 to someone who hasn't read it. What would be the most important points to include and why?

31
FACING THE CHALLENGES OF A CHANGING WORLD

SINCE 1989

> This chapter explores the changing nature of American politics and foreign policy from 1989 to the present. It examines the end of the Cold War during the presidency of George H. W. Bush, the domestic and foreign policies of the Clinton administration, and the George W. Bush administration's departures from previous U.S. policy in the wake of the September 11, 2001, terrorist attacks, and the election of Barack Obama.

> How did the United States respond to the end of the Cold War and tensions in the Middle East?

> What explains the Clinton administration's move to the right?

> How did President Clinton respond to the challenges of globalization?

> How did President George W. Bush change American politics and foreign policy?

> Conclusion: How have Americans debated the role of the government?

DID YOU KNOW?

By 2006, immigrants comprised 12.4 percent of the U.S. population.

New U.S. citizens. New citizens take the oath of allegiance at Monticello, Virginia, the historic home of Thomas Jefferson. July 4, 2008.

> How did the United States respond to the end of the Cold War and tensions in the Middle East?

The Gulf War These soldiers arriving in Dhahran, Saudi Arabia, were part of the massive military buildup in the Persian Gulf area before the U.S.-led coalition drove Iraqi forces out of Kuwait. For the first time, women served in combat-support positions piloting planes and helicopters, directing artillery, and fighting fires. Bettman/Corbis.

VICE PRESIDENT George H. W. Bush announced his bid for the presidency in the 1988 election, declaring, "We don't need radical new directions." As president, Bush proposed few domestic initiatives. Yet as the most dramatic changes since the 1940s swept through the world, Bush confronted situations that did not fit the simpler free world versus communism framework that had guided foreign policy since World War II. Most Americans approved of Bush's handling of two challenges to U.S. foreign policy: the disintegration of the Soviet Union and its hold over Eastern Europe, and Iraq's invasion of neighboring Kuwait. But voters' concern over a sluggish economy limited Bush to one term in the White House.

Gridlock in Government

The son of a wealthy New England senator, George Herbert Walker Bush served in Congress during the 1960s and headed the CIA during the Nixon and Ford years. In 1980, Bush adjusted his more moderate policy positions to fit Reagan's conservative agenda and accepted second place on the Republican ticket. At the end of Reagan's second term, Republicans rewarded him with the presidential nomination.

Several candidates competed for the Democratic nomination in 1988. The Reverend Jesse Jackson made an impressive bid, winning several primaries and seven million votes. But a more centrist candidate, Massachusetts governor Michael Dukakis, won the nomination. On election day, Bush won 54 percent of the vote, but the Democrats gained seats in Congress.

CHAPTER LOCATOR | How did the United States respond to the end of the Cold War and tensions in the Middle East?

President Bush promised "a kinder, gentler nation" and was more inclined than Reagan to approve government activity in the private sphere. For example, he signed the Clean Air Act of 1990, the most comprehensive environmental law in history. Some forty million Americans reaped the benefits of a second regulatory measure, the Americans with Disabilities Act, in 1990. Job discrimination against people with disabilities was banned, and private businesses and public facilities had to be made handicapped accessible.

Yet Bush also needed to satisfy party conservatives. His most famous campaign pledge had been "Read my lips: no new taxes," and he opposed most proposals requiring additional federal funds. Bush vetoed thirty-six bills, including those lifting abortion restrictions, extending unemployment benefits, raising taxes, and mandating family and medical leave for workers. Press reports increasingly used the words *stalemate*, *gridlock*, and *divided government*.

Continuing a trend begun during the Reagan years, states tried to compensate for this paralysis, becoming more innovative than Washington. States passed bills to block corporate takeovers, establish parental leave policies, improve food labeling, and protect the environment. In the 1980s, a few states began to pass measures guaranteeing gay and lesbian rights. In the 1990s, dozens of cities passed ordinances requiring businesses receiving tax abatements or other city benefits to pay wages well above the federal minimum wage. And in 1999, California passed a gun control bill with much tougher restrictions on assault weapons than reformers had been able to get through Congress.

A huge federal budget deficit inherited from the Reagan administration impelled the president in 1990 to abandon his "no new taxes" pledge, outraging conservatives. The new law authorized modest tax increases for high-income Americans and higher taxes on gasoline, cigarettes, alcohol, and luxury items. Neither the new revenues nor controls on spending curbed the deficit, which was boosted by rising costs for Social Security, Medicare, and Medicaid and spending on war and natural disasters.

Bush also continued Reagan's efforts to create a more conservative Supreme Court. His first nominee, federal appeals court judge David Souter, was a moderate. But in 1991, when the only African American on the Court, Justice Thurgood Marshall, retired, Bush set off a national controversy. He nominated Clarence Thomas, a conservative black appeals court judge who had opposed affirmative action as head of the Equal Employment Opportunity Commission (EEOC) under Reagan. Charging that Thomas would not protect minority rights, civil rights groups and other liberal organizations fought the nomination. Then Anita Hill, a black law professor and former EEOC employee, shook the confirmation process by accusing Thomas of sexual harassment.

Bush and Taxes

When George H. W. Bush accepted the Republican nomination for president in 1988, he addressed an issue central to conservative politics. "Read my lips," he told convention delegates: "No new taxes." When Bush was forced to break his promise, many Republicans were outraged. Here, conservative cartoonist Scott Stantis, then at the *Arizona Republic* in Phoenix, likens Bush to Pinocchio, whose nose grew when he lied. Scott Stantis/Copley News Service.

▶ FOR MORE HELP ANALYZING THIS IMAGE, see the visual activity for this chapter in the Online Study Guide at bedfordstmartins.com/ roarkunderstanding.

What explains the Clinton administration's move to the right?

How did President Clinton respond to the challenges of globalization?

How did President George W. Bush change American politics and foreign policy?

Conclusion: How have Americans debated the role of the government?

1988
- Republican George H. W. Bush is elected president.

1989
- Communism collapses in Eastern Europe.
- United States invades Panama.

1990
- Americans with Disabilities Act.
- Clean Air Act.

1991
- Persian Gulf War.
- Soviet Union dissolves.

1992
- Democrat William Jefferson "Bill" Clinton is elected president.

Colin Powell

▶ Chairman of the Joint Chiefs of Staff under President George H. W. Bush and secretary of state under President George W. Bush. In 2001, Powell became the first African American secretary of state. Disagreements between Powell and other members of the Bush administration over the Iraq War led to his resignation in 2005.

Saddam Hussein

▶ Iraqi dictator from 1979 to 2003. Hussein's decision to invade Kuwait in 1990 sparked the Persian Gulf War. In 2003, President Bush declared war on Iraq, citing Hussein's violation of UN resolutions and alleged connections to Al Qaeda. Hussein's government was quickly toppled, and he was eventually executed by Iraqi officials.

Before the Senate Judiciary Committee, Thomas angrily denied the charges, claiming that he was the victim of a "high-tech lynching for uppity blacks." Hill's testimony failed to sway the Senate, which voted narrowly to confirm Thomas, solidifying the Supreme Court's shift to the right.

Going to War in Central America and the Persian Gulf

President Bush won greater support for his actions abroad. In Central America, the United States had tolerated and, in fact, paid Panamanian dictator Manuel Noriega for helping the Contras in Nicaragua and providing the CIA with information about Communist activities in the region. But in 1989, after Noriega was indicted for drug trafficking by an American grand jury and after his troops killed an American marine, President Bush ordered 25,000 military personnel into Panama. In Operation Just Cause, U.S. forces quickly overcame Noriega's troops, sustaining 23 deaths, while hundreds of Panamanians, including many civilians, died. Chairman of the Joint Chiefs of Staff **Colin Powell** noted that "our euphoria over our victory in Just Cause was not universal." Both the United Nations and the Organization of American States censured the unilateral action by the United States.

In contrast, Bush's second military engagement rested solidly on international approval. Considering Iran to be America's major enemy in the Middle East, U.S. officials had quietly assisted the Iraqi dictator **Saddam Hussein** in the Iran-Iraq war, which began in 1980 and ended inconclusively in 1988. In August 1990, Hussein sent troops into the small, oil-rich country of Kuwait to the south (**Map 31.1**), and within days the invasion neared the Saudi Arabian border, threatening the world's largest oil reserves. President Bush quickly ordered a massive mobilization of American forces and assembled an international coalition to stand up to Iraq. He invoked principles of national self-determination and international law, but long-standing interests in Middle Eastern oil also drove the U.S. response.

The UN declared an embargo on Iraqi oil and authorized the use of force if Iraq did not withdraw from Kuwait by January 15, 1991. By then, the United States had deployed 400,000 soldiers to Saudi Arabia, joined by 265,000 troops from some two dozen other nations, including several Arab states. "The community of nations has resolutely gathered to condemn and repel lawless aggression," Bush announced. "With few exceptions, the world now stands as one."

With Iraqi forces still in Kuwait, in January 1991 Bush asked Congress to approve war. Considerable sentiment favored waiting to see if the embargo and other means would force Hussein to back down. In the end, Congress debated for three days and then authorized war by a margin of five votes in the Senate and sixty-seven in the House. On January 17, 1991, the U.S.-led coalition launched Operation Desert Storm, a forty-day bombing campaign against Iraqi military targets, power plants, oil refineries, and transportation networks. Having severely crippled Iraq by air, the coalition then stormed into Kuwait, forcing Iraqi troops to withdraw (see Map 31.1).

"By God, we've kicked the Vietnam syndrome once and for all," President George H. W. Bush exulted on March 1, 1991. Most Americans found no moral ambiguity in the **Persian Gulf War** and took pride in the display of military prowess. The

CHAPTER LOCATOR | How did the United States respond to the end of the Cold War and tensions in the Middle East?

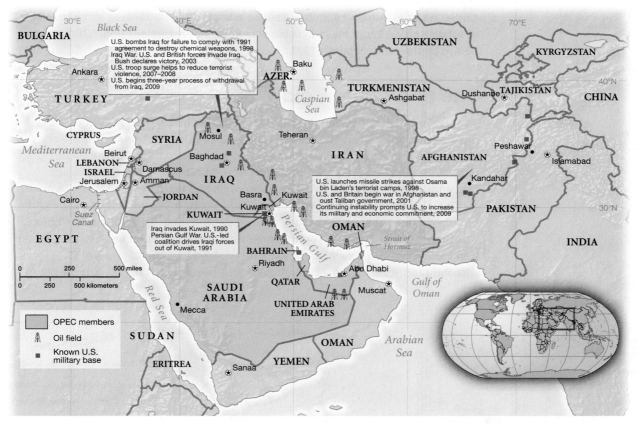

MAP 31.1 ■ **Events in the Middle East, 1989–2009**

During the Persian Gulf War of 1991, Egypt, Syria, and other Middle Eastern nations joined the coalition against Iraq, and the twenty-two-member Arab League supported the war as a means to liberate Kuwait. After September 11, 2001, the Arab League approved of U.S. military operations in Afghanistan because the attacks "were an attack on the common values of the world, not just on the United States." Yet, except for the countries where the United States had military bases—Bahrain, Kuwait, Qatar, and Saudi Arabia—no Arab country supported the American invasion and occupation of Iraq in 2003. Arab hostility toward the United States also reflected the deterioration of Israeli-Palestinian relations after 1999, as Arabs charged that the United States allowed Israel to deny Palestinians land and liberty.

> ► FOR MORE HELP ANALYZING THIS MAP, see the map activity for this chapter in the Online Study Guide at bedfordstmartins.com/roarkunderstanding.

United States stood at the apex of global leadership, steering a coalition in which Arab nations fought beside their former colonial rulers.

Some Americans criticized the Bush administration for ending the war without deposing Hussein. But Bush pointed to the UN mandate limiting the mission to driving Iraqi forces out of Kuwait and to Middle Eastern leaders' concern that an invasion of Iraq would destabilize the region. His secretary of defense, Richard Cheney, doubted that coalition forces could secure a stable government to replace Hussein and considered the price of a long occupation too high.

Yet Middle Eastern stability remained elusive. Israel, which had endured Iraqi missile attacks, was more secure, but the Israeli-Palestinian conflict remained intractable. Despite military losses, Saddam Hussein remained in power and

Persian Gulf War
► 1991 war between Iraq and an international coalition headed by the United States. The war was sparked by the 1990 invasion of Kuwait by Iraqi forces. Overwhelming American military superiority led to a quick victory for coalition forces. The Iraqi dictator Saddam Hussein was, however, left in power.

turned on Iraqi Kurds and Shiite Muslims whom the United States had encouraged to rebel. And he found ways to conceal weapons development from UN inspectors before he threw them out in 1998.

The End of the Cold War

The Soviet Union supported the American position in the Persian Gulf War, marking a momentous change in relations between the United States and the Soviet Union. The progressive forces that Gorbachev had encouraged in the Communist world (see chapter 30) swept through Eastern Europe in 1989, when popular uprisings demanded an end to state repression and inefficient economic bureaucracies. Communist governments toppled like dominoes (**Map 31.2**), virtually without bloodshed, because Gorbachev refused to prop them up with Soviet armies.

Unification of East and West Germany sped to completion in 1990, and former iron curtain countries such as Hungary and Poland lined up to join NATO. Although U.S. military forces remained in Europe as part of NATO, Europe no

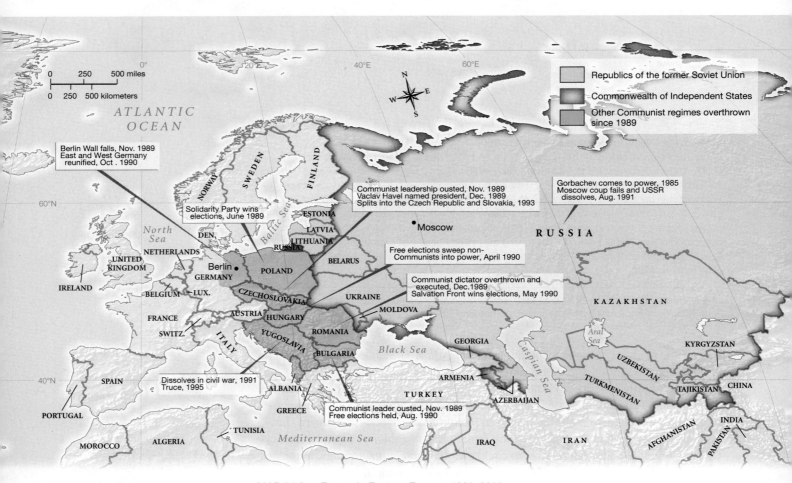

MAP 31.2 ■ **Events in Eastern Europe, 1989–2002**
The overthrow of Communist governments throughout Eastern Europe and the splintering of the Soviet Union into more than a dozen separate nations were among the most momentous changes in world history since World War II.

CHAPTER LOCATOR | How did the United States respond to the end of the Cold War and tensions in the Middle East?

CHALLENGES OF A CHANGING WORLD, SINCE 1989

longer depended on the United States for its security. Its economic clout also grew as Western Europe formed a common economic market in 1992.

Inspired by the liberation of Eastern Europe, republics within the Soviet Union soon sought their own independence. In December 1991, Boris Yeltsin, president of the Russian Republic, announced that Russia and eleven other republics had formed a new entity, the Commonwealth of Independent States, and other former Soviet states declared their independence. With nothing left to govern, Gorbachev resigned. The Soviet Union had dissolved.

China and North Korea resisted the liberalizing tides sweeping the world. In 1989, Chinese soldiers killed hundreds of pro-democracy demonstrators in Tiananmen Square in Beijing, and the Communist government arrested some ten thousand reformers. North Korea remained under a Communist dictatorship committed to developing nuclear weapons. "The post–Cold War world is decidedly not post-nuclear," declared one U.S. official. In 1990, the United States and the Soviet Union signed the Strategic Arms Reduction Talks treaty, which cut about 30 percent of each superpower's nuclear arsenal. And in 1996, the UN General Assembly overwhelmingly approved a total nuclear test ban treaty. Yet India and Pakistan, hostile neighbors, refused to sign the treaty, and both exploded atomic devices in 1998. Moreover, the Republican-controlled Senate defeated U.S. ratification of the test ban treaty. The potential for rogue nations and terrorist groups to develop nuclear weapons posed an ongoing threat to international peace and security.

The 1992 Election

In March 1991, Bush's chances for reelection in 1992 looked golden. With Bush's approval rating at 88 percent, most prominent Democrats opted out of the presidential race. But that did not deter William Jefferson "Bill" Clinton, who at age forty-five had served as governor of Arkansas for twelve years. Like Carter in 1976, Clinton and his running mate, Tennessee senator Albert Gore Jr., presented themselves as "New Democrats" and sought to rid the party of its liberal image.

Clinton promised to work for the "forgotten middle class," who "do the work, pay the taxes, raise the kids, and play by the rules." Disavowing the "tax and spend" label that Republicans pinned on his party, he promised a tax cut for the middle class, pledged to reinvigorate government and the economy, and vowed "to put an end to welfare as we know it." Bush was vulnerable to voters' concerns about the ailing economy, as unemployment reached 7 percent. The popularity of a third candidate, self-made Texas billionaire H. Ross Perot, revealed Americans' frustrations with government and the major parties.

Fifty-five percent of those eligible voted, just barely reversing the thirty-year decline in voter turnout. Clinton won 43 percent of the popular vote, Bush 38 percent, and Perot 19 percent—the strongest third-party finish in eighty years.

QUICK REVIEW

What were the achievements and failures of George H. W. Bush's presidency?

What explains the Clinton administration's move to the right?

How did President Clinton respond to the challenges of globalization?

How did President George W. Bush change American politics and foreign policy?

Conclusion: How have Americans debated the role of the government?

> # What explains the Clinton administration's move to the right?

Clinton and Gore on Tour
The gregarious Bill Clinton excelled at campaigning, and the youth of the first baby boomer candidates appealed to many. During the 1992 presidential election, Clinton and his wife, Hillary—with running mate Al Gore and his wife, Tipper—went out on bus tours as a way of demonstrating the Democrats' connection to ordinary people. Ira Wyman/Sygma/Corbis.

BILL CLINTON'S ASSERTION that "the era of big government is over" reflected the Democratic Party's move to the right that had begun with Jimmy Carter in the 1970s. Clinton did not completely abandon liberal principles. Yet his administration attended more to the concerns of middle-class Americans than to the needs of the disadvantaged.

Clinton's eight-year presidency witnessed the longest economic boom in U.S. history and ended with a budget surplus. Although various factors generated the prosperity, many Americans identified Clinton with the buoyant economy, elected him to a second term, and continued to support him even when his reckless sexual behavior resulted in impeachment. The scandal, however, crippled Clinton's leadership in his last years in office.

Clinton's Promise of Change

Clinton wanted to restore confidence in government as a force for good but also to avoid alienating antigovernment voters. The huge budget deficit that he inherited—$4.4 trillion in 1993—further precluded substantial federal initiatives. Moreover, Ross Perot's challenges denied Clinton a majority of the popular vote in both 1992 and 1996, and the Republicans controlled Congress for all but his first two years in office. Throughout most of his presidency, Clinton was burdened by investigations into past financial activities and private indiscretions.

Despite these obstacles, Clinton achieved a number of incremental reforms. He used his executive authority to ease restrictions on abortion and signed several bills that Republicans had previously blocked. Most significantly, Clinton pushed through a substantial increase in the Earned Income Tax Credit (EITC) for low-wage earners, a program begun in 1975. The EITC gave subsidies to people who worked full-time at meager wages in order to lift their family income above the poverty line. By 2003, some fifteen million low-income families were benefiting from the EITC, almost half of them minorities. One expert called it "the largest antipoverty program since the Great Society."

CHAPTER LOCATOR | How did the United States respond to the end of the Cold War and tensions in the Middle East?

Liberal Reforms under President Clinton

Family and Medical Leave Act of 1993

Violence against Women Act of 1994

Stricter air pollution controls and greater protection for national forests and parks

A minimum-wage increase

Expansion of aid for college students

Expansion of the Earned Income Tax Credit

CHRONOLOGY

1992
– Democrat William Jefferson "Bill" Clinton is elected president.

1993
– Clinton announces "don't ask, don't tell" policy for gays in the military.
– Family and Medical Leave Act.

1995
– Bombing of a federal building in Oklahoma City kills 169.

1996
– Personal Responsibility and Work Opportunity Reconciliation Act.
– President Clinton is reelected.

1997
– Tax cut is enacted.

1998
– President Clinton is impeached.

1999
– Senate trial fails to approve articles of impeachment.

Shortly before Clinton took office, the economy had begun to rebound, and the boom that followed helped boost his popularity through the 1990s. Economic expansion, along with budget cuts, tax increases, and declining unemployment, produced a budget surplus in 1998, the first since 1969. Despite a substantial tax cut in 1997 that reduced levies on estates and capital gains and provided tax credits for families with children and for higher education, the surplus grew.

Clinton failed, however, to provide universal health insurance or to curb skyrocketing medical costs. Under the direction of First Lady Hillary Rodham Clinton and with very little congressional consultation, the administration proposed an ambitious, complicated plan that the health care industry charged would increase taxes and government interference in medical decisions. Congress enacted piecemeal reform, such as underwriting health care for five million uninsured children, but affordable health care for all remained elusive.

Pledging to change the face of government to one that "looked like America," Clinton built on the gradual progress women and minorities had made since the 1960s, appointing the most diverse group of department heads ever assembled, including six women, three African Americans, and two Latinos. Secretary of Commerce Norman Y. Mineta became the first Asian American to hold a cabinet post. Janet Reno became the first female attorney general and Madeleine K. Albright the first female secretary of state. Clinton's judicial appointments had

Clinton's Appointments

Not only did President Clinton appoint more women to high government posts than any previous president, but he also broke new ground by appointing them to offices traditionally considered to be male territory. Here Secretary of State Madeleine Albright (left) and Attorney General Janet Reno (second from right) applaud Clinton's 1999 State of the Union address with other cabinet members. AP/Wide World.

What explains the Clinton administration's move to the right?	How did President Clinton respond to the challenges of globalization?	How did President George W. Bush change American politics and foreign policy?	Conclusion: How have Americans debated the role of the government?

a similar cast, and in 1993 he named the second woman to the Supreme Court, Ruth Bader Ginsburg, whose arguments before she became an appeals court judge had won key women's rights rulings from the Supreme Court.

The Clinton Administration Moves Right

The 1994 elections swept away the Democratic majorities in Congress and helped push the Clinton administration to the right. Led by Representative Newt Gingrich of Georgia, Republicans claimed the 1994 election as a mandate for their "contract with America," a conservative platform to end "government that is too big, too intrusive, and too easy with the public's money" and to elect "a Congress that respects the values and shares the faith of the American family."

The most extreme antigovernment sentiment developed far from Washington in the form of grassroots armed militias. They celebrated white Christian supremacy and reflected conservatives' hostility to such diverse things as taxes and the United Nations. The militia movement grew after government agents stormed the headquarters of an armed religious cult in Waco, Texas, in April 1993, killing more than 80. On the second anniversary of that event, a bomb leveled a federal building in Oklahoma City, taking 169 lives in the worst terrorist attack in the nation's history up to that point.

Clinton bowed to conservative views on gay and lesbian rights, backing away from a campaign promise to lift the ban on gays in the military. When military leaders and key legislators objected, he reverted to a **"don't ask, don't tell" policy** in 1993, forbidding officials from asking military personnel about their sexual orientation but allowing the dismissal of soldiers who said they were gay or engaged in homosexual behavior. In 1996, Clinton signed the Defense of Marriage Act, prohibiting the federal government from recognizing state-licensed marriages between same-sex couples.

Nonetheless, gays and lesbians continued to make strides as attitudes about homosexuality became more tolerant. By 2006, more than half of the five hundred largest companies provided health benefits to same-sex domestic partners and included sexual orientation in their nondiscrimination policies. More than twenty-five states banned discrimination in public employment, and many of those laws extended to private employment, housing, and education. By 2009, gay marriage was legal in Massachusetts, Connecticut, Vermont, and Iowa, and several states recognized civil unions and domestic partnerships, extending to same-sex couples the rights available to married couples in legal matters such as inheritance, taxation, and medical decisions.

Clinton's efforts to cast himself as a centrist were apparent in his handling of the New Deal program Aid to Families with Dependent Children (AFDC), which most people called welfare. Public sentiment about poverty had shifted since the 1960s. Instead of blaming poverty on the lack of adequate jobs or other external circumstances, more people blamed the poor themselves and insisted that welfare programs trapped the poor in cycles of dependency.

By vetoing two welfare reform bills, Clinton forced a less punitive measure, which he signed as the 1996 election approached. The Personal Responsibility and Work Opportunity Reconciliation Act abolished AFDC. The law provided grants to the states to assist the poor, but it limited welfare payments to two years, regardless of whether the recipient could find a job, and it set a lifetime

"don't ask, don't tell" policy

▶ Military policy announced by President Clinton in 1993 that barred officials from inquiring into the sexual orientation of military personnel but permitted the dismissal of personnel who admitted to being gay or engaged in homosexual behavior. The policy represented a retreat from Clinton's campaign promise to lift the ban on gays in the military and resulted in a significant increase in discharges of homosexuals from the armed forces.

CHAPTER LOCATOR | How did the United States respond to the end of the Cold War and tensions in the Middle East?

limit of aid at five years. Reflecting growing controversy over immigration, the law also barred legal immigrants from obtaining food stamps and other benefits and allowed states to stop Medicaid for legal immigrants.

Clinton's signature on the new law denied Republicans a partisan issue in the 1996 presidential campaign. The president ran as a moderate who would save the country from extremist Republicans, while the Republican Party also moved to the center, nominating Kansan Robert Dole, a World War II hero and former Senate majority leader. Clinton won 49 percent of the votes; 41 percent went to Dole and 9 percent to third-party candidate Ross Perot. Although Clinton won reelection, voters sent a Republican majority back to Congress.

Impeaching the President

Despite his continuing popularity, Clinton's presidency was hampered by scandals and an impeachment trial. Early in his presidency, charges related to firings of White House staff, political use of FBI records, and "Whitewater"—the nickname for real estate dealings that the Clintons had conducted in Arkansas—led to an official investigation by an independent prosecutor. The president also faced a sexual harassment lawsuit filed in 1994 by a state employee. A federal court threw out that case in 1998, but another sexual scandal more seriously threatened Clinton's presidency.

In January 1998, Kenneth Starr, independent prosecutor for Whitewater, began to investigate the charge that Clinton had had sexual relations with a twenty-one-year-old White House intern and then lied about it to a federal grand jury. After vehemently denying the charge, Clinton subsequently bowed to the mounting evidence against him. Starr prepared a case for the House of Representatives, which in December 1998 voted to impeach the president for perjury and obstruction of justice. Clinton became the second president (after Andrew Johnson, in 1868) to be impeached by the House and tried by the Senate.

The Senate trial took place in early 1999. Most Americans condemned the president's behavior but approved of the job he was doing and opposed removal from office. With a two-thirds majority needed for conviction, the Senate voted 45 to 55 on the perjury count and 50 to 50 on the obstruction of justice count. A majority, including some Republicans, seemed to agree with a Clinton supporter that the president's behavior, though "indefensible, outrageous, unforgivable, shameless," did not warrant his removal from office.

The investigation that triggered events leading up to impeachment ended in 2000 when the independent prosecutor reported insufficient evidence of illegalities related to the Whitewater land deals. Although more than 60 percent of Americans gave Clinton high marks on his job performance throughout the scandal, it distracted him from domestic and international problems and precluded the possibility of significant policy advances in his last years in office.

The Booming Economy of the 1990s

Clinton's ability to weather the impeachment crisis owed much to the prosperous economy, which in 1991 began its longest period of expansion in U.S. history. The president took credit for the thriving economy, and his policies did contribute to

| What explains the Clinton administration's move to the right? | How did President Clinton respond to the challenges of globalization? | How did President George W. Bush change American politics and foreign policy? | Conclusion: How have Americans debated the role of the government? |

the boom. He made deficit reduction a priority, and in exchange the Federal Reserve Board and bond market traders lowered interest rates, encouraging economic expansion by making money easier to borrow. Businesses also prospered because they had squeezed down their costs through restructuring and laying off workers. Economic problems in Europe and Asia helped American firms become more competitive in the international market. And the computer revolution and the application of information technology boosted productivity.

The Booming Economy of the 1990s

Gross domestic product grew by more than one-third.

Thirteen million new jobs were created.

Inflation remained in check.

Unemployment dropped to 4 percent.

The stock market soared.

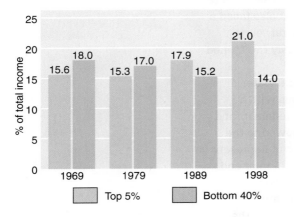

FIGURE 31.1 ■ **The Growth of Inequality: Changes in Family Income, 1969–1998**
For most of the post–World War II period, income increased for all groups on the economic ladder. But after 1979, the income of the poorest families actually declined, while the income of the richest 20 percent of the population grew substantially. Adapted from the *New York Times*, 1989.

People at all income levels benefited from the economic boom, but the gaps between the rich and the poor and between the wealthy and the middle class, which had been growing since the 1970s, failed to narrow (**Figure 31.1**). This persistence of inequality was linked in part to the growing use of information technology, which increased demand for highly skilled workers, while the movement of manufacturing jobs abroad diminished opportunities and wages for the less skilled. In addition, deregulation and the continuing decline of unions hurt less-skilled workers, tax cuts had favored the better-off, and the national minimum wage failed to keep up with inflation.

Although more minorities than ever attained middle-class status, in general people of color remained lowest on the economic ladder. For instance, in 2005 the median income for white households surpassed $50,000, but it stood at only $31,000 and $36,000 for African American and Latino households, respectively. In 2005, poverty afflicted about 25 percent of blacks, 22 percent of Latinos, and 11.1 percent of Asian Americans, in contrast to 8.3 percent of whites.

> ### QUICK REVIEW

What policies of the Clinton administration reflected the president's efforts to move his party to the right?

CHAPTER LOCATOR | How did the United States respond to the end of the Cold War and tensions in the Middle East?

<blockquote>**U.S. Troops in Kosovo** In 1999, American troops joined a NATO peacekeeping unit in the former Yugoslav province of Kosovo to assist the return of the ethnic Albanians after a U.S.-led NATO bombing campaign forced the Serbian army to withdraw. Here, an Albanian boy walks beside Specialist Brent Baldwin from Jonesville, Michigan, as he patrols the town of Gnjilane in southeast Kosovo in May 2000. Wide World Photos, Inc.</blockquote>

How did President Clinton respond to the challenges of globalization?

AMERICA'S ECONOMIC SUCCESS in the 1990s was linked to its dominance in the world economy. From that position, President Clinton tried to shape the tremendous transformations occurring in a process called globalization—the growing integration and interdependence of national citizens and economies. Clinton agreed with George H. W. Bush that the United States must retain its economic and military dominance over all other nations. Yet no new global strategy emerged to replace the containment of communism as the decisive factor in the exercise of American power abroad.

Defining America's Place in a New World Order

In 1991, President George H. W. Bush declared a "new world order" emerging from the ashes of the Cold War. As the sole superpower, the United States was determined not to let any nation challenge its military superiority or global leadership. (See "Global Comparison," page 870.) Yet policymakers struggled to define guiding principles for deciding when and how to use the nation's military and diplomatic power in a post–Cold War world. Combating Saddam Hussein's aggression seemed the obvious course of action in 1991, but dealing with other areas of instability proved more difficult.

Africa was a case in point. In 1992, guided largely by humanitarian concern, President Bush had attached U.S. forces to a UN operation in the small northern African country of Somalia, where famine and civil war raged. In 1993, President Clinton allowed that humanitarian mission to turn into "nation building"—an effort to establish a stable government—and eighteen U.S. soldiers were killed. The outcry at home suggested that most citizens were unwilling to sacrifice lives

| What explains the Clinton administration's move to the right? | How did President Clinton respond to the challenges of globalization? | How did President George W. Bush change American politics and foreign policy? | Conclusion: How have Americans debated the role of the government? |

869

Countries with the Highest Military Expenditures, 2005

During the Cold War, the military budgets of the United States and the Soviet Union were relatively even. For example, in 1983 U.S. military expenditures stood at $217 billion, compared to $213 billion for the Soviet Union. Even before the Iraq War, which began in 2003, the U.S. military budget constituted 47 percent of total world military expenditures. That proportion rose to 48 percent in 2005, with the United States spending nearly ten times as much as its nearest competitor. The U.S. defense budget reflects the determination of Democratic and Republican administrations alike to maintain dominance in the world, even while the capacities of its traditional enemies have been greatly diminished.

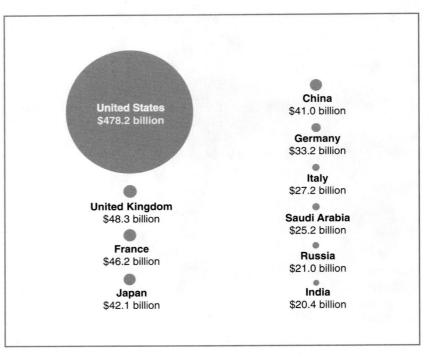

United States $478.2 billion

China $41.0 billion

Germany $33.2 billion

Italy $27.2 billion

United Kingdom $48.3 billion

Saudi Arabia $25.2 billion

France $46.2 billion

Russia $21.0 billion

Japan $42.1 billion

India $20.4 billion

when no vital interest seemed threatened. Indeed, both the United States and the United Nations stood by in 1994 when more than half a million people were massacred in a brutal civil war in the central African nation of Rwanda.

As always, the United States was more inclined to use force nearer its borders. After a military coup overthrew Jean-Bertrand Aristide, the democratically elected president of Haiti, thousands of Haitians tried to escape political violence and poverty, many on flimsy boats heading for Florida. In 1994, Clinton got the United Nations to impose economic sanctions on Haiti and to authorize intervention by U.S. troops. Hours before U.S. forces were to invade Haiti, the military leaders promised to step down. U.S. forces landed peacefully, and Aristide was restored to power. Initially a huge success, U.S. policy continued to be tested as Haiti faced grave economic challenges and political instability.

In eastern Europe, the collapse of communism ignited a severe crisis. During the Cold War, the Communist government of Yugoslavia held together a federation of six republics. After the Communists were swept out in 1989, ruthless leaders exploited ethnic differences to bolster their power, and Yugoslavia splintered into separate states and fell into civil war.

The Serbs' aggression under President Slobodan Milosevic against Bosnian Muslims in particular horrified much of the world, but European and U.S. leaders hesitated to use military force. Finally, in 1995, Clinton ordered U.S. fliers to join NATO forces in intensive bombing of Serbian military concentrations. That effort and successful offensives by the Croatian and Bosnian armies forced Milosevic to the bargaining table. After representatives from Serbia, Croatia, and Bosnia hammered out a peace treaty,

Yugoslavia 1945–1991

Breakup of Yugoslavia

CHAPTER LOCATOR | How did the United States respond to the end of the Cold War and tensions in the Middle East?

Clinton then agreed to send twenty thousand American troops to Bosnia as part of a NATO peacekeeping mission.

In 1998, new fighting broke out in the southern Serbian province of Kosovo, where ethnic Albanians, who constituted 90 percent of the population, demanded independence. The Serbian army retaliated, driving out one-third of Kosovo's 1.8 million Albanian Muslims. In 1999, NATO launched a U.S.-led bombing attack on Serbian targets that forced Milosevic to agree to a peace settlement. Serbians voted Milosevic out of office in October 2000, and he died in 2006 while on trial for genocide by a UN war crimes tribunal.

Elsewhere, Clinton remained willing to deploy U.S. power when he could send missiles rather than soldiers, and he was prepared to act without international support or UN sanction. In August 1998, bombs exploded at the U.S. embassies in Kenya and Tanzania, killing 12 Americans and more than 250 Africans. Clinton retaliated with missile attacks on terrorist training camps in Afghanistan and facilities in Sudan controlled by Osama bin Laden, a Saudi-born millionaire who financed the Islamic-extremist terrorist network linked to the embassy attacks. Clinton also launched air strikes against Iraq in 1993 when a plot to assassinate former president Bush was uncovered, in 1996 after Saddam Hussein attacked the Kurds in northern Iraq, and repeatedly between 1998 and 2000 after Hussein expelled UN weapons inspectors. Whereas Bush had acted in the Gulf War with the support of an international force that included Arab states, Clinton acted unilaterally and in the face of Arab opposition.

To ameliorate the Israeli-Palestinian conflict, a major source of Arab hostility toward the West, Clinton used diplomatic rather than military power. In 1993, due largely to the efforts of the Norwegian government, Yasir Arafat, head of the Palestine Liberation Organization (PLO), and Yitzhak Rabin, Israeli prime minister, recognized the existence of each other's states for the first time and agreed to Israeli withdrawal from the Gaza Strip and Jericho, allowing for Palestinian self-government there. In July 1994, Clinton presided over another turning point as Rabin and King Hussein of Jordan signed a declaration of peace. Yet difficult issues remained to be settled, and continuing violence between Israelis and Palestinians strengthened anti-American sentiment among Arabs, who saw the United States as Israel's ally.

Obstacles to Resolution of the Israeli-Palestinian Conflict

Control of Jerusalem

The fate of Palestinian refugees

200,000 Israeli settlers living in the West Bank

Debates over Globalization

Building on efforts by Presidents Reagan and Bush, Clinton sought to speed up globalization, the movement of products, capital, and labor across national borders. In November 1993, he won congressional approval of the **North American Free Trade Agreement (NAFTA)**, which eliminated all tariffs and trade barriers among the United States, Canada, and Mexico. Organized labor and others fearing loss of jobs and industries to Mexico lobbied vigorously against NAFTA, and a

CHRONOLOGY

1993
- Israel and Palestine Liberation Organization sign peace accords.
- North American Free Trade Agreement.

1994
- United States sends troops to Haiti.
- General Agreement on Tariffs and Trade establishes World Trade Organization.

1998
- United States bombs Iraq and terrorist sites in Afghanistan and Sudan.

1999
- United States, with NATO, bombs Serbia.

Israel and PLO sign accords, 1993
Israel and Jordan sign peace treaty, 1994
Progress of Israeli-Palestinian negotiations halts and violence escalates, 2000
Israel withdraws from Gaza, 2005
Israel at war with Hezbollah in Lebanon, 2006
Israel invades Gaza, 2008

Events in Israel since 1989

What explains the Clinton administration's move to the right?

How did President Clinton respond to the challenges of globalization?

How did President George W. Bush change American politics and foreign policy?

Conclusion: How have Americans debated the role of the government?

North American Free Trade Agreement (NAFTA)

▶ 1993 treaty that eliminated all tariffs and trade barriers among the United States, Canada, and Mexico. NAFTA was supported by President Clinton, centrist Democrats, and many Republicans. President Clinton's support of NAFTA reflected his desire to speed up globalization by seeking new measures to ease restrictions on international commerce.

Protests against the WTO

Environmentalists and animal protection advocates were among the diverse array of groups demonstrating against the World Trade Organization when it attempted to meet in Seattle, Washington, in November 1999. These activists dressed as sea turtles to protest WTO agreements permitting economic actions that they believed threatened the survival of the animals. Wide World Photos, Inc.

majority of Democrats opposed it, but Republican support ensured approval. In 1994, the Senate ratified the General Agreement on Tariffs and Trade, establishing the World Trade Organization (WTO) to enforce substantial tariff reductions and elimination of import quotas among some 135 member nations. And in 2005, Clinton's successor, George W. Bush, got Congress to lower more trade barriers with the passage of the Central American–Dominican Republic Free Trade Agreement.

The free trade issue was intensely contested. Much of corporate America welcomed the elimination of trade barriers. "Ideally, you'd have every plant you own on a barge," remarked Jack Welch, CEO of General Electric. Critics linked globalization to the loss of jobs, the weakening of unions, and the growing gap between rich and poor. Demanding "fair trade" rather than simply free trade, they wanted trade treaties to require decent wage and labor standards. Environmentalists wanted countries seeking increased commerce with the United States to eliminate or reduce pollution and to prevent the destruction of endangered species.

In November 1999, tens of thousands of activists dramatized the globalization debate when they gathered in Seattle, Washington, to protest a meeting of the WTO. Protesters charged the WTO with promoting a global economy that destroyed the environment, devastated poorer developing nations, and undercut living standards and wages for workers. Globalization controversies often centered on relationships between the United States, which dominated the world's industrial core, and the developing nations on the periphery, whose cheap labor and lax environmental standards caught the eye of investors. United Students against Sweatshops, for example, attacked the international conglomerate Nike, which paid Chinese workers $1.50 to produce a pair of shoes selling for more than $100 in the United States. Yet leaders of developing nations actively sought foreign investment, insisting that wages deemed pitiful by Americans offered people in poor nations a much better living than they could otherwise obtain. At the same time, developing countries often pointed to American hypocrisy in advocating free trade in industry while heavily subsidizing its own agricultural sector. "When countries like America, Britain and France subsidize their farmers," complained a grower in Uganda, "we get hurt."

Whereas globalization's cheerleaders argued that everyone would benefit in the long run, critics focused on the short-term victims. "International trade and global financial markets are very good at generating wealth," conceded American businessman George Soros, "but they cannot take care of other social needs, such as the preservation of peace, alleviation of poverty, protection of the environment, labor conditions, or human rights." The critics enjoyed a few successes. In 2000, President Clinton signed an executive order requiring an environmental impact review before the signing of any trade agreement. Beyond the United States, officials from the World Bank and the International Monetary Fund, along with representatives from wealthy economies, promised in 2000 to provide poor nations more debt relief and a greater voice in decisions about loans and grants. According to World Bank president James D. Wolfensohn, "Our challenge is to make globalization an instrument of opportunity and inclusion—not fear."

CHAPTER LOCATOR | How did the United States respond to the end of the Cold War and tensions in the Middle East?

The Internationalization of the United States

Globalization was typically associated with the expansion of American enterprise and culture to other countries, yet the United States experienced the dynamic forces of globalization within its own borders. Already in the 1980s, Japanese, European, and Middle Eastern investors had purchased American stocks and bonds, real estate, and corporations. Local communities welcomed foreign capital, and states competed to recruit foreign automobile plants. By 2002, the paychecks of nearly 4 million American workers came from foreign-owned companies.

Globalization was transforming not just the economy but American society as well, as the United States experienced a tremendous surge of immigration. By 2006, the nation housed 35.7 million immigrants, who constituted 12.4 percent of the population. Almost half of those who arrived between 1980 and 2005 were Asians, and nearly 40 percent came from Latin America and the Caribbean. Consequently, immigration changed the racial and ethnic composition of the nation. By 2004, Asian Americans numbered 13 million, while 41 million Latinos constituted—at 14 percent—the largest minority group in the nation.

The racial composition of the new immigration heightened the century-old wariness of native-born Americans toward newcomers. Pressure for more restrictive policies stemmed from beliefs that immigrants took jobs from the native-born, suppressed wages by accepting low-paying employment, or eroded the dominant culture and language. Americans expressed particular hostility toward immigrants who were in the country illegally—an estimated 12 million in 2008—even though the economy depended on their cheap labor.

The new immigration was once again making America an international, interracial society. The largest numbers of immigrants flocked to California, New York, Texas, Florida, New Jersey, and Illinois, but new immigrants dispersed throughout the country. Taquerias, sushi bars, and Vietnamese restaurants appeared in southeastern and midwestern towns; cable TV companies added Spanish-language stations; and the international sport of soccer soared in popularity. Mixed marriages also displayed the growing fusion of cultures, recognized in 2000 on Census Bureau forms where Americans could check more than one racial category.

Like their predecessors, the majority of post-1965 immigrants were unskilled and poor, seeking economic opportunity. They took the lowest-paying jobs, including farm and yard work, child and elder care, and cleaning services—work that employers insisted native-born Americans would not do. Yet a significant number of immigrants were highly skilled workers, sought after by burgeoning high-tech industries. For example, in 1999 about one-third of the scientists and engineers employed in California's Silicon Valley had been born abroad.

QUICK REVIEW <

How did President Clinton respond to globalization?

George W. Bush's Second Term

U.S. President George W. Bush (right) walks with Secretary of Defense Donald Rumsfeld, Secretary of State Condoleezza Rice, and Chairman of the Joint Chiefs of Staff Gen. Peter Pace at the White House in Washington, D.C., May 1, 2006. Jim Young/Reuters/Corbis

How did President George W. Bush change American politics and foreign policy?

THE ELECTION OF GEORGE W. BUSH in 2000 marked the second time that a son of a former president gained the White House. But the younger Bush pushed a domestic agenda that was closer to Ronald Reagan's than that of George H. W. Bush. Overseas, as Islamist terrorism replaced communism as the primary threat to U.S. security, the Bush administration adopted a policy of unilateralism and preemption.

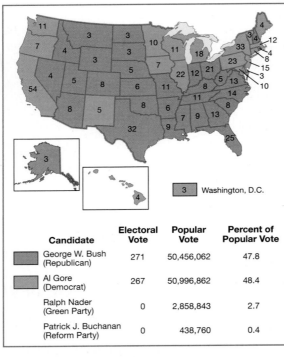

Candidate	Electoral Vote	Popular Vote	Percent of Popular Vote
George W. Bush (Republican)	271	50,456,062	47.8
Al Gore (Democrat)	267	50,996,862	48.4
Ralph Nader (Green Party)	0	2,858,843	2.7
Patrick J. Buchanan (Reform Party)	0	438,760	0.4

MAP 31.3 ■ The Election of 2000

The Disputed Election of 2000

George W. Bush won the Republican nomination after a series of hard-fought primaries. The son of former president George H. W. Bush, he had served as governor of Texas since 1994. Inexperienced in national and international affairs, Bush chose for his running mate a seasoned official, Richard B. Cheney, who had served in three previous Republican administrations.

Many observers predicted that the amazingly strong economy would give the Democratic nominee, Vice President Al Gore, the edge, and he did surpass Bush by more than half a million votes. Once the polls closed, however, it became clear that Florida's 25 electoral college votes would decide the presidency. Bush's tiny margin in Florida prompted an automatic recount of the votes, which eventually gave Bush an edge of 537 votes.

Meanwhile, the Democrats asked for hand-counting of Florida ballots in several heavily Democratic counties where machine errors and confusing ballots may have left thousands of Gore votes unrecorded. The Republicans, in turn, went to court to try to stop the hand-counts. The outcome of the 2000 election hung in the balance for weeks until a bitterly divided

CHAPTER LOCATOR | How did the United States respond to the end of the Cold War and tensions in the Middle East?

Supreme Court ruled five to four against further recounts, and Gore conceded the presidency to Bush on December 13, 2000 (**Map 31.3**). Despite the lack of a popular mandate, the Bush administration set out to make dramatic policy changes.

The Domestic Policies of a "Compassionate Conservative"

Bush's appointments, like Clinton's, brought significant diversity to the executive branch. He chose African Americans Colin Powell as secretary of state and Condoleezza Rice first as national security adviser and subsequently as secretary of state when Powell resigned in January 2005. Five of Bush's top-level appointees were women, including Secretary of Labor Elaine L. Chao, the first Asian American woman to serve in the cabinet.

Bush had promised to govern as a "compassionate conservative." A born-again Christian, he established the White House Office of Faith-Based and Community Initiatives to encourage religious and community groups to participate in government programs aimed at prison inmates, drug addicts, the unemployed, and others. The religious right praised the initiatives, but others charged that they violated the constitutional separation of church and state.

Bush's fiscal policies were more compassionate toward the rich than toward average Americans. In 2001, he signed a bill reducing taxes over the next ten years by $1.35 trillion. A 2003 tax law slashed another $320 billion. The laws heavily favored the rich by reducing income taxes, phasing out estate taxes, and cutting tax rates on capital gains and dividends. They also provided benefits for married couples and families with children and offered tax deductions for college expenses.

The administration insisted that the tax cuts would promote economic growth and jolt the economy out of the recession that had begun in 2000. The economy did recover, but opponents stressed inequities in the tax cuts and pointed to a mushrooming federal deficit—the highest in U.S. history—that surpassed $400 billion in 2004. The national debt rose to $9.6 trillion, making the United States increasingly dependent on China and other foreign investors, who held more than half of the debt.

Bush used regulatory powers that did not require congressional approval to weaken environmental protection as part of his larger goals of reducing government regulation, promoting economic growth, and increasing energy production. The administration opened millions of wilderness acres to mining, oil, and timber industries and relaxed environmental requirements under the Clean Air and Clean Water Acts. To worldwide dismay, the administration withdrew from the Kyoto Protocol on global warming, signed in 1997 by 178 nations to reduce greenhouse gas emissions.

Conservatives hailed Bush's appointment of two new Supreme Court justices. In 2005, John Roberts, who had served in the Reagan and George H. W. Bush administrations, was named chief justice. Bush then replaced the moderate Sandra Day O'Connor with Samuel A. Alito, a staunch conservative who won confirmation by a narrow margin.

In contrast to the partisan conflict over judicial appointments and tax and environmental policy, Bush won bipartisan support for the **No Child Left Behind (NCLB) Act** of 2002, marking the greatest change in federal education policy since the 1960s and substantially extending the role of the federal government in public

CHRONOLOGY

2000
- Republican George W. Bush is elected president.

2001
- **September 11.** Terrorists attack World Trade Center and Pentagon.
- United States attacks Afghanistan, driving out Taliban government.
- USA Patriot Act.
- $1.35 trillion tax cut.

2002
- No Child Left Behind Act.
- Department of Homeland Security is established.

2003
- United States attacks Iraq, deposing Saddam Hussein.
- Prescription drug coverage is added to Medicare.

2004
- President George W. Bush is reelected.

2005
- Hurricane Katrina.

2007
- Bush begins troop surge in Iraq.

2008
- Worst financial crisis since the Great Depression.
- Troubled Assets Relief Program is enacted.
- Democrat Barack Obama is elected president.

No Child Left Behind (NCLB) Act

▶ 2002 legislation championed by President George W. Bush that expanded the role of the federal government in public education. The law required every school to meet annual testing standards, penalized failing schools, and allowed parents to transfer their children out of such schools.

What explains the Clinton administration's move to the right?

How did President Clinton respond to the challenges of globalization?

How did President George W. Bush change American politics and foreign policy?

Conclusion: How have Americans debated the role of the government?

875

education. Promising to end, in Bush's words, "the story of children being just shuffled through the system," the law required every school to meet annual testing standards, penalized failing schools, and allowed parents to transfer their children out of such schools. NCLB authorized an increase in federal aid aimed primarily at the poorest districts, but not enough for Senator Paul Wellstone of Minnesota, one of the few critics of the education bill, who asked, "How can you reach the goal of leaving no child behind on a tin cup budget?" In addition to struggling to finance the new standards, school officials began to criticize the one-size-fits-all approach and pointed to family and community impoverishment as sources of student deficiencies.

The Bush administration's second major effort to co-opt Democratic Party issues constituted what the president hailed as "the greatest advance in health care coverage for America's seniors" since the start of Medicare in 1965. In 2003, Bush signed a bill authorizing prescription drug benefits for the elderly and at the same time expanding the role of private insurers in the Medicare system. Most Democrats opposed the legislation, charging that it left big gaps in coverage, subsidized private insurers with federal funds to compete with Medicare, banned imports of low-priced drugs, and prohibited the government from negotiating with drug companies to reduce prices. Overall, medical costs overall continued to soar, and the number of uninsured Americans surpassed 40 million in 2008.

One domestic undertaking of the Bush administration found little approval anywhere: its handling of **Hurricane Katrina**, which in August 2005 devastated the coasts of Alabama, Louisiana, and Mississippi and ultimately resulted in some 1,500 deaths. The catastrophe that ensued when New Orleans's levees broke, flooding 80 percent of the city, shook a deeply rooted assumption held by Americans, even conservatives devoted to limited government: that government owed its citizens protection from natural disasters.

New Orleans residents who were too poor or too infirm to flee the flooding spent anguished days waiting on rooftops for help; wading in filthy, toxic water; and enduring the heat, disorder, and lack of basic necessities at the convention center and Superdome, where they had been told to go for safety and protection. "How can we save the world if we can't save our own people?" wondered one Louisianan. Thousands of volunteers rescued the stranded, helped evacuees in distant cities, and traveled to the Gulf Coast to assist with reconstruction. Millions more opened their pocketbooks to aid the victims. Yet the immense private generosity and the superb response of a few groups, such as the U.S. Coast Guard, could not make up for the feeling that the nation had failed some of its citizens when they needed it most. Since so many of Katrina's hardest-hit victims were poor and black, the disaster also highlighted the severe injustices and deprivations remaining in American society.

The Globalization of Terrorism

The response to Hurricane Katrina contrasted sharply with the Bush administration's decisive reaction to the horror that had unfolded four years earlier on the morning of **September 11, 2001**. Nineteen terrorists hijacked four planes and flew three of them into the twin towers of New York City's World Trade Center and the Pentagon in Washington, D.C.; the fourth crashed in a field in Pennsylvania. The

Hurricane Katrina

▶ August 2005 hurricane that devastated the coasts of Alabama, Louisiana, and Mississippi and ultimately resulted in some 1,500 deaths, most of them among the region's poor. In the wake of the hurricane, New Orleans's levees broke, flooding 80 percent of the city. The inadequacy of the federal response to the disaster outraged the American public.

September 11, 2001

▶ Date on which nineteen terrorists hijacked four planes and flew three of them into the twin towers of New York City's World Trade Center and the Pentagon in Washington, D.C.; the fourth crashed in a field in Pennsylvania. The attacks took nearly 2,800 lives, including U.S. citizens and people from ninety countries. The attacks prompted President George W. Bush to initiate radical departures from long-standing American security and foreign policies.

CHAPTER LOCATOR | How did the United States respond to the end of the Cold War and tensions in the Middle East?

CHAPTER 31
876 FACING THE CHALLENGES OF A CHANGING WORLD, SINCE 1989

attacks took nearly 2,800 lives, including U.S. citizens and people from ninety countries.

The hijackers were members of **Al Qaeda,** an international terrorist network led by Osama bin Laden. Organized from Afghanistan, where the radical Muslim Taliban government harbored Al Qaeda, the attacks reflected several elements of globalization. Technological advances and increased mobility facilitated bin Laden's worldwide coordination of Al Qaeda. Moreover, Islamic extremists were

Al Qaeda

▶ Osama bin Laden's international terrorist organization, consisting of Islamic extremists who were enraged by the spread of Western goods, culture, and values into the Muslim world, as well as by the 1991 Persian Gulf War against Iraq and the stationing of American troops in Saudi Arabia, bin Laden's homeland. The group was responsible for the September 11, 2001, attacks on the World Trade Center and the Pentagon, which were organized from Afghanistan, as well as other attacks around the world.

▶ FOR MORE HELP ANALYZING THIS IMAGE, see the visual activity for this chapter in the Online Study Guide at bedfordstmartins.com/roarkunderstanding.

The Tribute in Light

Two pillars of light, projected by eighty-eight searchlights in the place where the World Trade Center's twin towers had stood, soared as a monument to the victims of the terrorist attacks of September 11, 2001. Turned on at the six-month anniversary of the attack, the "Tribute in Light" was dimmed one month later and has been illuminated every year since on September 11.
Daniel Derella/AP/Wide World Photos, Inc.

| What explains the Clinton administration's move to the right? | How did President Clinton respond to the challenges of globalization? | **How did President George W. Bush change American politics and foreign policy?** | Conclusion: How have Americans debated the role of the government? |

Afghanistan

USA Patriot Act

▶ 2001 law intended to increase America's ability to combat terrorism. The law gave the government new powers to monitor suspected terrorists and their associates, while allowing more exchange of information between criminal investigators and those investigating foreign threats. Critics charged that it represented an unwarranted abridgment of civil rights.

enraged by the spread of Western goods, culture, and values into the Muslim world, as well as by the 1991 Persian Gulf War against Iraq and the stationing of American troops in Saudi Arabia, bin Laden's homeland.

In the wake of the September 11 attacks, President Bush's public approval rating skyrocketed as he sought a global alliance against terrorism and won at least verbal support from most governments. On October 11, the United States and Britain began bombing Afghanistan, and American special forces aided the Northern Alliance, the Taliban government's main opposition. By December, the Taliban government was destroyed, but bin Laden had not been captured, and numerous Al Qaeda forces had escaped or remained in hiding throughout the world. Afghans elected a new national government, but although the United States still had 27,000 troops in Afghanistan seven years later, economic stability and physical security remained out of reach.

Throughout the United States, anti-immigrant sentiment revived, and anyone appearing to be Middle Eastern or practicing Islam was likely to arouse suspicion. Authorities arrested more than a thousand Arabs and Muslims, and a Justice Department study later reported that many people with no connection to terrorism spent months in jail, denied their rights. "I think America overreacted . . . by singling out Arab-named men like myself," said Shanaz Mohammed, who was jailed for eight months for an immigration violation.

In October 2001, Congress passed the **USA Patriot Act.** The law gave the government new powers to monitor suspected terrorists and their associates, while allowing more exchange of information between criminal investigators and those investigating foreign threats. It soon provoked calls for revision from both conservatives and liberals. Kathleen MacKenzie, a councilwoman in Ann Arbor, Michigan, explained why the council opposed the Patriot Act: "[A]s awful as we feel about September 11 and as concerned as we were about national safety, we felt that giving up [rights] was too high a price to pay." A security official countered, "If you don't violate someone's human rights some of the time, you probably aren't doing your job."

Insisting that presidential powers were virtually limitless in times of national crisis, Bush stretched his powers as commander in chief until he met resistance from the courts and Congress. In 2001, the administration established special military commissions to try prisoners captured in Afghanistan and taken to the U.S. military base at Guantánamo, Cuba. But in 2006, the Supreme Court ruled five to three that Congress had not authorized such tribunals and that they violated international law. That year, congressional leaders became openly critical of the administration for wiretapping phone calls made and received by U.S. residents without obtaining the warrants required by law.

The government also sought to protect Americans from future terrorist attacks through the greatest reorganization of the executive branch since 1948. In November 2002, Congress authorized the new Department of Homeland Security (DHS), combining 170,000 federal employees from twenty-two agencies that had responsibilities for various aspects of domestic security. During the new department's first six years, no terrorist attacks were launched in the United States, but doubts grew about its effectiveness when its subagency, the Federal Emergency Management Agency (FEMA), failed in the response to Hurricane Katrina.

CHAPTER LOCATOR | How did the United States respond to the end of the Cold War and tensions in the Middle East?

Chief Duties of the Department of Homeland Security

Intelligence analysis
Immigration and border security
Chemical, biological, and nuclear countermeasures
Emergency preparedness and response

Unilateralism, Preemption, and the Iraq War

The Bush administration sought collective action against the Taliban, but on most other international issues, it adopted a go-it-alone approach. In addition to withdrawing from the Kyoto Protocol on global warming and violating international rules about the treatment of military prisoners, it scrapped the 1972 Antiballistic Missile Treaty in order to develop the space-based Strategic Defense Initiative first proposed by Ronald Reagan. Bush also withdrew the nation from the UN's International Criminal Court, and he rejected an agreement to enforce bans on the development and possession of biological weapons—an agreement signed by all of America's European allies.

Nowhere was the new policy of unilateralism more striking than in a new war against Iraq, a war endorsed by Vice President Dick Cheney and Secretary of Defense Donald H. Rumsfeld, but not by Secretary of State Colin Powell. In his State of the Union message in January 2002, Bush identified Iraq, Iran, and North Korea as an "axis of evil." His words alarmed political leaders in Europe and Asia, who insisted that those three nations posed entirely different challenges and who preferred to emphasize diplomacy rather than confrontation.

Nonetheless, in June 2002 President Bush proclaimed a new policy for American security based not on containment but on preemption: "Traditional concepts of deterrence will not work against a terrorist enemy whose avowed tactics are wanton destruction and the targeting of innocents; whose so-called soldiers seek martyrdom in death and whose most potent protection is statelessness." Because nuclear, chemical, and biological weapons enabled "even weak states and small groups [to] attain a catastrophic power to strike great nations," the United States had to "be ready for preemptive action." The president's claim that the United States had the right to start a war was at odds with international law and with many Americans' understanding of their nation's ideals. It distressed most of America's great-power allies.

The Bush administration moved deliberately to apply the doctrine of preemption to Iraq, whose dictator, Saddam Hussein, appeared to be in violation of UN resolutions from the 1991 Gulf War requiring Iraq to destroy and stop further development of nuclear, chemical, and biological weapons. In November 2002, the United States persuaded the UN Security Council to pass a resolution requiring Iraq to disarm or face "serious consequences." When Iraq failed to comply fully with new UN inspections, the Bush administration decided on war. Making claims (subsequently refuted) that Hussein had links to Al Qaeda and harbored terrorists and that Iraq possessed weapons of mass destruction, the president insisted that the threat was immediate and great enough to justify preemptive action. Despite

| What explains the Clinton administration's move to the right? | How did President Clinton respond to the challenges of globalization? | **How did President George W. Bush change American politics and foreign policy?** | Conclusion: How have Americans debated the role of the government? |

879

Iraq War

▶ War launched by the United States, Britain, and a number of smaller countries in March 2003 against the government of Iraqi dictator Saddam Hussein. The U.S. invasion of Iraq proceeded in the face of considerable international opposition. Bush administration officials justified the invasion of Iraq by making claims (subsequently refuted) that Hussein had links to Al Qaeda and harbored terrorists and that Iraq possessed weapons of mass destruction. Although major combat operations in the war were declared over in May 2003, violence and instability continued to plague Iraq for years to come.

Iraq

opposition from the Arab world and most major nations, the United States and Britain invaded Iraq on March 19, 2003, supported by some thirty nations (see Map 31.1, page 861). Coalition forces won an easy and decisive victory, and Bush declared the end of the **Iraq War** on May 1. Saddam Hussein was ousted and remained at large until December 2003.

Chaos followed the quick victory over Hussein. Damage from U.S. bombing and widespread looting resulting from the failure of U.S. troops to secure order and provide basic necessities left Iraqis wondering how much they had gained. "With Saddam there was tyranny, but at least you had a salary to put food on your family's table," said a young father from Hussein's hometown of Tikrit. A Baghdad hospital worker complained, "They can take our oil, but at least they should let us have electricity and water." Five years after the invasion, continuing violence had caused 2 million to flee their country and displaced 1.9 million within Iraq.

The administration had not planned adequately for the occupation and sent far fewer forces to Iraq than it had deployed in 1991 in response to Iraq's invasion of Kuwait. The 140,000 American forces in Iraq came under attack almost daily from remnants of the former Hussein regime, religious extremists, and hundreds of foreign terrorists now entering the chaotic country. Seeking to divide Iraqis and undermine the occupation, terrorists launched attacks that resulted in the deaths of tens of thousands.

The war became an issue in the presidential campaign of 2004. Massachusetts senator John Kerry, the Democratic nominee, criticized Bush's unilateralist foreign policy and the administration's conduct of the war. The president eked out a 286 to 252 victory in the electoral college, winning 50.7 percent of the popular vote to Kerry's 48.3 percent and carrying Republican majorities into Congress.

In June 2004, the United States transferred sovereignty to an interim Iraqi government, and in January 2005 about 58 percent of Iraqis eligible to vote risked their safety to elect a national assembly. The daunting challenges facing the national assembly were to write a constitution, satisfy Iraq's sharply divided political blocs, and decide to what extent Islamic religious law would shape the new government. Violence escalated against government officials, Iraqi civilians, and occupation forces. A nineteen-year-old Iraqi confined to his house by his parents, who feared he could be killed or lured into terrorist activities, said, "If I'm killed, it doesn't even matter because I'm dead right now." By 2006, when U.S. military deaths approached 3,000 and Iraqi civilian casualties reached tens of thousands, a majority of Americans told pollsters that the Iraq War was a mistake.

By 2006, Bush's conduct of the Iraq War was subject to criticism that crossed party lines and included leading military figures. Critics acknowledged that the U.S. military had felled a brutal dictator, but coalition forces were not sufficiently numerous or prepared for the turmoil that followed the invasion, nor did they find the weapons of mass destruction or links to Osama bin Laden that administration officials had insisted made the war necessary. Rather, in the chaos induced by the invasion of Iraq, more than a thousand terrorists entered Iraq—the place, according to one expert, "for fundamentalists to go . . . to stick it to the West."

The war and occupation exacted a steep price not only in dollars but also in American and Iraqi lives, U.S. relations with the other great powers, and the nation's reputation in the world, especially among Arab nations. Revelations of

CHAPTER LOCATOR | How did the United States respond to the end of the Cold War and tensions in the Middle East?

CHAPTER 31

880 FACING THE CHALLENGES OF A CHANGING WORLD, SINCE 1989

prisoner abuse in the Abu Ghraib prison in Iraq and in the Guantánamo detention camp housing captives from the Afghan war further tarnished the United States' image. Anti-Americanism around the world rose to its highest point in history. The budget deficit swelled, and resources were diverted to Iraq from other national security challenges, including the stabilization of Afghanistan, the elimination of bin Laden and Al Qaeda, and the threats posed by North Korea's and Iran's pursuit of nuclear weapons.

Voters registered their dissatisfaction in the 2006 congressional elections, turning control of both houses over to the Democrats for the first time since 1994. President Bush replaced Secretary of Defense Donald Rumsfeld, and the administration displayed more willingness to work with other nations in dealing with Iraq, Iran, and North Korea. Yet Bush clung to the goal of bringing democracy to the Middle East. Despite opposition from Democrats in Congress, who wanted a timetable for withdrawal from Iraq, in 2007 the administration began a troop surge that increased U.S. forces there to 160,000. The surge, along with actions by Iraqi leaders, contributed to a dramatic reduction in terrorist violence, and the administration began planning for the eventual withdrawal of U.S. forces by the end of 2011.

Barack Obama and the Promise of Change

Despite the improving situation in Iraq, President Bush's approval ratings sank below 30 percent, posing severe difficulties for the Republican Party in the 2008 elections. The Republicans nominated Senator John McCain of Arizona. McCain chose Alaska governor Sarah Palin as his running mate, the second woman to run for vice president on a major party ticket. Even more historic changes occurred in the Democratic Party when **Barack Obama** edged out Hillary Rodham Clinton, the former First Lady, in closely contested battles that continued until the last primaries in June.

Born to a white mother and a Kenyan father and raised in Hawaii and Indonesia, Obama served in the Illinois Senate and in 2004 won election to the U.S. Senate. Obama won the Democratic nomination with a combination of brilliant campaign strategy based on grassroots and Internet organizing, a charismatic personality, and the ability to speak to deep-seated longings for a new kind of politics and racial reconciliation. He won 53 percent of the popular vote and defeated McCain 365 to 173 in the electoral college, while Democrats increased their majorities in the House and Senate (**Map 31.4**).

Obama promised a series of reforms in health care, education, and the environment, but by his inauguration, he faced more immediate problems. Fueled by a breakdown in financial institutions that had accumulated trillions of dollars of bad debt, a recession hit the economy in 2008. The financial crisis was so severe that Congress passed the Bush administration's $700 billion Troubled Assets Relief Program to inject credit into the economy and shore up banks and other businesses. Home mortgage foreclosures skyrocketed, major companies went

Barack Obama

▶ The first African American to win a major political party's nomination for president and the Democratic winner of the 2008 presidential election. Obama became the forty-fourth president of the United States on January 20, 2009, and immediately set to work on the country's severe domestic and international challenges.

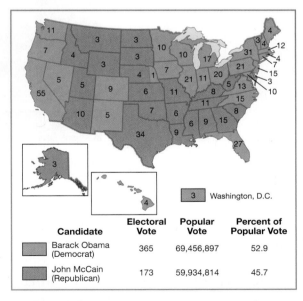

Candidate	Electoral Vote	Popular Vote	Percent of Popular Vote
Barack Obama (Democrat)	365	69,456,897	52.9
John McCain (Republican)	173	59,934,814	45.7

MAP 31.4 ■ The Election of 2008

What explains the Clinton administration's move to the right?

How did President Clinton respond to the challenges of globalization?

How did President George W. Bush change American politics and foreign policy?

Conclusion: How have Americans debated the role of the government?

881

bankrupt, and unemployment surpassed ten percent. Obama attacked the recession with $787 billion worth of spending to stimulate the economy and relieve unemployment; persuaded Congress to tighten regulations on Wall Street and protect consumers; and, over unanimous Republican opposition, signed a health care law extending health insurance to 30 million. Yet, in 2010 Republicans made strong gains in the mid-term elections, which took place amidst continuing high unemployment, a huge federal deficit, and the sentiment among a minority of voters that government was taking away their liberty.

The Inauguration of Barack Obama President Barack Obama and his wife, Michelle, walk down Pennsylvania Avenue after his inauguration at the Capitol on January 20, 2009. In his inaugural address, Obama spoke of "this winter of our hardship," referring to economic crisis, wars in Iraq and Afghanistan, and other challenges facing the nation. AP Images/Doug Mills/Pool.

> QUICK REVIEW

What impact did the terrorist attacks of September 11 have on U.S. domestic and foreign policy?

CHAPTER LOCATOR | How did the United States respond to the end of the Cold War and tensions in the Middle East?

Conclusion: How have Americans debated the role of the government?

THE END OF THE COLD WAR, the rise of international terrorism, and the George W. Bush administration's doctrines of preemption and unilateralism sparked new debates over the long-standing question of how the United States should act beyond its borders. Further, Americans had debated for more than two centuries what responsibilities the government could or should shoulder and what was best left to the private sector. The last three decades of the twentieth century had seen a decline in Americans' trust in government's ability to improve people's lives.

The shifting of control of the government back and forth between Republicans and Democrats from 1989 to 2008 revealed a dynamic debate over the role of government in domestic affairs. The reforms in some social areas built on a deep-rooted tradition that sought to realize the American promise of justice and human well-being. Those who mobilized against globalization worked internationally for what populists, progressives, New Deal reformers, and many activists of the 1960s had sought for the domestic population: protection of individual rights, curbs on laissez-faire capitalism, assistance for victims of rapid economic change, and fiscal policies that placed greater responsibility on those best able to pay for the collective good. Even the second Bush administration, which sought a more limited role for the federal government, expanded the government's role in public education and health care for the elderly, and a gigantic program to bail out failing businesses when a severe financial crisis hit the economy in 2008.

The United States became ever more deeply embedded in the global economy as products, information, and people crossed borders with amazing speed and frequency. Although the end of the Cold War brought about unanticipated cooperation between the United States and its former enemies, globalization also contributed to international instability and the threat of terrorism. In response to those dangers, the second Bush administration departed from the multilateral approach to foreign policy that had been built up by Republican and Democratic administrations alike since World War II. Toward the end of his second term, however, Bush worked to improve international relationships, and the unprecedented celebrations at home and abroad when Barack Obama won the presidency signaled the promise of a new era in American relations with the world.

SO NOW YOU KNOW

By 2006, the United States was home to some 35.7 million immigrants, 12.4 percent of the population. Although immigration has played a central role in the nation's history, globalization has changed the ethnic and cultural composition of the nation dramatically and has contributed to the presence of millions of illegal immigrants.

What explains the Clinton administration's move to the right?

How did President Clinton respond to the challenges of globalization?

How did President George W. Bush change American politics and foreign policy?

Conclusion: How have Americans debated the role of the government?

STEP
1
GETTING STARTED

Below are basic terms from this period in American history. Can you identify each term below and explain why it matters? To do this exercise online or to download this chart, visit bedfordstmartins.com/roarkunderstanding.

TERM	WHO OR WHAT & WHEN	WHY IT MATTERS
Colin Powell, p. 860		
Saddam Hussein, p. 860		
Persian Gulf War, p. 861		
"don't ask, don't tell" policy, p. 866		
North American Free Trade Agreement (NAFTA), p. 872		
No Child Left Behind (NCLB) Act, p. 875		
Hurricane Katrina, p. 876		
September 11, 2001, p. 876		
Al Qaeda, p. 877		
USA Patriot Act, p. 878		
Iraq War, p. 880		
Barack Obama, p. 881		

STEP
2
MOVING BEYOND THE BASICS

The exercise below represents a more advanced understanding of the chapter material. Reflect on the most important events and developments of the past two decades. Using the chart, describe the events that have had the most impact on recent American history. Consider events both within and outside the United States. When you are finished, consider the following questions: Were these events natural or orchestrated? What was the response of the administrations? How were these events and their effects viewed by Americans? By other nations? Which of the events and developments that you identified do you think will be most important in shaping the next twenty years of American history? Why? To do this exercise online or to download this chart, visit bedfordstmartins.com/roarkunderstanding.

Event/Development	Impact

Now that you've reviewed various parts of the chapter, take a step back and try to see the big picture by answering these questions. Remember to use specific examples from the chapter in your answers. To do this exercise online, visit bedfordstmartins.com/roarkunderstanding.

GEORGE H. W. BUSH AND THE END OF THE COLD WAR

▶ How did U.S. foreign policy change after the fall of communism in Eastern Europe and the breakup of the Soviet Union?

▶ Why did George H. W. Bush fail to win a second term as president?

THE CLINTON ADMINISTRATION

▶ Should Bill Clinton be considered a liberal? Why or why not?

▶ Why did Bill Clinton attract such intense animosity from the religious and political right?

LOOKING BACKWARD, LOOKING AHEAD

▶ Compare and contrast the place of the United States in the world in 1900 and in 2005. What explains the dramatic change in America's global stature?

▶ Based on your understanding of U.S. history, consider the follow question: In fifty years' time, will the United States still be the most powerful nation in the world? Why or why not?

THE GEORGE W. BUSH ADMINISTRATION

▶ What were the key components of George W. Bush's domestic agenda? How did his domestic priorities compare to those of Ronald Reagan?

▶ In what ways did Bush's foreign policy depart from that of previous administrations?

IN YOUR OWN WORDS

Imagine that you must explain chapter 31 to someone who hasn't read it. What would be the most important points to include and why?

SPOT ARTIFACT CREDITS

p. 427 (advertisement): Chicago Historical Society; **p. 429** (Bible): Anacostia Museum, Smithsonian Institution, Washington, D.C.; **p. 436** (ticket): Collection of Janice L. and David J. Frent; **p. 441** (plough): Courtesy Deere & Company; **p. 446** (election artifact): Collection of Janice L. and David J. Frent; **p. 455** (drum): © The Dorothea Lange Collection, Oakland Museum of California, City of Oakland. Gift of Paul S. Taylor; **p. 466** (silver bar): The Oakland Museum; **p. 481** (book): Beinecke Rare Book and Manuscript Library, Yale University; **p. 483** (telephone): Smithsonian Institution, Washington, D.C.; **p. 492** (cigarettes): Courtesy of Duke Homestead and Tobacco Museum; **p. 509** (trunk): National Park Service Collection, gift of Angelo Forgione/Picture Research Consultants & Archives; **p. 518** (typewriter): National Museum of American History, Smithsonian Institution, Washington, D.C.; **p. 528** (baseball glove): Smithsonian Institution, Washington, D.C.; **p. 537** (button): Picture Research Consultants & Archives; **p. 539** (ribbon): Collection of Janice L. and David J. Frent; **p. 543** (paycheck): Chicago Historical Society, Archives and Manuscript. Department; **p. 549** (poster): Nebraska Historical Society; **p. 551** (button): Collection of Janice L. and David J. Frent; **p. 555** (magazine cover): Granger Collection; **p. 567** (NAACP button): © Bettmann/Corbis; **p. 574** (token): The Western Reserve Historical Society, Cleveland, Ohio; **p. 590** (IWW poster): Library of Congress; **p. 597** (poster): Library of congress; **p. 605** (machine gun): National Museum of American History, Smithsonian Institution, Behring Center; **p. 609** (suffrage bird): Collection of Janice L. and David J. Frent; **p. 619** (IWW poster): Picture Research Consultants & Archives; **p. 627** (movie poster): Collection of Hershenson-Allen Archives; **p. 629** (Model T): National Museum of American History, Smithsonian Institution, Behring Center; **p. 636** (Hughes book): Picture Research Consultants & Archives; **p. 659** (Social Security card): Picture Research Consultants & Archives; **p. 661** (wheelchair): FDR Library/photo by Hudson Valley Photo Studio; **p. 664** (microphone): National Museum of American History, Smithsonian Institution, Behring Center; **p. 675** (WPA poster): Picture Research Consultants & Archives; **p. 681** (Grapes of Wrath): Granger Collection; **p. 689** (button): Collection of Janice L. and David J. Frent; **p. 695** (panzer): U.S. Army Ordnance Museum Foundation, Inc.; **p. 704** (flamethrower): National Museum of American History, Smithsonian Institution, Behring Center; **p. 708** (Double V button): Private Collection; **p. 713** (atomic bomb): National Archives; **p. 721** (button): Collection of Janice L. and David J. Frent; **p. 723** (Truman and Churchill button): Collection of Janice L. and David J. Frent; **p. 732** (baseball card): The Michael Barson Collection/Past Perfect; **p. 741** (Korean DMZ sign): Diana Walker/Time Life Pictures/Getty Images; **p. 747** (button): Central Intelligence Agency; **p. 749** (sign): Traffic Safety; **p. 758** (Homeowners Guide): State Museum of PA, PA Historical and Museum Commission; **p. 765** (The Feminine Mystique): W. W. Norton & Company, Inc. N.Y.C., © 1963; **p. 769** (NAACP button): Collection of Janice L. and David J. Frent; **p. 775** (button): Environmental Protection Agency; **p. 777** (food stamps): Getty Images; **p. 785** (pennant): Private Collection; **p. 790** (Indian resistance button): Collection of Janice L. and David J. Frent; **p. 803** (soldier): Catherine Leroy (Contact Press Images): **p. 806** (beret): West Point Museum, United States Military Academy, West Point, N.Y.; **p. 810** (Vietnam button): Picture Research Consultants & Archives; **p. 814** (antiwar button): Collection of Janice L. and David J. Frent; **p. 829** (soldier): © Bettmann/Corbis; **p. 831** (magazine): Young Americans for Freedom; **p. 844** (bumper sticker): Courtesy, Christian Coalition; **p. 857** (American flag): © Bettmann/Corbis.

INDEX

A note about the index: Names of individuals appear in boldface. Key terms and their locations are in boldface italic. Letters in parentheses following page refer to: *(i)* illustrations, including photographs and artifacts, as well as information in picture captions; *(f)* figures, including charts and graphs; *(m)* maps; *(t)* tables

AAA. *See* Agricultural Adjustment Act
Abington School District v. Schempp (1963), 782
ABMs. *See* Antiballistic missiles
Abolition and abolitionism, Lincoln and, 429
Abortion rights, 795, 796, 832, 848
Abstract expressionism, 766
Abu Ghraib prison, abuses in, 881
Accommodation
    by Indians, 458
    Washington, Booker T., and, 591, 592
Acheson, Dean, 725, 726, 735
Acquired immune deficiency syndrome (AIDS), 849
Action painting, 766
Activism. *See* Protest(s); Revolts and rebellions
Addams, Jane, 568–569, 568 *(i)*, 570
    peace movement and, 611
    woman suffrage and, 572
Adding machine, 520
Administrative Reorganization Act (1938), 682
Advertising
    in 1920s, 634
    on radio, 639
Aerospace industry, 759
Affirmative action, 786
    Nixon and, 797
    Reagan and, 847
    Supreme Court on, 832
    Thomas, Clarence, and, 859
Affluence. *See also* Prosperity
    in 1950s, 757–758
    of yuppies, 846
Afghanistan, 882
    bombing of, 878
    Soviets and, 842, 852
    terrorists in, 853, 871
    U.S. intervention in, 829, 851, 878, 881
AFL. *See* American Federation of Labor
Africa, 615
    Nixon and, 818
    U.S. involvement in, 851
African Americans. *See also* Africa; Civil rights movement; Freedmen; Race and racism; Slaves and slavery
    black codes and, 432 *(i)*, 433, 434
    black power movement and, 787

as buffalo soldiers, 468
in cabinet, 865, 875
churches of, 431
in cities, 514
citizenship and, 435
civil rights and, 734–735, 767–770
Colored Farmers' Alliance and, 539
as cowboys, 474
disfranchisement of, 439, 591
as domestic servants, 527
as Exodusters, 474
feminist movement and, 794
GI Bill and, 733–734
Jim Crow laws and, 514, 591
labor unions and, 524
lynchings of, 493–494, 514, 621
in middle class, 781
migrations by, 514, 618 *(i)*, 620–621, 642 *(m)*, 758
in New Deal, 678–679, 684
"New Negro" and, 635, 637–638
in New South, 493
in 1930s, 654
People's Party and, 552
poverty of, 868
as president, 881
in Progressive Era, 591–592, 593
racism against, 591–592
in reconstruction, 434
segregation of, 591
as soldiers in Vietnam, 812
Truman and, 743
university protests by, 790
voting rights for, 426 *(i)*, 438–439, 785–786, 786 *(m)*
in West, 468, 760
women and, 495, 519, 610–611, 758
in workforce, 519
in World War I, 605, 620–621
in World War II, 701–702, 709
African Methodist Episcopal Church, 431
Age. *See* Elderly
Agencies. *See also* Government (U.S.); specific agencies
    in World War I, 608–609
Agent Orange, 808, 813
Aggression
    Japanese, 697 *(m)*
    before World War II, 691, 692
Agnew, Spiro T., 834
Agrarianism, transformation of, 476
Agribusiness, 475, 476, 757–758
Agricultural Adjustment Act (AAA)
    first (1933), 668
    second (1938), 683
Agricultural domain, in geographic regions, 510, 511 *(m)*
Agricultural Marketing Act (1929), 648

Agriculture
    commercial, 474–476
    income (1920-1940), 651 *(f)*
    Japanese immigrants in, 470
    migrant workers and, 474
    in New Deal, 667–668, 671, 682–683
    price supports for, 629
    revolution in, 475
    sharecropping system of, 443–444
    in South, 493
    technology and, 757–758
    in West, 474–476
    workers in, 678
    in World War I, 609
    in World War II, 708
Aguinaldo, Emilio, 562
AIDS. *See* Acquired immune deficiency syndrome
Aid to Families with Dependent Children (AFDC), 781, 866
AIM. *See* American Indian Movement
Air-conditioning, 757 *(i)*
    in Sun Belt, 759, 760 *(m)*
Air force, in World War II, 697, 712–713
Airlines, deregulation of, 838
Air pollution
    Carter and, 840
    control of, 792
    Reagan and, 845
Alabama
    civil rights movement in, 784–785
    Hurricane Katrina and, 876
Alaska, Arctic National Wildlife Refuge in, 840
Albanians, ethnic, 869 *(i)*, 871
Albright, Madeleine K., 865, 865 *(i)*
Albro, Maxine, 674 *(i)*
Alcatraz Island, Indian seizure of, 788
Alcohol and alcoholism. *See also* Temperance
    prohibition and, 569–570, 635–636
    WCTU statement on, 548
    World War I and, 609
Algeciras, Spain, conference in, 581
Alien Land Law (California, 1913), 591
Aliens. *See* Illegal immigrants
Alito, Samuel A., 875
Allende, Salvador, 818
Alliance(s). *See also* specific alliances
    Tripartite Pact as, 696
    World War I and, 600, 601 *(m)*
    World War II and, 695, 722
Alliance for Progress, 806
Allies (World War I), 600, 601 *(m)*, 605, 606–607, 606 *(m)*. *See also* World War I
    loans to, 603, 647
    at Paris Peace Conference, 613 *(i)*, 614–616

Allies (World War II), 694 *(m)*, 701 *(f)*. *See also* World War II
  Casablanca meeting and, 706
  D Day and, 713
  NATO and, 728
  postwar Germany and, 724–725
  United Nations and, 713
  victory by, 712–717
Allotment policy. *See* Dawes Allotment Act
Al Qaeda, 877–878, 881
Altgeld, John Peter, 547
Amalgamated Clothing Workers, 676
Amalgamated Iron and Steel Workers, 542
American Communist Party. *See* Communist Party
American Equal Rights Association, 436
American Expeditionary Force (AEF), 605, 606 *(m),* 607
American Federation of Labor (AFL), 522, **524**–525, 526, 542, 546, 570, 619, 676. *See also* Labor unions; Strikes
  in Great Depression, 653
  merger with CIO, 758
  in World War I, 609
American GI Forum, 735–736, 761, 790
American Independent Party, 816
American Indian Movement (AIM), 789
American Indians. *See* Native Americans
American Liberty League, 671
  Social Security and, 677
American Medical Association, 637
  Social Security and, 677
American Psychiatric Association, gays classified by, 792
American Railway Union (ARU), 546–547
American Sugar Refining Company, 502
Americans with Disabilities Act (1990), 859
American Telephone and Telegraph (AT&T), 487
American Tobacco Company, 576
American Woman Suffrage Association (AWSA), 549
Ames, Adelbert, 449
Amusement parks, 527 *(i),* 528
Amusements. *See* Entertainment; Leisure
Anarchism, 525, 643
  unionism and, 543–544
Angel of the Waters (Stebbins), 529 *(i)*
Anglo-Americans, in West, 468
Anglo-Saxons, and scientific racism, 490
Angola, 851, 852
Animals, protection of, 872 *(i)*
Annexation
  of Hawaii, 555, 561
  after Mexican-American War, 468
  of Texas, 468
Anschluss, 693, 711
Anthony, Susan B., 436, 439, 494, **549**
Anthracite coal strike (1902), 576
Antiaircraft in Action (Cornwell), 688 *(i)*
Anti-Americanism, 881
Antiballistic missiles (ABMs), 818, 850
Antiballistic Missile Treaty (1972), 879
Anti-imperialists, 562
Antilynching movement, 494
  legislation and, 637
Antipoverty laws, 778–779, 864
Anti-Semitism. *See also* Jews and Judaism; Nazi Germany
  in Nazi Germany, 691

Antisodomy laws, 849
Antitrust activities
  Roosevelt, Theodore, and, 576
  Taft and, 584
  U.S. Steel and, 578
  of Wilson, 587
Antiwar protests, during Vietnam War, 790, 813–816
Antwerp, Belgium, 713
Apache Indians, 462–463
Apollo program, 805
Appeasement, before World War II, **693**
Appliances
  in 1950s, 762
  after World War II, 733 *(i)*
Apprenticeship laws, in black codes, 433
Arab-Israeli wars, 797, 819
Arab world, 615
  Clinton and, 871
  Eisenhower and, 755
  Israel-Palestine conflicts and, 729–730, 819, 871
  Nixon and, 797
  opinion of U.S. in, 880–881
  Persian Gulf War and, 860–862, 861 *(m)*
Arafat, Yasir, 871
Arapaho Indians, 463 *(i),* 464
Arbenz, Jacobo, 754
Arbitration treaties, of Taft, 584
Architecture
  Chicago school of, 529
  skyscrapers and, 529
Arctic National Wildlife Refuge, 840
Argonne Cemetery, 623
Arikara Indians, 462
Aristide, Jean-Bertrand, 870
Arizona (ship), 698 *(i)*
Arkansas, 429
  school integration in, 768 *(i),* 769
Armed forces. *See also* Military; Militia; specific branches
  African Americans in, 605
  Bonus Marchers and, 654
  desegregation of, 721, 735
  in World War I, 604–605, 605–606
  in World War II, 700–702
Armistice
  French in World War II, 695
  after Korean War, 742
  after World War I, 607, 614
Arms and armaments. *See also* Weapons
  "cash-and-carry" policy and, 692
  Iran-Contra and, 851–852
  Lend-Lease Act and, 696
Arms control, 818
Arms race. *See* Nuclear arms race
Army-McCarthy hearings, 749
"Arsenal of democracy," U.S. as, 695–696
Art(s). *See also* specific arts and artists
  in Harlem Renaissance, 637–638
  Johnson, Lyndon B., and, 780
Arthur, Chester A., 497
ARVN, 807–808, 819
Aryanism, in Nazi Germany, 709
Asia, 615
  Chinese civil war in, 729–730
  European colonies in, 696
  expansion into, 557
  immigrants from, 511, 514, 643
  Roosevelt, Theodore, and, 581

Taft and, 583
U.S. involvement in, 742, 851
Asian Americans
  bigotry against, 591
  in cabinet, 865, 875
  in New Deal, 679
  poverty of, 868
  in World War II, 700
Assassinations
  attempts on Castro, 836
  of Franz Ferdinand, 600, 601 *(m)*
  of Garfield, 497
  of Kennedy, John F., 777–778
  of Kennedy, Robert F., 816
  of King, Martin Luther, Jr., 787
  of McKinley, 575
Assembly lines, 631, 708
Assimilation
  of Indians, 456, 456 *(i),* 459, 679
  of new immigrants, 515
  of "nonwhite" groups, 470
Astronauts, Soviet, 805
Aswan Dam, 755
AT&T. *See* American Telephone and Telegraph
Atlanta, race riot in, 591–592
Atlanta Compromise, 591
Atlanta Constitution, 492
Atlantic Charter (1941), 696
Atlantic Ocean region. *See also* Exploration
  in World War I, 606
  in World War II, 704–705, 705 *(m)*
Atomic bomb. *See also* Nuclear weapons
  in World War II, 716, 716 *(i)*
Attorney general, 576
Audiotapes, in Watergate scandal, 833 *(i),* 835
Auschwitz, concentration camp in, 711
Australia, 511, 512
Austria, 615
  Hitler's *Anschluss* with, 693, 694 *(m),* 711
Austria-Hungary, 600, 615
Automobiles and automobile industry
  Ford and, 630–631
  in 1920s, 631 *(m)*
  UAW strike in (1937), 676
"Axis of evil," Bush, George W., on, 879
Axis powers (World War II), 694 *(m),* 698, 706
  surrender of, 717
  weapons production by, 701 *(f)*

Babbitt (Lewis), 640
Baby boom, 764, 764 *(t)*
Baker, Ella, 770, 783
Baker, Newton D., 605
Baker v. Carr (1963), 782
Balance of power, 581, 630
Balch, Emily Greene, 611
Baldwin, Brent, 869 *(i)*
Balkan region, 615
"Ballad of Pretty Boy Floyd, The," 652
Baltimore and Ohio Railroad, 522
"Banana republics," 557
Bank(s) and banking. *See also* Panics
  deregulation of, 845
  failures of, 648, 650, 665 *(f)*
  farmers and, 538
  Morgan and, 488
  national system of, 586–587

in New Deal, 665–666
Wilson and, 586–587
Bankruptcy
of Chrysler Corporation, 838
financial crisis of 2008– and, 882
in 1920, 629
of S&Ls, 845
Banks, Dennis, 789
Banky, Vilma, 640 *(i)*
Bannock Shoshoni Indians, 467
Baptists, 431
Barbed wire, 473, 474
Barrios, in California, 468
Barrow plantation (1861 and 1881), 444 *(m)*
Barry, Leonora, 524
Baruch, Bernard, 608
Baseball, 528, 638, 639 *(f)*
Bastogne, in World War II, 713
Bataan Death March, 703
Batista, Fulgencio, 754
Battle(s). See also Wars and warfare;
specific battles and wars
of Britain (1940), **695**
of the Bulge (1944–1945), 713
of Midway, **704**
Bay of Pigs invasion (1961), 804–805
Bayonet rule, in South, 448, 449
Beals, Melba Patillo, 769
Beat generation, 766
Begin, Menachem, 841–842
Beirut, Lebanon, 851
Belgium, Nazi invasion of, 694
Bell, Alexander Graham, 487
Belleau Wood, battle at, 606
Benefits
for labor, 758
Social Security, 677–678
Bentley, Elizabeth, 737
Berger, Victor, 620
Berkman, Alexander, 543
Berlin, Germany
division and occupation of, 724 *(m)*,
727 *(m)*, 806
in World War II, 714
Berlin airlift, 727
Berlin blockade, 727
Berlin Wall, 806
Berry, Chuck, 766
Bessemer, Henry, 483–484
Bethune, Mary McLeod, 678 *(i)*, **679**
Bible, in schools, 782
Bicycles, 548 *(i)*
"Big Bonanza," 467
Big business
railroads as, 482–483
regulation of, 587
tariffs and, 582–583
in West, 475
"Big stick" foreign policy, of Roosevelt,
Theodore, 580–581
"Big Three," in World War II, 713
"Billion Dollar Congress," 501
Bill of Rights (U.S.), Supreme Court on, 782
Bimetallism system, 503
Bin Laden, Osama, 871, 877, 878, 880, 881
Biological weapons, 879
"Birds of passage" (immigrants), 513
Birmingham, Alabama
iron and steel industry in, 493
racial violence in, 774 *(i)*, 784

Birth control, 589 *(i)*, 590, 637, 831
pill as, 791
Birthrate, after World War II, 733, 764
Bison. *See* Buffalo
Black Cabinet, of Roosevelt, Franklin D.,
678
Black codes, 432 *(i)*, **433**, 434
Black Elk (Oglala holy man), 461
Black Hills, 460, 466 *(m)*
"Black is beautiful," 787
Black Kettle (Cheyenne leader), 458
Blacklist(s), against union members,
544, 545
Black Panther Party for Self-Defense,
787
Black people. *See* Africa; African
Americans; Slaves and slavery
Black power movement, 787
Black suffrage
Fourteenth Amendment and, 435–436
Fifteenth Amendment and, 438–439
Black Thursday (October 24, 1929), 648
Black Tuesday (October 29, 1929), 648
Blaine, James G., 497, 498–499, 498 *(i)*,
499 *(m)*, 501, 557
Blitzkrieg ("lightning war"), 693–694
Blockades
of Berlin, 727
in World War I, 602, 603
Bloody shirt, waving the, 445
"Bloody Sunday," in civil rights movement,
784, 785
Blue-collar workers, 655
Boarding schools, for Indians, 459
Bolshevism
in Russia, 604, 606
after World War I, 619
Bombs and bombings
atomic bombs and, 716, 716 *(i)*
in Cambodia, 819
Haymarket, 524–525, 544
in Oklahoma City, 866
in Vietnam, 810, 811, 813, 815,
819–820, 821
in World War II, 712–713
Bomb shelters, 756
Bonfield, John ("Blackjack"), 526
Bonus Marchers, 654
Boomtowns, 466, 477
Bootblacks, 518, 519 *(i)*
Borah, William, 617 *(i)*
Border(s). *See* Boundaries
Bosch, Juan, 811
Bosnia, 600, 870–871
Bosses (political), 498, 530–531
Boston, 513
police strike in (1919), 619
school desegregation in, 830 *(i)*,
831–832
Boston Public Library, 530
Boundaries, after World War I (Europe),
615 *(m)*
Bow, Clara, 638
Boxer Protocol (1901), 556
Boxer uprising (China), 556
Boxing, 639
Boycotts
grape, 789–790
of Pullman cars, 546
of UN Security Council, 739–740

Boyer, LaNada, 788
Boys. *See also* Child labor; Children; Men
as bootblacks, 518, 519 *(i)*
Bozeman Trail, 460
Bracero program, 760, 761 *(i)*
Brains Trust, in New Deal, 664
Brandeis, Louis, 587
Bray, Rosemary, 780
Brest-Litovsk, treaty of (1918), 606
Briand, Aristide, 630
Bridge, Brooklyn, 508 *(i)*, 529
Brinkmanship, 753
Britain. *See* England (Britain)
Britain, Battle of (1940), **695**
British Empire. *See* England (Britain)
British Guiana, Venezuela and, 557
Brooklyn Bridge, 508 *(i)*, 529
Brooks, Gwendolyn, 734
Brotherhood of Sleeping Car Porters, 709
"Brown power," 790
Brownsville, New York, birth control clinic
in, 589 *(i)*, 590
Brown v. Board of Education (1954), **768,**
768 *(i)*, 782
Brunauer, Esther, 738
Bryan, William Jennings, **552**
election of 1896 and, 552–553, 563
election of 1904 and, 577
election of 1908 and, 582
Scopes trial and, 644
as secretary of state, 599
on U.S expansionism, 562
World War I and, 602
Buchanan, Pat, 797, 874 *(m)*
Buckley v. Valeo (1976), 836
Buddhists, in Vietnam, 756
Budget. *See* Federal budget
Buffalo
Indians and, 459
near extinction of, 459–460
Buffalo Bill (William F. Cody), 477
Buffalo soldiers, 468
Bulge, Battle of the (1944-1945), 713
Bull Moose Party. *See* Progressive Party,
of 1912
Bull Moose progressives, 587
"Bully pulpit," Roosevelt, Theodore, on,
575, 575 *(i)*
Bunche, Ralph J., 734
Bundy, McGeorge, 809
Bureaucracy, presidential control over,
682
Bureau of Indian Affairs, 464, 750 *(i)*
Indian takeover of, 789, 798
Bureau of Refugees, Freedmen, and
Abandoned Lands. *See* Freedmen's
Bureau
Burger, Warren E., 828 *(i)*, 832, 853 *(i)*
Burleson, Albert, 612
Burma, 696, 703, 714, 822
Burnham, Daniel, 532
Bus boycott, in Montgomery, 767 *(i)*,
769–770
Bush, George H. W.
election of 1988 and, 858–859
election of 1992 and, 863
Iran-Contra pardons by, 852
Iraq and, 860–861
taxation and, 859, 859 *(i)*
as vice president, 843

missionaries and, 555–556
of railroads, 483
Spanish-American War and, 558–562
U.S. overseas through 1900, 561 *(m)*
of U.S. trade (1870–1900), 555 *(f)*
in West, 455–477
Expatriates, in 1920s, 639–640
Exploration, space, 756, 805
Exports
expansion of, 555, 555 *(f)*
in 1930s, 691

Factionalism, 496, 497
Factories
welfare capitalism and, 632
women in, 519
Fair Deal, 731, 736–737
Fair Labor Standards Act (1938), 684
Fair trade, 872
Fall, Albert, 629
Falwell, Jerry, 844
Families
African American, 618
birth control movement and, 590
farm, 538 *(i)*
Farmers' Alliance and, 539
of freedmen, 430 *(i),* 431
in Great Depression, 651, 652
of homesteaders, 471–472
immigrant, 510 *(i)*
in 1950s, 764
in working class, 518–519
Farewell address, of Reagan, 853
Farm Board, 648
Farm Credit Act (FCA, 1933), 668
Farmers' Alliance, 538–540, **539,** 541
Farmers Friend Manufacturing Company, 475 *(i)*
Farms and farming. *See also* Agriculture;
Rural areas; Tenant farming
agribusiness and, 757–758
commercial, 474–476
consumer prices and farm income
(1865–1910), 539 *(f)*
cooperatives and, 540
electrification and, 666, 667, 667 *(m)*
expansion of markets for, 476
foreclosures in (1932–1942), 665 *(f)*
free silver issue and, 503
in Great Depression, 651, 653–654, 671, 671 *(m),* 672 *(i)*
on Great Plains, 538 *(i)*
migratory labor and, 474
in New Deal, 667–668, 680 *(i)*
in 1920s, 629, 647
railroads and, 475, 502
sharecropping and, 443–444, 474
tariffs and, 501
technology for, 475, 475 *(i)*
tenant, 474
in West, 472, 474–476
Wilson and, 587
World War I and, 609
Farm Security Administration (FSA, 1937), 682–683
Fascism. *See also* Nazi Germany
Roosevelt, Franklin D., and, 692
Faulkner, William, 640
FBI. *See* Federal Bureau of Investigation
FCA. *See* Farm Credit Act

Federal budget. *See also* Defense spending
Carter and, 838
deficit in, 845, 859, 875
Federal Bureau of Investigation (FBI), 836
Federal Communications Commission, 765
Federal Deposit Insurance Corporation
(FDIC), 665
Federal Election Campaign Act (1974), 835–836
Federal Emergency Management Agency
(FEMA), 878
Federal Emergency Relief Administration
(FERA), 666
Federal government. *See* Government (U.S.)
Federal Housing Administration, 759
Federal Republic of Germany. *See* West
Germany
Federal Reserve Act (1913), 586–587
Federal Reserve Board, 587, 838
Federal Surplus Commodities Corporation, 683
Federal Trade Commission (FTC), **587,** 629
FEMA. *See* Federal Emergency Management Agency
Females. *See* Feminists and feminism;
Women
Feminine Mystique, The (Friedan), 763
Feminists and feminism, 636
countermovement against, 795–796
Fifteenth Amendment and, 439
Friedan and, 763
goals of, 793–795
Nixon and, 798
protests by, 790
Reagan and, 848–849
Fences, ranching and, 468, 473, 474
Ferraro, Geraldine A., 845
Ferris, George Washington Gale, Jr., 532
Fertilizers, agricultural, 757–758
Fifteenth Amendment, 438–439
Filipino people, as farm laborers, 474
Films. *See* Movies
Filo, John, 821 *(i)*
"Final solution" (Hitler), 711
Finance capitalism, Morgan, J. P. and, 488–489
Finances. *See also* Business; New Deal;
Stock market
under Carter, 838
for Civil War, 501
crisis in 2008, 881–882
of presidential campaigns, 836
S&L scandal and, 845
tariffs and, 501
by U.S. government, 758
Finland, 724
Fireside chats, of Roosevelt, Franklin D., 665, 696
First Amendment, 738
First New Deal, 663–673
First strike capability, 807
First World War. *See* World War I
Fishing and fishing industry, in Sun Belt, 759–760
Fitzgerald, F. Scott, 640
Five Civilized Tribes, 456
Five-Power Naval Treaty (1922), 630
Flamethrowers, 703 *(i)*
Flappers, 635 *(i),* 637
Flexible response policy, 804, 806

Florida, 450, 642 *(m)*
election of 2000 and, 874
Food Administration, in World War I, 608–609, 647
Food stamp program, 779
Football, 639
Ford, Betty, 835 *(i)*
Ford, Edsel, 628 *(i)*
Ford, Gerald R., 834, **835**–836, 835 *(i)*
Ford, Henry, 628 *(i),* **630**–631
Ford Motor Company, 631, 676
Foreclosures
farm, 665 *(f)*
in Great Depression, 652, 654
Foreign aid
Marshall Plan and, 726–727
to South Vietnam, 807, 808
Foreign investment, 872
Foreign policy. *See also* Diplomacy
of Carter, 840–842
of Coolidge, 630
of Eisenhower, 752–756
of Harding, 630
of Johnson, Lyndon B., 809–812
of Kennedy, John F., 804–808
in late nineteenth century, 554–557
Marshall Plan and, 726
Monroe Doctrine and, 557
new world order and, 869–871
of Nixon, 817–824
Open Door policy, 554 *(i),* 557
of Reagan, 850–852
of Roosevelt, Franklin D., 691–692
of Roosevelt, Theodore, 580–581
of Taft, 583–584
of Truman, 725–730, 743
of Wilson, 598–600
Foreign Relations Committee (Senate), 617
Forests, 577, 578, 578 *(m)*
Fortas, Abe, 778 *(i)*
Four Freedoms, 696
"Four-Minute Men," 611
Fourteen Points, 613, 614, 616
Fourteenth Amendment, 435–436, 437
corporations and, 490
ratification by southern states, 442
segregation and, 768 *(i)*
voting rights and, 782
women's voting rights and, 436
France. *See also* World War II
in Indochina, 742
Morocco crisis and, 581
Nazi invasion of, 694
Ruhr Valley occupation by, 630
Suez Canal and, 755
U.S. war materiel and, 695
Vichy government in, 695
Vietnam and, 753
World War I and, 600, 603, 605–606, 606 *(m),* 609–610
World War II and, 695, 713
Franco, Francisco, 692
Frank Leslie's *Illustrated Weekly,* 544 *(i)*
Franz Ferdinand (Austria-Hungary), 600, 601 *(m)*
Freedmen, 427
black codes and, 432 *(i),* 433, 434
education and, 431, 442, 443
as Exodusters, 474
labor by women, 440 *(i),* 443

U.S. treaty with, 730
in World War I, 600
after World War I, 616
in World War II, 703–704, 714–715,
715 (m)
after World War II, 729
Japanese Americans
citizenship for, 679
discrimination against, 581
as farm laborers, 474
World War II and, 700, 700 (m)
Jazz, 638
Jefferson, Thomas, home of, 856 (i)
Jericho, 871
Jews and Judaism, 615. See also Israel
in Democratic Party, 492
Holocaust and, 707, 711, 711 (m)
as immigrants, 512, 513
mass execution of, 710 (i)
Nazi Germany and, 691
state of Israel and, 729, 729 (i)
Jim Crow laws, 442, 514, 591, 709
Jobs. See also Employment; Labor
discrimination against homosexuals, 849
Johnson, Andrew, 432, 436 (i)
assumption of presidency, 432
black codes and, 433
Fourteenth Amendment and, 436–437
Freedmen's Bureau and, 438
impeachment of, 438
reconstruction plan of, 432–433
Johnson, Hiram, 574, 585, 591, 617 (i)
Johnson, James Weldon, 638
Johnson, Lyndon B., 778, 778 (i), **809**
civil rights movement and, 784–785
election of 1964 and, 779
on environment, 792
foreign policy of, 809–812
Great Society and, 776
Latin America and, 811
as vice president, 776
Vietnam War and, 780, 809–810, 811–812
Johnson, Thomas Loftin, 573 (i), 574
Johnson-Reid Act (1924), **642**–643
Jones, William ("Billy"), 520
Jordan, 755
Joseph, Chief (Nez Percé), 462
Journalism. See also Newspapers
muckraking in, 577–578
women in, 494–495
yellow, 559
Judge magazine, 626 (i)
Judiciary. See also Courts; Supreme Court
revolution in, 782
Jungle, The (Sinclair), 578, 578 (i)
Juries, discrimination banned in, 761, 786
Justice Department, 619, 620

Kaiser, The: The Beast of Berlin (musical),
611
Kamikaze pilots, 714
Kansas
African Americans in, 468, 474
farm income and consumer prices in, 538
Katrina, Hurricane, 876, 878
KDKA radio, 639
Kearney, Denis, 470
Keating-Owen child labor law (1916), 587
Kelley, Florence, 572
Kellogg, Frank, 630

Kellogg-Briand Pact (1928), 630
Kennan, George F., 725, 727
Kennedy, John F., 804
assassination of, 777–778
civil rights movement and, 785
Cuban missile crisis and, 807
foreign policy of, 804–808
New Frontier of, 776–778
television and, 765
third world and, 806
Vietnam and, 807–808
Kennedy, Robert F., 784, 816
Kent State University, killings at, **820,**
821 (i)
Kenya, U.S. embassy in, 871
Kerouac, Jack, 766
Kerry, John, 880
Kettle Hill, 560
Keynes, John Maynard, 651, 682
Khomeini, Ayatollah Ruholla, 842
Khrushchev, Nikita, 755–756
Berlin Wall and, 806
Cuban missile crisis and, 807
nuclear arms race and, 752–753, 752 (i)
Kim Il-sung, 739
King, Martin Luther, Jr., 783
antiwar protests and, 813
assassination of, 787
Montgomery bus boycott and, 770
nonviolence principles of, 784
Kinsey, Alfred, 766
Kinship. See Families
Kiowa Indians, 460
Kissinger, Henry A., 817–818, 819
Klan. See Ku Klux Klan
Klir, Joseph, 480 (i)
Knights of Labor, 515, 522, **524,** 525, 526,
548, 549
Korea. See also Korean War; North Korea;
South Korea
labor in, 846
occupation zones in, 739
after World War II, 713, 739
Korean War (1950–1953), 737
Cold War and, 739–742
desegregation in, 743
Eisenhower and, 742
human toll of, 742
Korematsu decision, 700
Kosovo, 869 (i), 871
Ku Klux Klan, 441, 641 (i), **643**
Ku Klux Klan Act (1871), 447
Kurds, in Iraq, 862
Kuwait, Iraq and, 860
Kyoto Protocol, withdrawal from, 875

Labor. See also Free labor; Labor unions;
Slaves and slavery; Strikes; Workers
African American, 621, 678, 709
black codes and, 433
Chinese, 469–470
closed shops and, 629
contract labor, 541
contracts for, 629
farm, 474
in Great Depression, 653–654
industrial, 542
Mexican, 621
militancy in Great Depression, 653–654
minimum wage and, 684

NAFTA and, 871
in 1950s, 758
Reagan and, 845
Taft-Hartley Act and, 736
Wilson and, 587
in World War I, 608
after World War II, 732
Labor code, during reconstruction, 429–430
Labor Department, 583
Labor force. See Workforce
Labor unions. See also Labor; Strikes;
specific unions
blacks in, 524
closed shops and, 629
decline of, 868
membership in (1930–1939), 676 (f)
middle-class progressives and, 570–572
in mining, 467
in New Deal, 675
in 1930s, 675–676
Reagan and, 845
Sherman Antitrust Act and, 502
in steel industry, 544
trade unions and, 525, 526
welfare capitalism and, 632
women and, 524, 570–572
after World War I, 618–619
after World War II, 732–733
La Follette, Robert M., 574, 585, 609, 629
Laissez-faire, 490, 496, 550
Lakewood (housing development), 761
Lakota Sioux Indians, 458, 460
Land. See also Agriculture; Conservation;
Farms and farming
of Californios, 468
conservation of, 578
Dawes Act and, 461–462
for freedmen, 430, 433, 437–438, 443
Homestead Act and, 471
Indian, 456–458, 457 (m), 461–462, 750
public auction of, 428 (i)
for railroads, 483
return to ex-Confederates, 433
speculation in, 538
taxes on, 448
in West, 472
Land grants, to railroads, 472, 473 (m), 483
Landon, Alfred (Alf), 680–681
Lansing, Robert, 602, 614–615
Laos, 822
Laramie, Fort
Treaty of (1851), 457, 458
Treaty of (1868), 460, 461
La Raza Unida, 790
Latin America. See also Central America;
South America; specific locations
CIA and, 771
Good Neighbor Policy toward, 691
interventions in, 557, 754–755
Johnson, Lyndon B., and, 811
Kennedy, John F., and, 806
Nixon and, 818
Roosevelt Corollary and, 580–581
U.S. involvement in (1895–1941), 599 (m)
Latinos. See also Hispanic Americans
in cabinet, 865
equal rights struggle by, 735–736,
789–790
poverty of, 868
Law(s). See Legislation; specific laws

Patriot Act (2001). *See* USA Patriot Act
Patriotism, in World War I, 608, 611
Patronage, 491
Patrons of Husbandry. *See* Grange
Patton, George, 702
Paul, Alice, 590, 610
Pawnee Indians, 462, 464
Payne-Aldrich bill, 582–583
Peace. *See* Armistice; Disarmament
Peace Corps, 806
Peacekeeping forces, in Kosovo, 869 *(i)*, 871
Peace movement. *See also* Antiwar protests
  World War I and, 611
Peace talks, with Vietnam, 821–822
Pearl Harbor, Japanese attack on, *697*–698,
  698 *(m)*
Pell grants, 796
Pendleton Civil Service Act (1883), 498
Pennsylvania, September 11, 2001, attacks
  and, 876
Pennsylvania Railroad, 483
"Penny sales," in Great Depression, 654
Pensions
  as "bonus" in Great Depression, 654
  plans for, 632
Pentagon, September 11, 2001, terrorist
  attack on, 876
Pentagon Papers, 820
People of color
  economic status of, 868
  as immigrants, 511
People's Party (Populist Party), 540 *(i),*
  541, 547, 549, 563. *See also* Populist
  movement
  in election of 1892, 551, 552 *(m)*
  in election of 1896, 550, 552–553, 553 *(m)*
People's Popular Monthly magazine, 640 *(i)*
People's Republic of China (PRC). *See* China
People's Republic of North Korea, 739–740.
  See also North Korea
Peréz García, Héctor, 735
Perkins, Frances, 664
Perot, H. Ross, 863, 864
Pershing, John J. ("Black Jack"), *605,* 623
  in Mexico, 600
  in World War I, 605, 605 *(i),* 606
Persian Gulf region
  Carter and, 842
  military buildup before Iraq War, 858 *(i)*
Persian Gulf War (1991), 860–862, *861,* 861
  (m), 871
Pesticides, regulation of, 792
Peterson, Esther, 793
Petroleum. *See* Oil and oil industry
Philadelphia, 513
Philadelphia Centennial Exposition (1876),
  487
Philippines
  China trade and, 559
  human rights in, 841
  Spanish-American War and, 559, 560 *(m)*
  Taft in, 582
  U.S. expansion into, 560, 561–562
  in World War II, 696, 703, 814
Phillips, Wendell, 429, 439
Piecework, 546
Pinchot, Gifford, 579, 583
Pine Ridge Reservation, 460, 464
Pinkerton Detective Agency, 543, 544 *(i)*
Pinochet, Augusto, 818

Pittsburgh, 523
Pittsburgh Courier, 709
Plains Indians, 457–458, 460, 463–464
Planning, economic, 671
Planters and plantations
  labor code and, 430
  during reconstruction, 443, 444 *(m)*
Plastics, in 1950s, 746 *(i)*
Platt Amendment (1898), 561, 561 *(m)*
Playboy magazine, 765–766
Plenty Coups (Crow chief), 462
Plessy v. Ferguson (1896), *591,* 768 *(i)*
PLO. *See* Palestine Liberation
  Organization
Poets and poetry. *See* Literature; specific
  poets
Pogroms, against Jews, 513
Point IV Program (1949), 729
Poland
  Nazi invasion of, 693–694
  after World War I, 615
Police
  Haymarket bombing and, 526
  Red scare and, 620
  strike in Boston (1919), 619
  women as, 795
Polio, 661, 749
Political action committees (PACs), 836
Political machines, Tammany Hall as,
  530–531
Political parties, in Gilded Age, 491–492
Politics
  bosses in, 530–531
  farmers in, 541
  gays in, 849
  gender and, 493
  in Gilded Age, 491–492, 493, 496–499
  Klan in, 643
  in New South, 492, 493
  television and, 764–765
  Versailles treaty and, 616–617
  women and, 494–495, 636–637
  after World War I, 622
  during World War II, 710–711
Pollock, Jackson, 766
Poll tax, for voting, 591
Pollution. *See also* Air pollution; Environment; Water pollution
  environmental movement and, 792
  regulation of, 845
Polygamy, 469
Pools, 502
Poor people. *See also* Poverty
  leisure of, 528
Population
  baby boom and, 764
  of Chinese immigrants, 470
  in cities, 510
  Hispanics in, 468
  immigrants in, 511–512, 512 *(m),* 513, 642
  of Indians, 458
  of industrial wageworkers, 517
  Mexican-born in U.S., 621
  national, and economies, c. 1938, 683 *(t)*
  in rural areas, 474–475, 475 *(f)*
  shift from rural to urban (1920–1930),
    642 *(m)*
Populist movement, 540 *(i),* 541, 543. *See
  also* People's Party
  in election of 1892, 551, 552 *(m)*

  in election of 1896, 550, 552–553
  progressives and, 585
Pork barrel programs, 501
Port cities
  immigrants in, 510
  Jewish immigrants in, 513
Post office. *See* U.S. Post Office
Poverty
  antipoverty legislation and, 779–780
  in cities, 515, 516 *(i),* 568
  Clinton and, 866
  distribution of, 868
  in Great Depression, 651
  Kennedy, John F., and, 777
  in 1950s, 751
  in 1960s–1970s, 781 *(f)*
  in 1980s, 846
  prostitution and, 569
  on reservations, 458
  rural, 758
  social Darwinism and, 490
  wealth gap and, 505, 516 *(i)*
Powderly, Terence V., 515, *524,* 525
Powder River valley, 460
Powell, Colin L., 860
  Iraq War and, 879
  Panama and, 860
  as secretary of state, 875
Power (energy). *See* Electricity; Energy
  crisis; Oil and oil industry
Prager, Robert, lynching of, 612
Pratt, Richard Henry, 459
Preemption policy, 879
Prejudice. *See also* Discrimination
  abandonment of reconstruction and,
    447, 448
  against Asians, 700
  in West, 468
  in World War II, 709
Presbyterians, 491
Preservation, 578
President. *See* Elections; Executive;
  specific presidents
Presidential campaigns, financing of,
  835–836
Presidential debates, in 1960, 777
Presidential reconstruction, 432–433
President's Commission on the Status of
  Women (PCSW), 793
President's Committee on Civil Rights
  (1946), 735
Price controls
  Truman and, 732
  in World War II, 710
Prisons, 441
Private property, 461
Proclamation of Amnesty and
  Reconstruction (1863), 428–429
Proctor Electric Company, 733 *(i)*
Production, in World War II, 701 *(f),*
  702–703, 717
Productivity, between 1922 and 1929, 632
Professional Air Traffic Controllers Organi-
  zation (PATCO), strike by, 845
Progressive Era, 578, 591, 593
Progressive Party
  of 1912, 585, 585 *(m),* 587, 611
  election of 1924 and, 629
Progressivism, 570
  in city and state government, 574

election of 1912 and, 584–585
grassroots, 593
La Follette and, 574
limits of, 588–592
nativism and, 570
populism and, 585
reform and, 568–572
reform Darwinism and, 573
Roosevelt, Theodore, and, 574, 575–581
social engineering and, 573–574
Taft and, 582–584
Wilson and, 586–587
woman suffrage and, 572, 590
working class and, 570–572
World War I and, 605, 608–609
Prohibition, 569–570, 609, **635**–636, 644. *See also* Temperance
Prohibition Party, 495, 549
Propaganda, 611
in Cold War, 728
Property. *See also* Property qualifications
Confiscation Acts and, 429
return to ex-Confederates, 433
Property qualifications, for voting, 439, 441
Property rights, Homestead strike and, 543
Prosperity. *See also* Affluence
in 1920s, 647, 655
in 1950s, 757–761, 762–766
in World War II, 707
Prostitution, 528, 569, 605
Protective tariffs, 500–502, 648. *See also* Tariffs
Protest(s). *See also* Civil rights movement; Resistance
in China, 863
by environmentalists, 790
by farmers, 538–541
by feminists, 790
by gays and lesbians, 791–792
by Latinos, 789–790
by Native Americans, 788–789
in 1968, 815
by students, New Left, and Counterculture, 790–791
against WTO, 872
Protestants and Protestantism, in Republican Party, 491–492
Public debt. *See* Debts
Public education. *See* Public schools
Public libraries, 530
Public Opinion (journal), 515
Public parks, 529 *(i)*, 530
Public programs. *See also* Welfare programs
Carter and, 838
Public schools. *See also* School(s)
in cities and towns, 530
segregation in, 581
in South, 442
Public works, 551, 648–649
in cities, 530
Puerto Ricans, 789
Puerto Rico, 560, 561, 599 *(m)*
Pulitzer, Joseph, 559
Pullman (town), 542 *(i)*, 545
Pullman, George M., 542 *(i)*, 545–546, 547
Pullman boycott and strike, 546–547, 563, 570
Pullman Palace cars, 546 *(i)*
Pure Food and Drug Act (1906), 578
Pure food and drug legislation, 495, 578

Qaeda, Al. *See* Al Qaeda
Quotas, on immigration, 780

Rabin, Yitzak, 871
Race and racism. *See also* Civil rights movement; Segregation
against Chinese immigrants, 467, 469–470, 514
civil rights movement and, 767–770
Fifteenth Amendment and, 439
Great Society programs and, 781
Hispanics and, 468
immigrants and, 514–515
Indians and, 750–751
of Johnson, Andrew, 432
Ku Klux Klan and, 441
lynchings and, 493–494, 514
in New Deal, 678–679, 684
in 1930s, 654
Nixon and, 831–832
Populists and, 552
progressivism and, 591–592
reconstruction and, 441, 447–448
resistance to change, 831
scientific racism and, 490
social Darwinism and, 490
southern Democratic Party and, 448–449
U.S. imperialism and, 562
during World War II, 709
Race riots
in Atlanta, 591–592
in Harlem, 678
in 1943, 709
in North, 621
during reconstruction, 437
Racial segregation. *See* Segregation
Radar, 704
Radicalism and radicals. *See also* Communism
in Great Depression, 672
labor, 525–526
McCarthy and, 737–738
after World War I, 619–620
Radical reconstruction, 437–438
Radical Republicans, 434, 435, 437–438
Radio, 639
Radioactivity, from nuclear testing, 807
Railroad Administration, 609
Railroads
as big business, 482–483
buffalo hunting and, 460
cattle ranching and, 473
Chinese workers on, 469, 514
expansion of, 483–484, 484 *(m)*
farming and, 475
global mobility and, 511
land grants to, 472, 473 *(m)*, 483
mileage of, 486 *(f)*
in New South, 493
rate system of, 538
rebates from, 538, 576, 577
recruitment of settlers by, 470, 472
regulation of, 502, 583
reorganization of, 489
in South, 442
steel and, 483–484
strikes against, 522–524, 532, 545–547
telegraph communication and, 483
track mileage (1890), 486 *(f)*

transcontinental, 482
trusts in, 576
Ranching, 473–474
Ranchos, 468
Randolph, A. Philip, 709
"Rape of Nanking," 692
Rates, railroad, 538
Ratification, of Versailles treaty, 616–617
Rationing, in World War II, 710
Raw materials, tariffs and, 501
Raza Unida, La. *See* La Raza Unida
Readjusters, 493
Reagan, Nancy, 843 *(i)*
Reagan, Ronald, 828 *(i)*, **843**–848, 850–852, 853 *(i)*
budget deficit and, 845
as California governor, 843
conservative support for, 843–844
courts, Congress, and, 847–848
deregulation by, 845
economy and, 844–845, 846
election of 1976 and, 836
election of 1980 and, 842, 843
election of 1984 and, 845
feminism and, 848–849
foreign policy of, 850–852
Iran-Contra and, 851–852
Soviet Union and, 850–851, 852
Rebates, railroad, 538, 576, 577
Rebellions. *See* Protest(s); Revolts and rebellions
Recall, Populists on, 541
Recessions. *See also* Depressions; Economy; Panics
in 1937–1938, 681–682
of 2000s, 875
in 2008, 881–882
after World War I, 619
Reciprocal Trade Agreements Act (1934), 691
Reconstruction (1863–1877), 427–451
abandonment of, 446–448, 450
carpetbaggers and, 440–441
collapse of, 445–449
congressional, 434, 435–439
Johnson impeachment and, 438
Johnson's plan for, 432–433
labor code during, 429–430
Lincoln's plan for, 428–429
military rule during, 437–438, 437 *(m)*
North and, 434, 440, 446–448
politics in, 451
presidential, 432–433
radical, 437–438
Redeemers and, 448, 449
South and, 440–444, 449 *(m)*
southern Republican Party and, 440–441, 441–443, 448–449
wartime, 428–429
white supremacy and, 441, 448–449
Reconstruction Acts (1867), 438, 439
Reconstruction Amendments. *See* Thirteenth Amendment; Fourteenth Amendment; Fifteenth Amendment
Reconstruction Finance Corporation (RFC, 1932), 649, 665
Recovery, industrial, in New Deal, 664, 668–669
Recreation. *See* Leisure
Red Army (Soviet Union), 712, 713, 714

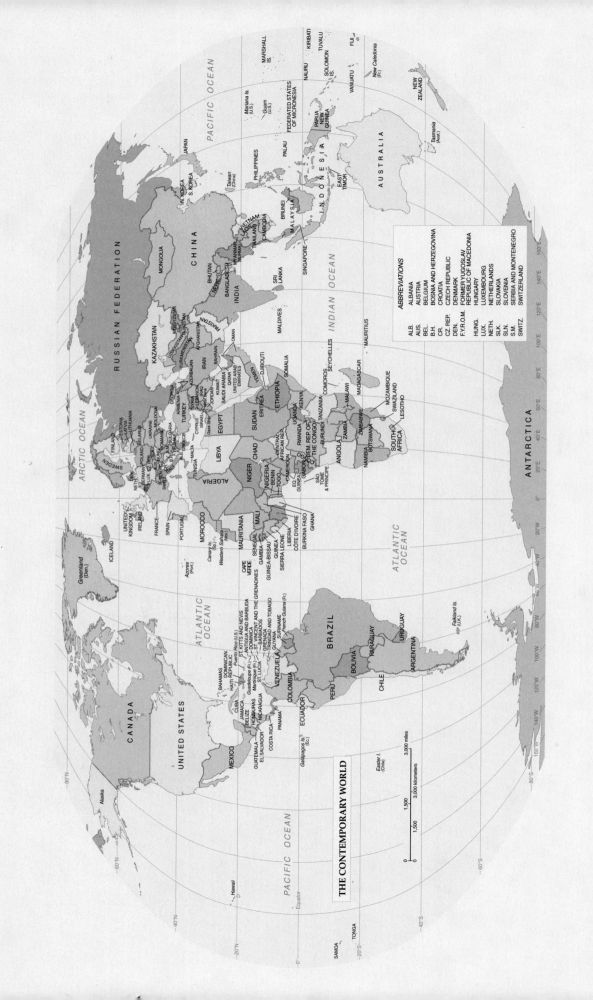

THE CONTEMPORARY WORLD

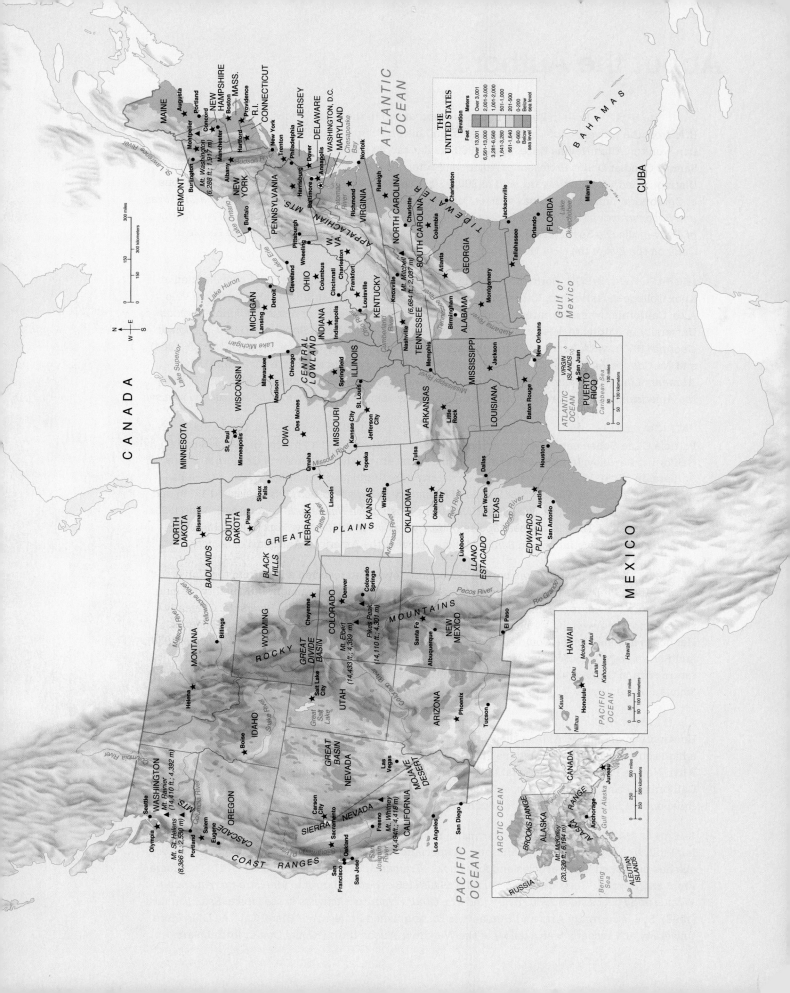

About the Authors

JAMES L. ROARK Born in Eunice, Louisiana, and raised in the West, James L. Roark received his B.A. from the University of California, Davis, and his Ph.D. from Stanford University. His dissertation won the Allan Nevins Prize. Since 1983, he has taught at Emory University, where he is Samuel Candler Dobbs Professor of American History. In 1993, he received the Emory Williams Distinguished Teaching Award, and in 2001–2002 he was Pitt Professor of American Institutions at Cambridge University. He has written *Masters without Slaves: Southern Planters in the Civil War and Reconstruction* (1977). With Michael P. Johnson, he is author of *Black Masters: A Free Family of Color in the Old South* (1984) and editor of *No Chariot Let Down: Charleston's Free People of Color on the Eve of the Civil War* (1984).

MICHAEL P. JOHNSON Born and raised in Ponca City, Oklahoma, Michael P. Johnson studied at Knox College in Galesburg, Illinois, where he received a B.A., and at Stanford University in Palo Alto, California, where he earned his Ph.D. He is currently professor of history at Johns Hopkins University in Baltimore. His publications include *Toward a Patriarchal Republic: The Secession of Georgia* (1977); with James L. Roark, *Black Masters: A Free Family of Color in the Old South* (1984) and *No Chariot Let Down: Charleston's Free People of Color on the Eve of the Civil War* (1984); *Abraham Lincoln, Slavery, and the Civil War: Selected Speeches and Writings* (2001); and *Reading the American Past: Selected Historical Documents*, the documents reader for *The American Promise*.

PATRICIA CLINE COHEN Born in Ann Arbor, Michigan, and raised in Palo Alto, California, Patricia Cline Cohen earned a B.A. at the University of Chicago and a Ph.D. at the University of California, Berkeley. In 1976, she joined the history faculty at the University of California, Santa Barbara. In 2005–2006 she received the university's Distinguished Teaching Award. Cohen has written *A Calculating People: The Spread of Numeracy in Early America* (1982; reissued 1999) and *The Murder of Helen Jewett: The Life and Death of a Prostitute in Nineteenth-Century New York* (1998). She is coauthor of *The Flash Press: Sporting Male Weeklies in 1840s New York* (2008). In 2001–2002 she was the Distinguished Senior Mellon Fellow at the American Antiquarian Society.

SARAH STAGE Sarah Stage was born in Davenport, Iowa, and received a B.A. from the University of Iowa and a Ph.D. in American studies from Yale University. She has taught U.S. history for more than twenty-five years at Williams College and the University of California, Riverside. Currently she is professor of women's studies at Arizona State University at the West campus in Phoenix. Her books include *Female Complaints: Lydia Pinkham and the Business of Women's Medicine* (1979) and *Rethinking Home Economics: Women and the History of a Profession* (1997). She recently returned from China where she had an appointment as visiting scholar at Peking University and Sichuan University.

ALAN LAWSON Born in Providence, Rhode Island, Alan Lawson received his B.A. from Brown University in and his M.A. from the University of Wisconsin. After Army service and experience as a high school teacher, he earned his Ph.D. from the University of Michigan. Since winning the Allan Nevins Prize for his dissertation, Lawson has served on the faculties of the University of California, Irvine, Smith College, and, currently, Boston College. He has written *The Failure of Independent Liberalism* (1971) and coedited *From Revolution to Republic* (1976).

SUSAN M. HARTMANN Susan M. Hartmann received her B.A. from Washington University and her Ph.D. from the University of Missouri. A specialist in modern U.S. history and women's history, she has published many articles and four books: *Truman and the 80th Congress* (1971); *The Home Front and Beyond: American Women in the 1940s* (1982); *From Margin to Mainstream: American Women and Politics since 1960* (1989); and *The Other Feminists: Activists in the Liberal Establishment* (1998). She is currently Arts and Humanities Distinguished Professor of History at The Ohio State University and recently was a fellow at the Woodrow Wilson International Center for Scholars.